D0903231

SHORT STORIES *for Students*

Advisors

Jayne M. Burton is a teacher of English, a member of the Delta Kappa Gamma International Society for Key Women Educators, and currently a master's degree candidate in the Interdisciplinary Study of Curriculum and Instruction and English at Angelo State University.

Mary Beth Maggio teaches seventh grade language arts in Schaumburg, Illinois.

Tom Shilts is the youth librarian at the Okemos branch of Capital Area District Library in Okemos, Michigan. He holds an MSLS degree from Clarion University of Pennsylvania and an MA in U.S. History from the University of North Dakota.

Amy Spade Silverman has taught at independent schools in California, Texas, Michigan, and New York. She holds a bachelor of arts degree from the University of Michigan and a master of fine arts degree from the University of Houston. She is a member of the National Council of Teachers of English and Teachers and Writers. She is an exam reader for Advanced Placement Literature and Composition. She is also a poet, published in *North American Review*, *Nimrod*, and *Michigan Quarterly Review*, among others.

Mary Turner holds a BS in Secondary Education from East Texas State University and a Master of Education from Western Kentucky University. She teaches English 7 and AP English 12 literature and composition at SBEC in Southaven, Mississippi.

Brian Woerner teaches English at Troy High School in Troy, Ohio. He is also a Program Associate of the Ohio Writing Project at Miami University.

SHORT STORIES for Students

Presenting Analysis, Context, and Criticism on Commonly Studied Short Stories

VOLUME 35

Sara Constantakis, Project Editor

Foreword by Thomas E. Barden

GALE
CENGAGE Learning

Detroit • New York • San Francisco • New Haven, Conn • Waterville, Maine • London

Short Stories for Students, Volume 35
Project Editor: Sara Constantakis
Rights Acquisition and Management: Jacqueline Flowers, Robyn Young
Composition: Evi Abou-El-Seoud
Manufacturing: Rhonda A. Dover
Imaging: John Watkins
Product Design: Pamela A. E. Galbreath, Jennifer Wahi
Content Conversion: Katrina Coach
Product Manager: Meggin Condino

Gale
27500 Drake Rd.
Farmington Hills, MI, 48331-3535

ISBN-13: 978-1-4144-8740-3
ISBN-10: 1-4144-8740-1

ISSN 1092-7735

This title is also available as an e-book.
ISBN-13: 978-1-4144-8743-4
ISBN-10: 1-4144-8743-6
Contact your Gale, a part of Cengage Learning sales representative for ordering information.

Printed in Mexico
1 2 3 4 5 6 7 15 14 13 12

Table of Contents

Why Study Literature At All?

Short Stories for Students is designed to provide readers with information and discussion about a wide range of important contemporary and historical works of short fiction, and it does that job very well. However, I want to use this guest foreword to address a question that it does *not* take up. It is a fundamental question that is often ignored in high school and college English classes as well as research texts, and one that causes frustration among students at all levels, namely why study literature at all? Isn't it enough to read a story, enjoy it, and go about one's business? My answer (to be expected from a literary professional, I suppose) is no. It is not enough. It is a start; but it is not enough. Here's why.

First, literature is the only part of the educational curriculum that deals directly with the actual world of lived experience. The philosopher Edmund Husserl used the apt German term *die Lebenswelt*, "the living world," to denote this realm. All the other content areas of the modern American educational system avoid the subjective, present reality of everyday life. Science (both the natural and the social varieties) objectifies, the fine arts create and/or perform, history reconstructs. Only literary study persists in posing those questions we all asked before our schooling taught us to give up on them. Only literature gives credibility to personal perceptions, feelings, dreams, and the "stream of consciousness" that is our inner voice. Literature wonders about infinity, wonders why God permits evil, wonders what will happen to us after we die. Literature admits that we get our hearts broken, that people sometimes cheat and get away with it, that the world is a strange and probably incomprehensible place. Literature, in other words, takes on all the big and small issues of what it means to be human. So my first answer is that of the humanist we should read literature and study it and take it seriously because it enriches us as human beings. We develop our moral imagination, our capacity to sympathize with other people, and our ability to understand our existence through the experience of fiction.

My second answer is more practical. By studying literature we can learn how to explore and analyze texts. Fiction may be about *die Lebenswelt*, but it is a construct of words put together in a certain order by an artist using the medium of language. By examining and studying those constructions, we can learn about language as a medium. We can become more sophisticated about word associations and connotations, about the manipulation of symbols, and about style and atmosphere. We can grasp how ambiguous language is and how important context and texture is to meaning. In our first encounter with a work of literature, of course, we are not supposed to catch all of these things. We are spellbound, just as the writer wanted us to be. It is as serious students of the writer's art that we begin to see how the tricks are done.

Seeing the tricks, which is another way of saying "developing analytical and close reading skills," is important above and beyond its intrinsic literary educational value. These skills transfer to other fields and enhance critical thinking of any kind. Understanding how language is used to construct texts is powerful knowledge. It makes engineers better problem solvers, lawyers better advocates and courtroom practitioners, politicians better rhetoricians, marketing and advertising agents better sellers, and citizens more aware consumers as well as better participants in democracy. This last point is especially important, because rhetorical skill works both ways when we learn how language is manipulated in the making of texts the result is that we become less susceptible when language is used to manipulate us.

My third reason is related to the second. When we begin to see literature as created artifacts of language, we become more sensitive to good writing in general. We get a stronger sense of the importance of individual words, even the sounds of words and word combinations. We begin to understand Mark Twain's delicious proverb "The difference between the right word and the almost right word is the difference between lightning and a lightning bug." Getting beyond the "enjoyment only" stage of literature gets us closer to becoming makers of word art ourselves. I am not saying that studying fiction will turn every student into a Faulkner or a Shakespeare. But it will make us more adaptable and effective writers, even if our art form ends up being the office memo or the corporate annual report.

Studying short stories, then, can help students become better readers, better writers, and even better human beings. But I want to close with a warning. If your study and exploration of the craft, history, context, symbolism, or anything else about a story starts to rob it of the magic you felt when you first read it, it is time to stop. Take a break, study another subject, shoot some hoops, or go for a run. Love of reading is too important to be ruined by school. The early twentieth century writer Willa Cather, in her novel *My Antonia*, has her narrator Jack Burden tell a story that he and Antonia heard from two old Russian immigrants when they were teenagers. These immigrants, Pavel and Peter, told about an incident from their youth back in Russia that the narrator could recall in vivid detail thirty years later. It was a harrowing story of a wedding party starting home in sleds and being chased by starving wolves. Hundreds of wolves attacked the group's sleds one by one as they sped across the snow trying to reach their village. In a horrible revelation, the old Russians revealed that the groom eventually threw his own bride to the wolves to save himself. There was even a hint that one of the old immigrants might have been the groom mentioned in the story. Cather has her narrator conclude with his feelings about the story. "We did not tell Pavel's secret to anyone, but guarded it jealously as if the wolves of the Ukraine had gathered that night long ago, and the wedding party had been sacrificed, just to give us a painful and peculiar pleasure." That feeling, that painful and peculiar pleasure, is the most important thing about literature. Study and research should enhance that feeling and never be allowed to overwhelm it.

Thomas E. Barden
Professor of English and Director of Graduate English Studies,
The University of Toledo

Introduction

Purpose of the Book

The purpose of *Short Stories for Students* (*SSfS*) is to provide readers with a guide to understanding, enjoying, and studying short stories by giving them easy access to information about the work. Part of Gale's "For Students" Literature line, *SSfS* is specifically designed to meet the curricular needs of high school and undergraduate college students and their teachers, as well as the interests of general readers and researchers considering specific short fiction. While each volume contains entries on "classic" stories frequently studied in classrooms, there are also entries containing hard-to-find information on contemporary stories, including works by multicultural, international, and women writers.

The information covered in each entry includes an introduction to the story and the story's author; a plot summary, to help readers unravel and understand the events in the work; descriptions of important characters, including explanation of a given character's role in the narrative as well as discussion about that character's relationship to other characters in the story; analysis of important themes in the story; and an explanation of important literary techniques and movements as they are demonstrated in the work.

In addition to this material, which helps the readers analyze the story itself, students are also provided with important information on the literary and historical background informing each work. This includes a historical context essay, a box comparing the time or place the story was written to modern Western culture, a critical overview essay, and excerpts from critical essays on the story or author. A unique feature of *SSfS* is a specially commissioned critical essay on each story, targeted toward the student reader.

To further help today's student in studying and enjoying each story, information on audiobooks and other media adaptations is provided (if available), as well as reading suggestions for works of fiction and nonfiction on similar themes and topics. Classroom aids include ideas for research papers and lists of critical and reference sources that provide additional material on the work.

Selection Criteria

The titles for each volume of *SSfS* were selected by surveying numerous sources on teaching literature and analyzing course curricula for various school districts. Some of the sources surveyed include: literature anthologies, *Reading Lists for College-Bound Students: The Books Most Recommended by America's Top Colleges*; Teaching the Short Story: A Guide to Using Stories from around the World, by the National Council of Teachers of English (NCTE); and "A Study of High School Literature Anthologies," conducted by Arthur Applebee at the Center for the Learning and Teaching of Literature and sponsored by the National Endowment for the

Arts and the Office of Educational Research and Improvement.

Input was also solicited from our advisory board, as well as educators from various areas. From these discussions, it was determined that each volume should have a mix of "classic" stories (those works commonly taught in literature classes) and contemporary stories for which information is often hard to find. Because of the interest in expanding the canon of literature, an emphasis was also placed on including works by international, multicultural, and women authors. Our advisory board members—educational professionals—helped pare down the list for each volume. Works not selected for the present volume were noted as possibilities for future volumes. As always, the editor welcomes suggestions for titles to be included in future volumes.

How Each Entry Is Organized

Each entry, or chapter, in *SSfS* focuses on one story. Each entry heading lists the title of the story, the author's name, and the date of the story's publication. The following elements are contained in each entry:

Introduction: a brief overview of the story which provides information about its first appearance, its literary standing, any controversies surrounding the work, and major conflicts or themes within the work.

Author Biography: this section includes basic facts about the author's life, and focuses on events and times in the author's life that may have inspired the story in question.

Plot Summary: a description of the events in the story. Lengthy summaries are broken down with subheads.

Characters: an alphabetical listing of the characters who appear in the story. Each character name is followed by a brief to an extensive description of the character's role in the story, as well as discussion of the character's actions, relationships, and possible motivation.

Characters are listed alphabetically by last name. If a character is unnamed—for instance, the narrator in "The Eatonville Anthology"—the character is listed as "The Narrator" and alphabetized as "Narrator." If a character's first name is the only one given, the name will appear alphabetically by that name.

Themes: a thorough overview of how the topics, themes, and issues are addressed within the story. Each theme discussed appears in a separate subhead.

Style: this section addresses important style elements of the story, such as setting, point of view, and narration; important literary devices used, such as imagery, foreshadowing, symbolism; and, if applicable, genres to which the work might have belonged, such as Gothicism or Romanticism. Literary terms are explained within the entry, but can also be found in the Glossary.

Historical Context: this section outlines the social, political, and cultural climate in which the author lived and the work was created. This section may include descriptions of related historical events, pertinent aspects of daily life in the culture, and the artistic and literary sensibilities of the time in which the work was written. If the story is historical in nature, information regarding the time in which the story is set is also included. Long sections are broken down with helpful subheads.

Critical Overview: this section provides background on the critical reputation of the author and the story, including bannings or any other public controversies surrounding the work. For older works, this section may include a history of how the story was first received and how perceptions of it may have changed over the years; for more recent works, direct quotes from early reviews may also be included.

Criticism: an essay commissioned by *SSfS* which specifically deals with the story and is written specifically for the student audience, as well as excerpts from previously published criticism on the work (if available).

Sources: an alphabetical list of critical material used in compiling the entry, with bibliographical information.

Further Reading: an alphabetical list of other critical sources which may prove useful for the student. Includes full bibliographical information and a brief annotation.

Suggested Search Terms: a list of search terms and phrases to jumpstart students' further information seeking. Terms include not just titles and author names but also terms and topics related to the historical and literary context of the works.

In addition, each entry contains the following highlighted sections, set apart from the main text as sidebars:

Media Adaptations: if available, a list of audiobooks and important film and television adaptations of the story, including source information. The list also includes stage adaptations, musical adaptations, etc.

Topics for Further Study: a list of potential study questions or research topics dealing with the story. This section includes questions related to other disciplines the student may be studying, such as American history, world history, science, math, government, business, geography, economics, psychology, etc.

Compare and Contrast: an "at-a-glance" comparison of the cultural and historical differences between the author's time and culture and late twentieth century or early twenty-first century Western culture. This box includes pertinent parallels between the major scientific, political, and cultural movements of the time or place the story was written, the time or place the story was set (if a historical work), and modern Western culture. Works written after 1990 may not have this box.

What Do I Read Next?: a list of works that might give a reader points of entry into a classic work (e.g., YA or multicultural titles) and/or complement the featured story or serve as a contrast to it. This includes works by the same author and others, works from various genres, YA works, and works from various cultures and eras.

Other Features

SSfS includes "Why Study Literature At All?," a foreword by Thomas E. Barden, Professor of English and Director of Graduate English Studies at the University of Toledo. This essay provides a number of very fundamental reasons for studying literature and, therefore, reasons why a book such as *SSfS*, designed to facilitate the study of literture, is useful.

A Cumulative Author/Title Index lists the authors and titles covered in each volume of the *SSfS* series.

A Cumulative Nationality/Ethnicity Index breaks down the authors and titles covered in each volume of the *SSfS* series by nationality and ethnicity.

A Subject/Theme Index, specific to each volume, provides easy reference for users who may be studying a particular subject or theme rather than a single work. Significant subjects from events to broad themes are included.

Each entry may include illustrations, including photo of the author, stills from film adaptations (if available), maps, and/or photos of key historical events.

Citing Short Stories for Students

When writing papers, students who quote directly from any volume of *SSfS* may use the following general forms to document their source. These examples are based on MLA style; teachers may request that students adhere to a different style, thus, the following examples may be adapted as needed.

When citing text from *SSfS* that is not attributed to a particular author (for example, the Themes, Style, Historical Context sections, etc.), the following format may be used:

"The Celebrated Jumping Frog of Calavaras County." *Short Stories for Students*. Ed. Kathleen Wilson. Vol. 1. Detroit: Gale, 1997. 19–20.

When quoting the specially commissioned essay from *SSfS* (usually the first essay under the Criticism subhead), the following format may be used:

Korb, Rena. Critical Essay on "Children of the Sea." *Short Stories for Students*. Ed. Kathleen Wilson. Vol. 1. Detroit: Gale, 1997. 39–42.

When quoting a journal or newspaper essay that is reprinted in a volume of *SSfS*, the following form may be used:

Schmidt, Paul. "The Deadpan on Simon Wheeler." *Southwest Review* 41.3 (Summer, 1956): 270–77. Excerpted and reprinted in *Short Stories for Students*. Vol. 1. Ed. Kathleen Wilson. Detroit: Gale, 1997. 29–31.

When quoting material from a book that is reprinted in a volume of *SSfS*, the following form may be used:

Bell-Villada, Gene H. "The Master of Short Forms." *García Márquez: The Man and His Work*. University of North Carolina Press, 1990. 119–36. Excerpted and reprinted in *Short Stories for Students*. Vol. 1. Ed. Kathleen Wilson. Detroit: Gale, 1997. 89–90.

We Welcome Your Suggestions

The editorial staff of *Short Stories for Students* welcomes your comments and ideas. Readers who wish to suggest short stories to appear in future volumes, or who have other suggestions, are cordially invited to contact the editor. You may contact the editor via E-mail at: **ForStudentsEditors@cengage.com.** Or write to the editor at:

Editor, *Short Stories for Students*
Gale
27500 Drake Road
Farmington Hills, MI 48331-3535

Literary Chronology

1804: Nathaniel Hawthorne is born on July 4 in Salem, Massachusetts.

1843: Nathaniel Hawthorne's "The Birth-mark" is published in *Pioneer* magazine. It is published in 1846 in *Mosses from an Old Manse.*

1850: Kate Chopin is born on February 8 in St. Louis, Missouri.

1858: Selma Lagerlöf is born on November 20 in Östra Emterwick, Sweden.

1864: Nathaniel Hawthorne dies in his sleep of unspecified causes on May 19 in Plymouth, New Hampshire.

1868: Adelaide Casely-Hayford is born on June 2 in Freetown, Sierra Leone.

1876: Jack London is born on January 12 in San Francisco, California.

1889: Ernest Hemingway is born on July 21 in Oak Park, Illinois.

1892: Ryunosuke Akutagawa is born on March 1 in Tokyo, Japan.

1894: Selma Lagerlöf's "The Outlaws" is published in Swedish as "De fagelfrie" in *Osynliga länkar*. It is published in English in 1899 in *Invisible Links*.

1897: Kate Chopin's "A Pair of Silk Stockings" is published in *Vogue*.

1901: Jack London's "The Law of Life" is published in *McClure's* magazine. It is published in 1902 in *Children of the Frost*.

1902: Juan A. A. Sedillo is born in New Mexico.

1904: Kate Chopin dies of a cerebral hemorrhage on August 20 in St. Louis, Missouri.

1904: Graham Greene is born on October 2 in Berkhamsted, Hertfordshire, England.

1909: Selma Lagerlöf is awarded the Nobel Prize for Literature.

1913: Josephina Niggli is born on July 13 in Monterrey, Nuevo Leon, Mexico.

1916: Jack London dies of uremia and other factors on November 22 in Glen Ellen, California.

1917: Gwendolyn Brooks is born on June 17 in Topeka, Kansas.

1919: Doris Lessing is born on October 22 in Persia (Iran).

1922: Ryunosuke Akutagawa's "In a Grove" is published *Sincho* magazine.

1925: Ernest Hemingway's "Cat in the Rain" is published in *In Our Time*.

1927: Ryunosuke Akutagawa commits suicide on July 24 in Tokyo, Japan.

1939: Juan A. A. Sedillo's "Gentleman of Rio en Medio" is published in the *New Mexico Quarterly*.

1940: Selma Lagerlöf dies of a stroke on March 16 in Östra Emterwick, Sweden.

1945: Josephina Niggli's "The Street of the Cañón" is published in *Mexican Village*.

1945: Tobias Wolff is born on June 19 in Birmingham, Alabama.

1946: Zhao Zenkai (Bei Dao) is born on August 2 in Beijing, China.

1950: Gwendolyn Brooks wins the Pulitzer Prize for Poetry for *Annie Allen*.

1951: Doris Lessing's "A Sunrise on the Veld" is published in England in *This Was the Old Chief's Country*. It is published in 1952 in the United States.

1953: Ernest Hemingway is awarded the Pulitzer Prize for Fiction for *The Old Man in the Sea*.

1953: Gwendolyn Brooks's "Home" is published as a chapter in *Maud Martha*.

1954: Ernest Hemingway is awarded the Nobel Prize for Literature.

1957: Graham Greene's "A Shocking Accident" is published in *Punch* magazine. It is published in 1967 in *May We Borrow Your Husband? And Other Comedies of the Sexual Life*.

1960: Adelaide Casely-Hayford's "Mista Courifer" is published in *An African Treasury*, edited by Langston Hughes.

1960: Adelaide Casely-Hayford dies on January 16 in Freetown, Sierra Leone.

1961: Ernest Hemingway commits suicide on July 2 in Ketchum, Idaho.

1981: Tobias Wolff's "Hunters in the Snow" is published in *In the Garden of the North American Martyrs*.

1982: Juan A. A. Sedillo dies.

1983: Josephina Niggli dies in Cullowhee, North Carolina.

1985: Bei Dao's "The Homecoming Stranger" is published in *Waves*.

1991: Graham Greene dies of leukemia on April 3 in Vesey, Switzerland.

2000: Gwendolyn Brooks dies of stomach cancer on December 3 in Chicago, Illinois.

2007: Doris Lessing is awarded the Nobel Prize for Literature.

Acknowledgements

The editors wish to thank the copyright holders of the excerpted criticism included in this volume and the permissions managers of many book and magazine publishing companies for assisting us in securing reproduction rights. We are also grateful to the staffs of the Detroit Public Library, the Library of Congress, the University of Detroit Mercy Library, Wayne State University Purdy/Kresge Library Complex, and the University of Michigan Libraries for making their resources available to us. Following is a list of the copyright holders who have granted us permission to reproduce material in this volume of *SSfS*. Every effort has been made to trace copyright, but if omissions have been made, please let us know.

COPYRIGHTED EXCERPTS IN *SSfS*, VOLUME 35, WERE REPRODUCED FROM THE FOLLOWING PERIODICALS:

African American Review, nos. 1–2, Spring/Summer, 2005. Reproduced by permission.—***America***, no. 11, March 30, 2009. Reproduced by permission of America Press, Inc.—***American Literary Scholarship***, pp. 295-333. Copyright 2006 Duke University Press. All rights reserved. Reprinted by permission of the publisher. www.dukeupress.edu—***American Literature***, Volume 1. Copyright 1991 Duke University Press. All rights reserved. Reprinted by permission of the publisher. www.dukeupress.edu—***American Transcendental Quarterly***, no. 2, June, 1989. Reproduced by permission.—***Americas*** no. 6, November/December, 2007. Reproduced by permission.—***Critique***, no. 4, Summer, 1984. Reprinted by permission of Taylor & Francis Ltd, http://www.tandf.co.uk/journals.—***Hartford Studies in Literature***, no. 2, 1981. Reproduced by permission.—***Hemingway Review***, no. 1, Fall, 1994; no. 2, Spring, 2000; no. 2, Spring, 2001.Reproduced by permission.—***Houston Chronicle*** (Texas), April 6, 2008. Reproduced by permission. via CCC.—***Kirkus Reviews,*** March 1, 2008. Reproduced by permission.—***MELUS***, no. 2, Summer, 1978. Reproduced by permission.—***Mississippi Quarterly***, no. 3, Summer, 2004. Reproduced by permission.—***New Centennial Review***, no. 2, 2009. Reproduced by permission.—***Nineteenth Century: A Monthly Review***, January-June 1900.—***Notes on Contemporary Literature***, no. 1, January, 2011. Reproduced by permission.—***Publishers Weekly***, no. 12, March 23, 1990. Reproduced by permission.—***Record***, May 17, 2008. Reprinted with permission.—***Research in African Literature***, no. 3, fall, 2004. Reproduced by permission.—***Scandinavian Studies***, no. 4, winter, 2009. Reproduced by permission of the Society for Scandinavian Studies.—***Studies in Short Fiction***, no. 2, Spring, 1993. Reproduced by permission.—***Tulsa Studies in Women's Literature***, no. 1, Spring, 1994. Reproduced by permission.—***World Literature Today***, no. 6, November/December, 2008. Reproduced by permission.

COPYRIGHTED EXCERPTS IN *SSfS*, VOLUME 35, WERE REPRODUCED FROM THE FOLLOWING BOOKS:

Barbara Bair, from "Pan-Africanism as Process: Adelaide Casely Hayford, Garveyism, and the Cultural Roots of Nationalism," in ***Imagining Home: Class, Culture and Imagining Nationalism in the African Diaspora***, Verso, 1994. Reproduced by permission.—Howard Hibbett, from "Introduction," in ***Rashomon and Other Stories***, Charles E. Tuttle, 1952. Reproduced by permission of the author.—Jane Hotchkiss, from "Coming of Age in Zambesia," in ***Borders, Exiles, Diasporas***, Stanford University Press, 1998. Reproduced by permission of Stanford University Press.—Kadiatu Kanneh, from "Coming Home: Pan-Africanism and National Identities," in ***African Identities: Race, Nation and Culture in Ethnography, Pan-Africanism and Black Literatures***, Routledge, 1998. Reproduced by permission of Taylor and Francis Books UK.—Richard Kelly, from "Short Stories," in ***Graham Greene***, Frederick Ungar, 1984. Reproduced by permission.—Mona Knapp, from "A Splendid Backdrop to a Disgraceful Scene: African Fiction, 1950-1965," in ***Doris Lessing***, Frederick Ungar, 1984. Reproduced by permission.—R. H. Miller, from "Short Stories, Plays, Essays," in ***Understanding Graham Greene***, University of South Carolina Press, 1990. Reproduced by permission of University of South Carolina Press.—Fred Lewis Pattee, from "The Prophet of the Last Frontier," in ***Side-Lights on American Literature***, Century, 1922.—Mary Ann Singleton, from "The City and the Veld: The Fiction of Doris Lessing," in ***The City and the Veld: The Fiction of Doris Lessing***, Bucknell University Press, 1977. Reproduced by permission.—Ilan Stevens, from "Foreword," in ***Mexican Village and Other Works***, Northwestern University Press, 2008. Reproduced by permission of Northwestern University Press.—Franklin Walker, from "London Mines Literary Gold from the Klondike," in ***Readings on The Call of the Wild from Jack London and the Klondike: The Genesis of an American Writer by Franklin Walker***, Huntington Library, 1994. Reprinted with the permission of the Henry E. Huntington Library.—Ruth Whittaker, from "The Colonial Legacy," in ***Modern Novelists: Doris Lessing***, St. Martin's Press, 1988. Reproduced by permission of Palgrave Macmillan.

Contributors

Bryan Aubrey: Aubrey holds a Ph.D. in English. Entries on "Hunters in the Snow" and "A Sunrise on the Veld." Original essays on "Hunters in the Snow" and "A Sunrise on the Veld."

Cynthia A. Bily: Bily teaches at Macomb Community College in Michigan. Entry on "The Law of Life." Original essay on "The Law of Life."

Catherine Dominic: Dominic is a novelist and a freelance writer and editor. Entries on "The Outlaws" and "A Pair of Silk Stockings." Original essays on "The Outlaws" and "A Pair of Silk Stockings."

Charlotte M. Freeman: Freeman is a writer, editor, and former academic living in small-town Montana. Entry on "The Homecoming Stranger." Original essay on "The Homecoming Stranger."

Diane Andrews Henningfeld: Henningfeld holds the rank of emerita professor of English at Adrian College and writes widely on literature and current events for a variety of educational publications. Entry on "Home." Original essay on "Home."

Michael Allen Holmes: Holmes is a writer with existential interests. Entries on "Gentleman of Rio en Medio" and "A Shocking Accident." Original essays on "Gentleman of Rio en Medio" and "A Shocking Accident."

Michael J. O'Neal: O'Neal holds a Ph.D. in English. Entry on "The Birth-mark." Original essays on "The Birth-mark" and "Gentleman of Rio en Medio."

April Dawn Paris: Paris is a freelance writer who has an extensive background working with literature and educational materials. Entry on "The Street of the Cañón." Original essay on "The Street of the Cañón."

Rachel Porter: Porter is a freelance writer and editor who holds a bachelor of arts degree in English literature. Entry on "Mista Courifer." Original essay on "Mista Courifer."

Christopher Dale Russell: Russell is a freelance writer fascinated by fiction. Entry on "Cat in the Rain." Original essay on "Cat in the Rain."

Bradley A. Skeen: Skeen is a classicist. Entry on "In a Grove." Original essay on "In a Grove."

The Birth-Mark

NATHANIEL HAWTHORNE

1843

"The Birth-Mark" (often written as "The Birthmark") is an allegorical short story by American author Nathaniel Hawthorne. The story was first published in 1843 in the *Pioneer*, a literary magazine edited by poet James Russell Lowell. It was later included in Hawthorne's 1846 collection of tales and stories *Mosses from an Old Manse*. "The Birth-Mark" tells of a scientist who becomes obsessed with an imperfection on the face of his beautiful young wife a small birthmark in the shape of a hand. The scientist tries to remove the birthmark, with tragic results. The story has remained relevant in the twenty-first century as scientists continue to push beyond the boundaries of medical science; Hawthorne's story was actually discussed at the 2002 meeting of the U.S. President's Council on Bioethics.

Hawthorne, best known for his classic novel *The Scarlet Letter*, was a major figure in the American romantic movement. He is often regarded as a writer in the tradition of "dark romanticism," a subgenre of romantic literature that features, among other elements, outcasts from society; the belief that the world is a dark, mysterious place; the conviction that humans are sinful, if not evil, and that they are often incapable of comprehending the realm of spirituality; and that the world cannot be reformed. At the extreme, the dark romantics—a group that included Edgar Allan Poe, Mary Shelley, and others—featured in their works vampires, ghouls, and manifestations of Satan. Shelley's

Nathaniel Hawthorne

gothic novel *Frankenstein* is probably the most widely known example of this phenomenon. In his novels and short stories, Hawthorne created allegories of the dark, irredeemable human condition, a point of view most likely traceable to the author's New England Puritan roots.

"The Birth-Mark" is widely available in anthologies of nineteenth-century American literature and in collections of Hawthorne's short stories, including *Nathaniel Hawthorne: Tales and Sketches*, published by the Library of America in 1982. The story is also available online at the Literature Network Web site (http://www.online-literature.com/hawthorne/125/).

AUTHOR BIOGRAPHY

Hawthorne was born on July 4, 1804, in Salem, Massachusetts, the second of three children born to Nathaniel and Elizabeth Manning Hathorne; he added the *w* to his name sometime after 1830 as a way of distancing himself from relatives he found embarrassing. Hawthorne was raised in Salem and in Raymond, Maine, before attending Bowdoin College in Maine from 1821 to 1825, where he described himself as an idle student. After graduation, he returned to Salem to live with his mother and sister and tried to launch a writing career. One of his earliest efforts was an 1828 novel, *Fanshawe*, which he later called a failure. He tried to collect and burn all copies of the book—and got help from a later warehouse fire that destroyed the book's remaining unsold copies. He had more success with short stories, several of which were published in literary journals during these years. His first collection of short stories, *Twice-Told Tales*, was published in 1837, but it was not until the 1840s that his writing brought him enough of an income to enable him to marry Sophia Peabody. The couple moved into a house called Old Manse in Concord, Massachusetts, giving rise to the title of his 1846 collection, *Mosses from an Old Manse*, which includes "The Birth-Mark."

Hawthorne was connected with the American transcendentalist movement and counted among his friends such figures as Ralph Waldo Emerson, Henry David Thoreau, and Bronson Alcott. Transcendentalism was a cultural and literary reformist movement that rejected orthodoxy and conformity and urged its followers to find an original relationship with creation, often through the natural world.

Because of growing debts, he and his family moved back to Salem, where in 1845 he took a position as a surveyor in the custom house (an official charged with collecting taxes on imported and exported goods). He lost this job in 1848, but in 1850 he published his major novel *The Scarlet Letter*, bringing him some measure of fame and financial security. He followed this novel with *The House of the Seven Gables* in 1851, *The Blithedale Romance* in 1852 (a novel based on his disillusionment with Brook Farm, a commune in Massachusetts where he lived in 1841), and *The Marble Faun* in 1860. Meanwhile, he produced dozens of short stories that are considered classics of American literature: "My Kinsman, Major Molineux," "Roger Malvin's Burial," the witchcraft story "Young Goodman Brown," "Rappaccini's Daughter," "Ethan Brand," "The Minister's Black Veil," and many others. He also wrote literature for children, including *A Wonder Book for Girls and Boys* (1852) and its sequel, *Tanglewood Tales for Girls and Boys* (1853).

In 1853 Hawthorne was appointed to a consulship in Liverpool, England, by his old college friend and classmate President Franklin Pierce.

After the position was eliminated in 1857, he toured Italy before returning home. He died in his sleep of undetermined causes on May 19, 1864, in Plymouth, New Hampshire.

PLOT SUMMARY

"The Birth-Mark" is set in the latter part of the eighteenth century. Aylmer is introduced as a highly proficient scientist and student of natural philosophy. He decides, though, to put aside his work in his laboratory to take a wife, Georgiana, a remarkably beautiful woman with one flaw, at least in Aylmer's estimation: she has a small birthmark in the shape of a human hand on her left cheek. Shortly after their marriage, Aylmer asks her whether she has ever considered having the birthmark removed. Georgiana replies that others have found the birthmark charming. Aylmer replies that on another, less perfect face, it might add to her beauty, but on hers, it "shocks" him "as being the visible mark of earthly imperfection." Georgiana is initially angry, but her anger turns to sadness as she wonders how Aylmer could love anything that shocks him.

As time passes, Aylmer becomes increasingly obsessed with the birthmark—an obsession Georgiana begins to share as she sees how much her husband dislikes it. Because the birthmark represents the imperfections of the natural world, Aylmer finds it entirely intolerable. Georgiana asks her husband about a dream he had the previous night. Aylmer talked in his sleep, and his wife heard him say, "It is in her heart now—we must have it out." Aylmer recalls the dream, in which he removed the birthmark with a knife and had to cut so deep that he had to cut his wife's heart out. Georgiana has no idea what the consequences of removing the birthmark might be, but she agrees to allow her husband to do so, believing that the birthmark has made her an object of disgust and horror to him.

So that he can better supervise his experiments, Aylmer moves Georgiana to an apartment connected with his laboratory. When Georgiana enters his laboratory, Aylmer "could not restrain a strong convulsive shudder," causing Georgiana to faint. At this point, Aylmer's assistant, Aminadab, appears and expresses his opinion that if Georgiana were his wife, he would allow the birthmark to remain.

MEDIA ADAPTATIONS

- "The Birthmark" is available on an audiocassette produced by DH Audio in 1998.
- Another audio version of "The Birthmark" was produced by Jimcin Recordings in 2007. Running time is 43 minutes.
- "The Birthmark" is available as a free MP3 download at several Internet sites, including BeeMP3 (http://beemp3.com/download.php?file=3259103&song=The+Birth+Mark).

Georgiana recovers, and Aylmer shows her the results of some of his scientific investigations. Among them is a flower that dies when Georgiana touches it. He also proposes to make a likeness of her through a scientific process that seems similar to early photography. The image, though, is blurry, except for the birthmark, so Aylmer destroys it. He then describes the history of alchemy and the quest to find "the Golden Principle," which "might be elicited from all things vile and base." He shows her a poison he has concocted, as well as a cosmetic for removing freckles. Georgiana asks whether he will use this cosmetic to remove the birthmark. Aylmer replies that the cosmetic can treat only surface imperfections and that he needs to use something that will reach more deeply. As Aylmer questions her about her physical sensations and comfort, Georgiana begins to suspect that her husband has already begun to drug her, either through the air or in her food.

As Aylmer works in the laboratory, Georgiana finds a book in which her husband has outlined his past experiments. The volume is "rich with achievements" yet is also "the sad confession . . . of the short-comings of the composite man—the spirit burthened [burdened] with clay and working in matter." Aylmer enters and finds his wife weeping over the book. He tells her that "it is dangerous to read in a sorcerer's books," but Georgiana replies, "It has made me worship you more than ever." Alymer then asks her to sing for him, which she does, pouring out "the liquid music of her voice."

As Aylmer works, Georgiana watches him. Alymer is irritated, accusing her of having no trust in him. Georgiana replies that she believes he has no trust in her. She then demands that he explain to her what he proposes to do. Aylmer concedes that he has tried various potions on her without her knowledge, but all have been unsuccessful. However, there is one more possibility, although it is dangerous. By now, Georgiana is willing to undergo any treatment before the birthmark drives them both mad. Aylmer sends his wife to her room and continues working.

Finally, Aylmer brings to his wife a drug, which she willingly drinks. She falls asleep, and her husband keeps watch over her. As he does, he notices that the birthmark is fading and is almost gone. At this point, he hears a low chuckle from Aminadab. Georgiana awakens, only to tell her husband that she is dying. She tells her husband not to repent the fact "that, with so high and pure a feeling, you have rejected the best that earth could offer." The hoarse laugh from Aminadab is heard again.

CHARACTERS

Aminadab

Aminadab is Aylmer's assistant. He is described as a man of "low stature, but bulky frame, with shaggy hair hanging about his visage, which was grimed with the vapors of the furnace." He is described as incapable of understanding any of the scientific principles that are Aylmer's stock in trade, but he is able to execute practical matters. He is said to "represent man's physical nature," in contrast to the intellectualism of Aylmer. Incidentally, the name Aminadab is taken from the Bible, appearing in the books of Exodus, Numbers, 1 Chronicles, Ruth, Matthew, and Luke.

Aylmer

Aylmer is the protagonist of "The Birth-Mark." He is a "man of science—an eminent proficient in every branch of natural philosophy." He is described as a pale, melancholy man totally absorbed by his scientific pursuits, perhaps hoping that he "should lay his hand on the secret of creative force, and perhaps make new worlds for himself." The essence of the story is his obsession with a birthmark—an imperfection—on the cheek of his new wife, Georgiana. To Aylmer, the birthmark is a symbol of human imperfection on an otherwise perfect face. He wants to remove the birthmark, which he tries to do with a potion, but the potion kills his wife. In the end, the narration says that Aylmer "reached a profounder wisdom," at last gleaning that "he need not thus have flung away the happiness, which would have woven his mortal life of the self-same texture with the celestial."

Georgiana

Georgiana is Aylmer's new wife. She is described as remarkably beautiful, although her beauty is marred, at least in the estimation of her husband, by a small birthmark in the shape of a human hand on her left cheek. She had begun to believe that the birthmark was charming, principally because others thought it so. But when she realizes that the birthmark "shocks" her husband and ultimately disgusts him, she agrees to allow him to try to remove it. She drinks a potion that appears initially to be successful in removing the birthmark, but the potion kills her: "As the last crimson tint of the birth-mark—that sole token of human imperfection—faded from her cheek, the parting breath of the now perfect woman passed into the atmosphere."

THEMES

Science

"The Birth-Mark" is set in the latter part of the eighteenth century. The reader is told that in those days "the comparatively recent discovery of electricity, and other kindred mysteries of nature, seemed to open paths into the region of miracle." Aylmer is a scientist who devotes himself to his research:

> Seated calmly in this laboratory, the pale philosopher had investigated the secrets of the highest cloud-region, and of the profoundest mines; he had satisfied himself of the causes that kindled and kept alive the fires of the volcano; and had explained the mystery of fountains.... He had studied the wonders of the human frame, and attempted to fathom the very process by which Nature assimilates all her precious influences for earth and air, and from the spiritual world, to create and foster Man.

TOPICS FOR FURTHER STUDY

- Investigate colonial American Puritans using traditional and online resources. Who were the Puritans? What did they want to "purify"? Why did they come to the New World? What impact did they have on American culture, literature, government, and values? What is the relationship, if any, between the Puritans and the Pilgrims? Focus on one or more of these questions in depth, and present the results of your investigation in an essay.
- Imagine that you have been given the task of providing illustrations for an edition of Hawthorne's stories, including "The Birth-Mark." Using the Internet, find illustrations that you think might represent the major characters, Aylmer's laboratory, and the like. Share your images with your classmates in a PowerPoint or Slideshare presentation.
- What do you think Hawthorne might have thought of cloning and other forms of bioengineering in modern life—all attempts to conquer nature and mortality through science? Write a brief short story that takes up the topic. Share your story on your social networking site and invite your classmates to comment.
- Among the characters in Theodora Goss's "The Mad Scientist's Daughter" (2010) is Beatrice Rappaccini, a character in Hawthorne's short story "Rappaccini's Daughter"—a story that bears comparison with "The Birth-Mark." Goss's story is available at the Strange Horizons Web site (http://www.strangehorizons.com/2010/20100118/daughter-f.shtml). Read the story, then imagine that Georgiana survived Aylmer's treatment to join the characters' discussions. Write a script that includes her, then share your script with your classmates, perhaps by acting it out.
- A series of stories that have remained popular with young-adult readers and fans of the "mad scientist" theme in science fiction are the "Herbert West—Reanimator" stories by H. P. Lovecraft, first published in 1922 but available in *Dagon and Other Macabre Tales*, edited by S. T. Joshi (Arkham House, 1986). Like Aylmer, Herbert West tries to conquer nature—in his case, by reanimating corpses. Read Lovecraft's tales, then write a review of them in the voice of Nathaniel Hawthorne. Share your review with your classmates on your blog or social networking site.
- "The Birth-Mark" makes reference to a number of scientific concepts, including electricity, photography, and of course drugs, including medicinal plants and poisons (much as Botox is a toxin used today for cosmetic purposes and as a cure for a variety of ailments). Research the history of medical science in the late eighteenth and early nineteenth centuries. Prepare a chart of scientific (and pseudoscientific) advances, perhaps with illustrations. Use Jing.com to assemble a presentation of your findings for your classmates.

That he is a "pale philosopher" married to a strikingly beautiful woman suggests a sexual theme, for Aylmer as an intellectual finds it difficult to accept the imperfections of his earthly, sexual wife, with her "liability to sin, sorrow, decay, and death," and thus, as a scientist, wants to correct them.

Nature

Closely related to the theme of science is that of nature, in particular, the imperfection of the material world and the efforts of scientists to conquer nature. Early on, the reader is told that "Aylmer possessed this degree of faith in man's ultimate control over nature." He searches for the "Elixir Vitae," or the "Elixir of Life," a substance that will defeat nature by conferring immortality. He also explains to his wife the history of alchemists,

> who spent so many ages in quest of the universal solvent, by which the Golden Principle might be elicited from all things vile and base. Aylmer appeared to believe, that, by the plainest scientific logic, it was altogether within the limits of possibility to discover this long-sought medium.

Perfection

The quest for perfection—or at least the eradication of imperfection—lies at the heart of "The Birth-Mark." Aylmer's wife, Georgiana, is described as a "living specimen of ideal loveliness," but she is flawed, in his view, by the presence of a birthmark on her cheek. Aylmer becomes obsessed with the birthmark, seeing it as emblematic of imperfection. As a scientist, he wants to erase the birthmark, but he fails to understand, despite his telling dream, that human imperfection extends far below the surface of the skin into the human heart. In trying to eliminate the birthmark, he kills his wife, for it is only through death that human imperfection can be ended.

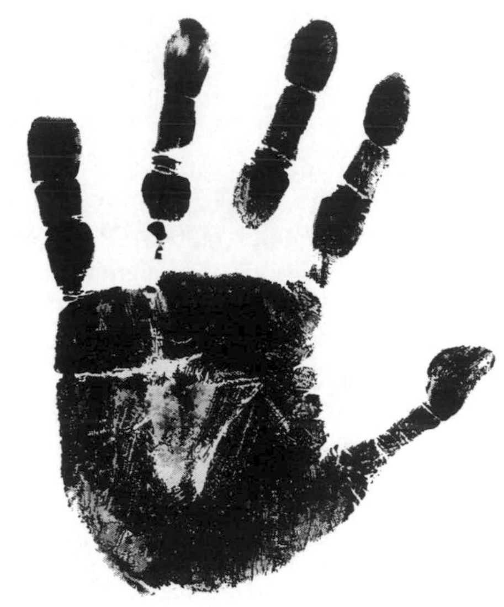

Georgiana's birthmark is shaped like a hand.
(ducu59us / Shutterstock.com)

Puritanism

"The Birth-Mark" does not make explicit reference to the nation's Puritan heritage, but Puritanism was part of Hawthorne's family and cultural origins. He grew up in Salem, Massachusetts, best remembered in American history as the site of the Salem witch trials in the seventeenth century. (Strictly speaking, the trials took place in a separate community, Salem Village, but the proximity of the two locales eroded the distinction over time.) Hawthorne's own ancestors were Puritans, and one of his great-great-grandfathers presided as a judge in the Salem witch trials.

While the early Puritans held to a number of theological tenets, an important one was their belief in the depravity of humans—in their essential sinfulness. This was a view that Hawthorne did not refute, and Harold Bloom quotes Hawthorne's journal as stating, "There is evil in every human heart." In "The Birth-Mark," Georgiana is never depicted as evil; quite the contrary. But she is human, and therefore she is weighted with the human imperfection wrought by original sin. This imperfection is signified by the "Crimson Hand," which suggests the mark of Satan. In contrast to his Puritan ancestors, though, Hawthorne calls implicitly for acceptance of human imperfection. At the end of the story, Aylmer achieves a "profounder wisdom," realizing that "he need not thus have flung away the happiness, which would have woven his mortal life of the self-same texture with the celestial."

STYLE

Allegory

"The Birth-Mark" is in many respects an allegorical story. An allegory is any symbolic narrative that suggests a secondary meaning that is not explicit on the surface. In this sense, an allegory is similar to a parable or a fable. Some allegories rely on personification, where the characters represent recognizable types. A good example from English literature is John Bunyan's *The Pilgrim's Progress*, in which characters, through their names—such as Christian, Despair, Feeble-mind, Evangelist, and Great-heart—represent abstract concepts and various Christian ideas.

Other allegories are described as symbolic allegories. In these, the characters have identities apart from the abstract concepts they represent. "The Birth-Mark" is an example of the latter type. Thus, Alymer might be regarded as symbolic of the arrogant scientist who wants to conquer nature, but within the confines of the story, he is a character, not purely an abstraction. The birthmark itself is an allegorical representation of human imperfection, of man's fall from grace. Aminadab, with his coarse, shaggy appearance and low chuckle, is said to "represent man's physical nature." In the end, when Aylmer's experiment on his wife fails, Aminadab can be heard chuckling, as though the earth is laughing at Aylmer for his arrogance.

Symbolism

As would be expected in an allegorical story, "The Birth-Mark" relies heavily on symbolism. The chief symbol is Georgiana's birthmark, which the narrator says is a mark of human imperfection. That the birthmark is in the shape of a hand is symbolic, for it suggests the hand of Satan. It is also significant that the birthmark is on her left cheek. In Latin, the word for "left" is *sinestra*, from which the English word "sinister" is derived. Thus, left-handedness and "left-ness" in general have traditionally been associated with evil, inauspiciousness, or ill luck (despite the fact that a disproportionate number of artists, musicians, U.S. presidents, and the like have been left-handed). By placing the birthmark on Georgiana's left cheek, Hawthorne suggests that it is somehow sinister, associated with the depravity and imperfections of the human condition.

Much of the action of "The Birth-Mark" is similarly symbolic. For example, as Aylmer is dreaming, he talks in his sleep and says, referring to the birthmark, "It is in her heart now—we must have it out." The clear implication is that Georgiana's imperfections extend below the surface into her heart. The only way to eradicate her imperfections is not to treat the surface manifestation but to root the evil out of her heart. Similarly, the chuckling and hoarse laughter of Aminadab can be thought of as symbolic of the earth, of matter, scoffing at the efforts of humans to conquer the natural world.

Allusion

An allusion is a reference, either direct or indirect, to another literary or artistic work. In "The Birth-Mark," Hawthorne alludes to the myth of Pygmalion, a story told in *Metamorphoses* by the classical Roman author Ovid. The myth concerns a sculptor, Pygmalion, who is convinced that women are faulty, so he resolves never to marry. But he winds up falling in love with one of his own marble sculptures, that of a beautiful woman. He then prays to the gods to send him a woman just like the statue to be his wife. In response, Venus, the goddess of love, imbues the statue with life. The sculptor, overjoyed that his marble creation has become real, marries her, with Venus's blessing. Like the sculptor in the Pygmalion myth, Aylmer cannot accept imperfection in the woman he marries; thus, he tries to change her.

"The Birth-Mark" also alludes very indirectly to the story of Adam and Eve in the Garden of Eden, as related in the first book of the Bible, Genesis. Aylmer, the intellectual scientist, is celibate. He is tempted away from his laboratory, though, by a beautiful woman, much as Adam was tempted by Eve. The woman, though, is earthly and human. She is marked by the hand of Satan with a birthmark. Like Eve, she is slightly vain; about her birthmark she says, "it has been so often called a charm, that I was simple enough to imagine it might be so." Aylmer, like Adam, is prideful and in his own way tries to improve on God's creation. In the process, he destroys the Edenic purity and simplicity of Georgiana's inner nature. In the end, she dies as a result of his efforts. Aylmer, though, achieves a "profounder wisdom," much as Adam and Eve achieve a kind of wisdom through their fall from grace and defiance of God. Like Adam, Aylmer has eaten from the Tree of Knowledge of Good and Evil (a reference to the source of the apple that Eve eats, then shares with Adam), leading to a recognition of human imperfection.

HISTORICAL CONTEXT

"The Birth-Mark" makes no reference to specific historical events. It was written, though, at a time when science was undergoing a radical transformation, and writers and intellectuals were thinking about the relationships among science, theology, philosophy, technology, and the social sciences. Of particular concern among many thinkers was that scientists, by attempting

COMPARE & CONTRAST

- **1700s:** Scientists, including physicians, study what is called "natural philosophy," meaning attempts to understand the natural world.

  1840s: New, more modern sciences have developed, spurred by advances in geology, physics (especially electromagnetism), and organic chemistry. Positivism is a leading intellectual trend that advocates use of the scientific method. Many scientists are gentleman amateurs.

  Today: The scientific method is firmly entrenched, with formally trained scientists and medical researchers conducting controlled experiments and submitting their results for publication and peer review.

- **1700s:** Scientists conduct experiments to study electricity. Benjamin Franklin conducts such experiments, and Luigi Galvani, Alessandro Volta, and others make major advances in the study of electricity.

  1840s: Electrical engineering becomes an important scientific field through the work of such figures as André-Marie Ampère, Michael Faraday (inventor of the electric motor), and Georg Ohm.

  Today: Electricity is part of the fabric of modern life, used in virtually every tool and appliance in homes and industry.

- **1700s:** Most of the scientific advances necessary for photography, including the discovery of such substances as silver nitrate and silver chloride, are in place.

  1840s: Photography is nearly two decades old, with the first photographs dating from the 1820s. The calotype process, which creates negative images, is just two years old.

  Today: Chemical film cameras, while still in use, have been rapidly replaced by digital cameras, which can produce, store, and transmit images electronically.

---

to unlock the secrets of the material universe, were in effect usurping the place of God.

In the eighteenth century, when "The Birth-Mark" is set, "science," as the term is understood in the twenty-first century, was in its infancy. The principles of the scientific method, with its emphasis on observation and experimentation, had been established by such earlier scientists as Galileo Galilei and Johannes Kepler in the late sixteenth and early seventeenth centuries. The eighteenth century came to be called the Enlightenment or the Age of Reason because thinkers began to adopt the scientific method in their quest to replace tradition and blind religious faith with skepticism and a quest for empirical truth—truth that could be ascertained by the evidence of the senses. By the late eighteenth century, many scientists were pursuing the study of what was then called "natural philosophy," in attempts to understand the workings of the universe through the study of astronomy, the elements, mechanics, motion, light, etiology (that is, causes), and the like. These scientists laid the foundation for experimental science, as the term is understood in the modern world. Wonder was to be replaced by understanding, faith by skepticism, belief by proof, priests by men of science.

In the early nineteenth century, scientific knowledge began to explode. Developments in such fields as physics (especially electricity and electromagnetism), biology, chemistry, anatomy, and other fields were reshaping people's understanding of the physical world. Achievements in geology were bringing into question traditional Judeo-Christian beliefs about the origin and age of the universe as reflected in the biblical book of Genesis: the fossil record was showing that the earth was much older than the Bible suggested, and it was beginning to suggest that creation was not an event but an evolutionary process stretching across vast expanses of time.

Many people, though, were growing increasingly disquieted by these developments. They saw the quest for scientific, empirical truth as a denial of creativity and the imagination. They believed that science took an overly mechanistic view of the natural order, attempting to reduce it to the clarity of mathematics. At its worst, science was an attack on nature, an endeavor that suggested that the human imperative was to conquer nature rather than to be part of it or to live in harmony with it. This was a point of view given expression in Mary Shelley's classic 1818 novel *Frankenstein*, which depicts the arrogance of science through the manipulation of nature.

The result of this backlash against Age of Reason science was the emergence of an intellectual trend that has been called romantic science, a trend that emerged at about the beginning of the nineteenth century and extended roughly to the time of the publication of "The Birth-Mark," or perhaps later, to the 1859 publication of Darwin's *On the Origin of Species*. There was no formal body of scientists who called themselves "romantic scientists," nor was there a text or manifesto to which these scientists adhered. "Romantic science" is a term that loosely describes a new attitude toward science. It was a view that resisted efforts to reduce the natural world to a set of mechanistic forces; for this reason, romantic science has often been described as antireductionist. Romantic scientists warned against the abuse of science to manipulate nature, and in particular to manipulate human beings, much as Aylmer manipulates Georgiana in "The Birth-Mark." Romantic scientists wanted to preserve the place of mankind within the natural order, and they argued that the natural order could be understood only in the context of self-understanding. The romantic scientists wanted not a cold, analytical, statistical understanding of nature but rather one that would reunite man with nature and the natural state. These views found their way into the romantic poetry of such British writers as William Wordsworth, Percy Bysshe Shelley, and John Keats and the prose of such American writers as James Fenimore Cooper (in the "Leatherstocking Tales"), Ralph Waldo Emerson (in numerous essays such as "Nature"), Henry David Thoreau (in *Walden)*, and Nathaniel Hawthorne.

Within romantic science, a handful of names stand out. Friedrich Schlegel wrote that "all art should become science and all science art; poetry and philosophy should be made one." Friedrich Schelling, the German idealist philosopher, referred to what he called *Naturphilosophie* (meaning, in throwback phrasing, "natural philosophy"), a philosophy of science that called for the reunification of man and nature. Sir Humphry Davy urged scientists to cultivate admiration for nature, even a sense of love and worship based on a highly personal response to nature. Biologist Jean-Baptiste Lamarck sought to replace mechanistic views of biology with views based on the belief that living organisms cannot be understood entirely by the laws of mechanics. Alexander von Humboldt tried to unite science and beauty. Johann Wolfgang von Goethe conducted experiments in which he claimed to prove that color was not a function of mechanistic optics but rather something inherent to human perception. Medical researchers adopted a view they referred to with the Latin phrase *vis medicatrix naturae*, or "healing powers of nature." Many believed that the source of health and healing lay within the natural world and that human intervention was of limited value.

In sum, the romantic scientists attempted to forge harmony between man and nature. Nature was no longer something to be parsed, analyzed, reduced, and conquered. It could be seen, perhaps, but not appreciated under a microscope. Rather, humanity and human perceptions were part of the natural order of things, and an understanding of nature required an understanding of harmony, connectedness, and human imagination—all elements that Aylmer denies in "The Birth-Mark."

The end of romantic science is often dated to the 1840s, when Auguste Comte was publishing his views on what he called positivism. Just as romantic science had been a backlash against Enlightenment views, positivism was a backlash against romantic science. Comte was a social scientist, but his goal was the application of the scientific method to social questions. His views gained ascendancy and continue to be applied to scientific questions today—although in the contemporary world, many people have adopted a more "romantic" view of science in the wake of such detrimental by-products of science as pollution, oil spills, atomic weaponry, biological and chemical weapons, bioengineering, cloning, and other applications of science that are destructive or perceived to be so.

Aylmer, a student of alchemy, wants to experiment to remove the birthmark. (Mirek Hejnicki / Shutterstock.com)

CRITICAL OVERVIEW

"The Birth-Mark" has been a rich mine for scholars and critics. In "The Genesis of Hawthorne's 'The Birthmark,'" Karl P. Wentersdorf traces the origins of the story in Hawthorne's personal life and in earlier literature. He notes, for example, that Shakespeare's *The Tempest*, like "The Birth-Mark,"

> is also an allegory on the eternal conflict between the spiritual and the sensual in humanity. Prospero, a man of science and reason, personifies intellectuality; his servant Caliban, a creature of brute ignorance and rank desire, typifies animality. They are paralleled in "The Birthmark."

John Gatta, Jr., focuses attention on the alchemical origins of the story. In "Aylmer's Alchemy in 'The Birthmark,'" he writes,

> The critical action of the tale is nothing less than an attempt on Aylmer's part to transmute the *prima materia* of Georgianna's human nature to a "golden" state of perfection, purging it of those normal earthly impurities that come to appear comparatively "vile and base" to the eye of the impassioned seeker.

Similarly, Robert D. Arner, in "The Legend of Pygmalion in 'The Birthmark,'" examines Hawthorne's use of the Pygmalion legend, noting that "the sculptor's story contains several key parallels to Hawthorne's tale. In the two protagonists . . . we have men whose work suggests the triumph of man's creative intellect over nature."

Still other critics explore the story's Puritan origins. In "Hawthorne's 'The Birthmark': Puritan Inhibitions and Romantic Appeal in the Context of the Faustian Quest," Roberto di Pietro concludes,

> In this tendency to exaggerate and make too much of a *real* but none the less *acceptable* flaw, Hawthorne takes the measure of Aylmer's Puritanism. That this particular aspect of the scientist's attitude reflects Hawthorne's idea of the Puritans' error of judgment one can hardly deny: like them, Aylmer shows a commendable amount of realism in detecting the basic "flaw"—but like them also, he is incapable of ascribing to it the proper degree of importance.

Other critics have focused on the imagery and symbolism of the story. A good example is Lewis B. Horne's essay "The Heart, the Hand and 'The Birthmark.'" As the title suggests, the writer examines the interplay of heart and hand images in the story and concludes that

> the journey into Aylmer's heart, is, in effect, what the reader makes with the unwitting and loving Georgiana when she moves into her husband's laboratory; and the clues to her danger appear in the references to Aylmer's hand.

Finally, some critics have looked at "The Birth-Mark" through a social and ideological lens. In "Eve's Daughter, Mary's Child: Women's Representation in Hawthorne's 'The Birthmark,'" Kary Meyers Skredsvig examines the issue of gendered identities in the story and notes,

> "The Birthmark" clearly revolves around a major concern of mid-nineteenth century U.S. society, the role of science in humans' lives, but in so doing it manifests crucial issues of gender identity and roles at personal and social levels.

Thus, she states, "Aylmer is not only introduced in the loftiest of terms, but is consistently associated throughout the story with the highest of intentions, standards, and worth." In contrast, "Georgiana herself describes her own level of comprehension as 'simple.'"

CRITICISM

Michael J. O'Neal

O'Neal holds a Ph.D. in English. In the following essay, he examines Hawthorne's use of imagery in "The Birth-Mark."

As an allegory, Nathaniel Hawthorne's "The Birth-Mark" might have run the risk of depicting characters and action in purely abstract terms, so that, for example, Aylmer would become little more than a pale, melancholy representation of a man of science bent on mastering the physical world. Perhaps one of the reasons that Hawthorne's work endures, though, is that he was able to root his fiction firmly in a sensory world, giving his stories a texture and depth that they might otherwise lack.

One way in which Hawthorne accomplishes this task is through his rich use of imagery. In literature, *imagery* refers to any language that evokes a sensory response. The most common type of imagery is visual: a visual image invites the reader to see the details of the setting. But other types of imagery, including sound, smell, texture, and the like, are common as well. The purpose of imagery, though, is not simply to create sensory effects. A person could toss off the word "scratchy" or "green," and these words, as far as they go, are images. In literature, imagery is an important way to create a train of associations or render an abstraction in concrete terms to elicit from the reader an emotional or intellectual response. The imagery of "The Birth-Mark" prevents the story from becoming simply an essay on science, or pride, or the futility of seeking perfection in humanity, or the depravity of the human heart, or any other theme that the reader might take away. The imagery places the characters in a physical milieu that guides the reader's response to the story.

Here, for example, is Hawthorne on Georgiana's birthmark:

> Had she been less beautiful . . . [Aylmer] might have felt his affection heightened by the prettiness of this mimic hand, now vaguely portrayed, now lost, now stealing forth again, and glimmering to-and-from with every pulse of emotion that throbbed within her heart.

The birthmark itself is not just a mark, but a "hand." The hand is a "mimic" hand, a word that suggests imitation and that is etymologically related to *mime*, referring to an actor, further suggesting that the birthmark is vital, not just a blotch of color. The birthmark is said to be sometimes "stealing forth," suggesting something furtive or underhanded. The birthmark is sometimes "glimmering," and Georgiana does more than simply have emotions: her emotions move in a "pulse," and they "throbbed." The imagery creates an almost sensual picture of Aylmer's young bride that contrasts sharply with his pale intellectualism. Aylmer thinks; Georgiana feels.

This distinction between thinking and feeling is one that is important to "The Birth-Mark." This distinction is reflected in a further distinction, between masculine and feminine. Aylmer lives in a masculine world of the intellect. It is a world of the *Transactions of the Royal Society*, of the laboratory, of beakers, furnaces, fire, and smoke. His world is the material world inhabited by the hoarse, shaggy Aminadab, "grimed with the vapors of the furnace," who wells up from the laboratory like a creature emerging from the earth—all images that reflect his earthly, "base" nature.

WHAT DO I READ NEXT?

- Hawthorne's major work is his 1850 novel *The Scarlet Letter*, an allegorical tale of sin, guilt, and redemption set in early colonial America. The novel is widely available.
- Hawthorne's "Rappaccini's Daughter" is a short story first published in 1844. It bears comparison with "The Birth-Mark" in that it, too, involves science—in this case, a medical researcher with a darkly mysterious daughter. The story is widely available, as is Hawthorne's "Dr. Heidegger's Experiment" (published in *Twice-Told Tales* in 1837), about a doctor who claims to have water from the Fountain of Youth and conducts an experiment with it on a group of friends.
- The Elixir of Life, a product of the Philosopher's Stone, plays a prominent role in J. K. Rowling's first young-adult "Harry Potter" novel, published in Great Britain as *Harry Potter and the Philosopher's Stone* and in the United States under the title *Harry Potter and the Sorcerer's Stone* (1999).
- Edgar Allan Poe's "The Oval Portrait," first published in 1842, is a mysterious story about an artist's obsession with his young bride as he is creating a painting of her.
- Readers who want to explore the history of nineteenth-century American medicine, both as a science and as a social science, might start with William G. Rothstein's *American Physicians in the Nineteenth Century: From Sects to Science* (1972).
- Readers interested in a modern take on the science of alchemy will find it in *The Alchemist* (1993), a young-adult novel by Brazilian author Paolo Coelho.
- "Pygmalion" is a story about a sculptor who falls in love with a statue he has created and who marries it after it is brought to life. The story originated in Ovid's *Metamorphoses* and was retold in the play *Pygmalion*, by George Bernard Shaw (first produced in 1913), which in turn became the basis for the modern musical *My Fair Lady*, by Alan Jay Lerner, produced first on the stage in 1956, then on film in 1964.
- A classic novel about the arrogance of scientific attempts to control creation that has been enjoyed by generations of young adults is Mary Shelley's *Frankenstein* (1818).
- Mary Pearson's *The Adoration of Jenna Fox* (2009) has emerged as a modern young-adult classic about the ethics of bioengineering.
- *Birthmarked* (2010), by Caragh M. O'Brien, is a young-adult fantasy novel about a girl, Gaia, with a burn scar on her face—which denies her entry to the gene pool in the walled city of the Enclave.

Georgiana, in contrast, inhabits a world that is overwhelmingly feminine:

> When Georgiana recovered consciousness, she found herself breathing an atmosphere of penetrating fragrance, the gentle potency of which had recalled her from her deathlike faintness. The scene around her looked like enchantment. Aylmer had converted those smoky, dingy, sombre rooms... into an abode of a lovely woman. The walls were hung with gorgeous curtains.... And as they fell from the ceiling to the floor, their rich and ponderous folds, concealing all angles and straight lines, appeared to shut in the scene from infinite space.... [Aylmer] now knelt by his wife's side, watching her earnestly, but without alarm; for he was confident in his science, and felt that he could draw a magic circle round her, within which no evil might intrude.

The sensory imagery creates a feminine world of enchantment, a fairy-tale world where Aylmer, the magician and sorcerer, can isolate Georgiana and protect her from evil. Here, "perfumed lamps" are "emitting flames of various hue, but all uniting in a soft, empurpled radiance." Aylmer wants to transcend mortality and the imperfect world of clay through science. One of his strategies is to isolate Georgiana, to wrap her in a feminine world of fragrance and hue. Georgiana, like many of Hawthorne's heroines, is willing to submit to Aylmer, in effect to sacrifice herself to his magic and sorcery.

It is possible to see a sexual theme in this imagery. Some of Hawthorne's women are characterized by a bit of a wild side, a vitality and sexuality that threatened both the underpinnings of Hawthorne's Puritan heritage and the social order in postcolonial America. The best example is Hester Prynne, the protagonist of *The Scarlet Letter*, who bears an illegitimate child fathered by a weak minister appropriately named Arthur *Dimmes*dale. She is a woman of fire and heat, in contrast to her appropriately named husband, Roger *Chilling*worth, and she pays a steep price for her humanity. In "The Birth-Mark," Georgiana is depicted as sexually attractive, and her very sexuality, enhanced by the birthmark, is tempting to "many a desperate swain" who "would have risked life for the privilege of pressing his lips to the mysterious hand." Aylmer, perhaps reflecting Hawthorne's own insecurities about his "manhood" and sexuality (Hawthorne was notoriously shy and conflicted about his vocation as a writer, sometimes expressing the view that writing and creativity were "feminine"), has to shackle and confine this sexuality, and ultimately to root it out. He thus converts a portion of his laboratory to a boudoir, where Georgiana learns to "worship" him—referring to the book in which he details his experiments, she says, "It has made me worship you more than ever"—and, in worshipping him, gives up her life.

Here is where literature diverges sharply from philosophy and history. The latter disciplines deal with the general. They explain. They take the raw materials of the world and squeeze out their essence in literal terms. Literature, in contrast, deals with the particular. Hawthorne could have written an essay about the arrogance of science, about the depravity of the human heart, about the connectedness of thought and feeling, about the admixture of the material and the celestial in the human makeup. And such an essay might have been interesting and thought provoking. But like creators everywhere, he was more interested in the particular—in a particular scientist who marries a particular wife under a particular set of circumstances, all described using a set of sensory images that convey to the reader the particulars of their drama in a way that suggests more than it says. Those particulars well up from the artist's own peculiar beliefs, motivations, psychological urges, and social attitudes. Readers, then, have to tease out the meaning of the particulars, just as they have to tease out meaning from their own particular lives and circumstances. It is this appeal to the particular, created in large part through imagery, that allows a story like "The Birth-Mark" to endure, for the impulses that drive the characters may also be our own.

Georgiana is given a potion by Aylmer. *(img85th / Shutterstock.com)*

Source: Michael J. O'Neal, Critical Essay on "The Birth-Mark," in *Short Stories for Students*, Gale, Cengage Learning, 2012.

Liz Rosenberg

In the following essay, Rosenberg argues that Hawthorne "suggests in 'The Birth-Mark' that human nature is its own proof of divinity and human love its highest expression."

"THE ONLY WAY TO EFFECT A CELEBRATION OF THE BODY IS NOT THROUGH DISTILLATION—SEPARATENESS, VOYEURISM, SCIENCE, ETC.—BUT THROUGH UNIFICATION, SYMPATHY AND LOVE."

"The Birth-Mark" is a love story, like most of Hawthorne's greatest fiction, concerned with the relation between men and women. The "love" in Hawthorne's fiction seldom takes any other form—his women are not mothers but wives, not angels but household saints: even in one notable exception, Hester's relation to her daughter Pearl comes to seem peripheral to her union (or disunion) with Reverend Dimmesdale.

This question of marriage—and the larger issue of union and separation—has a special piquancy in "The Birth-Mark," perhaps largely for biographical reasons. Written in 1843, it was Hawthorne's first work of fiction following his own marriage to Sophia. It remains clearly a newlywed's story, fresh with the author's anxieties, hopes, and fears. This very freshness helps make the story as peculiar in Hawthorne's oeuvre as it is characteristic. In "The Birth-Mark" Hawthorne takes to task his own "etherealizing" protagonist; he reveals a deep suspicion of mind/body theories current in his time; and, strangest of all, he ends by praising the imperfect and mortal quality of human nature.

The story's problematic "hero," Aylmer, is a scientist, artist, aesthete—and newlywed. An idealist by nature and profession, he falls prey soon after his marriage to a haunting awareness of "his wife's liability to sin, sorrow, decay and death," symbolized by the tiny birthmark on her cheek. This mark becomes to him "the spectral Hand that wrote mortally, where he would fain have worshipped." Aylmer's personality resists this: his lifelong search, Hawthorne suggests, has been for "ultimate control over nature."

"The Birth-Mark" examines Aylmer's dilemma chiefly by way of three systems of thought: alchemy, animism, and Emersonian Transcendentalism. All three systems address the issue of union versus separation—all three also bear upon "marriage," in its larger context of spirit and matter.

Alchemical references and imagery recur throughout "The Birth-Mark," as has been amply documented by Shannon Burns, David Van Leer and others. Aylmer's scientific aims are at one with alchemy, to "ascend from one step of powerful intelligence to another, until the philosopher should lay his hand on the secret of creative force, and perhaps make new worlds for himself." Aylmer relates to his wife "a history of the long dynasty of the Alchemists," and his library is filled with alchemical and other pseudo-scientific works.

The alchemists' fundamental project stems from an ambition to "peer beyond the experimental veil in their search for an all-embracing cosmical scheme" (Read 24) and further, to effect this transformation by human will. This kind of overweening pride renders Chillingworth—Hawthorne's most famous alchemist—"a demon," and Ethan Brand "a fiend," since it suggests not only a supplanting of God's powers but a violation of the "Mystery of life." For Aylmer, as for Chillingworth and Ethan Brand, this pride leads inevitably to the Unpardonable Sin: "an intellect that triumphed over the sense of brotherhood with man, and reverence for God, and sacrificed everything to its own mighty claims!" ("Ethan Brand").

Aylmer is not only an alchemist, which is bad enough: he is a bad alchemist besides. As Burns points out, "The old alchemists searched for an integrated, unified personality; Aylmer wants a perfect and pure distillation" (Burns 154). According to Burns, the alchemical process "was carried out by a man and woman working together" (Burns 148) and several alchemical texts point to alchemy as a kind of marriage: "The Great Work . . . being equivalent to the marriage of the King and Queen" (Read 19) and "the conjunction of the masculine and feminine principles . . . sometimes indicated as a hermaphroditic figure or androgyne" (Read 17).

What Aylmer effects is not a marriage but his own wife's death, the ultimate divorce. Distillation leads to separation, separation to loss. Aylmer's failures arise from his confusion about spirit and matter. In 1841, Hawthorne had written to Sophia, at that time his fiancée, regarding mesmerism: ". . . what delusion can be more lamentable and mischievous, than to mistake the physical and material for the spiritual?" In Aylmer's "delusion," he mistakes Georgiana's physical imperfection for a spiritual one, and, in trying to cure her of her human nature, he kills her.

Animism—a word coined in the mid-nineteenth century—is a system of thought that simultaneously conflates and divorces spirit and matter. The nineteenth-century animists believed that inanimate objects—stones, clods of earth—were imbued with spirit; they also believed it "the existence of soul or spirit apart from matter" ("Animism").

Aylmer's laboratory assistant or "under-worker" is Aminadab, whose name is a reverse anagram for "bad anima." He embodies man's physical nature in its lowest form. Aylmer calls him "thou human machine . . . thou man of clay!" and "Ah, clod! Ah, earthly mass!" Aminadab is a "clod" imbued with spirit, a "bad anima" of the almost-purely physical. Aylmer represents an opposite "bad anima," etherealized man who creates "Airy figures, absolutely bodiless ideas, and forms of unsubstantial beauty. . . . " Only in his repeated failures as a scientist does Aylmer reveal "the short-comings of the composite man—the spirit burthened with clay and working in matter. . . . "

Aminadab and Aylmer are alter-egos, mirror images. Aylmer is introduced to us as "an eminent proficient in every branch of natural philosophy," while Aminadab enters as one "issued from an inner apartment, a man of low stature." Aylmer possesses "the higher nature," Aminadab "the grunt or growl of a brute." To make matters perfectly clear, Hawthorne tells us in an authorial aside that Aminadab "seemed to represent man's physical nature; while Aylmer's slender figure, and pale, intellectual face, were no less apt a type of the spiritual element." What is "bad" in both is their lack of integration. Here, as elsewhere, Hawthorne reveals his distrust of polarizing extremes: "There is no surer method of arriving at the Hall of Fantasy, than to throw oneself into the current of a theory . . . " ("The Hall of Fantasy" 180). Fanaticism, Hawthorne suggests, kills the real.

Between Aylmer, the airy intellectual, and his "bad anima," the cloddish Aminadab, stands Aylmer's wife Georgiana—associated throughout the story with love, marriage, blood, and the heart. Her name, as Burns points out, is a feminized masculine, suggesting the "Two-thing" of the alchemical process, and perhaps also *geo*, "earth," poised between the "highest cloud-region" of Aylmer and the underworld "furnace" of Aminadab. Georgiana's birthmark is controlled by her heart's blood, as is Georgiana herself: she feels the effects of Aylmer's remedy as a "tingling, half painfully, half pleasurably, at her heart." In a story about the dangers of one-strandedness, Georgiana's failure of excessive heart—while to Hawthorne the most pardonable of sins—is ultimately deadly to her. As Barbara Eckstein has pointed out, "Romance is Georgiana's religion" (511) and she dies its martyr.

If the heart sees only the heart's truth, "The Birth-Mark" indicates that it is nonetheless closer to reality than either abstraction or cloddishness. Georgiana differs from Aylmer and Aminadab not only in the nature of her failure but in her clear-sightedness. Aylmer never truly *sees* his wife; even when she is dying, he misperceives the true import of her symptoms. Aminadab, on the other hand, feels only the physical: he says, "If she were my wife, I'd never part with that birth-mark" and expresses "delight" in a "gross, hoarse chuckle" while Georgiana lies dying. But Georgiana observes her husband's failures clearly, even while she admires him for his passionate convictions. She sees herself and her situation no less accurately: "Life is but a sad possession to those who have attained precisely the degree of moral advancement at which I stand. Were I weaker and blinder, it might be happiness. Were I stronger, it might be endured hopefully." It is Georgiana who proposes the operation, Georgiana who first observes its failure: "My poor Aylmer! . . . Do not repent, that, with so high and pure a feeling, you have rejected the best that earth could offer. Aylmer—dearest Aylmer—I am dying!"

Aylmer—failed scientist, failed husband—is the very type and symbol of Emersonian Transcendentalism at its worst. He appears, indeed, almost a caricature of Emerson himself. In his journals, Hawthorne described Emerson as "a great searcher for facts; but they seem to melt away and become unsubstantial in his grasp" (Mellow 208). Of Aylmer he writes, "He handled physical details, as if there were nothing beyond them; yet spiritualized them all. . . . In his grasp, the veriest clod of earth assumed a soul."

As E. Michael Jones points out in *The Angel and the Machine*, "The age of Emerson was pre-eminently the age of the opposition of mind and matter, the age of the great clash between the mechanist and idealist philosophies" (Jones 18). Emerson was, at least according to Hawthorne, the victim of both: "Mr. Emerson—the mystic, stretching his hand out of cloud-land, in vain search for something real; and the man of sturdy sense, all whose ideas seem to be dug out of his mind, hard and substantial, as he digs potatoes" (Mellow 208). Transcendentalists like Orestes A. Brownson addressed themselves directly to this "clash" and sought to "reconcile spirit and matter" (Miller 120):

> We cannot then go back either to exclusive Spiritualism, or to exclusive Materialism. Both these systems have received so full a development, have acquired so much strength, that neither can be subdued. Both have their foundation in our nature, and both will exist and exert their influence. Shall they exist as antagonist principles? Shall the spirit forever lust against the flesh, and the flesh against the spirit? Is the bosom of Humanity to be eternally torn by these two contending factions? No. It cannot be. The war must end. Peace must be made.
>
> This discloses our Mission. We are to reconcile spirit and matter, that is, we must realize the atonement. (Miller 120)

While Brownson proposes a reconciliation and an "atonement," Hawthorne proposes a marriage. Aylmer's failure to see, love, and accept Georgiana's imperfect, human nature is the failure to live "once for all in Eternity, to find the perfect Future in the present." What Aylmer has rejected is "the happiness, which would have woven his mortal life of the self-same texture with the celestial." The recommendation is so radical that Hawthorne—while often suggesting it again in his fiction's imagery or his sympathies with some of his "darker" characters—never again proposed it so directly. The ramifications of his own beliefs would—and did—appall him. There is no great leap from Georgiana's scarlet birthmark to Hester's scarlet letter. The difference is one of degree. Georgiana is not guilty, like Hawthorne's greatest heroines, of adultery or murder—she is guilty only of being human—liable to "sin, sorrow, decay and death." Yet if love between human beings, with all their innate imperfections and frailties, is "the best that earth could offer," then Hester's final question to Dimmesdale must be read in a new light—"Shall we not spend our immortal life together? Surely, surely, we have ransomed one another, with all this woe!" (*Scarlet Letter*)—as must the minister's response: '"Hush, Hester, hush!' said he, with tremulous solemnity. 'The law we broke!—the sin here so awfully revealed!—let these alone be in thy thoughts! I fear! I fear! . . . '"

What is it that Dimmesdale and Hester are guilty of, if not expressing their human nature? Is a pro-forma marriage a stronger link in the "magnetic chain of humanity" than love? What can their adultery be if not the very thing that Aylmer has tossed away, "the happiness, which would have woven his mortal life of the self-same texture with the celestial"? Miriam's speech to Kenyon goes still further:

> ". . . How wonderful is this! I tremble at my own thoughts, yet must needs probe them to their depths. Was the crime—in which he and I were wedded—was it a blessing in that strange disguise? . . . And may we follow the analogy yet farther? Was that very sin—into which Adam precipitated himself and all his race—was it the destined means by which, over a long pathway of toil and sorrow, we are to attain a higher, brighter, and profounder happiness, than our lost birthright gave?" (*Marble Faun*)

In *The Marble Faun*, Hawthorne's only answer is to "tremble" at the mystery, "the riddle of the Soul's growth, taking its first impulse amid remorse and pain, and struggling through the incrustations of the senses" (*Marble Faun*). But that is in 1860, after years of his own struggle, remorse and pain. In 1843, writing "The Birth-Mark" he was still the hopeful newlywed, critiquing not human nature but its critic, Aylmer.

"The Birth-Mark" proposes that human nature is a compound—a sacred mystery. The only way to effect a celebration of the body is not through distillation—separateness, voyeurism, science, etc.—but through unification, sympathy and love. "The Birth-Mark" is a hymn to earthly marriage, just as the story that immediately preceded it, "The Hall of Fantasy," is a hymn to the earth itself.

> "Oh, you are ungrateful to our Mother Earth!" rejoined I. "Come what may, I never will forget her! Neither will it satisfy me to have her exist merely in idea. I want her great, round, solid self to endure interminably, and still to be peopled with the kindly race of man, whom I uphold to be much better than he thinks himself. . . . " ("The Hall of Fantasy")

Aylmer's sin is in wanting "the ideal" instead of what Hawthorne in "The Artist of the Beautiful" would call "the enjoyment of the Reality." In 1843, Hawthorne's love of reality was inseparable from his love for Sophia. He told her as much, in his letters: "Thou art my reality; and nothing is real for me, unless thou give it that golden quality by thy touch" (*Love Letters*). She was, to use the alchemist's terms, his Active Agent, her love and understanding his Philosopher's Stone. Had these been his active agents, the author of *The Scarlet Letter* preface suggests, he might have come to better love this world, the Custom House of Earth:

> It was a folly, with the materiality of this daily life pressing so intrusively upon me, to attempt to fling myself back into another age; or to insist on creating the semblance of a world out of airy matter.... The wiser effort would have been, to diffuse thought and imagination through the opaque substance of to-day, and thus to make it a bright transparency; to spiritualize the burden that began to weigh so heavily; to seek, resolutely, the true and indestructible value that lay hidden in the petty and wearisome incidents, and ordinary characters, with which I was now conversant. The fault was mine. The page of life that was spread out before me seemed dull and commonplace, only because I had not fathomed its deeper import. A better book than I shall ever write was there; leaf after leaf presenting itself to me, just as it was written out by the reality of the flitting hour, and vanishing as fast as written, only because my brain wanted the insight and my hand the cunning to transcribe it. At some future day, it may be, I shall remember a few scattered fragments and broken paragraphs, and write them down, and find the letters turned to gold upon the page. (*Scarlet Letter*)

Here is the true alchemy of connection, a marriage between spirit and matter, the love of "the best that earth could offer." It has been said that the Romantics found proof of God in nature, while the Victorians found proof of God in human doubt. Hawthorne, poised as he was between the two, suggests in "The Birth-Mark" that human nature is its own proof of divinity and human love its highest expression. It was a daring supposition, one he himself could bear neither to sustain nor to follow out to its logical conclusions. But in 1843, he set out clearly enough the questions that were to haunt him all the rest of his life.

Source: Liz Rosenberg, "'The Best That Earth Could Offer': 'The Birth-Mark,' a Newlywed's Story," in *Studies in Short Fiction*, Vol. 30, No. 2, Spring 1993, pp. 145–51.

Ellen E. Westbrook

In the following essay, Westbrook illustrates that Hawthorne's "verisimilar fictional world" in "The Birth-Mark," as well as in some of his other works, "enable[s] us to perceive what familiarity masks."

> **"INSTEAD, HAWTHORNE'S NARRATIVE MAKES PERCEPTIBLE THE SUBTLE, HERE FATAL VIOLENCE OF BOTH CHARACTERS' REALITIES THAT WE TYPICALLY DO NOT SEE, PRECISELY BECAUSE OF THEIR FAMILIARITY."**

... But "The Birth-Mark" does not affirm norms of the everyday world that we breathing readers take for granted; it generates renewed values from the conflict among the three characters and from the interpretative guidance of the narrator. At issue, of course, are not the ethical implications of striving for one's notion of perfection in itself. Instead, the narrative exposes the potentially fatal implications of such an ambition when pursued at the expense of what the narrator identifies as a fundamental aspect of reality that too often is taken for granted: Georgiana's birthmark "was the fatal flaw of humanity, which Nature, in one shape or another, stamps ineffaceably on all her productions, either to imply that they are temporary and finite, or that their perfection must be wrought by toil and pain."

In light of the tale's events, this explicit moral is a resounding understatement of what already has been demonstrated with much greater power by the tale's confluence of drama and symbol. This confluence occurs within Hawthorne's narrative play between the particular and the general pattern, the mimetic and the seemingly marvelous, the historical and the explicitly fictive, a play authorized as probable by standard conventions of romance. The understated moral does remind us when we listen closely that we are in a fictional world and under the guiding influence of a narrator's ordering consciousness. The crown of that ordering in this particular tale is the narrator's anti-climactic moral statement. Paradoxically, that statement lends credibility to the authority of the lived (fictional) experience over which the narrator's moral seems to assert judging authority by the very contrast invoked between statement and drama, cool observation and fatal event. The narrator's moral provides a neat and safe closure to the tale, then, but it is deceptively so. The almost empty resonance of this moral's generalization against the particular, referential events of the tale directs us back to those events to decipher what the specific conflict is all about.

Glancing backward, we recognize the narrator's fictional challenge to fundamental cultural values by the tension he creates between the symbolic value of a natural phenomenon and its cultural context. By means of Georgiana's death, the narrator affirms the value of nature within everyday lived experience. He does so over and against Georgiana's perspective and that of her husband. Both of these perspectives are shaped by shared assumptions of what is natural as well as by shared cultural values that proscribe a deferential role to women and an assertive, controlling role to men. But if Aylmer's and Georgiana's fictional drama is fatally problematic, the narrator's affirmation of nature in the shape of Georgiana's death is equally so. As Georgiana lives out her role under Aylmer's tutelage, she is forced in effect to comply with her own death. The narrator's affirmation of nature, then, does not supplant Aylmer's magical endeavors with an alternative that the character of Georgiana can effectively embody. Indeed, the narrator's affirmation of nature shears those endeavors of their very physical and culturally-grounded material. He thereby allots character and reader sheer loss. Hawthorne's dramatized perspective of romance implicitly asks us a fundamental question: how can we live humanely within inescapably acculturated lives?

Hawthorne brings these fundamental contradictions between nature and culture before us in part by generating his perspective of romance from what we expect within our natural and acculturated reality. His mingling of the Actual and Imaginary dislodges our point of view from our taken-for-granted everyday world and dislodges our corresponding expectations for normatively mimetic narrative. But his method only displaces us superficially from our familiar world; finally it enables Hawthorne to direct us back with a horrific glance at the potential implications of our choices as we shape cultural values at the expense of humane motives. Hawthorne's "theatre" is indeed "a little removed." But to describe his process of romance accurately, and to recognize the nature of his commitment to unseating our taken-for-granted frameworks of perception, we need to recognize his theater's proximity to everyday experience as well as its departure from it.

Our methods for such recognition have become both problematic and enriched by our debate about the relationship between fictional and non-fictional experience, by our "focus on referentiality as a problem rather than as something that reliably and unambiguously relates a reader to the 'real world' of history, of society, and of people acting within society on the stage of history" (Miller 283). Hawthorne's tales invited us into this problem long before we separated, by our theoretical debates, lived experience from aesthetic artifact, before we considered language our singularly rich and resisting access to reality, and before we contemplated the inscription of history within fiction as our means to clarify the miasma of fictional and critical discourse.

Our sometimes heated explorations of the relationship between theory, reading, and meaning help us to understand Hawthorne's particular style, his aesthetic concerns, and his place within our literary and larger social culture. They also enable us to interpret more subtly the problem Hawthorne shapes by the form of romance that he develops in his short fiction. With our discrete theoretical filters, however, we also continue to risk rarefying the problem. Symptomatic of our discretion is our critical separating out of "the Actual" from "the Imaginary" in our analysis of Hawthorne's work, an interpretative strategy that assumes methodological authority in our historical, psychoanalytic, generic, and formalist discourse. We can comprehend the problems posed by Hawthorne's short fictions more clearly if our critical methods less insistently separate what Hawthorne's forms of narrative representation integrate. We can do so by confronting directly Hawthorne's use of what is verisimilar to our natural and cultural reality in the context of his use of literary conventions.

By focusing on such standard methods of nineteenth-century American romance as idealizing, as marvelous events, and as explicit fictionalizing, we have emphasized what Hawthorne referred to as the "Imaginary" in order to explicate narrative techniques that imaginatively transform everyday experience. By focusing on the historical (Colacurcio), we have emphasized Hawthorne's "Actual" in order to explicate what we think romance transforms, usually the historical underpinnings of the fictional artistry. Rarely in our criticism of Hawthorne's work have we considered the role of everyday objects or usual circumstances (Brodhead; Schlegel; DeJong). Shannon Burns does discuss five kinds of verisimilitude used by Hawthorne in his tales: present and actual circumstances, history, character, straightforward description of the physical world, and the realism of domestic, homey detail, especially the household hearth. These categories help considerably to establish Hawthorne's use of verisimilitude. But Hawthorne's practice is considerably broader than Burns's isolated examples of what is naturally and culturally verisimilar suggest. We have considered even less the relationships among the various types of references (Michael; Kinkead-Weekes; Carton).

Further segrating the Actual and the Imaginary, we have categorized Hawthorne's longer prose fictions as romances in contrast to novels, based on loose notions of their degree of mimetic representation, and we apply similar criteria to his short fiction. The mimeticism of novelistic styles asserts a correspondence between fictions and our assumptions about nature and our acculturated lives; the less mimetic form of romance asserts its ready departure from those assumptions. We are engaged by illusion as reality in novelistic styles, and in the nineteenth-century American romance by illusion as illusion. Novelistic styles create the illusion of reality in part by heightening the impression that what literature portrays in its unnatural, artificial form is natural or at least conventional. In contrast to novelistic styles, romance makes our everyday world appear unfamiliar in order to acquaint us with a different conception of reality, yet somehow probable nevertheless. Often we conclude that romance poses against our normative perspective an other reality that claims for itself a more authoritative world view. The generic distinctions that underlie such conclusions contrast sharply with how flexible the terms "novel" and "romance" were in the nineteenth century (Baym). They also disguise that period's concern with the distinction between fiction and fact and not between kinds of fiction such as novels and romances (Bell 9).

Hawthorne's use of different kinds of verisimilitude in a tale such as "The Birth-Mark" demonstrates an artistic style and project that are much more complex than our dichotomy between novelistic and romance styles suggests. Hawthorne himself draws our attention to the complexity of his method. Glancing backward to his tales as well as forward to *The Scarlet Letter*, Hawthorne states in "The Custom-House" that under the influence of moonlight, "The floor of our familiar room has become a neutral territory, somewhere between the real world and fairy-land, where the Actual and Imaginary may meet, and each imbue itself with the nature of the other.... " But "the somewhat dim coal-fire has an essential influence in producing the effect which I would describe.... This warmer light mingles itself with the cold spirituality of the moonbeams, and communicates, as it were, a heart and sensibilities of human tenderness to the forms which fancy summons up." Hawthorne's worlds of romance become credible not because we suspend our disbelief in the face of elderly women-become-witches, scientists/ministers-become-gothic-villains, or meteors-become-symbols radiating in the sky. Instead, Hawthorne generates the perspective of his other worlds of romance partly from the confluence of such apparent oppositions; for the imaginative activity of romance, Hawthorne's early method depends upon the transforming power of coal-fire as well as of moonlight.

Hawthorne's method in a tale such as "The Birth-Mark" suggests what is at stake in the frameworks of perception that characters enact in their fiction and that we choose as readers while we make sense of the theaters we enter. Georgiana embodies the values traditionally assigned to women and with which the narrator is most sympathetic; the narrator grants her the greatest potential to resolve the ethical conflicts raised by the tale. As a near-perfected representative of our imperfect sisters, she represents our potential to choose ethical lives within an everyday world. Conversely, Aylmer introduces a deviant reality that the narrator undermines in part by portraying him in less idealized, more referential terms. As a near-perfected representative of our less imperfect brothers, he too represents our potential choices within consensus reality but ones that we typically camouflage with our taken-for-granted modes of everyday perception—a world of judgment without compassion, of rational endeavor without humane purpose. "The Birth-Mark" does not promote the idealized reality of Georgiana. Nor of course does "The Birth-Mark" promote Aylmer's divergent reality that curiously reflects our own more than does Georgiana's. Instead, Hawthorne's narrative makes perceptible the subtle, here

"THE IMPORTANCE OF HAWTHORNE'S PSYCHOLOGICAL SYMBOL IS NOT THE SUSCEPTIBILITY OF MAN TO SIN AND DEATH, BUT THE SPECIAL MANNER IN WHICH THE MARKED WOMAN SUFFERS HER FATE: IT IS AYLMER WHO KILLS HER."

fatal violence of both characters' realities that we typically do not see, precisely because of their familiarity. He does so by drawing on a range of narrative conventions to shape a verisimilar fictional world. That world portrays our everyday lives in the unfamiliar, exaggerated form allowed by the license of romance. Because the techniques of this form of Hawthorne's romance reveal difference, the unfamiliar perspectives they create enable us to perceive what familiarity masks. From these different vantage points, we are better able to renew our ethical stance within both lived and fictional experience.

Source: Ellen E. Westbrook, "Probable Improbabilities: Verisimilar Romance in Hawthorne's 'The Birth-Mark,'" in *American Transcendental Quarterly*, Vol. 3, No. 2, June 1989, pp. 203–17.

James Quinn and Ross Baldessarini

In the following essay, Quinn and Baldessarini delineate how in "The Birth-Mark" Hawthorne utilizes the narrative device of offering various characters' responses to a particular symbol.

Hawthorne's art in the creation of character in many ways anticipates modern psychoanalytic psychology. As a literary psychologist, he excels at revealing unconscious sources of obsessed behavior. In "The Birth-Mark," Aylmer, a scientist whose ambition may be to control nature, provides an exceptionally good example of an obsessive character. He is obsessed with imperfection in human nature and is unable to achieve a mature human relationship.

In this tale, although we are presented with Aylmer's intense reactions to an apparently solitary imperfection in his bride, Hawthorne does not explicitly analyze them. Indeed, the reader is conditioned to accept ambiguity and multiplicity as inevitable features of human nature. Hawthorne evidently values a balanced view of a complex world and his appreciation of complexity is no more forcefully demonstrated than in his psychological analysis of character. As we noted earlier in our analysis of "The Minister's Black Veil," a crucial technique Hawthorne employs to achieve his psychological revelations is the literary device of multiple reactions of observers to a central symbol. Here the central symbol is a red nevus on the face of Georgiana, her birth-mark. Its power to evoke strong responses stems partly from the details which Hawthorne offers about its appearance. It is in the form of a hand appearing on her left (sinister and heart side) cheek. Hawthorne makes the red more vibrant by setting it off against Georgiana's changing complexion.

This method of the central symbol provides Hawthorne with a way to intrigue us by his revelations of the thoughts, feelings, and moods of leading characters as well as lesser observers. A short passage from "The Birth-Mark" illustrates his method:

> Some fastidious persons—but they were exclusively of her own sex—affirmed that the Bloody Hand, as they chose to call it, quite destroyed the effect of Georgiana's beauty, and rendered her countenance even hideous. But it would be as reasonable to say, that one of those small blue stains which sometimes occur in purest statuary marble, would convert the Eve of Powers to a monster. Masculine observers, if the birth-mark did not heighten their admiration, contented themselves with wishing it away, that the world might possess one living specimen of ideal loveliness, without the semblance of a flaw.

We also know that "many a desperate swain would have risked life for the privilege of pressing his lips to the mysterious hand" and, toward the end of the tale, Aylmer himself, while attempting to eradicate the mark, "by a strange and unaccountable impulse . . . pressed it with his lips." Reactions to Georgiana's birth-mark vary from the attraction of Aminadab and other men, to the ambivalence of Georgiana, to the negative reactions of Aylmer. In short, the chief narrative foci are the *perceptions* of the characters themselves. Hawthorne tells us that reactions to the hand-like blemish on Georgiana's cheek vary "according to the difference of temperament in the beholders." That is to say, the "meaning" of this symbol is complex and colored by the personality of the observer. This is one of the clearest revelations by Hawthorne of his method and psychology. Hawthorne shows that an object becomes what each viewer's personalized perceptions would have it become.

Hawthorne skillfully establishes the governing centrality of the birth-mark by describing its effect mainly from the standpoint of Aylmer's "sombre imagination." Specifically, Hawthorne gives overpowering sway to Aylmer's attitude toward the birth-mark and at the same time contrasts his view with Georgiana's initially more innocent perspective. We are told, for example, that before his marriage Aylmer had thought "little or nothing of the matter," while Georgiana had always imagined that the mark on her cheek was a kind of "charm" which, if anything, enhanced rather than detracted from her beauty. Soon after marrying, however, Aylmer discovers that he can think of little else but the birth-mark, "in spite of a purpose to the contrary," and that it has become a "frightful object, causing him more trouble and horror than ever Georgiana's beauty, whether of soul or sense, had given him delight." What has happened to make Aylmer feel this way? What indeed ails him? The question is a natural one, but useless. Hawthorne does not supply an answer and by this omission seems to suggest that insights into human behavior are likely to be subjective, imperfect, unsatisfying. What is important is not the cause of obsessive thought or compulsive behavior but the effects.

The dramatic situation here is that Aylmer, by marrying Georgiana, is forced to deal with a conflict between his earlier, somewhat distant view of her as an intellectualized feminine ideal and her present tangible reality. Clearly one meaning of the red hand is a mark of her accessibility to touch, that is, of her sexuality. It also includes conflict between personal idealization and reality—a classical and ubiquitous obsessional neurotic conflict. While Aylmer's struggle is virtually universal, his fixation on Georgiana's blemish approaches a symptom that is considered characteristic of obsessive-compulsive neurosis in modern-day psycho-pathological terms. The function of such neurotic symptoms in the psychic economy is to inhibit intolerable anxiety by focusing on an isolated and somewhat concrete representation so as to avoid a larger emotional conflict.

The psychoanalytic theorist Fenichel has written, "Many compulsive neurotics have to worry very much about small and apparently insignificant things. In analysis, these small things turn out to be substitutes for important ones." And further: "Compulsive neurotics try to use external objects for the solution or relief of their inner conflicts." As "the compulsive neurotic tends . . . to extend the range of his symptoms . . . " so Aylmer's reaction to the birth-mark grew "more and more intolerable with every moment of their lives," presumably as a result of Georgiana's unavoidable presence. What at first seemed a trifling matter "so connected itself with innumerable trains of thoughts and modes of feeling, that it became the *central point of all*" [Stress added]. Like Parson Hooper, Aylmer is another Hawthornian victim of morbid forces, largely internal, beyond his control. Surely Aylmer's aversion owes its intensity and its obsessive character precisely to the fact that it is not accessible to conscious examination.

In his morbid striving toward perfection for himself, Aylmer erects a monstrous structure to avoid engaging his bride directly and intimately. It is not clear that Aylmer has ever had a mature human relationship with Georgiana. Rather, his wife appears to be a wonderful possession meant to contribute to his own self-esteem. Having captured this object of desire, he then proceeds to isolate her in a setting of stagelike opulence.

> Aylmer had converted those smoky, dingy, sombre rooms, where he had spent his brightest years in recondite pursuits, into a series of beautiful apartments, not unfit to be the secluded abode of a lovely woman. The walls were hung with gorgeous curtains, which imparted the combination of grandeur and grace, that no other species of adornment can achieve; and as they fell from the ceiling to the floor, their rich and ponderous folds, concealing all angles and straight lines, appeared to shut in the scene from infinite space.

The description seems to reinforce the distance at which he wants to keep Georgiana. Again he is master and controller and isolates Georgiana from the real world in rooms unearthly and enchanted. Intimate and sexual desires he feels for Georgiana are presumably transferred to his efforts to create the perfect chamber for the perfect woman he desires. Yet Aylmer's attempt to "shut in the scene" hints at something concealed, secretive and perhaps guilty about his quest. This impression of Aylmer's aloofness is supported by his detached and icy approach toward life generally: "He had left his laboratory to the care of an assistant, cleared his fine countenance from the furnace-smoke, washed the stains of acids from his fingers, and persuaded a beautiful woman to become his wife."

Given the aloof nature of their relationship as well as Aylmer's obsession, it is perhaps not surprising that Georgiana is victimized by her husband's ill-disguised "horror and disgust." From Hawthorne's description of the birth-mark it is clear that it would not even be visible if Aylmer could accept Georgiana's humanity, her passion and sexuality:

> In the usual state of her complexion—a healthy, though delicate bloom—the mark wore a tint of deeper crimson, which imperfectly defined its shape amid the surrounding rosiness. When she blushed, it gradually became more indistinct, and finally vanished amid the triumphant rush of blood, that bathed the whole cheek with its brilliant glow. But, if any shifting emotion caused her to turn pale, there was the mark again, a crimson stain upon the snow, in what Aylmer sometimes deemed an almost fearful distinctness.

But rather than keeping her happy, he ironically unleashes a vicious circle: his discomfort infects her with anxiety; her pallor makes the birth-mark more obvious; and his heightened anxiety completes the vicious circle. His coldness makes the problem worse: "It needed but a glance, with the peculiar expression that his face often wore, to change the roses of her cheek into a deathlike paleness, amid which the Crimson Hand was brought strongly out, like a bas-relief of ruby on the whitest marble." Then Aylmer "so started with the intense glow of the birth-mark upon the whiteness of her cheek . . . could not restrain a strong convulsive shudder." This reaction clearly typifies a neurotic vicious circle: Aylmer's anxiety leading to neurotic compromise, leading to more anxiety.

Eventually Aylmer corrupts Georgiana into accepting his deluded quest for omnipotence and perfection. She never feels the birth-mark is evil as Aylmer does, but she suddenly realizes "you cannot love what shocks you." Rather than drawing the reasonable conclusion that Aylmer's feelings toward her are grotesque, she misleads herself into believing how much more "precious" was Aylmer's sentiment "than that meaner kind which would have borne imperfection for her sake. . . . " This feat of illogic closely resembles a shared delusion and paves the way for Georgiana's ultimate destruction.

The mocking laugh of Aminadab, an ordinary if somewhat peculiar man, suggests he realizes the irony of the situation and mocks his master, Aylmer, for trying to reach too high to attain perfection and reject humanity. He senses that escape from the human condition is hubris and death; that the attempt to scale the heights leads to descent into hell; that the more man struggles to be god-like, the more he makes misery for himself and others. In fact, the odd earthman Aminadab, an embodiment of humanity's long past, in contrast to Aylmer, has a rational and pragmatic attitude: "If she were my wife, I'd never part with that birth-mark."

Aylmer, unlike Aminadab, alternates between blacks and whites rather than accepting the grays of life. He draws distinct lines between good and bad as does Young Goodman Brown, who must see Faith, indeed all women, as Madonna or whore and who therefore remains immature and uncommitted. Aylmer, too, is like an adolescent, unable to find a point of equilibrium between two poles of thought, not realizing that "to be is to be imperfect, that the price of human existence is imperfection."

An ironic aspect of such obsessed and morbid behavior so often seen in Hawthorne's works, is that the more one struggles to attain perfection or to retain an unreasonable fixed idea, the more one is caught up in dealing with its opposite—imperfection and destruction. Obsessional behavior characteristically presents such ironies: those who seek perfect cleanliness are preoccupied with dirt. Elsewhere in Hawthorne, Endicott and the Puritans in "The Maypole of Merry Mount," in their attempt to deny sensual pleasure, are constantly preoccupied with it and deal with it sadistically. While Aylmer aspires to perfection, his daily world is a secret, hellish, smokey, fume-filled place of labor cloaked with heavy curtains and giving him a strong identification with the powers of darkness, a devilish and fiendish quality. As Georgiana found:

> The first thing that struck her eyes was the furnace, that *hot* and *feverish* worker, with the intense glow of its fire, which by the quantities of *soot* clustered above it, seemed to have been *burning* for *ages* . . . The atmosphere felt *oppressively* close, and was *tainted* with gaseous odors, which had been *tormented* forth by the processes of science. [Stress added]

The culmination of this diabolical side of Aylmer is Georgiana's destruction and death in the attempt to offer her the "elixir of immortality."

There are numerous foreshadowings of the ultimate outcome of Aylmer's crazed drive. There is Georgiana's discovery of her husband's past failures, of his inability to carry past experiments to fruition. The symbol itself is characterized by Hawthorne as a mark of Original Sin or the imperfection born with man as a race, as "the fatal flaw of humanity, which Nature, in one shape or another, stamps ineffaceably on all her productions . . . to imply that they are temporary and finite. . . . " Most significant is Aylmer's dream that explicitly suggests the intense, violent and remarkably sexual reaction the birth-mark evokes in Aylmer:

> He had fancied himself with his servant Aminadab, attempting an operation for the removal of the birth-mark. But the deeper went the knife, the deeper sank the Hand, until at length its tiny grasp appeared to have caught hold of Georgiana's heart; whence, however, her husband was inexorably resolved to cut or wrench it away.

This dream seems to arise from a waking fantasy ["for before I fell asleep, it had taken a pretty firm hold of my fancy"] of the vivid and often destructive and violent kind so typical in obsessional neurosis. Hawthorne makes an extremely perceptive statement for one living in the pre-Freudian world of 1843:

> When the dream had shaped itself perfectly in his memory, Aylmer sat in his wife's presence with a guilty feeling. Truth often finds its way to the mind close-muffled in robes of sleep, and then speaks with uncompromising directness of matters in regard to which we practise an *unconscious self-deception*, during our waking moments. [Stress added]

Again typical of obsessional neurotics, Aylmer goes on to act upon his omnipotent fantasies in a most compulsive and repetitious way by drawing Georgiana into a series of experiments with "drugs, elixers and concoctions" that eventually prove fatally toxic.

Up to this point we have been concerned with Hawthorne's presentation of Aylmer as one more neurotic and troubled obsessional soul More important, however, is Aylmer's dramatically exaggerated representation of a more general struggle to adjust the ideal and the real. Likewise the birth-mark can be viewed on more than one level. It is a mark of Georgiana's accessibility to touch, of her sexuality. It is suggestive of the scarlet letter—another public sign of secret and lustful sin, of "putting hands upon" in a sexual sense, of being touched, tainted, having sexuality and womanly characteristics. And, within the Judeo-Christian tradition, as noted above, it seems to Hawthorne to symbolize the fallen and sinful nature of man. In an even wider application, it symbolizes the mortality of all mankind.

We miss the point, however, if we connect the birth-mark solely with neurotic conflicts of atypical individuals or even with the hold death has on everyone, for the mark is also connected with sexuality and new life, indeed with aspiration to beauty and achievement and with the joy and energy for living. The importance of Hawthorne's psychological symbol is not the susceptibility of man to sin and death, but the special manner in which the marked woman suffers her fate: it is Aylmer who kills her. When the inward life concentrates narcissistically on self, demonic violence flares up in the lust to control and possess another person. Yet the first to be destroyed is Aylmer himself, who steps out of the procession of life, suffering from an incapacity to accept and integrate human emotions. The price of perfection is spiritual atrophy or death, a withdrawal from what Hawthorne called "the magnetic chain of humanity."

Source: James Quinn and Ross Baldessarini, "'The Birth-Mark': A Deathmark," in *Hartford Studies in Literature*, Vol. 13, No. 2, 1981, pp. 91–98.

SOURCES

Adler, Mortimer J., *The Four Dimensions of Philosophy: Metaphysical, Moral, Objective, Categorical*, Macmillan, 1993.

Arner, Robert D., "The Legend of Pygmalion in 'The Birthmark,'" in *American Transcendental Quarterly*, No. 14, Spring 1972, pp. 168–71.

Bloom, Harold, ed., *Nathaniel Hawthorne*, Chelsea House, 2001, p. 11.

Cunningham, Andrew, and Nicholas Jardine, eds., *Romanticism and the Sciences*, Cambridge University Press, 1990.

di Pietro, Roberto, "Hawthorne's 'The Birthmark': Puritan Inhibitions and Romantic Appeal in the Context of the Faustian Quest," in *Studi e Ricerche di Letteratura Inglese e Americana*, Vol. 2, 1972, pp. 239–57.

"Friedrich Wilhelm Joseph von Schelling," in *Stanford Encyclopedia of Philosophy*, http://plato.stanford.edu/entries/schelling/ (accessed July 19, 2011).

Gatta, John, Jr., "Aylmer's Alchemy in 'The Birthmark,'" in *Philological Quarterly*, Vol. 57, No. 3, Summer 1978, pp. 399–413.

Hawthorne, Nathaniel, "The Birth-Mark," in *Nathaniel Hawthorne: Tales and Sketches*, edited by Roy Harvey Pearce, Library of America, 1982, pp. 764–80.

"Hawthorne, Nathaniel," in *Merriam-Webster's Encyclopedia of Literature*, Merriam-Webster, 1995, p. 523.

"The History of Electricity—a Timeline," in *The Historical Archive*, http://www.thehistoricalarchive.com/happenings/the-history-of-electricity-a-timeline/ (accessed July 9, 2011).

"History of Photography," in *National Geographic*, http://photography.nationalgeographic.com/photography/photographers/photography-timeline.html (accessed July 9, 2011).

Horne, Lewis B., "The Heart, the Hand and 'The Birthmark,'" in *American Transcendental Quarterly*, No. 1, 1969, pp. 38–41.

May, William F., "Council Discussion of 'The Birth-Mark' by Nathaniel Hawthorne," in *The President's Council on Bioethics*, http://bioethics.georgetown.edu/pcbe/transcripts/jan02/jansession2intro.html (accessed July 15, 2011).

Nisbet, H. B., and Claude Rawson, *The Cambridge History of Literary Criticism: The Eighteenth Century*, Cambridge University Press, 2005, p. 613.

Pearce, Roy Harvey, "Chronology," in *Nathaniel Hawthorne: Tales and Sketches*, edited by Roy Harvey Pearce, Library of America, 1982, pp. 1471–76.

Skredsvig, Kary Meyers, "Eve's Daughter, Mary's Child: Women's Representation in Hawthorne's 'The Birthmark,'" in *Revista de Filologia y Lingüística de la Universidad de Costa Rica*, Vol. 26, No. 2, July/December 2000, pp. 95–105.

Wentersdorf, Karl P., "The Genesis of Hawthorne's 'The Birthmark,'" in *Jahrbuch für Amerikastudien*, Vol. 8, 1963, pp. 171–86.

FURTHER READING

Berkovitch, Sacvan, *The Puritan Origins of the American Self*, Yale University Press, 2011.

First published in 1975, this volume is a classic study of the influence of Puritanism on American culture and literature. As the title suggests, it explores the way that Puritanism helped define an American sense of identity.

Leeming, David Adam, and Kathleen Morgan Drowne, *Encyclopedia of Allegorical Literature*, ABC-CLIO, 1996.

Readers interested in allegorical literature will find in this volume discussion of all aspects of allegory in the Western tradition, from parts of the Bible to modern fiction. It also includes works from Africa, the Middle East, South America, and other cultures.

Marshall, Megan, *The Peabody Sisters: Three Women Who Ignited American Romanticism*, Mariner Books, 2006.

Marshall examines the lives of Elizabeth and Mary Peabody along with their younger sister, Sophia, who became Hawthorne's wife. Each of the sisters in her own way was influential in helping to forge and sustain the American romantic movement.

Meltzer, Milton, *Nathaniel Hawthorne: A Biography*, Twenty-first Century Books, 2006.

Meltzer has written a biography of Hawthorne suitable for young adults. The biography explores the drama and tragedy of Hawthorne's life and is made more appealing by its use of drawings, paintings, and photographs.

Miller, Edwin Haviland, *Salem Is My Dwelling Place: Life of Nathaniel Hawthorne*, University of Iowa Press, 1992.

Readers interested in a more comprehensive, scholarly biography of Hawthorne will find this entry satisfying. While steering clear of psychological jargon, the biography explores the suppression and anguish that marked much of Hawthorne's life.

Porte, Joel, *In Respect to Egotism: Studies in American Romanticism*, Cambridge University Press, 2009.

This volume is a wide-ranging study of American romanticism and places Hawthorne in the context of other American romantics, including Edgar Allan Poe, Walt Whitman, Herman Melville, Emily Dickinson, and others. A discussion of Hawthorne and his works, including "The Birth-Mark," is contained in chapter 5, "Hawthorne: 'The Obscurest Man of Letters in America.'"

SUGGESTED SEARCH TERMS

Nathaniel Hawthorne

Nathaniel Hawthorne AND The Birth-Mark

Hawthorne AND The Scarlet Letter

Hawthorne AND romanticism

American romanticism

dark romanticism

romantic science

nineteenth-century American science

natural philosophy

transcendentalism

elixir of life

alchemy

allegory

Sarah Peabody

Cat in the Rain

ERNEST HEMINGWAY

1925

"Cat in the Rain" is a short story by Ernest Hemingway, one of the most innovative and widely recognized American authors of the twentieth century. Hemingway wrote the story in 1924 while living with his first wife, Hadley, in France. It was first published in his 1925 debut collection, *In Our Time*. With this collection of short stories and vignettes, Hemingway changed the methods for writing and reading a short story more than any American author had before.

"Cat in the Rain" uses two of the major motifs in Hemingway's fiction: characters in a dissolving marriage and characters away from home or feeling out of place. Written with the abrupt sentence structure and ambiguous dialogue that defines Hemingway's style, "Cat in the Rain" is a story that demands to be solved like a riddle. Each sentence must be examined individually to gain an understanding of the whole structure. Written at a time when Hemingway's marriage to Hadley was disintegrating, the married characters in the story are suffering from an unseen and unacknowledged wedge between them. But like any couple trying to hide their disdain for each other, the problems between the couple shine through their veils of false contentment, and the setting—a hotel room on a rainy day—is perfect for the destruction of a marriage that cannot be maintained. "Cat in the Rain" is available in *In Our Time* as well as *The Complete Short Stories of Ernest Hemingway: The Finca Vigía Edition* (1987). Both of these

Ernest Hemingway (AP Images)

collections can be found in their entirety online at Google Books.

AUTHOR BIOGRAPHY

Hemingway was born on July 21, 1899, in Oak Park, Illinois, a suburb of Chicago. His father, Clarence Edmonds Hemingway, was a general-practice doctor, and his mother, Grace Hall Hemingway, was a housekeeper. He spent his entire childhood in Oak Park, and by the time he reached high school he was an avid boxer and the head of the school newspaper. After high school, Hemingway moved to Kansas City, where he worked as a journalist for the *Kansas City Star*. However, World War I was escalating in Europe at the time, and the news of the foreign affair attracted Hemingway's attention. In April 1918, Hemingway quit his job at the *Kansas City Star* and set sail for Europe. He joined the Italian army, where he worked as an ambulance driver on the front. On July 8, 1918, Hemingway was severely wounded when a bomb nearly destroyed his knee. After spending some time recuperating in Europe, Hemingway returned to America in 1919.

By this time, Hemingway's family had moved to Michigan, a place that would be profoundly influential to his fiction. During the summer of 1920, Hemingway met his first wife, Elizabeth Hadley Richardson, and spent most of his time traveling between his family's land in Michigan and her home in St. Louis, Missouri. On September 3, 1921, Hemingway married Hadley. At the time, he was working as a journalist for the Toronto *Star*. After their marriage, the Hemingways contemplated a move to Europe. They first considered moving to Italy, but Hemingway's earliest fiction-writing mentor, Sherwood Anderson, encouraged them to move to France instead. In December 1921, they moved to Paris.

In France, Hemingway decided to quit journalism to focus primarily on fiction. In his memoir, *A Moveable Feast*, Hemingway discusses the lack of money as a blessing for a fiction writer in the chapter "Hunger Was Good Discipline." After a few months in Paris, the Hemingways decided to travel to Italy. Hadley was ill at the time, so Ernest went first, and she met up with him after she had recovered. In traveling to Italy, Hadley decided she would surprise Hemingway by bringing all of his manuscripts with her so that he could work on them during their holiday together in December 1922. Sadly, the stories were stolen in the Gare de Lyon train station, and almost all of Hemingway's work was lost. When they met in Italy, Hadley told Hemingway about the loss, and that is when Hemingway began writing his new stories, including "Cat in the Rain."

Eventually, Hemingway was able to amass a new collection of stories, and he established his fiction-writing abilities with the short-story collection *In Our Time* in 1925. From there, his road to international fame began. In 1926, he published *The Torrents of Spring*, a farcical novel intended to dismantle his contract with the publishers Boni & Liveright. He wanted to begin a new contract with Charles Scribner, and he did; Scribner and Sons published every subsequent work by Hemingway for the rest of his life. His most influential works include his first serious novel, *The Sun Also Rises* (1926), *Men without Women* (1927), *A Farewell to Arms* (1929), *Winner Take Nothing* (1933), *For Whom the Bell Tolls* (1940), and *The Old Man and the Sea* (1952). Hemingway was awarded the

Pulitzer Prize for Fiction in 1953 for *The Old Man and the Sea* and the Nobel Prize for Literature in 1954.

During his later years, Hemingway was one of the most famous American authors, and the vast fortune he earned allowed him to travel the world. His experiences are hinted at in his fiction, which uses only settings that he was familiar with. On July 2, 1961, Hemingway took his own life with a shotgun. He died in Ketchum, Idaho.

PLOT SUMMARY

"Cat in the Rain" is an extremely short story, only three pages long. The first paragraph gives a lengthy description of the story's setting with a subtle undertone of isolation for the main characters. They are the only two Americans at their hotel, and they do not know any of the other guests there. They merely pass them "on their way to and from their room." This isolation limits the Americans to interacting only with each other and the employees of the hotel. The Americans are vacationing and have taken a room that faces toward the sea and looks out over a public garden and a war monument. Artists gather in good weather to paint pictures of the hotel buildings and palm trees by the sea. The narrator explains that Italians drive long distances "to look up at the war monument," providing the reader's first indication that the story takes place in Italy.

It is raining, a fact that is repeated many times in different ways as the narrator describes the scene. The bronze war monument glistens in the rain. The pools of water on the gravel paths reveal that it has been raining for some time, and no cars are parked before the war monument. The repetitive sea as it breaks and slips back shows the narrator's watchful, bored eye. The opening paragraph ends with a waiter standing in the doorway of a café, looking at the empty square, unable to serve any hungry tourists because of the oppressive rain.

The first scene of the story begins in the second paragraph, with the American wife looking at the rain through the hotel window. The story now focuses on her point of view, in third-person limited narration. That is, she is described from the outside, but the story gives her thoughts and feelings almost exclusively, being limited to her perspective. She notices a cat outside under a table, "trying to make herself so compact that she would not be dripped on." The wife says she is going to "get that kitty," and her husband—without bothering to get up from where he is lounging on the bed—says that he will do it for her. The wife says that she will do it, and the husband continues to read, "lying propped up with the two pillows at the foot of the bed." It would seem that there are only two pillows and he is using both of them, not making room for her. "Don't get wet," is all he says to her, and his lack of interest in his wife becomes more obvious as he continues to read his book.

The next scene follows the wife out to the hotel's lobby. Immediately, the hotel owner—called by the Italian word *padrone*, meaning "host" or "master"—who is old and very tall, stands and bows to her respectfully. They exchange a few words in Italian about the weather, and the American wife reflects that she likes the hotel-keeper. He "receives complaints" well, she thinks; he has dignity but wants to serve her. With his "old heavy face and big hands," he seems to be picturesque.

With the thought of liking the hotel owner on her mind, the wife opens the door to the hotel. The rain is more intense than it had been before. A man in a rubber cape quickly crosses the square, going toward the café. Standing in the doorway, the wife is devising a plan to rescue the cat in the rain when a maid opens an umbrella behind her. "You must not get wet," the maid says in Italian, and the wife assumes that the maid has been sent by the hotel-keeper. This is a sharp contrast to the husband's saying "don't get wet" without moving. The hotel-keeper and his employees use action to keep the American wife from getting wet.

With the maid carrying the umbrella, the two walk out into the square searching for the cat, but it is gone, and the wife is disappointed. The maid asks whether she has lost something, and she explains about the cat. Notably, she is described now as "the American girl" instead of "the American wife," as if her inability to find the cat has altered her title. When the maid laughs at the idea of a cat being out in the rain, the American woman switches to English: "I wanted it so much. I wanted a kitty." The maid becomes more distant and urges her to go back inside, and in response the American girl agrees. Again she is called "the American girl" in the text, as she is for the rest of the story.

Walking back into the hotel, the maid stays outside to close the umbrella. As the American girl passes the hotel-keeper, he bows his head. She feels "something... very small and tight inside" her. The hotel-keeper makes "her feel very small and at the same time really important." Her self-esteem grows as she leaves the lobby and eventually reaches the point of "supreme importance." She goes upstairs and into her room, where she finds George (the first time the husband's name is used) still reading, as before. He is the only character in the story with a name and not just a descriptive title. George asks whether she found the cat, and he puts his book down. She tells him it was gone. "Wonder where it went to," he says without a question mark, indicating his lack of interest in his wife's activity. Because this story is being told from the wife's point of view, her opinions of George's body language are all that will be given. This is apparent when he is described as "resting his eyes from reading," although he never says anything to confirm this, and there is no evidence in a person's body language that can prove such an activity. It is merely her interpretation of what he is doing, just as all of the hotel-keeper's actions are described through her opinion of what he intends to do. With George no longer reading, the wife sits down on the bed. She immediately begins to pout about *wanting*: "I wanted it so much.... I wanted that poor kitty. It isn't any fun to be a poor kitty out in the rain." George returns to his book.

Feeling ignored, the wife gets up from the bed and walks to the mirror. She studies her reflection from all angles. She asks George if he would like her to grow her hair long. George looks up and sees her neck, where her hair is "clipped close like a boy's." He responds that he likes it in this style, but again the wife is pouting. "I get so tired of it," she says. George begins to shift in his position on the bed, his first movement of the entire story other than setting down and picking up his book. Furthermore, he has not taken his eyes from her since she began talking. "You look pretty darn nice," he says, showing the first sign of interest between the married Americans. The wife gets up from the mirror and walks toward the window. Daylight is fading. Aloud, she wishes again for long hair, adding, "I want to have a kitty to sit on my lap and purr when I stroke her." George voices a bit of interest, and seeing her opportunity, the American girl rapidly lists the things she wants, which seem to signify the characteristics of a mother nesting but also signify a traveler wanting to go home: she wants her own table, her own silverware, candles, she wants the season to be spring, she wants to brush her hair, she wants a kitty (of course), and she wants some new clothes. Again annoyed, George replies, "Oh, shut up and get something to read." He goes back to reading again, and all of his interest in the American girl is gone.

After looking out the window, the American girl says, "Anyway, I want a cat.... I want a cat. I want a cat now. If I can't have long hair or any fun, I can have a cat." Clearly she is trying to be a nuisance. However, George is not listening to her at all, he is simply reading. There is a knock at the door: it is the maid, holding a tortoiseshell cat. The motion with which the maid brings the cat into the hotel room resembles a birth: she holds it "pressed tight against her," "down against her body." The maid explains that the hotel-keeper asked her to bring the cat for the American wife. The hotel-keeper has fulfilled all the expectations the American girl had of him, and George never once got out of the bed.

CHARACTERS

American Wife

Although her name is never given, the American wife is the focus of the limited third-person narration (that is, the narrator describes the characters as "he" or "she" and does not take part in the story) in "Cat in the Rain." She is staying in an Italian hotel with her husband, George, and is forced to stay mostly inside because of the rain. In the hotel room, she is ignored by George, who is preoccupied with reading a book and is lying across the entire bed. She sees a frightened cat outside in the rain; she longs to protect the cat (showing, arguably, her desire to have a child) and tells George her feelings. He ignores her. She leaves the hotel room and goes to the lobby, where she finds the hotel-keeper, also known as the padrone. The hotel owner represents a masculine father figure, the opposite of her uninterested husband. The American wife likes the hotel-keeper. She goes outside to find the cat, but it has disappeared. Disappointed, the American wife returns to her hotel room, where George continues to read and ignore her. After complaining to George about her appearance and their current situation, the married couple hears a knock at the door. The hotel owner has sent a maid to their room bearing a cat for the American wife.

George

George is the husband of the American wife. He is also staying in the Italian hotel during the rainstorm. For the entire story, he remains on the bed reading a book. His disinterest in his wife becomes apparent in the opening scene when he shows nonchalant interest in his wife's desire for a cat. The way he lays on the bed, propped up against the only two pillows in the room, shows that he is not interested in making room for her to sit. When she returns to the hotel room after her unfulfilled search for a cat, he sets his book down and rests his eyes, but after a short conversation with her he is back to reading again. When the American wife decides she is going to grow her hair long, George disputes her decision, telling her he likes the look of her short haircut. After his wife complains about their situation some more, George snaps at her, telling her to shut up and pick up a book to read, as he is doing.

Hotel-Keeper

The hotel-keeper, or padrone, is the American wife's favorite character in this story. He has very few lines of dialogue, but he is described in detail by the narration from the wife's point of view. His service is diligent, and his gesture of sending a cat to the Americans' hotel room at the end of the story shows his high level of professionalism, and possibly a paternal interest in the American wife.

The Maid

The maid holds an umbrella for the American wife while she searches for the cat in the rain. She also brings the cat, or perhaps another, to the Americans' hotel room.

Padrone

See Hotel Owner

THEMES

Dysfunctional Relationships

The dysfunctional relationship between the American wife and George is the wheel that turns the plot of "Cat in the Rain." In the opening scene, the American wife stares through a window in a hotel room, bored, watching the rain fall. George sits on the bed, reading, uninterested in anything his wife says. When the American wife sees the cat outside, she tells her husband. He does not ignore her, but he is not paying attention either. She leaves the room and runs into the hotel-keeper. Here, the third-person narrator following the American wife's point of view reveals her high opinion of the hotel-keeper and, in comparison to the previous scene with her husband in the hotel room, also reveals that she is perhaps losing interest in her husband and looking for a new man to love. When she is around the hotel-keeper, the narration gives multiple reasons why she likes him, but when she is around George she only speaks of things she wants. The American wife has lost interest in her husband, but George is far from being innocent with regard to their marital dysfunction. When he has heard enough from his wife, he tells her to shut up. Clearly, the distance between the two and their inability to communicate illustrate a dysfunctional relationship.

Fertility

In "Cat in the Rain," both fertility and infertility are suggested through multiple symbols. The American wife's desire to rescue the cat illustrates her motherly urge to take care of a small, living creature as she would take care of an infant. Her further interest in the masculine characteristics of the hotel-keeper may reveal her animalistic desire to find an adequate mate to produce a child. The setting of the story is filled with lush green plants, symbols of a fertile ecosystem. But the setting also contains a war monument, a symbol of death. The rain represents the life force for all living things, while the man running with a rubber cape to protect his body from the fertile rain is a humorous symbol of infertility (or, more accurately, the prevention of fertility). At the end of the story, the tortoiseshell cat that is given to the wife can be seen as a symbol of infertility because male cats of such coloring are almost always infertile. Hemingway is making a joke about the reproductive desires of the American wife and the disinterest of her husband George. The American couple can be compared to a doomed species because the male does not have any physical interest in the female. Furthermore, obtaining the cat may mean that the wife's motherly desires will be suppressed, at least for the moment.

Isolation

The young Hemingway is famously known as an American expatriate (someone living away from

TOPICS FOR FURTHER STUDY

- Research the modernist movement of the early twentieth century. Who were the authors and artists involved, and what were their goals? How can the stories and poems of the movement be compared to the art and architecture? Where they able to, in the words of poet Ezra Pound, "make it new"? If so, how were they able to accomplish this? If not, what did they do wrong? Write an essay explaining your findings and include at least one artist from each of the mediums of fiction, poetry, fine art, and architecture.
- Hemingway has been praised for his ability to write a story about a serious issue that is never directly mentioned in the narration but is understood by the reader. Using Hemingway's style, write a short story with an underlying message that is not addressed but that can be recognized by a perceptive reader.
- When reading "Cat in the Rain," a person who has never been married might wonder why the American couple stays together when there is such an obvious disconnection between them. Read several stories in the 2008 collection about teenage heartbreak *Breaking Up Is Hard to Do*. Write a persuasive essay comparing the breakups in the collection to the marriage in "Cat in the Rain." Do the teenage characters in *Breaking Up Is Hard to Do* have an easier time talking to each other about their problems than the married adults in "Cat in the Rain"? Your essay should explain your position and attempt to convince the reader that one approach (the teenagers' or the adults') is better than the other.
- Research the life of Ernest Hemingway and look for as many pictures from the different periods in his life as you can find. Keeping in mind that Hemingway wrote more fiction when he was young and that the fiction he wrote in later life is often his most critiqued work, compare the images that are easiest to find with the images you find only after more research. Create an interactive time line in which you place Hemingway's work and awards with pictures of him as he aged. Add excerpts from the critical reception for each work to the site.
- Hemingway served in the Italian army during World War I. When he wrote "Cat in the Rain," he was vacationing in Italy several years after the war had ended. Why do you think he chose to set the story in that particular nation? Does the narrator's description of the war monument have any importance with regard to Hemingway's personal history in Italy? Research the causes of World War I and find information on the Italians. After researching the stance of the Italians during World War I, remember that Hemingway was an American who chose to join the Italian army a few years before America became involved with the conflict. Why would Hemingway have done that? In your opinion, did the Italians have a just cause in World War I? Write an essay explaining your findings, and if you wish, include your opinion of Hemingway's decision to join another nation's army. Would you do the same for any reason?

one's country of birth) living in Europe. Furthermore, he is an author who is frequently confused with his characters and constantly accused of writing pseudo-autobiographical fiction. There are many reasons for this overlapping of the author's life and the author's fiction, but one of the main reasons is the displacement of many of his fictional characters. Many of Hemingway's characters who are older than twenty years old are found living far away from their hometowns (as Hemingway did). They are surrounded by people they do not know, often speaking a language other than English. "Cat in the Rain" is no exception to this motif in Hemingway's fiction. The Americans are identified as Americans. They are staying in a hotel in Italy. They do not know any of the people they pass in

George, the husband, is always reading and his wife feels ignored and unloved. (*Zurijeta / Shutterstock.com*)

the hallways other than the employees of the hotel. They are surrounded by a culture that is not their own, and because of this they are isolated, though they are not alone. The isolation of the characters becomes negative when their distaste for each other is revealed, but because of their distance from home they have no option but to stay with each other. To further illustrate the isolation of the Americans, Hemingway sets the story during a rainstorm. Whereas their relocation has created a mental isolation, the rain creates a physical isolation—they are trapped inside their hotel room. This theme helps Hemingway illustrate the dismantling of their relationship because the married couple's only option is to pick at each other. George is content with his isolation; it gives him a quiet place to read. However, the American wife is restless and discontented. She wants to go outside. She wants to save a cat. She interacts with the hotel-keeper and the maid because they are the only people who will talk to her in this land that is foreign to her. Ultimately, the American wife wants to go home. George does not. This leads the reader to the assumption that George has created this isolation, and the American wife has been forced to follow. She will follow until she has had enough, and then she will leave for a more comfortable place where she can know the people surrounding her.

Giving in to the urge many readers have to compare Hemingway's fiction to his life, Carlos Baker argues in his biography of Hemingway that "Cat in the Rain" is "about himself and Hadley and the manager and the chambermaid at the Hotel Splendide." This vacation took place during February 1923. In December 1922, while riding a train to meet Hemingway on vacation in Italy, Hadley lost all of Hemingway's stories in a briefcase she misplaced during her travels. It is interesting to compare the certain anger Hemingway felt toward his wife with the silent yet aggressive treatment George gives the American wife in "Cat in the Rain." Another point of interest is George's desire to read. And with regard to the theme of isolation, Hemingway said in his Nobel acceptance speech that "writing, at its best, is a lonely life." Isolation is something Hemingway desired, and it seems to be something George desires as well.

STYLE

Point of View

"Cat in the Rain" is written from a third-person point of view, but the narration is more heavily focused on the American wife than on any of the other characters. Because the story is written from her point of view, it feels as if she is the gravitational pull that is keeping the other characters circling around her. Never does the story leave her side, whether she is in the hotel room with her husband, in the lobby with the hotel owner, or outside with the maid holding an umbrella. Hemingway wrote the story from her point of view because she is the character most involved with the rest of the characters. She is also the character with the most inner strife, and a character with problems makes a more absorbing fictional character. Interestingly, this is the only short story in the *In Our Time* collection that is told from a female's point of view.

Ambiguity

Ambiguity is perhaps Hemingway's favorite writing device, especially in his early fiction. A thorough interpretation of his work is something the reader must earn, collecting sentences as a detective collects clues. The ambiguity of "Cat in the Rain" is subtle. The story is only three pages long, so each sentence must be read closely. Reading the story without paying special attention to the details could leave the reader in the dark. For example, a simple, uninterested reading of this story would be that the American wife wanted a pet cat, searched for a cat, and in the end received a cat. However, when the text is read with more careful attention, the reader will find a complicated web of interaction between the two American characters that can be interpreted in multiple ways. For instance, is the American wife pregnant? The symbols of infertility throughout the narrative and the lazy behavior of the uninterested husband would suggest that she is not, but the tight feeling in her stomach and her urge to build a nest for child bearing suggest that she is. Hemingway never confirms a pregnancy, nor does he deny one. Readers are left to apply their own opinions to the story. When a work is left ambiguous, it allows readers to become a part of the story, placing their own beliefs and opinions into the work, and in the end there is no correct interpretation. There are as many understandings as there are readers.

Modernism

The modernist movement began in the early twentieth century. It emphasized a break with the past, a rejection of tradition in the form and content of artistic and cultural works. "Make it new" was the slogan of modernism, and much of the literature produced was in direct response to humanity's collective experiences following World War I. Hemingway stands as one of the most prominent fiction writers of the modernist movement because his fiction (especially his short fiction) is written with a style unlike anything that had been written before. Often referred to as an iceberg, Hemingway's fiction is short, with abrupt sentence structures and small blips of dialogue, but beneath the surface of his tight sentences lies an immense body of pain, emotions, and scars. After Hemingway, the world of short fiction no longer favored long-winded paragraphs explaining every feeling inside the character; no longer could the first sentence of a short story be dull and without relevance to the rest of the story. Hemingway treated short fiction as if it were poetry—where every line must be interpreted individually to reach a firm understanding of the whole—and because of this completely original style Hemingway stands as the most innovative American author during the modernist movement. He certainly was able to "make it new."

HISTORICAL CONTEXT

The Roaring Twenties

"Cat in the Rain" was originally published in the short-story collection *In Our Time*. The title of the collection alone is symbolic of the era in which Hemingway wrote the story. In 1925, Hemingway was young, only twenty-six years old. Furthermore, he was a veteran of World War I, a historical moment that defined the culture and emotions of the world at the time. World War I had been a brutal war, a war in which the weapons overpowered all existing theories of warfare strategy. Many people died, and those who survived were witness to the mayhem. The war had an immense effect on the lives of the people of Hemingway's generation. The reference to World War I in "Cat in the Rain" is subtle, but it is important to understanding the mood of the characters in the story. The war monument in the courtyard outside the hotel stands as a symbol of death in this story, and the readers of the 1920s would have understood it as

COMPARE & CONTRAST

- **1920s:** If a couple wishes to live and travel together they are expected to be married. Living together out of wedlock is considered out of the ordinary and possibly offensive.

  Today: Many couples live together prior to marriage. Some couples live together for their entire relationship without being married.

- **1920s:** The fashions for women include short hair and small, revealing dresses. This is a vast change from the long hair and concealing outfits of prior generations, especially the Victorian era. Women dressing this way are called "flappers."

  Today: Women still wear revealing clothing and cut their hair short if they wish, but that is not the only fashion. Women also wear pants, as well as dresses and skirts.

- **1920s:** Hemingway is considered a bright young writer with a fresh style. His short fiction sells at a high volume, and he is quickly becoming the most famous American fiction writer in the world.

  Today: Hemingway is often remembered as a white-haired old man who drank too much alcohol, shot guns, fought people in bars, and committed suicide. His innovative short fiction is often overshadowed by his conveniently short novella *The Old Man and the Sea*. What is remembered of his short fiction is mimicked in contests where writers submit "bad Hemingway" stories, exaggerating the writer's short, abrupt style and often poking fun at his masculine persona.

- **1920s:** World War I is finally over, and the soldiers have returned to their homes throughout the world. Coinciding with the period of peace is an economic boom throughout most of the developed world. People (like the Americans in "Cat in the Rain") are traveling far and spending frequently.

  Today: Although there is no war involving the entire world, it is not exactly an era of peace. Small military actions involving many countries are happening all around the globe. The shape of the economy is in a fluctuating balance. There are few high moments, and there are few low moments. This contrasts sharply with the heavy spending of the 1920s, which led directly to the Great Depression of the 1930s.

- **1920s:** People stuck inside because of bad weather (like the Americans in "Cat in the Rain") have limited activities. Reading a book (as George does) is one of the most widely accepted things to do inside, but the American wife does not want to read, and she is bored. Listening to the radio is a new activity that is growing in popularity.

  Today: With so many easily obtained devices for entertainment indoors, the weather outside is inconsequential. While inside, people can watch television, surf the Internet on a computer, play video games, or listen to music. They can read a traditional book or a high-tech device with books stored electronically.

such. Also, remembering that Hemingway was a member of the Italian army, the setting of the story shines light on the autobiographical influence on his fiction. Hemingway's characters are in Italy after the war. To write such a story, it seems as though Hemingway would have had to also return to Italy following the war and revisit the memories of his service to that nation's army.

World War I was famously called "the war to end all wars," an expression of the hope that it would actually end war and bring a lasting peace. In the decade immediately following the war, an economic boom prevailed through most of the developed world. This economic boom was largely responsible for the carefree, party-filled lifestyle characteristic of the Roaring

Twenties. People had money, and they spent it as quickly as they could. This can be seen in "Cat in the Rain" in the traveling Americans. George and his wife evidently have enough money to travel throughout Europe. The wife embodies the Roaring Twenties more than George: she wears her hair short in the fashionable style called a bob, and she has an urge for fun.

Hemingway did as much to reflect and shape the culture of this decade as did other famous authors, including F. Scott Fitzgerald and Dorothy Parker. Hemingway's 1926 novel *The Sun Also Rises* tells the story of a group of young and rich Americans traveling through Europe and consuming as much as possible. "Cat in the Rain" is a perfect example of Hemingway writing what he knew: the roaring, affluent twenties.

Young Hemingway

Having a time period of one's own is an honor few writers have known. The author must be innovative, lasting, and involved. Many years after his death, Hemingway is still one of the most famous American fiction authors to have ever lived. His career spanned three decades, including both world wars (each being the subject of two different novels he wrote), and he remains a household name to such an extent that his first name is not needed to understand who is being talked about.

"Cat in the Rain" was a very early story in the young Hemingway era. It was included in his first collection, and it played a major role in the world's first glimpse of Hemingway's fiction. This is important because Hemingway began his career with what many scholars believe to be his best work. The stories published in *In Our Time* are inventive and game changing. Hemingway's fiction sought to challenge the reader with the iceberg technique. Each sentence is only a small block of ice floating above sea level, but when combined they reveal the massive block sunk beneath the surface. *A Moveable Feast*, Hemingway's memoir, was written when he was older and was published after his death, but it focuses on his life in Europe during the 1920s. In it he speaks about his "new theory that you could omit anything if you knew that you omitted and the omitted part would strengthen the story and make people feel something more than they understood." This theory was recognized by the reading world and accepted. It has since been the norm for strong, well-written, and scholarly fiction.

The young Hemingway era is defined by this theory of omission. "Cat in the Rain" is an excellent example of a story with a message buried beneath the surface. To the untrained eye, this story would seem dull and without any profound meaning. But when Hemingway's theory is understood, and when "Cat in the Rain" is compared with the other short stories in *In Our Time*, the reader can feel the emotions of the characters, and as Hemingway wrote in his memoir, that is what he sought to inspire. This era and this theory lasted from 1925 to 1933, including two novels, *The Sun Also Rises* (1926) and *A Farewell to Arms* (1929), and three short-story collections, *In Our Time* (1925), *Men without Women* (1927), and *Winner Take Nothing* (1933).

Following his young era, Hemingway would change his style, almost returning to his roots as a journalist. His 1939 novel *For Whom the Bell Tolls* gave the world a startling image of a murderous fascist party rising to power in Spain. It is a profound novel. However, the iceberg style was gone. Hemingway's short, stylized prose faded away, taking a back seat to his interest in using his fame to warn the world about the dangers of fascism.

The final era in Hemingway's life is morose. The celebrity-obsessed culture of America was budding in the 1950s, and Hemingway stood as one of America's largest celebrities of the time. He became a major target for magazine articles, which often depicted him as a drunkard or worse. Hemingway earned the nickname "Papa" during this era because he wore a large grey beard and because he seemed to be a grandfatherly figure. The final era of Hemingway's life was not as productive as his earlier career. His only notable publication during this era is *The Old Man and the Sea* (1952). In this novella, Hemingway attempted to return to the technique of omission with meaning that he had used in his earlier career but had fallen away from for over a decade. Some would argue it worked—he was awarded both the Pulitzer Prize and the Nobel Prize in literature with this novella. Others argue he was rather given both of these awards for his entire career. In his Nobel acceptance speech, Hemingway seemed to agree with the latter perspective. His final years were spent writing very little.

A wet cat represents the problems in the marriage. (Diana Taliun / Shutterstock.com)

CRITICAL OVERVIEW

Initially, "Cat in the Rain" was received as a small part of the greater whole that is the *In Our Time* collection. In fact, critical commentaries on *In Our Time* can be read in their entirety, and "Cat in the Rain" will only be briefly mentioned. It seems as if the earliest receptions of the story took it as a small chapter, overshadowed by Hemingway's more famous stories, including "Indian Camp," "Big Two-Hearted River: Part I," and "Big Two-Hearted River: Part II." Such stories stand as a representation of young people at the time of publication in the 1920s. They dealt with a generation gap that defined the beginning of a new century. Stories about married couples, such as "The Doctor and the Doctor's Wife," "Mr. and Mrs. Elliot," and "Cat in the Rain," were understood to be a secondary motif in Hemingway's fiction, and not as important as the stories that dealt with youth in America and war in Europe.

However, in 1962 (after Hemingway's death), John V. Hagopian wrote the essay "Symmetry in 'Cat in the Rain,'" in which he claims that "Cat in the Rain" is "probably Hemingway's best made short story." He argues that symbols such as the lush green landscape (a symbol of life) and the war monument (a symbol of death) create a setting in which polar opposites are being pushed together, though their magnetism inhibits any real connection. The American wife's multiple references to *liking* the hotel-keeper, compared with her many *wants* when alone with her husband, also represent a symmetry of opposites, according to Hagopian. The American wife's desire to grow her hair long compared to her husband's content attitude toward her short hair offers another example that Hemingway was writing a story of opposites forcing a connection that is not possible.

In his 2011 essay "Hemingway's 'Cat in the Rain': A Reproof of the Self," John V. McDermott illustrates that while this is the only story included in *In Our Time* that is written from the point of view of a woman, both characters are unable to see beyond their own vision of the situation. Hemingway reveals this through the symbolism of the Italians' appreciation of the war monument outside of the hotel.

McDermott's essay makes the same point that Seymour Chatman does in a 2001 essay, "'Soft Filters': Some Sunshine on 'Cat in the Rain.'" In this essay, Chatman argues that earlier critical interpretations of "Cat in the Rain" such as Hagopian's are dated, and though they may be relevant to the time Hemingway wrote the story, they have been succeeded by modern interpretations invoked by the culture of a new time. Chatman argues that Hemingway's manipulation of point of view in "Cat in the Rain" is what gives the story an ambiguity that leads to multiple relevant interpretations. Whereas earlier interpretations argued that "Cat in the Rain" is told from the American wife's perspective, Chatman contends that it is only told from her perspective through a majority of the story and not throughout the whole of the narration. For example, the second sentence of the story begins with "They did not know . . . ," and with an emphasis on *they*, Chatman illustrates that this story will sway from the collective narration of the couple to the wife's point of view. He concludes that "Cat in the Rain" is told by a third-person narrator, but at different moments in the story various characters' filters are applied to the narrator. The aforementioned example is that of the collective filters of the couple being placed over the narration. The husband does not have a filter that is not shared with the wife, so, according to Chatman, moments when the story seems to be from the wife's point of view are examples of the husband's filter being dropped from the narration.

Through these examples, the reader can understand how "Cat in the Rain" has transformed over time from an obscure story, often overlooked, to an acknowledged profound story with a controlled, singular understanding, and finally blossoming into an ambiguous story with profound interpretations based on gender roles, love, and cultural understanding. Critical reviews have aided in the opening of an extended debate over a story that seemed destined to a silent impact when first published.

CRITICISM

Christopher Dale Russell

Russell is a freelance writer fascinated by fiction. In the following essay, he examines the motif of affluent and dislocated American characters in Hemingway's short fiction, focusing on "Cat in the Rain."

"THE RAIN THAT TRAPS THE AMERICAN COUPLE INSIDE THE HOTEL IS SIMPLY THWARTING THEIR ATTEMPTS TO SAVE THEIR ROMANCE BY THROWING MONEY AT IT; THE CAT MAY BE IN THE RAIN, BUT SO ARE THEY."

Hemingway's early fiction follows a set of motifs based on the age and location of the characters. Young characters, like those in the stories about Nick Adams (Hemingway's autobiographical fiction character), are living in America and searching for peaceful guidance in a violent world. Teenage characters are at war or returning home and dealing with their conflicting memories of World War I. Characters in their twenties, like the married couple in "Cat in the Rain," are found living in Europe, traveling frequently, and spending money in abundance. The affluence of the characters in their twenties can be correlated to the younger characters for two reasons: the child characters longed to escape the isolated world their parents created, and the teenage characters—having traveled through Europe during battle, and sitting on large sums of soldier's pay—have gained access to the rest of the world and want to experience it as much as possible. This reasoning can be applied to the culture of the 1920s American in a discussion of both reality and fiction. In other words, the affluent nature of Americans during the Roaring Twenties is the result of two centuries of national isolation, the birth of a new generation forced to cross seas in battle, and an influx of money coming from a booming economy after a victorious war. The married couple in "Cat in the Rain" embodies the spirit of their generation, and therefore they embrace the affluence of an era that devoured so much and spent so freely that it led to the Great Depression one decade later.

"Cat in the Rain" is a story about tourists, as revealed with the first sentence: "There were only two Americans stopping at the hotel." To be a tourist is to spend money. Today, people take vacations frequently, but prior to the 1920s, people tended to stay at home. During earlier decades, a traveling family would need to be very rich.

WHAT DO I READ NEXT?

- *A Moveable Feast* (1964) is Hemingway's memoir about his life in Europe during the 1920s. It is an excellent companion while reading Hemingway's earliest fiction, offering the reader a glimpse into the creation of his style. Since it was not published until after Hemingway's death in 1961, it is unclear how long he worked on the text; however, to find the true passion of the author it is a necessary read.
- *The Sun Also Rises* is Hemingway's first serious novel, published in 1926. It tells the story of a young American man living in France and traveling to Spain for the annual running with the bulls. The novel made this custom known around the world and gave many people their first glimpse into the bullfights so revered in Spain. The novel is an excellent example of Hemingway at the top of his style.
- *The Great Gatsby* is the most famous novel by one of Hemingway's American friends, F. Scott Fitzgerald. Published in 1924, it is one of the most important American novels ever written. It is interesting to compare *The Sun Also Rises* with *The Great Gatsby*. The older, more famous Fitzgerald certainly had an effect on the young Hemingway.
- William Faulkner's 1930 novel *As I Lay Dying* is an excellent and challenging read. Faulkner's prose style uses stream of consciousness narration, heavy slang, and altered spellings of common words to show different accents; it is vastly different from Hemingway's stern, short sentences. Like Hemingway, Faulkner is a cornerstone of the modernist movement, but he is also considered one of the founding fathers of the postmodern movement.
- *The Portable Dorothy Parker* (1944) is an anthology of one of the most influential female authors of the 1920s. Known for her sass, wit, and humor, this anthology includes some of the best poetry, short fiction, journalism, and letters from Parker's vast body of work. Comparing the point of view of Parker's female characters to that of the American wife in "Cat in the Rain" can give the reader a more balanced view of the gender roles established in the 1920s.
- *The Road*, by Cormac McCarthy, was published in 2006. It is about a father and son wandering through a desolate dystopia (a ruined or nightmare society) searching for safety and food. It was published more than forty years after Hemingway's death, but the short sentences of the prose are an excellent example of how Hemingway's fiction continues to influence authors. The characters' desperation is reflected in the short, harsh sentences much in the same way that the separation of George and the American wife is shown in "Cat in the Rain."
- *Rage:A Love Story* (2009), by Julie Anne Peters, is a young-adult novel about a teenager's failed first attempt at love and the process of recovering after the loss. Comparable to the inevitable heartbreak for the characters in "Cat in the Rain," this novel is a fresh spin on the ancient feeling of lost love.
- Though Zora Neale Hurston's *Their Eyes Were Watching God* was not published until 1937, the author was famous during the Harlem Renaissance of the 1920s—a movement parallel to the modernist movement that was happening in Europe. While many white authors spent their time in Europe during the 1920s, Hurston and other members of the Harlem Renaissance remained in America and strove for the mainstream acceptance of art created by minorities. Because she was a black woman, Hurston's work can be read as a representation of a different worldview existing during the time of Hemingway's early career.

During the 1920s, the first wave of middle-class tourism began as a result of the strong economy of the decade. George and his wife seem to be examples of middle-class tourists with a little bit of extra money.

Now, the American wife stands as Hemingway's idea of an obnoxious tourist. She wants, she begs, she pouts, she complains, and she is outrageously repetitive. She wants to save the cat that is stuck outside in the rain. What will she do with the cat? It does not seem to be an issue for her or for George. If the cat needs food, they will buy it. If the cat needs shelter, they will buy it. This is an example of the affluence of the generation. All problems can be solved with money, especially when it has been easily earned. The direct opposite of a tourist is a local. The locals in "Cat in the Rain" are the employees at the hotel: the hotel-keeper and the maid. They serve the tourists to earn their own money, but not without dignity. If this story is seen as a joke on the far-fetched idealism of a spendthrift tourist, Hemingway made sure to let the locals keep their integrity. The hotel-keeper warns the American wife about the bad weather as she walks through the lobby toward the door. When he sees that she is bound to walk into the storm anyway, he sends a maid to keep her dry. The maid speaks Italian with the American wife, but when the American wife speaks English, and more specifically when she says the word *kitty*, "the maid's face tightened." Obviously uncomfortable with the American wife's unrealistic behavior, the Italian maid becomes the voice of reason: "Come, signora . . . we must get back inside. You will be wet." The American wife follows because she has been told to do so. The local holds the authority in a land that is foreign to the American wife.

When unable to recover the thing she wanted, the American wife is clearly upset. If one is searching this story for examples of affluence, her mood change during this scene is a glaring piece of evidence. When George asks the American wife about the cat, she immediately goes into a tantrum: "I wanted it so much. . . . I don't know why I wanted it so much. I wanted that poor kitty." Although her body language is not directly mentioned, the image conjured by this bit of dialogue is a child stomping her feet on the ground. She wants the cat, though she does not know why, and when she cannot have the cat she is upset. The affluence of her life has allowed her to receive everything that she desires, and when she is unable to get what she wants she does not know how to react in a plausible, calm manner. Upset over her wish not being granted, the American wife begins to pick apart her own life. She wants to grow her hair long. George tells her that he likes the way she looks. Now she is not hearing what she wants to hear, so what does she do? She repeats her desire to grow her hair long. She has felt the disappointment of not finding the cat, and she is not going to allow herself to be let down twice in such a short period of time. She then repeats that she wants a cat. Every character in this story knows the American wife wants a cat, the reader knows, Hemingway knows, yet she is still talking about wanting the cat. Her pouting has become a joke.

At this point in the story, the American wife has been denied in two apparent ways: she cannot find the cat, and George does not want her to grow her hair long. The third disappointment for the American wife in this story is never directly addressed, but because this is a story by Hemingway, a deeper meaning beneath the surface can always be found when he is using his iceberg writing style, and a close reading will reveal the neglect she receives from her husband. George ignores the American wife throughout most of the story. When he does talk to her, he speaks in short, uninterested sentences until the boiling point at the end, when he tells her to "shut up and get something to read." This division in their marriage is embodied by George's lack of interest in his wife—a desire of hers that cannot be quenched with money. However, the vacation they are taking in this story can be interpreted as an example of Americans trying to save their marriage by spending money on an exotic, international hotel. The rain that traps the American couple inside the hotel is simply thwarting their attempts to save their romance by throwing money at it; the cat may be in the rain, but so are they.

The American affluence embodied by the wife does not end with these three examples. Her inability to get any of the things she desires reaches a threshold inside the hotel room when she begins to talk about all the other items and things she wants:

> I want to eat at a table with my own silver and I want candles. And I want it to be spring and I want to brush my hair out in front of a mirror and I want a kitty and I want some new clothes.

Some of these desires—the table, the silver, the candles, the kitty, the mirror, and the new clothes—can be purchased with money. The other things—long hair and spring weather—will come with time.

Through the cat, the couple attempts to work out their marital angst. (Tatagatta / Shutterstock.com)

But another possible attribute of an affluent person is impatience. When all things can be purchased and when the money in one's pocket is abundant, waiting seems to be the most atrocious activity one can do. This outburst by the American wife leads to the outburst from George where he tells her to shut up. At this point she does not have any of the things she desires, and her marriage to George has deteriorated further. Hemingway, wanting to tap the joke that is the affluent American wife one more time, now has the character repeat herself: "Anyway, I want a cat. . . . I want a cat. I want a cat now. If I can't have long hair or any fun, I can have a cat." She wants and she wants now. Affluence and impatience are exemplified in her speech.

The affluence of the 1920s was succeeded by the depression of the 1930s. However, Hemingway wrote this story in 1925. The affluent had yet to find their ultimate disappointment at this moment in history. "Cat in the Rain" ends with the ultimate fulfillment of the American wife's desire. There is a knock at their hotel door. Waiting in the hallway is the Italian maid; the hotel-keeper has found a cat and sent it to them. The American wife has thrown a temper tantrum in her hotel room, possibly severing all ties to her husband, because she wanted a cat and could not find one. Although their marriage has lost one more leg to stand on, the American wife has finally received her cat. The age of disappointment has not yet reached these affluent Americans, and it will not reach them for another four years. The Great Depression will be their first serious disappointment, but it will not be their last.

Source: Christopher Dale Russell, Critical Essay on "Cat in the Rain," in *Short Stories for Students*, Gale, Cengage Learning, 2012.

John V. McDermott

In the following essay, McDermott argues that the theme of "Cat in the Rain" is what happens when a person's most important priority is "to please the self."

Ernest Hemingway's "Cat in the Rain" is not simply "a sympathetic portrayal of the woman's point of view" (Susan F. Beegal, *Hemingway's Neglected Short Fiction* [Ann Arbor: UMI Research Press, 1989]: 155). In its symphonic undertones, Expressionistic underpinnings and complex symbols, it suggests a story woven of many ideas that reveal the theme: one's number one priority to please the self.

It is the woman's words and actions that qualify the idea that "A Cat in the Rain" is "the only story in *In Our Time* from the woman's viewpoint" (Sheridan W. Baker, *Ernest Hemingway: An Introduction and Interpretation* [NY: Holt, Rinehart and Winston, 1967]: 26). In the opening paragraph the woman's vision is as myopic as her husband's; both cannot see beyond themselves. Neither is as sensitive as the "Italians [who] came from a long way off to look up at the war monument . . . made of bronze [that] glistened in the rain" (Ernest Hemingway, *The Complete Stories of Ernest Hemingway* [NY: Charles Scribner's Sons, 1987]: 129). The Italians' emotional memory of the selfless war dead contrasts sharply with the blasé attitude of the two Americans.

Hemingway's second reference to the Americans' concern for self is in the contrast he makes between them and the "Artists [who] liked the way the palms grew and the bright colors of the hotels facing the gardens and the sea" (*CS*). In their inability to recognize the wonders of nature or the creativity of others as artists do, the couple again reveals their insensitivity.

That George the husband is cast in an unfavorable light is beyond question. In his egotism he cannot recognize his spouse as a person; though his cold treatment of her elicits the reader's sympathy, it does not mitigate the idea that her main priority is pleasing herself. Hemingway counters the idea that the story is primarily a "sympathetic portrayal of the woman's point of view" (Beegal 155) by interjecting the Expressionistic element of "repetitive passages [that] are . . . as striking as the repeated lines and planes and masses of Cezanne or Picasso or Van Gogh, placed as they are on the canvas with extreme care with the conscious intention of arousing emotion in the viewer" (Raymond S. Nelson, *Hemingway: Expressionist Artist* [Ames: The Iowa State U P, 1979]: 66). This is obvious when one considers the wife's incessant litany of "I want . . . and I want . . . and I want . . . and I want" (*CS*), which prompts not sympathy for but rather agitation at her unabashed concern for self.

The idea that George is "only tangentially involved" (Carlos Baker, *Hemingway: The Writer as Artist* [Princeton: Princeton UP, 1963]: 135) seems untenable. Though apparently out of sight, he is the catalyst that evokes dramatically specific actions in the wife's belated realization that in his eyes she is an invisible presence, not someone of "supreme importance" (*CS*). Since George fails to see her as a person in her own right, she welcomed the attention of the sympathetic padrone and absorbs the "momentary feeling of supreme importance" (*CS*) he gives her; but she also felt "very small" (*CS*), knowing his ephemeral solicitude will evaporate under the persistent reality of her husband's refusal to see her worthy of his selfish world. It is in his "wide use of symbols" (Nelson 66) that we witness Hemingway's ability to strike the precisely right note to elicit the idea that some people do change themselves for the better. This is inferred by Hemingway's pointed movement from the positive to the comparative in conjunction with his stress on "light" (*CS*) and the "big Tortoise-Shell cat" (*CS*) in the culminating scenes. "It was raining" (*CS*), then "It was raining harder" (*CS*) equates in growing intensity the wife's pitiful feelings of neglect and near despair. Then, and with "dark" (*CS*), Hemingway moves from the positive to the comparative, "It was getting dark" (*CS*) to "It was quite dark now" (*CS*). However, all may not be lost for the woman, for the growing darkness may be pierced by "the light [that] had come on in the square" (*CS*), which may symbolize an answer to the wife's final plea, "I want candles" (*CS*). The light in conjunction with the gift of a "big tortoise-shell cat" (*CS*) suggests that the wife realizes the only way she can become her own person is by shedding her pathetic dependency on her husband.

In his story Hemingway's ingenious melding of symphonic tones, Expressionistic structures, and subtle, complex symbols effect his singular reflection that concern for self can lead only to depression and isolation.

If we listen, as Burton Roscoe did, to the "dialogue [that] is so naturally natural it . . . hardly seems to be written at all; one hears it" (Ernest Hemingway, *Literary Masters: Vol. 2* [Farmington Hills: The Gale Group, 2000]: 13), we will hear a voice that counseled going beyond the self to realize true and lasting satisfaction.

Source: John V. McDermott, "Hemingway's 'Cat in the Rain': A Reproof of the Self," in *Notes on Contemporary Literature*, Vol. 41, No. 1, January 2011.

Peter Griffin

In the following essay. Griffin explains how "Cat in the Rain" was conceived by Hemingway.

Hemingway's "Cat in the Rain" has been around a long time. Almost eighty years. Hardly a book on the author appears that doesn't include some information. Carlos Baker reports the story's genesis: "It was about [Ernest] . . . and Hadley and the manager and the chambermaid at the Hotel

Splendide" (107). Jeffrey Meyers sees in the American wife a "quest for a femininity that will arouse her husband ... [her] almost manic desire for a compensatory cat ... symbolizes her wish for a baby" (153). For Kenneth Lynn "Cat in the Rain" "manifested [Hemingway's] ... ability to look critically at the insensitive way in which men handled women" (252). And Michael Reynolds, after supplying some details of composition, asserts simply, "It was not a nice story ... it was a great story" (176).

"Cat in the Rain" was conceived by Hemingway in Rapallo, Italy, in February 1923. From the Hotel Splendide, he gave Gertrude Stein a sense of his mood:

> The sea is weak and dull here and doesn't look as though there was much salt in the water. The tide rises and falls about an inch. When the surf breaks it sounds like someone pouring a bucket of ashes over the side of a scow. (*Selected Letters*)

In fact, Hemingway and his wife were both depressed. Despite all precautions, Hadley had become pregnant (Lynn 191). There was little money, less work, and not much love. Now a baby was coming. And although three months earlier she'd been his "feather kitty" in Chamby (*SL*), Ernest had stopped making love to Hadley, claiming the altitude made his glands inoperative (*SL*). Yet, "The best-laid schemes o' mice and men/Gang aft a-gley." In Ernest's eyes—their gaze directly on his own needs, his career—now she'd been untrue.

To the eyes, the way men know the world, rain reveals vacancy, absence, sadness, and lingering regret. In "Cat in the Rain" the war monument drips; the big palms and green benches, the public gardens are sodden in the rain. "Across the square in the doorway of the café a waiter stood looking out at the empty square" (*Short Stories*).

The wife finds herself looking at the world, and herself, as if she were a man. And she doesn't like it.

"The American wife stood at the window looking out. Outside right under their window a cat was crouched under one of the dripping green tables. The cat was trying to make herself so compact that she would not be dripped on." The wife identifies. She's trying to keep dry herself. "'I'm going down and get that kitty,' the American wife said.... 'The poor kitty out trying to keep dry under a table.'"

But the female sense is touch, not sight. Hemingway knew this from the deep memories of infancy:

> Asked if he were afraid of the dark or of walking in the woods alone, Ernest would claim he was "afraid of nothing." But then he would cuddle around Grace's neck, asking to play "'Kitty,' where Mama be the Mama kitty and strokes him and purrs." "He pats my face in the night," Grace [his mother] wrote, "and squeezes up so close... and sings 'Ah' which is the way he loves" (Griffin 8).

In his surly mood, in Rapallo, in his twenties, Hemingway referenced a common slang, an easy play off well-lubricated vagina—"cat in the rain." On her way to the "poor kitty," the wife meets the hotel-keeper and the double entendre begins.

> "*Il piove*," the wife said. She liked the hotel-keeper.
>
> "*Sí, sí, Signora, brutto tempo*. It's very bad weather."
>
> He stood behind his desk in the far end of the dim room. The wife liked him. She liked the deadly serious way he received any complaints. She liked his dignity. She liked the way he wanted to serve her. She liked the way he felt about being a hotel-keeper. She liked his old, heavy face and big hands. (*SS*)

The American wife can't see the padrone too well. But how nice his "heavy face," his "big hands" make her feel. "Liking him" that way, she opens the door to the rain.

The padrone, however, is old, prewar, and can serve her only in his fashion: the comforts he provides, the small civilities he performs. On the other hand, her husband George only lies in bed, propped up on pillows, and reads. The American wife wants what should come to a young woman. And she speaks of it subconsciously.

> "I want to pull my hair back tight and smooth and make a big knot at the back that I can feel," she said. "I want to have a kitty to sit on my lap and purr when I stroke her."
>
> "Yeah?" George said from the bed.
>
> "And I want to eat at a table with my own silver and I want candles. And I want it to be spring and I want to brush my hair out in front of a mirror and I want a kitty and I want some new clothes." (*SS*)

The wife wants her hair to grow long. She's tired of looking like a boy. The American husband likes her to look like a boy. He likes what he sees. What irony there is in George's warning to the wife as she goes for the poor kitty. "'Don't get wet,' he said" (*SS*). But she does get "wet." When she returns, empty handed, and sits on the bed with George, she understands the uselessness of it all.

> "I wanted it so much," she said. "I don't know why I wanted it so much. I wanted that poor kitty. It isn't any fun to be a poor kitty out in the rain."

The American husband is dry, desiccated, unable or unwilling to act. "'I'll do it,' her husband offered from the bed" (*SS*). His generation, the postwar men, have a disgust for action, any action, except the action of the eyes. To read is to act without acting: Life caught by the eyes, passed directly to the imagination, and lived there. That's enough for George. In the four page story Hemingway has George "reading" a half dozen times. He tells his wife, bitchily, "'Oh, shut up and get something to read.'"

She gets something else. A cat. A gift from the padrone. But it's not the "wet pussy" (*A Moveable Feast*) she wanted. It's a "big tortoise-shell cat," a sterile male (Bennett 487). But then she's already got one of those. Outside the window it's quite dark, and raining. But George, and now his wife, are dry inside.

Source: Peter Griffin, "A Foul Mood, a Dirty Joke: Hemingway's 'Cat in the Rain,'" in *Hemingway Review*, Vol. 20, No. 2, Spring 2001, p. 99.

Hildy Coleman Neel

In the following essay, Neel claims that the monument in the short story is a "mute reminder of incomplete lives."

When Ernest Hemingway vacationed in Rapallo, Italy during the 1920s, he stayed at the Hotel Riviera Splendide, which today is simply called the Hotel Riviera. The present owners of the hotel have prepared a glossy advertising brochure, the first page of which pays tribute to its famous former guest by reprinting some opening lines from the author's signature tale, "Cat in the Rain" said to have been conceived "on a rainy day . . . that February [1923] at the Hotel Splendide" in Rapallo (Baker 133). The excerpt printed in the promotional brochure reads, in Italian:

> C'erano soltanto due clienti Americani alloggiati in quello albergo. . . . La lore camera era al secondo piano affacciata sul mare. Guardava anche sue giardini pubblici ed il monumento ai caduti. . . .

At the bottom of the page, the English text appears:

> There were only two Americans stopping at the hotel . . . Their room was at the second floor facing the sea. It also faced the public garden and the war monument.

It is significant, given Hemingway's minimalist locutions, that the war monument is mentioned two more times in the short scene-setting paragraph of fourteen sentences: "Italians came from a long way off to look up at the war monument. It was made of bronze and glistened in the rain" and "The motor cars were gone from the square by the war monument" (*SS*).

The actual monument featured in the story and clearly visible from Hemingway's Room 66 at the Hotel Riviera Splendide was the work of Giacinto Pasciuto. Pasciuto's sketch had won him the commission, following open competition among several artists, to create a *monumento ai caduti* (monument to the fallen) commemorating the sacrifices of Italian soldiers who died fighting in World War I. The sculpture was completed in late 1921 and unveiled near the Piazza IV Novembre in the public garden on 30 July 1922, months before Hemingway began to write his enduring tale.

A news item printed in the Rapallo tabloid *Il Mare* announced the unveiling along with a profile and photographs of Pasciuto's work, describing the prostrate figures of fallen soldiers as images of the sublime ideal, hugging each other in the last embrace of death: ". . . sono raggruppati nell'ultimo amplesso dalla morte le gloriose figure del Caduti abbracciantiai nella imagine de un sublime ideale." The dead warriors lay at the feet of a towering angel of victory stretching skyward, in one hand a conquering sword and in the other a triumphant crown. On the monument's stone base were inscribed the words "Affratelliati/ nel supremo sacrificio/ congiunti glorificati/ della piu grande/ Italia vittoriosa" (Brotherly soldiers in the supreme sacrifice, gloriously joined, in the greatest Italian victory).

For more than a decade, the Pasciuto monument graced the public garden at Rapallo, but in the late 1930s, it was dismantled so that the bronze figures that had "glistened in the rain" could be melted down for military hardware.

After World War II, the municipality of Rapallo commissioned a bronze replacement statue to memorialize those who died in all wars, this one created by the sculptor Alessandro Cherchi. In the vicinity of the public garden, near the sea and overlooked by the Hotel Riviera, the statue depicts "a mother complaining for her two children's sudden death because of war." On a white marble plate attached to the wall behind the monument, inscribed in bronze, an epigraph reads, Ai Caduti Di Tutte Le Guerre (To all those who died in wars).

However, whether we consider the original Pasciuto war memorial or the later Cherchi tableau, the essence of Hemingway's timeless vision in the story remains intact. As the central trope of "Cat in the Rain" the war monument is a mute reminder of the incomplete lives toward which the narrative's modalities point. Indeed, this concise little tale of a woman's thwarted yearnings coincides with the aborted dreams memorialized in the sculptures—both the "American girl" and the "fallen" Italian soldiers have been robbed of the natural fulfillment life might be expected to hold. Principal among the story's introductory references, the war monument not only corresponds with the succeeding incident between the couple in the parable, but renders and underscores a mood of universal human sadness.

Source: Hildy Coleman Neel, "The War Monument in 'Cat in the Rain': Then and Now," in *Hemingway Review*, Vol. 19, No. 2, Spring 2000, p. 102.

Edwin J. Barton

In the following essay, Barton notes that ambiguity about the possible pregnancy of the wife results in ambiguity about notions of fertility and maternity in the text, depending on the involvement of the reader.

In an influential essay, Gerry Brenner has identified what he takes to be "Hemingway's three epistemologic formulas for short fiction" (156). One of these formulas, according to Brenner, is the lexical riddle, which "pivot[s] upon a lexical crux, the unarticulated or ambiguous words [such as] abortion, lesbian, and corrupt. Hemingway's strategy here is to have readers so stew over the missing or ambiguous term that once they discover it or its meaning, they will feel they have solved the story and mosey along to the next one" (161). One finds among the examples he offers a brief reference to "Cat in the Rain": "... underlying the behavior of the American wife in "Cat" is the easy-to-come-by lexical crux, 'maternal instincts': her wish for a cat is the substitute for the domestic maternity she longs for" (161–62). Indeed, nearly every commentator would seem to agree that "domestic maternity" is in some sense the crux of the matter in this story. Yet no one, so far as I know, has managed to

"INDEED, CONSTRUCTING THE CLICHÉD READING THAT MAKES GEORGE THE ANTAGONIST PLACES THE READER IN THE SOMEWHAT HYPOCRITICAL POSITION OF FORMING AN INTERPRETATION BASED ON A BIAS AGAINST THE VERY ACTIVITY IN WHICH HE OR SHE IS ENGAGING."

explore the range of lexical riddles behind this "easy-to-come-by" crux. For if Hemingway's short fiction may be thought to depend in part upon such epistemologic formulas as these, we ought to explore the full extent to which the hermeneutics of the stories are multi-layered.

Writing of "Cat in the Rain," Warren Bennett observes that "present critical opinion has produced two disputes... One is the question of whether there are one or two cats in the story, and the second is the question of whether the wife wants to have a baby or whether she is already pregnant" (245). With respect to the former, Bennett argues that both textual and extra-textual evidence would seem to support the "two-cat theory." Whether or not some uncertainty in this matter remains is not my concern here; I am more interested in the latter question, which I believe has been improperly formulated. The better question to ask might well be whether or not we are meant to consider the possibility that the American wife/girl had been pregnant before. Still more to the point, we may wonder if the reader is meant to understand that she is incapable of bearing children, either because she (or her husband) has proved infertile or because of complications owing to a miscarriage or abortion.

Such questions, of course, arise from the assumption that Hemingway's fiction conforms to the conventions of realism, in which characters and actions are to be appreciated as sentient and meaningful. Answering the "easy-to-come-by" questions enables readers to arrive at a kind of clichéd diegesis. It is only when they continue to ask questions that the illusion of reality may begin to fall away, allowing them to appreciate how a text may contrive a number of competing fictions: the hermeneutics of the story.

The passage that seems to me to contrive the lexical riddle of fertility comes immediately upon the wife's seeing that "the cat was gone." Noticing that she "was suddenly disappointed," the hotel maid asks, "*Ha perduto qualque cosa, Signora?*" (*SS*). By having the maid ask it in Italian, Hemingway both disguises and emphasizes this question, which may be heard to resonate through the rest of the story. As there is no translation of the maid's question, we must translate it ourselves: Have you lost something, Madam? This question, I would assert, may well be pregnant in more than one sense.

In the logic of "realistic" fiction, such a question would require that the American wife translate it, too, in order to reply. And, significantly, her response gives evidence of transformation as well as translation, for it is immediately following this question that the narrator begins to refer to the wife as "the American girl."

> "There was a cat," said the American girl.
>
> "A cat?"
>
> "*Si, il gatto.*"
>
> "A cat?" the maid laughed. "A cat in the rain?"
>
> "Yes," she said, "under the table." Then, "Oh, I wanted it so much. I wanted a kitty."

At one level, the switch from wife to girl may be thought to signal a change in standing. The narrator seems here to key into the fictional consciousness of the maid: the American wife/woman is behaving like a girl. But if we identify the desire for a cat as a symbolic displacement of maternal instincts, the more subtle change indicated here may well be psychological. The maid's question, that is to say, may be thought to have tapped a latent desire or even a repressed memory of a primal scene; indeed the maid's query explicitly introduces the question of loss or lack, which both infers and implies a prior fulfillment of desire, whether physical or symbolic.

Hemingway marks this change with the adverb "Then, . . . " —creating a curious pause in the dialogue. Moreover, the retrospective tone and the verb tense shift, if ever so slightly, from "There was a cat" to "Oh, I wanted it so much. I wanted a kitty." The former refers to the recent past: what she saw from the window of her room. The latter, however, would seem to allude to a more distant past, as though she had lost a kitty she "wanted . . . so much" some time earlier. Moreover, she had wanted "a kitty," not the kitty. The perceptible trace of the perfect tense, as opposed to a more nearly simple past, intimates that her hopes belong exclusively to the past, though her desire remains sharp. Likewise, the insistence on an indefinite article may suggest that the object of desire was and remains an unknown quantity.

Yet, despite her seeming awareness of the anteriority of hope for fulfillment, the American girl finds a means for extending the aesthetic moment of desire:

> As the American girl passed the office, the padrone bowed from his desk. Something felt very small and tight inside the girl. The padrone made her feel very small and at the same time really important. She had a momentary feeling of being of supreme importance.

It would seem plausible here to discover in her feeling "very small and at the same time really important" a conflation of two apparently different states of being. One would seem to be the remembered state of virginity, the other an actual or imagined state of pregnancy. Bennett is no doubt right to insist that "the words 'small' and 'tight' do not gynecologically describe a condition of pregnancy" (248). But the "feeling of being of supreme importance," despite Bennett's objections, might very well describe the condition of being pregnant or, at least, the thought of being pregnant. Moreover, "small" and "tight" would seem to connote not so much a physical condition as a known and remembered feeling of virginity, which might itself bring on a momentarily recollected emotional state to which the American wife/girl appears to retreat. It is the deportment of the padrone, another word requiring translation, which appears to prompt these feelings.

As has so often been noted, the padrone may be thought to occupy the role of a surrogate father/suitor in the American wife's fictional consciousness:

> He stood behind his desk in the far end of the dim room. The wife liked him. She liked the deadly serious way he received any complaints. She liked his dignity. She liked the way he wanted to serve her. She liked the way he felt about being a hotel-keeper. She liked his old, heavy face and big hands. (168)

It has likewise become a commonplace in the criticism of this story to contrast the "dignity" and willingness to serve of the padrone with the unchivalrous behavior of George, whose sense of duty extends only to "offer[ing] from the bed" to retrieve the cat and assuring his wife that she "look[s] pretty darn nice" (169). But to read the story in this way is to ignore the possibility that Hemingway employs a variation on the "third epistemologic formula" of which Brenner speaks: namely, "extratextual reversal."

> In [some] stories Hemingway sets into action a character whose occupation or easily labelled role calls up cultural expectations of stereotypical behavior, ones Hemingway partly honors (to keep the stereotype intact) but primarily subverts (to violate the typecasting label and to render freshly the individual behind the stereotype). And by invoking these stereotyped labels Hemingway also welcomes the moral prejudgments that conventionally accompany them so as to maneuver his textual materials and subvert those judgments. (162–63)

The stereotyped labels here, then, are not only the sexually frustrated and unappreciated wife but also the impotent and insensitive husband. With these, one can easily reconstruct a clichéd diegesis: what a community of "readerly" (in Barthes' sense) readers might regard as the story as it should be.

I would contend that in "Cat in the Rain" Hemingway subverts these stereotyped labels through the lexical riddle of "fertility," which lies beneath or behind the lexical riddle of "domestic maternity." In this sense, "Cat in the Rain" would seem analogous to several of Hemingway's other stories—"Out of Season," "Hills Like White Elephants," and "The Sea Change" come to mind—in which domestic and sexual relations between men and women take center stage. These stories present highly complex, fluid, and dynamic relations between the sexes and suggest that Hemingway understood, like another American writer who went before him, that the stories of *eros tyrannos* are rarely just what we would expect:

> We tell you, tapping on our brows,
> The story as it should be,—
> As if the story of a house
> Were told, or ever could be;
> We'll have no kind veil between
> Her visions and those we have seen,—
> As if we guessed what hers have been,
> Or what they are or would be.
> (E. A. Robinson, "Eros Tyrannos")

Reading the story with this admonition in mind enables one to ponder the possibility that George's attitude and remarks are not wholly insensitive, though they may not be wholly justifiable either. His response to his wife's dissatisfaction with her hair, for instance, may be viewed as an attempt at consoling her—"I like it the way it is"—particularly if we appreciate the meaning of "it" in light of that "something" she has lost. Likewise, George's final response—"Oh, shut up and get something to read"—may be construed to be less a defense mechanism or a brutish cry of exasperation than an exhortation to acceptance of an existential reality. Getting "something to read" may indeed prove more efficacious than the wife's symbolic displacements:

> "And I want to eat at a table with my own silver and I want candles. And I want it to be spring and I want to brush my hair out in front of a mirror and I want a kitty and I want some new clothes."

These symbolic displacements appear unlikely to fill the void, as the arrival of a cat sent up by the padrone would seem to suggest. Indeed, treating her complaints in a "deadly serious way" might serve to sharpen rather than dull the edge of her desire.

The "readerly" reader, for whom the sense of closure and a determinate diegesis is essential, may fail to recognize the ways in which Hemingway's text is deliberately overdetermined. In the clichéd interpretation to which I have already alluded, the husband's preoccupation with reading may be seen as symbolic of his desire to escape the reality of his domestic life. That is to say, George is often understood to prefer the apparent plenitude of fulfilling fictions extrapolated from a written text to the actual world of human affairs, which is marked by loss and insufficiency. Yet this interpretation would seem to overlook the competing fictions that the American wife appears to have constructed for herself. In rereading the text of her body, she has created a diegesis in which the self-acknowledged tragic tenor of her life-story can be redeemed only by a wholly satisfying denouement: "And I want it to be spring and I want to brush my hair out in front of a mirror and I want a kitty. . . . " Her sense of an ending, which reveals her desire for a plenitude of presence, is in many ways no less desperate than George's exhortation to "shut up and get something to read." Indeed, one could argue that hers is more nearly the escapist fiction; George, at least, would seem to recognize the difference between reading and being.

Moreover, in coming to the specific question of George's reading, I would suggest that we are meant to recognize here that he and his wife are not the only ones engaged in making fictions. Indeed, constructing the clichéd reading that makes George the antagonist places the reader in the somewhat hypocritical position of forming an interpretation based on a bias against the very activity in which he or she is engaging. In reading, that is to say, we find fault with George, who prefers reading to looking in the mirror. Yet it is George's activity that mirrors our own. In this way, Hemingway's story serves to remind readers who continue to interrogate the text that they are engaged in an activity which encourages interpretation based on ambiguous signs.

As Brian McHale has suggested in *Postmodernist Fiction*, this vertiginous structure of riddles and interpretive activities foregrounds the epistemologic "dominant" that distinguishes high modernism (6–10). This would seem to agree with Brenner's assertion of the three "epistemologic formulas." By casting doubt on the story as it should be, Hemingway forces his readers to become less "readerly" and more "writerly" in their approaches to his stories; that is to say, he forces us to reread, as Barthes has put it, "Not the real text, but a plural text; the same and new" (16).

Source: Edwin J. Barton, "The Story as It Should Be: Epistemological Uncertainty in Hemingway's 'Cat in the Rain,'" in *Hemingway Review*, Vol. 14, No. 1, Fall 1994, pp. 72–78.

SOURCES

Baker, Carlos, *Ernest Hemingway: A Life Story*, Charles Scribner's Sons, 1969, pp. 102–33.

Chatman, Seymour, "'Soft Filters': Some Sunshine on 'Cat in the Rain,'" in *Narrative*, Vol. 9, No. 2, 2001, p. 217.

Cheville, Norman F., *Introduction to Veterinary Pathology*, 2nd. ed., Iowa State University Press, 1999, p. 267.

Hagopian, John V., "Symmetry in 'Cat in the Rain,'" in *Short Stories of Ernest Hemingway: Critical Essays*, edited by Jackson J. Benson, Duke University Press, 1975, pp. 230–32.

Hemingway, Ernest, "Cat in the Rain," in *In Our Time*, Scribner's Sons, 1925, pp. 89–94.

———, *A Moveable Feast*, Scribner, 1964, p. 75.

———, "Ernest Hemingway—Banquet Speech (Read by U.S. Ambassador to Sweden, John C. Cabot)," December 10, 1954, in *Nobelprize.org*, http://www.nobelprize.org/nobel_prizes/literature/laureates/1954/hemingway-speech.html (accessed November 7, 2011).

Lynn, Kenneth S., *Hemingway*, Harvard University Press, 1987.

McDermott, John V., "Hemingway's 'Cat in the Rain': A Reproof of the Self," in *Notes on Contemporary Literature*, Vol. 41, No. 1, 2011.

Tetlow, Wendolyn E., *Hemingway's "In Our Time": Lyrical Dimensions*, Associated University Press, 1992, pp. 78–81.

FURTHER READING

Benson, Jackson J., *Short Stories of Ernest Hemingway: Critical Essays*, Duke University Press, 1975.

The essays in this collection span a wide variety of Hemingway's short fiction and the critical reviews they have inspired. The collection is an excellent companion to the reading of Hemingway's short fiction, and the Hagopian essay on "Cat in the Rain" is one of the most frequently cited critical essays on that particular story.

Hipple, Theodore W., ed., *Twentieth Century American Short Stories*, Allyn & Bacon, 1977.

Hipple's collection of short stories includes some of the most famous works by authors such as Parker, Jack London, Fitzgerald, Faulkner, Hemingway, Steinbeck, Langston Hughes, and Kurt Vonnegut, Jr. It is an excellent resource for discovering the wide variety of American fiction that flourished in the twentieth century.

Humphrey, Carpenter, *Geniuses Together: American Writers in Paris in the 1920s*, Houghton Mifflin, 1988.

Part biography, part memoir, this book examines the vast movement of writers who migrated to Europe during the 1920s. As Gertrude Stein said and as Hemingway wrote, they were all part of a "lost generation," and Humphrey's book describes their cause. Authors in Europe at the time included Hemingway, Stein, Fitzgerald, T. S. Eliot, and Ezra Pound.

Mellow, James R., *Charmed Circle: Gertrude Stein and Company*, Houghton Mifflin, 1991.

Mellow's book looks at the group of writers who gathered around Stein in France during the 1920s. Hemingway was one of her followers, and many of their encounters can be found in Mellow's book, as well as in Hemingway's own writing. Since Hemingway was a part of this charmed circle, this book is essential to a thorough understanding of the author at the time he wrote "Cat in the Rain."

SUGGESTED SEARCH TERMS

Ernest Hemingway

Cat in the Rain AND Hemingway

In Our Time AND Hemingway

modernism

Hemingway AND modernism

Hemingway AND short fiction

Hemingway AND marriage

Hemingway AND World War I

modernism AND World War I

Hemingway AND expatriates

Hemingway AND F. Scott Fitzgerald

Hemingway AND Gertrude Stein

Gentleman of Rio en Medio

JUAN A. A. SEDILLO

1939

Juan A. A. Sedillo was a New Mexican attorney and politician who, in the middle of his career, wrote a story, "Gentleman of Rio en Medio," that would resonate with steady streams of readers through the remainder of the twentieth century and beyond. Much as he only dabbled in an acting career, Sedillo only dabbled in literature as well, ultimately earning his place in history as a judge on the International Court of Justice in Morocco. Sedillo certainly drew on a lawyerly objectivity and a judicial sense of fairness, in addition to his Spanish American roots, in writing "Gentleman of Rio en Medio," which was first published in the *New Mexico Quarterly* in 1939.

The story is an attorney's account of the purchase of the property of a dignified old gentleman in a small Hispano village. The old man defies the attorney's expectations both in completing the sale and in clearing up a certain matter afterward. Perhaps because of the poignancy with which the story captures the gradual historical ebbing of the village-level way of life, it has been republished many times, including in *We Are Chicanos: An Anthology of Mexican-American Literature* (1973), edited by Philip K. Ortego y Gasca; *Windows and Walls*, Vol. 1 (1980), edited by Theodore Clymer; and a great number of literature textbooks.

AUTHOR BIOGRAPHY

Sedillo was born in 1902 into a New Mexican family in which, by virtue of the father's devotion

Don Anselmo, a highly-respected figure, owns the land in question. (Breanne Schaap / Shutterstock.com)

to learning, education was highly valued. On both sides, his lineage was recorded as extending back to Spanish royalty. While attending law school at Georgetown University, in Washington, D.C., Sedillo happened to encounter an executive from Fox Studios who deemed his presence noteworthy, and he was cast as a Cuban detective in *Girl from Havana* (1929), but he did not pursue a film career. Back in New Mexico in the early 1930s, he practiced law and meanwhile served as secretary of the Progressive Party and as a state senator representing Santa Fe. In 1939, he published "Gentleman of Rio en Medio" in the *New Mexico Quarterly*.

In 1944, bearing the rank of lieutenant general in the military's Judge Advocate General Corps, Sedillo served on court-martial panels such as that which decided the fate of James Hendricks, who was convicted for an accidental murder. In *The Interpreter* (2005), her exploration of that case and a similar one, Alice Kaplan describes Sedillo as "a suave ambitious man" who "was an elitist who had always insisted on his white, European origins" (which did not bode well for the black defendant, Hendricks). In 1930, Kaplan notes, Sedillo had seen fit to write the *New York Times* to assert that, contrary to a book reviewer's statement, Colorado's first white child was born in the eighteenth century, not the nineteenth. He was fond of the sport of polo. He married and later divorced a French-speaking Danish countess, Eva Knuth.

Sedillo's achievements following World War II were in the field of law. In August 1946, he was named legal chief of the American military government in Stuttgart, Germany. In September 1948, he was a justice in occupied Germany's highest appeals court, and in 1953, he was appointed

American judge on the International Court of Justice in Tangier, Morocco. He wrote about the unique function of that court for the *American Bar Association Journal* in 1957. Sedillo died in 1982.

PLOT SUMMARY

"Gentleman of Rio en Medio" opens with a sentence that introduces the main protagonist, the old man. This sentence implies that the narrator is also a character within the story and hints at the central importance of a gulf of understanding between the two persons. The old man is portrayed as a rustic individual whose family, having lived on the same land for centuries, has become intertwined with their farm and the land itself. His property includes a wonderful orchard.

The old man visits what must be the narrator's office. By virtue of the narrator's role in conducting an estate sale, the reader may guess that he is an attorney or lawyer. The narrator describes the old man's garments in a somewhat condescending way. The reference to the New Mexico senator Thomas Benton Catron, who served in the mid-1910s, suggests that the story is rather set in the 1930s, contemporaneous with its publication, and that the old man's politics and wardrobe alike are severely outdated. (The "Prince Albert" was a double-breasted coat named after the English prince who later became King Edward VII.) Indeed, the old man seems to have been wearing his current ragged attire for decades. The description of the boy who comes with the old man reveals that their skin is relatively dark, suggesting Mexican or possibly Native American lineage—confirming, either way, the ethnic/cultural gap already suggested by the detached, analytical nature of the narrator's descriptions of the man. The mention of silent-film star Charlie Chaplin further depicts the old man as unintentionally comical in appearance.

After chatting about the weather and his family, the old man confirms that he will complete the sale as promised. The amount of $1,200 was quite a large sum in 1939—equivalent to roughly $19,000 in 2010. The fourth paragraph advances the reader's conception of the narrator, who now speaks in the first-person plural—that is, on behalf of the Americans he is representing—and in Spanish (which was a co-official language at this point in New Mexico history). Thus, Don Anselmo, the old man, is presumably Hispano, or a descendant of the Spaniards who settled the region before its acquisition by the United States. The use of "we" suggests that the narrator is truly a disinterested participant in this affair, with his own perspective melting into that of his client(s), while his knowledge of Spanish suggests that he can generally understand the old man, who perhaps speaks only Spanish, better than one might have guessed.

The attorney relates that his clients, who "are good people," wish to acknowledge the true extent of Don Anselmo's land by nearly doubling the amount to be paid. Responding after a sullen pause, Don Anselmo expresses indignity at the way he has been spoken to—perhaps specifically the suggestion that his foremost concern is money—and refuses to accept more than what he originally agreed upon. The lawyer argues, but the deal is concluded under the original terms, and Don Anselmo departs.

The narrator relates the ensuing activities of his clients, whom he actually refers to as "my friends." Moving onto Don Anselmo's property that summer, they fix things up and settle in, but they return to the attorney to protest the constant trespassing committed by the local children, who congregate freely around the trees even when instructed (in English) not to.

Don Anselmo returns to the lawyer's office when requested, in much the same manner and attire as before. The lawyer proceeds to carefully spell out the concern: his friends, who, he reiterates, are good people, are unable to enjoy their new home peacefully because of the activities of the children, and they are hoping that Don Anselmo might help the children understand the situation and respect the boundary of the property. His position as village elder should extend him this authority. Standing up to respond (as he did before), Don Anselmo agrees that the attorney's American friends are decent neighbors, but he asserts that the trees were not part of the bargain. The attorney recognizes that this could be a major problem and tries to explain why the trees, as part of the property, now belong to the Americans.

The speech that follows is Don Anselmo's longest. He explains that, being the oldest man in the small village, virtually everyone is related to him in some way. Ever since he inherited the house—around when the railroad first stretched to Santa Fe (which was in 1880)—he planted a tree for every person born into the village. Thus, the land was his, but the trees belong to the individual villagers, and they are not his to sell.

In the final paragraph of the story, the lawyer concedes that his clients had little choice but to accept Don Anselmo's argument. To object further, especially in light of his generosity regarding the sale price, would clearly upset him, and to use force to keep the children from their trees would surely ruin the Americans' reputation in the small village they now call home. Through the ensuing winter, the trees would have to be purchased one by one from all of Don Anselmo's kin.

CHARACTERS

Americans

The reader learns near the end of the story that the friends of the attorney who purchase Don Anselmo's property are Americans. It is interesting how effectively Sedillo prevents the Americans from actually entering the story. They may, conceivably, be present at either of the meetings in the lawyer's office, as the lawyer refers to Don Anselmo bowing to "all of us in the room" the first time and to how he "shook hands all around" the second time. It is unlikely that a disinterested party would be present in the room—perhaps a town clerk—but it is also unclear why, if the Americans are there, they are neither mentioned nor addressed throughout. However, if Don Anselmo only speaks Spanish and so can only converse with the attorney, and if he approaches the meetings as strictly legal concerns—that is, not social visits—he might very well ignore the Americans completely even if they are sitting before him. Regardless, Sedillo might have easily allowed the attorney/narrator a paragraph of physical description of the Americans, or he might have even introduced interaction with them—but he elected not to. This reflects their minimal relevance, as actual characters, to the content of the story. Indeed, the description of them as Americans and "good people" is enough to allow them to fulfill their function.

Although their race is not identified, the Americans' capitalist advantages (in an era when black citizens were still segregated and oppressed) and their evident inability to speak even the most elementary Spanish suggest that they hail from mainstream American society; the reader will likely conceive of them as white, despite the lack of any evidence to confirm this. (At the very least, there is no indication that these generic "Americans" are anything other than white.) Although one might easily disparage wealthy whites who, in a sort of micro-colonial manner, wield their riches to wrest property away from locals who have cherished their land for centuries, doing so is difficult when they are nonetheless "good people"—friendly, decent neighbors who try to be generous and respectful of local custom. The Americans' intent to offer Don Anselmo the fairest possible price for his land; their willingness to go to great lengths to acquire all the trees in a way that honors their assigned owners; and Don Anselmo's own affirmation of their decency all suggest that the Americans are indeed as benevolent as the attorney claims.

Don Anselmo

The title character of Sedillo's story, Don Anselmo is the central focus throughout. The narrator opens with a description of the old man's curious character and "quaint" property, then proceeds directly to his first visit. The attorney's comparisons of the old man with well-known personages, a senator and a film star, enhance Don Anselmo's image as a singular individual who has walked into the attorney's office straight out of history or a movie. The lawyer's descriptions are deliberately comical, but—like Chaplin in his frequent role as persevering everyman—Don Anselmo manages to retain a measure of human dignity.

Although his circumstances do not allow him the fanciest wardrobe, Don Anselmo carries himself as a gentleman and pays due heed to social propriety, greeting others formally and conversing politely. He takes great pride in his sense of honor, refusing to break his word by accepting anything other than the figure he originally agreed upon for his property, even though, as the lawyer points out, from a mathematical perspective revising the figure in accord with the extent of the land would be entirely reasonable. Don Anselmo also does not attempt to profit from the trees that he does not consider his own. Operating under moral principles that prefigure the laws under which the attorney and the Americans operate, the gentleman of Rio en Medio is indeed a man from a bygone era.

Attorney

As a character in the story, the attorney's relevance is minimal. He merely carries out the wishes of his American clients with regard to negotiating the purchase of Don Anselmo's land. As such, his spoken comments are very formulaic and deliberate, as intended to communicate as effectively as possible with the old man. The attorney's manner offends Don Anselmo during the negotiations—but there are two possible sources to this offense: it may be how the attorney implies that money is Don Anselmo's foremost concern, that he might be flattered or influenced by more of it, or it may be simply the suggestion that Don Anselmo go back on his word regarding the agreed-upon price.

The attorney's narrative comment during Don Anselmo's indignant reaction—"I kept still and let him have his say"—suggests that the attorney surmises that the old man needs to vent an emotional response despite his not fully understanding what he is being told. In fact, the attorney's role as narrator is where he plays the most significant part. The race of the lawyer is not clear; his name is not provided, and he does not describe himself in the least. However, his position contra Don Anselmo is made clear by his condescending descriptions of the old man's appearance and bearing. The lawyer may speak Spanish, but, whatever the color of his skin—and it seems most likely that he is a shade of white—he is clearly allied with the white culture represented by his friends, the Americans. It would be reasonable to regard the attorney as a stand-in for, if not the autobiographical equivalent of, Sedillo himself.

Boy

The boy who accompanies Don Anselmo to the lawyer's office is only briefly described. One of Don Anselmo's kin, the boy holds the old man's accoutrements and dutifully waits upon him. The boy's having "eyes like a gazelle" suggests the sense of wildness retained by him and by all the other young kin of Don Anselmo, whose village seems to subsist outside the bounds of modern Western civilization.

THEMES

Time

Over the course of his very brief story, Sedillo touches upon a number of themes that contribute to a broader contrast between the culture of the Americans and that of Don Anselmo. The first of these is time, a theme that is given pride of place in the story's first several sentences, which play a critical role in the reader's impression of the story as a whole. Don Anselmo is introduced as operating outside modern social bounds with respect to time, likely being hard to reach, slow to respond, and, in sum, "in no hurry." In the first sentence the lawyer, though primly diplomatic, hints at mild frustration with this quality of Don Anselmo's, pointedly noting his advanced age.

In present-day multiethnic American society, references to the deliberate pace of peoples from less technologically developed nations as being on "island time" or "African time," for example, are somewhat clichéd, but there is some truth to such conceptions. Don Anselmo, the reader may imagine, has no telephone, likely no electricity, and perhaps no mechanical timepiece ticking away. As such, he could live his advanced life never quite needing to care what time it is or even what day it is. He might only arrange meetings based on vague references to the portion of the day. Thus, he would never really have to worry about how late he is: how can one be late to an appointment that was never precisely scheduled to begin with? The lawyer, on the other hand, likely with a calendar on his desk and a clock on his wall, operating on a weekly schedule, can never be totally unaware of what day or time it is. The Americans of the story perhaps acquire Don Anselmo's property precisely, at least in part, in order to escape the temporal constraints of modernizing 1930s society.

Money

Don Anselmo further demonstrates a conception of money that differs from that of the lawyer and the Americans. In arranging the purchase of Don Anselmo's property, the Americans seem to have begun by proposing a figure, twelve hundred dollars, based on a presumed expanse of eight acres and a certain value per acre (as well as a certain amount for the small house). They then went to the trouble of having the land surveyed, to assess its proper size, and in finding the land much larger than imagined, they feel it just to offer a greater sum, "at the same rate per acre." Thus, the Americans arrive at their final offer by attaching a specific value to the land itself; each acre is worth a certain amount.

Don Anselmo approaches the transaction in a more holistic way. He, the reader may imagine, knows full well the extent of his own land, even if

TOPICS FOR FURTHER STUDY

- Write a parallel version of "Gentleman of Rio en Medio" from the perspective of Don Anselmo. (Although he would write in Spanish, write in English, as if your story were a translation of his.) While Sedillo's story is set primarily in the attorney's office, in relating the episode from Don Anselmo's perspective, it would be appropriate to include more detailed scenes from the village.
- Write a research paper on New Mexico's quest to be promoted from a territory to a state, which began in 1849 and concluded in 1910, after some fifty statehood bills had been proposed to Congress. Provide the political details, and also focus on how perceptions of New Mexicans throughout the United States were shaped by racism, xenophobia, and opposition to immigration. Conclude by conjecturing as to how attitudes that evolved within New Mexico during the statehood struggle might be reflected in Sedillo's story.
- Survey images on the Internet and in print resources that show what an old-time Hispano village in New Mexico would have looked like. Keep in mind that the village in "Gentleman from Rio en Medio" is understood to be "up there in the mountains," perhaps those around Santa Fe. Drawing on the few descriptions in Sedillo's story, paint a picture including such elements as Don Anselmo's house, his orchard (perhaps with children playing), and the creek; or use graphic-design software to create a digital reproduction of Don Anselmo's property and the rest of the village.
- Read "My Ancestor—Don Pedro," a short story suitable for young adults that can be found in *The Short Stories of Fray Angelico Chavez*. Chavez was a Franciscan priest from New Mexico. Both Don Juan in Chavez's story and Don Anselmo in Sedillo's story lived at turning points in history and culture. Write an essay comparing and contrasting the roles of these two characters, how they are portrayed, and their influence on those around them in changing times. Conclude by discussing how these two portrayals affect the tone and inherent messages of the two stories.
- Create a Web site on life and conditions within the Hispano community of New Mexico in the twenty-first century. Link to Web sites of nonprofit organizations and political movements, as well as any relevant blogs, to gauge prevailing opinions and worldviews among Hispanos, such as regarding traditional culture, the arts, state politics, national politics, and immigration trends.

---

he does not know precisely how many acres it amounts to. In agreeing to sell his property, he did not have in mind calculations based on a rate per acre but rather the value of the property as a whole. That he approached the transaction in this way is suggested by his refusal to revise the value assigned to his property. From a mathematical perspective, agreeing to the higher offer makes perfect sense. From a moral perspective, Don Anselmo has given his gentleman's word that he will sell all of his property for twelve hundred dollars, and his honor is evidently more important than mathematics or money.

Honesty

The major characters in this story, including the attorney, put on impressive displays of honesty. Don Anselmo foremost is represented as an honest person. He is so truthful in his dealings with the Americans, even when the circumstances of the property purchase change—the land is found to be more expansive than expected—that he cannot go back on his word; he cannot simply revise an agreement, or oral contract, that he has made, even when the other party to the contract suggests a revision in his favor. His sense of honesty restrains him.

The narrator's friends remodeled the homestead on the land. (Paul B. Moore / Shutterstock.com)

The Americans, too, are depicted as fundamentally honest people. While the attorney/narrator is being paid by them for his services and so would be expected to portray them positively in conversation, they were surely under no obligation to increase their offer based on the actual size of the property. The attorney was evidently instructed not just to propose the higher sum but also to do his best to persuade Don Anselmo to accept—"I argued with him but it was useless." When the Americans have a grievance in their new neighborhood, they do not try to avoid further interaction with Don Anselmo and forcibly remove the children from their property, but rather they appeal to him directly, hoping to resolve the situation peacefully.

The narrator also deals with Don Anselmo fairly. When Don Anselmo claims that he did not sell the trees, the attorney does not become officious and authoritative, as if speaking on behalf of the law itself, but rather continues to deal honestly with Don Anselmo, from person to person—in responding, the attorney did not simply declare, state, or assert, but "pleaded." After Don Anselmo explains his perspective on the trees, the attorney does not simply restate his previous assertion about the trees being part of the deal (as one imagines many a modern lawyer or government official would respond) but concedes, "There was nothing we could do"—and this in spite of the fact that "legally we owned the trees." The attorney, in representing the Americans, feels obligated to honor Don Anselmo's conception of the ownership of the trees, however contrary it is to the dictates of the law. The ultimate purchase of each tree individually, as related in the closing sentence, is the culmination of the prevailing honesty of Don Anselmo, the Americans, and the attorney alike.

Law and Order

Over the course of Sedillo's story, the various differences between the perspectives of Don Anselmo and the Americans coalesce into a collective statement on the differences between their two societies' approaches to law and social order. Don Anselmo's village is representative of centuries-old southwestern Hispano culture. The land that became the state of New Mexico was originally part of the colony of New Spain (mostly modern-day Mexico), whose roots were formed through the admixture of colonial Spanish and American Indian culture.

Hispano culture does not come to the fore in the story; no specific details are given that identify Don Anselmo's village as a Hispano one (other than the speaking of Spanish). Rather, it is more generally portrayed as an indigenous village, representing indigenous, "pre-civilized" culture. This is suggested especially by the wild-animal quality of the boy's eyes. In this indigenous culture, everything is conducted on a community-based, humanistic level. They speak with each other not over telephones but face to face; they treat land as belonging to everybody, to the community; and subjective agreements between individuals preserve the social order.

In the Americans' world, such a humanistic social order is in the process of being eclipsed. Not knowing Spanish (and evidently being unable or unwilling to learn even enough to talk with children), they conduct their business with Don Anselmo and the village through a mediator, a lawyer, who is paid for his efforts. As the attorney's comments suggest, the rhythm of the day in the Anglo-American world is determined not by the natural pacing of human activities in accord with the sun but by clocks and calendars. People do not directly exchange valuable goods with one another, as in the earliest barter economies, but use the mediating agent of currency, allowing all transactions to be carried out objectively.

In many ways, indigenous village society, marked by natural and sustainable survival on the same existential plane indefinitely, and modern American society, defined by progress and ever-increasing prosperity, are polar opposites. The arrival of these kind-hearted Americans in Rio en Medio is portrayed as harmless enough, but the reader may find in the story's conclusion the foreboding sense that the loss of Don Anselmo's property to outsiders signals the gradual takeover of the entire village by modern American civilization.

STYLE

Detached Narration

An aspect of Sedillo's narrative that affects the style of the presentation is the emotionally detached perspective of the narrator. Although the narrator is an individual who is participating in the action of the story, one who would presumably have biases or at the very least feelings, the narrator as attorney is strictly representing the interests of his clients, a role that does not necessarily involve his own feelings at all—a role that in fact largely excludes his feelings. This role is evident not only in the attorney's dialogue within the story but also in the story's narration, as he offers little to no subjective commentary on the action—that is, there is nothing that reflects his opinions; there is only the objective truth of the circumstances.

The story's opening paragraph is the closest the lawyer comes to offering value judgment, through words like "wretched," "quaint," and "beautiful," but even these might be considered objective assessments. In the second paragraph the narrator offers his personal thoughts, but he does not actually draw on these thoughts to form any opinions about Don Anselmo. Otherwise, the story is mostly a strictly factual account of the lawyer's relations with the gentleman from Rio en Medio—as if he had been asked to detail the episode for the sake of historical record.

With regard to stylistic effects, the detached narrative perspective can be said to lead the reader to put more faith in the narrative; the reader is not likely at any point to question the veracity of what is being said (in the context of the fictional story). That is, the attorney does not seem to be an unreliable narrator. The detached perspective also serves to highlight the unique character of Don Anselmo. Because the narrator is void of character—objective, unemotional, and never physically described—Don Anselmo's idiosyncratic traits stand out all the more starkly in relief.

Postcolonial Literature

Although Sedillo, whose literary output was not the focus of his career, might not be specifically identified as a "postcolonial" writer, the circumstances of this story are reflective of concerns typically addressed by such writers. Postcolonial literature may be said to include all that which addresses and reflects upon the conditions created and sustained by colonization and societies' responses to colonization. Most of the world's modern colonization occurred when the European powers of Spain, Portugal, France, Germany, and Great Britain laid claim to great expanses of land throughout Africa, South America, and Southeast Asia from the 1500s through the 1800s, using wealth and military force to subdue local populations. At different times in different regions, local populations eventually ousted the colonizing forces, usually through uprisings and revolutions, or at least achieved their equality within their newly heterogenous society (such as in South Africa). Many perceptive postcolonial works emerged after the colonizer's power had begun to wane, allowing the colonized populace opportunities to reflect on their oppression publicly—such as through literature. One highly regarded postcolonial author is V. S. Naipaul, who was born in Trinidad and Tobago, then part of the British Empire, to parents of Indian (South Asian) descent.

Sedillo himself, while his name suggests Hispanic lineage, evidently largely identified with Anglo-American culture. He would become better known as an attorney than as an author, and his own perspective might be imagined to coincide with the attorney's in "Gentleman from Rio en Medio." This story might be described as postcolonial because of the central focus placed on the cultural divide between Don Anselmo and the Americans (as well as the attorney himself). Although Great Britain's colonization of eastern North America ended with the American Revolution, the new nation's subsequent expansion across the continent might justly be described as the U.S. colonization of that land and of the peoples who previously occupied it, primarily Native Americans. Although Don Anselmo's village is Hispano rather than Native American, its roots are nonetheless centuries old, and it is representative of an indigenous relationship between community and land. In fact, Hispanos of the southwestern United States were subjugated much as American Indians were. Sedillo's story can thus be seen as a microcosm of the colonial U.S. occupation and seizure of the American Southwest.

HISTORICAL CONTEXT

The Hispanos of New Mexico

Though confined in scope to the proceedings of a single estate sale in one small New Mexican village, Sedillo's 1939 story can be seen to encapsulate the direction of historical progress in the state over the course of the preceding century—in particular, the arrival of Anglo-American culture and its eventual eclipsing of the deeply rooted Spanish American, or Hispano, culture. Native Americans occupied the modern American Southwest, one of the longest inhabited regions in the Western Hemisphere, for untold centuries before the arrival of Europeans. It was in the 1590s that settlers from New Spain first made their way north into what is now New Mexico. In 1609, Santa Fe was established as a capital of the Spanish colonial government; thus, the region's Spanish roots extend as far back as the British roots of Jamestown, Virginia. Although the Pueblo Indians drove the Spanish out in 1680, they returned in 1692 and forged more peaceable relations with the Pueblos. As was the case earlier in what is now Mexico, in New Mexico there was a fair amount of intermarriage between Spanish Americans and Indians. Life in newly established New Mexican villages, nonetheless, was more reflective of Hispano than Indian culture, as seen in the dominance of the Spanish language and the Roman Catholic faith.

Historian Suzanne Forrest traces the evolution of southwestern Hispano communities in *The Preservation of the Village: New Mexico's Hispanics and the New Deal*. Assessing Hispano villages as "unlike any other communities in the country," she describes them as having been typically populated by only a few hundred residents, with no commercial center, though a post office and/or general store might have been present. Other trades would be practiced by local individuals and advertised with only the simplest signs. In mountain villages—like the one in Sedillo's story—homes would be clustered around a plaza. The drawbacks of such villages would typically relate to the quality of the land, which was perhaps indeed only adequate to sustain a small village: farmland with nutrient-rich soil would be scarce and inefficient to farm, while hillsides would be eroded and overgrazed. "Many orchards," Forrest notes, were "old and scraggly." In sum, though persisting over time, such villages allowed for little more than subsistence-level farming and virtually no economic advancement for inhabitants. Yet this was not a strictly negative circumstance; as Forrest reports, even into the twentieth century, "New Mexican Hispanos, protected by their poverty and the inaccessibility of their mountain lands, still lived within the context of a tightly knit and richly textured village culture."

The New Mexican territory became the property of the United States as a result of the 1846–1848 Mexican-American War and the concluding Treaty of Guadalupe-Hidalgo, which specified that Mexican citizens could become U.S. citizens

COMPARE & CONTRAST

- **1930s:** As of 1930, New Mexico's population of just over 420,000 is 66 percent Hispano (of Spanish or Mexican American descent regardless of color), 7 percent Indian, and 27 percent Anglo-American.

  Today: As of 2010, New Mexico's population of just over 2 million is, using modern categories, 46 percent Hispanic, 9 percent Indian, 40 percent non-Hispanic white, and 5 percent other.

- **1930s:** During the Great Depression, New Mexico's minority communities are considered among the poorest sectors of the national populace. Accordingly, federal New Deal programs focus on reviving traditional crafts and increasing access to education and wage labor.

  Today: In the course of the economic downturn of 2008–2009, while New Mexico has the third-highest poverty rate in the nation, social safety-net programs like the state's General Assistance program and Medicaid actually preside over declines in the numbers of people benefiting, owing to constraints on government budgets.

- **1930s:** The infant mortality rate among Hispanos and Indians in New Mexico exceeds 140 deaths per thousand births, while the national rate is closer to 60.

  Today: Between 2004 and 2006, New Mexico's infant mortality rate of 5.8 deaths per thousand births is below the national rate of 6.8. Broken down by ethnic groups within New Mexico, the infant mortality rate among Hispanics is 5.3, whites 5.6, American Indians 7.8, and African Americans 13.0.

as they chose and would retain equal rights. In 1850, the territory's population was roughly 86 percent Hispano, 12 percent American Indian, and 2 percent Anglo-American. Through the rest of the century, the territory courted statehood and welcomed American investors—and meanwhile many Hispanos lost property as a result of litigation, fraud, government appropriation, and tax default. When the railroad came to Santa Fe in 1880—a development milestone that Sedillo highlights in his story—economic advancement, at least in urban areas, increased. New Mexico became a state in 1912. By 1930, Anglo-Americans constituted some 27 percent of the population, Hispanos 66 percent, and Indians only 7 percent, and the region's wealth had become concentrated in the hands of the white newcomers who had spurred the development. In the 1930s, the Hispanos of New Mexico's Rio Grande valley were considered one of the poorest segments of the national populace.

The 1930s proved to be a crucial period for New Mexican Hispanos, with the Depression exacerbating the dire poverty. By this time, Anglo-Americans were finally infiltrating even the villages; but rather than being culturally indifferent entrepreneurs, these whites, Forrest points out,

> wanted to escape from the driving forces of technological progress and economic gain. Rather than wishing to displace the villagers and their way of life, they wanted to merge with them, and learn from them, and preserve them from further change.

These Anglo-Americans "envisioned Hispanic village life as the ideal alternative to a mainstream society corrupted by a dehumanizing materialism." Political participation among such proponents of preserving village life contributed to the attention paid to the Hispanic population by the federal government. President Franklin Roosevelt's New Deal included emergency relief programs to provide food rations and generally improve health, education, and the standard of living in Hispano villages. These programs were intended to economically

The original sale did not include the orchard in which the Don had planted a tree for each child born in Rio en Medio. *(Agata Dorobek / Shutterstock.com)*

modernize the villages while yet sustaining community values.

Ultimately, the New Deal programs failed to achieve the intended effects, because when the programs ended, villagers still lacked adequate agricultural resources and otherwise had little to no recourse to wage labor. John R. Van Ness, editor of the "New Mexico Land Grant Series" and author of the foreword to Forrest's volume (the fourth in the series), notes that the New Deal programs failed largely because the agents in charge, mostly Anglo-Americans,

> failed to grasp the organic whole that was Hispanic village culture; that is, the fact that the means of gaining a livelihood, general patterns of social life, community beliefs, and values were all closely interrelated and interdependent.

Hispanos balked when the very agents who encouraged them to reinvigorate their traditional crafts and arts also sought, in Van Ness's words, "to eradicate what were deemed to be undesirable 'superstitions' and 'irrational' economic behavior that placed family and village solidarity above monetary gain." In other words, the trials of the villages exemplified the classic conflict between the humanistic values of small-scale rural communities and the law-based values of large-scale capitalist, industrial civilization.

Being intimately involved in state law and politics and writing in 1939, Sedillo would have been well aware of the circumstances in his state's impoverished Hispano villages. Although Sedillo does not give the government a role in his story, his juxtaposition of the shabbily dressed gentleman from Rio en Medio with the adequately wealthy Anglo-Americans who purchase his property—and even the trees of all his descendants—evokes the long, slow decline of the traditional Hispano village, which even the New Deal could not seem to stop.

CRITICAL OVERVIEW

While "Gentleman of Rio en Medio" has been anthologized countless times in literature textbooks, reflecting both its thematic significance and its accessibility, the story has not been the focus of much critical attention. This is due in part to the fact that Sedillo wrote little else besides this story—excluding legal articles and essays—and so did not offer a greater literary context in which his story could be considered. V. Y. Mudimbe devotes much attention to Sedillo's story in his scholarly *South Atlantic Quarterly* essay "*Et Nunc . . . Per Hoc Signum*: A Meditation on Genitives in Everyday Life Stories." Mudimbe focuses on how the characters' possession of land is used to illustrate "the basic relationship between nature and humanity," with the village-level appreciation of land as communal being evoked by the property nominally sold by the protagonist: "In the banality of wording—Don Anselmo's land—the genitive [possessive] attests a community's life." On the one hand, then, the story legitimizes "Don Anselmo's right to an attitude about a way of being and having, and the moral validity of his vision"; but on the other hand, as the story's conclusion implies, "The children must learn the meaning of property rights and privacy."

In his expansive survey "The Evolution of Chicano Literature," published in *MELUS*, Raymund A. Paredes situates Sedillo's story in the broader context of Mexican American literature. (He makes no reference to any other work by Sedillo.) Paredes cites "Gentleman of Rio en Medio" to illustrate his assertion that Hispano authors in 1930s New Mexico depicted a culture "locked in time and barricaded against outside forces. Here the New Mexican Hispanos passed their lives in dignity and civility, confronting the harsh environment with a religiosity and resolve reminiscent of the *conquistadores* themselves." Paredes notes that sadly, like Don Anselmo's cottage, Hispano culture by then "had fallen into a decadence that was perhaps quaint, but irreversible."

CRITICISM

Michael Allen Holmes

Holmes is a writer with existential interests. In the following essay, he probes the allegorical depths of Sedillo's short story "Gentleman of Rio en Medio."

Several aspects of Juan A. A. Sedillo's brief story "Gentleman of Rio en Medio" are likely to stand out in the reader's mind. Don Anselmo's moral perspective is highlighted by his unexpected refusal to accept additional money for his property, and by his conception of the trees on his property as belonging to all the respective villagers may be a heartwarming surprise. With the Americans feeling obligated to buy those trees individually, the reader may view this as a sort of financial victory for the villagers. But beyond the facts of the matter, the story seems to have certain allegorical implications that tend more toward the pessimistic.

> "IN PLACE OF THE COMPANIONSHIP OF THEIR BEAUTIFUL GNARLED TREES, WITH THEIR SHADING LEAVES ARRAYED IN RUSTLING COLLAGES OF SUNLIT GREENS AGAINST THE SKY, THE VILLAGERS GET UNIFORMLY RECTANGULAR PIECES OF GREENISH PAPER THAT CAN BE VERY NEATLY STACKED AND FOLDED."

Arguably, the best allegories are the subtlest ones, the ones that have the strongest subconscious effects on the reader; if the symbolism is too readily apparent, the story devolves from a humanistic story worthy of emotional investment into a schematic fictional construct with a specific message. In the best allegories, the reader's response to the story itself will correspond or resonate with whatever emotional reaction the author intends for the reader to have to the message or moral being conveyed symbolically. The circumstances in Sedillo's story are readily connected with the clash of civilizations represented by the (adequately) wealthy Americans and the (relatively) poor Hispano gentleman. Such an allegory is both materially supported and elevated to a universal plane by the details of the story.

Sedillo's characters are easily seen to stand for their cultures at large. Don Anselmo can be succinctly characterized as the Hispano village gentleman. Indeed, the story's title highlights his gentility, and his bearing is full of dignity. However, he is referred to only as "the old man," never as a gentleman, by the bourgeois attorney/narrator. The condition of his clothing makes clear that he leads a village-level existence; he is not invested in mere appearance and materialism, as is the modern urban gentleman. Indeed, the state of Don Anselmo's clothing links him not just with village life but

WHAT DO I READ NEXT?

- Published six years after Sedillo's story, Josephina Niggli's *Mexican Village* (1945), consisting of ten interrelated stories about the town of Hidalgo, is considered a milestone in Mexican American literature, drawing on folklore in framing one's cultural heritage as a part of one's essence.
- Mario Suárez is considered perhaps the first "Chicano" writer, identifying his characters as ethnic Mexicanos whose cultural has been partially diminished by their residence in the United States. His late-1940s stories set in a barrio in Tucson, Arizona, dubbed El Hoyo, or "The Hole," can be found in his *Chicano Sketches: Short Stories* (2004).
- José Antonio Villareal's first novel, *Pocho* (1959), is considered the first Chicano novel, portraying the trials of a boy born to a Mexican man who has been forced to accept a life as a migrant farmworker in California.
- In her first book, *The Last of the Menu Girls* (1986), which is appropriate for young adults, Hispano author Denise Chávez relates the experiences of a girl named Rocío growing up in a small town in southern New Mexico.
- The American literary giant John Steinbeck first achieved success with *Tortilla Flat* (1935), which follows a group of humble *paisanos*—men of the countryside—around Monterey, California.
- The Kenyan author Grace Ogot, one of Africa's first female English-language novelists, treats interactions and clashes between modern society and traditional village life among the Luos in her collection *The Other Woman* (1976).
- Kathleen Parthé's nonfiction volume *Russian Village Prose: The Radiant Past* (1992) explores the Russian movement in which authors between the 1950s and 1970s praised the traditional way of life that had been practiced in villages for a thousand years but that was disappearing during the Soviet era.
- Joseph Krumgold's young-adult novel *And Now Miguel* (1984) tells of the young son of a sheep rancher who longs to join the men when they herd the sheep up into New Mexico's Sangre de Christo Mountains.

directly with nature. His coat is green, the color of natural growth, and faded, reflecting a life lived out in the sunshine. Whereas a proper suit of clothes effectively insulates the wearer from the elements from neck to toe, Don Anselmo's outfit is the epitome of permeability. His old garments presumably have numerous holes, his gloves let his fingertips through, and for a walking stick he uses the skeleton of an umbrella, symbolizing his defenselessness against—and thus oneness with—nature. In conversation during the first visit, Don Anselmo speaks at length "about rain," and during the second visit he again "talked about the weather." Thus, Don Anselmo can be seen as symbolic not only of the moral integrity of communal, village-level life but also of the intimate connection with nature maintained in the village.

The Americans, in contrast, have diverging concerns. Don Anselmo and the reader are assured more than once that these Americans "are good people." They are not seeking to suppress or oppose life in the village—only to experience it for themselves. One is led to think of the pioneers who, from the establishment of the original thirteen American colonies through the ensuing several centuries, staked out claims and set up homesteads ever farther beyond the edge of established towns and cities, inexorably allowing American culture to fulfill its self-proclaimed "manifest destiny" and occupy the entire continent, as facilitated by the forced marches of defeated tribes of Native Americans ever westward or onto their designated reservations.

Although many of the pioneers themselves may have been "good people," their activities were part of the systematic American occupation of lands that had once belonged to entire communities, to everyone, or to no one person or group. Whereas American Indians over the centuries perfected the construction of domiciles with such virtually unlimited resources as adobe bricks, made of sun-baked earth, white Americans' primary house-building resource was timber—living trees cut down. Native Americans also used animal skins to make tepees, but they killed animals for food regardless, and so using the skin was a way of honoring the animal's life by not wasting any part of it. Also, since tepees are portable, Indian nations could favor an itinerant lifestyle that served as a natural safeguard against overhunting; if game became scarce in any given area, the people would move to another, allowing depleted species a chance to recover and thus maintaining a broader ecological balance. Trees, of course, grow back, but only over the course of decades—and not if they are cleared from the land for the sake of industrial-scale agriculture or urban development. Perhaps farming in some Hispano villages remained at subsistence levels because the people worked around the existing trees, instead of chopping them down to get them out of the way, uprooting the stumps, and letting machines barrel through.

The trees in Don Anselmo's old orchard become the focal point of Sedillo's story. In view of this, the first paragraph's last sentence—"His orchard was gnarled and beautiful"— takes on heightened meaning. On the one hand the trees, likely fruit trees, may not be as productive as they could be; perhaps the soil is too poor, or rainfall is inadequate, and so instead of growing straight and strong, the trees are bent and twisted. Yet they are beautiful; they are growing, breathing, living things, and how perfect their form is or how much they produce are irrelevant to their value as forms of life. Although Christianity accords humankind a special place in the world, man having been made, as the familiar dictum goes, in God's image, indigenous cultures have more often held the entire living world as infused with a divine presence, such that all of nature is sacred.

Sedillo's story directly reveals nothing about what Don Anselmo's religion or spirituality might be. The traditional religion of Spanish American settlers of the Southwest was Roman Catholicism, and even in small villages there would be a Catholic church. Yet if the fictional village of Rio en Medio is viewed not historically but allegorically, in particular, as representative of a sustainable indigenous community, the reader might look to the people's daily activities to find their spirituality in whatever has become ritualized in their lives, whatever they do on a regular basis. The most telling signal with regard to Christian practice (and others) would be prayer, a ritual many follow daily and devoutly, often before meals or at bedtime.

In Sedillo's very brief story, the reader learns only one important thing about what the people in Rio en Medio do: the children, at least, "came every day and played under the trees, built little play fences around them, and took blossoms." The way the children play in the orchard takes on the air of ritualized behavior: they bask in the presence of the trees and take blossoms so as to spread the natural beauty about the village. The fences they build may signify their conception of themselves as guardians of their trees, with each child surely knowing which tree is his or her own. Whatever the children's actual religion might be, such ritualized appreciation of trees effectively amounts to worship of nature. With each child having an intimate link with the tree that was planted at the very point in history when he or she first came into the world, child and tree become kindred spirits. These children thus have a spiritual connection with nature, with the earth, that perhaps cannot be fostered in any other equivalent way.

Considered in this light, the separation of these children from their trees would be tragic—as significant as a friend's moving away, or a death in the family, or the destruction of a house of worship. Curiously, when informed of the social relevance of the orchard, the Americans, however "good" they may be, do not demonstrate further benevolence by bequeathing the land on which the children's trees are growing back to the village. Nor do they seem to even consider simply allowing the children access to their trees in perpetuity. As it happens, the story concludes in such a fateful way that the reader is effectively denied the opportunity to imagine how the problem of the trees might have been solved differently. Don Anselmo's illuminating explanation about why the trees are not his own is so compelling, such a beautiful example of the sort of intimate connection that can be forged between man and nature, that the reader almost forgets that Don Anselmo's position is

Rio en medio literally means "between the rivers." (Jeff Banke / Shutterstock.com)

already compromised; technically speaking, the Americans already own these trees. Given the narrator's comically inflected depiction of this patchwork village gentleman, the reader intuitively is unlikely to expect the story to close with some resounding victory for such a (visibly) pathetic character.

Thus, while the opening line of the last paragraph, "There was nothing we could do," has a distinct air of inevitability about it, it still does not seem that the Americans will fail to get their way in the end. The following sentence does no more than clarify the current state of affairs. Thus, the supremely significant concluding action of the story is compressed into but a single sentence. The people may all be duly compensated for their trees, but this currency exchange only separates them from their trees even more definitively than did the mere sale of Don Anselmo's property, which did not prevent them from visiting the orchard. In place of the companionship of their beautiful gnarled trees, with their shading leaves arrayed in rustling collages of sunlit greens against the sky, the villagers get uniformly rectangular pieces of greenish paper that can be very neatly stacked and folded. The sorrowful conclusion of Sedillo's story, then, can be seen as allegorically chronicling how the slow crawl of American manifest destiny steadily eradicates the communal, spiritual relationship with nature fostered by indigenous ways of life, in favor of individual rights and legal possession of not just whatever man has made but even whatever naturally exists, all of which can be assigned a specific monetary value.

Source: Michael Allen Holmes, Critical Essay on "Gentleman of Rio en Medio," in *Short Stories for Students*, Gale, Cengage Learning, 2012.

Michael J. O'Neal

O'Neal holds a Ph.D. in English. In the following essay, he argues that in "Gentlemen of Rio en Medio," Sedillo combines two unique narrative elements—a first-person plural narrator and an antagonist who, in essence, is the reader—to create a story about a conflict between value systems.

In Juan A. A. Sedillo's "Gentleman of Rio en Medio," two narrative elements come together to provide the foundation of the story. One is the narrative voice. The other is the traditional

> "PUT THIS WAY, THE ANTAGONIST OF THE STORY IS THE READER; THE NARRATIVE VOICE SPEAKS FOR THE READER, AND THE FACT THAT THE NARRATOR, REPRESENTING THE INTERESTS OF COMMERCE, DOES NOT TREAT DON ANSELMO AS AN ADVERSARY MAKES THE LESSON OF 'GENTLEMAN OF RIO EN MEDIO' GO DOWN MORE EASILY."

concept of the antagonist in fiction (and drama). These two elements, combined, essentially define the story and give rise to its overall theme.

Perhaps the most significant feature of the narrative voice is that it is plural. The narrator's precise role is not defined, but he appears to be associated with a firm handling the purchase and sale of Don Anselmo's land and home to the narrator's friends. This narrator sometimes refers to himself in the first-person singular ("I"), but much of the narration uses the pronouns "we" and "us." For example, the narration says that "The old man bowed to all of us in the room"; "We would buy, and the money was ready"; "There was nothing we could do. Legally we owned the trees. . . . "

In this way, Sedillo adopts an unusual point of view, one that could be called first-person plural. The narrator is a unique character, but the reader never learns anything particular about him (with the possible exception of his interest in Charlie Chaplin films). Rather, the "narrator" of the story is a voice that represents the interests and values of a group. In this case, the group consists not only of the members of the firm but also, perhaps, of the larger business community, and even the community at large. The narrator speaks on behalf of this larger community. In this regard, it is noteworthy that the narrator is unnamed, for his identity is unimportant. Further, the reader never learns the names of any of the other people who make up the story's "we," nor does the reader ever learn the name of the firm the narrator represents. All the reader knows is "we" and "us."

Modern readers of fiction generally find the use of a first-person plural narrator disquieting; they are accustomed to the unique, singular point of view of a Huckleberry Finn or a Jim Hawkins or a Jane Eyre, characters who speak for themselves and whom the reader gets to know not just as an observer but as an actor in the drama. But while this form of narration is unusual, it is not unique. American author William Faulkner used the technique to good effect in his 1931 short story "A Rose for Emily," in which the values of the reclusive title character conflict with those of the community in which she lives. The narrative voice becomes a kind of collective voice, representing the point of view not just of a single narrator but of all the people who know Emily and have contact with her.

It also should be noted that this type of narration was commonly adopted by the ancient Greeks. Much of their earliest literature was in the form of the dithyramb, a chorus that was spoken in unison by as many as dozens of men. Later Greek drama continued to include not only individual characters but also a chorus that commented on the action. Thus, the use of a community point of view is not without precedent in the history of Western literature.

A second narrative element that is important in "Gentleman of Rio en Medio" is the traditional concept of protagonist and antagonist. Identifying the story's protagonist is easy. Don Anselmo is the principal actor in the story. It is *his* story that interests the reader. The story is a representation of his values and of the dignity of his personality as observed by another person. But typically, fiction involves conflict, and conflict implies an antagonist, a person or force opposed to the protagonist. (Note that these terms derive from the Greek, suggesting again continuity with the earliest Western literature. Both "protagonist" and "antagonist" in Greek refer literally to one who struggles or competes for a prize; the words are etymological cousins of the words *agony*—suggesting struggle—and *agent*—suggesting action.)

Sometimes, the antagonist in fiction is an abstract force such as nature; Jack London's *The Call of the Wild* is a classic example. Sometimes it is an institution, such as slavery and discrimination in Mark Twain's *The Adventures of Huckleberry Finn*. Most often, though, the antagonist is a particular person or perhaps group of people—persons with distinct identities and motivations (and who sometimes are more interesting than the protagonist). One immediately thinks of the villain Iago in Shakespeare's

Othello, or the various bad guys fought and foiled by Agent 007, James Bond.

"Gentleman of Rio en Medio" presents an interesting situation. Don Anselmo is the only named character in the story; the only other character in the story, other than the narrator, is the boy who stands behind Don Anselmo in the office and never speaks. No one emerges from the story as a "bad guy." No one fights with Don Anselmo, figuratively or literally. The collective "we" treats Don Anselmo with fairness and kindness. They do not try to cheat him or manipulate him in any way. Most readers would be delighted if any business professionals with whom they had dealings treated them in the way the "we" of the story treat Don Anselmo. Where, then, is the conflict? Who, then, is the antagonist?

To answer that question, consider the process readers go through when they read a work of fiction. Most readers are likely to ask themselves a number of questions. What is at stake here? Whose side am I supposed to be on? Who wins and loses? What is the outcome, and is the outcome one that is satisfying because it is consistent with the narrative arc and the nature of the characters?

The answers to these questions in "Gentleman of Rio en Medio" are fairly simple and straightforward. Clearly, Don Anselmo is the hero of the story, so it is his set of values that the reader is supposed to adopt. Don Anselmo "wins," but not in the sense of somehow "defeating" his "foes" but in the sense of quietly asserting his values over the commercial values of the narrative voice. He agreed to a price for his property, but when it is discovered that he owns more acreage than he thought he did, he insists on adhering to the original agreement. More importantly, he later insists that he cannot do anything about the children playing among the trees he planted, for the trees were planted for his many descendants. He does not regard them as part of the property in the same way that real-estate law does. Thus, a set of values pertaining to family, stewardship of the land, fair dealing, and sticking to one's word win out over the legalities of commerce.

The conflict of the story, then, is between competing sets of values. One set is represented by Don Anselmo, the other by the collective narrative voice. In this way, the antagonist of the story is not the narrator, and not his firm, but rather a societal view about conducting business to one's own advantage and according to legal principles rather than according to the imperatives of family and the community. In effect, the narrative voice adopts what is likely to be the reader's point of view. Nearly every reader of this story would have been delighted to accept the extra money for the extra acreage and would not have felt that doing so was in any sense unfair or a violation of his or her word. And nearly every reader would have recognized that, of course, the trees on a property are part of the property and belong to the owner, to do with as he or she wishes.

Put this way, the antagonist of the story is the reader; the narrative voice speaks for the reader, and the fact that the narrator, representing the interests of commerce, does not treat Don Anselmo as an adversary makes the lesson of "Gentleman of Rio en Medio" go down more easily. Sedillo does not launch a frontal assault on the values of the Anglo business community. Quite the contrary, his protagonist says that "I know these Americans are good people, and that is why I have agreed to sell to them." Later he says, "We have all learned to love these Americans . . . because they are good people and good neighbors."

The genius of the story, then, is in the interaction of point of view and the relationship between protagonist and antagonist. By adopting the narrative techniques he does, Sedillo prevents his story from becoming a preachy sermon against the Anglo community or against money-grubbing commerce. He gently leads the reader to see Don Anselmo and his value system in a sympathetic way. In this way, everyone "wins."

Source: Michael J. O'Neal, Critical Essay on "Gentleman of Rio en Medio," in *Short Stories for Students*, Gale, Cengage Learning, 2012.

Raymund A. Paredes

In the following excerpt, Paredes examines the evolution of New Mexican literature after 1848.

III

. . . For several generations after Guadalupe Hidalgo, the literary record of Mexican-Americans—or what we have of it—shows a considerably slower movement towards a distinctly Chicano perspective than does the folklore. The *corridos*, for example, as early as the 1860s focused on cultural conflict with the Anglos as the fundamental fact of the Mexican-American experience; much of the conventional literature, on the other hand, is nostalgic and oddly detached from contemporary issues, as if the present reality were too difficult to confront. Moreover, when writers did choose to treat current issues, their tone was not proud and defiant, but usually tentative and subdued, even submissive.

THE MEXICAN-AMERICAN LITERATURE IN ENGLISH THAT EMERGED FROM NEW MEXICO DURING THE 1930S EVOKES A PAST THAT, WHILE LARGELY IMAGINARY, IS PRESENTED WITH RIGID CONVICTION."

Although the southwestern territories were never as culturally isolated—either before or after the coming of the Anglo—as scholars have generally claimed, opportunities for formal education were scarce until well into the twentieth century. Before 1848, schooling, except in its most rudimentary form, was limited primarily to the privileged classes. After the region was absorbed by the United States, education for Mexican-Americans did not greatly improve for reasons of discrimination and differences over curricula and control of schools. But for those Mexican-Americans who had the tool of literacy, writing was a highly popular activity. Mexican-Americans kept diaries, journals, and "books of personal verses" to which several members of a family might contribute. For those writers interested in a larger audience there were Spanish-language newspapers throughout the Southwest that published creative works; in New Mexico alone, the period 1880–1900 saw the establishment of sixty-one such newspapers.

Of the published material, verse was by far the most popular form of literary expression. Mexican-American poets, clearly under the influence of prevailing Mexican literary conventions, demonstrated a taste for lyrical verse, especially in the generation after 1848 when romanticism was a powerful cultural movement in Mexico. Francisco Ramírez published love poetry in *El Clamor Público*, a Los Angeles newspaper from the period 1855–1859. A few of his verses have been reprinted, but these are of little interest, burdened as they are by evocations of "angels of love" and "enchanting nymphs." Another poet from *El Clamor Público*, José Elías González wrote these lines:

> Tu cabellera es de oro;
> Tu talle esbelto, ligero;
> Eres mi bien, mí tesoro,
> El ídolo que venero.

> Your long hair is golden,
> Your figure well-shaped, lithe;
> You are my love, my treasure,
> The idol I venerate.

The work of other Mexican-American poets of the period also suffers from sentimentalism and from an unwillingness to restrain romantic impulses. Undoubtedly, such verse was popular in its day, but it now seems precious, effete, and more than a little silly.

In New Mexico, where the literary record is less fragmentary than in other regions, several factors combined to create a distinctive Mexican-American perspective. Of all the southwestern states, New Mexico was the first colonized by the Spaniards, and its citizens took pride in the richness of their Spanish traditions. Of the three major centers of Mexican culture in the Southwest, New Mexico was the last to be affected dramatically by Anglo penetration. Texas began receiving large numbers of Anglos in 1822 and California in the 1840s, but New Mexico, with the exception of Santa Fe which prospered as a trading headquarters, was relatively undisturbed by Anglo influences until the arrival of the railroad in 1880. Consequently, the literature of New Mexico bears few signs of cultural conflict until the late nineteenth century. Even then, the prevailing tone was more accommodating than combative. Significantly, the *corrido* tradition, which flourished in the culturally-tense borderlands of south Texas, is undistinguished in New Mexico, dealing not with the exploits of *vaqueros* who defy Anglo oppression, but with more prosaic topics such as romance and family tragedy.

The custom of anonymous versifying, dating back to the earliest days of the Spanish colonization, remained vigorous in New Mexico long after the advent of the Anglo. Spanish-language newspapers were apparently inundated with this kind of poetry to the point where, in 1884, the exasperated editor of *La Aurora* in Santa Fe published an item entitled "Remedios para la Versomanía" (Remedies for Verse-mania). This poetry, in many cases virtually indistinguishable from folk verse, generally followed traditional Spanish forms such as the *canción* and the *décima*. Not surprisingly, much of this verse was of low literary quality, flawed by a lack of originality and excessive romanticism. One poem, obviously derivative of the Spaniard Bécquer, is a religious piece entitled "A la Virgen." It rhapsodizes about the poet's deliverance of his "affection, heart, and faith" to the Virgin "with all the trust of an innocent child." Not all the anonymous verse was trivial, however. In New Mexico, as in Texas and California, Mexican-Americans lamented the erosion of their heritage and the intrusion of Anglo technology. One talented poet, who signed his work "X.X.X.," dealt with such issues as the quality of the territorial educational system and the impact of the Spanish-American War on New Mexicans. The device of anonymity worked effectively for the New Mexican poets. It offered some protection from reprisal when they treated controversial subjects, but more importantly, anonymity gave their work a universal quality, as if each poem were a nameless cry from the collective consciousness.

Nothing exercised not only the poets but all the New Mexican writers like the question of Anglo prejudice. Writers particularly resented prevailing Anglo views that Mexican-Americans were backward and "alien," believing that these attitudes had postponed the admission of New Mexico to the Union for half a century. The poet X.X.X. complained that the United States had treated New Mexico like a "ragged beggar," yet still held out hope that statehood would come. When the Spanish-American War began in 1898, the New Mexican writers quickly proclaimed their allegiance to the United States and their willingness to take up arms against the "mother country." One New Mexican essayist expressed the view that, cultural differences notwithstanding, all "citizens and those who reside in this country, whatever their nationality, race or blood ties may be, must remember that they are living under this government and enjoying its beneficent protection." Certainly, there was plenty of room for debate about the quality and sincerity of the United States' "beneficent protection" of New Mexico, but still the writers rallied their people around the American flag.

As a group, the Mexican-American writers of New Mexico sought some sort of cultural compromise for their people. They encouraged the retention of Hispanic traditions and the Spanish language, but they also supported statehood, New Mexican participation in American wars, and the acquisition of English for practical purposes. In effect, these writers advocated the creation of a culture that was neither Hispanic-Mexican nor Anglo-American, but a synthesis of the two. Later Chicano writers would also advocate movement towards this goal.

But such a cultural synthesis was not easily attainable, as Mariano Vallejo, a California writer, made clear. A member of one of the most prominent families in the region, Vallejo had early supported statehood for California, maintaining that Mexico had neglected its northernmost territory and that the United States was the "happiest and most free nation in the world." His feelings began to change, however, after he was swindled by *yanquis* in various business deals. When H. H. Bancroft encouraged Vallejo to write a history of California, he plunged into the project, anxious to tell the Mexican side. He submitted his manuscript in five volumes to Bancroft in 1875.

"What a difference" wrote Vallejo in 1877, "between the present time and those that preceded the usurpation by the Americans. If the Californians could all gather together to breathe a lament, it would reach Heaven as a moving sigh which would cause fear and consternation to the Universe. What misery!" And so went the theme of Vallejo's massive history. The Anglos, propelled by their greed, swarmed into California, trampling everything in their paths. Vallejo wrote of Anglo "malefactors" to whom human life had no value. Ultimately, he regarded the Americanization of California as the despoilment of the "true Eden":

> When gold was discovered, the flag of stars already waved over Alta California. No longer were we ruled by the Mexican laws, under whose shadow some had advanced while others fell back, but under which no one had perished of hunger, and only two individuals had been by law deprived of their lives, a very common event during the early years of the North American domination in California.
>
> The language now spoken in our country, the laws which govern us, the faces which we encounter daily, are those of the masters of the land, and, of course, antagonistic to our interests and rights, but what does that matter to the conqueror? He wishes his own well-being and not ours!—a thing that I consider only natural in individuals, but which I condemn in a government which has promised to respect and make respected our rights, and to treat us as its own sons. But what does it avail us to complain? The thing has happened and there is no remedy.
>
> I ask, what has the state government done for the Californians since the victory over Mexico? Have they kept the promises with which they deluded us? I do not ask for miracles; I am not and never have been exacting; I do not demand gold, a pleasing gift only to abject peoples. But I ask and I have a right to ask for an answer.

Vallejo's history was an intensely personal work, written to show that the Californians "were not indigents or a band of beasts" as they were so frequently depicted by Anglo-Americans. But he held little hope that the Mexican culture of California could withstand the collision with that of the United States. Instead, he foresaw a day when his people might "disappear, ignored of the whole world."

Vallejo was not exactly writing for the whole world, but he did want to bring the "true history" of California to Anglo readers. In this endeavor he was exceptional, for in the nineteenth century, Mexican-American authors generally wrote for their own people. It was only after the first decade of the twentieth century that a few Mexican-Americans begin to publish stories and poetry in large circulation American magazines. This difference in audience dramatically affected the character of the literature itself.

María Cristina Mena published a series of Mexican stories and sketches in *The Century* and *American* magazines during the 1910s. Mena was a talented story-teller whose sensibility unfortunately tended towards sentimentalism and preciousness. She aimed to portray Mexican culture in a positive light, but with great decorum; as a consequence, her stories seem trivial and condescending. Mena took pride in the aboriginal past of Mexico and she had real sympathy for the downtrodden Indians, but she could not, for the life of her, resist describing how they "washed their little brown faces... and assumed expressions of astonishing intelligence and zeal." Occasionally, she struck a blow at the pretensions of Mexico's ruling class, but to little effect; Mena's genteelness simply is incapable of warming the reader's blood.

Her story-telling gifts are best displayed in "The Vine-Leaf." The main character is Dr. Malsufrido (impatient of suffering), a Mexico City physician more interested in the sins of his wealthy patients than their ailments. He talks about his first patient, a woman who comes to have a birthmark in the shape of a vine-leaf removed from her lower back. The surgery goes perfectly but throughout the operation the patient remains veiled. Malsufrido immediately falls in love with this mystery woman but never probes her identity. Five years later, he discovers by accident that the woman is a murderer, but when he encounters her again, this time face to face, he cannot think of bringing her to justice. The woman, now a *marquesa*, is as beautiful as the doctor had imagined and so, loving her still after all this time, he accedes to her secrecy. And there Mena's story ends, a charming and well-told piece, but nothing more.

In trying to depict and explicate Mexican culture to an American audience, Mena was undone by a strategy that would enervate the work of other Mexican-American writers. She tried to depict her characters within the boundaries of conventional American attitudes about Mexico. She knew what Americans liked to read about Mexico so she gave it to them: quaint and humble *inditos*, passionate *señoritas* with eyes that "were wonderful, even in a land of wonderful eyes," a dashing *caballero* or two "with music in their fingers." All these characters in a country Mena described as "the land of resignation." Mena's portrayals are ultimately obsequious, and if one can appreciate the weight of popular attitudes on Mena's consciousness, one can also say that a braver, more perceptive writer would have confronted the life of her culture more forcefully.

The fact that virtually all Mexican-American authors before 1900 wrote only in Spanish severely restricted their potential readership, Mena, of course, published in English although she tried, as later writers would, to capture in English the sound and feeling of Spanish; her work signalled the possibility that a new generation of Mexican-American writers would reach a larger audience. In the mid-1930s, for example, Robert Torres published stories about the Mexican Revolution in *Esquire*. A powerful writer in the Hemingway style, he focused on the pointless brutality of war. Roberto Félix Salazar also published in *Esquire*, but his stories are less interesting and less skillfully rendered than those of Torres; significantly, they have no ethnic content whatsoever. Salazar was concerned with ethnic affairs, but his most effective statement on the Mexican-American condition appeared not in a general interest magazine but in the *LULAC* (League of United Latin-American Citizens) *News*. The piece is entitled "The Other Pioneers" of which this is the first stanza:

Now I must write
Of those of mine who rode these plains
Long years before the Saxon and the Irish came.
Of those who plowed the land and built the towns
And gave the towns soft-woven Spanish names.
Of those who moved across the Rio Grande
Toward the hiss of Texas snake and Indian yell.
Of men who from the earth made thick-walled homes
And from the earth raised churches to their god,
And of the wives who bore them sons
And smiled with knowing joy.

Now this is a very mild expression of cultural affirmation and is characteristic of early Mexican-American work published in English. In learning the English language, Mexican-American writers invariably relinquished some part of their culture; their subdued tone when discussing their heritage suggests a certain cultural ambivalence or perhaps a lack of understanding of the extent of their cultural loss.

In confronting the prevailing Anglo stereotypes of their people, these writers tended not to demolish them but to assent to the least negative of such images. Mena's Mexicans are not swarthy, treacherous greasers, but charming—if artificial—creatures, very much in the popular tradition of Bret Harte, Helen Hunt Jackson, and Gertude Atherton. Undoubtedly, a good deal—if not most—of this sort of characterization can be attributed to popular taste and editorial control; it has only been in recent years, after all, that Americans have recognized honest expressions of minority consciousness.

Historically, the very term "Mexican" has had so harshly pejorative a connotation in the United States that a number of Mexican-American writers shrank from it and, ultimately, from their true heritage, creating in its place a mythical past of unsullied Europeanism. The New Mexicans particularly venerated and exaggerated the Spanish component of their heritage. For example, the influential folklorist, Aurelio M. Espinosa, determined that the oral traditions of New Mexico were essentially Spanish and had survived virtually untouched by other influences, whether Indian, *mestizo*, or Negro. It was only a short step to conclude that all of existing New Mexican culture was essentially Spanish: as one writer put it, "an echo of Spain across the seas."

The Mexican-American literature in English that emerged from New Mexico during the 1930s evokes a past that, while largely imaginary, is presented with rigid conviction. Much of the fiction is closely related to the oral traditions that Espinosa and his followers collected so assiduously. The writers described a culture seemingly locked in time and barricaded against outside forces. Here the New Mexican Hispanos passed their lives in dignity and civility, confronting the harsh environment with a religiosity and resolve reminiscent of the *conquistadores* themselves. But although the people struggled, they moved as if to a waltz and lived in villages with names like "Rio Dormido" (*Sleeping River*). A story by Juan A. A. Sedillo begins this way:

> It took months of negotiation to come to an understanding with the old man. He was in no hurry. What he had the most of was time. He lived up in Rio en Medio, where his people had been for hundreds of years. He tilled the same land they had tilled. His house was small and wretched, but quaint. The little creek ran through his land. His orchard was gnarled and beautiful.

Other New Mexican writers also stressed the continuity of the culture. But like the old man's cottage, it had fallen into a decadence that was perhaps quaint, but irreversible.

There is something profoundly disturbing about this body of work. It seems a literature created out of fear and intimidation, a defensive response to racial prejudice—particularly the Anglo distaste for miscegenation—and ethnocentrism. The New Mexican writers retreated from the contemporary world into nostalgia, and it is a striking quality of their work that there are so few Anglos in it, as if each one were a gross impertinence. The problem is that their literary past is so pathetically unreal. Nina Otero Warren, a chief advocate of New Mexico Hispanicism, defended the oppressive system of peonage by explaining that the peons "were not slaves, but working people who preferred submission to the *patrón* rather than an independent chance alone." She went on to observe that Hispanos "lived close to the soil and to nature. They cherished their traditions, inherited from Spain and adapted to their new life. Theirs was a part of the feudal age, when master and men, although separate in class, were bound together by mutual interests and a close community of human sympathy. Much of this life remains today." If some of the southern Anglo writers suffered from a plantation mentality, then we may say that New Mexican writers like Warren suffered from a *hacienda* syndrome.

In sum, the body of early Mexican-American literature that has survived—both in Spanish and English—is less interesting than the folklore and certainly less representative of the collective spirit. The vigor, the tone of defiance so typical of the *corridos* is lacking in the written materials. What we find instead, generally, is a rather ingenuous hopefulness, a submissiveness, and a contrived and derivative romanticism. Much of the early literature, especially that written in English, is so much persiflage. The reason for this dichotomy may be that until about 1940, most Mexican-American writers came from relatively privileged backgrounds, from families of position and property that had a considerable stake in cultural and political accommodation. The oral traditions in this period, on the other hand, were essentially a proletarian form of expression, articulating the sentiments of those who had little capital and few material goods to lose. These people sought to preserve their culture and were ready to defend it, as the expression went, "con pistola en la mano." All in all, an interesting twist to the stereotype of the humble Mexican as a docile, meek individual. . . .

Source: Raymund A. Paredes, "The Evolution of Chicano Literature," in *MELUS*, Vol. 5, No. 2, Summer 1978, pp. 71–110.

SOURCES

Anders, Patricia, "New Mexico Is Actually Making Matters Worse for State's Poor," in *New Mexico Independent*, March 27, 2009, http://newmexicoindependent.com/23346/new-mexico-is-actually-making-things-worse-for-states-poor (accessed September 28, 2011).

Beck, Warren A., *New Mexico: A History of Four Centuries*, University of Oklahoma Press, 1962, pp. 200–207, 226–30.

Forrest, Suzanne, *The Preservation of the Village: New Mexico's Hispanics and the New Deal*, University of New Mexico Press, 1989, pp. xi–xvi, 1–16, 33–35.

Gonzales, Felipe, *Forced Sacrifice as Ethnic Protest: The Hispano Cause in New Mexico and the Racial Attitude Confrontation of 1933*, P. Lang, 2001, p. 115.

Gonzales-Berry, Erlinda, and David R. Maciel, eds., *The Contested Homeland: A Chicano History of New Mexico*, University of New Mexico Press, 2000, pp. 1–9, 84–96.

Kaplan, Alice, *The Interpreter*, Simon & Schuster, 2005, pp. 49–50, 189.

Lee, Mike, "New Mexico's Population Shows Blending of American Demographics," in *Bloomberg*, March 16, 2011, http://www.bloomberg.com/news/2011-03-16/new-mexico-s-population-shows-blending-of-american-demographics.html (accessed September 28, 2011).

Mudimbe, V. Y., "*Et Nunc . . . Per Hoc Signum*: A Meditation on Genitives in Everyday Life Stories," in *South Atlantic Quarterly*, Vol. 108, No. 3, Summer 2009, pp. 419–47.

"New Mexico—Race and Hispanic Origin: 1850 to 1990," in *U.S. Census Bureau*, September 13, 2002, http://www.census.gov/population/www/documentation/twps0056/tab46.pdf (accessed September 28, 2011).

Padilla, Alex, *New Mexico Health Data Report 2011*, University of New Mexico Health Sciences Center, March 2011, pp. 4–6, 16, 21–22, http://hsc.unm.edu/research/ctsc/Docs/Edited%20NM%20Health%20Data%20Report%202011.pdf (accessed September 28, 2011).

Paredes, Raymund A., "The Evolution of Chicano Literature," in *MELUS*, Vol. 5, No. 2, Summer 1978, pp. 71–110.

Sedillo, Juan A. A., "Gentleman of Rio en Medio," in *New Mexico Quarterly*, Vol. 9, No. 3, August 1939, pp. 181–83.

Van Ness, John R., Foreword to *The Preservation of the Village: New Mexico's Hispanics and the New Deal*, by Suzanne Forrest, University of New Mexico Press, 1989, pp. vii–x.

FURTHER READING

Brysk, Alison, *From Tribal Village to Global Village: Indian Rights and International Relations in Latin America*, Stanford University Press, 2000.

Focusing on American Indians, Brysk's volume presents case studies on Indian rights movements in Mexico, Nicaragua, Ecuador, Bolivia, and Brazil to discuss the states of affairs among some of the most oppressed communities in the world.

Castro, Rafael, *Chicano Folklore: A Guide to the Folktales, Traditions, Rituals, and Religious Practices of Mexican Americans*, Oxford University Press, 2000.

Castro's volume delves into Chicano cultural history using an encyclopedic format, allowing the reader to explore whatever topics are of personal interest.

López, Tiffany Ana, *Growing Up Chicana/o*, HarperCollins, 1995.

This collection of narratives about life for young Mexican Americans includes stories by such renowned Latina/o authors as Helena Maria Viramontes, Sandra Cisneros, and Rudolfo Anaya.

Nostrand, Richard Lee, *El Cerrito, New Mexico: Eight Generations in a Spanish Village*, University of Oklahoma Press, 2003.

Nostrand consulted reams of public documents, including government and church records, and interviewed some sixty residents to compile this study of one Hispanic village since its founding in 1824, with the chapters historically parceled out generation by generation.

SUGGESTED SEARCH TERMS

Juan A. A. Sedillo AND Gentleman of Rio en Medio

Juan A. A. Sedillo AND biography

Juan A. A. Sedillo AND New Mexico

Hispano AND New Mexico

Hispano AND United States

New Mexico AND statehood

Mexican American literature AND history

Chicano literature AND history

Chicano AND short stories

Mexican AND short stories

Hispanic AND short stories

Home

GWENDOLYN BROOKS

1953

Although Gwendolyn Brooks is better known for poetry than for prose, she published one novel, *Maud Martha*, in 1953. Nestled within this tale of a young African American woman coming of age is the chapter titled "Home." This story, widely anthologized, paints a picture of a family fearful of losing their home, and everything with it, due to financial hard times. *Maud Martha*, including "Home," remains in print in the 1993 edition and is easily available at libraries, bookstores, and online.

In *Maud Martha*, *A Street in Bronzeville*, *Annie Allen*, *Blacks*, and many other volumes, Brooks demonstrates a rare talent for language that sings and social commentary that never preaches. The first African American to win a Pulitzer Prize, Brooks remained dedicated to her community and committed to helping young writers throughout her life. Anyone who had the honor of meeting Brooks could not fail to recognize her kindness, generosity, and humility.

AUTHOR BIOGRAPHY

Brooks was born on June 7, 1917, in Topeka, Kansas, to David Anderson Brooks (a janitor) and Keziah Corinne Wims Brooks (a teacher). The family moved to Chicago while Brooks was quite young. Her well-educated mother was a great influence on Brooks. Her father's ambition

Gwendolyn Brooks (AP Images)

had been to become a doctor, an ambition he was unable to fulfill due to a lack of money. The family highly valued education, and both parents encouraged their daughter to read and write. Brooks often told the story that when she was a child of nine or so, she presented her parents with her first poem. Her parents were lavish in their praise, predicting that she would become a female Paul Lawrence Dunbar. From that point on, Brooks never had to do dishes again because her parents wanted her to devote her time to writing poetry.

When she was thirteen, Brooks published her first poem in a children's magazine. By the time she was sixteen, she had published some seventy-five poems. Her mother took her to meet the famous African American poets James Weldon Johnson and Langston Hughes while Brooks was still in high school. The poets were generous with their encouragement and remained influential in Brooks's life as she grew as a writer.

In 1936, Brooks graduated from Wilson Junior College. She worked as a publicity director for the National Association for the Advancement of Colored People's Youth Council from 1937 to 1938. She married Henry Lowington Blakely II in 1938. The couple had two children, Henry Lowington Blakely III, born in 1940, and a daughter, Nora, born in 1951. During the early years of her marriage, Brooks continued to write poetry and attended formative poetry workshops. More and more, her work focused on the lives of the African Americans she saw living in the urban Chicago environment.

By the 1940s Brooks's work was appearing in such prestigious publications as the *Yale Review*, *Harper's*, and *Poetry*. She published her first collection of poems, *A Street in Bronzeville*, in 1945. In these poems, Brooks, as has Langston Hughes, reflects on the tension between dreams and realities. Poems from this selection, such as "The Mother," a first-person meditation by a woman who has experienced one or more abortions, continue to resonate in the years since the publication of this groundbreaking book.

A Street in Bronzeville was an immediate success, and Brooks was lauded as a new, important poetic voice. She was named one of the ten women of the year by *Mademoiselle* magazine in 1945, and she won a National Institute of Arts and Letters grant in literature in 1946. In addition, she won Guggenheim Fellowships in 1946 and 1947 as well as an American Academy of Arts and Letters Award for creative writing in 1946.

In 1950, Brooks won the Pulitzer Prize for Poetry for her collection *Annie Allen*. It was the first time this important award, in any category, was given to an African American. The poems in *Annie Allen* detail the life of an African American woman from childhood to adulthood as she tries to come to terms with her blackness and societal notions of beauty. This collection also won the Eunice Tietjens Prize from *Poetry* magazine.

Brooks's only novel, *Maud Martha*, was published in 1953. "Home," chapter 8 in the novel, is often anthologized as a short story. The novel traces the life of Maud Martha as she grows up in a family very much like Brooks's. In this novel, Brooks examines racism, both from the white community and within the African American community. As a darker-skinned African American, Maud Martha suffered from slurs, prejudice, and self-doubt. Although the work did not generate the critical praise and acclaim Brooks was accustomed to receiving for her poetry, in later years, the work has been closely examined by scholars and literary critics.

During the 1960s and 1970s, Brooks continued to produce important work. Her collection *The Bean Eaters*, released in 1960, includes her most anthologized poem, "We Real Cool." During the 1960s, Brooks became more political in her poetry, stating that she had reconsidered herself as a black woman. As a poet, she became more concerned with the social message of her poems than with the craft of the poetry. In the late 1960s and early 1970s, Brooks wrote the first volume of her autobiography, *Report from Part One*, published in 1972. She taught at colleges and universities that included Elmhurst College, Northeastern Illinois University, and the University of Wisconsin. In 1971, she was named as "Distinguished Professor of the Arts" by the City College of New York. Still, she continued to publish poetry and garner many prestigious awards. In 1968, she became the poet laureate of Illinois.

Brooks was well known for helping young poets. Throughout the 1980s and 1990s, she toured college campuses, reading her poems and working with young creative writers. She often met with African American students, mentoring them, giving them advice, and sometimes money, when she saw the need. From 1985 to 1986, she was the Library of Congress poetry consultant, and in 1988, she was inducted into the National Women's Hall of Fame. She won a Frost Medal from the Poetry Society of America in 1988 and a Lifetime Achievement Award from the National Endowment for the Arts in 1989.

Brooks was awarded more than seventy-five honorary degrees from colleges and universities worldwide. In 1994, she was chosen as the National Endowment for the Humanities Jefferson Lecturer, one of the most important awards in the United States.

Despite her busy calendar and the extraordinary time she spent giving lectures and helping young poets, Brooks continued to write prolifically. In 1992, she issued the important volume *Blacks*. Indeed, between 1981 and 2000 she published more than fourteen books, and in 1996 she completed the second volume of her biography, *Report from Part Two*.

In 1996, Brooks lost her husband of fifty-eight years when Henry Blakely died at the age of seventy-nine. Brooks died from stomach cancer on December 3, 2000, in Chicago.

At the time of her death, she was working on *In Montgomery, and Other Poems*, a collection published posthumously in 2003. Brooks was considered by many to be one of the most important writers of the twentieth-century. Her writing traces the African American experience, stretching from the Harlem Renaissance to the dawn of the new millennium.

PLOT SUMMARY

"Home" is a very short story of about a thousand words. Although "Home" often appears as a stand-alone short story in anthologies, it was originally published as chapter 8 of Brooks's novel *Maud Martha*. The novel follows protagonist Maud Martha from her childhood through young motherhood.

"Home" opens with Mama, Maud Martha, and Maud Martha's sister, Helen, sitting in rocking chairs on the front porch of their home in the late afternoon. The scene is described in beautiful detail, from the "snake plant in the jardiniere" to the "emphatic iron of the fence." The first sentence introduces a sad quality. The reader understands that although "what had been wanted" was for scenes like this to continue always, such might not be the case. This insight is confirmed at the end of the paragraph when the reader learns that the items so lovingly described might no longer belong to the family sitting on the porch.

The tension increases in the second paragraph. Papa was to have gone to the mortgage company during his lunch hour to try to get an extension on their mortgage payment. It is suggested that this is not the first time he has asked for an extension, implying that the family is just barely getting by. The family has lived in this house for fourteen years in spite of the struggle, but now, the girls and their mother sit on the porch and imagine what they will do if Papa is unsuccessful.

They try to make the best of it; Mama suggests that they will move into an apartment that is nicer than their house. However, the girls know that any apartment they move into will not be as nice as the one Mama mentions, since the rent would be far too high. Nonetheless, Helen agrees that the apartments her mother has described are much nicer than the house, and perhaps her friends will visit more often if she is living in a better neighborhood.

Mama adds that she's getting tired having to shovel coal all winter. Although Maud Martha has been silent until now, she cannot help but mention that she and her brother, Harry, have been helping with that. She continues to recall how nice it has been to have a little fire in the fireplace in the cold weather.

This comment makes them all very sad, and they try not to cry. Maud Martha can stand it no longer, and she bursts out that her father loves the house and that losing it will kill him. Helen immediately corrects her, telling her firmly that their father loves them, and that the only reason they even have a house is because of them. She also adds that losing the house might be preferable to just scraping along each month.

Mama says that losing the house might be the will of God, and that God could be directing their path. Maud Martha "cracked in" at this point and says that her mother always appeals to God as the reason for all things. The use of the term "cracked in" suggests that Maud Martha is not being serious, as does the fact that her mother looks at her to see if she is joking.

At this moment, Helen spots Papa walking up the street. There is significant tension through the relatively long paragraph that describes Papa's journey past each of their neighbors' homes. Mama and the girls can scarcely contain themselves, although they say nothing. When Papa arrives on the porch, he greets them, but his face gives nothing away. The girls remain on the porch as Mama follows Papa into the house.

Because it is not explicitly described, it is up to the reader to imagine the two girls waiting for word from their parents about whether the house will remain their home. Next, Mama sticks her head out the door, and she is elated. She tells the girls that Papa has arranged the extension. They will not lose the house.

Helen, who earlier said her friends do not like to visit her at the house, rocks on her chair quickly, as if the release of tension has given her a jolt of energy. She announces that she wants to give a party. She says that she wants her friends to know that they are home owners, not renters. The story ends here, and the reader is left to ponder Helen's change of heart.

CHARACTERS

Harry

Though Harry does not appear in this story, he is Maud Martha's brother. After Mama comments on being tired of shoveling coal, Maud Martha mentions that she and Harry have begun helping their mother with that chore recently.

Helen

Helen is Maud Martha's older sister. She is probably in her teens and is very concerned about what her friends think of her. (In the other stories of *Maud Martha*, readers learn that she is light-skinned and considered very beautiful.) She initially says that she is embarrassed about having her friends come to visit her home, and that some of her friends would not feel comfortable coming to her home except in a taxi, implying that they would not take a bus. This suggests that the neighborhood of the story is older, perhaps run down, and perhaps in transition. Helen participates with her mother in imagining that they could live in a better part of town and in a nicer dwelling if they were to lose the house. She also agrees with her mother that Papa loves the family more than the house, and that the only reason that they have the house is because of the family.

By the end of the story, Helen is very happy that they have not lost the house. She announces that she will have a party for her friends. She says that she would like to have some of her friends "just casually see that we're homeowners."

Helen's desire to live in a better part of town, as well as her desire to show off her family's home ownership, suggests that she is more concerned with what other people think of her than is perhaps healthy. She also demonstrates a degree of self-centeredness in assuming that the only reason her father has the house is because he loves his family. She considers neither his pride nor his needs.

Mama

Mama is the mother of the two girls with whom she sits on the porch. She tries to make the best of a bad situation by imagining that the family will be able to live in a nice flat in a better part of town if they lose the house. She does not consider that the flat will cost more than her husband earns. Mama is also a religious person who tries to find God's will in all things. In this case, she suggests that it may be God's will that they lose the house. She seems to be closer to her daughter Helen than to Maud Martha. She looks at Maud Martha sharply when her daughter mentions that she uses God's will to explain all events.

Maud Martha

Maud Martha is the protagonist of the story. Because the story is a part of a longer work that is semiautobiographical, it is easy to identify Maud Martha with Brooks. The character is smart, outspoken, and sometimes impatient with others in her family.

While Mama and Helen try to imagine how much better their lives will be if they lose the house in order to brace themselves for the pain, Maud Martha is the only one who speaks to the truth of the situation. She is not careful, however, in what she says: when she reminds her sister and mother how nice it is to have a fire in the fireplace in the winter, she realizes that she has saddened them, and herself, as they all feel like crying.

Maud Martha seems to be particularly close to her father. Her first concern over the potential loss of the house is that the loss will kill her father. She says, "He *lives* for this house!" She understands the pride he feels in being a home owner, the shame he must feel at having to ask for an extension on his mortgage, and the damage losing the house will do to his sense of self.

Maud Martha apparently has conflict with her sister, although this conflict is put aside when the family is under the stress of losing the house. She says that if Helen had said anything bad about their home on the day before or the day after, Maud Martha "would have attacked her." However, on this day, she says nothing. She knows that no matter what her mother or Helen might say, they are terribly worried about losing the house.

Maud Martha also seems to have a difficult relationship with her mother. When her mother says that perhaps losing the house is God's will, Maud Martha states that this is what Mama always says. Mama's reaction suggests that she does not always know when Maud Martha is being serious, when she's being funny, or when she's being disrespectful. In this case, Mama does not realize that Maud Martha is mildly making fun of her.

Papa

Papa is the father of the family. He works a job that barely provides a living wage, and he must go to the mortgage company to ask for an extension. In addition, the story suggests that this is not the first time he has had to ask for an extension. Maud Martha's comment that losing the house will kill their father suggests that he takes great pride in home ownership and that much of his sense of self-worth is tied up in owning his own property.

Although Papa is not present in the story except for a few short lines, his presence is felt throughout. Everything turns on his visit to the mortgage company over his lunch break. Because no one knows the result of the meeting until he comes home that evening, presumably after five o'clock, the girls and their mother have had a long day of tension.

Papa appears to be someone who carefully guards his emotions. When he comes walking up the street, the rest of the family is unable to tell from his walk or his face whether he has been successful or not. In addition, when he walks across the porch, he does not tell the girls or Mama what has happened; Mama must go inside the house to inquire. The reader is left to speculate why this is so. At some level, Papa could be feeling shamed that he had to ask for an extension on his mortgage. If this is the case, it is possible that the shame of the experience outweighs the joy of having the house. It might also imply that he is worried about the next time he will be unable to fully make his house payment.

THEMES

Home

Clearly, any story titled "Home" suggests strong thematic connections to the concept of home. In Brooks's story, there are two distinct interpretations of what constitutes a home.

Maud Martha and Papa equate home with the house. The story opens with a focus on the physical attributes of the home: the front porch, the plants, the rockers, the fence, and the gate. "What had been wanted was this always," the story opens, "this always to last." The solidity of the physical structure of the home is thus linked to the desire for permanence, to the desire that there always to be the house, and thus the home. Maud Martha's outburst that losing the home will kill her father links her to the opening narration of physical structure and permanence. For her, the well-being and attainment of the physical house are symbolic of the coherence and continuity of the family.

Likewise, Papa's choice to beg for an extension of their mortgage at the cost of his own pride suggests that he places the value of home ownership above all else. For him, if he is unable to provide a house for his family, he is also unable to provide a home.

TOPICS FOR FURTHER STUDY

- Research how to write a screenplay. Using screenwriting software such as Final Draft, write a screenplay for a short film of "Home." With a small group of students, produce a video of your screenplay and upload it to YouTube. Invite classmates to review your production.
- Read *Maud Martha*, the novel that includes "Home." Then read Sandra Cisneros's *The House on Mango Street*. Although both Maud Martha and Esperanza grow up in Chicago, they seem to be in different worlds. Write a brief essay in which you compare and contrast the two families from the novels. How are Esperanza and Maud Martha alike? How are they different?
- What was life like in the 1950s for an African American family living in a large city like Chicago? Using a computer to do research, compare the annual average salaries of white and black men. Identify the most common jobs held by white men and compare them with the jobs held by black men. Locate statistics on home ownership, comparing how many black families owned their own houses with how many white families owned their houses. What other statistics or facts can you find to help understand what life was like? Using the information you have gathered, develop a series of graphs and charts that illustrate your findings with a program such as Excel.
- Read George Kent's biography *A Life of Gwendolyn Brooks* (1990) and other biographical materials about Brooks. Using Glogster, create an interactive poster of Brooks's life, linking to reviews of her various works, showing the places she lived on a map, identifying her role in the Black Arts movement, and providing other important details. Share a link to your poster with other students and teachers and ask them to view and interact with your work.
- With a small group of students, read Mildred Taylor's 1976 young-adult novel *Roll of Thunder, Hear My Cry*. The story is about a Depression-era African American family living in Mississippi. What is the importance of land ownership in this novel? How does racism affect the main character and her family? Develop a list of reading and discussion questions based on the book and lead your small group in a meaningful discussion about the book.
- With your classmates, plan and execute a reading of works by important African American women writers such as Phyllis Wheatley, Zora Neale Hurston, Gwendolyn Brooks, Toni Morrison, Lucille Clifton, Audre Lorde, and Nikki Giovanni, among others. Use open-source project management software to keep track of assignments and tasks such as selecting and editing readings; rehearsing readings; creating displays and decorations for your reading space; creating invitations for other students, family, and community members; and planning refreshments, among other tasks.

Helen and Mama interpret the word *home* differently. They reply to Maud Martha's outburst with the contention that the home is wherever the family is together. They seem to subscribe to the old adage, "Home is where the heart is." They contend that Papa does not love the house but rather loves the girls and their mother above all else. Thus, if the family has to move because they lose the house, they will be able to establish a home elsewhere. Mama and Helen assert that Papa's desire to keep the house has nothing to do with the house itself, and everything to do with his love for them.

What Helen and Mama fail to take into account is that both Papa and Maud Martha need the solidity of the house to confirm the solidarity of the family. Without the house, the individual members of the family will be cut loose in the world, without a tether or anchor. They will be, in a sense, homeless, even if they have a rented roof over their heads.

Social Class

The family in this story are members of the working poor. Papa has steady employment, but the family is barely able to scrape by on his wages. Despite this, he has made a commitment to a mortgage in order to own real property. For him, his social standing is defined by home ownership. He is attempting to better the social standing of his family, and perhaps lift them into the middle class, through the vehicle of property. Whether he will be successful in the long run is in doubt; this is not the first time he has had to ask for an extension on his mortgage payment, and Helen mentions that they are just scraping along. But for Papa, hanging on to the house is the most important criterion for the social well-being of the family.

Mama and Helen also exhibit an awareness of social class that is tied up with the notion of house and home. When faced with the risk of losing their house, Mama dreams that they will take a flat on Washington Avenue, a more prestigious neighborhood. Although it is true that she is just trying to comfort herself about the potential loss of her dwelling, her willingness to entertain the thought that she might be able to improve her social standing as a result of defaulting on the mortgage suggests that she is dishonest with herself about the financial situation of the family. She equates social class with the geographical location of their dwelling rather than with the ownership of property.

Helen, on the other hand, moves from the position of her mother to the position of her father over the course of the story. Early on, she shares with her mother the dream of moving to a flat in a fancier neighborhood. She says that she will be happy to move to a flat uptown because her friends do not like to visit her where their house is located, implying that the house is located in a lower-class neighborhood. This statement implies that Helen is keenly aware of her own social class and cares deeply that her friends not look down on her because of the location of her dwelling.

However, by the end of the story, after it is clear that the family will be able to retain the house, Helen changes her tune. She says that she

In "Home," Maud's family is threatened with the loss of their house. *(Christina Richards / Shutterstock.com)*

wants to have a party and invite her friends visit her home. She wants her friends to see that her family owns property. Helen now seems to feel that although the house is old and not in the best neighborhood, owning the house places her in a superior social class to those of her friends who live in rented flats. At the very least, it appears that Helen will use the fact of home ownership to equalize her standing among friends who live in what she considers to be better neighborhoods.

STYLE

Genre

According to William Harmon and C. Hugh Holman's *A Handbook to Literature*, the word *genre* is "used to designate the types or categories into which literary works are grouped according to form, technique, or sometimes, subject matter." Traditionally, these categories include dramatic forms such as tragedy and comedy, as well as poetic forms such as lyric, pastoral, and epic. Through the eighteenth, nineteenth, and twentieth centuries, categories expanded to include the novel, short story, and screenplays, among others. Fictions have also been categorized along the lines of theme or setting, in groups such as romance novels or science fiction and fantasy.

The notion of genre is useful for several reasons. In the first place, it allows literary critics and scholars to categorize the huge quantity of available literature into smaller, more easily discussed units. In addition, readers have certain expectations of genre. If a novel is labeled as *western* fiction, then there had better be cowboys. If a novel is called *detective* fiction, then there will probably be a dead body.

Nonetheless, generic distinctions are purely arbitrary. A genre gets a new name when there are a sufficient number of works that bear some sort of similarity, be it in style, content, or form. For example, in the late twentieth century, very short stories began to appear in print. Many of these stories were a thousand words or less, and anthologies of this kind of story became quite popular. Consequently, the new form took on generic labels such as *flash fiction* or *sudden fiction*. That a name for this genre has not yet been agreed upon by scholars suggests its novelty.

Brooks chose to call *Maud Martha* a novel, and the story "Home," a chapter in *Maud Martha*, is often anthologized as a short story. However, neither the novel nor the story fit comfortably within the traditional generic definitions of novel or short story. Because, as Harmon and Holman note, "genre boundaries have been much subject to flux and blur in recent times," contemporary readers have little difficulty reading Brooks's prose as an interesting innovation in narrative technique. However, at the time of *Maud Martha*'s publication, reviewers and critics seemed at a loss; they were unable to fit the book into a neat generic slot. For example, in a 1954 review appearing in the *Journal of Negro Education*, Gertrude B. Rivers states, "The brevity and poetical jargon make it difficult to classify the work as a novel."

Indeed, it seems that most reviewers and critics were puzzled by why Brooks chose to write prose rather than poetry. Why switch genre at all when she had achieved such success with poetry? More recent critics realize that Brooks's choice to use prose was not a mistake in genre choice but rather an experiment in form, an attempt to expand the boundaries of what a novel could do and be. Her use of poetic imagery, her small vignettes such as "Home," and the fragmented chronology and episodic structure of her work demonstrate that a novel, written in prose, can examine and explore territory previously limited to poetry. As Asali Solomon comments in "Gwendolyn Brooks' Indispensable *Maud Martha*," in her novel, "Brooks collapses distinctions between poetry and prose, ending many of the chapters with elliptical but potent musings."

Unlike readers from the 1950s, used to longer, plot-driven novels, today's readers, familiar with works such as Tim O'Brien's *The Things They Carried* or Alan Lightman's *Einstein's Dreams*, have a more open and accepting attitude toward generic distinctions. It seems little wonder, then, that Brooks's sole novel is enjoying a resurgence in popularity among a new generation of readers.

Image

An image is a figure of speech that appeals to the reader's senses. Most commonly found in poetry, images also function in poetic prose such as "Home." By evoking the reader's senses, the writer can shape the tone, themes, and meaning of his or her work. Most readers are familiar with the notion of the visual image; in this case, the writer uses language that creates a picture in the reader's mind's eye. Less commonly considered are other sensory images: Auditory images insert sound into the reader's mind's ear. Olfactory images appeal to the reader's sense of smell and can evoke powerful emotional responses to a poem or story. Tactile images suggest a sensation of touch. Kinesthetic images provide a sense of movement, such as walking or running, within a poem or story.

As a poet, Brooks's use of images has been well noted by readers and critics alike. What renders stories such as "Home" so memorable is her choice to include poetic images in her prose. For example, the opening paragraph in the story sets a visual scene of plants, late afternoon light, the gate, and the girls and woman on the porch. In addition, the paragraph includes an auditory image, as the characters are "talking softly." The "late afternoon light" is not only a visual image: it also creates the feeling of warmth on the reader's skin, in that it is a tactile image. Finally, the rocking motion of the chairs creates a kinesthetic image. The soothing images in the first paragraph stand in stark relief to the tension built into the rest of the story as the family waits to learn if they will be turned out of their house. These images demonstrate what is at stake if Papa is not successful in getting the mortgage extended.

Likewise, near the end of the story, Papa's return is shot through with imagery. Brooks's narrator states, "It was that same dear little staccato walk, one shoulder down, then the other, then repeat, and repeat." The word *staccato* is a musical term, used to describe notes that are short and distinct one from the other. By using it to describe Papa's walk, Brooks provides an auditory image that says something important about both the sound of Papa's walk as well as Papa himself. The image allows the reader to sense Papa as a man with a purpose, with a walk that is quick and direct.

Later in the paragraph, the narrator relates, "They wanted to hurl themselves over the fence, into the street, and shake the truth out his collar." In this instance, Brooks employs a kinesthetic image through the use of the words *hurl* and *shake*. These are strong, active verbs that create movement within the story.

Through these examples and many others in "Home," Brooks uses images to create a finely wrought sense of first stability and comfort, then tension and fear, and finally palpable relief and joy. Brooks's talent as a poet enhances her ability to use images effectively in her prose.

HISTORICAL CONTEXT

The Great Depression

Although Gwendolyn Brooks published "Home" in 1953, a time of low unemployment and growing prosperity in the United States, her formative teenage and young-adult years were spent during the period in American history known as the Great Depression. This experience shaped her life and also shaped the story "Home." Moreover, her protagonist, Maud Martha, was born in 1917, which was also Brooks's birth year.

During the 1920s, the stock market rose dramatically, thriving on speculation and shaky business dealings. Everyone, it appeared, could get rich by investing in stocks and bonds. However, in October 1929, the U.S. stock market collapsed, and stock prices took a dramatic plunge that persisted for the next three years. The economic catastrophe started by Wall Street took ten years from start to finish. As a result, those who had invested in the stock market lost most, if not all, of their wealth. Even worse, banks and financial institutions that held stocks in their portfolios also lost nearly everything, forcing the closure of many banks. According to an article in *Modern American Poetry*, by 1933, 11,000 of the United States' 25,000 banks had failed. Thus, even those who had not invested in the stock market but had deposited their savings in banks were left destitute.

The loss of savings and of confidence led to a rapid decrease in demand for consumer goods. As a result, people involved in the production of these goods lost their jobs, making it even more difficult for them to purchase necessities. Manufacturing output tumbled downward, forcing unemployment upward. Most estimates place unemployment during the mid-1930s at about 25 percent. According to the PBS series *American Experience*'s Web site on the Great Depression, "African Americans suffered more than whites, since their jobs were often taken away from them and given to whites. In 1930, 50 percent of blacks were unemployed."

During the relatively prosperous period of the 1920s, more African American families had begun to purchase homes. However, because black breadwinners were often the first to lose their jobs, they found themselves in the difficult situation of not being able to keep up with their mortgage payments. Many lost their homes as a result.

According to the text of "Home," Maud Martha's family had owned their own home for more than fourteen years. Given that Maud Martha is an older teenager at the time of the story and that she was born in 1917, the family probably purchased the house during the early 1920s, shortly after Maud Martha's birth. The time frame of the story is likely 1932 or 1933. In 1933, according to David Wheelock's "Government Response to Home Mortgage Distress: Lessons from the Great Depression," 50 percent of all mortgages were delinquent during those years, and foreclosure rates reached a high of 1.4 percent in 1933.

Further, although it is fortunate that Papa has a job, it is also likely that he is not working full time, since many workers had only two or three days of work throughout the Depression. This would have reduced his already low wages. Since this character is based on Brooks's own father, it is possible that he works as a janitor. Further, the text suggests that his request for an extension of the mortgage from the Homeowner's Loan Company is not the first such request. In all likelihood, his mortgage would be considered delinquent, though not foreclosed.

The situation described in "Home" surely has its basis in the reality of the Great Depression. The fear that Mama, Helen, and Maud Martha experience about the possibility of losing their

COMPARE & CONTRAST

- **1930s:** The United States is in the grip of the Great Depression. Many are without work and lose their homes because they cannot pay their mortgages. Income levels fall drastically.

  1950s: In the years after World War II, the United States enjoys an improved and growing economy. Income levels rise.

  Today: A major recession affects the economy of the United States in the late 2000s. In 2010, median incomes fall to 1997 levels. This represents the largest decline in any single year since 1967.

- **1930s:** In 1933, more than 12 million Americans are unemployed, and the unemployment rate is about 25 percent.

  1950s: The Bureau of Labor Statistics records 1953 as the year of lowest unemployment in American history, with a rate of 2.93 percent.

  Today: The United States struggles with an unemployment rate of 9.1 percent.

- **1930s:** Overall, the home-ownership rate in the United States is about 47.8 percent in 1930. The year 1933 sees 14 foreclosures for every 1,000 mortgages, a rate of 1.4 percent, during the depths of the Great Depression.

  1950s: Overall, the U.S. home-ownership rate is about 55 percent. The foreclosures rate in 1953 is .04 percent.

  Today: Overall, the U.S. home-ownership rate is about 66 percent, having dropped from a high of 69 percent in 2005, according to the U.S. Census Bureau. The foreclosures rate is 2.5 percent in 2008 and continues to rise each year through 2011.

- **1930s:** By the end of the decade, slightly over 20 percent of African Americans are home owners

  1950s: Home ownership among African American families stands at 35 percent in 1950.

  Today: Home ownership among African American families stands at 44.8 percent. African Americans are more than twice as likely as whites to have lost their homes in the recession occurring in the late 2000s.

home was felt by many, many families during that time period.

Segregation

Although little is made of race in the short story "Home," it is an important concern in *Maud Martha*, as well as in most of Brooks's poetry. In addition, Helen's concern over her friends' reluctance to visit her house, located as it is in the inner city, suggests that the family lives in a segregated neighborhood. To understand the historical context from which this literature arose, it is important to investigate the situation in the early 1950s when Brooks was writing her novel.

Racial segregation in the largest sense means the separation of races. There were two primary forms of segregation in the 1950s: *de jure* and *de facto*. De jure segregation means segregation that has the force of law behind it. The passage of so-called "Jim Crow" segregation laws, especially in the South, required the complete separation of blacks and whites in public facilities. Therefore, there were separate sections for African Americans in theaters, on buses, in restaurants, and in public restrooms. Public facilities such as schools and swimming pools were completely separated.

In 1896, a challenge to segregation arrived at the U.S. Supreme Court in the case of *Plessy v. Ferguson*. The court ruled that segregation was legal so long as separate, but equal, facilities were provided for both blacks and whites. In reality, the facilities provided for African Americans were generally of very poor quality.

In the North, segregation was largely de facto. This means that although no laws required segregation, in reality, races were kept separate by custom and geographical location. As African Americans moved from the South in what

"Home" is set on the south side of Chicago. (*Henryk Sadura / Shutterstock.com*)

has been called the Great Migration between 1916 and 1970, cities such as Chicago were transformed, according to James Grossman in the *Encyclopedia of Chicago*. In Chicago and other cities, African Americans moved to the central city while white residents moved to the suburbs. As a result, schools and other social institutions became increasingly white or black. As Paul Auster writes in his article "De-Facto Segregation" from the *William and Mary Law Review*, "De-facto segregation in public schools refers to a situation in which schools are attended predominantly by one race, due to the racial composition of the neighborhoods served by those schools." One of the major problems of de facto segregation, according to Auster, is that it fosters "discriminatory practices in housing and employment."

In 1954, the U.S. Supreme Court overturned *Plessy v. Ferguson* by ruling against segregation in the case *Brown v. Board of Education of Topeka.* This ruling had far-reaching consequences, opening the door to the civil rights movement of the 1960s and eventually leading to the Civil Rights Act of 1964, which banned racially discriminatory practices, including segregation.

CRITICAL OVERVIEW

The short story "Home" was published in 1953 as chapter 8 of Brooks's only novel, *Maud Martha.* When the book appeared, Brooks was coming off the critical and popular acclaim of her 1949 success *Annie Allen*, a collection that won the 1950 Pulitzer Prize in Poetry. Brooks was the first African American to win a Pulitzer Prize.

Maud Martha, however, did not meet with immediate praise. Kenneth T. Reed, in his book *Gwendolyn Brooks*, reports that *Maud Martha* "was not very successful." In his opinion, the lack of success was due to the fact that Brooks was "still forming her ideas" in 1953. Although more recent critics cannot dispute Reed's claim that the novel did not receive strong early reviews, they do dispute Reed's reasoning for the lack of early critical success. For example, Valerie Frazier writes in *African American Review*, "Early critical analyses of *Maud Martha*... either dismissed it as an unsuccessful fiction and/or viewed it as a mere extension of Brooks's lyrical poetry." Frazier attributes this to a failure on the part of critics to recognize "the anger and tension below the narrative surface." Likewise, Mary Helen Washington notes in an essay for the *Massachusetts Review* that reviewers gave the novel "the kind of ladylike treatment that assured its dismissal." Like Frazier, Washington believes this is because "in 1953 no one seemed prepared to call *Maud Martha* a novel about bitterness, rage, self-hatred and the silence that results from suppressed anger."

By 1969, however, critics viewed Brooks's novel in a different light. John W. Connor, in a review appearing in the *English Journal*, applauds Popular Library for reissuing "this brilliant, brief novel." He further asserts that "*Maud Martha* is a poignant metaphor on the effects of poverty and racial inequality in our country." Bernard W. Bell, tracing the history and threads of African American literature in his 1987 book *The Afro-American Novel and Its Tradition*, argues that *Maud Martha* has played an important role in the evolution of the form:

> *Maud Martha* is one of the missing links between the poetic realism of [Jean Toomer's]

> *Cane* in the 1920s and [Toni Morrison's] *The Bluest Eye* and *Sula* in the 1960s. Gwendolyn Brooks . . . breaks with conventional plot structure and divides her novel into thirty-four impressionistic vignettes or slices-of-life.

This is high praise, linking Brooks to Jean Toomer, one of the giants of the Harlem Renaissance of the 1920s, and Toni Morrison, arguably one of the most important novelists in all of American literature.

Although abundant criticism of *Maud Martha* is now in print, few critics comment specifically on the chapter "Home." A notable exception is Frazier, who analyzes the novel in terms of "domestic warfare." She argues that it is in "Home" where the first evidence of domestic warfare can be found. In the scene where Maud Martha holds her tongue when Helen criticizes their house, Frazier argues that she is "silently defending the domestic space—the family home—from her sister Helen." Frazier reads Maud Martha's reference to building a fire in the fireplace as a covert attack rather than a slip of the tongue. She asserts, "Maud Martha pitches a battle by invoking thoughts about the positive qualities of the house. . . . She immediately makes a hit against her opponents, who look stricken and barely resist the temptation to cry." Further, Frazier argues that "The house, battle-weary yet solid, becomes the embodiment of Maud Martha's connection to her domestic identity. . . . The house . . . is a centrifugal force upon which she and her family pivot."

In the years since her death, Brooks's importance as a writer has only increased. She is well loved by readers of all ages, and critics continue to find ample room for analyses. Short-story writer Asali Solomon, in her essay "Gwendolyn Brooks' Indispensable *Maud Martha*," provides a key to the continued interest in Brooks's only novel:

> Like Gwendolyn Brooks' poetry, *Maud Martha* shows a passionate love for ordinary people: hairdressers, hoodlums, snobs, plainly pretty girls and homely little boys. And like her best-loved poems, this novella is not only the chronicle of one small life, but a mirror reflecting for each reader what shines and shimmers at the edges of his or her everyday existence.

WHAT DO I READ NEXT?

- Set in the same city, but many years later, than *Maud Martha*, Sandra Cisneros's *The House On Mango Street* (1984) is the story of young Latina girl growing up in inner-city Chicago in a neighborhood populated by Chicanos and Puerto Ricans.
- Like the main character in *Maud Martha*, the heroine of *April and the Dragon Lady* (1994), by Lensey Namioka, faces family struggle. This young-adult novel centers around a Chinese American teenager living in Seattle who must contend with her Chinese-born, traditional grandmother.
- David Robson's *The Black Arts Movement*, written for young adults, is a nonfiction examination of the literary and artistic arm of the Black Power movement of the 1960s and 1970s. Brooks became an important figure in the movement shortly after the publication of "Home."
- *Annie Allen* is Brooks's 1949 Pulitzer Prize–winning poetry collection, featuring many of the same themes and ideas she later developed in *Maud Martha*.
- In 1987 Brooks published *Blacks*, a large collection of her earlier works, among them *Maud Martha* in its entirety, including "Home," as well as selections from *A Street in Bronzeville*, *The Near Johannesburg Boy*, and other works. This is a must-have collection for those who appreciate Brooks's poetry and prose.
- Louis Hyman's *Debtor Nation* (2011) includes a chapter titled "Postwar Consumer Credit," detailing the financing of post–World War II home purchases. The chapter clearly delineates the differences in the kinds of mortgages available to white home buyers as opposed to African American home buyers.

CRITICISM

Diane Andrews Henningfeld

Henningfeld holds the rank of emerita professor of English at Adrian College and writes widely on literature and current events for a variety of educational publications. In the following essay, she considers how Brooks both uses and transcends biographical detail in her short story "Home" from Maud Martha.

"THE FAMILY DYNAMICS SURELY REVEAL DETAILS OF THE BROOKS FAMILY; HOWEVER, THE STORY SAYS MUCH MORE ABOUT THE STRAIN OF POVERTY, THE TENSIONS AMONG MOTHER AND SISTERS, AND THE DEEPLY ROOTED FEAR OF HOMELESSNESS THAN SIMPLE AUTOBIOGRAPHY CAN ACCOUNT FOR."

An autobiography is the story of a person's life written by the person himself or herself. Famous examples of autobiographies include those by Benjamin Franklin, Mark Twain, and Booker T. Washington. Sometimes, a work called an autobiography has actually been written by a so-called ghostwriter. In this case, the subject of the autobiography tells his or her story to a professional writer who writes it down. Generally a ghostwriter will organize, edit, and clean up the story as it is given to the writer. In some cases, the ghostwriter is more or less an amanuensis, that is, someone who writes down exactly what a speaker says. In others, the ghostwriter becomes a collaborator with his or her subject, in some cases shaping, changing, and creating the narrative. A good example of this is Alex Haley's *The Autobiography of Malcolm X*.

Nonetheless, most readers assume that if a work is called an autobiography, it is a true accounting of the writer's life, by the writer himself or herself. In recent years, however, this assumption has changed. Scholars realize that each person's interpretation of the events of his or her own life reflects the facts in a particular way, and that this interpretation may vary from the interpretations of others. Moreover, recent so-called memoirs or autobiographical writings, such as *A Million Little Pieces*, by James Frey, include events and circumstances made up by the writer, with little or no connection to the reality of his life.

Gwendolyn Brooks wrote two books that can be generically classified as autobiography: *Report from Part One* (1972), which covers her early years, and *Report from Part Two* (1996), an accounting of her later life. Each of these books includes material such as interviews, vignettes, and poems, items not generally a part of a formal autobiography. According to the Poetry Foundation's article "Gwendolyn Brooks, 1914–2000," which discusses the reception of *Report from Part One*, "some reviewers expressed disappointment that it did not provide the level of personal detail or the insight into black literature that they had expected." Instead, Brooks chose to trace her development as a writer, a woman, and an African American growing in political consciousness.

Thus, while her two-part autobiography is largely an account of her political and professional growth, Brooks turned to another genre to provide more details of her personal life. *Maud Martha*, and particularly the story titled "Home," is a fine example of autobiographical fiction.

Autobiographical fiction draws on the writer's life to provide structure and detail to the narrative. It does not purport, however, to be the *truth*; rather, autobiographical fiction allows the writer to explore, expand, or even exclude important moments in a life. It is also possible for the writer of autobiographical fiction to change the personal details of her characters to fit the story, rather than forcing the story to fit the facts. The fictionalization of events and people additionally allows the writer to protect her family and friends from uncomfortable scrutiny by critics and readers. In sum, writing autobiographical fiction gives the writer a great deal of freedom in using or discarding the bits and pieces of his or her life.

Initially, Brooks downplayed the autobiographical nature of her novel, although eventually she owned that many of the vignettes and characters were drawn from her own life. As she noted in an interview with Gloria T. Hull and Posey Gallagher, "*Maud Martha* is heavily autobiographical."

In the same interview, however, she added, "I've twisted many things and actually used my imagination here and there." Moreover, in an interview with George Stavros in *Contemporary Literature*, Brooks asserted that many of her characters in the novel have no counterparts in real life: they have been created specifically as characters in the book. Perhaps the most important of these characters is Helen. In reality, Brooks had no sister. Yet in *Maud Martha*, Helen is a necessary foil to Maude Martha's sense of herself as a dark-skinned, unattractive young woman. Thus, in twisting the details for "Home," Brooks fashioned a story that transcends her own history.

That said, the story "Home," appearing as chapter 8 in *Maud Martha*, appears to be based on several important events in Brooks's life. According to George E. Kent's *A Life of Gwendolyn Brooks*, the composition of *Maud Martha* coincided with the pregnancy and birth of Brooks's second child. In addition, Brooks was very interested in purchasing a home for her family in Chicago during this period. After the birth of her daughter in 1951, Brooks and her husband discussed the possibility of buying their own home. She hoped to turn a profit from her novel so that her desire for home ownership could be fulfilled. Kent notes,

> The idea became a goal for Gwendolyn, and they kept looking at houses. The endless moving about went against the grain of her desire to feel rooted—in place. Growing up in her parents' home had convinced her that "living in your own house" was the way to live.

Thus, it is not surprising that Brooks's thoughts on family and stability, while she was pregnant with her second child, coalesced around the desire for home ownership. Although she and her husband had been married for several years and already had a child, Brooks's desire to put down roots in Chicago, the same city where she had grown up, became firmer during this time. She wanted to replicate the secure, stable home life for her family that she had so enjoyed as a child.

However, according to Kent, "Gwendolyn was all too familiar with the pain of mortgage payments out of slim resources." Growing up during the Great Depression surely affected how she felt about the pressures of a mortgage. Thus, the situation of "Home" was one that Brooks felt deeply. The story plays on the closeness of Brooks's family life with her mother, father, and brother, as well as the firmly held idea that home ownership was of the utmost value.

At the same time, the story also illustrates the discomfort the young Brooks must have felt living in a family where the father, the breadwinner, was employed as a janitor because there was not enough money for him to pursue the education needed to become a doctor. Likewise, during the Depression, many people lost their jobs, or only worked a few days a week. In such a situation, worry over mortgage payments, utility bills, and other necessities must have been ever present. It is likely that her father's wages were stretched thin from trying to support his family and keep up with his mortgage payments. Despite these worries, Brooks always spoke of her home with great love and affection.

While it is instructive to examine the autobiographical details of "Home," it would also be a mistake to dwell exclusively on the story as autobiography. The family dynamics surely reveal details of the Brooks family; however, the story says much more about the strain of poverty, the tensions among mother and sisters, and the deeply rooted fear of homelessness than simple autobiography can account for. Indeed, Brooks uses autobiography as a vehicle, a way of structuring her narrative and providing vignettes. In a sense, the autobiographical detail is the jumping-off place for Brooks to explore themes that include familial love, fear, identity, and a strongly felt sense of place.

In a 2005 *African American Review* essay, Valerie Frazier suggests the house in "Home" is more than a physical place. Rather, she writes, "The house is a centrifugal force upon which [Maud Martha] and her family pivot." In other words, it is the house that keeps the family together rather than flying off, each in his or her own orbit. The house functions as the central place. Frazier continues,

> The longing for permanency in the domestic is evidenced in this scene, which juxtaposes the natural world with the physical markers of homeownership. In particular, the "emphatic iron" fence lends a proprietary air, inextricably linking the house with the family's identity.

Thus, for Frazier, the house is also a symbol, a physical representation of the abstraction of family. For there to be a family, there must be a house; for a house to be a home, there must also be a family.

Like all of Brooks's writing, "Home" is a highly polished, finely crafted literary creation. Through autobiographical fiction, Brooks shares with love the details of her early life while reaching out to offer the reader so much more. As Asali Solomon concludes in her article "Gwendolyn Brooks' Indispensable *Maud Martha*,"

> like her best loved poems, this novella is not only the chronicle of one small life, but a mirror reflecting for each reader what shines and shimmers at the edges of his or her everyday existence.

"FOR MAUD MARTHA, THE HOUSE SERVES DUAL ROLES AS THE SITE OF BOTH HER DISTRESS AND HER SUCCOR."

Source: Diane Andrews Henningfeld, Critical Essay on "Home," in *Short Stories for Students*, Gale, Cengage Learning, 2012.

Valerie Frazier

In the following excerpt, Frazier contends that the domestic warfare theme in Maud Martha *incorporates all aspects of the family and household.*

Early critical analyses of *Maud Martha*, Gwendolyn Brooks's sole novel, either dismissed it as an unsuccessful fiction and/or viewed it as a mere extension of Brooks's lyrical poetry. Those early critics, often in reviews of less than a single page, lauded the novel's "quiet charm and sparkling delicacy of tone" (Winslow 16) but didn't remark the anger and tension below the narrative surface. More recent criticism has centered on the undercurrents of rage and rebellion of the protagonist, Maud Martha Brown. This rage seethes beneath the surface of the novel's 34 vignettes of the seemingly common, everyday life experiences of a black woman living in the south side of Chicago in the 1940s. The shift in critical perspectives of the novel, then, is markedly different across generations. As Mary Helen Washington asserts in "'Taming All that Anger Down': Rage and Silence in Gwendolyn Brooks's *Maud Martha*": "In 1953 no one seemed prepared to call *Maud Martha* a novel about bitterness, rage, self-hatred and the silence that results from suppressed anger. No one recognized it as a novel dealing with the very sexism and racism that these reviews enshrined. What the reviewers saw as exquisite lyricism was actually the truncated stuttering of a woman whose rage makes her literally unable to speak" (453). Washington's watershed article is one of the first to acknowledge the protagonist's anger and internal revolt as Brooks weaves them into the tapestry of the novel; Washington recognizes a systematic pattern of suppressed rage and fury throughout the work.

Further sharpening the focus on one particular narrative conflict in *Maud Martha*, Harry B. Shaw explores the title character's "War with Beauty," as he subtitles a landmark essay, rendering militaristic the dark-skinned black woman protagonist's fight against Eurocentric paradigms of physical appearance. Shaw's essay delineates the effects of this biased, color-conscious system on Maud's psyche, and emphasizes its role in spawning internal battles with self-hatred and self-doubt (255–56).

While I agree with Washington's and Shaw's arguments regarding the psychological battles faced by Brooks's protagonist, I also find that the conflicts and turmoil that encapsulate Maud Martha's life coalesce into a comprehensive pattern of domestic epic warfare. This domestic epic warfare extends beyond Shaw's "war on beauty" and incorporates all areas of household and familial ties. Domestic warfare precisely describes Maud Martha's struggles to obtain and maintain her home and relationships with family members as she strives to retain a sense of identity within this confining structure.

Maud Martha captures the conventional literary epic's spirit of battle by encapsulating the metaphorical representations of domestic warfare as female epic with Maud Martha as the hero of her home/land. Like with traditional epic, *Maud Martha* emblematizes the cultural paradigms of a critical moment in history, revealing the struggles of post–World War II America to reconcile the roles of women, in particular African American women, within the public and private realms. Through the course of the novel, Maud Martha fights a war against sexism, classism, and racism to establish her identity. Winning this war is of paramount importance and of epic heroic dimensions because at stake for Maud Martha, as representative woman, are home and family, as well as autonomy, creativity, and self-expression.

Particularly during the early 1950s, the time in which *Maud Martha* was written and set, the domestic realm was one of tension and flux as women worked to balance their roles as wives, mothers, and artists. With World Wars I and II only recently past, and the Korean and Vietnam conflicts on the horizon, (white) women workers found their roles in society changing. They had entered the US workforce during the wartime era, providing the nation with a much-needed source of labor. Yet after the war, the return of their male counterparts forced working (white) women's return to the domicile and to domestic duties. The post-war decades of the 1950s and

60s also brought on the Red Scare—a crazed fear of worldwide domination by Communism. In reaction to these uncertain times, the nation placed increasing emphasis on maintaining the sanctity of the home. Elaine Tyler May reads this "containment ideology" as a defense in the wake of potential dangers of the Cold War and nuclear conflict (10–11). The US patriarchy mandated that women of all ethnic identities symbolize domesticity and concentrate their energies on the home.

To combat and counteract these scripts of domesticity, in *Maud Martha* Brooks encapsulates a distinctly feminine pattern of metaphoric warfare that destabilizes patriarchal and societal structures, and asserts the primacy of new visions of feminine growth and creative expression. To construct her epic of domestic warfare, Brooks employs such narrative strategies as encoded meanings within names, shifts in narrative voice, and conflations of birth and death imagery; thus, she subverts and redefines traditional definitions of domesticity, of marriage, and of motherhood. Significantly, for Brooks, these institutions become sites of both agency and complicity for women. She complicates the realm of the domestic beyond a sphere of binary and competing gender functions to critique the roles of men and women in creating and maintaining the social structures that limit female growth and to critique how race, class, and gender inform the relative perspectives of the heroine.

Notably, the tensions inherent in the domestic position are encoded within Maud Martha's name, with Maud representing the impetus towards warfare, as indicated by its Germanic derivative, meaning "powerful in battle" or "battlemaid." In contrast, the name Martha, with its Aramaic origins and meaning of "mistress" or "sorrowful," positions the protagonist within the realm of the domestic. In particular, the word *mistress* emphasizes the female's centrifugal position as domestic head of the household. Moreover, the descriptor "sorrowful" hints at the anguish and distress that are often byproducts of US women's domestic experience. Thus, with the juxtaposition of the two names Maud and Martha, Brooks lays the foundation for the domestic epic warfare at the core of the novel.

The novel's first mention of domestic warfare occurs in relation to the home, the quintessential heroic battleground, in a scene in which, when faced with the threat of losing their house to foreclosure, Helen supports her mother's falsely optimistic suggestion that living in a flat is more advantageous to living in a house. The narrator reveals Maud Martha's contentious thoughts: "Yesterday, Maud Martha would have attacked her. Tomorrow she might. Today she said nothing." In this scene, Maud Martha finds herself silently defending the domestic space—the family home—from her sister Helen, who had disparaged the house, saying: "They're [modern flats] much prettier than this old house." While the entire family is upset at the prospect of losing their home, the members mask their feelings of anxiety by overplaying the advantages of a potential move to more modern quarters. For Maud Martha there is no dissembling in this situation. She smarts at her mother's and sister's false camouflaging of feeling, and smolders in silence. Significantly, as Maud Martha's thoughts reveal, battle is a deferred activity, either a vestige of the past or a projection of the future. This holding pattern in terms of overt war finds an outlet in guerrilla-type tactics in which the attack is not direct but covert. Instead of addressing the slight toward her home directly, Maud Martha pitches a battle by invoking thoughts about the positive qualities of the house, such as the fact that they could build a little fire in their fireplace when "the weather was just right." She immediately makes a hit against her opponents, who look stricken and barely resist the temptation to cry.

The house, battle-weary yet solid, becomes the embodiment of Maud Martha's connection to her domestic identity. In the words of Mary Helen Washington, "The house, she understands, is like her" ("Plain, Black and Decently Wild" 275). The house, moreover, is a centrifugal force upon which she and her family pivot. Chapter eight of the novel, entitled "home," eloquently describes the domestic tranquility of the home: "What had been wanted was this always, this always to last, the talking softly on the porch.... Maud Martha and Helen rocked slowly in their rocking chairs, and looked at the late afternoon light on the lawn, and at the emphatic iron of the fence and at the polar tree." The longing for permanency in the domestic is evidenced in this scene, which juxtaposes the natural world with physical markers of homeownership. In particular, the "emphatic iron" fence lends a proprietary air, inextricably linking the house with the family's identity.

Throughout *Maud Martha*, family signifies an important part of the domestic. Maud Martha constantly fights to protect her family and secure a lasting place in their hearts, as evidenced in the scene in which Maud Martha protects her brother Harry against neighborhood bullies who chase him home, menacingly waving bats and throwing stones. As a defensive counterattack, Maud Martha brandishes a chair above her head and screams at the bullies: "Y'leave my brother alone! Y'leave my brother alone!" With this defense mechanism, she grants her brother enough time to reach the safety of the porch and then the front door. In this scene, Maud Martha acts as a sentinel for the house, maintaining the safety of the drawbridge from the marauding invaders, in this case, the bullies. Yet she receives little appreciation from her brother, who prefers their light-skinned sister Helen. Ironically, he holds doors open for Helen while slamming doors in the face of the sister who has acted as a buffer of safety for him. Even her father, with whom she shares an "almost desperate love" for the old house, shows favoritism toward Helen. Maud Martha's anguish results in her "crying in the pantry when no one knew. The old sorrows brought there!—now dried flattened out, breaking into interesting dust at the merest look. ..." For Maud Martha, the house serves dual roles as the site of both her distress and her succor. Yet at the end of the chapter, the tensions of fighting for parity with her sister within the family structure spur Maud Martha to set out on a quest to obtain a home of her own through the traditional avenue of obtaining a husband.

This quest challenges the values of Eurocentric beauty. Maud Martha feels that her dark skin is a hindrance in her relationship with Paul, her beau, who demonstrates society's Eurocentric standards of beauty. She locates the attraction of Paul as a site of battle, internalizing feelings of inferiority and doubt because she possesses African features. Continually she reiterates that she is not pretty due to her phenotypically African features and that no beautiful offspring will result from the union. She views her color as a wall that has to be scaled in order for Paul to meet her on a psychological level: "But he keeps looking at my color, which is like a wall. He has to jump over it in order to meet and touch what I've got for him. He has to jump away up high in order to see it. He gets awful tired of all that jumping." The metaphor of brown skin color as a wall heightens the immediacy of the domestic epic war to achieve fulfillment in the role of wife. Color remains an ever-present obstacle to the union.

Through a stream of consciousness–infused dialogue that places the two of them in oppositional positions as male and female, Maud Martha rationalizes that Paul will try to escape this union, but she imagines telling him: "your manhood will not let you concede defeat, and before you know it, you have let them steal you, put an end, perhaps to your career." Herein Maud Martha assigns Paul the role of an object of conquest, almost against his will, as a result of his masculine pride. She predicates his eventual defeat against feminine wiles with, "He will fight, of course," predicting a female victory: "But in the end I'll hook him, even while he's wondering how this marriage will cramp him or pinch at him."

Brooks inscribes Maud Martha's projections onto Paul her own thoughts about being "hooked" or circumscribed within marriage and by ritual of being obliged to capture a man. Hence, the actual victimization and role of the vanquished are subconsciously reversed. In particular, the clause "before you know it, you have let them steal you, put an end, perhaps to your career" speaks of Maud Martha's own hesitation regarding marriage and the stymieing effect it may have. Marriage usually does not signify a state that interrupts or discontinues the career of a man, but for a woman in the 1940s and 1950s, the union typically mandated a termination of any aspirations towards professional development; indeed, marriage was presumed to signify womanly fulfillment. Not surprisingly, marriage arouses conflicting desires within Maud Martha. On the one hand, she wants to earn the sobriquet of the "good Maud Martha" and to become the domesticated wife extraordinaire, excelling at cleaning, ironing, keeping house, all of the domestic arts. She imagines herself a self-sacrificing martyr, one of a breed of pioneer women "who would toil eminently, to improve the lot of their men. Women who cooked. She thought of herself, dying for her man. It was a beautiful thought." Momentarily, Maud is tempted by the fantasy of fulfilling a patriarchal script, the role of idealized womanhood. Yet, the desire to develop an autonomous self also tugs at her subconscious, such that she eventually determines that, in spite of the obligations attached to the domestic role, "She was going to keep herself to herself." ...

Source: Valerie Frazier, "Domestic Epic Warfare in *Maud Martha*," in *African American Review*, Vol. 39, Nos. 1–2, Spring/Summer 2005, pp. 133–41.

Malin Lavon Walther

In the following essay, Walther reports that in the chapter of Maud Martha *about the mouse, Brooks "affirms a nurturing and life-centered world view."*

In Gwendolyn Brooks's *Maud Martha*, the chapter "Maud Martha spares the mouse" rewrites Richard Wright's vision of the domestic in the rat scene in *Native Son*, thereby presenting an alternative, domestic aesthetic. Wright's rat scene, in the chapter entitled "Fear," opens *Native Son* with Bigger and his brother killing a rat, while his mother and sister look on in terror. The viciousness with which Bigger kills the rat and the inhumane way he taunts his sister with its crushed body lead to a family argument in which Bigger's mother rejects Bigger's cruelty, remarking bitterly, "Bigger, sometimes I wonder why I birthed you." She goes on to complain about his failure to get a job and her own unhappiness with her children and life. This wholly negative domestic scene, which depicts a home life of violence and antagonistic family relationships, is rescripted in Brooks's *Maud Martha*, revealing a revisionary motif that affirms nonviolence and recenters human and aesthetic value in nurturing relationships and traditionally maternal domesticity.

In fact, it is Maud Martha's esteem for the domestic that saves the mouse. Caught in the trap, the mouse waits for death.

> [Maud Martha] wondered what else it was thinking. Perhaps that there was not enough food in its larder. Perhaps that little Betty, a puny child from the start, would not, now, be getting fed. Perhaps that, now, the family's seasonal house-cleaning, for lack of expert direction, would be left undone.

Maud Martha's anthropomorphizing of the mouse is wholly in domestic terms and places emphasis and value on traditionally maternal domestic roles, such as providing meals and housekeeping. Her positive regard for domestic life causes her to release the mouse, saying, "'Go home to your children. . . . To your wife or husband.'" Maud Martha then returns to her own domestic tasks with "a new cleanness in her." While Brooks deliberately leaves the gender of the mouse open by allowing it either a wife or husband, its role in the family (as imagined by Maud Martha) emphasizes traditionally female tasks, an emphasis that highlights in Wright's text Mrs. Thomas's unnurturing maternal role.

Brooks's positive rendering of domesticity contrasts starkly with that of Wright, whose main character, Bigger, thinks, "He hated his family because he knew that they were suffering and that he was powerless to help them. He knew that the moment he allowed himself to feel to its fullness how they lived, the shame and misery of their lives, he would be swept out of himself with fear and despair." The fear of the chapter's title is thus not only the rat's fear, but also that of Bigger, to whom the rat is paralleled. Wright depicts a fatalistic cycle of fear and violence, a cycle Brooks circumvents in *Maud Martha*. Unlike Bigger's negative identification with the rat, which kills it (and ultimately Bigger, by the end of the novel), Maud Martha's positive identification with the mouse saves it. Turning Wright's rat into a mouse, of course, enables Brooks to diminish it as a physical threat, and thus allows a nonviolent response by Maud Martha. But perhaps Brooks is also suggesting that Wright makes a "rat" out of a "mouse," that he perhaps "protests" too much.

Brooks's "re-Wright" marks her delineation of new, uncharted aesthetic space in the context of Wright's dominance over Chicago Renaissance literary aesthetics, which emphasized a sociological perspective and "protest" literature. While Wright uses the opening domestic scene in *Native Son* as an entry to the "larger" socio-political issues at the center of his "protest" novel, Brooks places her domestic mouse scene at the very center of *Maud Martha* (chapter 17 in 34 chapters). The home and daily life are her artistic subject matter.

From within this domestic frame Brooks reevaluates beauty. While Harry Shaw astutely identifies *Maud Martha* as "a war with beauty and people's concepts of beauty," the rhetoric of war misreads Brooks's approach as excessively violent. Brooks, unlike Wright, depicts nonviolence, as the scene with the mouse suggests. Refusing to kill the mouse in her kitchenette, Maud Martha thinks, "A life had blundered its way into her power and it had been hers to preserve or destroy. She had not destroyed. In the center of that simple restraint was—creation. She had created a piece of life." Departing from Wright's naturalistic cycle of destruction, Brooks affirms a nurturing and life-centered world view in this chapter and specifically associates it with creativity, broadly defined. Letting the mouse go is presented as a greater aesthetic and ethical act than killing it. From this perspective, a "war" with beauty does not accurately characterize Brooks's stance in *Maud Martha*; rather, through the character Maud Martha, Brooks negotiates hegemonic aesthetic standards of physical and literary or artistic beauty and creates an alternative aesthetic space in the domestic.

Source: Malin Lavon Walther, "Re-Wrighting *Native Son*: Gwendolyn Brooks's Domestic Aesthetic in *Maud Martha*," in *Tulsa Studies in Women's Literature*, Vol. 13, No. 1, Spring 1994, pp. 143–45.

Patricia H. Lattin and Vernon E. Lattin

In the following excerpt, Patricia H. and Vernon E. Lattin suggest that Brooks presents a positive way of life in the characters of Maud Martha.

. . . Discussion of *Maud Martha* must begin with a recognition of what the novel is not. In 1940, Richard Wright told the story of Bigger Thomas growing up in black Chicago not far from where Maud Martha was to grow up. In 1953, the year *Maud Martha* was published, Ralph Ellison added the story of his protagonist harassed from the south to New York City. Judged by the standards of these two complex, powerful urban novels, *Maud Martha* could easily be dismissed. Maud does not experience the same intense search for identity that Bigger and Ellison's protagonist experience. Nor does the novel have comparable violent struggles between the black and white worlds, broad philosophical discussions of black nationalism, or tragic conflicts between characters. Maud Martha's stage is not the newspapers or courtrooms or Bigger's stage or the packed auditorium and street battles where Ellison's unnamed protagonist plays his role. Maud's stage is the home in which she grew up, the schools she attended, the kitchenette where she lives after marriage, and most often her own mind and heart as she struggles to be creative and to be an individual in a gray, oppressive world.

A reader cannot, therefore, approach *Maud Martha* expecting the epic or tragic dimensions of *Native Son* or *Invisible Man*. *Maud Martha* must be judged by its own standards. It is a unique work. With a very loose organization consisting of a series of short vignettes, and with lyrical language never far from poetry, this short novel has a deceptively light and simple exterior which belies the complexity of the interior. Although on the surface a comedy of the commonplace, *Maud Martha* is also a novel that looks directly at racial discrimination and its effects on Blacks, and anger often simmers underneath its calm surface. The protagonist, however, possesses a dual vision that allows her to see simultaneously beauty in ugliness, life in death, and a positive way of living by which one can maintain one's self-respect and creativity in the face of overwhelmingly negative forces.

Brooks's *Maud Martha* is first of all a comedy of the commonplace. Underlying the author's story is the constant recognition that the world is not populated with tragic or epic heroes. People generally exist in everyday settings, seldom reaching even the height of melodrama. Maud herself comments that "on the whole . . . life was more comedy than tragedy. Nearly everything that happened had its comic element . . . Sooner or later one could find something to laugh at . . . The truth was, if you got a good Tragedy out of a lifetime, one good, ripping tragedy, . . . you were doing well."

. . . It is not an overstatement to say that in *Maud Martha* Brooks suggests a positive way of life that can help one maintain one's self respect and creativity in the face of the racism and death which surround one. One can create in spite of the deadening realities of life. The novel is full of images of traps, walls, being cornered, and lying in a coffin-like bed. In the middle chapter of the novel (Chapter 17), Maud's marriage and life in her kitchenette have become a trap. As the reader focuses on Maud in her dingy apartment, the camera shifts, and we see Maud capturing a mouse that has been eluding her for days. Having captured the mouse, however, she begins to empathize with the creature, thinking that it may have a family and that it is regretting all the pleasure it will miss. She lets the mouse go. One can profitably contrast this scene with the opening scene of *Native Son*, where Bigger Thomas violently kills a fighting, frightened, cornered rat and then sadistically torments his sister with its dead body. In his limited, poverty-stricken, oppressed life, Bigger is as trapped as the rat. In contrast, Maud, at this midpoint in the novel, experiences an epiphany and "sees" that she has power "to preserve or destroy." She "sees" that she need not blindly succumb to circumstances but that she can in her own fashion create value and meaning. Through her "simple restraint" she has created. "She had created a piece of life." By letting the creature go, she has been not only an artist/creator but also a moral "good." Uniting art and morality, she sees herself as having "a godlike loving-kindness." Clearly for Brooks everyday existence can be invested with meaning and beauty.

Essential to the positive way of life Brooks suggests are the elements of love and the sense of place. Brooks seems to imply that these elements are not only necessary for the development of our "precious private identities" but also for the survival of Blacks as a people. Whereas Bigger Thomas grows up with little sense of "family," Maud grows up surrounded by love reinforced by an almost mythical understanding of her place in time and space. Her parents are always stable anchors for her. Going to the bathroom at night, the child Maud is reassured by seeing her parents lying close together in the bed, their earlier quarrel forgotten. "Why, how lovely!" Maud thinks. She was close to her grandmother alive, and the memory of her dead grandmother sustains her. Maud continues the line of love by showing deep care and concern for her own daughter, Paulette. Maud also developed a strong attachment for every detail of the house where she grew up, and the possibility of losing it during the depression was a frightening experience. Part of her unhappiness with the kitchenette apartment she lives in after marriage is that she is living with other people's furniture and the landlord will not allow her to use her own. One must, she knows, become familiar with places and things, possessing the sense of place that so many urban dwellers have lost. . . .

Source: Patricia H. Lattin and Vernon E. Lattin, "Dual Vision in Gwendolyn Brooks's *Maud Martha*," in *Critique: Studies in Modern Fiction*, Vol. 25, No. 4, Summer 1984, pp. 180–88.

SOURCES

"About the Great Depression," in *Modern American Poetry*, http://www.english.illinois.edu/maps/depression/about.htm (accessed September 30, 2011).

Auster, Paul, "De-Facto Segregation," in *William and Mary Law Review*, Vol. 6, No. 1, January 1965, pp. 41–57, http://scholarship.law.wm.edu/wmlr/vol6/iss1/5/ (accessed September 30, 2011).

Bell, Bernard W., *The Afro-American Novel and Its Traditions*, University of Amherst Press, 1987, pp. 188–91.

Brooks, Gwendolyn, "Home," in *Maud Martha*, Third World Press, 1993, pp. 28–32.

Callis, Robert R., and Melissa Kresin, "Residential Vacancies and Homeownership in the First Quarter 2011," in *U.S. Census Bureau News*, April 27, 2011, http://www.census.gov/hhes/www/housing/hvs/qtr111/files/q111press.pdf (accessed September 20, 2011).

Connor, John W., Review of *Maud Martha*, in *English Journal*, Vol. 58, No. 9, December 1969, p. 1378.

Elmer, Peter J., and Steven A. Selig, "The Rising Long-Term Trend of Single Family Mortgage Foreclosure Rates," FDIC Working Paper 98-2, in *Social Science Research Network*, October 5, 1998, http://papers.ssrn. com/sol3/papers.cfm?abstract_id = 126128 (accessed September 30, 2011).

Frazier, Valerie, "Domestic Epic Warfare in *Maud Martha*," in *African American Review*, Vol. 39, Nos. 1–2, Spring/Summer 2005, pp. 133–41.

Fisk, Donald, "American Labor in the 20th Century," in *Compensation and Working Conditions*, U.S. Department of Labor, Bureau of Labor Statistics, January 30, 2003, http://www.bls.gov/opub/cwc/cm20030124ar02p1.htm (accessed September 18, 2011).

"The Great Depression," in *American Experience: Surviving the Dust Bowl*, Public Broadcasting System, http://www.pbs.org/wgbh/americanexperience/features/general-article/dustbowl-great-depression/ (accessed October 1, 2011).

Grossman, James, "Great Migration," in *Encyclopedia of Chicago*, 2005, http://encyclopedia.chicagohistory.org/pages/545.html (accessed October 6, 2011).

"Gwendolyn Brooks, 1914–2000," in *Poetry Foundation*, http://www.poetryfoundation.org/bio/gwendolyn-brooks (accessed September 25, 2011).

Harmon, William, and C. Hugh Holman, *A Handbook to Literature*, 8th ed., Prentice Hall, 1999, p. 231.

"Historical Census of House Tables: Homeownership by Selected Demographic and Housing Characteristics," in *Census of Housing*, U.S. Census Bureau, 2004, http://www.census.gov/hhes/www/housing/census/historic/ownerchar.html (accessed September 30, 2011).

Hull, Gloria T., and Posey Gallagher, "Update on Part One: An Interview with Gwendolyn Brooks," in *Conversations with Gwendolyn Brooks*, edited by Gloria Wade Gayles, University Press of Mississippi, 2003, pp. 85–103; originally published in *CLA Journal*, Vol. 21, No. 1, September 1977, pp. 19–40.

Kellogg, Alex, "Racial Gap in Homeownership Widens in U.S. Slump," in *All Things Considered*, National Public Radio, August 24, 2011, http://www.npr.org/2011/08/24/139877687/racial-gap-in-homeownership-widens-in-u-s-slump (accessed September 30, 2011).

Kent, George E., "Gwendolyn Brooks," in *Dictionary of Literary Biography*, Vol. 76, *Afro-American Writers, 1940–1955*, edited by Trudier Harris-Lopez, Gale Research, 1988, pp. 11–24.

———, *A Life of Gwendolyn Brooks*, University Press of Kentucky, 1990, pp. 101–16.

Khimm, Suzy, "The Great Recession in Five Charts," in *Washington Post*, September 13, 2011, http://www.washingtonpost.com/blogs/ezra-klein/post/the-great-recession-in-five-charts/2011/09/13/gIQANuPoPK_blog.html (accessed September 30, 2011)

Lattin, Patricia H., and Vernon E. Lattin, "Dual Vision in Gwendolyn Brooks's *Maud Martha*," in *Critique: Studies in Modern Fiction*, Vol. 25, No. 4, Summer 1984, pp. 180–88.

Margo, Robert A., "Historical Perspectives on Racial Economic Differences: A Summary of Recent Research," in *NBER Reporter: Research Summary*, National Bureau of Economic Research, Winter 2005, http://www.nber.org/reporter/winter05/margo.html (accessed September 29, 2011).

McLendon, Jacquelyn, "Gwendolyn Brooks," in *African American Writers*, edited by Valerie Smith, et al., Charles Scribner's Sons, 1991, pp. 31–43.

Reed, Kenneth T., "*Maud Martha*," in *Gwendolyn Brooks*, edited by Harry B. Shaw, Twayne Publishers, 1980, pp. 164–75.

Rivers, Gertrude B., Review of *Maud Martha*, in *Journal of Negro Education*, Vol. 23, No. 2, Spring 1954, p. 156.

Solomon, Asali, "Gwendolyn Brooks' Indispensable *Maud Martha*," in *All Things Considered*, National Public Radio, October 10, 2006, http://www.npr.org/templates/story/story.php?storyId=6197361 (accessed October 6, 2011).

Stavros, George, "An Interview with Gwendolyn Brooks," in *Contemporary Literature*, Vol. 11, No. 1, Winter 1970, pp. 1–20.

Washington, Mary Helen, "'Taming All That Anger Down': Rage and Silence in Gwendolyn Brooks' *Maud Martha*," in *Massachusetts Review*, Vol. 24, No. 2, Summer 1983, pp. 453–66.

Wheeler, Lesley, *The Poetics of Enclosure: American Women Poets from Dickinson to Dove*, University of Tennessee Press, 2002, pp. 86–114.

Wheelock, David, "Government Response to Home Mortgage Distress: Lessons from the Great Depression," in *Federal Reserve Bank of St. Louis*, October 11, 2009, http://ppc.uiowa.edu/uploaded/Forkenbrock/Subprime/Slides/WheelockDavid.pdf (accessed September 30, 2011).

FURTHER READING

Brooks, Gwendolyn, *Report from Part One*, Broadside Press, 1972.

> Brooks details the first half of her life in an autobiography that includes significant commentary on the writing of *Maud Martha*.

———, *Montgomery, and Other Poems*, Broadside Press, 2003.

> Brooks was writing and assembling this collection of poems at the time of her death in 2000.

Bryant, Jacqueline, *Gwendolyn Brooks and Working Writers*, Third World Press, 2007.

> This book is a collection of recollections and anecdotes from people who knew Brooks. The entries speak to her language and work as well as her extraordinary kindness.

Evans, Mari, ed., *Black Women Writers (1950–1980): A Critical Evaluation*, Anchor Books, 1984.

> Evans has collected short writings by black women writers, following these with a chapter-length critical analysis of each writer's work. Writers include Maya Angelou, Gwendolyn Brooks, Toni Morrison, and Alice Walker, among others.

Melhem, D. H., *Gwendolyn Brooks: Poetry and the Heroic Voice*, University Press of Kentucky, 1987.

> Melhem offers a biographical and critical approach to Brooks's work and includes a chapter-length discussion of *Maude Martha* that mentions "Home," as well as other stories.

Wright, Stephen Caldwell, ed., *On Gwendolyn Brooks: Reliant Contemplation*, University of Michigan Press, 2001.

> In this collection, Caldwell gathers essays and reviews from an impressive variety of sources. The individual entries discuss Brooks's prose, children's collections, and essays, as well as her poetry.

SUGGESTED SEARCH TERMS

Gwendolyn Brooks

Gwendolyn Brooks AND novel

Gwendolyn Brooks AND prose

important African American writers

twentieth century African American writers

Maud Martha

Gwendolyn Brooks AND Maud Martha

Maud Martha AND Home

Pulitzer Prize winners

Chicago AND Gwendolyn Brooks

African American poets

Bronzeville Boys and Girls

autobiographical fiction

Annie Allen

family

mortgage default

The Homecoming Stranger

BEI DAO

1979

Although Bei Dao has been publishing poetry and fiction in his native China since the 1970s, it was 1990 before "The Homecoming Stranger" was published in English in the United States in *Waves*, as translated by Susette Ternent Cooke with the assistance of Bonnie S. McDougall. *Waves* was released simultaneously with Bei Dao's poetry collection *The August Sleepwalker*. Since the early 1970s, he has been known for his imaginative and avant-garde fiction and poetry and his political activism. He was a member of the Democracy Wall movement of the late 1970s, and his most famous poem, "The Answer," which was written during that period, became an anthem of dissent during the 1989 Tiananmen Square demonstrations in China. Although Bei Dao strenuously disowns having been a leader of any movement, particularly a political movement, it was in part because his poetry was used as a political anthem that he was exiled in 1989, and aside from a brief visit in 2001 to Beijing for his father's funeral, he has not been allowed to return to live in mainland China. Since 2006, he has lived in Hong Kong and taught at the Chinese University of Hong Kong. In the intervening years, Bei Dao has continued to write. Of his works, seven collections of poetry, one collection of short stories, and two collections of essays have been published in English translation.

Bei Dao wrote "The Homecoming Stranger" expressly for the second edition of his underground magazine, *Jintian* (Today), in 1979. The fiction Bei Dao both wrote for and published in *Jintian*

Bei Dao (© *Alberto Paredes / Alamy*)

became known as "ruins fiction." Unlike the earlier "scar fiction" published in the direct aftermath of the Cultural Revolution, ruins fiction exposed the toll that upheaval took on individuals as well as analyzing the political and social forces that underlay the revolution. It is because Bei Dao insisted in his work on the legitimacy of the individual experience in a political system in which all thoughts, feelings, and needs of the individual were supposed to be subordinated to the state that he has been considered both artistically and politically dangerous.

AUTHOR BIOGRAPHY

Bei Dao was born Zhao Zhenkai on August 2, 1949, in Beijing mere months before the People's Republic of China came into being. His was a prominent family: his father was an administrator and his mother was a nurse who later became a doctor. Like most children of the ruling cadre, he went to the best schools. In the 1960s, like many students, Bei Dao joined the Red Guards and participated in Mao Zedong's civil war against anyone declared a member of the liberal bourgeoisie. Bei Dao became disillusioned with the violent tactics of the Red Guards and was banished to the suburbs of Beijing, where he spent eleven years as a construction worker. During the Cultural Revolution, all literature on subjects other than Marxism and Mao's thoughts were banned. In an interview with Siobhan LaPianna in the *Journal of the International Institute* of the University of Michigan, Bei Dao explained, "Not only did I go into houses to look for things, I also organized the stealing of books from the libraries, because the libraries were all closed at that time." While in the suburbs, Bei Dao organized a group of friends who met every two weeks. He told LaPianna,

> We got together for reading, studying and writing. We would exchange our writings among ourselves. This was very important to me. One of the great motives for this secret writing was the tremendous pressure we were all experiencing, both political pressure and societal pressure. We were feeling very depressed. It all had to be done in secret.

In the late 1970s, after Mao's death, Bei Dao was allowed to return to central Beijing, where, along with his fellow poet Mang Ke, he founded *Jintian* (Today), China's first unofficial literary magazine. It was Mang Ke who gave the poet his pen name, Bei Dao, which means "Northern Island." This was a reference both to Bei Dao's origins in the northern city of Beijing and to his rather remote and cool personality. *Jintian*, which was often published as large broadsides pasted to empty walls in the capital, became increasingly popular. Although Bei Dao is primarily known as a poet who became famous as one of the "misty" poets, his fiction was also groundbreaking. Known as "ruins fiction" to distinguish it from the earlier but less politically engaged "scar fiction" that emerged just after the end of the Cultural Revolution, Bei Dao's fiction was revolutionary in that it sought to describe subjective experience and express the inner lives of individuals. "The Homecoming Stranger," written for the second issue of *Jintian* in 1979, was published in English in the United States in the translated collection *Waves* in 1990.

Although Bei Dao disavows being a leader of the democracy movement, his poetry became central both to the Democracy Wall protests of

1976 and to the students who led the 1989 protests in Tiananmen Square. Bei Dao was in Berlin during the 1989 uprising and watched from afar as students chanted lines from his poem "The Answer" at the soldiers in Tiananmen Square. Bei Dao has lived in exile ever since, and it was not until 1996 that his wife and daughter were allowed to join him. During his years of exile, he has taught at many American universities, and although he has been allowed to return to Hong Kong, where as of late 2011 he taught at the Chinese University of Hong Kong, he has not been allowed to return to live in mainland China.

Bei Dao was a Stanford presidential lecturer and has taught at the University of California at Davis, the University of Alabama in Tuscaloosa, and Beloit College in Wisconsin. Bei Dao's many awards include the Aragana Poetry Prize from the International Festival of Poetry in Casablanca, Morocco, a Guggenheim Fellowship, the Swedish PEN Tucholsky Prize, and the Jeanette Schocken Literary Prize in Germany.

MEDIA ADAPTATIONS

- The 92nd Street Y in New York City maintains a YouTube channel of authors reading from their work. Bei Dao read on March 31, 2011 (http://www.youtube.com/user/92ndStreetY#p/search/0/0XA3hBPBOOU).

PLOT SUMMARY

"The Homecoming Stranger" opens with a simple declarative sentence, "Papa was back." The succeeding paragraph, written in the passive voice, alludes to the lack of control any of these characters had over their fate or the fate of their father. And indeed, it is the same "leaders of the Theatre Association" who come to announce that the twenty-year sentence their father has served "was entirely a misjudgment, and he has been granted complete rehabilitation." Lanlan is incensed. It is only the sight of her mother's "calm yet suffering" eyes that keeps her from jumping up to confront their hypocrisy, that the same people who once condemned them all as enemies of the state expect that they will forget what they have suffered.

The ruling Communist Party moves the family from their tiny apartment into a new one with three bedrooms, palatial by the standards of the 1970s, when housing was perennially in short supply. Furniture appears, and Lanlan jokes to her mother that it must be props from the theater troupe. The joke, however, has basis in fact, for Lanlan feels that it is all somehow a show, all false, and that it has nothing to do with her. She feels that her father died a long time ago, when everyone she trusted as a child, her mother, the school officials, and "the whole social upbringing," conspired to convince her that her father was a bad man, a traitor to the state, and that she should not only forget him but "hate him, curse him." Lanlan's questions "What do you want me to do? Cry, or laugh?" can be read in this context as alluding to the theatrical nature of it all—the contradictory masks of tragedy and comedy are a classical trope of theater life, the life for which her father, as an intellectual, was banished.

Lanlan uses her work at school as an excuse to avoid her father's homecoming, and while grading a composition for a particularly bright student, one who reminds her of herself, she thinks that all adults deceive children, and that "teachers delineated life with haloes, but which of them does not turn into a smoke ring or an iron hoop?" This is exactly the sort of statement that made Bei Dao's fiction controversial, for the Chinese government had long declared that there must be no "middle characters" but only heroes and villains, and that the heroes should be wholly good and noble, the villains wholly bad and evil. To question the motives of teachers, who are figures of authority, was seen as questioning all authority, and therefore dangerous.

Lanlan reluctantly walks home, watching the many windows on the huge new apartment building into which they have been moved as they go on and off. She knows that her father is inside, the man she has not seen in twenty years, the man whose letters she burned and whose photographs she threw away. She has a recurring memory of her father riding an elephant, and that he wrote plays "that once created a sensation and a thick book on dramatic theory."

When she enters the apartment, her younger brother, whom she partially raised in the wake of her mother's sorrow after their father was taken away, rushes to take her coat. The sight of her father paralyzes her. He is so small, so shriveled. He takes her hand and they sit down on the sofa. Lanlan contemplates an inflatable doll sitting on the window-sill, a doll that seems to reflect her inner turmoil. At first she thinks it will burst into a million pieces; then she feels perhaps it will fly away, like a balloon. Finally, she breaks down, rushes into her room, and flings herself onto her bed. She does not cry, however, and when her mother enters to comfort her, she thinks that "if I could still cry the tears would surely be red, they'd be blood."

When her mother tells her that "everything will pass," Lanlan wonders how that can be. How can memories just pass, like the one she has of the dying old man tied to the pommel horse, who asked her for water she was too frightened to give him because she was just a child herself, huddling in a corner, her knees cut to ribbons by the broken glass she had been forced to kneel upon as punishment for believing her father was wrongly accused. How, she wonders, does one recover not only from the physical punishment but further from the disillusionment of believing in adults who repudiate her attempts to prove the truth? How does one recover from a childhood spent in a web of deceit and fear and lies?

When Lanlan awakes early the next morning, after a nightmare in which there appear both the image of her father and that of the bloody old man, she finds her father in the kitchen, going through the garbage, picking out those bits that might still be edible. He is still haunted by the habits of the prison camps, worried that the "team leader" will find something he has written, and Lanlan is shaken by this image of her father as a broken old man.

Lanlan returns home later and later over the next few nights. Her mother comes into her room to confront her and reminds Lanlan that she is not the only one in the family who has suffered, and that for her father to have survived required a great deal of courage. Lanlan claims she cannot "make a false display of affection." When her mother accuses her of being selfish, Lanlan agrees. Selfishness was what saved her during the hard years when she was marked by her father's fate. "In those years," she thinks, "selfishness was a kind of instinct, a means of self-defense."

The next day, Lanlan calls her fiancé, Jianping, and asks him to come home with her to help. Jianping, Lanlan notes, "has the ability to head off disaster," and although Lanlan thinks of herself as self-sufficient, she relies on his "broad shoulders whenever there's a crisis." They set to making dumplings together, and when Lanlan's parents come home, there is an awkward moment before Jianping greets Lanlan's father with warmth as "Uncle." Because Lanlan's father was in disgrace for so long, he is delighted to be greeted in the polite and appropriate manner, and they all settle in for a pleasant domestic evening together. However, Lanlan comes to feel that they are acting a scene from a play, that there is a falseness to everyone's actions, that they are "acting happiness, acting calmness, acting glossed-over suffering." This feeling separates her from Jianping and her parents, and she begins to doubt them all. She walks Jianping to the bus, but estrangement settles between them.

At school, Zhang Xiaoxia begs Lanlan to come see her run the one-hundred-meter dash the following day, but Lanlan does not want to go, so she lies to the child, telling her she will be there. She does not go to school at all, and when she gets up late, her father suggests they go for a walk in the park. He points out that the last time they were at the park together, the tall trees were just saplings, and he muses about the overturned boats. He tells her that she liked to kick her feet imitating a motor, and that she was an active child, like a boy. He apologizes to her for the trouble she has had all these years on his account and tells her that he turned himself in, in part to protect her, even though it did not work. He relates how he had lied to her, telling her he would take her rowing even though he knew he was leaving. He apologizes for deceiving her, and Lanlan's heart opens to him, and for the first time she bursts into tears.

After all this time, she can finally feel his struggle. She imagines his life all these years, and his isolation. That is when he pulls a present for her from his pocket, a "beautiful green necklace" that he made for her from old toothbrush handles. He apologizes for the crude nature of the gift while she shushes him, thinking it beautiful. Finally she thinks of Zhang Xiaoxia, to whom she lied. In her mind's eye, she sees the child flying across the finish line, winning the race.

CHARACTERS

Jianping

Jianping is Lanlan's fiancé, classmate, and a natural leader of the "educated youth." He breaks the ice during dinner with Lanlan's family with his warmth and by addressing Lanlan's father as "Uncle." However, this causes Lanlan to feel that they were all merely "acting happiness, acting calmness, acting glossed-over suffering." She walks him to the bus stop after dinner, and they feel estranged, although the relationship is not ruptured in any way. Lanlan's inability to feel connected even to Jianping is evidence of her own alienation.

Lanlan

Lanlan is a young woman in her midtwenties whose father was sentenced to exile when she was four or five. As a young girl she tried to vindicate her father, only to be "struggled against, given heavy labor, and punished by being made to kneel on broken glass." During this punishment she was locked up with an old man who had been savagely beaten, and whom she denied a dying request for water. Blaming her parents for the suffering she had to overcome, she finds it difficult to accept the return of her father. She feels alienated from her family, from her fiancé, and from her students, and it is only when she feels true empathy for her father that she breaks out of her shell of isolation.

Mama

Mama is the mother of Lanlan; she urges her to get past her resentment and show love to her father. Lanlan cannot forgive her mother for repudiating her as a child. In a moment of weakness, Mama admitted to Lanlan that her father had been falsely accused. Relieved, Lanlan ran to all the other authority figures in her life to share this news, assuming that they would help her free her father. Instead, they confronted Mama, threatening her, too, with exile and punishment. She told them that she never said any such thing to Lanlan, and as a result, Lanlan was punished. Their relationship remained difficult ever after.

Papa

After twenty years of exile and "reform through labor" Lanlan's father, Papa, returns to Beijing. A playwright, he was, like most intellectuals, sentenced to hard labor during the Cultural Revolution. Belatedly, the authorities have declared his sentence erroneous. They return him to his family, whom they give a much larger apartment. Papa has taken on the habits of a prisoner; he wakes very early, sifts through the garbage to salvage potential edibles, and compulsively saves and burns random scraps of paper so he will not be caught by the authorities. He is a stranger to his children, and it is only when he takes Lanlan for the same walk to the same park they visited when she was a child that he can break through her alienation and resentment and they are truly reconciled.

Younger Brother

Lanlan's younger brother is nineteen years old and "still full of a childish attachment to" her, in part, she thinks, because "I had given him the maternal love which had seemed too heavy a burden for Mama in those years." The younger brother seems largely unaffected by Papa's return, which Lanlan credits to the fact that Papa was exiled when the boy was just an infant.

Zhang Xiaoxia

Zhang Xiaoxia is a small girl at the school where Lanlan teaches. She reminds Lanlan of herself at that age. She wants Lanlan to come see her race, but Lanlan lies to her, telling the child she will come when she knows full well that she will not. At the story's end, she thinks of Zhang Xiaoxia running toward the finish line and finds happiness in this image of childish freedom and joy.

THEMES

Totalitarianism

The term *totalitarianism* describes a political system in which the individual is completely subordinated to the control of the state. Totalitarian regimes enforce their views through the use of extensive surveillance by secret police, often reinforced by the systematic use of spies and informers. In a totalitarian society, every level of social interaction, from the workplace to the family, is undermined by spying in order to subordinate the citizenry to the absolute control of a single party and a single leader. The modern phenomenon of totalitarianism relies on technologies of surveillance and the systematic erosion of family and community bonds.

Bei Dao is almost exactly as old as the People's Republic of China. However noble the initial goals of the revolution, by the time Bei Dao reached young adulthood, a cult of personality had grown up around Chairman Mao Zedong. Following the lead of Joseph Stalin in Russia and the long Chinese history of autocratic rulers, Mao set himself up as the "Great Leader." The

TOPICS FOR FURTHER STUDY

- In "The Homecoming Stranger," Lanlan loses her father to political exile when she is a young girl and is forced to witness her mother's denunciation of her father and to denounce him herself. In Dave Eggers's novel *What Is the What* (2007), Valentino Achak Deng loses his family and finds himself marching across the desert as one of Sudan's "Lost Boys." Although Eggers has called his book a novel, it is based on over one hundred hours of interviews with Deng, who is an actual person. Read the novel, and write a paper comparing the concepts of abandonment, home, and grief in Bei Dao's short story and Eggers's novel.
- Poetry, music, and painting are all integral to the Chinese sense of cultural history. Interview your parents and grandparents about your own ethnic background and the role that stories, poetry, or music play in their cultures. Then build a Web site whose elements include video interviews with your family, visual representations of important artistic works in your own heritage, recordings of traditional performers, and links to research about ethnic organizations working to keep those traditions alive.
- During the Chairman Mao era of Chinese history, ordinary language was very specifically subordinated to the political aims of the ruling party. In an interview for *Agni* magazine, Bei Dao stated that "for creative writers the goal has been to create a *new language* that would put some distance between them as members of the *literati* and the government in power." We are all confronted every day with language that has been subverted to specific purposes, whether by the government, by popular culture and advertising, or by religions and the military. Working in small groups and using the Internet, newspapers, and magazines as sources, collect ten examples of phrases that exemplify this subversion. Write a poem that explores the ways that these phrases have been used to express something other than their ordinary meaning.
- One of Lanlan's happiest moments in "The Homecoming Stranger" is when she is making dumplings with Jianping. Food is central to Chinese culture, as it is to many ethnicities, and the recipe for making dumplings is one Lanlan seems to know by heart. Many families have traditional dishes that have been passed down from one generation to the next. Interview your parents, grandparents, aunts, or uncles and ask them to tell you about a family dish. Ask them to teach you how to cook this dish. Take notes and write up a recipe for the dish, complete with ingredients, measurements, and instructions. Pretend you are producing a cooking show, and create a video presentation that explains the origins of your family dish and that can be used to teach someone else how to make it.
- Bei Dao has lived in exile since 1989. For the first seven years of that exile, he had only fleeting visits with his daughter and his wife, and his marriage ultimately did not survive the ordeal. Team up with several classmates and write a play in which you dramatize the experience of being exiled. Where is your protagonist when he or she is exiled? Why does the government declare that this person can never return home? What loved ones does your character leave behind? Your play should have at least three scenes. When it is complete, perform it for your class or post it to your Web page or YouTube and invite comments.

Cultural Revolution was an expression of this totalitarianism, one in which the leader urged the masses to enforce his definitions of moral and political purity, and much of Bei Dao's fiction is written as a response to the ways the state sought to infiltrate all levels of language and the violent means by which that infiltration was enforced.

One of the best examples of how a totalitarian state functions occurs in "The Homecoming Stranger" when the young Lanlan does not understand that when her mother tells her that her father is a good man who was unjustly accused, she is telling her a secret. Lanlan, with the innocence of a young person who believes that those in authority all tell the truth, runs to tell her teachers and the officials in the theater troupe, assuming they will free her father. Instead, they nearly arrest her mother as well, forcing Mama to renounce Lanlan. As a result, Lanlan is punished, forced to kneel on broken glass and to witness the death of the beaten old man. The central conflict of "The Homecoming Stranger" is the manner in which the characters struggle to surmount the trauma that totalitarianism has inflicted upon them and to relate to one another in a sincere manner.

Alienation

Throughout his career, Bei Dao has sought to express the inner imagination of the individual and to explore the political, social, and linguistic forces that alienate the individual from the self. In the totalitarian society of Maoist China, the state explicitly demanded total loyalty of thought as well as action.

In "The Homecoming Stranger," Bei Dao dramatizes the alienating effects of these policies as he dramatizes Lanlan's struggle to understand the implications of her father's return from exile. Lanlan experienced her father's banishment as a betrayal by the authorities she trusted—her parents, her teachers, society at large. While her father was gone, the repercussions of his banishment were something that separated her not only from her family but from her true inner self. She suffered repudiation by her mother, was beaten, was forced to kneel on broken glass, and had to overcome the stigma of being the daughter of an intellectual exile, all of which forced her to learn to put on a false front for other people. When her father returns, Lanlan must come to grips with his suffering, the suffering of her mother, and the suffering that the Cultural Revolution imposed on the entire nation. She must break through the alienation these experiences induced in her and discover true empathy for the man who stands before her now, the man who loved her, who sacrificed himself for her, and who has suffered terribly.

Maoist China demanded total loyalty to the state and viewed individuals solely as representatives of class or historical forces, forces that needed to be overcome for the good of the nation. The family unit was considered a bourgeois extension of the individual, and so, during the Cultural Revolution, the state sought to destroy it by encouraging children to turn against their parents, breaking family bonds. Lanlan is alienated as a result of the manner in which the state smashed her family unit, and it is not until she breaks out of that alienation and truly rejoins her family that she is set free.

Love

The central conflict in "The Homecoming Stranger" is Lanlan's struggle between isolated individualism and allowing herself to truly love her family members, her fiancé, and even her students. At the beginning of the story, she reels from what she perceives to be the cavalier attitude the authorities have toward her father's crimes. During the twenty years of her father's exile for the crime of being an educated intellectual, Lanlan was told to consider him a dead man and encouraged to hate him and to curse him, and she feels that the adult world of authority would even "have given me a whip so I could lash him viciously!" Now, those same authorities have changed their minds, have declared that her father's verdict "was entirely a misjudgment" and that he has been "granted complete rehabilitation." In exiling her father, the state effectively broke Lanlan's family. They broke her love not only for her father but for her mother, too. When Lanlan's mother, in a moment of weakness, admitted that her father had been wrongly accused, Lanlan ran to all the authorities, and as a result, her mother repudiated her words and left Lanlan to take the punishment alone.

Hence, Lanlan has come to feel that any display of emotion toward her parents is a "false display of affection," a feeling that creeps over her even during the one evening when it seems the family is on its way to reuniting. When her parents and Jianping are finally relaxing and enjoying one another, the sense comes over her that "surely this was a scene from a play?" Lanlan has become so jaded by a world in which all authority figures have lied to her that she cannot recognize genuine affection and happiness when it is offered, and she retreats further into her own cocoon of individualistic isolation.

Lanlan's father finally breaks through her sense of isolation by telling her several small stories about herself that she had not known; hearing these stories enables her to free herself from the sense of estrangement that has plagued

The theme of Bei Dao's story is the adjustment of the family to Papa's return. (Li Chaoshu / Shutterstock.com)

her. She can finally feel once more the love she had for her father, a love she was forced to hide away when he was exiled. She bursts into genuine tears and cries for a long time on her father's shoulder. The parent-child relationship, which was shattered by the Cultural Revolution, is restored. Her father's return has also restored Lanlan's ability to love, an ability that is turned outward in the final lines of the story, when Lanlan thinks not only of herself and her father but of her student Zhang Xiaoxia, who is at that very moment racing toward a finish line.

STYLE

Modernism

Although modernism became the predominant mode of literary expression in the West in the early decades of the twentieth century, it has always been condemned by the People's Republic of China as an expression of bourgeois liberalism. The purpose of fiction was rather said to be to disseminate uplifting stories of proletariat heroes who demonstrate the virtues of the Chinese Communist Party. As D. E. Pollard outlines in "The Controversy over Modernism, 1979–84," published in *China Quarterly*, the standard Chinese view was that

> modernism was spawned in Europe at a time when European civilization had collapsed from within . . . monopoly capitalism began to crumble; the foundations of society were shaken by the vibrations of the marching feet of workers; religion and philosophical certainties were undermined.

In the Chinese view, the carnage of World War I confirmed the end of Western civilization, after which

> writers and artists came to see the world as chaos or wasteland, and, mistrustful of or repelled by objective reality, turned in on themselves. The only thing they could be sure of was the subjective truth of what went on in their own heads.

In answer to this chaos and negativity, China's ruling party offered certitudes and expected fiction writers to do the same. However, after the Cultural Revolution, Deng Xiaoping, in part to discredit his eclipsed rival Mao Zedong, loosened the strictures on modernist technique in fiction.

The result, as Pollard notes, was that while writers were still expected to be realistic, they were now allowed "to include subjective reality, slipping off the harness of chronological sequence which ties the rendering of mental states to the events that give rise to them." While "The Homecoming Stranger" is narrated in the third person, it is narrated exclusively through Lanlan's point of view, and although a story filtered through the consciousness of a character who is working her way through a confusing personal situation hardly seems radical to the Western reader, for Chinese fiction this was a new and revolutionary means of telling a story. Lanlan's story is not a cautionary tale, there is no explicit moral spelled out, nor is she a heroic figure who demonstrates the righteousness of the ruling party. She is a confused young woman who has suffered through trauma, trauma that was a direct result of actions taken by the government, and who struggles to come to grips with that trauma. Her story is personal and individual, and although it represents the experiences of many young people who lived through that period, it is not didactic, that is, it is not intended to teach a lesson. Later, when the political tides turned again, it was for his modernist portraits of the subjective human experience that Bei Dao was castigated and exiled.

Middle Characters

One argument the post-revolutionary Chinese governments gave for the rejection of modernism was that it reflected the very nihilism, chaos, and subjectivity of the West from which the Chinese government sought to protect its citizens. Chinese fiction, which was controlled by the government, could be trusted to reflect only the ideals of the revolution and to uphold the righteousness of the cause. That modernist Western fiction was decadent was proved by its confusing lack of chronology, by the murkiness of its portraits of internal subjective realities, and by the way writers experimented with language. It was in order to spare the Chinese reader from these distracting confusions that the state claimed its right to define what was and was not the proper subject matter and technique for artistic literary expression. One hallmark of official Chinese fiction during these decades was the rejection of what were called middle or mixed characters. These were characters who were neither heroes nor villains but contained elements of each type. This mix was to be avoided. Heroic characters were to model behavior for the citizens. Heroes were, as Bonnie McDougall and Kam Louie note in *The Literature of China in the Twentieth Century*, "mostly unmarried young men or women; they were invariably from a humble peasant or working-class background and had limited formal education." Not only were they from the correct class, but also their physical descriptions had to exemplify Mao's conviction that it was in the peasant classes who demonstrated the true China. These characters

> were portrayed as perfect specimens, physically and morally: tall and strong, with marked facial features, abundant and glossy hair, bright eyes and red lips, they also shared qualities such as generosity, honesty, modesty, reasonableness, level-headedness and courtesy.

And because all official fiction was didactic, these characters had to demonstrate perfect loyalty to the Communist Party: "they were loyal and submissive; to obstructionists within the Party they showed rebelliousness; and to the enemy they were implacable."

Bei Dao's "The Homecoming Stranger" is composed almost entirely of "middle characters." None of the characters in this story are entirely brave and heroic, neither are they craven and villainous. Lanlan, the protagonist of the story, is certainly not heroic in the traditional sense. She is alienated from her family and her fiancé. She has rebellious thoughts, and she resists showing her father the filial piety that Chinese custom demands. She scandalously kisses her fiancé on the sofa for a while before starting to make dinner, and she lies to the student who looks up to her. And yet, Lanlan is not a villain. She is simply a human being working her way through a confusing and emotionally complicated situation. Since Bei Dao is not a didactic writer, even Lanlan's eventual breakthrough is presented as an individual, not a moralistic, one. That she eventually comes to accept her father once again, and can accept his humble gift of the toothbrush necklace, is portrayed as a singular experience, as the experience of one woman, not as a lesson that everyone should emulate. Although this portrait of individual experience does not seem revolutionary to the Western reader, to write in this way was a real risk for Bei Dao, one for which he paid dearly.

HISTORICAL CONTEXT

The Cultural Revolution

The Cultural Revolution began in 1966 and ushered in a decade of violence and chaotic upheaval in China. In the early 1960s, more practical and

COMPARE & CONTRAST

- **1970s:** While the most violent aspects of the Cultural Revolution ended with the Party Conference in 1969, the cultural and political repressions of the Cultural Revolution continue until Mao Zedong's death in 1976.

  1990s: Although purged twice during the Cultural Revolution, Deng Xiaoping takes leadership of the Chinese Communist Party after Mao's death and introduces the "socialist market economy," a series of reforms that open the country to foreign investment and limited private competition. Deng continues to crack down on artistic freedom and political dissent. He leads the country until his death in 1997.

  Today: Building on the reforms set in place by Deng Xiaoping, China is now the second-largest economy in the world, right behind the United States. It is the world's fastest-growing economy, and where Mao sought to export revolution, the current People's Republic of China deploys its huge reserves of cash to build relationships of "soft power" around the world. While per capita income has risen, artistic and political dissent continue to be suppressed.

- **1970s:** In the wake of the violence of the Cultural Revolution, a widespread underground literary movement arises. In order to distance himself from Mao's crackdown on artists and intellectuals during the Cultural Revolution, Deng Xiaoping does not crack down on the use of poetry either as an expression of personal subjectivity or as a vehicle for political protest. Underground magazines arise, often publishing on posters plastered on public spaces.

  1990s: After the Tiananmen Square massacre, most poets, intellectuals, and writers flee to the West. Those who do not are often arrested. Literary critic, writer, and human rights activist Liu Xiaobo does the opposite. Returning to China from his teaching post at Columbia University, he is imprisoned for two years, then spends another three years being "re-educated through labor."

  Today: Liu Xiaobo wins the Nobel Peace Prize in 2010 and is first placed under house arrest, then in May is transferred to Jinzho prison in his home province of Liaoning. Because Liu Xiaobo is under arrest, the Nobel committee represents his absence with an empty chair at the awards ceremony.

- **1970s:** Seeking to control population growth, China institutes the one-child policy, which limits most urban couples to one child only. Strictly enforced, with only a few exceptions for rural families, the one-child policy is intended to curb China's rapid population growth in the wake of the famines of the Great Leap Forward.

  1990s: As a result of strong Chinese cultural preferences for male children, who carry on the family name and care for parents in their old age, China is faced with millions of baby girls who are abandoned at birth. Foreign adoption becomes one solution to this problem, and thousands of Chinese girls are adopted by American families.

  Today: The Chinese authorities make clear that they intend to continue the one-child policy. Owing to the ingrained cultural preferences for boy children, China now faces a serious gender imbalance, with boys outnumbering girls by a ratio of 120 boys for every 100 girls. The situation is particularly dire in rural areas as girls migrate to the cities, seeking better employment.

---

less ideological officials who sought to modernize China posed a threat that Mao Zedong was unable to fend off from within the Communist Party. In order to defeat those who he felt threatened his control of the party and the state, in 1966 Mao closed the schools and universities and tasked the "Red Guards" with fighting the "four olds," referring to thought, culture, customs, and habits. Red Guard units reached throughout the nation, denouncing anyone they suspected Mao would want purged. Often, they first turned on teachers in the schools, beating them savagely and parading them through the streets wearing tall dunce caps, then turned even on their own parents. Anyone who was educated or who possessed books or artwork or who worked as a professional was in danger. Although Bei Dao himself was a member of the Red Guards in the early days of the Cultural Revolution—he later denounced the movement, sickened by the violence and rampant manipulation of young people by the state—it was the books he stole from libraries and private homes that provided his education not just in Chinese poetry and fiction but in world literature as well. As the eldest son and main support of his family, Bei Dao escaped true exile to the countryside, being sent instead to the western suburbs of Beijing to work construction for a decade. There Bei Dao formed an underground group of fellow students for the purposes of writing and self-education. While the most violent phase of the Cultural Revolution came to an end with the Ninth Party Congress in 1969, the Cultural Revolution lingered on until Mao's death in 1976.

Democracy Movement of 1976–1978

In the wake of the Cultural Revolution and the death of Mao, a period of political uncertainty ensued between 1976 and 1978. During this period, young writers like Bei Dao who had been publishing underground via mimeographs and hand copies began to emerge aboveground. In the autumn of 1978, "big character" posters, a traditional form of Chinese dissent, began to appear on a wall near the Xidan intersection in Beijing. It was at this time as well that Bei Dao and Mang Ke began publishing *Jintian*, which appeared both as a traditional bound magazine and in the form of big character posters. The Democracy Wall movement continued throughout the winter of 1978–1979 as people gathered to discuss the effects of the Cultural Revolution, to criticize Mao's mistakes, and to demand democratic reforms. Although Deng had supported the democracy protesters who gathered in Tiananmen Square in 1976, it became clear when he cracked down on the Democracy Wall movement in 1978 that his earlier support was less for democratic reform than it was in opposition to the "Gang of Four," whom he sought to depose. It was during this time that Bei Dao wrote what is probably his most famous poem, "The Answer." In the spring of 1979, the Democracy Wall movement was crushed by Deng, who jailed many dissenters.

Tiananmen Square Demonstrations of 1989

By the late 1980s in China, economic reform was under way, outside investment was becoming common, the agricultural communes were being dismantled, and students and intellectuals returned to Tiananmen Square to demonstrate for democratic reform. They were seeking freedom of speech and of the press, increased funding for education, economic growth unhindered by political corruption, and a move toward democracy. Protests grew in intensity, and students took to chanting Bei Dao's poem "The Answer" at television cameras, soldiers, and party officials. When the Chinese government's tanks rolled in on June 6, 1989, to disperse the protesters, the world was riveted by still and video photographs of a lone man dressed in a white shirt and black pants and carrying an ordinary plastic shopping bag who stepped into the street, raised his hand, and halted the moving tanks. No one has ever discovered the identity of this lone protester who stopped the tanks temporarily before being whisked away by the Chinese authorities. During the Tiananmen protests, Bei Dao was in Germany, and he has never been allowed to return to live in mainland China. Many of the student protesters were jailed, although a few, including Wuer Kaixi, managed to escape the country. Televised internationally in real time, the student protests provided a rare glimpse into the internal divisions that still roil the nation.

Chinese Authoritarian Censorship in the Twenty-first Century

China has seen enormous growth in consumer culture since Mao's death. While the Communist Party has increasingly opened the country to private enterprise, it remains an authoritarian system with a nearly complete hold over political and artistic expression, and censorship is common. Growth of the Internet, fueled in part by the thriving telecommunications industries centered around Shanghai, has been a particular challenge for both the Chinese government and for

Papa's gift to Lanlan is a necklace made of discarded toothbrushes. (qvist / Shutterstock.com)

American companies like Google whose products provide worldwide access to information. Google was allowed entry to the Chinese market in 2006 after agreeing to strip out search results of topics the government wanted censored. Investors and human rights activists were appalled that the company whose corporate motto is "Don't Be Evil" would collude with the Chinese government in this way, and in January 2011, after a series of cyber attacks, Google announced that it would no longer censor search results. In March 2011, Google moved its Chinese search engine to Hong Kong. Access remains limited within China, and discussions about the future of the search site are ongoing. The Chinese government also continues to censor artists and dissidents. In 2010, the Nobel committee bestowed the Peace Prize on the dissident Liu Xiaobo, who had been sentenced to eleven years' imprisonment for subversion. Enraged, the Chinese government urged other nations not to attend the ceremony and cut off all Internet coverage of the event inside China.

CRITICAL OVERVIEW

While "The Homecoming Stranger" was not reviewed individually, the collection *Waves* did attract significant critical acclaim. Bonnie McDougall first brought Bei Dao's work to the West in the early 1980s when she began publishing translations of his poetry, for which he is primarily known, in academic publications. In 1990, New Directions published translations of two collections, poetry in *The August Sleepwalker* and short stories in *Waves*. *Waves* was one of the first examples of "ruins fiction" to appear in English. Distinguished from the earlier "scar fiction," which appeared right after the Cultural Revolution, by the manner in which it emphasized not only the personal damage caused during those years, "ruins" fiction went further, adding a level of political analysis that had been lacking in the first narrative responses to that upheaval. During the tumultuous years after the death of Chairman Mao, a small period opened up in which the Chinese people were encouraged to express their political opinions, and Bei Dao and Mang Ke took advantage of this opportunity to start China's first underground literary magazine, *Jintian*. It was at this time that Mang Ke gave Zhao Zhenkai his pen name, Bei Dao ("Northern Island"), by which he has been known ever since.

Bei Dao's work has most often been reviewed autobiographically and politically. That is, his work has been seen, even in English translation, as the expression of someone who experienced very specific political and social oppression and whose writing answers to that oppression. Gregory Lee, for example, reviewing *Waves* for *China Quarterly*, notes that

> *Waves* maintains a fresh, disturbing bite born of the times of which it tells. In short, *Waves* shows Bei Dao to be not only a gifted poet who can write an enthralling story, but also a guardian of common, and precious, decency.

Kandice Hauf, in the *Harvard Book Review*, notes that Bei Dao "probes the wounds which the betrayal and dislocation of the Cultural Revolution has left in the tissues of human relationships." For Hauf, the core of these stories rests in Bei Dao's examination of "how . . . truth, love, trust, communication [are] to be recovered among the ruins of lies and conformity." The China scholar Jonathan Spence, who subsequently became a close friend of Bei Dao's, reviewed the book for the *New York Times* and noted that fiction "lets Bei Dao explore his own self and his own society with more leisure." He observes that "Bei Dao's vision is not totally despairing," but "it is certainly dark, and the flashes of light that cut through the haze of anguished memory seem at times too frail to make up for all the loss."

While the realistic portrait of a family dealing with the trauma of their father's return from exile in "The Homecoming Stranger" might not seem revolutionary to the Western reader, it is this very subjectivity and nuanced portraiture that was revolutionary by Chinese standards. Chinese fiction, even in the period just after the Cultural Revolution, was still bound by the requirement that the protagonist be heroic. The purpose of fiction, like all other arts, was to directly support the state, and thus fiction, like drama, was required to portray heroes and villains, and not to dwell on "middle characters." Heroes were, as well, to come from humble peasant or working- class backgrounds, were perfect physical specimens, and demonstrated only noble qualities of honesty, generosity, and loyalty to the party. The characters in "The Homecoming Stranger," by contrast, are intellectuals who have formerly been disgraced and who do not immediately rise to the occasion and mouth party platitudes. This alone marks Bei Dao's work as new, different, and potentially subversive and is, in part, the reason for his ongoing exile.

Bei Dao has not published any fiction in English translation since *Waves*, but he has published two volumes of essays, *Blue House* (2000) and *Midnight's Gate* (2005). In the years since his exile from China, he has continued to write and publish poetry to great acclaim, and he has twice been in serious consideration for the Nobel Prize in Literature.

CRITICISM

Charlotte Freeman

Freeman is a writer, editor, and former academic who lives in Montana. In the following essay, she examines the ways in which "The Homecoming Stranger," in using commonplace techniques of literary modernism that might not seem radical to a Western audience, would seem very radical to a Chinese audience.

To a Western reader, Bei Dao's "The Homecoming Stranger" seems like a fairly ordinary story of a traumatized young woman coming to terms with a confusing emotional situation. However, to Chinese audiences used to the strict limitations on subject matter and technique imposed by the Communist Party, it was revolutionary for several reasons. In the West, the novel genre has always concentrated on expressing the inner lives of individuals, often using experimental language and form as well as social and political critique. In the Chinese tradition, poetry has always been the central form of literary art, while fiction was usually considered entertainment. Since the Chinese Revolution of 1949 and the imposition of Maoist Communism, writers had been required to write stories in the service of the revolution. This meant stories that extolled the heroic virtues of the peasantry and that upheld the values of the party and the revolution. Chinese writers were restricted to didactic stories that divide people into two types, the entirely heroic and the entirely villainous. It was explicitly forbidden to write middle or mixed characters, that is, characters that contained both good and bad qualities. "The Homecoming Stranger" was revolutionary because it is made up of exactly this sort of mixed or middle characters. These are people who love one another, who have betrayed one another, and who learn to forgive one another; none of them are entirely good, and none of them are entirely bad. Using a subjective point of view, one that reflects the interior experience of the individual rather than the state-dictated reality, is also a technique that is ordinary to a Western reader but that would have seemed revolutionary to a Chinese reader. While "The Homecoming Stranger" is told in the third person, it is told almost exclusively through Lanlan's point of view and reflects her subjective experience of reality, including those things about which she is mistaken. Another hallmark of twentieth-century Western fiction is social and political critique. Not only was overt social and political critique forbidden in China, but the Chinese censors, in their zeal to root out subversive thought, were prone to interpreting ordinary fictional situations as encoded political subversion. While "The Homecoming Stranger" does not seem particularly political to a Western audience, to Chinese readers raised in a totalitarian society, this realistic portrait of the aftereffects of the government's actions during the Cultural Revolution was shocking, and refreshing, and dangerous. Although Bei Dao was exiled largely for his poetry, and especially for the

WHAT DO I READ NEXT?

- In 2010, Bei Dao published *The Rose of Time: New and Selected Poems.* Introduced by the noted translator Eliot Weinberger, this volume brings together in one place poems from 1990's *The August Sleepwalker* to 2010. Like most volumes that collect poems from such a wide time span, it gives an excellent overview of Bei Dao's development as a poet and of the work he has done in exile. The volume is published *en face*, with the Chinese on one page and the English on the facing page, affording even the casual reader a glimpse at the characters that form the original.
- Gene Luen Yang's prizewinning graphic novel for young adults *American Born Chinese* (2008) is the story of Jin Wang, a lonely Taiwanese American boy navigating the challenges of middle school in San Francisco. The novel filters Jin Wang's feelings of being born in the wrong body through the story of a Chinese folk hero, the Monkey King, and through the figure of Chin-Kee, an amalgamation of every ugly Chinese American stereotype. This lively and emotionally affecting book was the first graphic novel nominated for the American Book Award.
- Bei Dao's first book of essays translated into English is *Blue House* (2000). This deceptively simple collection of essays gives a portrait of the poet in exile, a man without a home who drifts from the safe haven of one academic position to another. Written with the same lucid eye, attention to physical detail, and tenderness toward the people he loves as found in his poetry, this volume portrays the life of a man wrenched against his will from his home and his determination to keep writing.
- Marjane Satrapi is Iranian, and her memoir in graphic-novel form, *Persepolis* (2004), tells the story of her family's struggle to find a life in a repressive society. The story begins when Satrapi is a child during the Iran-Iraq War, follows her through her teenage years in an Austrian boarding school, and then returns to Iran, where she attends college, marries, and divorces. By the book's end, Satrapi has fled Iran for Paris, where she begins work on the manuscript that becomes *Persepolis.* Satrapi's art is minimalist and shot through with humor. Her volume was made into an animated film in 2007.
- Moying Li was only twelve years old when the Cultural Revolution swept across China. In *Snow Falling in Spring: Coming of Age in China during the Cultural Revolution* (2010), written for a young-adult audience, she tells the story of that traumatic time. One day she arrives at school to find her headmaster being beaten in the street, then returns home only to find her beloved grandmother being denounced while her father and his precious library are taken away by the Red Guards. Li takes refuge in books, but in a nation where all reading not specifically sanctioned by the party has been banned, even this activity puts her in danger.
- In *The Search for Modern China* (1999), Jonathan Spence covers the last four centuries of Chinese history. Written in a narrative style that brings events to life, Spence covers the British attempts to subdue the Chinese with opium, the brutal Japanese occupation of World War II, and the rise of Mao and the devolution of the nation into chaos during the Cultural Revolution. With more than two hundred illustrations and a generous glossary that explains terms, this is a comprehensive single-volume guide to the period.

manner in which his most famous poem, "The Answer," became the anthem of the 1989 Tiananmen Square protests, his nuanced fictional portraits of individual Chinese characters and their struggles to survive are also seen by the government as deeply problematic.

"WHILE 'THE HOMECOMING STRANGER' DOES NOT SEEM PARTICULARLY POLITICAL TO A WESTERN AUDIENCE, TO CHINESE READERS RAISED IN A TOTALITARIAN SOCIETY, THIS REALISTIC PORTRAIT OF THE AFTEREFFECTS OF THE GOVERNMENT'S ACTIONS DURING THE CULTURAL REVOLUTION WAS SHOCKING, AND REFRESHING, AND DANGEROUS."

Since the 1940s, Chinese fiction writers had been required to write about heroic characters locked in battle with villainous forces. As Bonnie McDougall and Kam Louie note in *The Literature of China in the Twentieth Century*, during the period of the Cultural Revolution, this tendency became even more exaggerated than in earlier decades. She notes that in the 1960s

> the major emphasis in fiction was on the creation of heroic characters as models: whether they were true to life was a secondary consideration, and "middle characters" disappeared in the extreme polarization of heroes and villains.

It was also not enough simply to show people acting heroically; heroes were required to demonstrate specific qualities. McDougall and Louie state that "heroes were mostly unmarried younger men and women; they were invariably from a humble peasant or working-class background and had limited formal education." That is, the heroes had to demonstrate Mao's preference for the peasantry over the intelligentsia and the bourgeoisie, a preference, of course, that came to such a disastrous head during the Cultural Revolution when young people like Lanlan were forced to denounce and attack their parents, teachers, and elders. McDougall and Louie also note that it was not enough for the heroes to act heroically, and to come from the correct class background, but they also had to be

> portrayed as perfect specimens, physically and morally: tall and strong, with marked facial features, abundant and glossy hair, bright eyes and red lips, they also shared qualities such as generosity, honesty, modesty, reasonableness, level-headedness and courtesy.

These cartoon-like characters were also required to demonstrate perfect fealty to the party; McDougall and Louie state that the key traits of these heroic characters were that "With unerring instinct, to the Party they were loyal and submissive; to obstructionists within the Party they showed rebelliousness; and to the enemy they were implacable."

That Bei Dao does not include a single character in "The Homecoming Stranger" who could be described as heroic was a real breakthrough in modern Chinese fiction. "The Homecoming Stranger" was written expressly for the second issue of *Jintian* (Today), the underground literary magazine that Bei Dao founded with Mang Ke in late 1978. It was never intended to go through the official channels of Chinese publication, and so he was not bound by the ordinary rules of censorship. He also published this story during the brief period between the end of the Cultural Revolution and the crackdowns that began in the 1980s and culminated with the Tiananmen Square massacre of 1989. What is notable is how invisible the really quite radical approach he took to characterization is to a Western reader. We are so used to realistic stories about the interior lives of characters that it would never occur to most Western readers that such a portrait could be considered an act of rebellion. That Lanlan is not heroic, but rather a realistic portrayal of a traumatized young woman who struggles with the conflicted emotions elicited by her father's return, seems ordinary to us, but it was an audacious artistic risk on Bei Dao's part. In fact, all the main characters in this story are mixed characters. The father is a mix of heroic survivor, a man who willingly turned himself in to try to shield his family from harm, and broken ex-prisoner, one who cannot shake the rhythms and habits of the prison camps. The mother is heroic in the way she kept the family together but villainous in the way she renounced Lanlan as a child. Lanlan is heroic in her determination to get ahead despite the poverty and repression of her childhood but villainous in her rejection of her parents. And yet, none of these characters is a villain or a hero; they are human beings, struggling to do the right thing by one another, which is perhaps the most radical thing about this story.

The subjective point of view was seen by China's party officials as an expression of all that was decadent about Western capitalist societies, and thus it was expressly forbidden throughout most of the history of modern Chinese fiction. As D. E. Pollard notes in "The Controversy over Modernism, 1979–84," published in *China Quarterly*, in the wake of the Cultural Revolution, the ruling party, as part of its effort to repudiate the policies of that time, loosened the strictures on what was allowed as both subject matter and technique in fiction. The result was that "the major new trend was towards opening out 'reality' to include subjective reality." During the Cultural Revolution, Bei Dao, among others, had managed through various means, including raiding the libraries of exiled intellectuals, to find modern novels in translation and to circulate them among his fellow writers. In this period of liberalization, they took eagerly to the literary techniques of modernism, which included, as Pollard notes,

> slipping off the harness of chronological sequence which ties the rendering of mental states to the events that give rise to them, and giving the role of principal to the mind itself, as it ranges back and forward, integrating events into its own unique system.

In "The Homecoming Stranger" Bei Dao uses previously forbidden modernist techniques like flashback (which breaks "the harness of chronology") and internal monologue. In a society where the state was the only organ of interpretation, merely to portray a young woman seeking to interpret the events of her own life for herself was a daring venture. Although this story is not told in the strict stream of consciousness style of Western modernists like Virginia Woolf or James Joyce, the story does stick to reality as Lanlan experiences it, and the arc of the narrative concerns not external events but Lanlan's internal subjective struggle to accept her father's return from exile. The revolutionary aspect of the story is that it takes as its subject the interior life of an individual and portrays a realistic reflection of Chinese life as it is actually lived rather than portraying the external actions of an idealized and unrealistic character for didactic purposes.

The modernist impulse in Western fiction always contained an element of social and political critique, and it was largely for this reason that it was condemned by the party. As Pollard notes, as far as the party was concerned, modernism was evidence of the end of civilization, brought on by the breakdown of monopoly capitalism, and the subsequent undermining of religious and philosophical certainties. It was further evidence of the instability of the Western capitalist system, a system in which "writers and artists came to see the world as chaos or wasteland, and, mistrustful of or repelled by objective reality, turned in on themselves." This turning inward resulted in an artistic and philosophic worldview in which "the only thing they could be sure of was the subjective truth of what went on in their own heads." Repelled by this individualism, and wedded to a Marxist interpretation of history, the Communist Party sought to free the Chinese people from this confusion by the rigorous application of a version of reality as they interpreted it. Mixed characters and the use of a subjective point of view were forbidden in fiction because the only correct interpretation was the one the party had decided upon. To the Chinese government in those decades, the certitude of totalitarian authoritarianism was far preferable to the chaos and confusion of individual, subjective experience.

The rigor with which political and social critique was scrubbed from fiction in the decades after the Chinese Revolution resulted in a literature in which the heroic characters always and only support the party, extol the party's goals, and dramatize the rectitude of the revolution. While "The Homecoming Stranger" is hardly a scathing critique of the effects of the Cultural Revolution, it is quite open about Lanlan's father's innocence and the fact that he was a scapegoat sacrificed to placate the party. Publishing the story, even underground, would have been impossible had it not come out during the period when the government of Deng Xiaoping was distancing itself from those events by blaming the recently deceased Mao for the Cultural Revolution.

It is exactly the things that seem unremarkable to a Western reader about "The Homecoming Stranger" that mark it as a truly noteworthy addition to the history of modern Chinese fiction. That Bei Dao used his years in forced labor to learn the techniques of modernist literature and that he had the opportunity to experiment with it in this way make this story revolutionary in a manner that might not be readily apparent to a Western reader. For just as Western literature was largely unavailable to the Chinese reader, contemporary Chinese literature has only become available to Western readers in the last several decades.

Source: Charlotte Freeman, Critical Essay on "The Homecoming Stranger," in *Short Stories for Students*, Gale, Cengage Learning, 2012.

Walking along the river by the old boats finally allows Papa and Lanlan to rebond. (Maugli | Shutterstock.com)

Bei Dao and Tang Xiaodu

In the following excerpt, Bei Dao reflects on his odyssey as a writer and the role of critical thinking and creativity in literature. The excerpt also includes an interview by Tang Xiaodu in which Bei Dao discusses his status as an "expatriate."

. . . In his speech at the Puterbaugh banquet last spring, Bei Dao reflected on his odyssey as a writer and the role of critical thinking and creativity as "a driving force for culture."

I was born in 1949 in Beijing. As Chairman Mao declared the birth of the People's Republic of China on the rostrum in Tiananmen Square, I was lying in my cradle no more than a thousand yards away. My fate seems to have been intertwined with that of China ever since.

I received a privileged but brief education. I was a student at the best high school in Beijing, until the Cultural Revolution broke out in 1966. All the schools closed, and three years later I was assigned to work in the state-run construction industry. I worked as a concrete mixer for five years, and then another six years as a blacksmith. This experience of laboring hard and living low at the bottom of society eventually

> "WHILE I BELIEVE IN FATE, I DON'T MUCH BELIEVE IN NECESSITY; FATE, LIKE POETRY, IS A KIND OF INTERACTION BETWEEN THE PERSON AND THE WORLD, AND ALSO A MUTUAL CORRESPONDENCE."

benefited me a great deal, it broadened my understanding of life in a way that was tangible and material, something that books could hardly be capable of achieving. It was under those kinds of harsh life circumstances that I began my creative writing. I finished the first draft of my novella *Waves* in a darkroom, while supposedly developing photos for a propaganda exhibition of the construction site. That was one of the darkest periods of contemporary China, when reading and writing were forbidden games.

Yet underground creative writing was breaking through the frozen shell of the earth. On December 23, 1978, I, together with some friends, launched the first non-official literary journal in China since 1949, *Today*. The "misty" or "obscure" poetry—a pejorative term applied by the authorities—that appeared in *Today* was able to challenge the dominance of the official social discourse, by opening a new space and possibilities for the modern Chinese language. Inevitably, the journal was banned after two years of existence, but it opened a new phase in the history of Chinese literature.

On June 4, 1989, I was in Berlin, as tanks were rolling through Tiananmen Square. Nevertheless, the Chinese authorities claimed that I was one of those who had incited the student demonstrations, for I had written an open letter to the government, signed by thirty-three intellectuals, in February of that year, demanding the release of political prisoners.

Berlin in 1989 marked the beginning of my life in exile. For the next four years, I lived in six countries in Europe. *Today* was revived in 1990 and has continued to be published abroad ever since. It remains the only Chinese avant-garde literary journal whose existence transcends geographic boundaries. As its chief editor, I have been engaged, alongside writers within China, in a long-term "literary resistance"—not only to the hegemony of the official discourse but also to the level of commercialization throughout the world. A once-mimeographed journal floating across the oceans has managed to survive in environments where other languages are spoken. Perhaps this is another example of the so-called globalization of our times. In this connection, I see two kinds of globalization taking shape at the moment: one is the globalization of power and capital that is carving up the world; the other is the globalization of the seeds of language and the spirit that are settling on fertile ground wherever the storm may take them.

Critical thinking and creativity constitute a driving force for culture. A prerequisite for creativity is critical thinking, without which creativity cannot be sustained or grow. Without creativity, national culture is doomed to perish; without creativity, a nation, no matter how wealthy or powerful, in essence is poor and weak.

Whenever I reflect on my own life path, I feel fortunate. The fact that my fate has been intertwined with Chinese modern history not only has conferred a sense of mission to my existence, but it has also demanded that I overcome the heavy shadow that modern Chinese history has projected over my being. Literature guides me through the darkness, just as a drifter floats around the world. . . .

AN INTERVIEW WITH BEI DAO

From the late 1980s to now, in both your personal life and your writing, you've constantly occupied—let's be careful in our use of terms here—a "floating" position (as an expatriate). From the state or emergency at the beginning to the more regular conditions of later years what influence has this situation had on your writing? If change is unavoidable has this kind of change contributed primarily to your new attitude to your mother tongue? Brodsky once said about the mother tongue in this kind of situation that it "simultaneously becomes a person's sword, shield and space vehicle." What do you think?

While abroad I've often been asked this kind of question. "When you've been an expatriate for a long time, hasn't your mother tongue become a strange and remote thing?" Actually it's just the reverse: I've become even closer to the mother tongue, or to be more precise, it's a changed relation. When you're writing in Chinese while living abroad, your mother tongue is the only reality.

I once wrote in a poem: "I float amid languages / the brasses in death's music / full of ice." I think that to Brodsky's three metaphors another has to be added: the mother tongue becomes a "wound." Exile is a kind of fate. While I believe in fate, I don't much believe in necessity; fate, like poetry, is a kind of interaction between the person and the world, and also a mutual correspondence. But necessity makes one think of so-called objective history.

Everyone has his or her own "history of the event" concerning their writing, and to some degree everyone forms their own personal poetics, their own individual poetic genealogy. But for the vast majority of readers, you seem to be a riddle in this regard. Could I ask you to talk briefly about how you began to write poetry? Roughly what stages have you gone through up to now? What are the corresponding emphases in the realm of poetics? With which poets do you have the feeling of closest spiritual kinship? It's been said that in your early years you were influenced by the Soviet poet Yevtushenko; would you agree?

It's a riddle for me too, just as a river flows but can't explain itself. I've tried to explain how I got my start in writing, but every time I give up the effort of tracing the stream to its source. I think writing is a hidden flow in one's life, it either comes to the surface or dries up, always unpredictably. External circumstances don't make much difference. When I was young I read a book in the yellow-covered translation series, *The Valley of the Maidens and Other Poems*, and so I liked Yevtushenko. In the early 1980s he came to give a reading in Beijing; I left when he'd read about three poems. He disgusted me. That was because of the biases imposed on reading at the time. There are plenty of poets in the world, and they form different schools on account of their spiritual kinships; language and nationality don't matter. Many of the poets I like are from the first half of the twentieth century—for example, Dylan Thomas, Lorca, Trakl, Celan, Mandelstam, Pasternak, Gennady Aygi, Tomas Transtromer. The last two are still with us, and I've had the good fortune to meet them. The first half of the twentieth century was a golden age for poetry, and since I'm so attached to these figures, I sometimes think I'll write a book just on this topic.

You've always been obsessive about choosing words and shaping lines. Some of the startling lines in your early poetry that still stick in the mind are not only a personal triumph of yours but also a triumph of the Chinese poetic tradition. In your more recent poetry, you seem to have moved on to an obsession with shaping "poetic space," and the penetrating power of the lines always comes forth most strongly in the last words of a poem. At the same time, your poems still have an incremental quality of concentration, repetition, and a highly personal way of handling certain images. For the interpreter, these images and ways of speaking have a "keyword" character, just like, in your early work, "stone," "sky," and later, "child," "flower," and so on. Stephen Owen thinks your poetry "may sum up the Chinese poetic tradition." How is it that the author of *The Great Age of Chinese Poetry: The High T'ang* can give you this kind of accolade, while in China your name is a byword for antitraditionalism? In this absurdity, there are clearly the signs of a complex understanding of "tradition." How would you describe, from your personal point of view, the relation of your poetry to traditional Chinese poetics?

In the last few years, there's been a certain rediscovery of tradition outside of China. It's like blood calling to blood: at a certain moment, you're suddenly aware of it. Compared to an individual's poor powers and scanty accomplishments, the breadth and beauty of the tradition is like a huge wind pressing down on a tiny sail, a sailor has to know how to use the wind if the boat is going to go far. And the problem is that the tradition arises from causes as complex as those that produce the wind—you can seek them but you won't find them, you can feel them but not know them. The emphasis Chinese traditional poetry lays on imagery and poetic space is in the end our own wealth (sometimes it comes to us by twisted paths, as when we get it by way of the American Imagist school). When I do readings abroad, I sometimes feel that Li Bai, Du Fu, and Li Yu are standing right behind me. When I hear Gennady Aygi read, I seem to sense Pasternak and Mandelstam behind him, not to mention Pushkin and Lermontov, even though the differences among them are very great. That's what tradition means. If we have the capability, we can enter into this tradition and enrich it; otherwise we're just failures.

In the realm of poetics, there's no doubt that your tendency is minimalism. The aspiration of minimalism is toward the Daoist ideal: "the great image is without form," "the supreme music is nearly silent." But that can easily slip into mannerism, where the poetry becomes too "poetic," or into intentional vacuity. How do you manage to preserve the boundaries and tensions amid these tendencies? To guard against mannerism, or to open up more possibilities, some contemporary poets no longer care if what they write turns out to be poetry, or intentionally write poetry that isn't "poetic." Do you ever feel this kind of impulse?

I'm aware of this problem: it's one aspect of the irony and self-mockery you've noticed in my poems. Mannerism is always a cerebral game, and it's a dismal swamp or a dead-end street for poetry. I've learned from this error myself. The way to guard against mannerism is to write more straightforwardly, not to write poetry that's antipoetic. Naturally, antipoetic experiments are a good thing, a way of reminding ourselves that poetry has its limits.

I've noticed that you've written only one poetic sequence: "Daydream" (from *The August Sleepwalker*). That's unusual for a contemporary poet. Most distinguished poets, or poets who try to be distinguished, have paid a lot of attention to the long poem or the poetic sequence, as a way of erecting their own "monuments." Are you just uniquely devoted to the short, self-contained poem? In your plans for future writing, is there room for a long poem?

For me, "Daydream" was a failed attempt. For the moment, let's put that aside. There's virtually no long poem I really like. From the Homeric epics on, the narrative function of poetry has been steadily eroding, and contemporary poets find it hard to keep up enough tension for a long poem. I truly only like short poems—for me, they are the only vehicle for contemporary lyricism, since they release the greatest poetic richness in the smallest space. Modern lyric poetry has not gone out of style; its latent power is waiting to be discovered. These days, "lyric" is practically a derogatory term: that's a complete misunderstanding.

In the last few years, international Sinology has been continually on the search for "Chineseness," "Chinese literary roots," "the essence of the Chinese language," and the like. This seems to have become a piece of the cultural landscape, against the background of globalism. And quite a few poets and writers from within China have had their say. But I don't believe we've heard from you yet. Do you see this as a problem for your own writing? Or is it a false problem, a false question?

Ten or fifteen years ago I wrote an essay about this question of "the translation style." My main point there was that after 1949 a whole group of important poets and writers were forced to lay down their pens and go into translating, and thereupon they created a new style of writing that stood apart from official discourse: that was the "translation style." The emergence of underground literature of the late 1960s was based on this style. In the early days, we were all profoundly marked by this style, and later we had to work hard to break free from it. In that sense, I think it's a real question, at least for me. I find it hard to talk abstractly about "Chineseness"; that's the critics' business.

In "Background," you wrote the lines: "the background needs revising / you can return to your hometown." As I interpret them, the words "background" and "return" have many layers of meaning. Now that the "background" of your "hometown" has been considerably "revised," the possibility of "return" is greater than before. But the question is, the homecoming may not be the homecoming you had expected. It could be a false position, nothing more. If that were to be true, would you feel disappointment?

Actually, it's an absurdity. "Revising the background" refers to reestablishing an already changed background, which is Impossible, and so returning home is also Impossible. The poem is built on this absurdity: because you want to go home, the road to home doesn't exist. So that it isn't even a disappointment but confusion and loss at the absurdity of human life.

And correspondingly, it seems that you would find it easier to understand the progress in the Chinese poetic situation in the last few years. Could you give us your opinion on that situation?

These last few years, I haven't been on the scene and I feel a certain remoteness from it all, but this distance may give me an outsider's privilege. One thing I find very comforting is that some important poets, including younger ones, are not deserting their posts, and their work forms a fulcrum for contemporary Chinese poetry. My feelings about the poetry of the 1990s are complicated. I often think that the new poetry that emerged in the modernist May Fourth Movement of 1919 fermented, after a long period of general blockage, in the underground writings of the 1960s and '70s and then burst forth suddenly at the beginning of the 1980s and became a climate unto itself. Then it entered the commercial 1990s. When you look at this tradition, what were its motivations and what were its inbuilt defects? To tell the truth, the problems of the 1990s can be traced back to the 1980s—they started with my generation. We lacked self-awareness, and we didn't fully understand the tradition. This is a problem at the very root of contemporary Chinese poetry. If we don't go to the roots, we won't be able to sustain our forward movement. I remember in the mid-1980s, when it seemed the whole country was arguing about "Misty Poetry," a blank appeared in my writing and this went on for several years. If it hadn't been for exile, loneliness, and reflection, my own writing would have regressed or simply stopped. The "victorious great escape" of the 1980s buried the signs of danger and filled those who came after with delusions and idols. When you add in the collapse of standards, the absence of poetry criticism, the conformism of little cliques and their struggles for discursive authority, the crisis just gets deeper. Sometimes when I open a poetry journal or read a literary website and see the cheap and flashy poems people publish, I sweat from embarrassment. I think we conscientious poets and critics need to start with the ABCs of poetry, do some real work, and put some effort into the rebirth of Chinese poetry.

Let's try to get a grasp of what you call the problem of "motives and defects" in the tradition of modern poetry. I think this is extremely important. Could you be more explicit about your personal views?

Antonio Machado thought poetry was a vehicle for melancholy. Maybe this is where the problem of "motives and defects" resides: the modern Chinese poetic tradition being what it is, either lacks real melancholy or lacks a vehicle. Put this way, it sounds a little like a blind man describing colors, but if you think about it, it makes sense. Look at it this way: if a poet's never been overcome by sadness, what is he going to write about? But those people overcome by sadness keep on failing to find a formal vehicle. The history of modern poetry in China in the last hundred years ought to make us pause and reflect. I think this has to do with the Chinese nation's collective lack of religious faith, our desire for advantage, and our carpe diem tendencies. . . .

Source: Bei Dao and Tang Xiaodu, "Bei Dao," in *World Literature Today*, Vol. 82, No. 6, November/December 2008, pp. 20–36.

Penny Kaganoff

In the following review, Kaganoff describes the "intense reality" of the stories in the collection Waves.

"Our generation's dream is too painful, and too long; you can never wake up, and even if you do, you'll only find another nightmare waiting for you," says a young woman in this collection of six stories and a novella written between 1974 and 1982. The tension between the dead-end despondency the characters see in post–Cultural Revolution China and the passion, hope and anger they express gives *Waves* its intense vitality. The author, a Beijing resident who is know for his poetry, draws upon an impressive range of literary styles to explore and critique contemporary life under Communism, from the realism of "The Homecoming Stranger," (a father returning after "exactly twenty years of reform through labor") to the surrealism of "13 Happiness Street," in which a journalist seeking to learn who lives in a mysterious house is accused as an "ideological criminal." Bei Dao never mitigates the horrors he recounts by pointing to easy solutions or obvious villains, and his evocation of a troubled marriage in "Melody" suggests that some of the obstacles to human happiness in China may not be so foreign to Americans after all.

Source: Penny Kaganoff, Review of *Waves*, in *Publishers Weekly*, Vol. 237, No. 12, March 23, 1990, pp. 72–73.

SOURCES

Barth, Kelly, Introduction to *The Tiananmen Square Massacre*, edited by Kelly Barth, Greenhaven Press, 2003, pp. 10–13.

Bei Dao, "The Homecoming Stranger," in *Waves*, translated by Susette Ternent Cooke and Bonnie S. McDougall, Sceptre, 1989, pp. 9–26.

"Bei Dao," in *Poets.org*, http://www.poets.org/poet.php/prmPID/774 (accessed August 10, 2010).

"China: Liu Xiaobo," in *PEN: American Center*, http://www.pen.org/viewmedia.php/prmMID/3029/prmID/172 (accessed October 7, 2011).

"Chinese Gender Imbalance Will Leave Millions of Men Without Wives," in *Telegraph* (London, England), January 10, 2010, http://www.telegraph.co.uk/news/worldnews/asia/china/6966037/Chinese-gender-imbalance-will-leave-millions-of-men-without-wives.html (accessed October 7, 2011).

Fenby, Jonathan, *Modern China: The Fall and Rise of a Great Power, 1850 to the Present*, Ecco, 2008, pp. 22–23, 441, 451.

Hauf, Kandice, Review of *Waves*, in *Harvard Book Review*, Nos. 19–20, Winter/Spring 1991, pp. 27–28.

Helft, Miguel, and David Barboza, "Google Shuts China Site in Dispute over Censorship," in *New York Times*,

March 22, 2010, http://www.nytimes.com/2010/03/23/technology/23google.html (accessed September 25, 2011).

Jacobs, Andrew, and Miguel Helft, "Google, Citing Attack, Threatens to Leave China," in *New York Times*, January 13, 2010, http://www.nytimes.com/2010/01/13/world/asia/13beijing. html?sq=Google%20China&st=Search&scp=2&pagewanted=print (accessed September 25, 2011).

LaPianna, Shannon, "An Interview with Visiting Artist Bei Dao: Poet in Exile," in *Journal of the International Institute*, Vol. 2, No. 1, Fall 1994, http://hdl.handle.net/2027/spo.4750978.0002.102 (accessed September 10, 2010).

Lee, Gregory, Review of *Waves*, in *China Quarterly*, No. 117, March 1989, pp. 152–54.

Liu, Binyan, "The Chinese Government's Opposition to Reform," in *The Tiananmen Square Massacre*, edited by Kelly Barth, Greenhaven Press, 2003, p. 24.

McDougall, Bonnie, *Fictional Authors, Imaginary Audiences: Modern Chinese Literature in the Twentieth Century*, Chinese University Press, 2003.

McDougall, Bonnie, and Kam Louie, *The Literature of China in the Twentieth Century*, Columbia University Press, 1997, pp. 325–44, 368–71, 397–98.

Pollard, D. E., "The Controversy over Modernism, 1979–84," in *China Quarterly*, No. 104, December 1985, pp. 641–56.

Ratiner, Steven, "Reclaiming the World, a Conversation with Bei Dao," in *Agni Online*, Vol. 54, 2001, http://www.bu.edu/agni/interviews/print/2001/ratiner-beidao.html (accessed August 16, 2010).

Spence, Jonathan, "On the Outs in Beijing," in *New York Times*, August 12, 1990, http://www.nytimes.com/1990/08/12/books/on-the-outs-in-beijing.html (accessed September 25, 2011).

Wong, Edward, "Official in China Says Western-Style Democracy Won't Take Root There," in *New York Times*, March 20, 2010, http://www.nytimes.com/2010/03/21/world/asia/21china.html (accessed September 4, 2010).

Wright, Edmund, "Cultural Revolution," "Gang of Four," and "Totalitarianism," in *Oxford Dictionary of World History*, Oxford University Press, 2006, pp. 164, 239, 641.

FURTHER READING

Bei Dao, *August Sleepwalker*, New Directions, 1990.
Bei Dao's first collection of poems published in the West came out simultaneously with *Waves*. Translated by Bonnie McDougall, this is the volume that made Bei Dao's reputation in the West. Many of these poems date from his days running *Jintian* (Today). The volume contains his most famous poem, "The Answer," which became an anthem for the Tiananmen Square protesters of 1989.

———, *Midnight's Gate: Essays*, New Directions, 2005.
In this collection of essays and meditations, Bei Dao describes the experience of exile. Like his poetry, his essays rely on allusive language and elliptical narrative structure to recount experiences as diverse as the destruction of Palestine, a baseball game in Sacramento, California, and a conflagration in New York. In this volume, Bei Dao also writes about his eleven years as a concrete mixer and ironworker during his internal Chinese exile, as well as his travels among writing programs and poetry workshops around the world.

Chang, Leslie T., *Factory Girls: From Village to City in a Changing China*, Spiegel and Grau, 2008.
Chang, formerly a reporter for the *Wall Street Journal*, documents one of history's largest migrations, with some 130 million people leaving the Chinese countryside to seek work in the factories of the coastal cities. For three years Chang followed two village girls, Min and Chunming, who migrated to the new factory town of Dongguan. This is a portrait of both individual and collective ambition that Chang filters through her own experience as a first-generation Chinese American.

Finkel, Donald, *A Splintered Mirror: Chinese Poetry from the Democracy Movement*, North Point Press, 1991.
One of the only anthologies in English to cover the "misty poets" as a group, this collection gives an overview of the many poetic approaches this group took contra the political and linguistic repression with which they were faced. While some of the poetry may seem obscure to Western readers, the collection's value lies in the overview it gives of this artistic and political moment in Chinese history.

Huss, Ann, and Jianmei Liu, *The Jin Yong Phenomenon: Chinese Martial Arts Fiction and Modern Chinese Literary History*, Cambria Press, 2007.
Jin Yong is the most prolific and popular martial arts novelist in twentieth-century Chinese history. His novels are beloved by Chinese readers both in the People's Republic of China and around the world. They have been adapted for film, television, comic books, and video games. In this volume, the authors put Jin Yong in the context of Chinese literary history and consider important theoretical issues arising from such matters as modernity, gender, nationalism, East/West conflict, and high literature versus low culture.

Zhang, Wei, *The Ancient Ship*, Harper Perennial, 2008.
Originally published in Chinese in 1987, this epic novel spans three generations of the Sui, Zhao, and Li families and the fictional town of Wali, located in the north of China. Beginning in 1949, this nonlinear narrative follows the families as China undergoes the upheaval of the revolution and an oppressed people struggle to take control of their own fate and to negotiate the clash of tradition and modernization.

SUGGESTED SEARCH TERMS

Bei Dao

Waves AND Bei Dao

The Homecoming Stranger AND Bei Dao

The Homecoming Stranger AND Waves

big character posters

Democracy Wall AND China

Cultural Revolution AND China

Jintian AND Today

Tiananmen Square AND 1989

totalitarianism AND China

authoritarianism AND China

modern Chinese fiction

socialism AND Chinese characteristics

Hunters in the Snow

TOBIAS WOLFF

1981

"Hunters in the Snow" is a short story by American writer Tobias Wolff. It was published in Wolff's first collection of stories, *In the Garden of the North American Martyrs*, in 1981. In the British edition of this collection, published in 1982, "Hunters in the Snow" is the title story. The story is also available in Wolff's *Our Story Begins: New and Selected Stories* (2008) and *The Art of the Tale: An International Anthology of Short Stories* (1987), edited by Daniel Halpern.

The story is about a group of three friends, Kenny, Frank, and Tub, who go on a hunting trip during a snowstorm in Spokane, Washington. There are tensions between the three men, and when the hunt goes badly—they fail to even catch sight of any deer—the trip takes an ugly turn. Kenny gets bad-tempered and shoots a dog, and when Tub thinks Kenny is about to turn the gun on him, he shoots Kenny. As Frank and Tub attempt to get the wounded Kenny to a hospital, a series of events further reveals the tenuousness of the friendships between the men. As one of the first published stories by an acknowledged modern master of the short-story form, "Hunters in the Snow" is an excellent introduction to Wolff's spare, realistic, and sometimes disturbing fictional world.

Tobias Wolff (*AP Images*)

AUTHOR BIOGRAPHY

Wolff was born on June 19, 1945, in Birmingham, Alabama. His mother, Rosemary, was a secretary and waitress, and his father, Arthur, was an aeronautical engineer. Wolff's parents were divorced when he was ten, and he went to live with his mother in Chinook, Washington, near Seattle. His mother remarried, but her second husband developed into an abusive stepfather, and Wolff's teenage years were troubled. He won a scholarship to the Hill School, a prestigious prep school in Pottsdown, Pennsylvania. It later turned out that the fifteen-year-old Wolff, showing a highly developed writing ability, had written all the recommendations required by the school himself. He attended the school from 1961 to 1963 and enjoyed his stay there as a refuge from his turbulent home life. By that time, he was already writing stories, and his early literary heroes were figures such as Leo Tolstoy, Anton Chekhov, Guy de Maupassant, Sherwood Anderson, Ernest Hemingway, and Jack London. His brother, Geoffrey Wolff, who was seven years older than Tobias and would also become a writer, encouraged him in his efforts.

In 1963, Wolff was expelled from the prep school. A year later, in 1964, he enlisted in the U.S. Army and trained as a Green Beret. In 1967, during the Vietnam War, he began a tour of duty in Vietnam, and when he left the army in 1968 he held the rank of first lieutenant. He later wrote that he always knew he would join the armed forces because his literary influences, such as Hemingway, William Faulkner, and Norman Mailer, had all had military experience.

After leaving the army, Wolff was accepted into Oxford University in England, where he earned a bachelor of arts in English language and literature in 1972 and a master of arts in the same subject in 1975. In that year, his first novel, *Ugly Rumours*, was published in England. This year was particularly eventful for Wolff: upon his return to the United States, he married Catherine Dolores Spohn (they would later have two sons and a daughter), worked as a reporter for the *Washington Post*, and became a Wallace Stegner Fellow in creative writing at Stanford University. He earned a master of arts in English from Stanford in 1978 and in that year taught fiction writing at Goddard College, in Vermont. In 1980, he began teaching at Syracuse University, in New York.

In 1981 Wolff published his first collection of short stories, *In the Garden of the North American Martyrs*, containing "Hunters in the Snow." This collection received the St. Lawrence Award for fiction in 1982. In 1984, he published the novella *The Barracks Thief*, which was awarded the PEN/Faulkner Award for fiction in 1985. A second volume of short stories, *Back in the World*, was followed in 1989 by *This Boy's Life: A Memoir*, which won the Los Angeles Times Book Award in 1990. A second memoir, *In Pharaoh's Army: Memories of the Lost War*, was published in 1994. His later work includes the short-story collection *The Night in Question* (1996), the novel *Old School* (2003), and *Our Story Begins: New and Collected Stories* (2008). As of 2011, Wolff was the Ward W. and Priscilla B. Woods Professor in the School of Humanities and Sciences at Stanford University.

PLOT SUMMARY

As "Hunters in the Snow" opens during a morning snowstorm in Spokane, Washington, a young man named Tub waits on the sidewalk for his two friends, Frank and Kenny, to pick him up in Kenny's truck. They are going on a hunting trip.

Frank and Kenny arrive an hour late, driving fast and almost knocking Tub down. When Tub chides them, Frank dismisses his complaints.

They drive into the country as the snow eases off and reach the woods where they are going to hunt. As they cross a field, Tub, who is overweight, has difficulty in getting through the fences, but the other two do not help him. They hunt for two hours but see no deer or even deer tracks. They stop to eat. Tub eats a hard-boiled egg and a stick of celery, even though he also has sandwiches and cookies with him. The others mock him for being fat, and he claims it is only because of his glands.

They hunt along the creek, moving slowly through snowdrifts, Kenny and Frank on one side and Tub on the other. Tub gets left behind but catches up. It is now late afternoon, and they go back toward the road, but then Kenny spots some deer tracks. He reproaches Tub for not having seen them, since they cross the route Tub took. (Tub had not seen them because he had lost interest and stopped looking.) They follow the tracks, but when they come upon a No Hunting sign in the woods, they decide to head back to the truck. Tub again gets left behind and sits down to eat. He just manages to catch up to Kenny and Frank as they are pulling away in the truck.

They go to the nearby farmhouse to ask permission to hunt. While Kenny goes into the house, Tub tries to get Frank to be more friendly toward him and to find out what secret Frank and Kenny are keeping from him, which is something to do with a babysitter. Frank tells him to mind his own business.

Kenny returns with permission to hunt. As they walk toward the woods, a big old dog barks at them.

They go into the woods but eventually lose the deer tracks. Kenny gets upset, blames Tub, and snaps at Frank. As they walk back, he shoots at a post, then at a tree. When the dog emerges from the barn, Kenny shoots it dead. He turns to Tub and says he hates him, which is exactly what he just said about the post, the tree, and the dog. Tub, not unreasonably thinking that Kenny is about to shoot him, too, shoots Kenny in the stomach. Kenny falls, wounded. He shows Frank the wound, and Frank tells Kenny he is lucky the bullet did not go into his appendix. Then Frank vomits.

Tub and Frank walk to the farmhouse, intending to call an ambulance. While Frank makes the call, the owner of the house tells Tub that he had told Kenny to shoot the dog, because it was old and sick; he did not have the heart to kill it himself.

Franks returns and says the nearest hospital is fifty miles away and no ambulance is available. They will have to take Kenny to the hospital themselves, in the truck. The farmer's wife gives Tub directions, and he writes them down.

It is now dark. Tub and Frank take some boards, put Kenny on them and take him to the truck. Tub slips, dropping Kenny, and Frank insults Tub because of it. Tub fights back, telling Frank not to talk to him like that. Frank apologizes.

Kenny is placed in the bed of the truck, covered with blankets. As they depart for the hospital, Frank apologizes again to Tub and says that the shooting was not his fault. Kenny had been asking for trouble by acting so aggressively.

There is a hole in the windshield and the heater does not work, so Frank and Tub get too cold to continue. They decide to stop at a tavern so they can warm up. Kenny complains he is cold, and the other two replace the blankets that had blown off him.

Inside the tavern, they order coffee. Frank makes more conciliatory remarks to Tub and takes him into his confidence, saying he may be leaving his wife, Nancy. He is in love with a girl named Roxanne Brewer, who is not yet sixteen. Roxanne babysits for Frank and Nancy. Defending himself against Tub's incredulity, Frank insists that Roxanne is special. He has not yet told his wife of the affair. Tub says he is not going to judge Frank harshly because Frank is his friend, a remark that greatly pleases Frank.

After they have returned to the truck and traveled a few miles, Tub realizes that he has left the paper on which he wrote the directions to the hospital in the tavern. Frank says not to worry because he can remember them.

They get very cold again and stop at the next roadhouse, where they warm themselves by using the hand-dryer in the bathroom. They exchange some friendly talk, and Tub decides to reward Frank for telling him about Roxanne with a confession of his own. He admits that the reason he is fat is nothing to do with his glands but is due to overeating. He cannot stop himself. Not even his wife knows this, and he tells Frank he is fed up with leading a double life, pretending to eat abstemiously and then indulging in great amounts of food when no one is around.

Frank responds sympathetically and takes Tub into the restaurant that adjoins the bar, where over Tub's protests he orders four orders of pancakes with plenty of butter and syrup. When the food arrives, he insists that Tub eat all of it.

When they return to the truck, they find that the blankets have blown off again, and Kenny is mumbling and barely conscious. Frank and Tub take the blankets into the cab of the truck and use them themselves. They drive off again, not realizing that they have taken a wrong turn and are headed in the opposite direction from the hospital.

CHARACTERS

Roxanne Brewer

Roxanne Brewer is the fifteen-year-old girl with whom Frank is having an affair. She babysits for Frank and his wife. Roxanne does not appear directly in the story.

The Farmer

The farmer gives the three men permission to hunt on his property. He also asks Kenny to shoot his old, sick dog for him, because he is too soft-hearted to do it himself. The farmer allows the men to use his telephone to call the hospital, and the woman who is also in the house (presumably his wife) gives them directions for how to get there.

Frank

Frank is a young man, probably about the same age as Tub and Kenny. He is married to a woman named Nancy and has children. However, he is having an affair with their fifteen-year-old babysitter. Frank treats Tub badly, mocking him for being fat and insulting him in other ways. When Tub first confronts him about it, Frank is unsympathetic. But when Tub confronts him a second time, after Kenny has been shot, Frank is more sympathetic toward him and behaves in a more conciliatory way. He takes Tub into his confidence regarding his affair with the babysitter, which before he had only confided to Kenny. He sides with Tub against Kenny, saying that the shooting was Kenny's fault because of his aggressive behavior. When Tub a bit later confesses that his weight problem has nothing to do with his glands, Frank and Tub solidify their newfound trust in each other.

Kenny

Kenny is friends with Tub and Frank. He owns the truck they use to go hunting. Kenny is aggressive from the beginning, almost running Tub down with the truck. He and Frank act like best friends, excluding Tub, to whom Kenny is sarcastic and generally contemptuous. When things do not go Kenny's way, he becomes morose and even more aggressive. He is upset when after spending most of the day hunting they remain empty-handed. He shoots at a post and a tree, saying he hates them, and then shoots the dog, saying he hates it, too. When he turns to Tub, saying he hates him, Tub becomes alarmed, fearing that Kenny is about to shoot him, so Tub shoots first, wounding Kenny in the stomach. Kenny denies he was about to shoot Tub, saying it was just a joke. Kenny is then placed in the bed of the truck, and the others promise they will take him to the hospital. The previously aggressive Kenny now becomes a pathetic, helpless figure, and the relationships among the three men change. Kenny, rather than Tub, becomes the outsider.

Nancy

Nancy, Frank's wife, is referred to but does not appear directly in the story.

Tub

Tub is a young man, possibly in his twenties or early thirties. He is called Tub because he is overweight. He is married to a woman named Alice, who does not appear in the story, and has children. Because of his weight he is cruelly teased by Frank and Kenny. When they go hunting, Tub has difficulty keeping up with the others. He misses some deer tracks, for which Kenny later reproaches him. Tub shoots Kenny in what he thinks is self-defense. Later, he stands up to Frank, telling him not to be so cruel to him regarding his weight. After this, he and Frank become closer, exchanging mutual confidences about their lives, including Tub's confession that he is fat because he eats too much. He snacks all the time and cannot control his appetite. He feels bad about this because he tells everyone his weight problem is due to his glands, not to overeating. His confession to Frank is an act of trust in the man who formerly mocked him, a kind of reward to Frank for apologizing and telling him, Tub, about his affair with the babysitter.

THEMES

Friendship

An important theme of the story is friendship, but the type of friendship shown is largely shallow and fickle, devoid of real feeling. The old saying "Two's company, three's a crowd" seems to apply in this situation. At no point do the three men form a happy group or share genuine camaraderie. At the beginning of the story, Frank and Kenny act like pals, and they gang up on Tub, making him the butt of cruel jokes about his weight. Tub is the outsider, the one who gets victimized. When they begin the hunt, the other two men go on ahead, and Tub struggles to keep up, but they do not help him. Tub is repeatedly separated from his companions physically as well as in the lack of friendship and concern the other men show him.

By the end of the story, however, the dynamic between the three men has altered. Kenny, having been shot and now lying in the bed of the truck, has become the outsider, while Frank and Tub have reached a better mutual understanding, a result of Tub's forceful rebellion against the contemptuous treatment he has been receiving. Frank sides with Tub over the shooting incident. They later exchange confidences and spend their time in a tavern and then a restaurant while Kenny lies freezing outside. The aggressor has now become the victim. Frank and Tub even take Kenny's blankets away and use the blankets themselves, a visible sign of Kenny's exclusion and the new solidarity between Frank and Tub.

It will be apparent that these are not mature friendships but are more reminiscent of high-school cliques, complete with episodes of cruelty, bullying, and sudden switches in allegiance. Cruelty, a result of a lack of empathy, is apparent throughout, first in the treatment of Tub and later in the treatment of Kenny.

Even at the beginning, when Kenny and Frank appear to be close friends who both pick on Tub, Kenny and Frank soon fall to bickering between themselves, with Kenny hinting that he will spill the beans regarding Frank's affair with the babysitter, and Frank telling him to keep his mouth shut (since Tub does not at this point know about Frank's affair). There appears to be an underlying hostility between the two men, despite their appearance of friendship. Frank hints that Kenny is "asking for it," which foreshadows the events of later in the day.

TOPICS FOR FURTHER STUDY

- Search YouTube and watch the videos that some young people have created with their own versions of "Hunters in the Snow." Get together with some classmates and make a video of the story yourselves, and then upload it to YouTube or a social networking site. Provide a published source or an online link to the short story and invite classmates to review your production after reading the short story.
- Select another short story by Wolff and compare it to "Hunters in the Snow" in an essay. Comment on elements such as theme, style, and character development.
- Research the problem of obesity in the United States. Why are so many people overweight? Why is the problem getting worse? What causes obesity? Consult *Am I Fat? The Obesity Issue for Teens*, by Kathlyn Gay, a 2006 book written for young adults. Give a class presentation with your findings.
- Wolff's form of realism is very different from the characteristic postmodern short story, for which he has expressed disdain. Read "The Babysitter," a well-known story by one of the most noted of American postmodern short-story writers, Robert Coover. Write an essay in which you explain how differently these two writers go about their tasks. What fictional techniques does Coover use that are outside the scope of realism?
- Read the young-adult book *Fat Kid Rules the World*, by K. L. Going (2004). Create a chart that compares the characters in this book with those in "Hunters in the Snow" using descriptions and dialogue from the book and the short story to illustrate your comparisons. Focus specifically on the theme of friendship and the role of the settings in the two pieces of fiction.

In truth, there is no real understanding or empathy between any of these men, as is shown by how Kenny is treated after he is shot. Frank

Kenny, Tub, and Frank set out on a fateful winter hunting expedition. *(Pierdelune | Shutterstock.com)*

and Tub do make an attempt to get him to a hospital, but Frank talks to Kenny as if he were a child who has to be given comforting words, and he and Tub, in the wake of their new trust in each other, seem to forget about Kenny altogether when Frank buys pancakes for Tub in the restaurant. Frank, it seems, has taken a kind of pity on Tub following Tub's tale of woe about his weight problem, and he indulges in a sentimental show of warmth and generosity while his wounded friend freezes outside. Even the newfound accord between Tub and Frank seems fragile and temporary, the product mostly of the cowardly Frank's realization that he can no longer bully Tub, and of Tub's desire to make Frank like him so he will no longer be the outsider.

Weakness

All three characters appear to be emotionally brittle, weak, and unhappy. They appear not to have much in their lives that would allow them to form solid, deep relationships. A hunting trip is often a way in which men bond together and affirm their masculine identity, but if that is the intention, whether conscious or unconscious, of these three men, the result is a dismal failure that reveals only their inadequacies, insecurities, and hollowness. There is no bonding, only hostility.

Kenny is frustrated and angry from the beginning, taking out his bad feelings on Tub. His bullying is just a result of his own unhappiness, although Kenny, unlike the other two characters, does not directly reveal anything of his inner life and conflict during the course of the story. When they fail to shoot any game, Kenny relapses into a childish sulk and then tries to make up for his disappointment by firing his gun at things that do not move—and then at things that do move.

As for Frank, he appears to be trapped in a marriage he no longer wants, but he feels guilty about deceiving his wife, Nancy, because she has been good to him. He entertains a fantasy that he can be happier by taking up with a fifteen-year-old girl. His emotional duplicity makes him preoccupied and unsure of his direction in life. He is at the mercy of his emotions.

Tub, too, is divided against himself. His weight problem is caused by overeating, but he dares not admit this, even to his wife, so he sets up an elaborate smoke screen of appearing to eat very lightly while devouring large quantities of junk food on the sly. He cannot stop this habit, and he is as helpless in the face of his desire for food as Frank is in his emotional desire for new excitement in his life and as Kenny is regarding his anger and aggression. No one in the story has any real control over his own life or emotions. They are all helpless in one way or another.

The story ends with the sentence, "They had taken a different turn a long way back." At the literal level, this refers to the fact that they have unknowingly become lost and are now driving away from the hospital, but it also suggests something deeper: at some point much earlier, something went wrong in the lives of these men. They started moving in the wrong direction, and now they are powerless to change direction and start living more rewarding lives.

STYLE

Irony

Irony—in general, an intended meaning that is opposite what is said—can take many forms in a literary work. Irony can, for example, show an incongruity (an inconsistency) between what might be expected in a situation and what actually happens. In this story, many of the situations are ironic in the sense that the words and actions of the characters are incongruent with what the situation actually requires and what they might normally be expected to do or say. Irony in this sense is so pervasive in the story that it might be called structural irony: it is fundamental to the way the story is told. Through this device, the author shows the extent to which the characters are disconnected from each other and oblivious to the needs of the situation they are in. For example, after Frank tells Tub about his affair with the babysitter and fears adverse judgment from Tub, Tub reassures him by saying, "When you've got a friend it means you've always got someone on your side, no matter what." Frank responds that it makes him feel good to hear such a sentiment. Both men appear to forget that as they are sitting there talking casually and taking their time, Kenny, their friend, is lying in the bed of the truck in freezing weather, bleeding from a gunshot wound and in urgent need of medical attention. Poor Kenny does not really have "someone on [his] side," even though his two friends are supposed to be taking care of him. Later, when they are using the hand-dryer to warm themselves, Frank says that trust is important because "no man is an island." He is quoting the famous phrase of the poet John Donne, about how every human being is connected with every other one. Frank is oblivious, but the reader is not, to the irony in his words. Kenny is at that very moment an island to himself, stuck in the bed of a truck with a bullet in his stomach, waiting for his so-called friends to get him to the hospital.

Earlier than that, when they first go inside the tavern, Frank says after the waitress brings him coffee, "Just what the doctor ordered." There is an almost comic irony in this statement, bearing in mind that outside, Kenny is the one who is really in need of what a doctor might order. The irony is due to the contrast between the trivial meaning of the speaker and the real but ignored need of the man waiting outside.

Indeed, the entire hunting trip might be considered ironic, since it is not the hunted that gets shot but the hunter. The hunted, the deer, does not even show up. The irony is presented in the scene when Frank and Tub pull up to the parking lot of the tavern. In the parking lot they see the results of more successful hunting endeavors, in the form of deer strapped across the hoods of the parked jeeps and trucks. In contrast, their hunt has resulted not in a dead deer on a hood but in a wounded man in the flatbed.

Setting

The setting is described in pervasive images of cold and bleakness. It is snowing, at times heavily. There are snow drifts the men wade through. It is cold. Even the truck is cold, since the heater does not work and there is a hole in the windshield, so the cold and snow come inside. Tub and Frank get so cold driving after Kenny is shot that they have to stop twice to go inside and get warm. Kenny complains he is cold, but the blankets keep blowing off him. The following description conveys the bleakness of the landscape and its effect on the men:

> The snow let up, but still there was no edge to the land where it met the sky. Nothing moved in the chalky fields. The cold bleached their faces and made the stubble stand out on their cheeks and along their upper lips.

The coldness of the setting acts as a metaphor for the emotional coldness at the heart of the story. The hearts of the men are as bleak as the landscape that envelops them.

COMPARE & CONTRAST

- **1980s:** In the United States in 1980, slightly less than one adult in two is overweight, with about one person in seven considered obese. This figure rises as the decade goes on.

  Today: Two of every three adults in the United States are overweight, and one in three are obese. Obesity takes a toll on people's health, and according to a 2010 report by the National Bureau of Economic Research, complications arising from obesity account for an estimated 17 percent of medical costs. Obesity adds over $2,800 to a person's annual medical costs.

- **1980s:** Raymond Carver, Ann Beattie, Andre Dubus, and many other American writers of short stories produce what some consider a renaissance of the short story in American literature.

  Today: In addition to many well-established writers, younger American writers, such as Tao Lin, Belle Boggs, Lori Ostlund, Anne Sanow, Marisa Silver, Alyson Hagy, Sherrie Flick, Ben Greenman, Blake Butler, Justin Taylor, Deb Olin Unferth, and Laura van den Berg, make rich contributions to the short-story genre.

- **1980s:** Hunting deer is a popular activity in Washington state whitetail deer country. November and December are good times to hunt, as snow falls then and deer are easier to track in fresh snow. The deer population increases across the United States.

  Today: Deer hunting has lost none of its popularity. Despite hunting and increasing development of rural areas, the deer population in the United States continues to rise, to an estimated twenty million.

HISTORICAL CONTEXT

Dirty Realism

In 1983, two years after Wolff published his collection *In the Garden of the North American Martyrs*, Bill Buford, editor of the fiction magazine *Granta*, coined the term "dirty realism" to refer to some of the emerging writers of short fiction in the United States. Realism is a long tradition in literature in which writers attempt to represent life as it really is, as opposed to the extravagances of adventure tales and other genres. Dirty realism, then, would be a subdivision of realism in which authors present certain subjects and themes in a distinctive manner. Buford offered the following definition of dirty realism:

> Dirty realism is the fiction of a new generation of American authors. They write about the belly-side of contemporary life—a deserted husband, an unwed mother, a car thief, a pickpocket, a drug addict—but they write about it with a disturbing detachment, at times verging on comedy.

This description might well be applied to Wolff's "Hunters in the Snow." Indeed, Wolff was one of the fourteen writers whose work appeared in that issue of *Granta*, which was dedicated to dirty realism. Wolff's included story, "The Barracks Thief," was later expanded and published as a novella. Other writers published in that issue, and thus classed as authors of dirty realism, included Carver, Richard Ford, Frederick Barthelme, Bobbie Ann Mason, Elizabeth Tallent, Jayne Anne Phillips, and Angela Carter. The American novelist and short-story writer Charles Bukowski (1920–1994), with his fiction about life in Los Angeles at the lower end of the socioeconomic scale, is sometimes considered the originator of dirty realism. Of the writers published in that issue of *Granta*, Carver is the greatest figure, and Wolff has expressed admiration for Carver's work. Carver began publishing short stories in the 1970s. His work in the 1980s included *What We Talk About When We Talk About Love* (1981) and *Cathedral* (1983).

Other prominent writers of short stories in the 1980s, though not associated with the "dirty"

A horrible accident requires the trio to head to the emergency room. (sepavo / Shutterstock.com)

aspect of realism, were Beattie, notably in *The Burning House* (1982) and *Where You'll Find Me, and Other Stories* (1986), and Dubus (another writer admired by Wolff), in collections such as *The Times Are Never So Bad* (1983) and *The Last Worthless Evening* (1986).

Set against the realistic short fiction of Wolff and others during this period was a different kind of fiction known as postmodern fiction. This experimental form moved away from the traditional focus on storytelling through plot and character toward an examination of the process of writing fiction itself. Wolff disliked the average postmodern short story. In 1994, when he edited *The Vintage Book of Contemporary American Short Stories*, he described such fiction in his introduction, as quoted by James Hannah in *Tobias Wolff: A Study of the Short Fiction*, as "resolutely unrealistic, scholastic, self-conscious—*postmodern*—concerned with exploring its own fictional nature and indifferent if not hostile to the short story's traditional interests in character and dramatic development and social context." The postmodern short story is associated with writers such as John Barth, Donald Barthelme, and Robert Coover, who published much of their work in the 1960s and 1970s. Wolff saw the new interest in realism in the 1980s as a reaction against these postmodernists. In the anthology he edited, he drew on the work of Carver, Beattie, Ford, Phillips, and Dubus, as well as writers such as Dorothy Allison, Frank Conroy, Stuart Dybeck, Richard Ford, Thom Jones, Jamaica Kincaid, Joyce Carol Oates, Mona Simpson, Robert Stone, and Amy Tan. He included no work by Barth, Coover, or other postmodern writers of the short story, such as William H. Gass, or, among the younger writers at the time, T. Coraghessan Boyle, Lydia Davis, William Vollmann, or David Foster Wallace.

CRITICAL OVERVIEW

"Hunters in the Snow" was well received by reviewers and critics as part of Wolff's successful first collection of stories, *In the Garden of the North American Martyrs*. For example, in words that could certainly be applied to this story, Bruce Allen, in the *New England Review*, comments, "The twelve quietly realistic, beautifully detailed and subtle stories collected here are about moments of crisis in the lives of tightly coiled, introspective, self-distrusting (sometimes self-despising) people."

Dean Flower, in the *Hudson Review*, comments on the characters in "Hunters in the Snow," describing Kenny as "sadistic" and Frank as "a typical Wolff character in that he fails to take any stand, siding with Kenny at first and getting drunk with Tub later, apparently because the confusions of his personal life . . . have made him covertly vengeful." (Actually, Frank and Tub do not get drunk; they stop at a bar but they order coffee.) Hannah, in *Tobias Wolff: A Study of the Short Fiction*, describes "Hunters in the Snow" as

> a disturbing story about the vagaries of and cruelties of superficial friendships, about masculine camaraderie that appears sympathetic and fulfilling but that is in the end destructive and as barren as the frozen landscape in which the story takes place.

Hannah also regards the story as "surreal in its atmosphere and its conclusion."

Marilyn C. Wesley, in her essay on Wolff in the *Dictionary of Literary Biography*, describes the story's three characters as "poor and sad." They are a group of men who desire "an image of themselves that they can begin to respect. They try to establish that image through the assertion of masculine power ritualized in hunting, but they fail." Wesley concludes that "Hunters in the Snow"

> is a superb example of structural irony used to suggest, rather than deny, the complexity of experience. During the course of the story, each character reverses his former psychological role by acting out its buried contradiction.

CRITICISM

Bryan Aubrey

Aubrey holds a Ph.D. in English. In the following essay, he examines the characters in "Hunters in the Snow" and their relationships with each other.

In rejecting the experiments of the postmodern short story, which he thought did not sufficiently engage the reader in believable characters and settings, Tobias Wolff built on the tradition of realism in the short story. This tradition began with Anton Chekhov in the late nineteenth century and continued in writers such as Ernest Hemingway in the mid-twentieth century and Raymond Carver and others in the 1970s and 1980s. This was the tradition to which Wolff felt he belonged. Wolff's stories aim to present ordinary people who are not especially good or bad, or exceptional in any way, in such a convincing manner that readers feel some connection with them. This "sense of kinship" between reader and character, Wolff wrote in his introduction to *The Vintage Book of Contemporary American Short Stories*, as quoted by James Hannah in *Tobias Wolff: A Study of the Short Fiction*, "is what makes stories important to us. . . . We need to feel ourselves acted upon by a story, outraged, exposed, in danger of heartbreak and change."

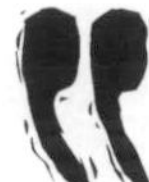

THERE IS NOTHING ESPECIALLY REMARKABLE ABOUT ANY OF THESE THREE CHARACTERS: KENNY, FRANK, AND TUB COULD BE FOUND IN JUST ABOUT ANY MALL OR BAR OR SPORTS EVENT IN AMERICA, AND WOLFF'S EAR FOR DIALOGUE IS SUCH THAT MOST CONTEMPORARY AMERICAN READERS WILL RECOGNIZE THIS."

In light of those comments, how might "Hunters in the Snow" strike the average reader? It certainly fits the common Wolff mold. Three very ordinary guys go off together on a little hunting trip in Spokane County, Washington, the sort of trip that thousands of men do every year in different parts of the country, partly as a way of getting out of the house and doing something "with the guys." There is nothing especially remarkable about any of these three characters: Kenny, Frank, and Tub could be found in just about any mall or bar or sports event in America, and Wolff's ear for dialogue is such that most contemporary American readers will recognize this. They have heard this kind of everyday, casual talk before. These characters speak casually in short, colloquial phrases, and as with real people, the dynamics that take place between them are quickly apparent to the observer. One man, Tub, is the butt of the cruel humor of the others, although neither Kenny nor Frank think of it as cruel. For them it is just banter, a chance to show off their wit. They are probably unaware that Tub actually has any particular feelings, let alone feelings that could be hurt by their remarks.

WHAT DO I READ NEXT?

- In his highly praised *This Boy's Life: A Memoir* (1989), Wolff recalls his childhood and adolescence up to the age of about eighteen. Wolff's mother was divorced, and the man who became her second husband was an abusive stepfather. Wolff of necessity became skilled at lying, surviving through cunning and resourcefulness. He also managed to fake the recommendations that got him admitted to an elite prep school, although he was expelled before he graduated. Reviewers praised the memoir as being as gripping as any novel.
- Raymond Carver was one of the most important writers of short stories in the United States in the 1970s and 1980s. His collection *Cathedral* (1983), which contains twelve stories, is one of his finest. Some of the stories, including the moving title story and "A Small, Good Thing," express a more hopeful, optimistic point of view than was apparent in Carver's earlier work.
- Argentine writer Julio Cortázar was one of the most noted of twentieth-century story writers. His collection *Blow-Up, and Other Stories* (1967), translated by Paul Blackburn, is a representative selection of his work in this genre. Cortázar was part of what is known as the Latin American boom of the 1960s, a highly productive period in which many high-quality works were published. Writers such as Cortázar favored nonrealistic modes, such as the absurd and the fantastic, often in the form of magical realism, as well as psychoanalytical stories. These stories are therefore very different from the realism of Wolff and others.
- *No Easy Answers: Short Stories about Teenagers Making Tough Choices* (1999), edited by Donald R. Gallo, is a collection of sixteen original stories by prominent writers of young-adult fiction. The stories show teenagers grappling with moral and ethical dilemmas regarding issues such as peer pressure, teen pregnancy, and self-censorship.
- *A Doctor's Visit: Short Stories*, by Anton Chekhov, edited and with an introduction by Tobias Wolff (1988), is a collection of short stories by one of the founders of the modern realistic short story. This is Wolff's own selection from Chekhov's stories, and his introduction reveals what he finds most valuable in the work of the great Russian master.
- *The Best American Short Stories of the Century* (2000), with an introduction by John Updike and a foreword by Katrina Kenison, contains fifty-five stories. The table of contents reads like a who's who of American literature of the twentieth century. Writers represented include Sherwood Anderson, Hemingway, Willa Cather, Katherine Anne Porter, William Faulkner, F. Scott Fitzgerald, Eudora Welty, John Cheever, Flannery O'Connor, Philip Roth, Joyce Carol Oates, Raymond Carver, Beattie, and Alice Munro, as well as some newer voices from the 1990s, including Gish Jen, Pam Durban, Annie Proulx, and Pam Houston.

Even though their sense of humor is laced with hostility (especially in the case of Kenny), they expect Tub to take it in good fun.

Kenny is the most superficial of the characters. He is never shown in reflective mode, unlike Tub and Frank. Kenny is the kind of man who is brash and confident on the exterior, with an aggressive edge to his conversation, but on the inside is undeveloped and brittle, a prey to his darker emotions when things suddenly do not go his way. When he realizes he is not going to bag any deer this time, he throws a petulant, childish fit, swearing, throwing down his hat, and saying, "This is the worst day of hunting I ever had, bar none." Kenny is good company, one might imagine, as long as things do not go wrong and no one challenges him. It is Kenny's self-centeredness, his failure to gauge the mood of his companion Tub or the effects of the words he speaks, that leads directly to his downfall. He appears to directly threaten Tub with his gun, but after Tub shoots him in what Tub is sure is self-defense, Kenny claims that he was just "kidding around.... It was a joke." This is the common response of the bully or the person whose humor always has a cruel edge to it when he is finally confronted by someone regarding his behavior. The irony here is that Kenny is probably telling the truth as he sees it; he got his kicks from threatening and scaring Tub, just because Tub was there and Kenny felt bad and wanted to let off a bit of steam. Little did Kenny guess Tub would react as he did.

Kenny can be thought of as a man who lacks what is called "emotional intelligence." A person's emotional intelligence measures not intellectual ability, like the better-known IQ, but a person's ability to recognize, understand, and manage his or her own emotions and those of others in a way that makes for harmonious social interaction. Emotional intelligence also involves understanding body language and facial expressions, the ability to correctly read the cues that others provide as to how they feel and how they are likely to behave. Kenny, as any reader can see, is not going to win any medals in this department. Indeed, what happens to him during the course of the story is rather revealing about his inner condition. Lying helplessly in a truck on a journey to nowhere—the truck ends up going in the opposite direction to the hospital—is a metaphor for the true condition of his being; it shows the hollowness, the fragility, the lack of control that lies behind the surface swagger.

If the reader may recognize a character type in Kenny, he or she will surely know a Tub, too. Poor Tub. Even the name itself gives away his discomfort, defining him entirely by his weight. He has probably had this nickname for a long time, and he is used to being the butt of jokes, but they hurt nonetheless. No one ever really gets used to being regularly humiliated without some resentment simmering away inside. Tub's resentments and pain come out early, after Frank and Kenny deliberately pull away in the truck before he is even inside it. It is all he can do to scramble into the flatbed. Kenny thinks this is a terrific joke and looks back through the window at Tub, grinning. As soon as the truck stops and as Kenny goes to the farmhouse, Tub says plaintively to Frank, "I used to stick up for you," which is at once a reproach and a plea to Frank to treat him better, even if only out of a sense of fairness. But fairness is not something that Frank is given to thinking much about. Instead, he merely deflects the point with the ridiculous statement, "You're a grown-up, Tub. You can take care of yourself." (Kenny is not the only one who lacks emotional intelligence.)

This little exchange also suggests that Tub and Frank have known each other a long time, perhaps since childhood, and Tub may well have been enduring taunts about his weight for many years. In Tub's need to lie about his condition, saying it is due to a glandular problem rather than overeating, the reader will see immediately the stigma that is attached in American society to being fat. Tub has to cover up, to pretend, "to lead a double life," which leaves him full of shame and guilt and self-reproach: "Always having to think about what you say and do. Always feeling like people are watching you, trying to catch you at something. Never able to just be yourself." Tub is so worn down by the strain of living like this that he is only too happy to blurt out the truth to Frank when he sees that Frank has softened his attitude toward him.

By this point, Tub and Frank seem to have reached an accord in the sense that they are now making a show of each not judging the other. Frank, expecting condemnation from Tub for his affair with the babysitter, is surprised when Tub has the opposite reaction; then when Tub, expecting Frank to agree that Tub's gluttony is "pretty disgusting," is surprised to find Frank expressing a more compassionate attitude. For the reader, of course, the effect is one of irony, because while Frank and Tub share their confidences and bask in the warm glow of knowing what true friendship is all about, Kenny, cold and bleeding outside, is experiencing the truth of what their friendship is really worth to him: not very much. Not even enough to get him to the hospital when he has a bullet in his stomach.

As for Frank, his creator Wolff gives him a distinguishing feature, revealed in his words, that sets him apart from his two companions. Frank appears to have some intellectual interests, even an aspiration to a spiritual kind of life—at least, when he is not misbehaving with the fifteen-year-old babysitter. The clue to Frank's aspirations comes early, when he steps out of the truck when they first arrive at the woods. He closes his eyes, breathes deeply, and says, "Tune in on that energy." Then he tells Tub to "get centered." Frank is speaking in the jargon of popular so-called New Age thought, with its emphasis on developing one's spiritual potential and living in harmony with nature.

In the story, the trip to the hospital is delayed by stops at various places, including a diner. *(Laura Stone / Shutterstock.com)*

Kenny recognizes this immediately, and his retort, though cruel, is dead-on: "Next thing you'll be wearing a nightgown, Frank. Selling flowers out at the airport." (He is probably referring to the orange-robed devotees who could often be seen in the 1980s in groups chanting the praises of Lord Krishna, one of the revered gods in Hinduism.) A little later, when they are delayed by the No Hunting sign and Kenny thinks it may get dark before they can resume the hunt, Frank tells him to relax: "You can't hurry nature. If we're meant to get that deer, we'll get it. If we're not, we won't." If one were inclined to be unkind, one might call a comment like that half-baked New Age nonsense. The truth is that Frank does not have a clue what he is talking about in this area, so he comes out with a series of meaningless clichés. After they realize they are not going to kill any deer, Frank tries to tell Kenny that the expedition is not just about killing deer, but having the experience of hunting: "There are all these forces out here and you just have to go with them." Kenny responds that he has no time for "a bunch of hippie [nonsense]." The point here is that in a few deft slices of dialogue, Wolff has created a character who exhibits a painfully obvious gap between the philosophy to which he appears vaguely and inadequately to aspire and the reality of the life he lives.

Does the reader feel some connection with these not very inspiring characters, as Wolff wanted the readers of his short stories to feel? Each reader has to answer that for himself or herself, but the chasms revealed in the personalities of these three disappointed hunters—the way the author lays bare their inner conflicts and their weaknesses—might arouse in reflective readers a feeling that though these characters may not be the finest specimens humanity has ever produced, the frailties and turmoil that Kenny, Frank, and Tub cannot help but reveal are not so far removed from what those same readers experience within themselves. In that, one must suppose, is the "sense of kinship" that Wolff has referred to between character and reader.

Source: Bryan Aubrey, Critical Essay on "Hunters in the Snow," in *Short Stories for Students*, Gale, Cengage Learning, 2012.

Robert Reid

In the following review, Reid contends that Our Story Begins *allows for readers to see both what Wolff is about and how he compares with other great short-story authors.*

If you want to know what Tobias Wolff is all about, all you have to do is read his short story, The Liar. However, if you want to understand why he compares favourably to fellow American masters of short fiction, Raymond Carver and Richard Ford, not to mention Canadian masters Alice Munro and Alistair McLeod, you need to read *Our Story Begins* cover to cover.

The volume brings together 10 new stories, which are reason enough to celebrate, with 21 stories gleaned from three earlier collections: *In the Garden of North American Martyrs*, *Back in the World* and *The Night in Question*. All were first published in prestigious American magazines.

The notion that lying reveals deeper truths is central to the Wolff esthetic. It defines all his writing, whether fictional memoir, novella, novel or short story. The Liar is about a teenager who knowingly lies about his mother's health as a means of coping with the insufferable pain of his father's death. Lying is an expression of grief.

Many of the characters in *Our Story Begins* lie as a means of revealing their deeper selves which otherwise would remain buried in dark recesses of unconsciousness. They are ordinary men and women, sometimes caught up in predicaments that become extraordinary, if only momentarily. Most are unsavory in mundane ways. They are not the kind of people we want as neighbours, but, unfortunately, most of us have made their acquaintance in real life.

Wolff blurs the line between personal history and imagination. Consequently, many of the stories have an autobiographical element—whether male coming-of-age, military service or campus life—which recurs throughout his writing.

In a postmodern age, Wolff is something of a throwback to an earlier time when character and narrative were the engines that drove fiction. He takes a storyteller's delight in weaving tales. He eschews metafiction. Rather, his stories often veer off and meander down unexpected roads that surprise and delight as they unsettle our equilibrium. It's not unusual to want to return to a story immediately after reading it for the first time.

Many of the stories in *Our Story Begins* are road stories, which becomes a unifying metaphor for the accelerated displacement of contemporary life. This is not the celebratory whelp of Kerouac, but the quiet desperation of Thoreau. The stories are as commonplace as newspaper headlines, but some slip behind the partition of the surreal.

The widely anthologized Bullet in the Brain, about a thorny book critic who is shot during a bank heist, concludes by tracing the path of the bullet. Similarly, Hunters in the Snow follows a pair of hunters as they leisurely transport a mortally wounded partner in the back of a pickup truck. After stopping to wet their whistles with a few beers in a rural bar, the mindless pair head off in the opposite direction of the hospital.

Although the stories in *Our Story Begins* span a quarter century, they are amazingly consistent in vision, accomplishment and effect. All that we readers can hope for with respect to Tobias Wolff is that the story continues.

Source: Robert Reid, "Short Stories Reveal a Deeper Truth behind Lies," in *Record* (Kitchener, Ontario), May 17, 2008, p. W10.

Lisa Jennifer Selzman

In the following review, Selzman points out the surprises found in Wolff's adept collection of short stories Our Story Begins.

Theresa, a college student two decades older than her classmates, comes upon her art history professor in a campus smokers' area. Professor Landsman speaks with an exotic accent and carries herself with an elegance and drama that set her apart from others at the school.

"Today she wore a black coat draped over her shoulders and another of her long, beautiful scarves; in class she restlessly tugged and rearranged them as she spoke." Though Theresa has never had a personal conversation with her before, she finds herself talking with the professor about war, subterfuge, the slanting, easy edge between courage and the abuse of power.

Throughout the story, Landsman confides key events in her history, but it is in an offhand detail that we learn the most: She "closed her eyes and blew out a stream of smoke, exposing a splotchy purple birthmark on her neck . . . eyes still closed, she twitched the scarf and the birthmark vanished."

Those fabulous signature scarves are, after all, just camouflage for this seemingly aloof woman and her self-perceived shame. This revelation of vulnerability is a tender surprise, one of many offered up in the first collection of short fiction by Tobias Wolff in more than a decade. *Our Story Begins: New and Selected Stories* contains 21 of his classic pieces, the oldest written close to 30 years ago, and 10 newer stories.

A professor of creative writing at Stanford University, Wolff is the recipient of numerous honors, including the O. Henry Award, the PEN/Malamud Award and the Rea Award, all for the short story, and the PEN/Faulkner Award for Fiction. One of our wisest, most highly lauded contemporary American writers, Wolff uncannily documents cultural mood via the briefest interactions, the quietest decisions made by ordinary people, and thus he holds a place alongside other masters of the spare voice such as Raymond Carver and Ann Beattie.

He is known, in fact, for his achingly adept short short stories—whole worlds evoked in just a few pages. Yet, several entries in this collection—particularly those about the adventure and melancholy of boyhood, and a few of his more recent works—have in them the heft and density, the unexpected beauty, of Alice Munro, of Chekhov. Author of three previous story collections, two memoirs—including the harrowing *This Boy's Life*—a novella and most recently the well-regarded novel *Old School*, Wolff is a deserving candidate for this kind of career-navigating anthology. Originally published in journals such as *Antaeus* and *Story*, or in larger-circulation venues such as the *New Yorker*, the *Atlantic* and *Esquire*, the 31 stories are testament to the author's literary bravery.

The works are segregated chronologically—a section of older stories, followed by a section of newer ones. This distinction between the two allows the reader to witness Wolff's progression in tone and richness over time. Is there anyone else who has his ability to write so succinctly of desolation, so fervently of human impulse? And to also be, sometimes, very funny?

Each and every Wolff story has a distinct inevitability. No matter their length or subject matter, they coil up and deliver repeatedly. Many evoke unpleasant characters and situations, including domestic unease or violence, neglectful mothers, or despairing references to war and its bitter aftereffects on a soldier's psyche. Among the earlier stories, brief entries such as "Next Door," about having to endure the neighbors' constant fighting, or "Say Yes," which takes place almost entirely while a married couple is washing dishes, shatter with a breezy ruin. They stay with you for days. "Hunters in the Snow" is a stark tale of hunting buddies who, when one of their own is shot, display a startling disrespect for life.

In "Mortals," a young journalist, saddled with writing obituaries for four months, is "full of the consciousness of death. It puffed me up with morbid snobbery, the feeling that I knew a secret nobody else had even begun to suspect. It made me wearily philosophical about the value of faith and passion and hard work, at a time when my life required all of these. It got me down." This sort of prodigious ennui, the sense that there is something better out there, just beyond grasp, runs through the collection. And though the stories often build on an individual's capacity for mean-spiritedness, they succeed because of a parallel longing and the author's acutely honed insights.

Some of the seemingly bleakest pieces are the most poetic: "Witness Desert Breakdown," 1968, which observes a couple and their toddler—on their way to Los Angeles, city of dreams—as they end up stranded at a lone gas station with an eerily menacing group of people. While the husband sets out to find a car part in another town, and questions if he should return at all, the pregnant wife's deep love for her little boy is cruelly mocked. In the end, the young family will reconstitute, but with a tarnished innocence.

What a pleasure, then, to discover "Flyboys," a lovely, searing story about childhood—again, the subject matter with which Wolff consistently soars—the words cut diamond-sharp from guilt and a profound collective nostalgia. Mourning the razed woods behind his friend's house where they had once played, a young boy muses at the short-sightedness, the undependability, of the adults all around him. "This place had been Iroquois wilderness to me, English forest and African jungle. It had been Mars. Now gone, completely. I was a boy who knew that this lake of mud was the work of a fool."

While the earlier works contain details that date them, such as a lack of car seats and cell phones, a plethora of cigarettes, numerous references to Vietnam, they exist as indestructible snapshots of a time even as they successfully transcend that confine. The war stories make us shiver and think, ah, here we are again. And it is thrilling to read the newer pieces, noting their deepening dimensions. In "Down to Bone," a grown son escapes "the long hours of useless witness to his mother's dying"—a woman he truly loves—in order to keep an appointment at a funeral home. On the verge of an empty seduction with the woman who works there, he rushes home just in time to hear his mother whisper words that constitute an unbearably sad and satisfying ending to the piece.

"The Benefit of the Doubt" is certainly one of the most complex stories. An Illinois businessman visiting Rome first punishes and then becomes a spontaneous advocate for a pickpocket, in a series of unusual and heartbreaking events. We learn that three years prior, his daughter, 11 at the time, survived a brain tumor—but his marriage did not. In a kind of trancelike desire for something primordial, something sweet, he embraces children we assume are those of the pickpocket, oblivious to the darker implications. However, despite a disappointing world, the man maintains a faith in personal principles—even as he acknowledges the luxury of making mistakes that his wealth allows him. "During his daughter's sickness he had become intensely conscious of life as something good in itself, his own as well as hers," the American thinks as he rides through this ancient city.

It is that fierce life force resolute throughout these narratives, in the face of Wolff's detonating truths, that makes this collection so important.

Source: Lisa Jennifer Selzman, "Evoking Whole Worlds in a Few Pages," in *Houston Chronicle*, April 6, 2008, p. 17.

Kirkus Reviews

In the following review, a contributor to Kirkus Reviews *remarks on the "impressive range of contemporary experience" in this collection of short stories.*

An impressive range of contemporary experience is distilled into crisp, urgent little dramas in this story collection from Wolff (Old School, 2003, etc.).

The book features 21 previously published stories and ten new stories. A number of the entries, Wolff notes, have been slightly revised for the purposes of the collection. Troubled families are a recurring subject: "The Liar," for example, concerns a teenaged boy whose compulsive prevarications are both defense mechanisms and strategies for achieving a necessary maturity, and the beautifully paced, Cheever-like "The Rich Brother" depicts the frustrating bond between two contrasting adult siblings. Wolff reaches convincingly beyond the quotidian in a sinuously plotted tale about three men ("Hunters in the Snow") whose taunting horseplay whiplashes into an explosion of rage and violence, and an equally tense account of an underachieving career soldier whose screw-ups are echoed in varied relationships with his buddies, superior officers and married girlfriend ("Soldier's Joy"). Even when comic detail predominates, these are dark visions, animated and accelerated by a sense of ever-present danger and general unconcern (e.g., a hitchhiker passed by cars bearing numerous different state license plates "felt like the whole country had turned its back on him"). Both the new and old stories display Wolff's versatility: his mastery of oddly angled viewpoints ("Her Dog"); an incisive understanding of how inchoate teenage emotion can distract and alienate ("Deep Kiss"—which compares quite interestingly with "The Liar"); and a potent grasp of how lives replete with event and adventure may expand generously when touched by others' lives ("A Mature Student").

Richard Yates, Raymond Carver and Robert Stone are the modern masters whom Wolff most resembles. Like their best work, his own exhibits classic richness and depth, and it's built to last.

Source: Review of *Our Story Begins*, in *Kirkus Reviews*, March 1, 2008.

SOURCES

Allen, Bruce, "American Short Fiction Today," in *New England Review*, Vol. 4, No. 3, Spring 1982, pp. 486–88.

Buford, Bill, "Dirty Realism," in *Granta*, No. 8, http://www.granta.com/Magazine/8 (accessed September 16, 2011).

Campbell, James, "Brutal Beginnings," in *Guardian* (London, England), July 18, 2008, http://www.guardian.co.uk/books/2008/jul/19/fiction2 (accessed September 15, 2011).

Cheng, Terrence, "Interview with Tobias Wolff," in *Crazyhorse*, No. 52, Spring 1997, pp. 116–24.

Cherry, Kendra, "What Is Emotional Intelligence? Definitions, History, and Measures of Emotional Intelligence," in *About.com*, http://psychology.about.com/od/personalitydevelopment/a/emotionalintell.htm (accessed September 23, 2011).

Flower, Dean, "Fiction Chronicle," in *Hudson Review*, Vol. 35, No. 2, Summer 1982, pp. 278–79.

"General Deer Population Facts," in *Wildlife Control Information*, Cornell University Cooperative Extension, http://wildlifecontrol.info/deer/pages/deerpopulationfacts.aspx (accessed September 25, 2011).

Hannah, James, *Tobias Wolff: A Study of the Short Fiction*, Twayne Publishers, 1996, pp. 3–5, 7–9.

Mason, Wyatt, "Stifled Truth," in *London Review of Books*, Vol. 26, No. 3, February 5, 2004, pp. 19–20, http://www.lrb.co.uk/v26/n03/wyatt-mason/stifled-truth (accessed September 15, 2011).

"Obesity Costs U.S. $168 Billion, Study Finds," in *USA Today*, October 18, 2010, http://www.usatoday.com/yourlife/fitness/2010-10-18-obesity-costs_N.htm (accessed September 15, 2011).

Shivani, Anis, "Short Stories: Writers Talk about the Form to Anis Shivani," in *Huffington Post*, August 28, 2010, http://www.huffingtonpost.com/anis-shivani/short-stories-writers_b_667550.html (accessed September 15, 2011).

"Washington State Whitetail Deer Tips," in *HuntWashingtonState.com*, http://www.huntwashingtonstate.com/hws/big%20Game/whitetail_tips.htm (accessed September 17, 2011).

Wesley, Marilyn C., "Tobias Wolff," in *Dictionary of Literary Biography*, Vol. 130, *American Short-Story Writers since World War II*, edited by Patrick Meanor, Gale Research, 1993, pp. 314–22.

Wolff, Tobias, "Hunters in the Snow," in *In the Garden of the North American Martyrs: A Collection of Short Stories*, Ecco Press, 1981, pp. 9–26.

———, ed., *The Vintage Book of Contemporary American Short Stories*, Random House, 1994.

FURTHER READING

Charters, Ann, ed., *The Story and Its Writer: An Introduction to Short Fiction*, 6th ed., Bedford/St. Martin's, 2002.

This wide-ranging collection of short stories also contains writers' reflections on their own creative processes, readings that provide commentary on a story, and some critical essays. It includes Tobias Wolff's story "The Rich Brother."

Gelfant, Blanche H., and Graver, Lawrence, eds., *The Columbia Companion to the Twentieth-Century American Short Story*, Columbia University Press, 2000.

This collection includes eleven thematic essays that discuss many aspects of the short story, including development, type, and ethnic group, such as African American, Asian American, Chicano, Latino, and Native American. The essays in the remainder of the book focus on 113 individual authors.

Goleman, Daniel, *Emotional Intelligence*, Bloomsbury Paperbacks, 2010.

First published in 1995, this book by *New York Times* science writer Goleman popularized the concept of emotional intelligence, a way of assessing how well people handle their emotional life, a skill which is important for successful relationships.

Lyons, Bonnie, and Bill Oliver, "An Interview with Tobias Wolff," in *Contemporary Literature*, Vol. 31, No. 1, Spring 1990, pp. 1–16.

Wolff discusses his life and work in this wide-ranging interview.

SUGGESTED SEARCH TERMS

Tobias Wolff

Hunters in the Snow AND Tobias Wolff

In the Garden of the North American Martyrs: A Collection of Short Stories AND Tobias Wolff

dirty realism

realism

irony

white-tailed deer

emotional intelligence

obesity

Tobias Wolff AND short story

Tobias Wolff AND dirty realism

In a Grove

RYŪNOSUKE AKUTAGAWA

1922

Ryūnosuke Akutagawa's "In a Grove," published in 1922 in *Sincho* magazine, is a detective story set in ancient Japan. It has become well known throughout the entire world as the basis of Akira Kurosawa's breakthrough 1950 film *Rashomon*. The story appears in *The Essential Akutagawa*, edited by Seiji M. Lippit, published in 1999.

"In a Grove" tells its story through the testimony of three witnesses in a murder investigation, each of whom confesses to the killing. The third witness is the victim himself, claiming to be a suicide, speaking from beyond the grave through a spirit medium. Through this device, Akutagawa evokes the ancient shamanic traditions of Japan, as well as the spiritualist movement that swept over the world in the late nineteenth and early twentieth centuries. The impossibility of reconciling the three versions of events suggests the impossibility of finding truth and meaning in an irrational cosmos. In a turn of events its author could never have envisioned, the technique of telling the same story from different and irreconcilable viewpoints has become one of the mainstays of the entertainment industry, forming the skeleton of countless films and television programs, from art film to sitcoms.

AUTHOR BIOGRAPHY

Akutagawa was born on March 1, 1892, in Tokyo, Japan. According to traditional Chinese astrology, he was born in the year, month, day,

A wooded area is the scene of the crime in "In A Grove." (sharon hitman / Shutterstock.com)

and hour of the dragon, so he was give the name Ryunosuke, which means "son of the dragon." The Akutagawa family had been court nobles of the Tokugawa, responsible for conducting the culturally and spiritually significant tea ceremony, so his family life was steeped in tradition. Akutagawa was given a first-class education based equally on the Japanese and Chinese classics and Western literature.

While at Tokyo Imperial University, Akutagawa became an editor of the student literary magazine, *Shinshicho* (New Currents of Thought), as well as a frequent contributor of both original short stories and translations of Western poetry. He became a disciple of Natsume Sōseki, who was at the time the most prominent novelist in Japan. Akutagawa wrote more than one hundred fifty short stories, only some of which have been translated into English, but never produced a full-length novel. His first short story, "Rashomon," was published in 1915. "In a Grove" was originally published in the magazine *Sincho* in January 1922.

Akutagawa taught English briefly at the naval engineering school in Yokosuka before becoming a full-time writer. During his life, Akutagawa was popular and well accepted by Japanese critics, but his work was nevertheless seen as old fashioned because of his reliance on traditional narrative forms and his reluctance to indulge in the autobiographical revelations that dominated the literature of his era. Only later was his interest in pure aestheticism (devotion to beauty and the arts) used to elevate him to the first rank of Japanese literature.

His later work became more ambitious, including the film script for *San Sebastian* (1927), which showed the strong influence of the surrealist movement, and *Kappa* (1927), a novella presenting a satire of Japanese society as seen through the eyes of a mental patient. As he approached middle age, Akutagawa became uneasy about the future, because of his seeming inability to produce a novel and because of an obsessive fear that he would become insane as his mother had. His health also declined, producing constant pain and hallucinations. After at least one previous suicide attempt, Akutagawa killed himself on July 24, 1927, at the age of thirty-five. He died of an overdose of medicinal drugs, so his death was unrelated to the tradition of ritual suicide in Japan.

PLOT SUMMARY

"In a Grove" consists of seven sections of transcribed testimony from a trial or investigation. No narrative framework is provided to tie them together or give context. The witnesses frequently respond to questions, but these questions are not recorded (though their nature can be inferred from the answers), so there is only one speaker in each section. Actions on the part of each witness are sometimes described in parentheses, as in a script. In the three main narratives, Tajomaru and Masago both confess to killing Takehiro, while his ghost claims he committed suicide, and there are many other mutually exclusive details in their stories.

The Story of a Woodcutter Questioned by the Grand Magistrate

This testimony establishes the basic facts of the crime under investigation throughout the story. The woodcutter, going about his work in the forest, discovered the body of a samurai in a bamboo grove or thicket in the mountains, well off the road. He had been stabbed once in the heart and had evidently been tied up by some ropes found near his body. Trampled grass in the grove suggested a struggle. The woodcutter confirms that the samurai's horse could not have entered the grove because of the thick growth of bamboo and was nowhere to be found.

The Story of a Traveling Priest Questioned by the Grand Magistrate

The priest saw the samurai about noon on the day before his body was discovered. Armed with a bow (although they carried swords, samurai in this period were primarily horse archers), the samurai had been traveling with his wife, leading a horse, on which she rode.

The Story of a Police Official Questioned by the Grand Magistrate

The police official testifies that he has captured the notorious local outlaw Tajomaru. He believes that Tajomaru is the killer because he had a horse similar to the one the priest had seen and because he has a bow and a quiver of arrows, which he was not known to have had before and which the priest saw the samurai carrying. The policeman also says that Tajomaru is the worst of all the local bandits for interfering with women and is suspected in several kidnappings and murders of women, but as yet, the official does not know what happened to the samurai's wife. At the end of his testimony, he begs the magistrate to investigate the wife's disappearance as a possible kidnapping or murder by Tajomaru also.

The Story of an Old Woman Questioned by the Grand Magistrate

The woman is the mother of the missing wife. She supplies the name of the dead samurai—Kanazawa no Takehiro—and of her daughter, Masago. She also does not yet know what happened to her daughter.

MEDIA ADAPTATIONS

- Akira Kurosawa's 1950 film *Rashomon* is an adaptation of "In a Grove," using Akutagawa's short story "Rashomon" to provide part of the setting.
- Mayako Kubo's opera *Rashomon*, which premiered in 1996, is an adaptation of Kurosawa's film and includes a full adaptation of "In a Grove." It is available on a 1996 CD performed by the Grazer Philharmonisches Orchester conducted by Stefan Lano.
- In 1996, Akutagawa's short story was adapted as a film by Hisayasu Sato under its original title, *Yabu no naka*. The film has not been released outside of Japan.
- The Japanese playwright Nomura Mansai adapted Akutagawa's short story for the stage in 1999. The play's title is usually translated as *In a Thicket*, although the Japanese is the same as the short-story title (*Yabu no naka*). The play exists in two forms: one adapted for the Western stage and one that is a traditional Noh play.

Tajomaru's Confession

Threatened with torture, Tajomaru agrees to tell the whole story of what happened, but not without mockery of the police official and the magistrate. Tajomaru happened to meet the samurai couple on the road, he says, and, catching a glimpse of the exceptional beauty of the wife's face, he decided to take her for herself, even if he had to kill the husband (though he wanted to avoid that). He lured the husband into the grove by appealing to his greed. He told the samurai that he had found a buried cache of antique swords (ancient burials of warriors and nobles often included caches of weapons, as though they could use them in the next world) and offered to sell them to him cheap. Telling the samurai he had reburied the swords in a grove, Tajomaru led him into the thicket and, taking him by surprise, overcame him and bound him, gagging him by stuffing his mouth with grass.

He then lured the wife into the grove by saying her husband had fallen ill. Boasting of his fighting skill, Tajomaru says that he wrestled the woman's knife away from her and raped her in front of the husband, but without having to kill him. When the outlaw started to leave, Masago stopped him, saying that her shame was too great for both of the men to live: either her husband or her rapist had to die, and she would willingly go with the other. Although this was clearly an invitation for Tajomaru to kill the bound samurai, he considered this dishonorable. Instead, he untied the man and fought a duel with him. Tajomaru claims the samurai was a highly skilled fencer, but his own skill was greater, and he killed the samurai. When the fight was over, the woman had fled, so Tajomaru took the samurai's horse and weapons.

The Confession of the Woman Who Came to Kiyomizu Temple

After the rape, Masago had evidently sought refuge in this famous temple, built about 780 in the mountains above Kyoto and considered one of the most beautiful in Japan. Her story picks up just after the rape. She says she had passed out, and when she came to, the outlaw was gone, with her husband still tied up. She felt that she could not live with the shame of what happened to her. Seeing the contempt for her in her husband's eyes, she does not untie him or remove his gag but tells him: "I am resigned to die. Yet—yet I ask you to die as well. You have witnessed my shame. I cannot leave you alive this way." She claims she read in her husband's eyes that he wished her to kill him as well. She did so, promising to kill herself afterwards. However, she failed in the effort to take her own life. She says that Kannon, the Buddhist saint of mercy, declined to help her.

The Story of the Ghost Told by a Medium

Takehiro, the victim of the murder, is, of course, dead at the time of the investigation, but the magistrate interrogates his ghost through the use of a spirit medium, a woman whose body is possessed by his ghost and who speaks in his voice. Although the lack of narrative framework in the story leaves the matter unresolved, it is possible the magistrate decided to take the extreme step of interrogating a ghost because of the impossibility of resolving the stories of the wife and bandit.

Takehiro's story also begins after the rape, with Tajomaru trying to talk Masago into going away with him. She agreed but insisted that the bandit must kill her husband. That a wife would so shamelessly want to see her own husband dead was too much even for the bandit, and he asked the bound husband whether he wanted Tajomaru to kill her for her impudence or spare her. The samurai hesitated to give a reply, and his wife ran off. Tajomaru cut the samurai free and ran off himself. Unable to go on after being dishonored in this way by his wife, Takehiro killed himself by plunging his wife's dagger into his heart. After a while, certainly after he was dead, his spirit perceived someone—he cannot see who—pull the knife out of his chest. After that, there is only wandering in darkness.

CHARACTERS

Grand Magistrate

The magistrate does not technically appear as a character in the story, but most of the documents are tagged as being transcripts of testimony delivered before him. Such a figure would be in charge of the legal process in a group of villages, each of which he might visit one day a month. In turn, he would answer to a superior official in the government. He is presumably the one asking the questions that the witnesses sometimes answer.

Masago

Although the other characters in the story have a great deal to say about Masago, their views seem self-interested and unreliable. Her own mother seems to prefer her son-in-law to her daughter, whom she considers difficult: "strong-willed like a man" and therefore flawed as a woman. Because of Masago's class, Tajomaru idealizes her past the point of providing reliable witness to her character. Her husband's ghost reports seeing her transformed after the rape and after listening to the outlaw's persuasive speech that seemed, to him, to put a spell on his wife. He blames her for shamelessly agreeing to go off with Tajomaru and even demanding that the outlaw kill him, her husband, which seems an inversion of using murder to restore lost honor.

But an explanation for this comes from Masago's own story. After she was raped, Takehiro looked on her with contempt, as though she had done something wrong. Indeed, in the view of the traditional culture, she had. Her relation with a man other than her husband was an act of betrayal of her marriage and a stain on her honor that could only be erased by her killing herself or by her husband or another male relative killing her. In Takehiro's version of events, Masago rebels against the traditions of her society that would blame and punish her for merely being violated against her will, becoming an outlaw like Tajomaru.

Masago's own version can readily be seen as a repressed fantasy beneath the account of her failure to live up to the expectations of honor. The fact that Masago had been raped was immaterial compared to the fact that the sanctity of marriage had been violated. Society expected her to share this view of herself and kill herself. This is what she imagines her husband is wordlessly ordering her to do, to kill both him and herself, because their honor could never be restored in life. However, in her account she kills him but fails to kill herself. Perhaps this is a fantasy representing her response to the injustice of her situation; perhaps she wished to kill her husband because his reaction to her violation was to hold her in contempt and condemn her. Although the story says nothing about what happens to Masago after the hearing, if she did not become a nun in the Kiyomizo temple where she had sought sanctuary, it is very likely that the magistrate or her male relatives would have executed her.

Medium

Although the medium does not appear in the story, her role can be understood in the context of traditional Japanese culture. Each village or country district would have had a ritual expert charged with communicating with the dead, so this character is a recognizable type. One must imagine the ghost of Takehiro has taken possession of her body and is speaking through her. How to take her story is left entirely to the reader. Does it carry, in its context, the authority of supernatural powers, or is the medium fabricating a story to please the magistrate?

Old Woman

The old woman is the mother of Masago and mother-in-law of Takehiro. The fact that she does not know that her daughter is still alive (information the magistrate would hardly have concealed from her) suggests that the depositions of the various characters were taken over several days in the course of the investigation.

Police Official

The man who arrested Tajomaru is an experienced local police officer who knows the bandit and his reputation very well. He deduced that Tajomaru was the murderer from the fact that he had a samurai's bow and quiver with him, which he could only have stolen. The bow was the traditional weapon of the samurai, to be supplanted in prestige by the sword only after the Heian period.

Priest

The priest was the last person to see Takehiro alive before the crime. His ignorance of weapons suggests the social separation of the priestly and samurai classes (something that was to change in the chaotic time following the Heian period, when many priests had to take up arms to defend their temples). The priest has a literary bent and offers a poetic comment on the murder—"Truly, human life is as ephemeral as dew and as brief as lightning"—although this rather hackneyed verse may be interpreted as the priest showing off his limited knowledge.

Tajomaru

As an outlaw, Tajomaru stands outside of the hierarchical system of Japanese society. Thus, it is impossible for him to find any legitimate place. His reaction to his place in society is to boast and exaggerate his achievements in an attempt to create a better status for himself. This attitude is so ingrained in him that he persists in his boasting even after he has been captured and his execution is eminent. This is why he describes the murder as an epic sword duel: "No one else has ever crossed swords with me twenty times. (Energetic laughter.)" Tajomaru knows that, as an outlaw, he would be executed if captured, as he says, "All along I knew I would hang from the gallows one day, so go ahead and do your worst. (A defiant attitude.)" The investigation is only to find out what happened to the dead samurai, not to determine Tajomaru's guilt or innocence. His very status condemns him to death, not any particular action. This is why Tajomaru makes no effort to defend himself or protest his innocence. The most he can hope for is to avoid further torture, so he is happy to talk, especially so that he can criticize the society in which he lives.

While the reader cannot know why Tajomaru became an outlaw, the excessive taxation of the peasantry to concentrate wealth in the hands of a small class of nobles is the generally accepted reason for the societal crisis that ended the stability of the Heian period. Certainly Tajomaru is keenly aware of class inequalities and responds to them with hostility. For instance, he says that he led the samurai on by appealing to his greed, but his contempt for the social hierarchy above him is brought out most strongly in his criticism of the magistrate:

> But you—you don't use swords, you kill with power and money. Sometimes you even kill with words that sound like they're full of kindness. There may be no blood, and the man may still breathe, but you've killed him all the same. When you think about it, it's not so easy to tell who is guiltier, you or I. (An ironic smile.)

Tajomaru's sudden and excessive desire for Masago, the samurai's wife, may also be conditioned by his class consciousness. On the one hand, he idealizes her beauty and says she looks like a boddhisatva—a saint—but at the same time, when he sees her eyes "lit up like fire," he not only desires her but also wishes to marry her, that is, to take legal possession of her as if he might gain a higher social position through her. He wants not only to rape her, but to control her, as a sort of compensation for whatever social forces made him an outcast. Takehiro's characterization of Tajomaru as a mere thief and a liar is, conversely, an attempt to dismiss his class concerns.

Kanazawa no Takehiro

Takehiro is the samurai who is the victim of the murder that forms the centerpiece of the plot of "In a Grove." He appears directly in the story only as a ghost speaking through a spirit medium. According to his mother-in-law, "he had a gentle nature, so he wouldn't have any enemies." Tajomaru depicts him as easy to trick because of his greed but also as a noble fighter, though this was meant to build up Tajomaru's own image as an even greater swordsman. Takehiro's ghost says that once he was freed of his bonds and could act, he was so overwhelmed by the humiliations of seeing his wife raped and then her betrayal of him that his only reaction was to sob and then to kill himself, suggesting that he was as emotionally overwhelmed at the end of his life as he is in death, sinking "into the blackness of the abyss." His wife's account gives still a different depiction of Takehiro. According to Masago, Takehiro acted in conformity with the traditional honor code of Japanese society, blaming his wife for the transgression of being raped (as opposed to his ghost, who blames her for plotting with Tajomaru afterward) and desiring to wipe out their disgrace with her death and his own.

Woodcutter

In a preindustrial society, wood fires must be used to cook food and heat homes. The woodcutter in a village goes into the forest beyond the fields to gather the wood that everyone else needs in exchange for a share of their crops. His relatively lowly status is indicated by the fact that his name is not given and by the reflexive deference he shows to the magistrate at the beginning of his testimony.

THEMES

Storytelling

About a quarter of Akutagawa's stories, and a much higher proportion of his translated ones, take place in past eras of Japanese history. "In a Grove" is among these, set during the Heian period (794–1185 CE). In fact, the story, like many of Akutagawa's, is based on a folktale from the collection *Konjaku monogatari-shū* (Anthology of Tales from the Past), which was composed by an anonymous scholar about the year 1200. In this original version (translated by Marian Urys in *Tales of Times Now Past*), the outlaw trades his antique sword to Takehiro for his bow and arrows, but at the moment Takehiro is lifting his wife down from her horse, the outlaw draws the bow and threatens to shoot him if he does not put off his swords. He then ties Takehiro up and proceeds to rape his wife in front of him. When the outlaw leaves, the wife unties her husband but denounces him as a coward for failing to protect her.

Akutagawa's stories, of course, cannot be considered simple historical fiction, and he does

TOPICS FOR FURTHER STUDY

- *The Kurosagi Corpse Delivery Service*, written by Wiji Otsuka and illustrated by Hosui Yamazaki, is an unusually sophisticated *manga* (Japanese comic book) in which a group of young men studying to become Buddhist monks discover that they have the power to use traditional rituals to help the spirits of the newly dead move on to their appointed place in the afterlife. It was translated into English and published in a twelve-volume set in the United States in 2006. Draw your own *manga* adaptation of one of the three main sets of testimony from "In a Grove."
- *Hyakumonogatari kaidankai*, or "gathering of one hundred supernatural tales," was a popular party game in Japan during Akutagawa's youth. It consisted of lighting one hundred candles and extinguishing them one by one as each player told a ghost story or fairy tale. Supposedly when the last candle is snuffed out and the room plunges into total darkness, a supernatural apparition would appear. Organize such a game in your class (perhaps with fewer than one hundred candles). Alternatively, write a short story in which an account of such a game is used as a framework for a few ghost stories or fairy tales of your own invention.
- Shamanism still survives in many countries around the world (including in the United States, especially among Native Americans). Use the Internet and traditional library resources to write a research paper comparing shamanic practices in Japan with those in one or two other cultures. Be sure to cite all sources.
- Read Akutagawa's "Rashomon," and view Kurosawa's film *Rashomon* (which is based on that story and "In a Grove"). What elements are unique to the film and therefore Kurosawa's own inventions? How do these additions attempt to unravel the contradictions and logical difficulties in "In a Grove"? How does it add to them? Set up an online blog explaining your interpretation of these issues and invite your classmates to debate your conclusions.

far more than simply repeat this traditional tale. He is not interested in telling a simple story dressed up in the trappings of the past but rather uses historical material as a connection to Japanese tradition, which for him is aesthetic and spiritual more than historical. Moreover, Akutagawa's technique is to take historical material and transform it through psychological exploration into a distinctly modern literature. Akutagawa also used earlier historical periods to justify the introduction of supernatural elements into his work, which he used as psychological symbols and which were importations from Western writers like Ambrose Bierce and Edgar Allan Poe.

Suicide

The ritual suicide performed by the samurai is a well-known element of Japanese culture and history. There is some controversy about the name of the practice. It is pronounced as *hara-kiri* in spoken Japanese, but the characters used to write that term have the value in Chinese of *seppuku*; this term is preferred in writing and ought to be used in English. *Seppuku* simply means "cutting the belly" and refers to a technique of suicide in which a samurai would plunge his short sword or dagger into his stomach, while his second would behead him with the long sword (ideally only the spine would be severed, leaving the body intact).

The practice was originally introduced on the battlefield as a means of escaping capture by the enemy (which would most likely have meant protracted torture), but it came, within the samurai code of Bushido, to be a way of restoring honor lost through cowardice or some other personal failure (often at the order of a samurai's feudal lord) and a means of protesting dishonorable actions by a superior. This kind of ritual suicide

The victim in "In a Grove" is a young samurai named Kanazawa no Takehiko. (Ivan Demyanov / Shutterstock.com)

has very little to do with suicides committed because of mental illness like depression. A samurai committing seppuku would frequently write a poem expressing the new perspective he had found in facing his impending death. Women of the samurai class sometimes committed suicide for the same type of reasons as their male counterparts, but they were permitted to cut open their own jugular veins, considered a means of suicide both less physically and emotionally demanding than the ritual followed by men.

Seppuku came into practice with the rise of the samurai only during the Gempei War at the end of the Heian period. Accordingly, it would be anachronistic to see the report of suicide from the samurai's ghost in "In a Grove" as describing an act of seppuku: "My wife's fallen dagger glinted on the ground before me. I took it in my hand and stabbed myself once in the chest." The ritual form of seppuku was not followed, and it takes place before the custom had developed. On the other hand, the concept became so ingrained in Japanese culture that it is hard to separate any suicide by a samurai from the concept of seppuku in a piece of modern literature, however anachronistic.

Nevertheless, Takehiro commits suicide because the events of the story had stained his honor in an overwhelming way that had destroyed his own sense of identity, in a way that could not be repaired by any other action. (Killing the bandit would have had little value in the Japanese honor system because he stood outside the social hierarchy.) Therefore the act resolves an otherwise impossible and intolerable circumstance and takes on many of the social features of classical seppuku. Ritual suicide was outlawed in Japan in 1873 as part of the modernizing reforms of the Meiji era. Akutagawa's own suicide seems to have been undertaken for entirely personal and psychological reasons (such as fear of going mad as his mother had) and cannot be considered seppuku.

STYLE

Documentary Story

Although the most popular books read and written today are generally fiction, the idea of purposefully writing false stories is a later development in world literature. Stories like those in the thirteenth-century Japanese *Konjaku monogatari-shū*, from which the story used in "In a Grove" descends, were collected by scholars from folk sources who most likely believed they were narrating events that actually happened. This was true in general of older forms like epic and drama. Works that now would be called fiction seem to have first developed in China from this same scholarly activity of collecting folktales that grew out of historical events. This is represented in works like the fourteenth-century Chinese classic *Shuihu zhuan*, or *Water Margin*, a collection of independent stories given a single narrative framework by a scholarly editor who gradually composed more and more material until something like a modern novel came into existence.

"In a Grove," however, is also based on Western sources, and its character as a collection of documents is distinctly Western. Fiction first developed in Greece within the context of higher education. Students studying law and oratory would be asked in assignments to create forensic speeches, or draft letters, in connection with hypothetical legal cases. Eventually this practice left the schools and became a way of writing fiction and eventually evolved into the novel, of which the earliest is Chariton's *Callirhoe* (first century BCE).

When the novel form was revived in the West during the eighteenth century, many early examples, like Samuel Richardson's *Pamela*, were epistolary novels, consisting entirely of the text of manufactured letters. Perhaps more relevant is a novel like Bram Stoker's *Dracula*, which is told entirely through a collection of fictional documents in various genres, including letters, newspaper articles, transcripts of meetings, and journal entries. This was the form taken by Ambrose Bierce in "The Moonlit Road," one of Akutagawa's sources for "In a Grove," which consists of two depositions and the stenographic record of a séance. Akutagawa adopted this Western form, producing his story from the transcripts of testimony given at a trial, or at least during a criminal investigation, without any explanatory or connective material providing a context or a framing narrative.

Intertextuality

Critics of Akutagawa's fiction in his own time often found fault with his work because it drew so heavily on source material that it seemed to lack originality. His stories were compared to a mosaic composed of tiles drawn from his predecessors' work, leaving Akutagawa as no more than an arranger. "In a Grove," for instance, takes its basic plot from a folktale of the Heian period collected in the *Konjaku monogatari-shū* (Anthology of Tales from the Past), and it also draws on two Western works. Robert Browning, in *The Ring and the Book* (1868–1869), created the form of telling a story through the court testimony of various characters, all of whom narrate the same event but from different perspectives and with great ambiguity in that each character twists the narrative to his own advantage, creating mutually irreconcilable versions. Ambrose Bierce's short story "The Moonlit Road," in which a woman's strangulation by a supernatural apparition is described through discrete blocks of testimony from the father and son and through a medium from the ghost of the wife who was killed, is another direct inspiration for "In a Grove."

Today this technique would be considered not a weakness in Akutagawa's prose but rather a strength. He engages in an intertextual discussion with classic literature, interrogating his sources to find new meaning through understanding them. He creates a new and original work by recombining the fragments of his source material in an original way. An artist composing a mosaic from existing tiles still has the responsibility of creating a picture or design by arranging the fragmentary tiles into a coherent whole. It is also generally recognized that no literature, even if it represents itself as original, can be free from close dependency on its author's tradition. Even the plays of Shakespeare, where they are not explicitly historical, draw on tropes and themes from classic literature at every level of detail. For example, the plot of *Hamlet* is based on a legendary version of the history of Denmark, and in Prospero's farewell speech at the end of *The Tempest*, many of the lines are translations from the Roman poet Ovid.

Akutagawa anticipates the postmodern in more clearly pointing his readers to his sources through a more direct dependency and in more self-consciously creating new literature by transforming the old, interpreting his sources to find new psychological and philosophical meaning. The folktale that Akutagawa begins with is partly comic and mildly obscene: a diversion. "In a Grove," using the techniques of more sophisticated literature, addresses the central issue of the meaninglessness of life.

COMPARE & CONTRAST

- **Heian Period:** Traditional Japanese shamans fill the social role of interacting with the spirit world, including communicating with the dead.

  1920s: Beginning in the 1850s, modern spiritualists in the West claimed that they could communicate with the dead, sparking a worldwide movement. Though past its prime in the 1920s, this kind of spiritualism is introduced into Japan.

  Today: Spiritualism still persists as a fringe practice with little social significance.

- **Heian Period:** The integrity of women's bodies is viewed by society only as an index of masculine honor, and women's lives are carefully controlled by their male relatives and husbands.

  1920s: The only prospect allowed to a middle-class woman is to make a good marriage, which is arranged by her father. A woman must carefully guard her reputation or bring shame on her family and ruin her chances for marriage.

  Today: Women in Japan receive less education than men and are more poorly represented in the labor force. Their lives still revolve around marriage prospects to a much greater degree than, for example, in the United States.

- **Heian Period:** Heating and cooking are carried out with fires fueled by wood collected in forests.

  1920s: Japan is rapidly being electrified, while coal provides most of the fuel for heating and cooking.

  Today: Japan has the most advanced power system in the world, with much of the electricity provided by nuclear power, as well as a sophisticated infrastructure for delivering natural gas to homes and businesses.

HISTORICAL CONTEXT

The Heian Period

"In a Grove" is based in part on a folktale from *Konjaku monogatari-shū*, a collection of stories from the Heian period (794–1185 CE) of Japanese history. The Heian period is seen as the end of a golden age of Japanese history (beginning about 500 CE) when the land was generally at peace and was managed by a central government based in Kyoto, first under the emperors and then under the Fujiwara clan, who ruled as regents under emperors who had become mere figureheads. However, during the Heian period, the special military class of the samurai emerged, and regional clans became more powerful until the central government dissolved in the civil conflict of the Gempei War, beginning the feudal period of constant regional warfare with no strong central authority that lasted until the seventeenth century. The lack of an adequate police force maintained by the central government, leading to rampant brigandage, as well as huge economic differences between classes eventually led to social and political collapse. The Gempei War is the subject of a famous folk epic, the *Tale of the Heiki. The Tale of Genji*, the earliest novel written in Japan, was produced at the height of the Heian period. Numerous later plays and other works of literature are set during the Heian period.

Rashomon

Akira Kursowa's film *Rashomon* is an adaptation of "In a Grove." It is set within a larger frame story borrowed from "Rashomon," another Akutagawa story, allowing the testimony of the various witnesses to be repeated and discussed in a narrative framework. Kurosawa added a fourth version of the story, told by the woodcutter to his acquaintances in the framing story but not to the investigating magistrate. This narrative casts the events

A traveling Buddhist priest testifies that he met the victims of the attack that is the subject of "In a Grove." *(MaxPhoto / Shutterstock.com)*

in the grove into a pathetic light, with the samurai, wife, and bandit all acting out of moral insufficiency and personal failure. While this is presented as an objective account, meant to resolve the impossible difficulties in the three versions gathered by the magistrate, its hearers cast doubt on it, suggesting that the woodcutter saw nothing and is merely trying to make sense out of the senseless nature of existence.

At the end of the film, the woodcutter finds and adopts a baby exposed at the Rashomon temple. Although the abandonment of the child is presented as a symbol of cosmic dissonance, confirming the pessimistic and irrational results of the investigation, the adoption suggests that hope can still be found in love. The film, widely considered among the best ever made, won the Golden Lion at the 1951 Venice Film Festival, marking the introduction of Japanese cinema to the West. This film version is largely responsible for the popularity of Akutagawa's story, and several other adaptations, such as Western remakes (including Martin Ritt's 1964 *The Outrage*, which resets the story in the American West) and operas, are based on the film rather than directly on the short story. The generic technique of having the events of a story narrated from three or more viewpoints in a television program or comic book is generally known as the Rashomon style.

Akutagawa Prize

The Akutagawa Prize was established in 1935 in honor of the recently deceased author. It is awarded to a story published in each calendar year in a magazine or newspaper by a first-time or at least young author. It is considered one of the most prestigious literary awards in Japan. The prize carries a cash award of one million yen (about thirteen thousand dollars).

CRITICAL OVERVIEW

Although Akutagawa is important in Japanese literature, he has been relatively neglected by Western scholars. Many of his works have never been translated, particularly his theoretical essays. There is only one monograph on Akutagawa in English, Beongcheon Yu's *Akutagawa: An Introduction*, from 1972. Yu reads "In a Grove" as an assertion that the passions are stronger than reason in human beings, a condition that leaves people uncertain and blindly searching for unattainable truth. Yu sees this as a modern meaning built on an ancient setting.

Seiji M. Lippit, in the introduction to his edited collection *The Essential Akutagawa*, observes that the most proximate model for "In a Grove" is Ambrose Bierce's story "The Moonlit Road," but Akutagawa's tale differs in that the three versions are impossible to reconcile. Also, the three main characters in "In a Grove," rather than trying to deflect guilt from themselves, all confess to the killing. Lippit points out more generally that Akutagawa considered his work to be an equal reconciliation of the ancient and the modern and that "In a Grove" in particular concerns the relationship between history (the murder in this case) and narrative, as seen in people's necessarily imperfect efforts to represent what happened.

Jorge Luis Borges, the acclaimed Latin American writer, wrote the foreword to Lippit's collection. Borges considers that Akutagawa tried to hold the influences of Eastern and

Western literature in balance in his work and that he saw it as his principal task to express Japanese tradition in modern psychological terms. In general, Borges finds that Akutagawa's subjects and sentiments are Oriental, but his rhetorical structures are European.

Susan J. Napier, in *The Fantastic in Modern Japanese Literature* (1996), develops the theme of historical ambiguity further. In traditional literature, a supernatural element is often introduced into a narrative to give finality or certainty. In "In a Grove," Akutagawa uses the supernatural for precisely the opposite effect, to create further confusion and suggest that certainty and even intellectual stability are impossible in this world, anticipating the postmodern worldview and the techniques of magic realism (a genre in which magical elements blend with the real world).

Alan Tansman, in his 2009 *The Aesthetics of Japanese Fascism*, argues that, though Akutagawa can hardly be described as a political author, his aesthetic vision lay the foundation for the literary style assumed by fascism in Japan during the 1930s and 1940s. There was a general sense among intellectuals of Akutagawa's generation that Japanese literature was exhausted by the effort to be modern: digesting Western literature and paring away subject matter until nothing was left but the writer's self. Akutagawa hoped to overcome this by making a new connection with tradition. He viewed language as an incantation, prose as something to be possessed by the spirit of poetry, and he sought to create lyric fragments that did not yield the discursive meaning of Western prose. Akutagawa's creation of a style of lyric imagery that could only be understood by reference to tradition paved the way, in Tansman's judgment, for the irrational evocations typical of fascist literature.

Hisaaki Yamanouchi, in *The Search for Authenticity in Modern Japanese Literature*, explores the ways in which the combination of "In a Grove" and "Rashomon" in Kurosawa's 1950 film *Rashomon* strengthens both stories through an exploration reinforcing mutually supporting themes between them.

CRITICISM

Bradley A. Skeen

Skeen is a classicist. In the following essay, he examines the theme of spiritualism and shamanism developed in "In a Grove."

"AKUTAGAWA HAD AMPLE PRECEDENT IN THE WIDESPREAD FOLK PRACTICE OF SHAMANIC MEDIUMSHIP THROUGHOUT JAPANESE HISTORY AND EVEN IN A FEW INSTANCES WHERE OFFICIALS AS HIGH AS THE EMPEROR TURNED TO THIS KIND OF DIRECT INTERROGATION OF THE SPIRITS."

Ryūnosuke Akutagawa's composition of "In a Grove" combines into a literary mosaic elements from many sources, of which the two most important are the Heian period folktale "How a Man Who Was Accompanying His Wife to Tanba Province Got Trussed Up at Oeyama" and Ambrose Bierce's short story "The Moonlit Road." Akutagawa applies the structure of Bierce's story to the folktale, introducing into it the testimony of the dead man found in the grove from beyond the grave through a medium. Because of this mosaic of story elements, the fantastic element can be, or even must be, accounted for from two different perspectives. The first is the modern context of Bierce's story and the time of Akutagawa's own writing, which requires an explanation for the fantastic, one that is supplied by the modern phenomenon of spiritualism. At the same time, the conjuration of the dead must function within the historical context of the Heian period in the twelfth century (or earlier), and that is justified by the shamanic practices embedded in traditional Japanese religion.

The influence of European literature on the leading Japanese writers of the 1920s lagged behind by about a generation, so the greatest impact on them came from the French decadent movement of the 1890s (which is reflected in English literature, for example, in Oscar Wilde's *The Picture of Dorian Gray*). Working at the end of the nineteenth century, decadent writers like Joris Huysmans embraced civilization as a sick and dying organism, one of whose fatal symptoms was the belief in magic and the occult. This is the background in which Akutagawa would have understood spiritualism.

Modern spiritualism began in the 1840s in the small town of Hydesville, New York, where two teenage sisters, Kate and Margaret Fox, began to

WHAT DO I READ NEXT?

- Ambrose Bierce's short story "The Moonlit Road," first published in *Cosmopolitan* in 1907, was a direct inspiration for "In a Grove." It gives testimony from three witnesses relating to a death caused by an attack from a supernatural creature, of which the third comes through a spirit medium from the woman who was killed. It is widely available in collections and anthologies.
- *The Legends of Tono* is a collection of Japanese folklore originally published in 1910 by Kunio Yanagita. The work is considered the Japanese equivalent of *Grimms' Fairy Tales* and is suitable reading for all ages. The work was translated into English by Ronald A. Morse in 1975 and reissued in 2008.
- *The Tale of Genji* is a novel written during the Heian period by Shikibu Murasaki, a courtier at Kyoto. It is the most famous work of literature from the period in which "In a Grove" is set. It has been frequently translated, including an edition by Richard Bowring in 2004.
- *The Tale of the Heiki* is a folk epic describing the civil war that ended the Heian period. It was collected by scholars in the fourteenth century from a collection of songs performed by bards of that time. There are several translations in print, including one by Helen Craig McCullough, published in 1988.
- *The Way of Kinship: An Anthology of Native Siberian Literature*, edited and translated by Alexander Vaschenko and Claud Clayton Smith in 2010, is a collection of literature in every genre produced over the last two centuries by members of the native tribes of Siberia. The collection shows a traditional shamanic culture in conflict with the encroaching modern world.
- The second volume of *The Cambridge History of Modern Japan*, edited by D. H. Shively and W. H. McCullough in 1999, offers a general overview of the Heian period.
- Henry Scott Tokes's 2000 biography *The Life and Death of Yukio Mishima* takes as it subject one of the most important Japanese writers of the mid-twentieth century (had he lived it is probable he would have won the Nobel Prize for Literature), who killed himself in the last formal act of traditional ritual suicide in 1970 as an act of political protest.
- Dianne Salerni's 2007 volume *High Spirits: A Tale of Ghostly Rapping and Romance* is a historical novel for young adults based on the lives of the Fox sisters, the founders of spiritualism.

---

claim that they could communicate with the spirits of the dead. Patronized by the newspaper publisher Horace Greeley, they soon found themselves consulted by the richest and most powerful people in America and made very advantageous marriages. Soon hundreds of women began to imitate them. Mediums, as they were called, claimed to be able not only to communicate with the spirits of the dead but also to exhibit a wide range of what eventually came to be called psychic powers: telepathy (the ability to read minds), telekinesis (the ability to move objects without physically touching them), and precognition (foretelling the future). Mediums also claimed to have the ability to cause the spirits of the dead to physically manifest themselves to human sight and hearing.

During and after the Civil War, when millions of Americans whose sons or husbands had been killed in the war suddenly had an urgent desire to speak with the dead, spiritualism became an important and enduring social phenomenon. The fact that the Fox sisters eventually confessed that everything they had done had been a fraud did very little to stop the growth of spiritualism. The immediate forms that spiritualism took were the séance and the more public spirit-cabinet show, in which the medium would demonstrate her mind-reading abilities and other psychic powers. Some mediums not only spoke in the voices of the dead, but even affected an off-stage costume change into the flowing robes that angels wore in Victorian paintings and passed themselves off as physical apparitions of spirits. Frequently the medium would enter a small cabinet (i.e., a coffin) and be handcuffed or placed in a straitjacket by a member of the audience in order to guarantee that there was no trickery involved, but this merely allowed them to use the techniques of the escape artist to carry out their deceptions. The spirit-cabinet show was the ancestor of the modern stage magician's show and was virtually identical in form, except the spiritualists claimed that everything they did was being accomplished by miracles.

Once the spirits began to be interrogated about the nature of the afterlife (and gave answers strikingly different from mainstream religions like Christianity), spiritualism became a religious movement, with church organizations in the English-speaking world and in France using spiritualist practices as religious rites. Most mediums came from liberal, middle-class families and so associated their movement with the most progressive causes of the nineteenth century, including women's suffrage and the movements for the abolition of slavery and the prohibition of alcohol. At the same time, spiritualism presented itself as a science whose miracles were no greater or more mysterious than the technological miracles that transformed nineteenth-century life, such as the telegraph and steam-powered trains and ships, although whenever spiritualists' claims were subjected to legitimate scientific scrutiny, they were found to be false. Spiritualism arrived in Japan after World War I, and by 1925, the church known as the Society for Psychical Science Research (named as if it were a typical scientific society) had been founded there.

Spiritualism was introduced into Japan mainly through France. Akutagawa had a collection of about a half dozen French books on spiritualism in his private library, by authors like Camille Flammarion, an important astronomer who was also a spiritualist and one of the chief supporters of spiritualist psychic research as a pseudoscience. Akutagawa's mentor, the prominent novelist Natsume Sōseki, had a much larger collection, frequently used spiritualist themes in his own works, and eagerly participated in pseudoscientific tests of psychic powers. The extent of Akutagawa's personal belief in spiritualism is not known, but it could hardly have been very great without leaving more evidence in his writing and personal papers. The spiritualist episode in Bierce's "The Moonlit Road," was meant to capitalize on the popularity of spiritualism, but the theme appealed to Akutagawa because it bound together his personal connection to spiritualism through Sōseki, his decadent interest in the occult and the fantastic, and traditional shamanic practices that are superficially similar to spiritualism.

The word *shaman* comes from the Tungus language of Siberia, where Europeans first encountered shamanism, but it describes a general set of beliefs and a practice that is as old as the human species and spread all over the world. Shamanism probably grew out of the evolutionary tendency of the human mind to experience and interpret the external world in comprehensible, even personal, terms. Shamanism can be understood from its practice in the contemporary world and provides an explanation for a good deal of archaeological evidence from prehistory. The practice of burying family members with flowers and with tools and weapons (which is at least fifty thousand years old) indicates a belief that death is not an end but a transition to another place. If that is the case, many believed, then it ought to be possible to go there and come back, as to any other place. The shaman claims to be able to do so and to be able to interact with the spirits (i.e., the dead) there to influence the things on earth that they control.

In shamanism, the spirits are responsible for all good fortune and misfortune: they cause illness and drought but also the fertility of the land and its herds. Through the spirits, the shaman can control all these things. The shaman acquired the power to journey to the other world, as he believed, and intervene on behalf of humanity through a set of ascetic practices (controlling things like eating, sex, and the reaction to cold in ways that ordinary people do not) that brought about a vision, which can be understood as a descent into his own mind in a state of trance, but which he understood as an actual journey to a real place. The thirty-thousand-year-old cave paintings of Lascaux, Chauvet, and other sites in Europe are believed to be records of such shamanic journeys, and the paintings of game animals are a sign of the fecundity the shamans brought about.

Once human life was transformed by the agricultural revolution, the new cities and kings took religion under their control and founded institutions that, although founded on old shamanic practices, were hostile to actual shamans and marginalized them. In Europe, for example, myths like the descent of Orpheus to the underworld or the harrowing of hell point to some survival of shamanism, but the cults associated with the these myths were marginalized as magic by religious authorities and could function only on the fringes of society.

Shamanism in Japan is described in the magisterial work of the Cambridge anthropologist Carmen Blacker titled *The Catalpa Bow: A Study of Shamanic Practices in Japan*. Although Japanese religion is much closer to older shamanic practices, the same marginalization occurred there, and traditional shamans either became ritual functionaries in temples stripped of any concept of shamanic powers or else were pushed to the margins of society. The *miko*, or female medium, for example, came to be either a dancer in temple ceremonies or a figure of village life, marginal to the imperial court, temples, and other institutions. A *miko* would have been married to a male shaman, who would help to induce her trance through playing a musical instrument as she danced herself into an ecstatic state. He gained this power by making the shamanic voyage to the other world (conceived in Japan to be either at the bottom of the sea or at the place of sunrise or sunset), but only the *miko* herself was capable of receiving a spirit from there. As Blacker explains,

> the medium or the *miko*... can enter a state of trance in which the spiritual apparition may possess her, penetrate inside her body and use her voice to name itself and to make its utterance. She is therefore primarily a transmitter, a vessel though whom the spiritual beings, having left their world to enter ours, can make their communications to us in a comprehensible way.

Once the *miko* was speaking in the voice of a spirit, she could be interrogated, usually about the likelihood of the success or failure of that year's crop. Accordingly, the *miko*'s trances usually took place during the spring planting festival, but there are cases in which government officials would have a *miko* enter a trance to provide information about government business. The *Kojiki* chronicle describes the emperor Keiko consulting a *miko*. The emperor asks the spirit whether he ought to attack a certain rebellious hill tribe but is instead ordered to invade Korea. When he refuses, he drops dead on the spot, but his successor makes sure to obey the spirit's command.

The consultation of a *miko* or medium by a Heian magistrate in "In a Grove," then, is exceptional, but it must be motivated by the impossibility of resolving the contradictory evidence offered by the witnesses, both of whom confessed to the same murder, and the desire to get at the truth, even if by unorthodox means. Akutagawa had ample precedent in the widespread folk practice of shamanic mediumship throughout Japanese history and even in a few instances where officials as high as the emperor turned to this kind of direct interrogation of the spirits. Thus the addition of the medium's testimony to his story seems to grow out of an authentic tradition. At the same time, the shamanic practice introduces an irrational and antisocial element that heightens the effect of the confusion readers of "In a Grove" feel before its ambiguities and contradictions and evokes the decadent pessimism of Western literature. It exploits the conjunction of traditional shamanism in Japan, which survives even today, with the Western phenomenon of spiritualism, which was making inroads into Japan and into Akutagawa's own intellectual circle just at the time the story was written in the early 1920s.

Source: Bradley A. Skeen, Critical Essay on "In a Grove," in *Short Stories for Students*, Gale, Cengage Learning, 2012.

Howard Hibbett

In the following excerpt, Hibbett discusses the themes used by Akutagawa in the short stories in the collection Rashomon and Other Stories.

To sketch the background and temperament of Akutagawa Ryūnosuke is to risk a melancholy cliché. He was brilliant, sensitive, cynical, neurotic; he lived in Tokyo, went to the University, taught briefly, and joined the literary staff of a newspaper. Even his early suicide (in 1927, at thirty-five) only heightens the portrait of a modern Japanese intellectual, the double victim of an unsympathetic society and a split culture. But it is a vague composite portrait. For Akutagawa himself, aloof, elusive, individual, remains withdrawn behind the polished facade of his collected works. All that needs to be known about their author, besides the name stamped on the binding, may be found within these poems, essays, miscellaneous writings, and more than a hundred beautifully finished stories.

The stories have a dazzling and perhaps deceptive sheen. Superficial critics called Akutagawa precious, or decadent, or dismissed him as a fatiguingly clever dilettante. Unprepared for the strength of his later satires, they supposed him to care only for the superb texture of his prose. Translation protects us from the seductions of this style, yet encourages a similar error, since the nuances of Akutagawa's prose are what conveys the essence of his thought. Like Natsume Sōseki and Mori Ōgai, whom he admired, Akutagawa used his language delicately, precisely, and with a richness enhanced by a knowledge of several literatures. It is significant that his first published writings were translations of Yeats and Anatole France. He remarked once that words must yield more than the bare dictionary meanings; he had a poet's feeling for their shapes and flavors, as well as their ambiguities, and he combined them with such freshness and economy that his phrasing never lacks distinction. Like Picasso, Akutagawa often varied his style, but always, whatever the particular blend of vernacular and mandarin, he controlled it with scrupulous precision. A master of tone, he gave his stories a cool classic surface, colored but never marred by the wit and warmth underlying that perfect glaze. The composure of his style is undisturbed even by vivid accents of the sordid or the bizarre.

Detachment was a key strategy to Akutagawa. As a narrator, he liked to be unseen, impersonal; he cultivated the oblique glance. When he did enter his stories, it was usually in the slight role of the observer or the suave self-effacing compiler. Old tales and legends, historical settings of the remote Heian Period or the feudal ages which followed—these he used not to turn his elaborate erudition to account, but to enrich and extend the implications of his themes, and to maintain aesthetic distance. The early era of Christian conversion in Japan, in the sixteenth century, was a favorite of his; in *Hōkyōnin no shi (The Martyr)* he exploited it to the point of hoax by supporting an archaic style with a source reference which, after an interval for learned controversy, he acknowledged to be fictitious. It suited his ironic taste to play the illusionist who leaves his audience staring blankly into a mirror.

But Akutagawa did more than deceive scholars and baffle the unwary: he antagonized ruling critical opinion. His attention to style, his preference for techniques of indirection and restraint, his indifference to current dogma—such attitudes were heresy to both the leading literary schools. The Proletarian writers, flourishing in the '20's, found nothing in common between Akutagawa's subtle stories and their own carefully chosen but grossly cut slices-of-life. The Naturalists, their rivals, had moved toward romantic individualism, forgetting Zola's concept of social inquiry. Dominant since the Russo-Japanese War, they sanctioned only the literary method to which, in the name of the first-person-singular *shishōsetsu*, their successors still adhere. This was the Confession, ranging from the sentimental memoir to the clinical report of an author's sexual life. Despite the exhaustion of the autobiographical form of fiction after Proust, these novelists went on eagerly probing their wounds and laying themselves open to reproach; while Akutagawa, unmoved by the exhibition of so many tedious egos, went his own way. A few of his stories suggest maliciously that confession itself may be false. *Yabu no naka (In a Grove)*, for example, converts an old melodramatic tale into a series of conflicting statements which undermine our prosaic confidence in distinguishing between subjective and objective, truth and fiction. Even the dark testaments which he left before suicide contain flashes of mockery to perplex the straightforward reader.

There are enough Swiftian touches in Akutagawa to show his hatred of stupidity, greed, hypocrisy, and the rising jingoism of the day. But Akutagawa's artistic integrity kept him from joining his contemporaries in easy social criticism or naive introspection. If, too often, his finely enameled miniatures seemed cold, over-subtilized, worn thin by an obsessive critical sense, still they are never merely decorative. What he did was to question the values of his society, dramatize the complexities of human psychology, and study, with a Zen taste for paradox, the precarious balance of illusion and reality. He developed a variety of techniques—from realism to fantasy, symbolism to surrealism—and used all of them in the search for poetic truth. Akutagawa was both intellectual and artist, and it was the quality of his artistry that enabled him to explore these difficult problems as deeply as he did, and to give his perceptions such exquisite and durable form.

Source: Howard Hibbett, Introduction to *Rashomon and Other Stories*, Charles E. Tuttle, 1952, pp. 9–13.

SOURCES

Akutagawa, Ryūnosuke, "In a Grove," in *The Essential Akutagawa*, edited by Seiji M. Lippit, Marsilio, 1999, pp. 103–14.

Blacker, Carmen, *The Catalpa Bow: A Study of Shamanic Practices in Japan*, 2nd ed., Mandala, 1992, pp. 49–63, 161–250.

Borges, Jorge Luis, Foreword to *The Essential Akutagawa*, edited by Seiji M. Lippit, Marsilio, 1999, pp. vii–ix.

Boyer, Pascal, *Religion Explained: The Evolutionary Origins of Religious Thought*, Basic Books, 2002, pp. 1–168.

Clottes, Jean, and David Lewis-Williams, "Paleolithic Art and Religion," in *A Handbook of Ancient Religions*, edited by John R. Hinnells, Cambridge University Press, 2007, pp. 7–45.

Ikegami, Eiko, *The Taming of the Samurai: Honorific Individualism and the Making of Modern Japan*, Harvard University Press, 1999, pp. 95–117.

Keene, Donald, *Dawn to the West: Japanese Literature of the Modern Era*, Vol. 1, *Fiction*, Holt, Rinehart and Winston, 1984, pp. 556–93.

The Kojiki: Japanese Records of Ancient Matters, translated by Basil Hall Chamberlain, Asiatic Society of Japan, 1883, pp. 284–85.

Kurachi, Tsuneo, "Akutagawa Ryūnosuke and Spiritualism," in *Comparative Literature Studies*, Vol. 28, No. 3, 1991, pp. 259–70.

Lippit, Seiji M., Introduction to *The Essential Akutagawa*, edited by Seiji M. Lippit, Marsilio, 1999, pp. xi–xxviii.

Napier, Susan J., *The Fantastic in Modern Japanese Literature: The Subversion of Modernity*, Psychology Press, 1996, pp. 14–15.

Smith, Robert J., *Ancestor Worship in Contemporary Japan*, Stanford University Press, 1974, pp. 39–68.

Tansman, Alan, *The Aesthetics of Japanese Fascism*, University of California Press, 2009, pp. 39–42.

Urys, Marian, ed., "How a Man Who Was Accompanying His Wife to Tanba Province Got Trussed Up at Oeyama," in *Tales of Times Now Past: Sixty-two Stories from a Medieval Japanese Collection*, translated by Marian Urys, University of California Press, 1979, pp. 184–85.

Yamanouchi, Hisaaki, *The Search for Authenticity in Modern Japanese Literature*, Cambridge University Press, 1978, pp. 88–89.

Yu, Beongcheon, *Akutagawa: An Introduction*, Wayne State University Press, 1972, pp. 26–36.

FURTHER READING

Browning, Robert, *The Ring and the Book, with the Author's Latest Corrections*, Houghton, Mifflin, 1895.

Originally published in 1868–1869, this verse novel tells the story of a murder case among the Roman nobility of the seventeenth century. At the time, testimony in criminal cases in the Papal States was given in written form, and Browning bought documents relating to the case at a used-book stall. He fictionalized and versified his source. Each of the twelve chapters goes over the same facts from the point of view of a different witness, with great variation in specifics. This work may have been an inspiration for "In a Grove."

Flammarion, Camille, *Mysterious Psychic Forces: An Account of the Author's Investigations in Psychical Research, Together with Those of Other European Savants*, Small Maynard, 1907.

This is an English translation of one of the spiritualist books that Akutagawa was familiar with and which provided a background for the séance conducted in "In a Grove."

Hearn, Lafcadio, *Kwaidan: Stories and Studies of Strange Things*, Houghton, Mifflin, 1904.

Kwaidan (more properly *kaidan*) is Japanese for "strange tales," roughly meaning fairy tales, and is the title of a genre that was widely collected by Japanese scholars and writers from peasants at the end of the nineteenth century. Hearn re-collected several such stories from written sources and published them in popular English editions, including *Kwaidan*, which has been frequently reprinted. Four of the stories were exquisitely filmed in 1964 by Masaki Kobayashi and released in the United States under the title *Kwaidan*.

Kelsey, W. Michael, *Konjaku monogatari-shū*, Twayne's World Author Series, No. 621, Twayne Publishers, 1982.

This is a critical study of the collection of Heian period folktales that contains the original version of "In a Grove."

Poe, Edgar Allan, *Poetry and Tales*, Library of America, 1984.

Poe exerted considerable influence on Akutagawa through his tales of mystery and the supernatural and his romantic view of the past in, among other tales, "The Gold Bug," "Ligea," and "The Murders in the Rue Morgue."

SUGGESTED SEARCH TERMS

Ryunosuke Akutagawa

In a Grove AND Ryunosuke Akutagawa

Rashomon

spiritualism

shamanism

Ambrose Bierce AND Moonlit Road

Edgar Allan Poe

Akira Kurosawa

Japanese literature

Heian period

Kojiki

The Law of Life

JACK LONDON

1901

"The Law of Life" is a short story by the American writer Jack London, one of the most famous and most commercially successful fiction writers of the late nineteenth and early twentieth centuries. The story was first published in the March 1901 edition of *McClure's* magazine, an influential monthly that printed serious works of literature as well as investigative journalism and illustrations. The story appeared in book form for the first time in London's third collection, *Children of the Frost* (1902), and has been reprinted in countless collections of London's work, as well as in multiple author anthologies, in the intervening years, including the Library of America's 1982 collection, *Jack London: Novels and Stories*.

"The Law of Life" is set in the Klondike region of Canada's modern Yukon Territory, where London himself and thousands of others went between 1896 and 1899 to look for gold. (Until 1898, the Yukon River region was part of the Northwest Territories.) London set many of his early stories in the Klondike, including the novel that many consider to be his master work, *The Call of the Wild* (1903). The main character of "The Law of Life" is Koskoosh, an elderly former chief of an Inuit tribe. As the story begins, Koskoosh sits alone in the frozen winter with a small fire, listening to his tribe packing up their camp and preparing to move to a place where there might be more food. Koskoosh, weak and blind, waits for the fire to go out and for death to slowly take him. He knows that he

Jack London *(The Library of Congress)*

can no longer contribute to his tribe, and he accepts his isolation and death as the natural way of things.

AUTHOR BIOGRAPHY

London was born John Griffith Chaney on January 12, 1876, in San Francisco, California. Many critics believe that his father was William Henry Chaney, but London never knew for sure, and the two only met on one occasion. His mother, Flora Wellman, married John London the year her son was born, and the writer later took his stepfather's last name. During his own lifetime, London was as well known for his adventurous life as for his writing. In his teens, he did odd jobs and factory work, bought his own small boat, and found work stealing oysters; later, he became an agent with the California Fish Patrol, joined a seal-hunting expedition, and then traveled around the country for several months on his own—all before graduating high school. He was a reader and a writer from the beginning, spending his spare time in the Oakland Public Library and publishing his first story, "Story of a Typhoon off the Coast of Japan," when he was sixteen. He enrolled in the University of California at Berkeley in 1896, but he ran out of money after one semester and turned his energies to writing.

In July 1897, London joined thousands of others in heading for the Klondike River in Canada's Yukon region, where gold had been discovered. He found the Klondike thrilling and absorbed all he could from the rough men and women he met prospecting, from the Inuit people of the region, and from the brutal landscape. A bout of scurvy forced him to return home in the summer of 1898, no wealthier than when he had arrived. But his memories of the northland stayed with him for the rest of his life, and several of his most famous works, including "The Law of Life" (1901), *The Call of the Wild* (1902), *White Fang* (1906), and "To Build a Fire" (1908), drew on those experiences. It took him a while to earn a living writing; having married Bessie Madden in 1900 and fathered two daughters with her, he had several mouths to feed. But after*The Call of the Wild* was established as a success, he quickly became famous and wealthy.

In 1904, London began something of a second writing career with the novel *The Sea Wolf*, the first of many stories and novels populated by sailors and fishermen. His marriage to Madden ended, and in 1905, he married Charmain Kittredge. For the next several years, he returned again and again to the sea. He built a sailboat, the *Snark*, and he and Charmain sailed to Tahiti, Hawaii, and Australia.

London lived a short life, but he sought adventure and continued to write nearly until the end. As a reporter he covered the Boer War in southern Africa, the Russo-Japanese War, the San Francisco earthquake, and the Mexican Revolution. He published more than four dozen books, lectured at major universities, and involved himself for a time in socialist politics. When he died on November 22, 1916, on his ranch in Glen Ellen, California, he was mourned as a national hero. The reason for his death at the age of forty seemed to be a combination of dysentery contracted in Mexico, alcohol abuse, and kidney failure.

PLOT SUMMARY

The main action of "The Law of Life" takes place during the last few hours of an old man's life. It is told by a third-person narrator but follows the thoughts and sensations of one character, Koskoosh, an old man who was formerly the chief of an Inuit tribe in the Klondike region of Canada's Yukon Territory. As the story opens, old Koskoosh sits alone outside the tribe's camp. He is nearly blind, but his hearing is still sharp, and he listens to the sounds of the women packing up the camp, preparing to move on to a place where the hunting might be better. He hears his granddaughter, Sit-cum-to-ha, struggling to harness the sled dogs, which will drag the lodges and other supplies across the snow; he hears individual lodges being taken down and packed on the sleds; he hears Koo-tee, a weak and sick child who will probably not live long, fussing and being comforted by the mother.

Koskoosh plays no part in the packing, and it soon becomes clear that he will not accompany the tribe on their journey. Instead, he will sit alone, with only a small fire and a small pile of firewood, and wait for death. This is the way it has always been done, and Koskoosh does not resist his fate. As he thinks to himself, "Death wait[s]," and there is no avoiding it. He imagines that the sick child, Koo-tee, might die on the journey, his body buried beneath the frozen tundra, but he imagines it with no emotion. He hears the last sled, and the last bark from the dogs, and then he is alone to face his "last bitter hour."

However, he hears a soft footstep of a moccasin in the snow, then feels a hand rest on his head. His son, the current chief, has come to say goodbye. Not all sons do this for their fathers, and Koskoosh is quietly grateful and proud. The son asks, "Is it well with you?" The people have left, the son explains, and they are moving quickly because they have not eaten well for some time. Koskoosh assures him that all is well, that he knows he is old and near death, and that he is ready. The son walks away, and now Koskoosh is truly alone. He reaches out his hand to check his woodpile and thinks about how the fire will slowly die out, and he will slowly freeze to death. "It was easy," he thinks. "All men must die."

Koskoosh thinks about the relationship between nature and humans as he has been brought up to understand it. Nature is concerned only with the perpetuation of each species, he thinks, not with the survival of any individual person or other individual creature. The purpose of humans is to bring forth children to keep the species going, and once that purpose is achieved, nature has no interest in them. Women in their youth are pretty and lively so that they will attract the attention of men, who will father their children. Once they have raised their children, nature has no purpose for them, and when the tribe faces famine or a long journey, old women will be left behind. Men who are too old to contribute to their tribe are also useless, as Koskoosh is now. Koskoosh remembers leaving his own father behind one winter, and he thinks about the life cycles of mosquitoes, squirrels, and nature's other creatures. Death is a part of life, and it will come in its own time, no matter what a person might do. This inevitability is "the law of life."

He remembers a time when his people faced a famine that lasted for years, when many people—including his own mother—starved to death. And he remembers times when there was plenty to eat, the women produced many children, and the men

MEDIA ADAPTATIONS

- "The Law of Life," read by William Dufris, was released as an MP3 download by Word of Mouth in 2009.
- "The Law of Life" is included in several audio collections of Jack London short stories on CD, including Tantor Media's 2011 collection *To Build a Fire, and Other Stories*, read by Patrick Lawlor; Audio Book Contractors' 2009 collection *Jack London Short Stories*, read by Flo Gibson; and Request Audiobooks' 2006 collection, *Love of Life, and Other Stories*, read by David Birney and Arte Johnson.
- Russian film director Rishat Gilmetdinov filmed an animated adaptation of "The Law of Life" in 2009, with music by Douglas Blue Feather. The short film was screened at the Cannes Film Festival in 2009 and is available to be viewed on YouTube.

were well enough fed to fight with other tribes. Next his thoughts wander to his childhood, when he and his best friend, Zing-ha, tracked an old moose that was being pursued by a pack of wolves. Following the trail, they were able to read the story of how the old moose was cut out of the herd and chased for hours; they could see where the moose fell down and fought his way back to his feet, and where he succeeded in trampling one of the wolves to death. Eagerly, the boys followed the trail, finally creeping along on their bellies and reaching the clearing in time to see the last moments of the moose's life. The narrator does not describe the moose being torn apart by wolves but reveals that Koskoosh can still picture it clearly; though the reader cannot see the scene, the old man's "dim eyes watched the end played out." He remembers other vivid moments from his time as chief, when he led his people, gave good advice, killed many members of the Pelly tribe, and once killed a white man in hand-to-hand combat.

The fire continues to burn, and Koskoosh slowly adds his remaining sticks. For a fleeting moment he wishes his Sit-cum-to-ha had been more attentive and left him a larger pile of wood, but then he remembers that in his own youth he did not pay much attention to the older folks, either. In another quickly passing thought, he wonders if his son might change his mind and come back for him. But he is alone, and he knows it.

Suddenly he hears the cry of a wolf, and the picture of the wounded, bloody moose from long ago comes back to his mind. This time, the narrator describes those last awful moments—the blood, the eyes and fangs of the wolves, and the way they circled the moose, slowly drawing their circle smaller and smaller until they were upon him. Koskoosh feels the cold muzzle of a wolf against his cheek, and with his instinct for survival he brandishes a flaming stick at the wolf to make him back away. The wolf retreats, but calls out to his pack, and soon there are many wolves gathered around Koskoosh in a circle. Koskoosh remembers the moose, remembers that death will come whether he fights against it or not, and drops the stick into the snow. He rests his head on his knees and waits.

CHARACTERS

The Beaver

The Beaver is the grandson of Zing-ha. He is attracted to Sit-cum-to-ha, Koskoosh's granddaughter.

The Chief

The chief is Koskoosh's son, described as "stalwart and strong, head man of the tribesmen, and a mighty hunter." He shouts orders to the women as they pack up the camp, and before he leaves for the last time, he stops next to his father to be sure that the old man is well and that he has a supply of firewood. The sound of the chief's footsteps fading away is the last human sound Koskoosh hears.

Koo-tee

Koo-tee is a small, sickly child of the tribe. As he listens to the tribe packing to leave, Koskoosh hears Koo-tee whimpering and pictures the child's probable death and burial in the frozen ground.

Koskoosh

Koskoosh, the story's protagonist, is a former chief of his tribe, replaced in his old age by his son. As the story opens he is sitting alone next to a small fire; old and blind, he listens to the tribe packing up the camp and preparing to move on to a place where they hope to find more food. As is the custom—the law of life—Koskoosh will not accompany the tribe when they leave; he is too old to contribute to the hunting and would only slow the tribe down as they hurry to a new home. Instead, he will sit as long as his firewood lasts, and when the fire dies down he will slowly freeze to death. Koskoosh accepts his fate, as his father did before him.

Waiting to die, Koskoosh thinks about his relationship with nature and contemplates his life. He remembers times of plenty and times of famine; he remembers his old friend Zing-ha; he remembers the great deeds he did as chief. Finally, the fire begins to die down and Koskoosh feels the cold. For the first time, he can hear wolves howling and gathering in a circle around him. For a moment he considers trying to fight them off with a flaming stick, but, remembering the law of life, he drops the stick and waits for the end.

Sit-cum-to-ha

Sit-cum-to-ha is Koskoosh's granddaughter, his daughter's daughter. She works so busily helping the other women pack up that she has no time to think about her grandfather. It was her job to gather firewood for Koskoosh to keep near him at the end. As unconcerned with the old folks of her tribe as Koskoosh was himself as a youth, Sit-cum-to-ha is consumed with thoughts of the young man whose attention she has attracted, and she has gathered only a small pile of wood for her grandfather.

The Son

See The Chief

Zing-ha

Zing-ha was Koskoosh's childhood friend. As he waits for his death, Koskoosh remembers a day in his youth when he and Zing-ha tracked a moose who was being pursued by wolves, and found him in time to see the wolves drag him down and kill him. Throughout his life, Koskoosh remembers, Zing-ha was an unusually skilled tracker and hunter. He died one winter in an accident, falling through an airhole as he hunted on the Yukon River.

THEMES

Death

Although the title of this story is "The Law of Life," the overriding theme of the story is death. The theme is introduced, as theses often are in formal essays, at the end of the first paragraph, where the narrator reports of Koskoosh, "he was very close to death now." The story, of course, follows Koskoosh in his last hours, but most of his thoughts are of the deaths of others as he awaits his own: the impending death of the sickly child Koo-tee; the long-ago deaths of "other old men whose sons had not waited after the tribe"; the old women, their years of child rearing behind them, who had also been left behind; the mosquitoes, tree squirrels, and rabbits; his own father and his mother; a missionary; members of other tribes killed in battle; the moose Koskoosh and Zing-ha watched being torn apart by wolves; Zing-ha himself, who "fell through an air-hole on the Yukon"; and a "strange white man he had killed, knife to knife, in open fight."

The deaths represent a range of causes. The child will die of weakness and illness; several of the old people effectively commit suicide to avoid being a drain on their community; Koskoosh's mother and several members of the tribe die of starvation; the moose is killed for its meat; Zing-ha dies in an accident; the white man loses what seems to be a fair fight. Yet all of the deaths are equal—and all equally unimportant. There is no sense in struggling to stay alive, Koskoosh thinks, because death is always waiting, and death does not care about individual creatures, human or animal. A person's only task is to produce offspring, and fulfilling this task will preserve the group, but not the individual. As Koskoosh explains to himself, "Did he not perform it, he died. Did he perform it, it was all the same, he died. Nature did not care."

Although he thinks only of death, Koskoosh does not fear it. He plans, as his own father did, to slowly feed his small fire until he runs out of wood, and then to slowly freeze to death. He expects to feel "numbness" and then to "rest." "It was easy," he thinks; "all men must die." But life is a strong force within him, and even as he acknowledges its futility, he admires the ferocity of the moose's struggle for life against a host of strong, well-rested opponents. Koskoosh remembers that the moose "had done his task long since, but none the less was life dear to him." Why is this the most vivid memory in Koskoosh's last hours? Is he considering that he, too, might rise up and struggle against death? In the end, his struggle is only instinctive, as the moose's was. Koskoosh does not think about resisting, but his body responds instinctively. When the narrator describes Koskoosh's instinctive sensations, it is as though his body is acting on its own: "A chill passed over his body," and then, "His hand shot into the fire and dragged out a burning faggot." Both actions are automatic, not guided by Koskoosh's conscious mind. But it is with his conscious mind that he gives up the struggle; when he "drop[s] the blazing stick" and "drop[s] his head," the verbs are active. In the end, Koskoosh accepts the law of life. He accepts his own death.

Inuit Culture

Children of the Frost was London's third collection of short stories about the people who lived in and passed through the Alaska Peninsula and the Klondike region of Canada's Yukon Territory, and many of the stories include characters who belong to Inuit culture. But *Children of the Frost* is different from the other collections in that many of the stories, including "The Law of Life," have Inuits as the main characters and are told from the point of view of an Inuit narrator. This story depicts a custom of self-sacrifice that London believed—rightly or wrongly—to be common among the Inuit. The story presents this custom as an act of bravery and attempts to explain the reasoning behind it. As Koskoosh sits and waits for death, he thinks back over his life, and through his thoughts London offers glimpses of the life of Koskoosh's tribe for a

TOPICS FOR FURTHER STUDY

- Watch the short animated film version of "The Law of Life" by Rishat Gilmetdinov (available on YouTube). List the major differences between the film and the story. For example, in the film there is more ceremony involved in leaving Koskoosh behind, and more attention is paid to Koskoosh's history with the wolves. Write an essay in which you examine the important differences and explain whether the adaptation changes London's essential message about the relationship between human life and nature.
- If "The Law of Life" were to be filmed with human actors, it would likely contain more dialogue than London provides in his story. Imagine that you were going to film the scene in which the young Koskoosh and his friend Zing-ha track the injured moose and watch him die. Write out the dialogue of the two boys as they pursue and then watch the moose. Alternately, write a scene in which the two boys have returned to camp and are telling their story to their friends. If you wish, film the scene and post it to your Web page or YouTube and invite classmates to review your work.
- Research the Inuit people who have lived in the Yukon region of Canada (formerly part of the Northwest Territories). Prepare a PowerPoint presentation in which you illustrate traditional forms of housing, clothing, and food preparation of the tribes. Include historical information about the tribes as well.
- Think about how a faith or ethnic community you belong to treats its oldest members. Interview an elderly member of that group to find out how she or he sees the role of elders. With your classmates, create a shared Wiki or blog on which you present and discuss the different ideas generated. Be sure to include your understanding of Koskoosh's tribe.
- Read through picture books that reflect the relationship between a young person and a grandparent. Examples include *Halmoni and the Picnic*, by Sook Nyul Choi (1993); *Grandmother's Dreamcatcher*, by Becky Ray McCain (1998); and *Farolitos for Abuelo*, by Rudolfo Anaya (1998). Prepare a picture book about your own relationship with a grandparent, using paper and art materials or computer software.
- Research the growing famine of the early 2010s in East Africa, where a long drought has brought millions of people to the point of starvation. Find out what is being done to help feed them. Write a paper in which you explore whether people in the twenty-first century are better able to handle periods of famine than Koskoosh's tribe was at the end of the nineteenth century. Alternately, organize a debate or panel discussion presenting a range of ideas on this topic.

readership hungry for information about the frozen North. There are small details about sleds and sled dogs, about how clothing and lodges are made of hides and skins, and about the landscape, and there are references to a chief and a shaman. Koskoosh refers to the Pellys and the Tananas, or the various tribes who lived along the Pelly and Tanana rivers, tributaries of the Yukon. As London captures it, the language Koskoosh and his son speak is deliberate, formal, and poetic. London depicts Koskoosh and his tribe having a closer connection with and a deeper understanding of nature than a typical European city dweller. Koskoosh's son can tell that snow is coming, Koskoosh is aware of the life cycles of the rabbit and the mosquito, and the tribe's fortunes rise and fall with those of the salmon and the caribou. Through "The Law of Life," London introduces his readers to Koskoosh's tribe and to their ways of life and death.

A North American Indian in full dress in a teepee
(Elena Shchipkova / Shutterstock.com)

There is also one small comment that reveals the bias inherent in London's understanding of the indigenous tribes of the Yukon Territory. When Koskoosh ponders nature's indifference to the individual in favor of the survival of an entire species, the narrator comments, "This was the deepest abstraction old Koskoosh's barbaric mind was capable of, but he grasped it firmly." This remark, made by an omniscient narrator in a story written by a white man, published in a magazine with an overwhelmingly white readership, reflects a sense of white superiority that was not uncommon at the beginning of the twentieth century. Throughout the rest of the story the tone is dignified and respectful, and surely readers are intended to admire Koskoosh's understanding and acceptance of his duty. The story presents a people and a way of life that is undoubtedly striking to most readers, and through its unquestioning presentation of the law of life it invites readers to see that in the eyes of nature—if not in the eyes of men—all people are the same.

STYLE

Naturalism

"The Law of Life" is an example of a work growing out of the literary movement known as naturalism, which flourished at the end of the nineteenth and the beginning of the twentieth centuries in Europe and the United States. American writers of naturalism, who included Stephen Crane, Theodore Dreiser, Jack London, and others, were influenced by the writings of biologist Charles Darwin and of one of his colleague's, the economist and philosopher Herbert Spencer, who had used the phrase "survival of the fittest" to explain why some groups succeeded and others failed in the struggle for life. Naturalist writers depicted a world in which humans were not elevated above the other animals and in which nature—not any supernatural being—was in control and was indifferent to humans and animals alike. The only struggle that mattered was the struggle to survive, and that struggle was typically seen as a violent fight against nature itself.

"The Law of Life" announces by its very title that it is formed with the philosophy of naturalism. As Koskoosh well understands, there is nothing he can do to change what is going to happen to him. Some years there is plenty to eat, and the people are happy and healthy; in other years there is famine, and people die. Nothing they do can ensure an ideal outcome. It may have been easy for people to accept this philosophy in the remote wilderness, in a society without technology; indeed, there is little that people dependent on natural cycles can do to increase their food supply. But the notion of only the fittest surviving applies, in London's stories, to the individual as well as to the tribe. Koskoosh reflects on the indifference of nature and realizes that "Nature was not kindly to the flesh. She had no concern for that concrete thing called the individual." Nature calls humans to perform only the task of producing children, but even fulfilling that task will not save one's life; both those who have children and those who do not die eventually. Because Koskoosh is old, weak, blind, and tired, it is his time to die, just as the moose that he and Zing-ha followed died at his proper time, when he was "an old one.... An old one who cannot keep up with the herd."

For a moment, in his inevitable terror, Koskoosh thinks he will try to defy the law of life and fight for his own survival. He believes for a quick, instinctive moment that he can choose his own fate. But he is wrong and quickly realizes it. "Why should he cling to life?" he asks himself, and he drops his torch. Koskoosh's death is not meant to be seen as a failure. The world is the way it is. The important struggle here is not against an indifferent universe—that is a battle humans can never win. Instead, knowing the kind of world he inhabits, Koskoosh struggles to control his own emotions and fears, and he succeeds in overcoming his instinctive terrors, to die with grace and dignity.

Point of View

One of the key structural aspects of "The Law of Life" is London's decision to narrate the story from a third-person limited point of view. The story's narrative voice is called third-person because it is a voice observing the story from outside the action, referring to Koskoosh as "he"; it is limited because the narrator can see only into Koskoosh's mind and has no knowledge of what other characters—Koskoosh's son, for example—are thinking and feeling. The narrator is sympathetic to Koskoosh and reveals his changing thoughts with deep insight. This is demonstrated in the story's first sentence, "Old Koskoosh listened greedily." A dispassionate narrator, or another character observing Koskoosh sitting on the ground, could perhaps tell simply by looking that he was listening, but only a narrator able to peer into the man's mind could know that he listened "greedily." In the same way, the narrator is able to relate Koskoosh's moments of panic and reassurance, his contentment, his memories of famine and feast, his momentary resentment of Sit-cum-to-ha's careless disregard, and his ultimate loneliness and surrender.

The use of the third person solved one practical problem for London: if he had told the story in the first person, having Koskoosh narrate his own story, it would have made the ending somewhat ridiculous. Who would he be telling his story to? How could he describe his own last moments? But the third person also gives Koskoosh a standing that he might not otherwise attain. By having an outside narrator calmly relate Koskoosh's struggles and his ultimate acceptance of death, London creates an Inuit protagonist of dignity and strength—a type of character that was a rare achievement in American literature at the turn of the twentieth century.

HISTORICAL CONTEXT

Klondike Gold Rush

The brief period between 1897 and 1903 was a remarkable time in the history of North America: it may have been the last time hoards of people cast aside their former lives and raced off to a largely uncharted wilderness to find fortune and fame. It began in 1896, when gold was discovered near the Klondike River in the Alaska Peninsula. As soon as word got out, tens of thousands of people—most, but not all, men, and most, but not all, American—made their way to the area looking for gold. Most returned with nothing, and the Klondike gold rush did not last long.

As Jeanne Campbell Reesman explains in her study *Jack London*, London was perfectly positioned to take part in the gold rush. In July 1897, he was healthy, single, twenty-one years old and struggling to make a living as a writer, having withdrawn from an unsuccessful attempt at college. He was not the only one struggling. During the 1890s the United States was in what would now be recognized as a recession. Banks were failing, and unemployment was high. For unattached young men like London, the lure of leaving the site of past failures and finding gold was irresistible. News of the discovery of gold reached San Francisco, where London was living, on July 14, 1897, when a group of miners arrived on a ship transporting a ton of newly discovered gold. Eleven days later, London sailed out of San Francisco bound for the Klondike.

London's trip was difficult and dangerous, especially because he was among the first to go, and improvements in the trails had not yet been made, nor had the towns that welcomed and launched later miners been established. Reesman describes London's "400-mile trek from Dyea Beach [Alaska] over the rugged Chilkoot Pass, through the dangerous White Horse Rapids, and downriver to the mouth of the Stewart River" as "the adventure of a lifetime." Would-be miners carried hundreds of pounds of gear with them and had to use sleds and make several small trips back and forth because horses could not climb the steep mountain trails. After spending the winter

COMPARE & CONTRAST

- **1901:** Living in an inhospitable landscape with few natural resources, most Inuit peoples of Canada and the Alaska Peninsula have little or no contact with people of European descent.

  Today: After decades of being overwhelmed and absorbed by European culture, most of the Inuit peoples in Canada live in largely autonomous communities, and many feel that their hold on traditional culture is growing stronger again.

- **1901:** The population of the Yukon Territory is approximately 31,000 people.

  Today: The population of the Yukon Territory is still 31,000 people.

1901: Although wolves are being killed in great numbers in the western United States as farming and ranching expand, the wolves in the Alaska Peninsula and in the Yukon Territory remain largely undisturbed. Wolves are hunted for their fur by indigenous peoples, but only in limited numbers.

Today: There are approximately 4,500 to 5,000 wolves living in the Yukon Territory, according to the Wolf Conservation and Management Plan Review Committee, approximately the same number that have lived in the area for the last ten thousand years.

---

prospecting for gold, London returned home by way of a 2,000-mile raft trip on the winding Yukon River, "punctuated by occasional stops at Indian villages and trading posts ashore." Many people died in the pursuit of Klondike gold, freezing or falling to their deaths in the harsh landscape. London was one of many who suffered from scurvy, a disease that is caused by a lack of Vitamin C, normally obtained from fresh fruits and vegetables, and which causes painful swelling, fever, and loss of teeth.

London did not strike it rich in the Klondike, and his illness cut his adventure short. But he spent many nights listening to stories around the campfire, and he met the miners and Inuit and First Nations peoples who would later populate his most important works of fiction. When he returned home, he had journals filled with notes, tales, and character sketches that provided material for *The Call of the Wild*, *White Fang*, "To Build a Fire," "The Law of Life," and dozens of other stories. Hundreds of books were published about the gold rush, but only London's stories and the poems of Robert Service have endured. A small number of miners were more successful at finding gold. Reesman reports that by the end of the gold rush in 1903, "$100 million in gold dust and nuggets had been milked from the cold, muddy tributaries of the Yukon."

For the native peoples of the Alaska Peninsula and northwestern Canada, the Klondike gold rush meant a sudden influx of white people. The various tribes referred to as the Inuit, living in Alaska and Canada's Yukon and Northwest Territories, inhabited regions so remote that they were largely isolated from the western expansion that had so drastically affected the lives of native peoples in the United States. Except for the occasional missionary or prospector, their contact with whites was rare, and for the most part, the local Inuit peoples did not participate in the gold rush except as guides. Instead, they were able for several years to carry on with their lives as they had before gold was discovered. Although most of the whites left when the gold or their luck ran out, enough stayed behind that the Inuit way of life gradually changed, new technologies were adopted, and the indigenous peoples were eventually outnumbered and pushed aside.

A vintage portrait of an elderly American Indian man and his blanket (ChipPix / Shutterstock.com)

CRITICAL OVERVIEW

Although "The Law of Life" is frequently studied in middle-school and high-school literature courses—second among London's stories only to "To Build a Fire"—it has not attracted much critical attention; no major journal of literature has published a critical article devoted entirely to this story, and the major collections of critical essays on London ignore the story or devote only a paragraph or two to analyzing it. Perhaps the qualities that make "The Law of Life" a popular choice for classrooms, including its simple plot line and its bold treatment of theme and imagery, have given critics little to wrestle with, even as the story has proven popular with readers for more than a century.

After its 1901 magazine appearance, "The Law of Life" was published in London's third short-story collection, *Children of the Frost* (1902), a volume of stories featuring the indigenous peoples of the Alaska Peninsula and Canada's Yukon and Northwest Territories. London had attracted a following by this point, and *Children of the Frost* was reviewed in major newspapers and magazines. B. G. Lathrop, a regular book reviewer for the *San Francisco Call*, wrote about the book when it was published in 1902, calling London "the recognized authority in fiction dealing with the peoples of the frozen zone." The *New York Times* reviewed the book twice in 1902, introducing a controversy that continues to circle around London's work into the twenty-first century. The reviewer for the "Recent Fiction" column of the *New York Times*, published on October 25, praises London's portrayal of the native peoples who are at the heart of the stories as "ethnographical," surmising that "he must have listened 'viva voce' [by word of mouth] to the stories, the legends of the long past, as told him of the Indians." Weeks later, on December 6, the *New York Times* published a letter from Alaskan explorer William H. Dall, who declared, based on his personal experience in the Yukon, "There is absolutely no local color or verisimilitude in Mr. London's stories. His alleged Indians are not only absolutely unlike the Yukon Indians, but they are unlike any Indians whatsoever."

The degree to which London portrayed his indigenous characters (and, later in his career, other nonwhite characters) accurately and sympathetically has been much discussed by critics, most notably by Jacqueline M. Courbin in a 1978 *Jack London Newsletter* article, "Jack London's Portrayal of the Natives in His First Four Collections of Arctic Tales," and by Jeanne Campbell Reesman in a 2009 book, *Jack London's Racial Lives.* Courbin calls "The Law of Life" "certainly one of London's better stories" and includes it among a list of stories from *Children of the Frost* that are "complex, deeply human and universal in their implications." But she acknowledges that London had a conflicted understanding of the native peoples he encountered and portrayed, seeing their lives sometimes as "simple, peaceful and even idyllic," sometimes as "miserable and beastly." Reesman devotes her entire book to exploring how London could, on the one hand, believe strongly in white superiority and, on the other hand, portray nonwhites nobly; and she finds in *Children of the Frost* "some of London's most racially sensitive works."

Many critics have recognized the stories of *Children of the Frost* as being among London's best short fiction. James I. McClintock, in his

White Logic: Jack London's Short Stories (1976), singles out the collection for special praise, remarking, "no single volume of short stories is as consistent in quality of artistry and control of theme," and he identifies "The Law of Life" as "the most economically, and dramatically, conceived and written story in this volume." Reesman, this time in *Jack London: A Study of the Short Fiction* (1999), calls the volume London's "most compelling collection of Klondike stories." She makes only a brief reference to "The Law of Life," describing how the story conveys "nobility in the old man's death," unlike many of London's stories that show native peoples in defeat. Reesman notes, "It is unfortunate that this story is so often reprinted in anthologies without any related London tales."

CRITICISM

Cynthia A. Bily

Bily teaches at Macomb Community College in Michigan. In the following essay, she examines the narrator's careful diction in "The Law of Life."

When old Koskoosh faces death in Jack London's "The Law of Life," it is with an active understanding and acceptance of the laws of nature. He knows as he sits beside his small fire that he has only hours to live, and yet he sits there. He does not get up; he does not argue with his son or struggle to be included in the journey. Instead, he sits quietly, near enough to the rest of the tribe that he can distinguish voices and actions, even recognizing by sound alone the individual lodges being taken down. The others must be able to see him, though no one speaks to him or pays him any attention. It would be merely cruel if this forced isolation was personal, but this is the tradition—how it is always done. Koskoosh remembers other old men who have yielded their lives this way, including his own father, whom "he had abandoned . . . on an upper reach of the Klondike one winter." Because he knows his tribe's history and traditions, and because he knows the laws of Nature, Koskoosh accepts that this is the time he will die. But if it were that simple, that straightforward, there would be no story: a man accepts that it is time, waits patiently, and dies. What London has created is more complicated and more interesting than that. Koskoosh makes no serious outward or physical attempt to save his life, because he is a chief; but because he is also a man, he faces internal struggles that shape the story into a heroic battle.

> "IN THE LAST PARAGRAPH OF THE STORY, THE LANGUAGE IS A SWIRL OF ECHOES OF WHAT HAS COME BEFORE, AND MAN AND BEAST ARE SEEN AS TWO IMAGES OF THE SAME THING."

The story's third-person limited narrator gives few clues to Koskoosh's state of mind, but those brief clues are telling. As the story opens, Koskoosh is still attached to his tribe; the first sentence is "Old Koskoosh listened greedily." He is greedy—eager to hear what he can, to know what he can about the people with whom he has spent his life. Although the narrator states that Koskoosh's eyes "no longer gazed forth upon the things of the world," his mind is still on earthly things, and he "strain[s] his ears" to gather every detail about what the other people are doing. But although he is listening "greedily" for every detail about his people's activities, they are not so concerned about him; this contrast is emphasized in the opening paragraph, when the narrator explains that Koskoosh's granddaughter Sit-cum-to-ha is "too busy to waste a thought upon her broken grandfather." In the minds of the people, Koskoosh is already gone, and even to think of him while there is life-saving work to do would be a "waste." Koskoosh knows this, and for the moment he is not simply alone but "forlorn." In the opening paragraphs of the story, then, Koskoosh is physically ready for death—he is seated obediently out of the way next to his small fire—but he has not yet broken his emotional and psychological ties with his people.

In the second paragraph, Koskoosh reacts instinctively to his approaching death: the thought makes him "panicky," but only "for the moment." He is not consciously resisting his fate, and he is able to fight down the panic in an instant. With the comfort of a small fire that will die out gradually, he will freeze to death relatively painlessly, as the elderly among his people have done for generations. Koskoosh controls his momentary panic by touching the little pile of wood, which makes him feel "reassured" that his encounter with death will be peaceful.

WHAT DO I READ NEXT?

- In London's "To Build a Fire," originally published in 1908, an inexperienced white man in the Klondike falls through ice and is soaked while out on the trail alone, with only a dog for company. His life is at stake. It can be found in *Jack London: Novels and Stories*, a 1982 Library of America issue, as well as many other anthologies.
- *The Call of the Wild* (1902), London's most famous work, is a short novel written in the formula of a heroic quest. The protagonist is Buck, a domesticated dog who is brought against his will to the Klondike and gradually recovers his essential wildness.
- *Two Old Women*, by Velma Wallis, is a dramatic and inspirational novel about two women left behind by their tribe during a time of famine in the Yukon River valley in Alaska. The story, published in 1994, is based on a traditional legend of the Athabascan Indians.
- *Northern Voices: Inuit Writings in English* (1992) is a rich, extensive collection of tales, myths, poems, historical documents, and memoirs by Inuit writers and storytellers of northern Canada. The editor, Penny Patrone, introduces each item and establishes its historical context.
- Jenny Downham's *Before I Die* is a novel told in the first person by sixteen-year-old Tessa, a girl dying of leukemia. The novel, published in 2007, is surprisingly humorous and optimistic, following Tessa's internal life as she faces death.
- The best biography of London for young readers is Daniel Dyer's *Jack London*, published in 1997. Dyer is a former eighth-grade teacher, and with his son he traveled to the Klondike to see the places London visited.
- *Never Cry Wolf: The Amazing True Story of Life among Arctic Wolves*, by Canadian writer Farley Mowat, is now thought to be a lightly fictionalized account of Mowat's studies of wolves' natural behaviors in the wild. Although some scientists find the work to be outdated due to its 1963 publication, it is beautifully written and was an important force in changing public opinion in favor of wolves in the 1960s.
- *Nory Ryan's Song* (2000), by Patricia Reilly Griff, is a historical novel about the struggle of twelve-year-old Nora of western Ireland, who seeks to help her family survive the great Irish potato famine of the 1840s.

The second and third paragraphs, like the first, emphasize the differences between Koskoosh and the people he has separated from. As the old man, sitting immobile, listens to the movements of his tribe, the words used to describe the others are noticeably loud or active: "rammed," "jammed," "toiled," "chiding," "grunt," "piled," "whimpered," "lashing," "drawing tight," "snarled and bit," and, finally, "churned slowly away into the silence." It would appear that Koskoosh has withdrawn from his people and is ready for his last solitary journey, except for one new word that the narrator introduces, describing the man's last hours as "bitter."

When Koskoosh's son, the current chief, comes up and lays his hand on Koskoosh's head, something unexpected happens: instead of reaffirming Koskoosh's bonds to his family and his present life, the gesture instead helps him break those bonds. Rather than clutching his son's hand or asking for another chance at life, Koskoosh's thoughts fall "away into the past," toward other men who faced what he now faces, many without the assistance of a son's gestures. Readers do not know how long the old man thinks about his past while his son stands guard, but his reverie lasts "till the young man's voice [brings] him back." A brief conversation follows, during which the younger man shows his respect for his father and his sense of duty toward the tribe, and then the son leaves. Now the bitterness and the panic are gone. Koskoosh is described as "content," and again the narrator highlights the key word through contrast: while Koskoosh is "content," it is the snow under his son's footfalls that is "complaining." Koskoosh is ready. He considers the gradual numbness that will overtake his body as he slowly freezes, picturing that "his head would fall forward upon his knees, and he would rest. It was easy. All men must die." The narrator echoes the contrast that has just been presented, saying that the old man "did not complain."

Now begins the story's longest passages of memory, as Koskoosh remembers what he has learned of the laws of Nature, the great task of procreation, the Great Famine and the periods of abundance his people experienced. These memories stir no apparent emotion in Koskoosh; he runs through his philosophy and his memories in a matter-of-fact way. When he remembers the death of his mother there is no hint of sorrow or regret, and the story of his father's death is given simply, directly, and enfolded in the same sentence as another, unrelated event: "He remembered how he had abandoned his own father on an upper reach of the Klondike one winter, the winter before the missionary came with his talk-books and his box of medicines." Koskoosh demonstrates no emotion over his father's death. He remembers that those medicines used to fill him with longing, but now he feels nothing.

The only memory that stirs emotion in Koskoosh is that of the moose he and Zing-ha tracked in their youth. In this passage, the language is vivid, the verbs active, and the sentences punctuated with exclamation points. The old man remembers that when they first realized that they might see the final moments of the moose's life, "Zing-ha and he felt the blood-lust quicken!" Koskoosh himself is not sure why this memory is so "strong with him"—even stronger than his own encounters with fighting and death. It is the only memory he recounts with such detail—although he does not picture the moose's final moments—and when he has finished with it he again falls back into recalling "the days of his youth."

As the cold takes him, Koskoosh's thoughts and emotions become duller. The pile of wood is getting ever smaller, but he can summon only the barest suggestion of resentment toward Sit-cum-to-ha, who might have provided a larger pile if she were not so typically young and careless. But the thing that has distracted her is a young man, the Beaver, and attracting his attention is part of her one true task, so he cannot sustain his resentment. Next he wonders for a moment whether his son will come back for him, but he knows the answer; he knows that he is alone. "It was very lonely," the narrator says.

The rest of the story passes quickly, as the significance of Koskoosh's train of memories is revealed. One of the first things Koskoosh considers after his son walks away is "the way of life," "the law of all flesh," "the law of life." He knows that Nature is indifferent to individuals, interested only in "the species, the race." And he knows that there is no sense in resisting, or disobeying. A human's task is to procreate and then get out of the way, and "Did he not perform it, he died. Did he perform it, it was all the same, he died. Nature did not care." Koskoosh's memories are of humans and animals that have died, most of them yielding up their lives without complaint. Only two creatures in Koskoosh's memory resisted: Zing-ha, who made it halfway out of the hole in the ice before he froze to death, and the old bull moose, who "fought desperately," taking three wolves down with him before finally being torn to pieces with his "great branching horns, down low and tossing to the last." His disjointed scraps of memory resolve into a clear lesson for Koskoosh: there is no sense in resisting. Zing-ha, "the craftiest of hunters," excelled at killing and tracking but died in the kind of accident that Nature could call down on anyone. The moose fought bravely—or was it foolishly?—with his last bit of energy, but the result was the same. Nature did not care. Koskoosh's death is not to be as he had planned. Instead of a slow slipping away into numbness and a quiet death—followed, to be sure, by his body becoming food for other creatures—he sees now that he will be torn apart alive.

In the last paragraph of the story, the language is a swirl of echoes of what has come before, and man and beast are seen as two images of the same thing. Feeling the wolf's muzzle on his face, Koskoosh instinctively responds with fear, and grabs a flaming stick from the fire; the wolf also instinctively responds, with "his hereditary fear of man," and pulls back for a moment. When the wolf calls his brother wolves, they respond "greedily," echoing Koskoosh listening "greedily" in the story's first sentence. One wolf approaches

Elderly American Indian man in full dance ceremony regalia (Jose Gil / Shutterstock.com)

Koskoosh by "worm[ing] his chest forward," calling to mind Zing-ha, who "bellied it through the snow" to watch the moose's last battle. Koskoosh calls up the image of the old moose once again. Now the men and the moose and the wolves are indistinguishable. All have killed; all will die. Remembering what he had forecast for his last moments—"His head would fall forward upon his knees, and he would rest"—Koskoosh accepts his fate and stops resisting. But rather than the passive motion of his head falling forward, he makes his last action a choice, an act of will, as "Koskoosh drop[s] his head wearily upon his knees." And Nature does not care.

"The Law of Life" is in some ways a simple story. But London skillfully uses diction to add complexity to the idea of Nature's indifference. If Koskoosh accepted the law without struggle, it would be too easy to read the story as an example of a mysterious awareness of Nature and her laws that indigenous people, being spiritually closer to the earth, share, and which London's original Anglo readers could only admire across the cultural divide. But Koskoosh's changing emotions, leading eventually to a willful acceptance of the law of life, make his story more universal, more applicable to the world of the reader. In a very short story, every word counts. This is particularly true in "The Law of Life," where individual words widely separated demonstrate that Koskoosh is not merely a stereotypical indigenous chief, but a very real human.

Source: Cynthia A. Bily, Critical Essay on "The Law of Life," in *Short Stories for Students*, Gale, Cengage Learning, 2012.

Donna M. Campbell

In the following excerpt, Campbell summarizes the critical response to Jack London during the early twentieth century.

II. JACK LONDON

. . . Essays on Jack London's racial and political beliefs comprise much of this year's work on the author. Jeffory A. Clymer provides an important contextual reading of *The Iron Heel* and *The Assassination Bureau* in *America's Culture of Terrorism: Violence, Capitalism, and the Written Word* (No. Car., 2003). London early displayed a fascination with terrorists as evidenced in stories like "The Minions of Midas" and journalistic pieces like "Something's Rotten in Idaho" (1906), his protest at the framing of Big Bill Haywood and other labor organizers for the assassination of former governor Frank Steunenberg. In the tense political climate for labor and socialism in 1906, as Clymer shows, *The Iron Heel*, with its vision of a totalitarian state, and the never-finished *Assassination Bureau*, with its model of corporate efficiency applied to murdering those who exploit labor, resonate as works that show the essential parallels, if not symbiosis, between a capitalist state and the terrorist agencies that seek to destroy it. In writing of London and racial politics in the South Pacific, Christopher Mark McBride in *The Colonizer Abroad: Island Representations in American Prose from Herman Melville to Jack London* (Routledge) argues that although the stories in London's *The House of Pride* seem initially to suggest racial tolerance and to protest prejudice (as in "Chun Ah Chun"), the deeper messages are more disturbing. They include a dual attitude toward the treatment of lepers on Molokai, which London describes as relatively humane for the natives sent there but unfit for his white protagonist Kerndale of "Good-by, Jack"; a vision of leprosy itself as a contamination attributable to racial others; and the publication of the stories themselves as an act participating in colonialism, since London's popularity ensured that tourists would visit their setting, the Hawaiian Islands. Laurie Hergenhan's "Jack London and the Never Never" (*Overland* 177: 88–89) reprints London's unpublished brief preface to the American edition of Australian memoirist Jeannie Gunn's *We of the Never Never* (1908); there London casts Gunn's work as a pioneer saga and also praises Australian works such as *For the Term of His Natural Life*, *Jim the Penman*, and the works of Henry Lawson and G. B. Lancaster. Classing London with other popular naturalists such as Frank Norris and David Graham Phillips in *Homelessness in American Literature: Romanticism, Realism, and Testimony* (Routledge), John Allen argues that despite the warnings they contain, "tramp autobiographies" like London's *On the Road* romanticize homelessness by focusing on adventure, intellectualism, and individualism, presenting an optimistic view of the life and failing to challenge the practices of capitalism in a sustained way.

A special issue of *Eureka Studies in Teaching Short Fiction* (5, i) focuses on teaching Jack London's short stories. In "Jack London and Some of His Short Fiction: A Genuine Quarrel with Colonialism?" (pp. 40–53) Reinaldo Francisco Silva challenges recent critics such as Jeanne Campbell Reesman, Earle Labor, and Andrew Furer who have read London's South Seas stories as presenting a more sympathetic view of the racial other than his earlier work. In addition to quoting theorists from Richard Rorty to Toni Morrison on the inability of whites to be objective about racial others, Silva uses as evidence incidental phrases from the stories, "momentary outbursts of ethnocentrism" such as a character's wishing that he were king or the description of Mauki's ears in "Mauki" as implicitly conjuring up visions of an elephant's ears, to support his argument. Miriam J. Shillingsburg's "Jack London's Boxing Stories: Parables for Youth" (pp. 7–15) focuses on the narrative and symbolic use of boxing in "The Mexican" and "A Piece of Steak," both of which preserve suspense through their descriptions of boxing strategy and illustrate larger London themes of strength and survival. Kenneth K. Brandt also focuses on theme in "London's Fiction Technique and His Use of Schopenhauer as the 'Motif under the Motif' in 'The Law of Life'" (pp. 54–66), which argues that the clarity of London's prose causes students to overlook the complexity of his ideas. When teaching "The Law of Life" Brandt discusses London's theories of fiction and his use of Schopenhauer. By granting Koshkoosh, the point-of-view character and tribal elder left to die in that story, the same perspective on life as Schopenhauer, London allows the reader to critique the worldview that it engenders. Thomas R. Tietze focuses instead on aesthetics and the title character's relationship to the aesthetic object as a means of engaging student interest in "Teaching Aesthetics: Art and the Artist in Jack London's *Martin Eden*" (pp. 78–88). Also linking London with Schopenhauer is Paul Goetsch, whose "Shipwreck with Spectator: Norris, London, Crane," pp. 149–62 in Klaus Benesch et al., eds., *The Sea and the American Imagination* (Stauffenburg), examines three incidents of shipwrecks in naturalistic fiction—Stephen Crane's "The Open Boat," Norris's *Vandover and the Brute*, and London's *The Sea-Wolf*—in light of the principal character's dual positioning as participant and spectator in the event. Goetsch finds that instead of serving as the traditional providential sites of salvation, shipwrecks become for naturalistic writers the site of initiation into disbelief and disillusionment. . . .

Source: Donna M. Campbell, "Fiction: 1900 to the 1930s," in *American Literary Scholarship*, 2004, pp. 295–333.

Franklin Walter

In the following excerpt, Walter discusses the "survival of the fittest'" motif in Children of the Frost, *particularly in "The Law of Life."*

SURVIVAL OF THE FITTEST

. . . With *The Children of the Frost* London did better. This volume, made up of ten stories, most of which were published during 1902, concerns itself with Indians or with Indians in contact with whites. The tales are presented from the Indian's point of view. Though they show, as Dall pointed out, very little professional knowledge of the aborigines of Alaska and the Canadian North-west, scarcely discriminating between Indians and Eskimos and differing from the picture of red men elsewhere principally through the emphasis on cold and blubber, they embody effectively two of the themes which London could handle well: the struggle for survival in a primitive environment, and the weakening of a native culture by contact with the predatory Anglo-Saxons. . . .

The best of the stories in *Children of the Frost* are 'The League of the Old Men' and 'The Law of Life.' The former tells of a plot entered into by some old men among the Indians of the upper Yukon to murder all the whites they meet in camp or on the trail, hoping thereby to discourage the Anglo-Saxons from coming into the region and thus to prevent the disintegration of their native culture. Of course they fail, but something of their dignity and tragedy is embodied in the last survivor, one Imber, who turns himself over to the law in Dawson City. He tells his story in dramatic terms to a shocked audience. After a number of killings he has reluctantly come to the conclusion that the newcomers are much too numerous to be picked off one by one, that they are much too resourceful to succumb to guerilla tactics, and that, because they live by the law, they are certain of victory in the end.

London always affirmed that this was the favourite among his stories. 'I incline to the opinion that "The League of the Old Men" is the best short story I have written,' he stated. 'It has no love-motif, but that is not my reason for thinking it is my best story. In ways, the motif of this story is greater than any love-motif; in fact, its wide sweep includes the conditions and situations for ten thousand love-motifs. The voices of millions are in the voice of old Imber, and the tears and sorrows of millions are in his throat as he tells his story; his story epitomizes the whole vast tragedy of the contact of the Indian and white man.' It is not hard to understand why London favoured this story, for it combined his sympathy for the Indians, and underdogs generally, with his belief in the survival of the fittest through the operation of manifest destiny acting through the Anglo-Saxons. But the story has little action and less atmosphere; it is too talky to hold its own with London's best stories.

Much closer to his true forte is 'The Law of Life,' which tells of the approach of death to Old Koskoosh, once an able warrior, now abandoned in the snow by his tribe to meet the fate of the decrepit. As the cold moves up and the wolves close in, he stoically dreams of the old days, particularly of his experience with a grand old moose who had eventually been forced to give up just as he was doing.

This story is told effectively by a writer who had learned a great deal about his craft in two years. In a letter to Cloudesley Johns, London used it to illustrate points he wished to make about universality, objectivity, and control of point of view in writing.

> It is short, applies the particular to the universal, deals with a lonely death, of an old man, in which beasts consummate the tragedy. My man is an old Indian, abandoned in the snow by his tribe because he cannot keep up. He has a little fire, a few sticks of wood. The frost and silence about him. He is blind. How do I approach the event? What point of view do I take? Why, the old Indian's, of course. It opens up with him sitting by his little fire, listening to the tribesmen breaking camp, harnessing dogs, and departing. The reader listens with him to every familiar sound; hears the last draw away; feels the silence settle down. The old man wanders back into his past; the reader wanders with him—thus is the whole theme exploited through the soul of the Indian. Down to the consummation, when the wolves draw in upon him in a circle. Don't you see, nothing, even the moralizing and generalizing, is done, save through him, in expressions of his experience.

In 'The Law of Life' the Indian was forced to accept the principle that: 'Nature was not kindly to the flesh. She had no concern for that concrete thing called the individual. Her interest lay in the species, the race.' In this way London continued to dramatize his interpretation of Darwin, feeling that here the biological theory of survival of the fittest applied to the extinction of the moose and the old man just as in 'The League of the Old Men' it applied to the success of the virile,

"UNQUESTIONABLY [LONDON] WAS NOT A NOVELIST: HE WAS TOO IMPATIENT, TOO HEADLONG, TO ROUND OUT A LARGE PLAN. HE HAD NOT THE PATIENCE TO REVISE; HE REFUSED TO READ HIS EARLIER CHAPTERS DAY BY DAY AS HE PROCEEDED."

imaginative races like the Anglo-Saxons, 'the salt of the earth,' as he liked to call them. He wedded Darwin and Kipling in this fashion—not as difficult a union to manage as the union of Darwin and Marx, effected in his later fiction by assuming that the survival of the fittest applied to classes as well as to individuals and that the proletariat was the class most fit to survive. . . .

Source: Franklin Walter, "London Mines Literary Gold from the Klondike," in *Readings on "The Call of the Wild,"* edited by Katie de Koster, Greenhaven, 1999, pp. 50–58.

Fred Lewis Pattee

In the following excerpt, Pattee asserts that London's fiction is highly romanticized, despite the claims of previous critics who characterize his work as essentially realistic.

It was [London's] Alaska stories that gave him his first hearing. He had the good fortune to speak at the one moment when all would listen. In 1898 the imagination of the world had been stirred by the Klondike gold strike, and everywhere there was demand for material that was concrete, circumstantial, hot from first-hand observation. Of London's first six books all save one, a juvenile in *St. Nicholas*, were tales of the Alaska gold fields, vivid with pictures, breathing everywhere actuality; and it is upon these five—*The Son of the Wolf*, *The God of His Fathers*, *A Daughter of the Snows*, *Children of the Frost*, and *The Call of the Wild*, the last issued in 1903—that his ultimate fame must rest. All are of short story texture: even the novel *A Daughter of the Snows* is a series of episodes, and *The Call of the Wild* might have for its sub-title "Seven Episodes in the Life of the Dog Buck."

His method was the method of Kipling, as Kipling's had been that of Bret Harte. He would present a field new to literature by means of startling pictures; swift scenes flashed upon a screen with emphasis, even to exaggeration, upon the unique and unusual. Everywhere Bret Harte paradoxes: Hay Stockard is accused by the missionary of breaking all the commandments, and he is a blasphemer until "From the slipping of a snowshoe thong to the forefront of sudden death his Indian wife would gauge the occasion by the pitch and volume of his blasphemy," and yet he dies rather than renounce the God of his Puritan fathers. In all this early fiction the rush of the narrative is compelling and the seeming fidelity to nature in the background convincing. . . .

We are won at the start by the positiveness of the author. We must take him on faith: few of us know how civilized men behave in the areas beyond the bounds of civilization, how men die of starvation, how does deport themselves in the Arctic night. He tells us in minute detail, with Defoe-like concreteness of touch upon touch. But are we certain it *is* the truth? We are not. He is no more a realist than was Harte. Like Harte he is writing from memory and imagination the story of a vanished period, a brief and picturesque day in a new environment, where youth is supreme and alone, and his fancy hovers over it fondly, and paints it and exaggerates it and idealizes it even to romance. . . .

His characters are not actual men whom he has himself seen and known: they are demigods, the unsung heroes of a heroic age now put into epic setting. . . .

Moreover, he adds to this the romance of a fading race. He dates "The God of His Fathers" at "the moment when the stone age was drawing to a close." His Indian women are a remarkable group: Ruth, wife of Mason, in "The White Silence"; Madeline in "An Odyssey of the North"; Unga in "The Wife of a King"; Passuk, wife of Sitka Charley; Zarniska, wife of Scruff Mackensie; Sipsu, the Chief's daughter, in "Where the Trail Forks"; and Killisnoo, wife of Tomm, introduced with the remark: "Takes a woman to breed a man. Takes a she-cat not a cow to mother a tiger." By no means are they realistic studies. They are drawn from imagination rather than from notes made after observation, they are the type of primitive super-woman their author's imagination delighted in—Jees Uck for instance, with her "great blazing black eyes—the half-caste eye, round, fullorbed, and sensuous...."

Romanticized and overdrawn as unquestionably they are, nevertheless these women are the most vital and convincing of all Jack London's characters. They are his only additions to the gallery of original characters in American fiction. Their doglike fidelity and honesty, their loyalty and self-sacrifice, their primitive resourcefulness in danger and privation, excite unconsciously our admiration and our pity.

It is not too sweeping to say that the primary purpose of all London's early fiction was pictorial. He would reproduce for us the White North. Everywhere pictures, flash-lights not only upon the surfaces of the scene but into the heart and meaning of it....

His affinity is with Conrad; with him he might have said, "My task which I am trying to achieve is, by the power of the written word, to make you hear, to make you feel—it is, before all, to make you *see*...."

[The causes for London's eventual decline] lay in the author's temperament and in the nature of his literary field. In reality, after the first five books, he exhausted his Alaska claim; his lode petered out. Harte and even Kipling had discovered that to confine oneself to the recording of a primitive society is soon to run out of material. London had added nothing to Harte's outfit save a new set of drop scenery, a new fresh vigor of treatment, and a Gogol-like gruesomeness of detail, and these now had grown familiar. But the enormous vogue of *The Call of the Wild* gave him at once new latitude. He cleared his desk of early material—"The Faith of Men," *The War of the Classes*, "Moon Face," and the like—and then began to write as he pleased: his market allowed it. By nature and training he was an extreme idealist; a revolutionist, indeed.... From this time on he was constantly astride of hobbies, some of which he rode furiously. He had discovered in his tumultuous reading the evolutionary theory, the recapitulation theory, Gogol, Spencer, Karl Marx, Nietzsche. At the time of his death he was, to quote his wife's words, "enormously interested in psychoanalysis," and had he lived would have written a series of novels concerned with "research into the primitive, into the noumenon of things, in order to under stand the becoming of what man is to-day," novels undoubtedly of the type of *The Star Rover*....

Unquestionably [London] was not a novelist: he was too impatient, too headlong, to round out a large plan. He had not the patience to revise; he refused to read his earlier chapters day by day as he proceeded. As a result, the novels grew by accretions, and became, like *The Little Lady of the Big House*, masses of loosely-bound material for novels. Had patience been granted him, and restraint, he might, perhaps, have enlarged his vignettes into careful wholes; into novels even....

His range, however, is small. Of one whole rich area of human society he knew only the surface. The sordid misery of his childhood had warped his sense of values and narrowed the circle of human characters that he knew intimately enough to portray as a novelist should portray characters. His world, therefore, is lopsided and misleading. His socialism, unrelieved as it is by humor, is often ludicrous. His gospel, as one finds it in *The Sea Wolf*, for instance, and *Martin Eden*, is frankly and outspokenly materialistic, and materialism is the antipodes of all that we denominate art.

Moreover, within his own chosen field he is limited of range. After the voyage of the *Snark* he added the South Seas to his literary area and tried to do for them what he had done for Alaska, but it was only a changing of scenery. Instead of intense cold, intense heat; instead of the aurora, the glamour of the tropic night. The novel *Adventure* is *A Daughter of the Snows* transferred to the Solomon Islands, and Frona Wilse changes her name to Joan Lackland. Smoke Bellew becomes the David Grief of "A Son of the Sun." But there is a falling off in zest and vision. The South Sea tales do not leave so wholesome an impression as the earlier tales of the Arctic. He has chosen only the loathsome, the sensational, the unique; and one feels that he has chosen them simply to make salable copy....

[London's] sea tales are contemporary with Conrad's and at many points there is parallelism. Both deal largely with outcasts, both exalt their leading characters into super-men—Captain Mac Whir in *Typhoon*, Razumov with his "men like us leave no posterity"; both tell graphically of typhoon and violence; both are sonorous and gorgeous of diction. But Conrad is objective and London is prevailingly subjective; Conrad knows the sea better and he loves it with his whole soul....

The final literary style of Jack London—and doubtless it is true of all men—was the product of his own temperament. He was too individualistic, too impatient long to follow the lead of other men. Directed as he was at first by Kipling and Gogol and O. Henry, he soon divested himself of their mannerisms and voiced only himself. He was writing now furiously for money and only for money. In an interview published with his sanction at the height of his career, he declared that he did not write because he loved writing. He hated it.

> Every story that I write is for the money that will come to me. I always write what the editors want, not what I'd like to write. I grind out what the Capitalist editors want, and the editors buy only, what the business and editorial departments permit. The editors are not interested in the truth.

Everything in his life during the last decade of his work called aloud for money, and his only source of income was his pen. For a man of his temperament there could be but one result: one finds almost nothing in his writings that has been brooded over, that, like ripened wine, has body to it and bouquet. One thousand words a day, every day in the week, without vacation or rest, excited work unrevised and unreturned to, is journalism, the ephemerae of the Sunday supplement.

His temperament is everywhere visible. His sentences are short, often mere members of a sentence—the unit of measure of one excitable and headlong. There is no reserve, no restraint: everywhere exaggeration, superlatives; everything in extreme. In his later work he used the adjective "abysmal" until it became a mannerism that could even creep into one of his titles: *The Abysmal Brute*.... Even on literary topics he can render tongue-tied and silent Humphrey Van Weyden "the Dean of American Letters the Second," Van Weyden "the cold-blooded fish, the emotionless monster, the analytical demon." Are we convinced? On the contrary we begin to doubt the accuracy even of his autobiographical confessions. *Can* this man tell the truth? Will his imagination and melodramatic impulses permit him, even if he tries? Can we believe, for example, that a healthy country boy—not a De Quincey under the influence of drugs—can have dreams as extreme and as circumstantial as those he describes in the autobiographical parts of *Before Adam*?

That London devoutly believed that he was a realist and that his extreme pictures came only from his thoroughness, there can be no doubt. In *Martin Eden* he has said: "Realism is imperative to my nature, and the bourgeois spirit hates realism. The bourgeois is cowardly. It is afraid of life." But realism is science, and scientist London was not. Surely his is not the realism of the French school that filled endless note-books with careful observations before it began to write. He has been on the spot, to be sure, and the reader is never allowed for a moment to lose sight of the fact, but he works not from scientifically collected data. He can weave a glorious web of impressions of an era over which time is throwing a mellowing haze, he can heighten its picturesque places and exaggerate its lights and shades, but this is not realism. Wherever he touches the things that we know, we are likely to find him even grotesquely unrealistic. His dialogue seldom rings true, never, indeed, in his later novels....

In the field of action, however, especially action in the primitive areas of life, he stands with the masters. Few have surpassed him in power to present vivid moving-pictures: records of fights—dog-fights, prize-fights, bull-fights, the fight of a bull moose with a wolf pack, the battle of a Scruff Mackensie with a whole Indian tribe, the over-powering single-handed of a mutinous crew by a Wolf Larsen, the stand of a band of island lepers against the authorities. Scenes of battle and tempest arouse his imagination as nothing else: typhoons in the Solomon Islands, races with the Yukon mail, mutinies at sea, Arctic heroes conquering single-handed a whole firm of Wall Street sharpers....

At one time—about 1903 it was—O. Henry threw his influence over London's short stories, notably those in *The Faith of Men* and *Moon Face*, but between London and O. Henry there is this fundamental difference: London was passionately in earnest; he wrote without humorous intent; he wrote with a motif, and this he never forgot even in his most headlong moments of copy production. Behind his work was a principle that he fought for, a conviction that was Puritanic in its intensity. O. Henry, and also Bret Harte, lacked this element, and lacking it, they are in danger, despite their literary cleverness and their humor, of falling among the mere entertainers, useful people but not a class to be placed high in the major scale of values.

Source: Fred Lewis Pattee, "The Prophet of the Last Frontier," in *Side-Lights on American Literature*, Century, 1922, pp. 98–160.

SOURCES

Courbin, Jacqueline M., "Jack London's Portrayal of the Natives in His First Four Collections of Arctic Tales," in *Jack London Newsletter*, Vol. 10, 1978, pp. 129–30.

Dall, William H., "Jack London's 'Local Color,'" in *New York Times Saturday Review of Books* December 2, 1902, p. BR23.

Labor, Earle, and Jeanne Campbell Reesman, "Chronology" and "The American Adam," in *Jack London*, rev. ed., Twayne Publishers, 1994, pp. xv–xvii, 15, 17.

Lathrop, B. G., "Books of the Week and Literary Chat," in *San Francisco Call*, November 9, 1902, p. 12.

London, Jack, "The Law of Life," in *Jack London: Novels and Stories*, Library of America, 1982, pp. 365–71.

McClintock, James I., "Alaskan Nightmare and Artistic Success, 1898–1908," in *White Logic: Jack London's Short Stories*, Wolf House Books, 1976, pp. 100, 107.

"Quick Facts and Yukon History," in *Yukon Info*, http://www.yukoninfo.com (accessed September 4, 2011).

"Recent Fiction," in *New York Times Book Review*, October 25, 1902, p. BR4.

Reesman, Jeanne Campbell, *Jack London's Racial Lives: A Critical Biography*, University of Georgia Press, 2009, p. 66.

———, "The Klondike," in *Jack London: A Study of the Short Fiction*, Twayne's Studies in Short Fiction Series, No. 75, Twayne Publishers, 1999, pp. 53, 56.

Spencer, Herbert, *Principles of Biology*, Vol. 1, Williams and Norgate, 1864, p. 444.

"The Status of Wolves," in *Wolf Conservation and Management Plan Review: Fact Sheet 2*, 2011, http://www.yfwcm.ca/YukonWolfPlanReview/going/documents/4146-052-WolfConsSheets_FACTSHEET2_02_WEB.pdf (accessed September 4, 2011).

FURTHER READING

Auerbach, Jonathan, *Male Call: Becoming Jack London*, Duke University Press, 1996.

This critical biography explores how London created and manipulated an image of himself as rugged and masculine to appeal to publishers and readers. Two chapters focus on London's brief time in the Klondike; particularly pertinent here is "The (White) Man on Trail: London's Northland Stories."

Cassuto, Leonard, and Jeanne Campbell Reesman, eds., *Rereading Jack London*, Stanford University Press, 1996.

Although this collection makes only passing reference to "The Law of Life" as an example of a story that has been used to force London into a narrow critical framework, several of the fifteen essays address issues that are reflected in the story, including masculinity and London's treatment of people of different cultures.

Haley, James L., *Wolf: The Lives of Jack London*, Basic Books, 2010.

This admiring biography emphasizes London's political life, casting him as a complicated man whose many adventures, literary successes, and too-brief life are underscored by and attributable to his identity as an activist for social justice. This book is a good introduction to London's colorful life and rich body of work.

Tavernier-Courbin, Jacqueline, ed., *Critical Essays on Jack London*, G. K. Hall, 1983.

This collection of twenty-two essays, though somewhat dated, demonstrates the significance of London's large body of work and the many ways he has been read. Though it makes only the smallest references to "The Law of Life" and to *Children of the Frost*, the book features appreciations by London's contemporaries written as early as 1906, two brief biographical studies, several critical pieces, and a section of "Notes and Documents" that includes letters, clippings, and photos of rough drafts with London's revisions.

Wilson, Graham, ed., *The Klondike Gold Rush: Photographs from 1896–1899*, Wolf Creek Books, 1997.

In 1899, two years after London made a similar journey, the steamship *Thetis* sailed from San Francisco to the Alaska coast, encountering shipwrecked sailors, native peoples, gold prospectors, and beautiful and frightening landscapes. This book collects photos taken during that journey, with descriptive text written by one of the men aboard.

SUGGESTED SEARCH TERMS

Jack London

The Law of Life AND Jack London

Children of the Frost AND Jack London

realism

naturalism

Jack London AND Klondike

Jack London AND Northland

Jack London AND nature

Koskoosh

Inuit culture

Mista Courifer

ADELAIDE CASELY-HAYFORD

1960

Adelaide Casely-Hayford was a Sierra Leonean feminist, activist, educator, philanthropist, writer, and advocate of African unity. She did not start writing until later in her life, producing a memoir and a handful of short stories. "Mista Courifer" is the best-known work of her fiction writing. The story was first published in a 1960 anthology of writings by black Africans called *An African Treasury*, edited by Langston Hughes.

Set in Freetown, Sierra Leone, in the 1950s, the story explores how the presence of British culture in the city influences one Sierra Leonean family. Casely-Hayford uses wit and situational irony to demonstrate how a father and son adhere to and stray from social conventions. The work has been well received by critics for its simultaneously subtle and incisive exploration of culture.

AUTHOR BIOGRAPHY

Casely-Hayford was born as Adelaide Smith on June 2, 1868, in Freetown, Sierra Leone, to William Smith, Jr., and Anne Spilsbury. Her father was of English and royal Fanti parentage, and her mother was a Creole of English, Jamaican Maroon, and Sierra Leone liberated African heritage. Her wealthy family was part of the Creole elite in Freetown. When Casely-Hayford was four years old, her family migrated to England, where she spent the majority of her youth. Casely-Hayford's

Mista Courifer is a coffin maker and priest who has embraced western culture. *(Christy Thompson | Shutterstock.com)*

mother died in England when Casely-Hayford was still very young. She was mainly raised by her father, who made sure that she received a strong education. At the age of seventeen, she left to study music in Germany, but a few years later she returned to her family in England.

When Casely-Hayford was twenty-four, she moved back to Freetown, Sierra Leone, to start a teaching career. After a few years, she moved back to England to open a boarding home for African bachelors with her sister. In England, she married Joseph Ephraim Casely-Hayford, an advocate of Pan-Africanism and cultural nationalism, after a very brief courtship. It is probable that her husband's influence contributed to Casely-Hayford's later career as a Pan-African nationalist. Their daughter, Gladys, was born in 1904 with a hip defect. The marriage ended in divorce in 1909.

After twenty-five years in Europe, Casely-Hayford returned to Freetown. Having been deeply affected by the work done by Marcus Garvey's Universal Negro Improvement Association (UNIA), Casely-Hayford joined the ladies' division of the Freetown branch and eventually became its president. In 1920, she left the organization and traveled around America giving lectures to educate Americans about Africa. When Casely-Hayford returned to Freetown once again, she worked to organize a girls' vocational school. It opened in 1923 in Casely-Hayford's own home, and she served as the principal. One of her goals was to instill a sense of national pride in young girls. She ran the school until she retired in 1940, when the school was forced to close.

Casely-Hayford did not start writing literature until later in her life. Her work usually addresses topics relating to cultural and national identity. "Mista Courifer" is her best-known short story. It was published in 1960, the same year that Casely-Hayford died. She died on January 16, 1960, in her native Freetown.

PLOT SUMMARY

"Mista Courifer" is set in Freetown, the capital city of Sierra Leone, in an unspecified time that is most likely sometime in the 1950s. As the story opens, an omniscient third-person narrator describes a coffin-making workshop that is the workplace of the story's main character, Mista Courifer. The shop is directly attached to Mista Courifer's house in the middle of Freetown. In the shop and in his home, Mista Courifer is almost always silent because he sees no point in speaking in the presence of his loquacious wife, who can easily out-talk him. According to Mista Courifer, there is no point in arguing with a woman. It is clear that Mista Courifer does not have very much respect for his wife's opinions.

Mista Courifer's reticence at home is in stark contrast with his behavior at the local church, where he serves as preacher, leader of prayer meetings, and sometimes even the Sunday school teacher. At the church, he is known for being a dynamic speaker who gives elaborate sermons in varying pitch and tone. However, the narrator informs the reader that Mista Courifer sometimes takes the liberty of imposing unlikely interpretations on the Bible stories he discusses.

Mista Courifer idealizes anything and everything European and believes that all Africans should try to emulate European culture as much as possible. Having heard somewhere that English undertakers wear somber clothing, he began wearing black all the time. After a visit to England, he acquired an English-style house that his family finds uncomfortable and cramped compared to Freetown's typical outdoor compounds with huts. In short, Mista Courifer strives to be as European as possible in his daily life.

Mista Courifer has tried for a long time to instill his appreciation of European culture in his son, Tomas, but it is not an issue on which the two men see eye to eye. Another point of disagreement for Mista Courifer and his son is his son's job. Mista Courifer is proud that his son woks for the government and has high hopes that he will move up the chain of command in government service. Tomas, on the other hand, does not think much of his job, though he does not say so in front of his father. Determined to make his son into the perfect Englishman, once a year Mista Courifer orders clothes from England for Tomas to wear. Once Tomas became an adult, he began to resent this practice. Tomas is a great favorite, and Mista Courifer does not dote equally on his homely daughter Keren-happuch, who wishes that she could have European clothes to wear as well.

One day, Tomas tells Keren that he intends to leave his job with the government as soon as possible because he does not enjoy it and because they do not allow him his due benefits, such as vacation time. Keren urges him not to quit, for he will surely invoke the rage of their father, but he assures her that he intends to act up at work so that he is fired and it appears that he did not have a choice in the matter.

Tomas arrives at work an hour late for a week straight before he is reproached by Mr. Buckmaster, a supervisor. Tomas is upset by Mr. Buckmaster's scolding, because Mr. Buckmaster is one of the few white men whom he respects and is the reason he had put up with ill treatment at work thus far. When Mr. Buckmaster asks Tomas why he has been behaving so poorly lately, Tomas explains his reasoning.

Six weeks later Mr. Buckmaster comes to visit Mista Courifer at his workshop. Mista Courifer is delighted by the sight of him, thinking that surely he has come to order a coffin. Mista Courifer prefers European clients to African clients, because generally European clients will pay the full cost of a coffin up front, while African clients will negotiate, haggle, or withhold payment. Mista Courifer is even more excited when Mr. Buckmaster explains that he is not visiting to purchase a coffin but to discuss Tomas's job with the government. Mista Courifer speculates that they are giving Tomas an important promotion that will bring glory and honor to the Courifer family. However, Mista Courifer is sorely disappointed when Mr. Buckmaster explains that he just came to say that he will be leaving the country soon, but that he would be happy to give Tomas a letter of recommendation for potential future employers, if ever he should need it. Mista Courifer reasons that a letter from a European would be valuable and asks Mr. Buckmaster to compose one on the spot.

The following Monday morning, Tomas excitedly walks into his father's workshop and tells his father that he has been granted two month's vacation time. At this news, Mista Courifer tells Tomas that this will be the perfect opportunity for him to learn how to construct coffins. Tomas sharply disagrees and states that he will be spending the time learning "how to make love" and constructing a mud hut for his bride. Tomas explains that he has met a nice girl whom he wishes to marry and who reads and writes beautifully but might not know how to cook. Disgusted, Mista Courifer tells Tomas that he absolutely cannot marry a woman who cannot cook well, because the heart and the stomach are interrelated. Tomas replies that it is irrelevant whether or not she can cook, because he would not want his wife to spend all of her time slaving away in the kitchen. Tomas says that he does not approve of the way the women in Sierra Leone spend all of their time serving the men.

Mista Courifer responds that he only wanted his son to *look* like a European, not *act* like a European. Tomas says that he will never truly be able to look like a European, but he does appreciate some European customs, such as the way European men treat their wives. Mista Courifer is further outraged when Tomas explains that he and his wife will live in a traditional mud hut, not a European-style house such as the one he was raised in. Mista Courifer is so upset by this he bursts into a yelling fit and accuses his son of being ungrateful. Tomas explains that his entire life he has tried to live up to his father's European standards, but he will not try any longer. He claims he is going to live in the style of his native culture from now on.

The next Sunday during Mista Courifer's sermon at the church, he is so shocked to see his son and his bride walking up the aisle in traditional dress that he forgets everything he had planned to preach about. The story ends with simple sentences explaining that Mista Courifer no longer serves as the local preacher and instead only works on his coffins.

CHARACTERS

Accastasia

Accastasia is the young woman that Tomas Courifer, Jr., marries at the end of the story. Tomas describes her as being "quiet and gentle and sweet." She is also well read and can write beautiful letters. Tomas is not sure whether she possesses skills, such as cooking, that are traditionally valued by Sierra Leonean men, but he does not care whether she does or not.

Mr. Buckmaster

Mr. Buckmaster is Tomas's boss at his government job. He is one of the few white men whom Tomas respects, because he is perceptive and fair. Mr. Buckmaster also seems to respect Tomas, for he allows him leeway at work, listens to his problems, and even works to fix them. After Tomas complains that he never receives any vacation time, Mr. Buckmaster gives him two full months of vacation. Mr. Buckmaster even visits the Courifer household to write Tomas a personal letter of recommendation.

Keren-happuch Courifer

Keren-happuch Courifer, also referred to as Keren, is Mista Courifer's daughter and Tomas's younger sister. She is not considered attractive but has a large heart. Keren is usually overlooked by people, including her parents, because of her small stature and lack of typical beauty. She completely adores her brother Tomas, though she is a bit jealous of the English clothes her father buys for him, because he never buys such things for her.

Mista Courifer

Mista Courifer, the story's namesake, is a coffin maker who is completely obsessed with European culture. More specifically, he is obsessed with the *appearance* of European culture. He wears European-style clothes and lives in a European-style house, but he does not have any interest in engaging in European cultural customs. Mista Courifer believes that his wife's role in the household should be to cook food and take care of the house. He feels that his wife talks too much and does not see any point in talking to her. According to Mista Courifer, there is no use in arguing with women or teaching them mechanical skills such as carpentry, because they always miss the point. Mista Courifer also serves as the local preacher, though he tends to produce elaborate interpretations of Bible stories that are not always convincing to his parishioners. Perhaps Mista Courifer's defining characteristic is his rigidity; he has very specific opinions, especially about how his son, Tomas, should live his life, and is appalled by any variance from his expectations.

Mrs. Courifer

Mrs. Courifer is hardly mentioned in the story, except at the beginning. She is described as a woman who talks a great deal, although her husband never bothers to listen to her.

Tomas Courifer, Jr.

Tomas is the eldest child in the Courifer family and the only son. He is a young man, most likely in his late teens or early twenties. Though his father has planned the course of Tomas's life since he was a child, he is freethinking and

TOPICS FOR FURTHER STUDY

- Read the young-adult novel *The Roller Birds of Rampur*, by Indi Rana. In this book, Indian-born teen Sheila Mehta, who has been raised in London, returns to her family's farm in India after her British boyfriend dumps her. Like Tomas in "Mista Courifer," she has to learn to reconcile two very different cultures, both of which have influenced her. Write a paper explaining how Sheila is different from Tomas and how she is similar. How do both of these characters reconcile their native heritage with the culture in which they are raised? How do they justify their choices to their parents in situations where they choose to go against social conventions or their parents' wishes?
- Sierra Leone was one of many countries that the British colonized. In fact, at the height of the British Empire, the British claimed ownership of land on every continent of the world. Using the Internet and print sources, research the evolution of the British Empire. Choose one country that the British invaded that particularly interests you, and create a digital multimedia time line that gives a political, economic, and cultural overview of Britain's influence on that country. Be sure to address how British occupation affected the social conventions of the country you have chosen.
- Casely-Hayford was a prominent feminist and national activist. Her values and opinions are often not only evident but actively explored in her fiction writing. Choose a writer, artist, musician, filmmaker, or dancer whom you admire. How are their personal values reflected in the art that they create? Create a digital multimedia presentation that introduces the work of the person you have chosen to your classmates. Be sure to show how their personal values are reflected in their work. Also be sure to include video and photo representations of the work or works you are discussing.
- In "Mista Courifer," Casely-Hayford uses "pronunciation spelling" or nonstandard spelling that is used to draw attention to pronunciation, to represent Mista Courifer's particular way of speaking. Many short-story writers, including Mark Twain, William Faulkner, Charles Dickens, and Flannery O'Connor, frequently use pronunciation spelling in their stories. Choose and read a story that incorporates the use of pronunciation spelling. Translate the passages that are written in dialect to standard English. Using a computer, create a chart that compares the words in the story that are deliberately misspelled with the words that they are meant to represent. Under your chart, type a paragraph that explains, to the best of your knowledge, the region and/or culture that the author is trying to represent by using pronunciation spelling.

chooses to do things his own way. His father wants Tomas to wear English clothes, live in an English house, and advance to a prestigious position in the government, but Tomas would rather wear traditional African clothes and live in a mud hut. Tomas is very progressive in his attitude towards women. He deplores the way women in his country are treated as cooks and housekeepers for the men and explains that he would rather have an equal relationship with his spouse.

THEMES

Social Conventions

Social convention is the theme that is most visibly explored in "Mista Courifer." Both of the main characters, Mista Courifer and his son Tomas, challenge, break, and adhere to social conventions in interesting ways. They are both indigenous natives of Sierra Leone. Yet Mista Courifer breaks several of the social conventions of his society. Casely-Hayford writes, "He was one of the Sierra Leone gentlemen who consider everything European to be not only the right thing, but the *only* thing for the African." This statement indicates that Mista Courifer's eccentricities are not altogether unheard of in Sierra Leone.

He, presumably like some of the other gentlemen of Freetown, chooses to wear European dress exclusively. He has also built his family a European-style house that is impractical for the tropical climate of Sierra Leone. Although it is not explicitly stated in the story, it is probable that Mista Courifer tries to emulate British men because he views them as respected and powerful. Having grown up at the height of British colonialism, Mista Courifer has probably only encountered a handful of powerful men who were not British. Mista Courifer goes against the social conventions of his people in order to classify himself as someone who is wealthy, well respected, and powerful.

Mista Courifer tries to pass an affinity for British clothes and houses on to his son Tomas, but Tomas wholeheartedly rejects these things in favor of native dress and a traditional mud hut. In many ways, Tomas wants a conventionally normal life, but he rejects the social conventions of his people in other ways. He tells his father,

> The style in our country is not at all nice, Sir. I don't like to see a wife slaving away in the kitchen all times to make good chop for her husband who sits down alone and eats the best of everything himself, and she and the children only get the leavings. No thank you!

Tomas chooses to go against the Sierra Leonean social conventions regarding husbands and wives. He chooses his wife not for her ability to perform domestic functions but for her personality and because he fell in love with her. Despite his adoration of the British, Mista Courifer thinks this method of choosing a spouse is absolutely crazy.

British Colonialism

Another theme addressed in the story is that of British colonialism. Sierra Leone was a British colony until 1961, and from the way both Mista Courifer and Tomas challenge the social conventions of their people, it is evident that another culture has impressed its influence on their own in a substantial way. If Sierra Leone had not been a British colony, this story would not exist, for the main action in the story involves the clash of two

Mista Courifer's son Tomas still embraces the traditional African culture. *(lenetstan / Shutterstock.com)*

distinct sets of social conventions. Tomas's boss Mr. Buckmaster and the other men he works for are administrators of British colonialism. Tomas explains that he hates working for the government because the white British officials are allowed to work for short spurts of time while receiving large paychecks, yet in all the time Tomas has worked for the government he has never even received a vacation. Despite this bleak view of the government, Tomas has a great deal of respect for Mr. Buckmaster, making the view of British colonialism in the story all the more complicated.

STYLE

Situational Irony

Irony occurs in a situation in which actions have an effect that is opposite from what was intended, so that the outcome is contrary to what was expected. In literature, situational irony is frequently used to add humor or depth of meaning to a story. In "Mista Courifer," Mista Courifer strives to make his son, Tomas, into a respectable English gentlemen despite his African heritage. He takes deliberate actions, such as buying Tomas European clothes and pressuring him to take a job with the government, to ensure this outcome.

Situational irony is apparent at the end of the story when Tomas reveals to his father that his father has in fact succeeded in his mission to make him an English gentlemen, but in the exact opposite of the way he had intended. Mista Courifer explains to Tomas that he had only ever wanted Tomas to appear to be an Englishman, he never wanted him to actually act like an Englishman. Tomas, on the other hand, rejects everything that is English in appearance. He hates his English clothes and would prefer to wear traditional African garments. He also refuses to build an impractical European-style house, in favor of traditional mud huts. Yet Mista Courifer's attempts to make Tomas English in appearance have had the unexpected consequence of exposing him to English culture, many aspects of which Tomas has found himself attracted to. Tomas appreciates the way that European men treat their wives. He claims that in his own culture women are undervalued by their husbands, and he intends to treat his wife differently. Though Mista Courifer only wanted to make Tomas European in appearance, to his dismay he ended up making him somewhat European in his actions.

Foil

When speaking of literary devices, a foil is a character whose attitudes and behaviors contrast with those of a main character, in order to highlight important or distinctive aspects of the main character's personality. In "Mista Courifer," Mr. Buckmaster serves as a foil to Mista Courifer. The existence in the story of this character makes the inherent hypocrisy and absurdity of Mista Courifer's desire to appear European more apparent than it would be otherwise.

In a way, Mr. Buckmaster serves as an alternative father figure to Tomas. He is Tomas's boss at work, and Tomas respects him and highly values his opinion, perhaps more highly than he values that of his own father. While Mista Courifer simply dresses like an Englishman, simultaneously rejecting English culture and values, Mr. Buckmaster actually is an Englishman. The existence of an actual Englishman in the story, especially as an alternative father figure to Tomas and in direct contrast with Mista Courifer, makes it all the more apparent that Mista Courifer is simply playing dress up with his English clothes. His imitation of British life does not go any deeper than the surface.

Pronunciation Spelling

Pronunciation spelling is the intentional use of incorrect or nonstandard spellings to indicate alternative pronunciations of words. In literature, pronunciation spelling is often used in lines of dialogue that are spoken by a character with a regional accent. When pronunciation spelling is used in dialogue, it indicates to the reader that the character speaking does not pronounce things according to standard English pronunciation guidelines. It also indicates to the reader that it is an important fact that the character does not use standard English pronunciation. Typically, pronunciation spelling is used to tell the reader something about the background of the character who is speaking.

In "Mista Courifer," Casely-Hayford uses pronunciation spelling in Mista Courifer's lines of speech to indicate that he speaks with a thick Sierra Leonean accent. For example, when Mista Courifer is speaking, Casely-Hayford replaces the word "them" with "den," "very" with "berry," and "other" with "odder." By using these alternative spellings, Casely-Hayford ensures that her readers can hear what Mista Courifer's speech sounds like.

Poetic Justice

Poetic justice is imposed as a literary device when the good characters are rewarded, while the bad characters are punished. In "Mista Courifer," there are not necessarily good or bad characters, but the characters' fates at the end of the story are indications of whose behavior is deemed more acceptable. Tomas's open-mindedness and freethinking are rewarded with a promotion and a wedding, while Mista Courifer's empty imitation and stubborn rigidity are punished by his losing his position as the town's preacher.

HISTORICAL CONTEXT

From Crown Colony to Independence

Sierra Leone did not gain independence until 1961, a year after Casely-Hayford's death. During the time she was alive, the country was a colony of

COMPARE & CONTRAST

- **1950s:** Sierra Leone is a colony of the British Empire, although the 1953 election of Sir Milton Margai as Sierra Leone's first prime minister marks the beginning of the nation's journey toward becoming a free and independent state, a feat that is finally achieved in 1961.

  Today: Sierra Leone is an independent, self-governing constitutional republic with a directly elected president. The current constitution, adopted in 1991, established three branches of government: the legislature, the executive, and the judiciary.

- **1950s:** Since Sierra Leone was founded, there has been an absence of laws that protect women from discrimination and violence. A woman living in Sierra Leone is not allowed to own property, annul a marriage, or seek the government's protection from an abusive spouse or family member.

  Today: Three bills protecting women, collectively known as the "gender bills," become law on June 14, 2007. The Registration of Customary Marriages and Divorce Act, the Domestic Violence Act, and the Devolution of Estates Act are unanimously adopted by the parliament. The Marriages and Divorce Act protects girls under eighteen from being forced into marriage. The Domestic Violence Act criminalizes domestic violence and provides protection for women and children who are victims of violence. The Devolution of Estates Act allows women the legal right to inheritance of land and property in the event that they are widowed.

- **1950s:** Pan-Africanism, or the idea of unity among the African countries, begins to spread across the countries of West Africa. Kwame Nkrumah, who becomes the leader of Ghana in 1957, advocates an independent West African federation. Nkrumah is a founding member of the Organisation of African Unity, a group that seeks to promote unity among the African states and drive colonialism out of Africa.

  Today: The Organisation of African Unity has been replaced by the African Union, a union of fifty-four African states. The primary goal of the African Union is to promote "an integrated, prosperous and peaceful Africa, driven by its own citizens and representing a dynamic force in global arena."

England. The capital of Sierra Leone, Freetown, was first settled by the British in 1787 as a refuge for emancipated slaves from England and America. Despite several civilian uprisings, such as the Hut Tax War of 1898, Sierra Leone remained firmly in England's grasp until 1953, when Sir Milton Margai became its first chief minister and began laying the groundwork for independence.

Until that time, the British controlled the country using both direct and indirect rule. Indirect rule was a power structure implemented by the British government wherein local authorities, such as Sierra Leone's tribal chiefs, would remain in their positions of power but would be incentivized to rule according to the demands of the British government. This structure made it easier and more efficient for the British to maintain control of an entire country, because they were able to utilize the power structure that was already in place for their own purposes. Of course, it was necessary for a few British administrators to live on site in Sierra Leone to maintain control. In the story "Mista Courifer," Tomas Courifer's boss, Mr. Buckmaster, is a fictional example of such an administrator.

Margai was perhaps the most instrumental figure in the dismantling of colonial rule in Sierra Leone. In 1951, he supervised the drafting of a new constitution for the country that included a plan for decolonization. In 1953, when the country was granted ministerial powers, Margai was elected the first chief minister of Sierra Leone. He was easily reelected in 1957. On April 20, 1960, Margai led twenty-four other well-known Sierra Leonean politicians to a constitutional conference in London, where they met with Queen Elizabeth II and the British colonial secretary Iain Macleod to negotiate for independence. Almost exactly one year later, on April 27, 1961, Sierra Leone became politically independent of Great Britain. Margai was elected as the country's first prime minister. Sierra Leone retained a parliamentary system of government and became a member of the Commonwealth of Nations.

Pan-Africanism and the Universal Negro Improvement Association and African Communities League

The Universal Negro Improvement Association and African Communities League (UNIA-ACL, or simply UNIA) is a black nationalist fraternal organization founded by Marcus Garvey. Garvey was a Jamaican journalist and activist. He was a strong supporter of the black nationalism and Pan-Africanism movements, and his writings had a profound impact on Casely-Hayford. Proponents of the black nationalism movement supported the definition of an indigenous national identity based on race. Pan-Africanism is a movement whose proponents sought unification among all of the African states and African peoples.

Garvey believed that the unification of all black people was the only thing that could improve the lives of the race as a whole. He formed the UNIA-ACL in 1914 in an effort to promote and strengthen his causes. The UNIA-ACL was inclusive of all blacks everywhere, and by 1920 the association had over eleven hundred divisions in more than forty countries. In 1920, Casely-Hayford became the president of the ladies' division of the Freetown branch of the UNIA. These branches dedicated themselves to the advancement of people of African descent all over the world. For the entire month of August 1920, the UNIA-ACL held its first international convention at Madison Square Garden in New York City. There, the members in attendance drafted a document called the Declaration of Rights of the Negro Peoples of the World.

Although Garvey was incontestably a significant figure in the history of Pan-Africanism, some of his actions have been considered controversial. Garvey was investigated by the Bureau of Investigation (a predecessor of the Federal Bureau of Investigation) of the United States. As a result of the investigation, he was accused of mail fraud and taken to trial. In June 1923, he was convicted and sentenced to five years in prison, of which he served three months before posting bail. Garvey claimed that the trial and conviction were politically motivated and biased. In 1927, he was deported from the United States and sent back to Jamaica. After his deportation, the popularity of the UNIA-ACL significantly declined.

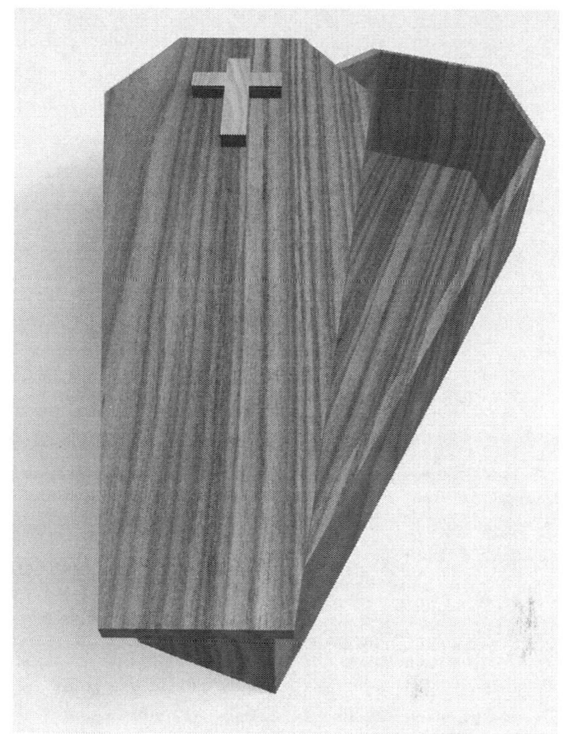

The coffin in "Mista Courifer" has several connotations. (Alfonso de Tomas / Shutterstock.com)

CRITICAL OVERVIEW

Because Casely-Hayford's fiction writing was limited to a handful of short stories, her fiction did not receive a great deal of critical attention. However, "Mista Courifer," being her best-known story, has been discussed by several critics.

Most commentators agree that in this story, Casely-Hayford cleverly addresses cultural issues. In an essay called "Clothes Philosophy and

African Literature: A Mirror for Typologists," Austin J. Shelton claims that "Mista Courifer" exemplifies "British Woolens" literature,

> a phase of literature and development which is largely passé—a stage occurring with the settling-in of colonialism and missionarism when some Africans ("Uncle Toms" or "Oreos" in the United States) seemed truly to believe in assimilation or integration.

Shelton notes that "Casely-Hayford's wonderfully imitative Mista Courifer is a perfect example of this type."

In an article published in the journal *Phylon*, reviewer Rina Okonkwo explains that in "Mista Courifer," Casely-Hayford combines the cultural concepts of feminism and cultural nationalism in a different way than most of her contemporaries. Of the story, Okonkwo states,

> It is interesting to see the way Hayford combined feminism and cultural nationalism. Tomas could wear African dress, but he also adopted the English family structure. Although most cultural nationalists believed the extended family system to be at the heart of African culture, Hayford rejected it.

In the essay "Gendered Self-Fashioning: Adelaide Casely-Hayford's Black Atlantic," Gaurav Desai argues that Casely-Hayford, and African women writers in general, have been unjustly overlooked by critics and scholars. He claims that a study of Casely-Hayford's life and work can "help us thicken our accounts of colonialism and nationalism in Africa and the ways in which it was mediated through gender, class, and race." Discussing "Mista Courifer," Desai describes the story as "an acerbic critique of the English pretensions of Sierra Leonian Creole society." Desai also calls "Mista Courifer" "perhaps the most aesthetically accomplished of [Casely-Hayford's] writings."

CRITICISM

Rachel Porter

Porter is a freelance writer and editor who holds a bachelor of arts in English literature. In the following essay, she demonstrates how Casely-Hayford's feminism and cultural nationalism are simultaneously apparent in Tomas, the character fashioned as the story's true hero in "Mista Courifer."

Before Adelaide Casely-Hayford was a writer, she was an activist. She spent the majority of her life promoting feminist and nationalist causes. She traveled back and forth between England and Sierra Leone, opened and ran a girl's vocational school in Freetown, served as the president of the ladies' division of the Freetown branch of the Universal Negro Improvement Association, completed two extended lecture tours through the United States, and managed to raise her daughter, Gladys, as a single parent. It was only toward the end of her life, after she had retired from her other posts, that she began writing literature. As is to be expected, the work that she produced during this time was deeply steeped in her life experience and saturated with her beliefs and passions.

"THE WORK CULMINATES IN A DISAGREEMENT BETWEEN A FATHER AND A SON THAT CASELY-HAYFORD BRILLIANTLY USES AS A PLATFORM TO PROBE THE CULTURAL AND GENDER-RELATED TENSIONS THAT WERE ABUNDANTLY PRESENT IN SIERRA LEONE IN THE 1950S."

"Mista Courifer," a short story that was published in 1960, is Casely-Hayford's best-known, and, according to critics, most accomplished work of fiction. The work culminates in a disagreement between a father and a son that Casely-Hayford brilliantly uses as a platform to probe the cultural and gender-related tensions that were abundantly present in Sierra Leone in the 1950s. In her biographical article "Adelaide Casely Hayford, Cultural Nationalist and Feminist," Rina Okonkwo briefly mentions the story "Mista Courifer." Okonkwo comments, "It is interesting to see the way Hayford combined feminism and cultural nationalism. Tomas could wear African dress, but he also adopted the English family structure." Okonkwo's suggestion that Casely-Hayford's feminism and cultural nationalism are symbolically melded together in the character of Tomas is a legitimate claim.

First, however, it is important to understand why the simultaneous exploration of these two movements is unusual and significant, particularly for the time period (the 1950s) during

WHAT DO I READ NEXT?

- *No Condition Is Permanent*, by Cristina Kessler, published in 2000, is a young-adult novel about a fourteen-year-old protagonist named Jodie. Jodie's anthropologist mother moves the family from California to Sierra Leone so that they can stay together while she completes a study on African tribal customs. In Africa, Jodie must adjust to a completely new way of living. This novel provides ample background information on the history and customs of Sierra Leone.
- "The Good Deed," by Pearl S. Buck, published in 1969, presents an intergenerational culture clash that is similar to the dispute between Mista Courifer and his son Tomas. In Buck's story, an elderly Chinese woman who has been moved to New York disagrees with her son's American way of living.
- *Mother and Daughter: Memoirs and Poems*, by Adelaide Casely-Hayford, published in 1983, is a collaborative memoir written by Casely-Hayford with help from her daughter, Gladys. This work provides insight into Casely-Hayford's personal life from her own perspective. Gladys Casely-Hayford was an accomplished poet in her own right and was deeply influenced by her mother's work.
- *The Krio of Sierra Leone: An Interpretive History*, by Akintola J. G. Wyse, published in 1991, is a lengthy study of the Krio people of Sierra Leone. The Krio, who are sometimes incorrectly called "Creole," are the descendants of the first colonists of Sierra Leone. This book provides a summary of Sierra Leone's complicated and culturally diverse history.
- *Nehanda*, by Yvonne Vera, published in 1994, is the story of a Zimbabwean spiritual leader named Nehanda who is prosecuted and eventually executed by the British. Although this story is fiction, it is based on the life of a woman named Nehanda Charwe Nyakasikana. This story is an extreme example of the cultural divide between the British and African peoples that Casely-Hayford explores in "Mista Courifer."
- *The Turning*, by Ron Terpening, published in 2000, is a young-adult novel that involves a father-son conflict similar to the one exemplified in "Mista Courifer." Sixteen-year-old Artie Crenshaw is the son of a stern preacher. Artie and his father have very different ideas of how Artie should live his life. As in "Mista Courifer," the son is buoyed by his love for a woman and eventually works up the courage to confront his father.
- *Poems from Black Africa: Ethiopia, South Rhodesia, Sierra Leone, Madagascar, Ivory Coast, Nigeria, Kenya, Gabon, Senegal, Nyasaland, Mozambique, South Africa, Congo, Ghana, Liberia*, published in 1963 and edited by Langston Hughes, is a collection of poems by black African poets, including natives of Sierra Leone, where "Mista Courifer" is set.

which Casely-Hayford was writing. Feminist writers use literature as a tool to expose and critique the oppression of women. Through myriad different techniques and varying degrees of subtlety or overtness, writers who purport feminist values reveal how patriarchal beliefs are unjust. Similarly, writers who espouse cultural nationalism use their writing to promote the belief that a strong sense of cultural identity should be associated with the people of a given nation. Historically there has been something of a divide between those who fight against gender discrimination and those who fight against racial discrimination. This is because it is easier and more straightforward to advocate for one distinct group of people at a time. For example, many African American women who participated in the civil rights movement viewed second-wave feminism as a potentially debilitating, divisive force in the African American community.

Casely-Hayford would not have shared this viewpoint. She was never afraid to advocate for two social causes at once. She ran a vocational school for girls in which she sought to instill her pupils with a sense of both female empowerment and national pride. She also served president of the ladies' division of the Freetown branch of the Universal Negro Improvement Association, a black nationalist organization. African nationalism and feminism could easily be viewed as mutually exclusive causes, because African culture is traditionally patriarchal. To this day, this is very much the case in Sierra Leone. Casely-Hayford was in the minority that believed that feminism and Sierra Leonean nationalism could advance concurrently.

This viewpoint is very much apparent in "Mista Courifer" in the character of Mista Courifer's son, Tomas, who, like Casely-Hayford, is simultaneously a feminist and a Sierra Leonean cultural nationalist. Tomas's feminism is apparent in his interactions with the women in his family and his attitude toward marriage. Unlike his father, who believes that women are not worth speaking to, Tomas has a close relationship with his little sister, Keren. He discusses his frustrations with her and is sensitive to her needs and emotions. When Keren hints that she is jealous of the European clothes her father buys for Tomas but never for her, Tomas takes it upon himself to buy her a frilly European dress that she wears to church with relish.

Tomas exposes his feminist values most explicitly near the story's close, when he discusses with his father how he intends to build his own family. When describing the positive characteristics of his chosen spouse, Accastasia, Tomas states, "She has been to school for a long time. She reads nice books and she writes, oh, such a nice letter." To this Mista Courifer scoffs and asks what is to him the most important question: whether or not she can cook well. Tomas responds that he does not know or care whether or not she can cook. He elaborates:

> The style in our country is not at all nice, Sir. I don't like to see a wife slaving away in the kitchen all times to make good chop for her husband who sits down alone and eats the best of everything himself, and she and the children only get the leavings. No thank you!

Tomas continues, "I like the way white men treat their wives; I like their home life; I like to see mother and father and the little family all sitting down eating their meals together." It is obvious that Tomas wants his wife to be more than a cook and a maid: he wants her to be an emotional and intellectual companion.

It is in this crucial debate with his father that Tomas's feminism comes together with his cultural nationalism, for, though he intends to adopt the more feminist family structure of the British, he also rejects other aspects of British culture in favor of his own culture. Despite his father's lifelong efforts to make Tomas appear to be an Englishman, Tomas rejects English attire in favor of traditional dress. At this point it is important to note that Casely-Hayford saw it as absolutely essential that Africans wear African dress rather than European dress. She believed that wearing traditional clothing was essential to the promotion of cultural nationalism, as it fostered a sense of racial pride and national unity. She herself always appeared in African dress, even when she traveled in the United States. When she opened her girls' vocational school, she wanted to make it mandatory for the girls to wear African dress every day. In addition to donning African dress, Tomas also rejects his father's wish for him to live in a European-style house in favor of a traditional mud hut. By implementing the aspects of British culture that he thinks are worthwhile and at the same time preserving the aspects of his native culture that he enjoys, he is a feminist and a cultural nationalist at once.

Thus, Tomas stands for everything that Casely-Hayford believed in, while his father, Mista Courifer, stands for the exact opposite. Mista Courifer is the stereotype of the "African Englishman." By wearing English clothes and living in an English-style house in the hope that it will make him look like a well-respected gentlemen, Mista Courifer buys into the notion of English superiority that was spread by English imperialists. At the same time, Mista Courifer thoughtlessly rejects all aspects of English culture, without even the slightest consideration that he might find some English cultural practices preferable.

By the end of the story, there can be no mistake as to which character Casely-Hayford would rather people emulate. For Tomas's good behavior, he earns a promotion at work, a raise, two full months of vacation time, and a marriage to a woman that he loves. On the other hand, Mista Courifer is left unhappy at the end of the story, having been, in his mind, undermined, betrayed, and disrespected by his son. Additionally, he loses

Casely Hayford wrote extensively from her experiences in Freetown, Sierra Leone.
(Pontus Edenberg / Shutterstock.com)

his job as the local preacher after becoming speechless on the pulpit at the sight of his son in native dress. While Mista Courifer is punished for his narrow-mindedness, Tomas's progressive freethinking attitude is rewarded, and he emerges as the true hero of the story.

Source: Rachel Porter, Critical Essay on "Mista Courifer," in *Short Stories for Students*, Gale, Cengage Learning, 2012.

Gaurav Desai

In the following excerpt, Desai argues that a study of Casely-Hayford's life and work is essential to understanding African colonialism and nationalism and how each was "mediated through gender, class, and race."

. . . It is toward such a task of deepening the literary history of women in Africa that this paper gestures. I turn, then, to one African woman whose life and work may help us thicken our accounts of colonialism and nationalism in Africa and the ways in which it was mediated through gender, class, and race. Adelaide Casely Hayford is generally known to Africanist literary critics as the author of the much anthologized short story "Mista Courifer." While this story, an acerbic critique of the English pretensions of Sierra Leonian Creole society, is perhaps the most aesthetically accomplished of her writings, it is important to note that Casely Hayford also published at least three other short stories that unfortunately have escaped critical attention. These stories. "Kobina, a Little African Boy," a morality tale about the virtues of commitments, "Two West African Simpletons," a semi-autobiographical story of two Creole orphans returning to West Africa to set up a girls' school, and "A Black and White Encounter, a Tale of Long Ago," about the racially fraught encounter between a young black girl and a white boy on a sandy beach, were all published in 1949 in the *Sierra Leone Weekly News*. The stories are not easily available, having never been reprinted since their publication in newspaper form, and hence, they are reproduced here for the benefit of other scholars interested in pursuing Casely Hayford's work. In addition to these stories, in 1953 and 1954, the *West African Review* published Casely Hayford's autobiography in serial form. It is to this text, a wonderful window on her life, that I will

UNDERTAKEN FROM A PERIOD OF THE RAPID EUROPEAN COLONIZATION OF WEST AFRICA THROUGH TO THE PERIOD OF AN INSURGENT NATIONALISM, THESE TRAVELS WERE ALSO FOR ADELAIDE LESSONS IN THE ECONOMY OF BLACK FEMALE SUBJECTIVITY IN A RAPIDLY CHANGING WORLD."

now turn. I should note that while my aim is to read the autobiography as a text that speaks to the author's own self-fashioning, I am also indebted in my reading to the work of Adelaide M. Cromwell who remains Casely Hayford's most authoritative biographer.

Adelaide Casely Hayford was a pioneer of women's education in Sierra Leone and the story of her life, involving several sojourns in the Euro-American world, makes for a fascinating read in the context of our recent critical attention to the world of the Black Atlantic. She was born on 27 June 1868 in Freetown, Sierra Leone. Her lineage is of some importance to understanding her status in the Creole society in which she was born. Her grandfather was a white man from Yorkshire who came to the Gold Coast around 1820 to work with the African Company. Moving to Sierra Leone over the course of his career, he became, at the time of his retirement, the Commissary Judge for the Mixed Courts in Freetown. He had two marriages, one with an Englishwoman and the other with the daughter of a Fanti chief. Adelaide's father, William Smith, Jr., was the offspring of the marriage between the Yorkshireman and the Fanti woman. Adelaide's maternal grandmother. Hannah Carew Spilsbury, was the progeny of a recaptive Bambara butcher and a shrewd Hausa trading woman who, by all accounts, made so much money that she had to hire "a young clerk of Maroon (half West Indian) origin" (1) to manage her affairs. This young man, Joseph Spilsbury, married Hannah, who gave birth to Anne Spilsbury, Adelaide's mother. What is important to note is that even though they themselves had no formal education, Adelaide's great-grandparents had sent their daughter Hannah to study in England and had made it possible for her to have a very financially secure married life. Hannah's husband, Joseph Spilsbury, too, was of no small stature. When he died in 1853, he was deemed to be "one of the nineteen biggest land and home owners in Freetown" (Cromwell 30).

Adelaide was born, then, into family circumstances that, by any definition, would be considered elite. Upon her father's retirement from the Government Service in 1871, the Smith family prepared to move to England, arriving there in 1872, when Adelaide was four years old. They first settled in a suburb of London but later moved to St. Helier on the Isle of Jersey. When Adelaide was a mere seven years old, she lost her mother. At the age of seventeen, encouraged by one of her teachers at school, Adelaide moved to Germany to study music at a branch of the Stuttgart Conservatory. The presence of African students was not unknown at the time, and, in fact, at one point in her memories, Adelaide describes a rendezvous with two of her stepnieces who were studying at the Catharinenstift. In 1888, Adelaide returned to England to a household with a new stepmother, an Englishwoman whom her father had married. Adelaide's older sister Bea had already been married and had settled in Freetown, and her younger sister Nettie was engaged to marry the following year. After Nettie's marriage, feeling somewhat out of place in her father's new household, Adelaide decided to return to Freetown to try her hand at teaching. She was soon recalled to England on the death of her stepmother in 1894. Not too long thereafter, Adelaide's father too passed away, leaving behind a very meager inheritance for his two unmarried daughters, Adelaide and Emma.

With no family left in England, Adelaide and Emma decided to migrate to Freetown. But they did so with some apprehension. "Africa at that time had no attraction for us because by now England seemed more like our real home. Although our parents did a wonderful thing by giving us the chance of an excellent European education, we had become strangers to the African environment," writes Casely Hayford (19). Their reception in Freetown was not warm: "It took us a long time to settle down. Most of the educated Africans were definitely hostile to us" (20). The environment did not suit Adelaide's health, and when the opportunity arose to go back to England, this time with her recently widowed sister Nettie and her two children, the three sisters retraced their steps back to England. Life in England seems to have been frugal, with paying guests taken on to supplement income, but this was also a time when the sisters made acquaintance with some important dignitaries, the most prominent being the musical composer Samuel Coleridge Taylor, of half Sierra Leonean and half-English heritage. It was also then that Adelaide was wooed by her husband-to-be, the barrister Joseph Ephraim Casely Hayford—West African patriot—best known to us for his remarkable works, *Gold Coast Native Institutions* and what is allegedly the first African novel in the English language, *Ethiopia Unbound*. The story of this marriage, which so sadly went awry, was to preoccupy Adelaide's consciousness for the next several years.

The first three years of married life were spent by the couple in Axim where Joseph had a lucrative practice. While Adelaide surely felt a little out of place in these new surroundings, she seems to have made the best of it. But when their daughter Gladys was born with a malformation of the hip joint, something that would best be treated in England, Adelaide, reluctant as she was to leave her husband, knew that it was her duty to ensure the best for her child. Her estrangement from her husband began during these years of Gladys's treatment in England where she waited in vain for a visit from a husband who was by then in the midst of a thriving legal practice, a nationalist cause, and a career in writing and journalism. The letters between husband and wife, which her biographer Adelaide Cromwell draws upon, reveal a whole range of human emotions—from desperation to anger, from loneliness to a sense of betrayal.

It is ironically perhaps precisely the failure of her marriage that led in some measure to the future public rise to prominence of Adelaide Casely Hayford. Moving to Freetown in May 1914 with her daughter Gladys, Casely Hayford was determined to do something to improve the education of girls in the country. Despite her own European education, Casely Hayford insisted on a more "relevant" form of education for girls, which in practical terms meant a kind of schooling that would prepare them for domesticity. Recognizing her own financial dependence on her husband, Adelaide was convinced that a proper education for young girls would involve a vocational component—such as mastery of traditional crafts or basket weaving—which could, in times of need, be relied upon as a source of revenue. Along with this turn towards an educational philosophy that was based on practical training, Adelaide Casely Hayford also began to insist on the importance of taking pride in one's own race. It was at this point in her life that this English-raised woman would begin to don traditional African attire as a source of pride and would ridicule, as Kobina Sekyi was doing elsewhere, the Victorian pretensions of elite Creole society. Some of this was undoubtedly also influenced by her marriage—albeit ultimately estranged—with Joseph Casely Hayford. For he, himself influenced by Edward Blyden, had in *Ethiopia Unbound* made an explicit plea for a return to African traditions and especially to African dress.

Yet it was not always easy for a descendant of the Creole elite to take such a stance and be read as being entirely honest. A remarkable moment in Adelaide Casely Hayford's life was when the Prince of Wales visited Freetown in April 1925. Casely Hayford wrote a column about the visit in *West Africa* entitled "The First Impression of the Prince in West Africa to reach this country from the pen of a West African" The column aroused a certain amount of controversy because Casely Hayford suggested: "A few days before the Prince's arrival, frenzied women were rushing about trying to beg, borrow or steal gloves for the grand reception at Government House on that gala night" (Cromwell 142). While the intent of the piece was allegedly to point out the absurdity of Africans having to cater to European codes of dress (Adelaide herself showed up, much to the consternation of others, in African attire), the statement was read by some as mockery on the part of a society woman of others of lesser social standing who had been caught off guard. This incident serves rather well as a symptom of the larger sense of unease with which Casely Hayford had to negotiate her own identity and her project of the education of young girls in a Creole society that was slowly but surely beginning to show its own internal fissures.

What for us must remain the most remarkable achievements of Adelaide Casely Hayford are her two fund-raising trips to the United States. The first was in 1920 when she visited thirty-six cities and towns, some more than once. Accompanied by her niece Kathleen Easmon, Casely Hayford made a home base in Harlem. Her autobiography is rife with details about their various contacts with African-American churches throughout the Northeast and the South. She writes about a week in Washington, DC, visiting a school for girls, and remarks on the pleasures of seeing the "White House, the Capitol, Lincoln's Memorial and other world famous buildings" (39). She writes of a visit to Chicago's Hull House and reads it as a great symbol of American philanthropy. She also notes her presentation at the annual National Convention of Colored Women in Indianapolis. During what was arguably the first fund-raising visit ever of an African woman to the United States, Adelaide Casely Hayford took every opportunity to advance her cause for women's education in Sierra Leone. She saw Kathleen and herself as important ambassadors of African culture and custom: "The Negroes had expected to see two half-civilized, illiterate women, but after they had heard us speak, they were overwhelmed with enthusiasm. Our address had dwelt on the good points of our down-trodden race instead of the usual descriptions of barbaric fetish practices and devil-worshipping rites to which they were accustomed" (38). Presenting themselves in traditional African dress, the women were conscious of the fact that they were in some senses a curiosity, but they were undeterred. Adelaide began to recognize that the fact that she was Joseph Casely Hayford's wife was in no small part responsible for her favorable reception in the United States and, despite her own marital difficulties, she realized the importance of keeping these difficulties away from the public. In one of her letters to her husband in 1921 she writes, "Of course no one here has any idea of the relationship between us. I act as if everything is all right" (Cromwell 124).

Of her many visits to colleges and churches, her meeting with the widow of Booker T. Washington seems to have made a deep impression. Tuskegee Institute, with its warm reception of Adelaide, was also a place that she felt knew how to "dignify labor," and the pedagogical lessons of this institution were to further her own ideas about the "appropriate" education for girls in Sierra Leone. After about two and half years in the United States, Casely Hayford returned home to start her school, which throughout its early years faced several detractors. Indeed, Adelaide may well have been referring to this struggle to set up the school when she wrote at another point in her autobiography of the "anguish of soul and disillusionment that we suffered on our return to our native shores years later" (8). The school suffered from lack of sufficient enrollment, and when an English-woman joined the staff and abruptly left, taking with her some of the newly enrolled students, Adelaide felt betrayed and disillusioned. She decided nevertheless to undertake a second fund-raising trip bolstered by the financial success of the first one. It was during this trip that she met, among others, Paul Robeson, whom she persuaded to sing a couple of songs at a fund-raising event at which she was scheduled to speak. While her autobiography does not dwell on it, letters between her and Langston Hughes in the Hughes archives at the Beinecke suggest that she attempted to secure Hughes's interest in her work and the poetry of her daughter. The letters that begin during this second visit to the States indicate that they met at least once in the early twenties and continued to correspond (with greater frequency on her part) until the end of her life. The result of this correspondence was the publication of her short story "Mista Courifer" in a collection edited by Hughes, but later on in her life Casely Hayford seems to have been disappointed that Hughes could not muster enough interest on the part of publishers in publishing her autobiography.

It was during this trip that Casely Hayford also secured financial assistance from a wealthy woman who agreed to sponsor a young white American woman, Beth Terry, who came to Freetown as a teacher at Adelaide's school. The autobiography has nothing but kind and grateful words about Beth Terry, who stayed with the school for sixteen months. But once again, upon returning to Sierra Leone, Adelaide received a cold reception. Somehow, though, with annual financial support coming from across the Atlantic, the school survived. Despite all the detractors, Casely Hayford kept it running until 1940, when, facing her retirement at the age of seventy and with no one else to take over the helm, the school had to close.

"Traveling is no new experience to me," writes Casely Hayford in her autobiography, "because I have crossed the Atlantic at least twenty-one times" (56). Despite her blasé attitude, however, it is clear from reading her autobiography that her travels were also in many ways personal trials of strength and endurance. Undertaken from a period of the rapid European colonization of West Africa through to the period of an insurgent nationalism, these travels were also for Adelaide lessons in the economy of black female subjectivity in a rapidly changing world. As she looks back on the innocence of her childhood, the older, now much traveled writer recognizes the internalization of racial hierarchies even within her own family.

She writes about her sister Nettie: "Like Emma, she inherited our father's very light complexion and beautiful silky hair. Consequently, they got all the cream, while we others, who had inherited our mother's dark skin subsisted on skimmed milk" (3, 4). In keeping with her own perceptions at the time, she writes about her schooling in England: "We were happy in spite of our color, or perhaps because of it, since we were singled out for extra tidbits of love, kindliness or goodwill. What did we know of racial prejudice and an inferiority complex? Nothing" (8). But being noticed as racially other, even if to beneficial effect, is still to be noticed as other, and this is a recognition that Adelaide has as a teenager in Germany. She feels that she is on display: "In 1885, when I first went to Germany, very little was known of Africans there; so I occupied the priority place of curio No. 1" (11). It comes to the point where she is always alert to the German gaze—when she is at a wedding, for instance, she is quick to note: "Nobody seemed to notice either my color or my morning dress" (13). Toward the end of her stay in Germany she confesses:

> I suffered acutely from self-consciousness, not so much because I was black but because I was so conspicuous. I could never withdraw and was always in the limelight. I remember on one occasion I went into a shop to buy something and everyone of the assistants fled, leaving me monarch of all I surveyed. Fortunately, my sense of humor came to the rescue and I was able to joke about it; but nevertheless it hurt. Now I realize that because I was only a girl at that time, I was not sufficiently sensible to see things in their right light. I now know that God never makes mistakes, and that my black skin was part of the equipment with which he had endowed me to make good in life. I therefore 'took fate by the throat' and decided to turn this liability into an asset by facing up to life and carrying on with my career. This decision was the right one—the only one. (14, 15)

If her race was a liability, it was perhaps most so in a painful experience she describes on board a ship between Sekondi and England. On her way to England with Gladys during her early years of marriage while carrying a second pregnancy, she experiences the most explicit kind of racism. Despite being booked in a first-class cabin, she is shuttled because of her race to what she remembers as the "worst second class cabin on the boat" (29). Unable to persuade the Chief Steward that she is entitled to the first-class accommodations, she storms to the Captain, who is taken aback by her flawless German and concedes to her occupation of a first-class cabin on the condition that she agree to vacate it were it to be needed by someone else (presumably white). She gives birth to a stillborn child in that cabin, and when a fellow passenger arrives, the latter expresses surprise: "I can't understand why you are here at all. When I boarded the ship at Calabar I was told that at Sekondi I would have to share a cabin with a Mrs. Hayford and child" (30). Casely Hayford writes with a bitter irony that speaks to her larger predicament: "The combination of a black skin and an English name can prove a terrible handicap" (30).

It is important to realize, nevertheless, that while Adelaide Casely Hayford suffered such injustices on account of her race, she too nurtured prejudices, often against the indigenous (non-Creole) Africans who are, in her autobiography, no more than a backdrop for the unfolding of events. Thus, for instance, we learn that one of the reasons she cannot cope with her husband's surroundings in the Gold Coast is because she is "surrounded by illiterate peasants who spoke a different language altogether" (29) and when, most tellingly, the Temne leader Bai Bureh resists the colonial Hut Tax, Casely Hayford allows herself to be swept up by the prevalent rhetoric of an exceedingly brutal uprising: "The Temne Chief Bai Bureh, staunchly supported by his people, determined to kill all white people and educated Africans as well. Fortunately," she continues, "the rising was put down before it reached Freetown, but many missionaries were killed, and many Africans were plunged into mourning because of it" (22). Positioning herself starkly on the side of the colonial authorities against a dangerously encroaching savage hinterland, Adelaide Casely Hayford here casts her lot with the English rather than with the indigenous peoples.

While we cannot, then, glorify everything about Adelaide Casely Hayford, she nevertheless is an important figure for us to reconsider. For if, as Paul Gilroy has suggested in the *Black Atlantic*, Western modernity is best understood not as an exclusively European phenomenon but one that has depended upon a traffic of bodies, commodities, and ideas across the Atlantic, and if, furthermore, this modernity has engendered a black counterculture, then it is increasingly relevant to ask about the role of women such as Adelaide Casely Hayford in this enterprise. It was indeed the very same Black Atlantic history that Gilroy refers to that produced the Creolized societies of West Africa, primarily in Sierra Leone and Liberia but also, by extension, in the neighboring lands of what was then the Gold Coast and Nigeria. Historians such as E. A. Ayandele, J. A. Langley, Jean Herskovits Kopytoff, Christopher Fyfe, and Akintola Wyse have enriched our understanding of the cross-pollination between the New World and Africa and the role of the African diaspora in the rise of West African Nationalism. In the majority, this work has focused on the lives of eminent men such as Adelaide's husband, Joseph Casely Hayford. But it is somewhat ironic that in a curious reversal of gender stereotypes, in this particular case at least, the greater Atlantic traveler, and arguably the more cosmopolitan subject, was not the more rooted Joseph, but rather his wife, Adelaide. To read Adelaide Casely Hayford's autobiography is to understand that travels are oftentimes also trials—physical and emotional—but that they can also be liberatory, as they ultimately were for this remarkable woman who was at once an orphan, an estranged wife, a single mother, a fundraiser, an educator, a cultural ambassador, and indeed, an African patriot. . . .

Source: Gaurav Desai, "Gendered Self-Fashioning: Adelaide Casely Hayford's Black Atlantic," in *Research in African Literatures*, Vol. 35, No. 3, Fall 2004, pp. 141–60.

Kadiatu Kanneh

In the following excerpt, Kanneh contends that Casely-Hayford's short story is representative of the metropolitan character of Creole nationalism in Freetown.

. . . This radical disparity between a fixed colonial idea of Sierra Leone as an 'Africa' of distinct developmental stages—from 'primitive' to 'civilised'—and the alternative mapping of the colony as a region of multiple and contested cultural identities becomes more complicated on examining how colonial ideology shifted during the nineteenth century. The changing colonial idea of 'the African' was determined by mid-nineteenth-century pseudo-Darwinism impacting upon the notion of cultural revolution to produce the new idea of racial evolution (*Lives In Between*, pp. 69–70). The violence of this conceptual change is illustrated by the fact that, in 1853, the liberated Africans, or second-generation recaptives, had been officially declared British subjects. The subsequent slide from being subjects to inferior conquests contributed to the rise of pan-Africanist responses among the Creoles. These serve to indicate how cultural issues were central to nationalist concerns, and how nationalism—emerging among the Freetown Creole elite—firmly negated any identification with the interior. The name reform movements and the Dress Reform Society of 1887 presupposed and hoped to create the acknowledgement of an African identity that embraced modern ideas of progress and enlightenment and also insisted on African difference. This perceived and avowed 'difference' could not be conflated with the radical 'unknowingness' of pre-enlightenment Sierra Leone. The indigenous Sierra Leonean population, at one remove from British colonial education, was also understood by nationalist Creoles to be historically removed from national consciousness. In this way, the reform movements sought to create a reinvented African within a re-invented Sierra Leonean nation. The fashion for taking Yoruba names revealed a more powerful emotional link with another area of the West coast, Nigeria, and the African dress of Creole nationalism was a creative *departure* from 'bush' fashions (*Lives In Between*, p. 159).

The exclusively metropolitan character of this nationalism, powerfully influenced by the teachings of the pan-Africanist Edward Wilmot Blyden (pp. 157–8), is illustrated by the Creole writer Adelaide Casely-Hayford, born in Sierra Leone in 1868 into the Freetown Creole elite. Her short story 'Mista Courifer' expresses the cultural nationalism which began to define Creole identity. Structured as the triumph of nationalist consciousness over colonial repression, styles of fashion and architecture emerge as significant metaphors for the struggle between European and Africanist ideologies. Mr. Courifer, a Creole preacher and coffin-maker, represents the anachronistic, colonial mentality of the Creole middle class, whose adulation of Englishness is made apparent by his choice of housing, furnishing and clothes. The arguments against his 'European house' and 'English' clothing raise questions of appropriateness and 'nature' that logically condemn the hot, carpeted house as 'unsanitary' and his clothing as simply 'anti-nationalist':

> So Mr Courifer wore Black. It never struck him for a single moment that red would have been more appropriate, far more becoming, far less expensive and far more national.

This evocation of national appropriateness is linked directly to racial particularity. African racial difference is absolute, both physically and qualitatively. Mr Courifer's choices for his son become not only unfitting but impossible:

> From start to finish, Tomas's career had been cut out, and in spite of the fact that nature had endowed him with a Black skin and an African temperament, Tomas was to be an Englishman. He was even to be an Englishman in appearance.

Blyden's influence on Creole nationalism emphasized this belief in racial particularity and its relationship with occupation, social organisation and dress (see *Lives In Between*, pp. 157 8). Racial being manifested itself in terms of separate racial destinies and, in this way, race had to become the basis of African nationalism. Blyden's Sierra Leone lecture of April 1884 (in *Christianity, Islam, and the Negro Race*) emphasizes this passionate belief in racial determinism as the essence of nationalist development: 'It is the feeling of race—the aspiration after the development on its own line of the type of humanity to which we belong' (p. 197). The support which Blyden gained from Creole nationalists is evident in Samuel Lewis' 'Introductory Biographical Note' to Blyden's *Christianity, Islam, and the Negro Race*, in which he is at pains to advertise both his own qualifications for introducing Blyden and Blyden's own racial qualities.

Claiming his identity as 'a Negro . . . of unadulterated African blood,' and pointing to Blyden's 'purest Negro parentage' (pp. vii and viii), Lewis is careful to associate himself with Blyden's understanding of African nationalism in its most dedicated and separatist form, as the continuation of an abhorrence for racial hybridity.

Adelaide Casely-Hayford's narrative follows this identification of race with nationalism with a sustained concentration on dress codes. The significance of dress for the Creole middle and upper classes was directly conditioned by the desire to differentiate themselves from slaves and 'primitives' or 'up-country natives.' Richard West's analysis of this pre-nationalist approach to fashion emphasizes an earlier reading of 'freedom':

> The Creoles dressed somewhat after the English fashion. Since nakedness was the badge of a slave, an abundance and even an excess of clothes was seen as the proof of freedom. The wealthier men wore jackets, waistcoats and trousers of cloth, sometimes torturing themselves with suits of wool because this was more 'English' than cotton. Top-hats and spats were often seen in the last decade of the century. (*Back to Africa*, p. 176)

West also outlines the primary importance of religion and church-going for Creole identity: 'At innumerable churches and chapels, all day and most of the night, the Lord's Word was preached, chanted, calypsoed and yelled' (p. 176).

Tomas Courifer's liberation into a man of independence and authenticity occurs via his rejection of English fashions in favour of African dress. His father's exhortation that he 'look like an Englishman' is exposed as absurd through Tomas' direct appeal to the natural difference of race: 'Well, sir, if I try till I die, I shall never look like an Englishman.' Tomas' final choice to be true to his African identity by appearing in 'pantaloons and the bright loose overjacket of a Wolof from Gambia' reveals how Creole nationalism identified itself with tribal origins *outside* Sierra Leone, making links with a metropolitan-based pan-Africanism rather than a notion of specifically Sierra Leonean unity. The endorsement of feminist ideas within the narrative, while making concessions to 'some English customs,' remains its reliance on 'natural' personality and inclination. The role of women within the household is judged with reference to a lifestyle perceived to be particularly English in origin, but which also has a sympathetic place within Tomas' own nature. Tomas' sympathy for women's equality is immediately revealed as an innate quality and therefore reflected in his 'feminine' style of clothing. . . .

Source: Kadiatu Kanneh, "Coming Home: Pan-Africanism and National Identities," in *African Identities: Race, Nation and Culture in Ethnography, Pan-Africanism and Black Literatures*, Routledge, 1998, pp. 48–108.

Barbara Bair

In the following excerpt, Bair recounts Casely-Hayford's return to Freetown and her subsequent involvement in the Universal Negro Improvement Association and the creation of a girls' school.

SISTERHOOD AND SELF-RESPECT: FEMINIST PAN-AFRICANISM

Female Education and Involvement in the UNIA: When Adelaide Casely Hayford left her husband and returned to Freetown with her young daughter in the spring of 1914, she became a music teacher at the Annie Walsh Memorial School, where she had volunteered years before. In addition to finding work, she also became active in community affairs, much as she had been in England. Soon after her arrival she spoke at the Wesleyan church on 'the Rights of Women and Christian Marriage' and thereafter made 'frequent public addresses' in women's forums, including a talk to the Ladies

"

CASELY HAYFORD WROTE THAT SHE HAD COME TO A REALIZATION ABOUT THE IMPORTANCE OF APPRECIATING AND PRESERVING AFRICAN HERITAGE, AND OF INSTILLING THE KIND OF FIRM RACE CONSCIOUSNESS THAT GARVEY PREACHED TO HIS FOLLOWERS."

Pastoral Aid Association on the 'social troubles in the family, industrial troubles (labor vs. capital), economic war (war between producers and consumers); disease, health problems and finally racial war.'

By October 1919, she was president of the local YWCA and was teaching YWCA classes for young women along with her niece Kathleen Easmon. During this period of her involvement in the YWCA, she also became a member of the local Freetown branch of the UNIA. There is no direct documentation of Casely Hayford's reasons for becoming a leader in the UNIA; however, her membership coincided with her desire to start a school for girls with a curriculum that stressed many of the same elements that were central to the educational program of Garveyism. Garvey had begun the UNIA as a benevolent association in Jamaica, with plans to begin an industrial training school for Blacks in the West Indies on the model of Booker T. Washington's Tuskegee Institute. When he traveled to the United States to raise funds for the UNIA and its proposed school, the organization took on broader economic and political goals. Although the Jamaican institute was not built, education remained a mainstay of the Garveyite platform. Unlike W.E.B. Du Bois and other advocates of a liberal or classical education for Blacks, Garvey endorsed a combination of industrial/vocational training and a curriculum that would heighten student awareness of African history and an appreciation of African arts. According to the UNIA Constitution, each local UNIA division would plan a series of classes for children, with mostly women from the ladies' wings of the divisions serving as teachers. The women's auxiliaries also sponsored classes, with Mothers' Clubs meetings, Black Cross Nurse instruction on home nursing and nutrition and the teaching of practical arts such as dressmaking and millinery. Women's divisions also sponsored exhibits of African art and clothing. UNIA division meetings and special events also relied heavily on the arts, with choral music, elocution performances, debates, drama events, pageants and dances among regular division activities. Music and oratory were also important functions within the UNIA's African Universal Church. The UNIA briefly opened the Booker T. Washington University, a classroom building in Harlem, and in the mid 1920s invested in Liberty University, a former high school in Virginia that was converted to a UNIA curriculum. In 1937 Garvey taught eleven students in the African School of Philosophy, a training course for UNIA organizers and officers. The lessons from Garvey's training sessions were later made available to Garveyite men and women as a home study correspondence course.

While West African men were attracted to the UNIA's economic program, particularly to the promise of the Black owned and operated Black Star Line, it is likely that Adelaide Casely Hayford came to the organization because of its dual-sex structure, which afforded women a separate sphere of influence as well as leadership roles within the hierarchy of the women's wings of the divisions, and because of the divisions' cultural and educational programs. Explaining her desire to build the school, Casely Hayford wrote that she had come to a realization about the importance of appreciating and preserving African heritage, and of instilling the kind of firm race consciousness that Garvey preached to his followers. In her article 'A Girl's School in West Africa,' she wrote a critique of colonial education as social control:

> the education meted out to us had, either consciously or unconsciously taught us to despise ourselves, and that our immediate need was an education which would instill into us a love of country, a pride of race, an enthusiasm for the Black man's capabilities, and a genuine admiration for Africa's wonderful art work. We needed an education more adapted to our requirements, which while assimilating all that was good in European education, would help us to maintain our natural heritage of African individuality, and to become the best type of African we could be.

In addition to this cultural nationalist agenda, which challenged the hegemony of Eurocentric teaching in colonial and missionary schools, Casely Hayford also had feminist reasons for beginning a school for girls. She envisioned that her school would train young adult women for positions in the work force previously reserved for men, particularly as white-collar and clerical workers within the civil service and in business enterprises. At the same time that she would better prepare girls to support themselves as producers in the labor force, she would also obey the class dictates of her own background, planning to train them in the domestic and fine arts in order to make them more companionate wives for well-educated husbands. Rina Okonkwo has noted that Casely Hayford's ideas for the school grew out of her personal awareness of her need to support herself and her child, and by extension, the need for other women to learn a trade and to foster their talents and self-respect independent of their relationships with men. The educational curriculum advocated by Casely Hayford thus had a compensatory nature: it would overcome the cultural deprivation inflicted by colonial educational systems, and it would offer the same opportunities for advancement to girls that had been previously made available to boys.

By the spring of 1919, Casely Hayford was the lady president of the Freetown UNIA division and as the leading female officer, had enlisted the women of the division in raising funds for her proposed school for girls. The plan was initially endorsed by both the ladies' division and the larger male and female membership. In April 1919 Casely Hayford delivered a UNIA address about the school, telling her audience that the 'purpose underlying the idea of the Technical Training School for Girls was to enable the female section of our country to get their livelihood by honourable means and independently.' Kathleen Easmon devised a strategy for grassroots campaigning on behalf of the school. Placards were posted in the streets and announcements about the school were read from Freetown pulpits. UNIA women went door-to-door with collection boxes to solicit funds; leading Europeans in the colonial infrastructure were also approached for financial support. Controversy arose in Freetown when news spread that Casely Hayford had approached members of her husband's NCBWA for support and had not only been rebuffed, but reprimanded for beginning a scheme that would compete with the NCBWA's own limited ability to win financial support for its programs. When Casely Hayford contacted a NCBWA member and told him of her plan to travel down the West African coast to raise funds for the school, he 'gave her distinctly to understand that any such move by her would be countered by him: that he would cable to the various centres down the coast, warning the people of her probable activities among them.... If, however, she would sit tight for a while and throw in her lot with the Congress,' then perhaps 'she and her scheme would be favourably entertained in the near future.' Soon after, the Freetown barrister C.D. Hotobah-During wrote a letter to the editor of the *Sierra Leone Weekly News* stating that the proposed school was unnecessary since there were no jobs for trained women. Kathleen Easmon replied that jobs would be created if there were skilled women to fill them and if the colonial Civil Service was opened to female employees. Meanwhile, a dispute arose within UNIA ranks over Casely Hayford's management of the funds collected by female UNIA members and over the legal question of whether Casely Hayford or the UNIA leadership would have direct authority over the proposed school. In response to these internal politics and the recalcitrance of community members who opposed the training of girls, Casely Hayford resigned as lady president of the UNIA, returned the funds collected by women UNIA members, canceled the fund-raising trip down the coast and made alternative plans to travel to the United States with Kathleen Easmon. Having been stymied by African male Pan-Africanists, she turned instead to African-Americans, particularly to African-American women, for the aid and expertise she needed....

Source: Barbara Bair, "Pan-Africanism as Process: Adelaide Casely Hayford, Garveyism, and the Cultural Roots of Nationalism," in *Imagining Home: Class, Culture and Imagining Nationalism in the African Diaspora*, edited by Sidney F. Lemelle and Robin D. G. Kelley, Verso, 1994, pp. 121–44.

SOURCES

"Africanism," in *New Internationalist*, August 2000, http://www.newint.org/features/2000/08/05/simply/ (accessed September 30, 2011).

Casely-Hayford, Adelaide, "Mista Courifer," in *Unwinding Threads: Writing by Women in Africa*, edited by Charlotte H. Bruner, Heinemann, 1994, pp. 11–19.

Cromwell, Adelaide M., "Adelaide Smith Casely Hayford as a Widow: The End of a Dream," in *An African Victorian Feminist: The Life and Times of Adelaide Smith Casely Hayford, 1868–1960*, Howard University Press, 1992, pp. 182–99.

Dagnini, Jérémie Kroubo, "Marcus Garvey: A Controversial Figure in the History of Pan-Africanism," in *Journal of Pan African Studies*, Vol. 2, No. 3, March 2008, http://www.jpanafrican.com/docs/vol2no3/MarcusGarveyAControversialFigureInTheHistoryOfPanAfricanism.pdf (accessed September 30, 2011).

Desai, Gaurav, "Gendered Self-Fashioning: Adelaide Casely Hayford's Black Atlantic," in *Research in African Literatures*, Vol. 35, No. 3, Fall 2004, pp. 141–60.

"Foil," in *The Bedford Glossary of Critical and Literary Terms*, edited by Ross Murfin and Supriya M. Ray, Bedford/St. Martin's Press, 2003, p. 168.

"Gender Equality and Social Institutions in Sierra Leone," in *SIGI: Social Institutions & Gender Index*, http://genderindex.org/country/sierra-leone (accessed September 30, 2011).

"Legal Protection at Last for the Women of Sierra Leone," in *UN Women*, July 5, 2007, http://www.unifem.org/news_events/story_detail.php?StoryID=606 (accessed September 30, 2011).

Murfin, Ross, and Supriya M. Ray, "Foil," in *The Bedford Glossary of Critical and Literary Terms*, Bedford/St. Martins, 2003, p. 168.

Nazareth, Peter, Review of *Stories from Central and Southern Africa*, in *World Literature Today*, Vol. 58, No. 4, Fall 1984, pp. 650–51.

Okonkwo, Rina, "Adelaide Casely Hayford, Cultural Nationalist and Feminist," in *Phylon*, Vol. 42, No. 1, Spring 1981, pp. 41–51.

Rogers, Brittany Rose, "Hayford, Adelaide Smith Casely (1868–1960)," in *BlackPast.org*, http://www.blackpast.org/?q=gah/hayford-adelaide-smith-casely-1868-1960 (accessed September 30, 2011).

Sesay, Bhai D., "Adelaide Casely Hayford (1868–1960): Cultural Nationalist and Educationist," in *Sierra Leone Live*, http://www.sierraleonelive.com/adelaide-casely-hayford-1868-1960-cultural-nationalist-and-educationist (accessed September 30, 2011).

Shelton, Austin J., "Clothes Philosophy and African Literature: A Mirror for Typologists," in *Transition*, No. 47, 1975, pp. 12–16.

"Sierra Leone Information," in *Art & Life in Africa Online*, University of Iowa, October 15, 1998, http://www.uiowa.edu/~africart/toc/countries/Sierra_Leone.html (accessed September 30, 2011).

"Sierra Leone: Women Need Rights and Protection," in *Amnesty International*, August 1, 2006, http://www.amnesty.org/en/library/asset/AFR51/009/2006/en/a6a5b7cb-d40b-11dd-8743-d305bea2b2c7/afr510092006en.html (accessed September 30, 2011).

FURTHER READING

Cromwell, Adelaide M., *An African Victorian Feminist: The Life and Times of Adelaide Smith Casely Hayford, 1868–1960*, Routledge, 1986.

An African Victorian Feminist is, to date, the only full-length biography of Casely-Hayford that has been published. Cromwell covers Casely-Hayford's entire life and work in this 236-page tome. She provides separate chapters for each of Casely-Hayford's major projects, including her school for girls, her advocacy work, and her writing.

Esedebe, P. Olisanwuche, *Pan-Africanism: The Idea and Movement, 1776–1991*, Howard University Press, 1994.

Pan-Africanism is a major movement whose advocates seek the unification of all African people or people living in Africa. It originated in the late 1800s and still has proponents today. Esedebe provides a comprehensive overview of the movement.

Hughes, Langston, ed., *An African Treasury*, Crown, 1960.

An African Treasury is a collection of articles, essays, poems, and short stories by black African writers, selected by Langston Hughes. "Mista Courifer" was first published as a part of this collection. Many of Casely-Hayford's peers and contemporaries are included in this book.

Newell, Stephanie, *West African Literatures: Ways of Reading*, Oxford University Press, 2006.

Newell's study contextualizes West African literature within the broader culture. This account summarizes the literature of the entire West African region and provides cultural insights into its literary tradition.

Oyewumi, Oyeronke, ed., *African Women and Feminism: Reflecting on the Politics of Sisterhood*, African World Press, 2004.

All of the essays included in this volume were written by African women who were born and raised in Africa but are now university professors in the United States. This book sheds light on the antifeminist attitudes exhibited by Mista Courifer in his treatment of his wife.

SUGGESTED SEARCH TERMS

Adelaide Casely-Hayford

Adelaide Casely-Hayford AND feminism

Adelaide Casely-Hayford AND Pan-Africanism

Adelaide Casely-Hayford AND nationalism

Adelaide Casely-Hayford AND activist

Adelaide Casely-Hayford AND Mista Courifer

Adelaide Casely-Hayford AND fiction writings

Adelaide Casely-Hayford AND African women writers

Mista Courifer AND feminism

Mista Courifer AND Pan-Africanism

Mista Courifer AND nationalism

The Outlaws

SELMA LAGERLÖF

1894

Renowned as the first woman to be awarded the Nobel Prize in Literature, Swedish author Selma Lagerlöf was a novelist and short-story writer. The short story "The Outlaws," originally published in 1894, concerns the fate of a peasant named Berg who flees into the forest after killing a monk. There, Berg joins forces with a young fisherman, Tord, and the two help one another survive in the wilderness, while Berg continues to escape capture by the villagers who wish to see him punished for his crime. Berg learns that Tord, who lives in exile and is believed to be a thief, took the blame for a crime his father committed. As the story progresses, Tord learns of Berg's adulterous history with a woman named Unn. He also discovers that the monk slain by Berg had publicly accused Unn and Berg, in front of Berg's wife, of having an affair.

After Berg finishes this account, he grows alarmed that Tord seems to have no moral compass; he does not condemn Berg for his actions. Berg then undertakes to teach Tord about the nature of God, morality, and justice. Tord later hears voices in a storm that compel him to seek justice for Berg's sin. Throughout the story, Lagerlöf explores the nature of justice, friendship, and betrayal. Like many of her works, "The Outlaws" employs supernatural elements and conveys a sense of moral ambiguity and complexity. Religiosity, spiritualism, and mysticism are interwoven into the fabric of the story, yet Lagerlöf avoids any overt moralizing or preachiness.

Selma Lagerlof *(© Lebrecht Music and Arts Photo Library / Alamy)*

"The Outlaws" was originally published as "De fagelfrie" in Swedish in 1894 as part of the short-story collection *Osynliga länkar*. This collection was translated by Pauline Bancroft Floch in 1899 and published by Little, Brown as *Invisible Links*. A 1907 translation of "The Outlaws" by Grace Isabel Colbron was published in 1927 in the collection *The World's One Hundred Best Short Stories, Part Eight: Men*, edited by Grant Overton. A reprint of this volume was reissued in 2005.

AUTHOR BIOGRAPHY

Born on November 20, 1858, in Östra Emterwik in the province of Värmland in Sweden, Lagerlöf was the fourth of five children. Her father, Erik Lagerlöf, was a retired army lieutenant and a farmer, and her mother, Lovisa Wallroth Lagerlöf, came from a wealthy family. Lagerlöf was raised on the family estate with her sisters, while her brothers received a formal education and went on to university studies. Lagerlöf remained at the family estate for much of her youth. Economic troubles plagued the family during a period of national recession in the 1870s, and Lagerlöf served as the governess for her sisters for some time.

In 1881, after securing a loan for her education, she departed for a teachers' college in Stockholm. After she completed her schooling in 1885, Lagerlöf began teaching at a girls' secondary school in Landskrona. She began writing during this time as well and in 1891 published the well-received novel *Gösta Berlings saga*. Several years later, in 1894, she published her second work, a collection of short stories, *Osynliga länkar* (*Invisible Links*, 1899).

Over the next several years, Lagerlöf traveled and wrote, accompanied by her friend and companion, fellow writer Sophie Elkan. Having received financial backing in 1895 from both the Swedish royal family and the Swedish Academy, Lagerlöf devoted herself to her writing and gave up teaching. In 1897, after traveling to Italy, Lagerlöf published *Antikris mirakler* (*The Miracles of Antichrist*, 1899), a novel set in Sicily. She went on to publish several other novels and in 1909 was awarded the Nobel Prize for Literature. At this point in her career Lagerlöf was both a critical and popular success, but her productivity declined during World War I.

Following the war, she became involved in a variety of women's causes and began writing again, publishing short fiction and a trilogy, along with her autobiography. After many years together, Lagerlöf lost Elkan to a cerebral hemorrhage in 1921. During World War II, Lagerlöf worked with the resistance movement against Nazi Germany, aiding in the escape of German artists and intellectuals from Nazi forces. Later, Lagerlöf donated her Nobel Prize medal to the Finnish resistance to Soviet military aggression. Lagerlöf suffered a stroke and died at her home on March 16, 1940.

PLOT SUMMARY

"The Outlaws" opens with a brief description of how two outcasts found each other and became companions. After a peasant who has murdered a monk escapes into the woods, he meets a young fisherman, also a fugitive, who had been accused of stealing fishing net. The two make a home in a cave in the mountainside and hunt and fish for sustenance. Occasionally the fisherman ventures into the village with the game he and the peasant kill and trades it for supplies. The men are hunted by the villagers who would see them punished for their crimes. The murderer sometimes taunts his pursuers by allowing himself to be seen and then, being strong, fast, and agile, leading them on a chase. He takes great risks, climbs to enormous heights, and manages to elude capture.

The young fisherman, named Tord, is sixteen years old and has been living in the woods for a year when the story begins. The peasant, the reader is now informed, is named Berg. Tall and strong, he is sometimes called "the Giant." Berg is described as fit and handsome, and Tord seems to worship him. Happy to serve Berg by performing the menial chores around their camp, Tord appears unaware of Berg's contemptuous attitude toward him. Tord is repeatedly approached by villagers who hope to persuade him to betray Berg's whereabouts, but Tord refuses.

Later, Tord becomes ill after having slept in the entrance to the cave, exposed to the elements, the better to guard Berg. Tord becomes feverish for days, but Berg cares for him until he is once again well. As the two begin to speak more openly with one another, Berg is impressed with Tord's knowledge of Berg's family history and the wealth his ancestors once possessed. When Berg asks Tord about his own family, Tord states that his father is a thief who plunders wrecked ships and that his mother is a witch who eats corpses. The conversation continues, and Berg learns that Tord, at his mother's urging, claimed responsibility for his father's crimes and then fled to the woods to avoid punishment. Berg is astonished and angry that a young man would throw his life away in such a manner.

One day, Berg and Tord explore the ponds in a remote region of the mountain's forest and become entranced by its stillness and beauty. As they fish, they imagine they see a water spirit, a nixie, in the depths, but when she vanishes, they are unsure whether what they had seen was real. Just after this incident, the two men see a woman rowing a boat and gathering water lilies. They remain hidden from her sight until she has gone. Tord later dreams of the young woman, and he asks Berg if he knew the woman's name. Berg identifies her as Unn and tells Tord that he is related to her. Soon Tord realizes that the woman was the cause of Berg's exile in the forest. He recalls having heard about the incident that precipitated Berg's murder of the monk.

Berg relates the events that led to the murder, describing the banquet he hosted with his wife. Unn was at the banquet with Berg, his wife, and their extended family. Between his own recollections and Berg's discussion of the matter, Tord gathers the full story. Berg's wife, who suspected that Berg and Unn were having an affair, had invited a monk to the banquet in hopes that the monk would be able to teach Berg the error of his actions. The monk made the affair known to all at the banquet, hoping to shame Berg into ending his relationship with Unn. When Unn turned to leave the banquet, Berg followed her and asked her what she wanted him to do, so that she would continue to be with him. Berg then murdered the monk. Unn thanked him and then urged him to flee and save himself.

When Tord's comments about the incident reveal a deepening of his appreciation for Berg, rather than an understanding of the moral wrongness of his actions, Berg feels compelled to teach Tord about Christianity and culpability, about sin and justice. Sometime later, when Tord is alone in the forest during a storm, he begins to hear voices. He comes to believe that God is speaking to him, telling him that he must reveal Berg's location to the villagers. Tord states that he longs for Berg to repent, that he fears for Berg because he will ultimately suffer God's judgment. Tord then sees the ghost of the monk that Berg murdered and believes that the monk, like God, is urging him to betray Berg in order for Berg's soul to be saved.

When Tord returns to Berg, he tells him of his vision of the monk and how the monk and the ghosts of other monks tried to persuade Tord to turn Berg in. Tord expresses his love for his friend and describes the way he insisted to the ghosts that Berg is a good man, despite his deed. Berg tells Tord he must return to the village and go to the priest there and tell him the truth, yet Tord insists that Berg must go himself, in order to repent his sin. Berg feels the weight of his misdeed growing within him, and he tells Tord of his deep regret. Tord grows joyful with the knowledge that Berg is indeed sorry for his sin. He then tells Berg to escape, before the villagers find him, for Tord has already gone to them and told them where Berg might be found.

Berg is furious that Tord has betrayed him. He reaches for his ax, but Tord responds quickly, grabbing his own ax and striking Berg at once. The villagers then arrive at the cave and praise Tord for his actions, informing him that he will be pardoned for his past crimes. Tord cries over the body of his friend but with the speech that closes the story announces that he acted in the name of justice.

CHARACTERS

Berg

Berg is a peasant who kills a monk prior to the opening of the story. After fleeing into the forest, he joins forces with sixteen-year-old Tord, who is a fisherman and allegedly a thief. Berg is described as tall, handsome, strong, and fit. Berg and Tord hunt and fish together, and Tord, by acting as a scout, helps keep Berg safe from the villagers who wish to capture and punish him. Berg is initially disdainful of Tord, regarding him "with contempt, as a common thief," but their businesslike companionship gradually evolves into something of a friendship. Berg's views on Tord soften because of Tord's adoration of him and following Tord's revelation that he committed no crime but rather took the blame for his father's thievery.

In the course of their conversations, Berg describes to Tord the way he slew the monk, telling Tord he acted in deference to the wishes of Unn, with whom he was having an extramarital affair. Alarmed at Tord's apparent lack of a sense of morality, Berg lectures his young companion on God, religion, the nature of sin, and the importance of justice. The lecture proves to be Berg's undoing, because Tord becomes tormented with thoughts of Berg's sin. When confronted by Tord, Berg becomes increasingly aware of his own sense of regret about his murder of the monk. The sin becomes "monstrous" in his estimation, and he begins to see the way that his actions have led him to stand "in conflict with the Will that rules the world," that is, God's will, according to Berg's earlier stated beliefs. At this point, "remorse entered his heart." However, when Tord confesses that he has already betrayed Berg, Berg resorts instantly to violence, drawing his ax, prepared to murder Tord. Instead, Berg is slain by Tord.

Berg's Wife

Berg's wife appears in the story only through Berg's recollection. The unnamed wife asked the monk to attend a banquet she and Berg were hosting. She had hoped that the monk would be able to persuade Berg to be faithful to her. After Berg kills the monk, Berg's wife forces her children to look at Unn, so that they can know the person whom Berg's wife believes is ultimately responsible for Berg's actions.

Monk

The unnamed monk is slain by Berg prior to the story's main action. As is revealed later, the monk was invited to a banquet hosted by Berg and his wife in order to shame Berg into ending his affair with Unn. As a result of his public condemnation of Unn and Berg's relationship, the monk is murdered by Berg.

Tord

Tord is a sixteen-year-old fisherman who is discovered by Berg in the woods. Accused of stealing fishing net, Tord, like Berg, has escaped into the forest to avoid capture and prosecution; he has been living in the forest for a year when Berg finds him. The men work together to sustain themselves through hunting and fishing. Because Tord's crime is a minor one, he is not universally reviled in the village, as is Berg, who has killed a man of God. Tord occasionally returns to the outskirts of the village and trades with the more isolated of the villagers. Tord brings game he and Berg have hunted and in return brings back to the cave such supplies as clothing, arrowheads, and dairy products, which he shares with Berg.

Tord regards Berg with some awe, having "never seen any one so magnificent and so mighty before." Tord treats Berg with extreme reverence, serving him and honoring him like a god. After Tord reveals that his mother is a witch and his father plunders shipwrecks as a means of survival, he further alludes to the fact that at his mother's urging, he fled to the forest as if he had committed the theft of the fishing net rather than his father. Sparing his father punishment and possible execution, Tord takes on those risks himself. Berg grows angry with Tord for having confessed to crimes he did not commit. He subsequently begins to treat Tord more kindly, and when Tord questions him about Unn, whom they have seen in the forest, Berg explains to Tord Unn's role in his murdering of the monk.

When Tord describes Unn has having been "ennobled" by Berg's deed, Berg is surprised and frustrated that Tord "never condemned that which was wrong. He seemed to know no sense of responsibility." Berg teaches Tord about such things, and Tord grows increasingly agitated. He becomes convinced that the ghost of the slain monk has spoken to him and told him to betray Berg, which he does. After compelling Berg to admit his remorse, Tord admits that he has told the villagers where they may find Tord. When Berg despairs and rages at this betrayal, he moves to attack Tord, but Tord kills Berg first. They are soon discovered by the villagers, who regard Tord as a hero. Tord mourns the loss of his friend but insists that his actions were just.

Unn

Unn is the young woman with whom Berg engaged in an affair before the action of the story commences. After Berg and Tord spy Unn in the forest, her relationship to Berg is revealed through Berg's recollections. She compels Berg to kill the monk after he has revealed their affair publicly.

THEMES

Divine Justice

In "The Outlaws," the notion of divine justice plays a significant role in the story. Divine justice refers to punishments meted out by God or in God's name for wrongdoing against God's will. Berg begins to suspect that Tord has little understanding of moral behavior and responsibility when he tells Berg about his mother and father. Tord states that his mother is a witch who utilizes the bodies of drowned children for ointments or even for food. Berg is horrified, but Tord replies calmly that it might seem horrible, but it is not horrible for a witch. She cannot help what she is, Tord suggests, and she cannot therefore be blamed or punished the way someone else might be.

Berg's frustration and pity for Tord's moral ignorance culminate when Tord fails to find fault with him for his murder of the monk. The murder, in Tord's eyes, brought Unn a sense of greater dignity because Berg defended Unn's honor. Berg is "astonished at the same thing that had before now surprised him in the boy. Tord was a heathen, or worse than a heathen; he never condemned that which was wrong." Aware that Tord's mother taught her son "to believe in the spirits of the dead," Berg takes it upon himself to provide Tord with moral instruction. "He opened the eyes of this ignorant boy to the power of God, the Lord of all Justice, the avenger of wrong, who condemned sinners to the pangs of hell everlasting."

Berg's teachings make a great impact on Tord, who becomes tormented by the voices he hears in the forest. He dwells on the notion of sin and on Berg's sin and becomes convinced that "God, the Great Avenger, the Lord of all Justice" is speaking to him, demanding "that he should give up the murderer of the monk to vengeance." Because Tord learned from Berg of the nature of sin and of God's role as the punisher of sin and as the champion of justice, Tord begins to believe fervently that Berg must be brought to justice for his crime. Tord tells the villagers where Berg may be found, so that justice may be delivered by their hands, through whatever punishment they see fit.

Before the villagers can reach Berg, Tord compels Berg to express his remorse for his crime. Berg begins to understand the weight of his actions, and Tord feels relief that Berg is morally capable of feeling guilt and remorse over the murder of the monk. When Tord confesses that he has set the villagers on Berg, Berg turns on his friend. Tord is prepared, however, and kills Berg. As he stands over the body of his friend, Tord states that he "slew Berg because Berg had taught him that justice is the cornerstone of the world." Ironically, Tord had previously been ignorant of this notion of justice before being tutored by Berg. Essentially, Berg is slain, or in Tord's eyes, brought to justice, because of Berg's own moral convictions.

Friendship and Betrayal

As fugitives from justice, Tord and Berg develop a relationship built upon the aid they can offer one another. Tord leads possible pursuers away from Berg, thereby protecting him from the law. Berg assists Tord with hunting and fishing and cares for Tord through his illness. Tord is additionally able to venture into the outskirts of town and trade with the villagers, bringing back additional supplies. Yet the balance of the friendship is skewed. Tord regards Berg with adoration and devotion: "He served him humbly as he would have served a master, he revered him as he would have revered a god." Berg, however, seems to think Tord is somewhat beneath him. Berg's attitude toward Tord begins to shift after he discovers that Tord has refused the villagers' promises of reward for turning Berg in. Berg tells Tord he

TOPICS FOR FURTHER STUDY

- *The Saga of Gösta Berling*, originally published in Swedish in 1891 as *Gösta Berlings saga*, is one of Lagerlöf's best-known works. In it, through the character of a disgraced minister, Lagerlöf explores the conflict between human urges and moral responsibilities, a theme also examined in "The Outlaws." Read *The Saga of Gösta Berling* (a 2009 English translation is available) and study the way Lagerlöf treats this theme in a full-length novel. Consider as well the style the author uses. Is the novel similar in tone to the short story? Write an essay in which you examine this and the other thematic concerns of *The Saga of Gösta Berling*. Be sure to discuss the ways in which other formal elements, including characterization, language, and imagery, aid the author in the exploration of her themes.
- Hahn Moo-sook's 1992 novel *Encounter: A Novel of Nineteenth-Century Korea*, translated by Ok Young Kim Chang, explores the tensions between the Catholic missionaries brought to Korea and traditional pre-missionary Korean culture. Set during roughly the same time period as when Lagerlöf was writing, the novel considers the evolving role of Christian religion in a non-Christian country. Read Moo-sook's novel, and contemplate the way the various religions (Catholicism, Taoism, and Buddhism) are treated by the author. Write a review of the novel, summarizing its plot and characters and providing an overview of its treatment of the role of religion in Korean culture in the nineteenth century.
- Swedish novelist Per Nilsson's 2005 young-adult novel *You & You & You*, geared toward a more mature teen audience, is a modern example of Swedish fiction. The work, translated by Tara Chance, employs elements of magical realism (incorporating supernatural, fantastic, or absurd elements within an otherwise realistic narrative) in its exploration of the relationships among three friends. With a small group, read Nilsson's novel. Consider the way the author employs the use of the supernatural in the novel. Are religious themes or figures incorporated into the plot? In what way does the author's use of a third-person omniscient narrator shape or affect the characterizations? Discuss these issues, as well as the story's basic plot and the balance of dark themes and whimsical elements in the story, in an online blog your group creates.
- Lagerlöf wrote during a time in which naturalism and realism were the prevalent modes in literature, and she introduced into this literary world a return to the romantic ideals of the earlier portion of the nineteenth century. Research these trends in Swedish nineteenth-century literary styles, examining the way each period dovetailed into the next. Were Swedish writers influenced by movements elsewhere in Europe or in the rest of the world? Were there historical events that triggered or contributed to the evolution of these movements in Swedish literature? Write a research paper in which you analyze the trends in Swedish nineteenth-century literature. Be sure to cite all your sources. Share your findings with the class via a PowerPoint summary of your paper or through a Web page in which you highlight your findings and provide links to related materials.

---

is a "fool," but Tord continues to treat Berg with faithful devotion.

Berg gradually becomes close enough to Tord to ask Tord about his family. Upon learning that Tord's parents have treated the boy unjustly by encouraging Tord to accept blame for a crime committed by his father, Berg grows angry, outraged on Tord's behalf: "Here this strong, beautiful boy had thrown away his whole life for another. Neither love, nor riches, nor respect of his fellow

Tord and Berg are both hiding from the law in the wilderness. (Raywoo / Shutterstock.com)

men could ever be his again." Berg also now comprehends that however foolish Tord may be, he is not the "common thief" Berg once believed him to be.

After Berg, out of deep concern for what he believes to be Tord's complete ignorance of morality, teaches Tord about God's justice and moral responsibility, Tord begins to fear for his friend. Understanding now how Berg has sinned against God, Tord fears for his soul. Tord, compelled by the voices he has heard in the forest, tells the villagers where they may find Berg and then persuades him to repent. Tord is deeply moved that he has been able to "move [Berg's] heart," but the thing that Berg has feared throughout the course of the story has come to pass, as he realizes that Tord has already betrayed him. "I trusted you," Berg tells Tord; "I loved you." After Tord kills Berg, he "crouched beside the body, spoke amid his tears to the dead, and begged him to awake." Tord, so moved by love for his friend that he resorted to betrayal in order to save his soul, weeps over Berg's body before he rises and proclaims that the justice Berg has taught him to respect is "the cornerstone of the world."

STYLE

Folktale

Like many of Lagerlöf's works, "The Outlaws" has the tone and style of a folktale. Lagerlöf uses an omniscient third-person narrator to relate the story. An omniscient narrator is an all-knowing one, able to relate the thoughts and feelings of any of the characters in the story. Lagerlöf's narrator uses the third-person voice, that is, speaks of the other characters by name or the pronouns "he" or "she," in contrast to a first-person narrator, who would refer to himself as "I." A third-person narrator often exists outside the action of the story. Third-person narrators, while not typically characters in the story, do relate events in a variety of ways; some use an objective, journalistic tone.

In "The Outlaws," whether associated or not with Lagerlöf herself, the narrator comes across as an oral storyteller, describing events in lyrical language and weaving in elements of foreshadowing, as when the narrator informs the reader that Tord "had been accused of the theft of a herring net." The reader, like Berg, believes for some time that Tord is "a common thief," yet Tord later reveals that he has shouldered the blame for his father's crime. The setting of the story is repeatedly described in dark and threatening terms, as in a folktale. The cave in which the outlaws live is "gloomy." When pursued they hide there, "panting in terror." Berg traverses a "gaunt, bare hilltop." Tord is fearful "in the night darkness of the wood" and trembles in the "gloom of a thicket" even during the day.

Lagerlöf also incorporates elements of the supernatural into the story, another aspect that underscores its relationship to the folktale. Tord, for example, claims his mother is a witch, and Berg believes that she has taught Tord to listen to voices of the dead. Through these methods, Lagerlöf conveys the sense that a story is being told to a listening audience, and she captures her reader's attention and builds suspense by incorporating an atmosphere of darkness and danger. The way Lagerlöf approaches the nature of moral behavior, of right and wrong, in the story suggests that Lagerlöf will, in folktale fashion, provide a moral, yet the message remains ambiguous, because both men were moved in some way by their love for another, but both were capable of murder as well.

Supernaturalism

In "The Outlaws," the supernatural aspects of the story are vital to the progression of the narrative. There are several elements of the supernatural early in the story: Tord says that his mother is a witch, and Tord and Berg believe they see a nixie, or a half-human, half-fish water spirit, sleeping in the water. A more significant example of Lagerlöf's supernaturalism occurs when Tord begins to hear voices in the forest. He hears laughing, threats, and curses, and to Tord the sounds he hears are alternately perceived as a multitude of voices and as a single voice speaking to him. Terrified, he also believes he hears an army of men crashing through the woods.

Initially ascribing the voices and sounds to "ghosts and sprits," Tord eventually comes to believe that he is hearing the voice of God. He believes that "God pursued him because of his comrade." Tord tells God that he wants to plead with Berg to "make his peace with God," but he is unable to because of his embarrassment and his love for his friend. Next, Tord sees the ghost of the monk, the man Berg slew. He envisions the man covered in blood and with an ax wound in his forehead. The monk implores Tord to betray Berg and thereby save Berg's soul.

After doing what the monk asks, Tord returns to Berg, and he tells him of what he saw, mentioning specifically the bloody ax wound in the monk's head. Berg, attempting to convince Tord that he has only imagined the spirits, informs Tord that he slew the monk with a knife, not an ax. However, when Berg learns that Tord has betrayed him and attempts to attack him, Tord kills Berg with his ax. When he sees the fatal wound in Berg's head, the significance of his earlier vision is underscored. The wound he saw in the ghost of the monk was that which he himself would create in Berg. The presence of spirits in "The Outlaws" and Tord's firm belief in them bring about the climax of the story by causing Berg's death. These elements also lend the work its dark tone and supply the grim and suspenseful tale with the threat of otherworldly danger and doom.

HISTORICAL CONTEXT

Neoromanticism in Swedish Literature

During the 1890s, some Swedish writers increasingly turned away from the realism and naturalism that had prevailed in Swedish literature for some time and instead embraced many of the ideals of romanticism, creating a literary school of thought described as neoromanticism. Realism and naturalism both focus on the accurate depiction of individuals, society, and environments. Naturalism differs from realism in its scientific approach to human behavior, which is regarded as a part of the fabric of the natural world; humans are seen as devoid of free will but are rather acted upon, like other animals, by the forces of nature, instinct, and the environment.

As Adolph B. Benson observes in the *Columbia Dictionary of Modern European Literature*, "The demand for a more elevated style, whether in verse or prose, for idealism, beauty, imagination, and the sovereign rights of the individual artist were resuscitated during the last decade of the 19th century." The lyricism and the idealization of the individual and the imagination that characterized the romanticism of the early nineteenth-century literature became vital once again for Swedish neoromantics. Writers such as Lagerlöf and Verner von Heidenstam have been

COMPARE & CONTRAST

- **1890s:** Popular styles in Swedish literature include naturalism and realism, both of which focus on the unidealized, accurate portrayal of individuals and society. Some writers, such as Lagerlöf and Verner von Heidenstam, begin to move away from these modes, embrace romantic styles of the past, and incorporate elements of the fantastic or supernatural in their works, along with a sense of mysticism and a focus on the individual and the imagination.

  Today: Popular Swedish literature includes a variety of genres, including historical fiction, by writers such as Kerstin Ekman and Carl-Johan Vallgren; coming-of-age stories, often set in the recent past, as in the works of Torbjörn Flygt and Mikael Niemi; and works incorporating magical realism, as seen in the fiction of Per Nilsson.

- **1890s:** The established state religion of Sweden is the Lutheran Church of Sweden. Dissatisfaction with the church, along with the popular perception of the church as an unfair institution that favors the wealthy, are factors that lead to the growth of independent, or free, Christian churches in Sweden.

  Today: About 75 percent of the Swedish population consider themselves members of the official Lutheran Church of Sweden. About 5 percent of the population practice other Protestant religions, and 5 percent are Muslim. The remainder of the Swedish population are generally Roman Catholic, Jewish, Buddhist, Pentecostal, Baptist, or Orthodox.

- **1890s:** Capital punishment (or execution) for crimes such as murder is legal in Sweden. A crime such as that committed by Berg in Lagerlöf's "The Outlaws" (the murder of a monk) is punishable by death. Historically, commoners are hanged, while nobles are beheaded, but by the later nineteenth century, beheading by ax is used on criminals of all social classes for crimes punishable by execution.

  Today: Capital punishment is no longer legal in Sweden, having been abolished for capital crimes committed during peacetime in 1921 and for all crime in 1976.

credited with engendering the neoromantic movement in Sweden. Lagerlöf employs the elements and style of the folktale in many of her works in a way that exemplifies the neoromantic emphasis on the imagination and the emotional and psychological struggles of the individual.

Lagerlöf's 1891 novel, *Gösta Berlings saga*, for example, reshapes Swedish folk legends "in an effusive, personal, spontaneously lyric prose," according to Alrik Gustafson in the *Columbia Dictionary of Modern European Literature*. At the time, this style was markedly different from most Swedish fiction, and the work helped to initiate the neoromantic movement in Sweden. Heidenstam made a similar impact with his poetry, novels and essays, in particular his essay "Renascence" (1889), which attacks the realism of the 1880s. Poet Ola Hansson likewise is counted among Sweden's neoromantics and wrote in a colorful lyric style. Hansson's works are characterized by idealism, mysticism, and eroticism. Sweden's neoromanticism of the 1890s was paralleled by similar movements in Denmark, though in Denmark the neoromantic movement was largely confined to poetry.

Christianity in Sweden in the 1890s

In "The Outlaws," Lagerlöf uses the characters of Berg and Tord to explore and question a sense of moral responsibility that is rooted in Christianity. Berg lectures Tord about God and teaches Tord to "love Christ and His Mother, and all the saintly men and women who sit before the throne of God," yet these teachings eventually compel

Berg was known as "the giant" in the villages. (Katie Dickinson / Shutterstock.com)

Tord to kill Berg. During the time Lagerlöf's story was written, the Christian church in Sweden was undergoing an era of conflict. Until the mid-nineteenth century, the state church, that is, the official Church of Sweden, was the Lutheran Church. The rigid doctrines that had become associated with this church began to be a source of contention for some Swedes, who protested the fact that religious gatherings that involved the taking of Communion (the eating of a wafer or bread-like product believed to be transmuted into the body of Jesus Christ) in places other than church were banned until 1858. Some Swedish Christians increasingly sought greater religious freedom; the Christian organization Christian Assemblies International states,

> It is estimated that more than one and a half million, or a third of the [Swedish] population, moved to America from the mid 19th century to the beginning of the 20th century, because of poverty and for political and religious reasons.

Christian denominations such as the Baptist Church and the Missionary Church were founded in Sweden during the late-nineteenth century; this period came to be known as the revivalist movement, in that these newly founded independent churches advocated a revival of interest in Christians developing a more personal relationship with Jesus Christ than that which was being cultivated in the Lutheran Church. Kenneth-Scott Latourette explains in *Christianity in a Revolutionary Age* that the growth of such "free" churches (those independent of the Lutheran Church of Sweden) was influenced by several social factors, including the fact that many "humble folk regarded the state church as allied with the wealthy." Latourette also maintains that the rise to prominence of the Social Democratic Workers Party, which was sparked by the industrialization of urban Sweden, contributed to the move away from the Church of Sweden by many Christians. The social democrats, focused on the rights of the working class, perceived the established state church as being an elite, classist institution. In the wake of this increasing disregard for the state religion, the free churches continued to gain followers and shaped the religious attitudes of Swedish Christians well into the twentieth century.

CRITICAL OVERVIEW

"The Outlaws" is not often discussed individually by modern critics. However, an early review of the work appeared in the 1899–1900 volume of the journal *Catholic World*, after the 1899 translation of the story was published. The *Catholic World* critic focuses on the relationship between Berg and Tord and the way their love for one another shapes their actions in the story: Tord's love for Berg is the driving force behind his betrayal, as he longs for Berg to repent, while Berg is able to repent only by seeing the horrific nature of his crime through his friend's eyes. After summarizing this relationship, the reviewer concludes, "It is a very roundabout way of reaching a fundamental principle of human nature, that the esteem of one loved is valued."

In a 1910 issue of *Review of Reviews and World's Work*, Edwin Björkman offers an assessment of Lagerlöf's work, commenting that each tale in the collection *Osynliga länkar* (*Invisible Links*), in which "The Outlaws" appears, "is characterized by a play of fancy and fascination of style that at times suggest [Nathaniel] Hawthorne." Björkman also praises the "power and charm" of the works, noting that this style is consistent with Lagerlöf's earlier novel, the fairytale-like *Gösta Berlings saga*.

Later critics have commented favorably on Lagerlöf's body of work as a whole. Helena Forsås-Scott, for example, states in *Swedish Women's Writing, 1850–1995* that Lagerlöf's "novels and short stories have consistently had a wide popular appeal, but their complexity and sophistication have only begun to come to light as the result of scholarly work from the 1950s onwards." In reviewing the collection *Osynliga länkar*, *Dictionary of Literary Biography* contributor Karin Petherick observes that in this collection of short stories, Lagerlöf focuses on "the conflict between Old Norse heathendom and Christendom." Petherick asserts that Lagerlöf intentionally avoided the tone of her first book and "applied herself to another diction—sparer, more laconic, and inspired by the simplicity of the Old Norse sagas."

CRITICISM

Catherine Dominic

Dominic is a novelist and a freelance writer and editor. In the following essay, she explores Lagerlöf's incorporation of naturalist and neoromantic elements in "The Outlaws."

> **"'THE OUTLAWS,' WITH ITS FOLKTALE ELEMENTS, LYRICAL LANGUAGE, MYSTICISM, AND SUPERNATURAL ELEMENTS, EXEMPLIFIES THE NEOROMANTICISM WITH WHICH LAGERLÖF CAME TO BE ASSOCIATED."**

Lagerlöf was writing at a time in Swedish literature in which both realism and naturalism prevailed. Her fiction grew out of those traditions and at the same time embraced the romantic ideals common earlier in the century. "The Outlaws," with its folktale elements, lyrical language, mysticism, and supernatural elements, exemplifies the neoromanticism with which Lagerlöf came to be associated. At the same time, it is also imbued with characteristics of naturalism.

Nineteenth-century naturalism, like realism, reflected a move toward depicting individuals and society in an unvarnished, accurate manner. Unlike realism, nineteenth-century naturalism was rooted in the philosophy that human activity is governed by natural forces, such as instinct, heredity, and the environment. A certain degree of pessimism was further associated with naturalism in its assumption that humans were essentially victims of both their internal instincts and their external environment. Lagerlöf exploits these ideas in "The Outlaws" and sets them in opposition to the governing principles of Christian morality. Through Berg's and Tord's desire for Unn, Lagerlöf underscores the conflict between the base urges of man and the Christianity that Berg professes and teaches to Tord.

Unn appears in the story when Tord and Berg have gone to a remote series of ponds in the mountains in order to fish. The men become lost in their daydreams and believe they see a water spirit sleeping at the bottom of the pond. Not long after, a pale young woman paddles near them in her own small boat. The men do not address her, although she rows near them. They do this not "from fear of discovery," the narrator informs, but because of their voyeuristic "desire to look at her undisturbed." They laugh together after the woman leaves, and Berg asks Tord if he thought the girl was

WHAT DO I READ NEXT?

- *Memories of Mårbacka*, published in 1996 as edited by Greta Anderson, includes selections from several of Lagerlöf's earlier autobiographical works. This anthology also features essays on her childhood and young adulthood and the history of her family estate, Mårbacka.
- Lagerlöf's *Jerusalem*, originally published in 1901–1902, is a novel concerned with a group of Swedish peasants who emigrate to the Holy Land. The work is based on the author's travels to Jerusalem in 1900. A 2010 reprint is available.
- *The Wonderful Adventures of Nils*, originally published by Lagerlöf in Swedish as *Nils Holgerssons underbara resa genom Sverige* (1906), is one of Lagerlöf's best-loved works. The book is a collection of children's stories featuring a young boy, Nils, who travels on the back of a goose.
- Lagerlöf's contemporary and fellow neoromantic Verner von Heidenstam published *The Charles Men* in two volumes in 1897 and 1898. A historical novel that has been praised for its poetic language, the work is available in a 2003 reprint edition.
- Henning Mankell is a popular twenty-first-century Swedish author of crime fiction and of young-adult fiction. His 2009 young-adult novel *When the Snow Fell* is a coming-of-age story set in rural Sweden. Students of "The Outlaws" will note similarities between the isolation and conflict experienced by sixteen-year-old Tord and by the fourteen-year-old protagonist of *When the Snow Fell.*
- Mexican American novelist Luis Alberto Urrea's 2005 novel *The Hummingbird's Daughter* incorporates elements of magical realism in a narrative set in late-nineteenth-century Mexico. The work focuses on a fourteen-year-old Indian girl who allegedly possesses mystical powers but is denounced by the Catholic Church as a heretic. Like Lagerlöf, Urrea explores conflicts between mysticism and Christianity in this work.
- Swedish literature has reemerged with the popularity of the "Millennium" series of books by Stieg Larsson, published posthumously. *The Girl with the Dragon Tattoo*, *The Girl Who Played with Fire*, and *The Girl Who Kicked the Hornet's Nest* combined to sell twenty million copies by 2010.

beautiful. He skirts the issue, saying she passed by too quickly for him to notice.

Later, Tord dreams of her, and in his visions he "had time enough to see that she was beautiful." He dreams of her repeatedly, and in one dream, she kisses him. Tord now thinks of the girl often, and he resolves to ask Berg if he knew her name. In this section of the story, Tord does not yet know Unn by name but is entranced with her beauty, so much so that he dreams of her nightly in an increasingly erotic fashion. To Tord, the girl is almost otherworldly, believed at one point to be a water spirit and later described as almost inhumanly pale. With Berg, Tord secretly watches Unn, not wanting to interact with her so that his hungry gazing can continue for as long as possible. The men grow unnerved by Unn's presence, and feel "a strange desire to laugh" after she departs. Their nervous laughter diffuses the arousal Unn inspired, a desire heightened by Berg's and Tord's secretive spying.

After Tord asks Berg if he knows the girl whom they watched, Berg reveals his history with Unn, some of which Tord realizes he recalls from his previous life in the village. Tord learns that Berg's wife suspected her husband of being unfaithful, and in an effort to demonstrate to Berg his wrongdoing, the wife invited a monk to their banquet. In Berg's retelling, the monk speaks to the group at large, stating, "Here sits a man who takes no care for his house and his children, and who seeks his pleasure with a strange woman. Him I will call the vilest of men." In response, Unn turns to Berg, insisting, "Berg, this is said to you and to me." She goes on to bemoan the fact that her father is not there to protect her from the public shaming she has received. After she tells Berg that she does not wish to see him any longer, he pleads for a way for the two of them to remain together, and she tells Berg that "he himself should know best what he must do."

Berg then kills the monk. Unn remains at the scene, looking "so beautiful that the men who saw her trembled." Berg's wife makes her children look at Unn as she curses the young woman and seeks to inspire her children to "always remember the woman for whose sake their father had become a murderer." After thanking Berg, Unn tells him to flee and to never rob or kill again. Upon hearing this story, Tord tells Berg, "Your deed had ennobled her," thereby emphasizing Tord's idealized notion of Unn.

Tord realizes now why Berg acted as he did. Unn's plea to Berg, "Never have I been so shamed, but my father is not here to protect me," seems to justify, in Tord's mind, Berg's murder of the monk, because Berg was defending the honor of his lover. It is in this way that Unn is "ennobled" by Berg's action, in Tord's estimation. Further, Unn's status in the story as an object of desire is first underscored by the way in which Berg and Tord stare at Unn secretly, and later by the way the men at the banquet stare at Unn after Berg has killed the monk. They look at her, trembling in response to her beauty.

Berg appears offended or in some way troubled by Tord's response to his story of Unn and the killing of the monk. He seems to feel that Tord lacks any understanding of morality. Although Berg then takes it upon himself to tutor Tord, providing lectures on morality, sin, damnation, justice, and Jesus Christ and his mother Mary, among other topics, Berg himself does not express any remorse for his murder of the monk. He faults Tord for his lack of understanding regarding moral values and lectures Tord as if he, Berg, has not committed two horrendous sins in the eyes of the church: adultery and murder. Tord is clearly moved by Berg's words, as his later torment in the forest will reveal. Nevertheless, there is no evidence in the story that his views on Unn, who also was a willing participant in acts of adultery, have changed.

As Tord wanders through the storm in the forest and begins to hear voices, he becomes increasingly tormented by the ghosts he believes are following him and calling out to him. The voices become those of God, telling him to betray "the murderer of the monk." Berg then hears the voice of the monk himself, telling him to betray Berg. As Tord flees, the voice once again becomes the voice of God, and even in his terror, Tord begins to contemplate the nature of Berg's crime, which now seemed to Tord "more horrible to him than ever it had seemed before. A weaponless man had been murdered, a servant of God cut down by the steel. And the murderer still dared to live." Tord is focused only on Berg and the murder of the monk. His thoughts and visions do not implicate Unn in the least; her culpability is not considered by Tord.

When Tord confronts Berg, Berg feels the weight of his misdeeds only after seeing how much his wrongdoing torments Tord. But learning of Tord's betrayal is more than Berg can bear. Whatever remorse he had for the murder of the monk dissolves, as Berg is prepared to murder again. He draws his ax to kill Tord and, in doing so, emphasizes the way in which he is moved only by his animal-like instincts to kill when provoked. He is driven to kill the monk out of his own desire to keep Unn, as evidenced by his asking her "what he should do that she might stay with him." She tells him that he "should know best what he must do" and his response is to kill. Threatened by Tord, his response is again to kill, but Tord kills Berg first.

When Tord slays Berg, he mourns the loss of his friend but insists that he acted righteously, that Berg's death was just. Interestingly, it is Unn that Tord focuses upon when proclaiming the just nature of his actions. "Tell Unn," he states, "for whose sake Berg the Giant became a murderer, that Tord the fisherman . . . slew Berg because Berg had taught him that justice is the cornerstone of the world." Tord's actions appear to have been contemplated deeply and to have been motivated by the sense of Christian justice Tord believes Berg instilled in him. Yet his invoking of Unn seems to point to his continued obsession with the young woman. It is unclear whether Tord wishes Unn to know of Berg's death out of a desire to punish her for her own role in compelling Berg to kill or because he wishes Unn to regard him (Tord) as "ennobled" by his killing of the murderer Berg, in the same way that Unn was "ennobled" by Berg's killing of the monk. Tord is driven by some impulse to draw Unn's attention through his actions. Furthermore, Tord's betrayal and murder of Berg were inspired by his own sense of natural spirituality, evidenced by the spirits he heard in the forest and by the sense of justice he speaks of in his final speech, a notion clearly engendered within him by Berg's lectures on Christianity and moral responsibility.

In mingling Tord's motivations in this manner, Lagerlöf highlights man's helplessness in the face of his own desires and blood lust, but she also underscores man's apparent desire to use both spirituality and religion to rise above the baser elements of his psyche. In this way, the literary naturalism prevalent in Swedish literature at this time is confronted by both Christian morality and Lagerlöf's neoromantic mysticism. Moral ambiguity reigns at the close of the story, as Tord's notion of justice has been derived from such a variety of sources.

Source: Catherine Dominic, Critical Essay on "The Outlaws," in *Short Stories for Students*, Gale, Cengage Learning, 2012.

The conclusion of "The Outlaws" is reminiscent of the Old Testament story of Cain and Abel.
(aragami12345s / Shutterstock.com)

Christopher P. Oscarson

In the following review, Oscarson discusses the problems of translating Lagerlöf's work, focusing on her most famous novel, The Saga of Gösta Berling.

During her lifetime, Selma Lagerlöf enjoyed a considerable audience and reputation not only in Sweden but also abroad. She was the first woman and first Swede to win the Nobel prize 100 years ago (in 1909) and behind Strindberg is Swedish author most widely translated into English. But sadly, her reputation in the English-speaking world is now largely at the mercy of often inadequate translations that do little justice to the creativity and complexity of her work. Furthermore, the out-dated translations that are available make it difficult for twenty-first century audiences to grasp the relevance of Lagerlöf's work in contemporary cultural discourse and discussions. Very few of Lagerlöf's works are currently available in modern, up-to-date English editions (*The Lowenskjold Ring* translated by Linda Schenck being at least one notable exception), and while it is safe to say that Lagerlöf's reputation in Sweden is unquestioned, her work clearly deserves more attention among non-Swedish speaking audiences. Strangely, she is probably best known abroad for her most Swedish of works, *Nils Holgerssons underbara resa genom Sverige*. Among these same audiences, however, knowledge of her other literary contributions is seriously limited. With this in mind, Paul Norlen's most recent effort to translate Lagerlöf is most welcome, and his edition of *Gösta Berlings saga* fills a significant gap in the understanding of Swedish culture. One can only hope that just as *Gösta Berlings saga* put Lagerlöf on the cultural map in Sweden in the 1890s, Norlen's translation might have a similar effect in facilitating a rediscovery of Lagerlöf in the non-Swedish speaking world as one of Sweden's most singular and important literary voices.

Gösta Berlings saga is an important work as the debut novel of Lagerlöf's long and distinguished career, and it is arguably one of the single most widely analyzed works of Swedish literature in Sweden. For its contemporary audience, *Gösta Berlings saga* represented a significant break with the socially-oriented realism of the 1880s and an embrace of a more fanciful, symbolist artistic ideal. Some of Lagerlöf's early supporters such as Oscar Levertin helped to open the path for her work but did so by characterizing Lagerlöf as a naive storyteller—a reputation she both embraced and fought against her whole life. While the label is decidedly unfair as it confuses simplicity with naivete, it highlights the important fact that part of what made *Gösta Berlings saga* so appealing was its accessibility and the pleasure readers experience as they are drawn into the stories of Gösta Berling and his fellow cavaliers, a pleasure replicated in Norlen's excellent new, 2009 translation, *The Saga of Gösta Berling*.

The first two translations of *Gösta Berlings saga* both appeared in 1898, one by Lillie Tudeer and the other by Pauline Bancroft Flach. The Tudeer translation—still widely circulated in an edition re-printed by Penfield Press (1997) and other small publishers re-issuing books in the public domain—is most notable for the liberties it takes with Lagerlöf's novel. Tudeer, for example, quite inexplicably left eight chapters out (later to be restored in a revised, 1918 edition by Velma Swanston Howard) in addition to making numerous significant departures from the original Swedish text. An example of such a detour is found in the beginning of the early chapter "Landskapet." The Lagerlöf text reads quite simply, "Nu maste jag beskriva den langa sjon, den rika slatten och de blaa bergen, eftersom de voro den skadeplats, dar Gösta Berling och Ekebykavaljererna framlevde sin lustiga tallvaro." Tudeer's "revised translation" from 1918, however, reads,

> Now I must beg those of my readers who know this lake, this fertile plain, and those blue mountains, to skip a few pages. They can do this without compunction, for the story will be long enough without them. But you will understand that I must describe the country for those who do not know it, as it was the scene where Gösta Berling and the gay cavaliers of Ekeby spent their lives; and those who have seen it will understand too that the task surpasses the power of one who can only wield the pen.

The complete willingness to re-write Lagerlöf's text makes it difficult to even refer to this as a translation in the strict sense of the word. Norlen takes a slightly more direct approach with his translation of the same passage: "Now I must describe the long lake, the fertile plain, and the blue hills, because this was the setting where Gösta Berling and the cavaliers of Ekeby lived out their eccentric existence." This faithfulness to both the text and replication of the tone of the narrator's voice in clear, flowing prose distinguishes this translation.

But really, one does not need to turn past the first page of the book to notice the differences in the translations of Lagerlöf's text. The famous first line of the novel, "Antligen stod prasten i predikstolen" is rendered by Tudeer/Swanston Howard as "The pastor was mounting the pulpit steps" (1918, 3). Flach's 1898 translation is better, "At last the minister stood in the pulpit" (1898, 1), but Robert Bly's 1962 reworking of Flach's translation (although in other parts, superior to earlier translations) is in this case deficient as it lessens the impact of the opening statement by unnecessarily changing the word order: "The minister at last stood in the pulpit" (1962, 9). Norlen's translation is quite clearly best, "At long last the minister stood in the pulpit" (2009, 1). The "at long last" captures the anticipation of the moment while at the same time remaining faithful to Lagerlöf's style. Norlen's translation is prefaced by an introduction written by George Schoolfield that provides a brief biography of Lagerlöf along with a basic introduction to her works. Written with typical Schoolfieldian wit and breadth of knowledge, this short introduction places both Lagerlöf and her texts within a broader Swedish and European cultural context. This summary should be helpful especially for the non-specialist in getting a sense of the significant work at hand as well as its relationship to other important writers and trends of its era. The short summary of the secondary literature should also prove most helpful for anyone wishing to dig deeper into this fascinating and complex text and author.

While the translation is to be praised for its faithfulness to Lagerlöf's text and narrative voice, one improvement might have been the inclusion of short notes along with the text explaining some of the more culturally-specific references in the story that might not be apparent to audiences unfamiliar with the original Swedish context. But this seems like a fairly minor point and should not overshadow the overall significance of the contribution at hand.

In a prefatory note, Norlen describes the difficulty of translating Lagerlöf's work and identifies one particular challenge to be "capturing the various registers in her narrative voice (from deceptively simple to passionately lyrical with more than an occasional touch of unabashed melodrama)" (xxix). In this regard, however, Norlen has been

"COMPARED WITH OTHER WRITERS, SELMA LAGERLÖF HAS WRITTEN VERY LITTLE, NOT MORE THAN THREE BOOKS IN EIGHT YEARS; BUT WHAT SHE HAS WRITTEN IS THOROUGHLY GOOD—THERE IS NOTHING IMMATURE IN IT."

decidedly successful in rendering Lagerlöf's unique voice as readable in English as it is pleasurable in Swedish. "At long last" we have available to us a viable translation of one of the truly great works of Swedish literature sure to attract attention again to one of the region's most significant authors and works.

Source: Christopher P. Oscarson, Review of *The Saga of Gösta Berling*, in *Scandinavian Studies*, Vol. 81, No. 4, Winter 2009, pp. 542–45.

Hermione Ramsden

In the following excerpt, Ramsden makes a case for the turn-of-the-twentieth-century declaration that Lagerlöf is the best mystical writer from Sweden.

IV

Sweden: Selma Lagerlöf is not only the most mystical writer in Sweden, but she is also the best. There is absolutely no difference of opinion on the subject. Ask a Norwegian or a Dane whom they consider the best among their younger writers, and they will hesitate, some naming one and some another; but put the same question to a Swede, and the answer is invariably the same: 'Selma Lagerlöf.'

It is not that Selma Lagerlöf is by any means the only writer of importance in Sweden, for there are several. At the time when Norway first boasted of Ibsen, Björnson and Jonas Lie, and Denmark of Georg Brandes and Schandorph, Sweden possessed only one writer of importance, August Strindberg, and although he was a realist of the coarsest type she was compelled to make the most of him for want of a better. At the present time, however, Sweden takes the foremost rank in the modern literature of the three Scandinavian countries. There is Verner von Heidenstam, the historian and novelist, Per Hallström and Gustaf af Geijerstam, all of whom show a decided mystical tendency as opposed to the 'realism' of former days. Even Strindberg's writings have undergone a change since he became a Roman Catholic and wrote a book called *Hell.*

Women have occupied a prominent position in Swedish literature since the days of Frederica Bremer. Ernst Ahlgren and A. C. Edgren-Leffler, the friend and collaborator of Sonya Kovalevsky, have written several very good novels, while Ellen Key occupies a position of considerable influence as a lecturer and writer of essays.

Selma Lagerlöf's first book, *Gösta Berlings Saga*, was published in Sweden in 1891, and two English translations have appeared this year. It is a collection of stories relating to Wermland, one of the Swedish provinces, and each story is linked with the next, thus forming a kind of historic novel; but the manner of writing is so original that at first the foreign reader does not know what to make of it or how to class it. 'Is it a fairy story or a novel?' he asks—'a collection of legends or an allegory?' But gradually, as he perseveres, the style grows upon him, and without quite understanding it he proclaims the book to be a very fascinating one.

Selma Lagerlöf was determined not to follow in the footsteps of any previous writer, and she has succeeded admirably. In these days, when her style is considered especially good, it is interesting to learn that her chief difficulty as a beginner lay in her want of style. In her school-days the childishness of her composition was the despair of her teachers, and she was many years at work upon *Gösta Berlings Saga* before she was able to produce it in a style that satisfied her; but as this book has been translated into English I will not dwell upon it, but prefer to pass on to her next work, *Invisible Links*.

In spite of the opinion of her countrymen that *Gösta Berlings Saga* is her masterpiece and a true national picture of Sweden in the past, I cannot help thinking that her style is better adapted to the short story than to a longer work. In *Gösta Berlings Saga*, as in her latest work, *The Miracles of Antichrist*, the reader's interest is apt to flag for want of a more positive link of connection between the chapters, whereas in the short stories we are kept spell-bound from beginning to end, and are forced to confess that each one is a little masterpiece. The writer possesses the touch of human nature which makes all the world akin, no matter whether she places the scene of her story in the old days of serfdom in Sweden, or whether her hero is a man of modern times and a convert to the Salvation Army. A story in which the latter is the case is very vividly told; the title is "A Fallen King," bearing this motto:

> Mine was the realm of fantasy,
> And now I am a fallen king.

The hero, the owner of a small shop, becomes a great preacher in the Salvation Army on the strength of certain wrongs of which he believes himself to be the victim, but which turn out to be purely imaginary. The discovery robs him of his power to preach, and at the moment when he finds himself reinstated in the good opinion of his fellow men he loses the sole object of his life and the joy of his existence. There is no longer anything for him to preach about.

> He was a painter without hands, a singer who had lost his voice. He had only spoken of his sorrow. What should he speak of now?
>
> He prayed. 'O God, since honour is dumb, but dishonour speaks, give me dishonour once more! Since happiness is dumb, but sorrow speaks, give me sorrow once more!'
>
> But the crown had been taken from him. There he sat, more miserable than the most wretched, for he had fallen from a great height. He was a fallen king.

Selma Lagerlöf has the power of telling the most commonplace tale in a manner which makes it interesting, while a romantic and almost impossible story assumes an air of probability when told by her.

The best story in the book is called "The Cairn of Stones." In it a young married couple set up house in a little hut which they build for themselves near a cairn in the forest where King Atle (Attila?) is supposed to be buried. They have no children of their own, and after some years have gone by they undertake the charge of a little orphan, but they are not quite as careful of this child as they should be, and he dies. Jofrid feels that she is to blame, but she will not confess it even to herself, and one night, when she stands at the door of the hut looking at the cairn, she seems to recognize in it, as she has often fancied before, the stone face of the king.

> He was watching her with calm indifference. The strange, unfathomable look, which is found in large stone faces, had taken possession of his features. There he sat, sombre and mighty, and Jofrid had a vague indistinct impression that he was the representation of something that was to be found in herself and in all human beings, something that has been buried for many centuries, weighed down with many stones and is yet not dead. She saw him, the old king, sitting in the centre of the human heart. He had spread his royal mantle over its unfruitful soil. There pleasure-seeking held sway, vanity and pride disported themselves. He was the great giant whose heart was not touched when want and poverty passed him by. 'The gods have willed it so,' he said. He was a strong stone man who could bear the load of unrepented sin without betraying himself. He always said: 'Wherefore sorrow over that which thou hast done, predestined by the Immortals?'
>
> Jofrid's breast heaved with a deep sigh. There was feeling within her, which she could not express in word, a feeling that she too would have to fight with the stone man, if she was ever to be happy. But at the same time she realised her utter helplessness.
>
> Her impenitence and the stone giant out on the heath seemed to her to be one and the same, and if she were not able to conquer them first they would be sure sooner or later to obtain the victory over her.

Jofrid knew that to confess would mean that she would lose her liberty, and she would sooner die than lose it; thus of the two evils she chose death. She throws herself upon the cairn and receives a death-blow as her head falls upon the hard stones.

Selma Lagerlöf must be read thoroughly to be enjoyed: her style does not lend itself to short extracts, and the plots of her stories are too fantastic to bear repeating. Another very good story of hers is called "The Outlaws," where the scene is laid in romantic times, one of the chief characters being a boy whose father was a wrecker and his mother a witch. But the most popular story in the whole collection is the little sketch written in memory of Frederica Bremer, and called "Mamsell Fredrika." It describes her last Christmas Eve, with the dreams she had of the past, and the good that her example had done for the women of Sweden, ending with a description of the great book she had meant to write, but which remained unwritten because Death, the dark knight, had come to fetch her away.

Compared with other writers, Selma Lagerlöf has written very little, not more than three books in eight years; but what she has written is thoroughly good—there is nothing immature in it. Her first work is a masterpiece, and the two which have appeared since have not disappointed the public expectation.

The *Miracles of Antichrist* is a Sicilian novel, in which she has collected a number of tales and legends and woven them into a latter-day romance. Here again her allegorical gift is apparent; for

Antichrist is Socialism, whose kingdom is 'only of this world,' but the connecting links, as in *Gösta Berlings Saga*, are sometimes entirely missing, and one cannot help feeling that the short story, not the novel, is Selma Lagerlöf's *forte*.

Source: Hermione Ramsden, "The New Mysticism in Scandinavia," in *Nineteenth Century: A Monthly Review*, edited by James Knowles, Vol. 47, January–June 1900, pp. 293–96.

SOURCES

Benson, Adolph B., "Swedish Literature," in *Columbia Dictionary of Modern European Literature*, edited by Horatio Smith, Columbia University Press, 1947, pp. 796–800.

Björkman, Edwin, "Selma Lagerlöf, a Writer of Modern Fairy Tales," in *Review of Reviews and World's Work*, Vol. 41, January/June 1910, pp. 247–50.

Forsås-Scott, Helena, Introduction to *Swedish Women's Writing, 1850–1955*, Athlone Press, 1997, pp. 1–8.

Gustafson, Alrik, "Vernor von Heidenstam," in *Columbia Dictionary of Modern European Literature*, edited by Horatio Smith, Columbia University Press, 1947, pp. 373–74.

———, "Selma Lagerlöf," in *Columbia Dictionary of Modern European Literature*, edited by Horatio Smith, Columbia University Press, 1947, pp. 463–64.

Lagerlöf, Selma, "The Outlaws," translated by Grace Isabel Colbron, in *The World's One Hundred Best Short Stories, Part Eight: Men*, edited by Grant Overton, 1927, reprint, Kessinger Publishing, 2005, pp. 70–91.

Larsen, Hanna Astrup, "Danish Literature," in *Columbia Dictionary of Modern European Literature*, edited by Horatio Smith, Columbia University Press, 1947, pp. 192–96.

Latourette, Kenneth-Scott, "Protestantism: The Nineteenth-Century Story in Sweden," in *Christianity in a Revolutionary Age: A History of Christianity in the Nineteenth and Twentieth Centuries*, Harper, 1958, pp. 167–87.

"Naturalism," in *NTC's Dictionary of Literary Terms*, edited by Kathleen Morner and Ralph Rausch, National Textbook, 1994, pp. 145–46.

Nylander, Johan, "Sweden Enjoys 100 Years without Executions," in *Swedish Wire*, November 23, 2010, http://www.swedishwire.com/politics/7344-sweden-enjoys-100-years-without-death-penalty- (accessed October 4, 2011).

Petherick, Karin, "Selma Lagerlöf," in *Dictionary of Literary Biography*, Vol. 259, *Twentieth-Century Swedish Writers before World War II*, edited by Ann-Charlotte Gavel Adams, The Gale Group, 2002, pp. 119–33.

Review of *Invisible Links*, by Selma Lagerlöf, in *Catholic World*, Vol. 70, October 1899/March 1900, pp. 844–46.

"The Revivalist Movement," in *Swedish Christian History*, Christian Assemblies International, http://www.cai.org/bible-studies/swedish-christian-history (accessed October 4, 2011).

"Sweden," in *Diplomacy in Action*, U.S. Department of State, July 19, 2011, http://www.state.gov/r/pa/ei/bgn/2880.htm (accessed October 4, 2011).

FURTHER READING

Berendsohn, Walter Arthur, *Selma Lagerlöf: Her Life and Work*, Kennikat Press, 1931.

Berendsohn's is one of the few biographies of Lagerlöf published in English.

Blecher, George, ed., *Swedish Folktales and Legends*, Pantheon, 1994.

Blecher provides a selection of Swedish tales. The stories include the comic, the bawdy, and the moralistic and offer examples to the student of Lagerlöf's work of some of the traditions upon which the author drew.

Brantly, Susan, "Into the Twentieth Century: 1890–1950," in *A History of Swedish Literature*, edited by Lars G. Warme, University of Nebraska Press, 1996, pp. 273–380.

Brantly explores the major movements in Swedish literature at the close of the nineteenth century and during the first fifty years of the twentieth century, discussing naturalism and realism and describing the romantic elements of Lagerlöf's work in terms of nostalgia and escapism.

Edgren, Lars, and Mangus Olofsson, eds., *Political Outsiders in Swedish History*, Cambridge Scholars Publishing, 2009.

Edgren and Olofsson present a series of essays on the social and political movements that subtly shaped Sweden's modern culture in the shadow of the dominance of the Social Democratic Party.

Waddams, Herbert Montague, *The Swedish Church*, Greenwood Press, 1981.

Waddams offers an overview of the history of the Church of Sweden beginning with an account of the nation's gradual conversion to Christianity.

SUGGESTED SEARCH TERMS

Selma Lagerlöf AND The Outlaws

Selma Lagerlöf AND Invisible Links

Selma Lagerlöf AND naturalism

Selma Lagerlöf AND realism

Selma Lagerlöf AND neoromanticism

Selma Lagerlöf AND Swedish literature

Selma Lagerlöf AND folktales

Selma Lagerlöf AND Nobel Prize

Selma Lagerlöf AND Christianity

Selma Lagerlöf AND mysticism

A Pair of Silk Stockings

KATE CHOPIN

1897

Known in her lifetime as a writer of local color for her realistic portrayals of the habits, dialect, and culture of American southerners in Louisiana, Kate Chopin established her reputation as a popular author of short stories, including "A Pair of Silk Stockings," published in *Vogue* magazine in 1897. Chopin was keenly focused on the experiences, frustrations, and psychology of women, particularly within the context of marriage and motherhood. These interests are explored in "A Pair of Silk Stockings," in which the protagonist unexpectedly finds herself fifteen dollars richer. A wife and mother, Mrs. Sommers contemplates the practical ways the money should be spent. Her need to make sure these few dollars are spent as wisely as possible underscores the family's struggling economic status and lower class standing. Shoes must be repaired, and fabric purchased for the making of shirts.

Mrs. Sommers thoughts reveal her struggles as a mother and her memories of a time in the recent past, before she was married, when she was much better off financially. Although apparently dedicated to her frugal and practical plan, Mrs. Sommers happens upon a bin of silk stockings, and her budget-conscious concerns evaporate. At a turning point in the story, she buys herself a pair of silk stockings. From this point on, Mrs. Sommers spends the rest of the day treating herself, to new shoes, to a pair of gloves, to expensive magazines, and to lunch in an upscale restaurant. After lunch, Mrs. Sommers takes in a play at the

Kate Chopin *(The Library of Congress)*

theater. In concise language, Chopin depicts a woman overwhelmed with responsibilities who, given the chance for a momentary escape from her domestic burdens, seizes upon a course of action that runs counter to her intentions at the beginning of the story. The brief narrative conveys Mrs. Sommers's intense dissatisfaction with her current existence and her attempt to flee her troubles, if only for a short while. "A Pair of Silk Stockings" is also available in a 1996 collection of Chopin's work, *A Pair of Silk Stockings, and Other Stories*.

AUTHOR BIOGRAPHY

Chopin was born on February 8, 1850, in St. Louis, Missouri. Named Catherine O'Flaherty at birth, she lost her father, who died in a railway accident, when she was just five years old. She entered Sacred Heart Academy in St. Louis that same year. During the years she attended the academy, the Civil War raged, from 1861 through 1865. Her brother died of typhoid while enlisted in the Confederate Army. She graduated from the academy in 1868. Not long after, in 1870, she married Oscar Chopin. The couple moved to New Orleans after traveling through Europe for their honeymoon. Over the next several years, Chopin gave birth to five sons and a daughter. After moving to Cloutierville, Louisiana, in 1879, the well-off family lived on a small plantation. In 1882, Chopin's husband died of swamp fever. Within two years, Chopin moved with her children back to St. Louis, where she suffered the loss of her mother in 1885.

Beginning in 1888, Chopin began to write professionally, in part to provide for her family. She published her first works, a poem and a short story, in 1889. Her first novel, *At Fault*, was published the following year. For the next several years, Chopin focused on her short fiction, publishing stories in *Vogue* and *Harper's*. Her short story "A Pair of Silk Stockings" appeared in an 1897 issue of *Vogue*. She additionally published two short-story collections: *Bayou Folk* in 1894 and *A Night in Acadie* in 1897. Chopin fell out of favor with critics and audiences, however, in 1899 with the publication of her novel *The Awakening*, which was condemned both for its sexually explicit nature and for its thorough questioning of contemporary notions of femininity and gender roles. Her short-story collection *A Vocation and a Voice* was rejected by her publisher in 1900. Chopin published only one more story in her lifetime, "Polly," in *Youth's Companion*. Chopin continued to pursue—unsuccessfully—publication of *A Vocation and a Voice* until her death; the stories were collected in 1969 for the first time with the publication of *The Complete Works of Kate Chopin*. Chopin died in St. Louis of a cerebral hemorrhage on August 20, 1904.

PLOT SUMMARY

"A Pair of Silk Stockings" opens with the announcement that Mrs. Sommers has received, unexpectedly, fifteen dollars. Although Mrs. Sommers considers this to be quite a large sum of money, the reader is not informed how this sudden influx of cash has made its way toward Mrs. Sommers, and the story unfolds in the absence of this information. Feeling important with this sum in her possession, Mrs. Sommers reveals herself to be practical and frugal as she considers how the money should be spent. Some nights, she is unable to sleep because she is so consumed with carefully plotting her intended expenditures. Lying awake, Mrs. Sommers devises plans designed to ensure a "proper and judicious use of the money." Referring to an unspecified

MEDIA ADAPTATIONS

- "A Pair of Silk Stockings" is available as an MP3 download from the audio collection *Kate Chopin: The Short Stories*, produced by Word of Mouth in 2010. The selections on this album are read by Richard Mitchley, Liza Ross, and Ghizela Rowe.

number of male children along with two girls, Janie and Mag, Mrs. Sommers plans to use a good proportion of the money on items of clothing the children need, or the materials with which the industrious Mrs. Sommers can make the clothing herself. She speaks of shoes for Janie, fabric for shirts for all the children, a new gown for Mag, new stockings for everyone, and "caps for the boys and sailor-hats for the girls." Mrs. Sommers envisions her children looking well turned out "for once in their lives," and this notion fills her with excitement. Mrs. Sommers's compulsive need to repeatedly review her budgeted expenditures with regard to the unexpected funds underscores the pervasiveness of the privation endured by the Sommers family.

This sense of dearth, heightened by the loss of a previous higher standing of living, is never clearly explained as the story continues, but the emotional context of adjusting to that loss is emphasized. Mrs. Sommers does not specifically contemplate the journey from wealth to destitution, but reference is made to the past, when times were not so hard. As the third-person narrator notes, Mrs. Sommers spends little time thinking about the past. Despite her fears about the future, she is entirely occupied by her family's needs in the present. As she embarks upon her shopping trip, Mrs. Sommers, who is used to patiently waiting in line for a bargain or fighting her way through a crowd to reach the sale bin, notices that not only does she feel a little tired, but she also feels weak and somewhat faint. Eventually she realizes she has not eaten any lunch. Sitting on a stool at a counter where she tries to regain her composure, Mrs. Sommers notes that her hand is resting upon something "very soothing, very pleasant to touch." When Mrs. Sommers looks down, she sees beneath her hand a pile of silk stockings, which she quickly observes are on sale. When the sales girl asks if she would like to examine the stockings, Mrs. Sommers does not answer immediately. Rather, she simply smiles, and enjoys the feel of the fabric against her fingertips. With a rush of blood to her cheeks, Mrs. Sommers abruptly asks the sales girl if they have her size in the stockings. After she is shown several pairs in her size, in a variety of colors, Mrs. Sommers selects a black pair, which she purchases. She notes the almost insignificant weight of the parcel in her otherwise empty "shabby old shopping-bag."

Mrs. Sommers's purchase marks a turning point in her day and in the story: "Mrs. Sommers after that did not move in the direction of the bargain counter." She instead takes the elevator to the ladies' dressing rooms. Everything Mrs. Sommers does in the story after the purchase of the stockings is focused on her own pleasure. Alone in a dressing room, Mrs. Sommers removes her own cotton stockings and replaces them with the new silk pair. Mrs. Sommers spends some time in the changing room, reclining in the cushioned chair in the room and "reveling for a while in the luxury" of the feel of the raw silk on her legs. Mrs. Sommers then proceeds to the shoe department, where she flummoxes the clerk there. He, with some confusion, compares her old, worn shoes to her fine, new stockings. Mrs. Sommers takes pains to find just the proper pair of new boots and tells the clerk than an extra dollar or two in cost is nothing to her, "so long as she got what she desired." Next, Mrs. Sommers is fitted with a new pair of kid gloves (*kid* refers to the soft leather made from the skin of a young goat). After purchasing her gloves, Mrs. Sommers buys two expensive magazines, such as those she used to read "in the days when she had been accustomed to other pleasant things." Mrs. Sommers now feels a sense of confidence in her inclusion in the finely dressed crowd with whom she mingles on her way to lunch. Rather than waiting until she returns home to eat, as she normally would do, Mrs. Sommers enters an upscale restaurant, observing that no one looks at her with displeasure, as if she might be out of place in such an establishment. She then orders oysters, a cut of meat, dessert, wine, and coffee. She marvels at the whiteness of the damask tablecloth and the sparkle of the crystal chandelier. Having thoroughly enjoyed an expensive lunch in decidedly elegant surroundings, Mrs. Sommers opts next to take in a play. She drinks in everything eagerly, observing the sights and sounds of the stage, the players, and the other theater-goers. She even laughs and cries throughout the play with the woman next to her, an extravagantly dressed woman who shares her candy with Mrs. Sommers.

As the story ends, Mrs. Sommers is aware of the fact that the man sitting opposite her in the cable car is staring at her, studying her face. Riding toward home, she wishes "the cable car would never stop anywhere, but go on and on with her forever."

CHARACTERS

Clerk

The clerk sells Mrs. Sommers a pair of boots and seems confused by the fact that, although Mrs. Sommers's old pair of shoes is quite worn, Mrs. Sommers wears new silk stockings and carries herself as a woman with some wealth.

Man in the Cable Car

The man riding the cable car with Mrs. Sommers watches her intently, and she wishes that she could ride the cable car forever instead of returning home.

Sales Girls

There are two sales girls with whom Mrs. Sommers interacts. The first sales girl shows Mrs. Sommers the silk stockings she eventually purchases. The second sales girl sells Mrs. Sommers a pair of gloves, helping her find the perfect fit and admiring with Mrs. Sommers the look of the glove on her hand.

Sommers Boys

Not mentioned by name, the boys are Mrs. Sommers's children. The story does not specify how many male children Mrs. Sommers has. The boys do not appear directly in the story but are present in Mrs. Sommers's thoughts.

Janie Sommers

Janie Sommers is one of Mrs. Sommers's daughters. Janie, Mag, and their brothers do not appear directly in the story, but their mother thinks of them as she does her shopping.

Mag Sommers

Mag is one of Mrs. Sommers's daughters. Like her siblings, Mag does not appear directly in the story but crops up in her mother's thoughts.

Mrs. Sommers

Mrs. Sommers is the protagonist of the story. She is referred to as "little" at several points in the story, indicating either her stature or her youth. She has several children, two girls and an unspecified number of boys. As the story progresses, it becomes clear that Mrs. Sommers was once better off financially than she is now. References are made to better times and to the fact that she was once accustomed to having fine things. Her thriftiness is the focus of the first several paragraphs of the story. She seems determined to make the fifteen dollars she possesses go a long way toward making certain her children look well dressed and presentable. Her eagerness to purchase new clothing for them is apparent; she cannot sleep at night because she is figuring out how much she can get for her money and how lovely her children will look. Yet Mrs. Sommers does not proceed with her plan to use the fifteen dollars on her children. Having tired quickly, in part at least because she has not eaten any lunch, Mrs. Sommers sits down at a counter to rest. Realizing suddenly that her hand has come to rest on a pile of silk stockings, Mrs. Sommers is overcome with the desire to purchase something for herself rather than spend all the money on the children. She purchases, and quickly changes into, the silk stockings. Mrs. Sommers now strikes out on a new course entirely. She purchases a new pair of boots, new gloves, magazines, lunch at an expensive restaurant, and a ticket to a play. Having spent the afternoon pampering herself, Mrs. Sommers boards a cable car to return home and fantasizes about never returning to her family.

Waiter

The waiter serves Mrs. Sommers her lunch in an expensive restaurant. Mrs. Sommers is pleased by the waiter's deferential attitude when he bows to her before her departure.

Woman in the Theater

In the theater, Mrs. Sommers sits next to a "gaudy woman," with whom she laughs and cries through the play. The woman shares her candy with Mrs. Sommers.

THEMES

Motherhood

As "A Pair of Silk Stockings" opens, Mrs. Sommers is depicted as a mother to at least four children, although the number of boys is never

TOPICS FOR FURTHER STUDY

- Like "A Pair of Silk Stockings," Chopin's short stories "A Point at Issue!," published in 1889, and "The Storm," written in 1898 but not published until 1969, are among her works that focus on married women. Read these two stories and compare them with "A Pair of Silk Stockings." How does Chopin treat the institution of marriage in these stories? How are the protagonists of the stories similar? Consider the ways in which Chopin characterizes the male figures in the story. Does motherhood figure into all of the stories? How does it shape the female protagonist? Write a comparative analysis in which you discuss these issues, along with the plot, secondary characters, and themes of the stories.
- Written from 1903 to 1904 and subsequently published in serial form, Chinese novelist Liu E's *The Travels of Lao Can* is set in 1890 in China. Although vastly different from Chopin's fiction in subject matter, Liu E's novel, like much of Chopin's work, utilizes realistic, detailed descriptions and observations and incorporates an element of social commentary. Read *The Travels of Lao Can* (available in a 2001 English-language edition) and study the ways in which Liu E employs realistic narration to explore the novel's themes. Write a report in which you summarize the novel's plot, characters, themes, and style.
- Padma Venkatraman's 2008 young-adult novel *Climbing the Stairs* is set during India's struggle for independence from British rule. The young protagonist, Vidya, struggles, like Mrs. Sommers in "A Pair of Silk Stockings," against a sense of familial obligation and societal expectations. With a small group, read *Climbing the Stairs* and discuss the author's stance on the rights of women in India. How does Vidya's desire for an education conflict with her family's expectations of her? In what ways does Vidya challenge those expectations? Create an online blog in which you discuss such topics with members of your group. When you have fleshed out the main conflicts of the story, create a presentation for your class in which you provide an overview of the novel and its plot, characters, and themes.
- In many of her works, Chopin depicts women who struggle in some way against the expectations of them as wives and mothers in American society. Due to her depiction of the dissatisfaction of women in these roles, Chopin has been associated with the early feminist movement in America. Research the history of feminism in America during the late nineteenth and early twentieth centuries. Who were the key figures in the movement at this time? What role did authors such as Chopin play in the movement? What were the goals of these early feminists? Create an interactive time line that illustrates the major events and figures of the movement up to the ratification of the Nineteenth Amendment. Include links to Web sites about the feminist movement.
- Most of Chopin's works are set in Louisiana, where she resided for a portion of her marriage. Research the history of Louisiana in the decades following the Civil War. How did issues of class and racial tensions influence daily life during this time? In what ways did the economy of the region evolve from the late 1860s through the 1890s? How did the economic recession of the 1890s affect the people of Louisiana? Consider the social and political atmosphere of this region as you conduct your research. Write a research paper in which you analyze race, class, politics, and the economy in post–Civil War Louisiana. Be sure to cite all of your sources.

specified; there are at least two, as they are spoken of in the plural sense. Two girls are identified by name: Janie and Mag. Having come into some money unexpectedly, Mrs. Sommers cannot sleep at night as she frets over the ways she might most efficiently use her unexpected small fortune. A full paragraph in this very short story is devoted to Mrs. Sommers's speculations regarding what she will purchase for her children. She contemplates their individual needs, wondering what she can make, what she can mend, and what needs to be purchased in order to have "her little brood looking fresh and dainty and new." Although she acknowledges in passing that there was a time when she had no need to worry so much about the family finances, Mrs. Sommers does not dwell on this happier past, as her family's present needs are so prominent and pressing.

Yet Mrs. Sommers's persistent focus on her children evaporates when, in a moment of self-indulgence, she purchases a pair of silk stockings for herself. The moment evolves into an afternoon, and the hats and shoes and dresses and fabric for shirts that Mrs. Sommers had intended to buy for her children are all but forgotten. Mrs. Sommers allows herself to forget for a short while that she is a mother with extensive responsibilities toward her family and home. A "mechanical impulse" has taken over and has "freed her of responsibility." For the rest of the afternoon, thoughts of her maternal duties do not intrude. On the cable car, Mrs. Sommers is overcome with "a powerful longing that the cable car would never stop anywhere, but go on and on with her forever." The extent to which Mrs. Sommers embraces the fantasy that she can ignore the needs of her children and spend the resources of time and money on herself, combined with this desire to never return to her family, underscore the notion of a mother completely overwhelmed by the expectations placed upon her. As the impulse toward maternal self-sacrifice is rebuffed, and Mrs. Sommers turns instead toward a day of indulgence, she is carried along by a sense of instinct, drawn to activities in which she is both insulated by a sense of solitude and admired as a woman of stature. A mother's need to escape into a different life, an existence less burdened by responsibility, becomes the driving force of the story. Although the bulk of the story centers around Mrs. Sommers's escaping her role of mother, the opening paragraphs so strongly stress her dedication to her children that her sense of internal conflict cannot be overlooked.

Female Identity

Mrs. Sommers is a woman who embodies a dual sense of identity. At the onset of the story, she is a devoted mother, eager to spend an unexpected gift of money on her children, who are in desperate need of new clothing. Yet her identity as a mother is something from which Mrs. Sommers practically flees when provided both the opportunity—a day alone to shop and the funds with which to do so—and the inspiration, in the form of a luxurious pair of black silk stockings. Once Mrs. Sommers has embarked on the path of pursuing her own desires, she makes a series of choices that illuminate further what her notion of self as a woman is. As the story progresses, it becomes clear that Mrs. Sommers's sense of her identity as a woman has been perpetually buried beneath her identity as a mother. Shedding the role of mother, her reconnection with herself as an independent woman becomes the focus of the story. Mrs. Sommers buys the silk stockings and puts them on as quickly as she can find a changing room; the narrator makes a point of stating that Mrs. Sommers chooses the elevator instead of the stairs. Her urgency dissolved, she now takes time to enjoy the tactile pleasure of silk on her skin.

Next, Mrs. Sommers creates an opportunity in which her leg, now beautifully garbed in silk, can be viewed publicly, when she proceeds to try on new boots. She does not rush this process, however. The clerk examines the old shoes and her new stockings, attempting to figure her out. With a new boot upon her foot, she holds back her skirts and admires the look of the boot upon her foot. She takes the time to find just the right pair; "she wanted an excellent and stylish fit." The narrator draws attention to the clerk's focus on Mrs. Sommers and to her own intensity in regarding the look and fit of the boots. When Mrs. Sommers tries on new gloves, both she and the sales girl admire the fit of the glove upon her hand. She later notices the way the waiter bows to her before she departs, and then the gaze of the "man with keen eyes" upon her. Being seen, being admired, are integral to Mrs. Sommers's notion of herself as a woman. When she divests herself of her role of mother, however temporarily, Mrs. Sommers steps into another role, another sense of female identity in which she defines herself by how she is viewed by others. She is thought stylish by other women, she is bowed to and studied by men, and, as the story concludes, Mrs. Sommers becomes lost in the desire to be this woman—admired and free of responsibility—indefinitely.

Mrs. Sommers begins the story by shopping for bargains for her struggling family. (Donna Beeler / Shutterstock.com)

STYLE

Omniscient Third-Person Narrator

Chopin employs the use of an objective third-person narrator in "A Pair of Silk Stockings." A third-person narrator refers to the characters in the story as *he* or *she* or by their names and is not a character in the story. This is in contrast to first-person narration, in which the narrator is typically a character in the work who refers to himself or herself as *I*. Third-person narrators are often associated with the author, but they may or may not represent the author's views. In "A Pair of Silk Stockings," the narrator is omniscient, or all-knowing, and largely relates the story from Mrs. Sommers's point of view but additionally conveys to the reader the thoughts of the other minor characters in the story, as when the narrator states that the "clerk could not make [Mrs. Sommers] out; he could not reconcile her shoes with her stockings, and she was not too easily pleased." By revealing the unspoken opinions of other characters, the narrator allows the reader a broad overview of the characters and events occurring in the story. By using an omniscient third-person narrator, Chopin underscores the story's sense of realism; her narrator reports on the events in the story in an almost journalistic fashion, describing, for example, the colors of stockings from which Mrs. Sommers's chooses her black pair, or informing the reader what Mrs. Sommers eats for lunch. The reader is left to form his or her own judgments about Mrs. Sommers's choices—to deduce, for example, that black is a practical color for stockings, but silk is a luxurious fabric, or that Mrs. Sommers's lunch, including oysters, a chop, wine, and dessert, is indulgent. Chopin's narrator simply conveys an array of details objectively, yet it is the author who determines what details are pertinent enough for her narrator to relay.

Realism

Chopin employs the use of realism in her narrative. The story avoids the sentimentalism traditionally associated with romanticism, a mode of writing prevalent in the mid-nineteenth century. While romanticism focuses on individualism, emotion, imagination, and the subjective impressions of characters, realism embraces objectivity, reason, and accuracy in conveying the details of everyday life. Social realism focuses on the straightforward presentation of a society's problems, whereas psychological realism centers on the depiction of an individual's thoughts and responses to his or her environment.

Through her use of specific details, Chopin attempts to portray the story's events in a straightforward, objective manner. Mrs. Sommers's actions are narrated as if by an observer; although her thoughts are revealed, her feelings are not explored in detail. As is the case with many realist works from the nineteenth century, "A Pair of Silk Stockings" focuses on everyday life, in this case, for one woman in particular. The narrative relates Mrs. Sommers's actions and thoughts and is primarily concerned with character, rather than plot. On the surface of the story, not much happens; a woman goes shopping. Yet Mrs. Sommers's shift in focus from her children to herself is a key point in the story, and through it, Chopin draws attention to the notion of a mother's divided sense of identity. Mrs. Sommers's sense of self as a mother stands in conflict with her sense of personal identity, and this struggle between various aspects of a woman's notion of selfhood is the focus of much of Chopin's writing. As Patricia

Penrose discusses in "American Realism: 1865–1910," American realism from the late nineteenth century often focuses on a particular group or subject; Chopin's work explores marriage and women's roles in society. Chopin realistically depicts the conflict between a mother's instinct to provide for her children and her simultaneous desire to indulge in the rare opportunity to be who she once was. In this way, Chopin comments on the experience of women in late nineteenth-century American society and incorporates elements of both social and psychological realism into the work.

HISTORICAL CONTEXT

Economic Recession of the 1890s

Following a period of rapid industrialization in the 1870s and 1880s, the United States suffered a severe economic recession in the 1890s, beginning with the depression of 1893. In the decades after the Civil War (1861–1865), the industrial manufacturing sector rapidly expanded. David O. Whitten observes in "The Depression of 1893" that U.S. industrial production rose by approximately 296 percent between the close of the Civil War and 1890. The expansion of railroad construction contributed to this industrial growth, as the railways opened new markets for such commodities as lumber, coal, iron, and steel. By 1892, however, this vigorous economic growth began to slow. Demand for building construction declined, spurring similar downturns in related industries. Investment in railway construction similarly began to decline, and growth in the agricultural sector was hampered by a variety of factors, including natural disasters such as storm and drought as well as overproduction. A financial panic, spurred in part by these downturns in agriculture and manufacturing, in part by depression conditions in Europe in the early 1890s and the withdrawal of European investors from American markets, struck the United States in 1893. Business failures increased rapidly and were paralleled by high unemployment rates that lasted throughout much of the decade. Whitten observes that although unemployment data was not directly measured until 1929, estimates suggest that following the depression of 1893, the unemployment rate "exceeded ten percent for five or six consecutive years." Low unemployment and the consequent reduced incomes of many families resulted in years of reduced consumption and general economic stagnation, which persisted until about the middle of 1897, when recovery slowly began. "Full prosperity," Whitten contends, "returned gradually over the ensuing year or more."

Realism, Regionalism, and Local Color in Late-Nineteenth-Century American Literature

In the late nineteenth century, American literature was moving away from the romanticism that had dominated the middle portion of the century. Writers focused increasingly on society over the individual, on reason over emotion and the imagination, and on the objective representation of the world around them rather than on their characters' subjective interactions with their world. American writers often associated with late-nineteenth-century realism include William Dean Howells, Mark Twain, Henry James, Chopin, and Sarah Orne Jewett.

In attempting to realistically capture a particular environment, some writers came to be associated with a particular geographic region. Twain and Chopin, for example, were considered specifically southern writers, as their works were typically set in southern locales, and their characters exemplified attributes typically associated with people from the region. Twain and Chopin were also writers who were described as local colorists, for the precision with which they depicted the dialect and cultural characteristics of particular communities, with Twain focusing on whites and African Americans in Mississippi and Chopin centering many of her stories in Louisiana and populating them with creole and Cajun characters. The lines between the literary distinctions of regionalism and local-color writing were often blurred, and they are now commonly regarded as subgenres of realism. Local-color writing was sometimes regarded as caricaturization of a particular region and its inhabitants; when it was done well, it was regarded as realistic. As Kate McCullough observes in *Regions of Identity: The Construction of America in Women's Fiction, 1885–1914*, writers were aware of the hierarchical nature of these categories, and Chopin "aligned herself with Realism, ridiculing both provincial writers and generic plots as limited and partial, and calling instead for a mimetic depiction of life." At the same time, McCullough goes on, Chopin "exploited the 'provincial' form of Local Color fiction to get

COMPARE & CONTRAST

- **1890s:** The United States undergoes a prolonged period of economic recession sparked by a sharp economic decline in 1893. Unemployment rates and business failure rates are high, and a corresponding recession in Europe contributes to the financial struggles in the United States. A slow recovery begins in 1897.

  Today: The United States endures a severe economic recession in 2008, one that is mirrored by a global economic downturn. After bank failures, a debt crisis, and the subsequent government bailouts of a number of financial institutions, unemployment rates remain high. In 2011, a number of protestors join an "Occupy Wall Street" demonstration designed to draw attention to continued economic struggles faced by many Americans and to protest the perceived inequitable treatment banks received to the detriment of the American people.

- **1890s:** American literature is marked by an emphasis on the realistic portrayal of individuals and society. Some authors, including Chopin and Mark Twain, focus in particular on capturing the dialect and culture of specific areas of the country. Consequently, they are described as regional or local-color writers.

  Today: Twenty-first-century American literature is marked by a merging of literary and popular elements, while works written in traditional genres continue to enjoy wide readership. Regionalism remains a relevant category in American fiction. Elizabeth Strout is associated with twenty-first-century New England regionalism, while Tim Gautreaux writes regionalist fiction centered in Louisiana.

- **1890s:** The early feminist movement has been sparked by women who criticize traditional gender roles and demand equal rights with their male counterparts. In 1848 a Women's Rights Convention was held, and from this grew the women's suffrage movement. Through protests, marches, and hunger strikes in the 1890s, women's rights advocates demand that voting rights be extended to women.

  Today: Having won the right to vote with the ratification of the Nineteenth Amendment in 1920, American feminists in the twenty-first century focus their political efforts on protecting the reproductive rights of women, advocating economic equality, ending discrimination based on gender and sexual orientation, and campaigning to protect women from domestic violence.

published." In "American Regionalism," Susan K. Harris similarly observes the tensions created over literary categories, citing realist author and editor Howells as establishing the notion that regionalism existed as "a subcategory of realism, and that realism is, or should be, America's predominant literary mode." Harris goes on to observe that such staunch supporters of literary realism were at odds, in late-nineteenth-century America, over how regionalism should be valued. Harris states, "They tended to waver between celebrating it, especially as manifested in the stylistically elegant work of Sarah Orne Jewett, and denigrating it as vulgar, pedestrian and static." Nevertheless, these genres—local-color writing and regionalism—remained linked with realism in that all served what Michael A. Elliott describes in *The Culture Concept: Writing and Difference in the Age of Realism* as "the realist agenda of ushering into print so-called natural productions, free of artifice and sentiment." The publication of such materials, Elliott goes on, "provided to the urban, middle-to-upper-class reader a diversity of peoples and manners of expression."

Mrs. Sommers buys some fitted gloves, a luxury item, on her shopping expedition. *(Katrina Brown / Shutterstock.com)*

CRITICAL OVERVIEW

Chopin enjoyed a successful career as a writer before her 1899 publication of the sexually explicit novel *The Awakening*, which earned her a black mark in the literature community. Until that time however, her work was well received. As Mary Ellen Snodgrass notes in the *Encyclopedia of Feminist Literature*, Chopin garnered her first critical and popular accolades with the 1897 publication of the short-story collection *A Night in Acadie*, "a story collection," states Snodgrass, "that ventured beyond regionalism to examine social and sexual differences in Louisiana's rich ethnic mix." Snodgrass describes "A Pair of Silk Stockings" as Chopin's lament for women who sought reprieve "from housewifery and penury."

Allen F. Stein examines Mrs. Sommers's escapism in *Women and Autonomy in Kate Chopin's Short Fiction*. Stein maintains that despite Mrs. Sommers's "brief sojourn in the fantasy realm of consumerism," she "never has any more autonomy than she has had at any recent point in her married life." Her escape, Stein asserts, "is futile and devoid ultimately of anything approximating meaningful freedom."

Doris Davis, in an essay in *Kate Chopin Reconsidered: Beyond the Bayou*, maintains rather that Mrs. Sommers "uses the money to nurture her sense of aesthetics, an action that Chopin seems to suggest is important for this character's development." Furthermore, Davis states, Mrs. Sommers is able to cultivate a "feeling of independence and fulfillment in her judicious use of money."

Other critics have focused on the effect of the story on the reader. Linda Wagner-Martin and Cathy N. Davidson, for example, in the *Oxford Book of Women's Writing in the United States*, describe the work as a "brief but startling story" in which the author "involves the reader in both questioning the actions of the character, and empathizing with her."

Mrs. Sommers's actions are depicted in the story as rebelling against "the cultural expectation of selflessness for Victorian womanhood," Charlotte Rich states in *A Companion to the American Short Story*. Rich asserts that Chopin's protagonists, including Mrs. Sommers, "must mediate the gap between cultural expectations of selfless absorption in husband and children and the fulfillment of their own desires."

CRITICISM

Catherine Dominic

Dominic is a novelist and a freelance writer and editor. In the following essay, she explores the implications of Mrs. Sommers's materialist impulses in "A Pair of Silk Stockings."

In "A Pair of Silk Stockings," Kate Chopin depicts a mother who temporarily flees from her responsibilities by spending the money she had allocated for her children's needs on herself instead. Critics such as Allen F. Stein, in *Women and Autonomy in Kate Chopin's Short Fiction*, regard Mrs. Sommers's actions as an ultimately futile grasp at independence, an escape into "the fantasy realm of consumerism." Stein suggests that Mrs. Sommers's motivations are driven by a need to

WHAT DO I READ NEXT?

- *The Awakening*, published in 1899 and reissued in 2011, is Chopin's best-known, and most controversial, work. Taking place in Louisiana, the work focuses on one woman's struggle to come to terms with views on womanhood and motherhood that stand in stark contrast to the norms of her society.
- Chopin's collections of short stories *Bayou Folk*, published in 1894, and *A Night in Acadie*, published in 1897, exemplify Chopin's work as a regionalist or local-color writer in that they present detailed portraits of the women and men of nineteenth-century New Orleans and Natchitoches Parish. The works were published together in a single volume in 1999.
- Mark Twain was a contemporary of Chopin's whose work, like hers, was often described in terms of its regionalism. Twain's depiction of Mississippi is seen in such works as *The Adventures of Tom Sawyer* (1876) and *The Adventures of Huckleberry Finn* (1884). Both novels were published together in 2002.
- Japanese novelist Kyoko Mori's 1994 young-adult novel *Shizuko's Daughter* centers on the struggles of a twelve-year-old Japanese girl whose mother committed suicide to escape a bitter marriage. Students of Chopin will see a similarity in Mori's indirect critique of modern marriage and societal expectations of women.
- Somali-born Muslim writer Ayaan Hirsi Ali offers a feminist critique of Islam in her 2007 nonfiction book *Infidel.* In the work, Ali recounts her experiences after having been forced into an arranged marriage. Ali uses this and other incidents as examples of unrealistic and unfair restrictions that strict adherents to the Muslim faith place upon women.
- Julie Anne Peters's young-adult 2007 short-story collection *grl2grl: Short Fictions*, offers a reexamination of notions of gender roles, expectations, and sexuality in the twenty-first century.
- Sandra M. Gilbert and Susan Gubar's seminal work *The Madwoman in the Attic: The Woman Writer and the Nineteenth-Century Literary Imagination*, originally published in 1979, was reissued in a second edition in 2000. The work explores the way women writers in the nineteenth century used their fiction to examine and critique the nineteenth-century's patriarchal society and its expectations about women, marriage, motherhood, gender roles, and sexuality.
- *The Southern Middle Class in the Long Nineteenth Century*, edited by Jonathan Daniel Wells and Jennifer R. Green and published in 2011, is a collection of critical essays concerned with the social, economic, and class-based issues that affected the middle class in the South before, during, and after the Civil War.

cultivate, through repeated acts of consumerist self-indulgence, a sense of autonomy that, in reality, she does not possess. Yet a close reading of the text reveals another layer of her character, another dimension to the acquisitiveness she displays in the story. Although Mrs. Sommers is clearly overwhelmed by her duties as a mother, and while she does seem to revel in a sense of freedom, however short lived it may be, her materialism seems to be directed at reestablishing a sense of self-worth and of belonging to a social class from which she has been excluded by her impoverished circumstances. Repeated references are made to better times, when Mrs. Sommers was not yet Mrs. Sommers—when she enjoyed life's luxuries. The silk stockings, which her hand brushes against, serve as a trigger that compels Mrs. Sommers along a course of action described as virtually instinctual. With the unexpected wealth of fifteen dollars in her pocket, Mrs. Sommers, sagging under the twin burdens of

> "WITH THE UNEXPECTED WEALTH OF FIFTEEN DOLLARS IN HER POCKET, MRS. SOMMERS, SAGGING UNDER THE TWIN BURDENS OF NECESSARY FRUGALITY AND MOTHERHOOD, REVERTS TO A FORMER VERSION OF HERSELF, ALLOWING HER CONFIDENCE IN HER SOCIAL WORTH, HOWEVER FLEETINGLY, TO BE RESTORED."

necessary frugality and motherhood, reverts to a former version of herself, allowing her confidence in her social worth, however fleetingly, to be restored.

From the opening of the story, Chopin clearly delineates Mrs. Sommers's relationship with and attitude toward money. The fifteen dollars that have suddenly come into her possession seem to Mrs. Sommers to be a large sum, and she relishes the way the money "stuffed and bulged her worn old *porte-monnaie*." Having a full purse provides Mrs. Sommers with "a feeling of importance such as she had not enjoyed for years." In this first paragraph, Chopin demonstrates the way wealth, for Mrs. Sommers, does not simply symbolize comfort, or the ability to provide for her family. Rather, money makes Mrs. Sommers feel *important*. Significantly, Mrs. Sommers has not felt this way for some time; her sense of worth is wedded to the notion of wealth, and without money, Mrs. Sommers does not feel, and has not felt, valued. Her keen sense of insignificance becomes a motivating factor as the story progresses.

How to spend this newfound money—how to get the most out of it—occupies Mrs. Sommers's thoughts for some time before she embarks on her shopping trip. Her calculations even keep her awake at night. She outlines how she will spend the money most efficiently, and her mental list, shared with the reader, includes only items for the children: shoes, fabric for shirts, a gown, stockings, caps, and hats. Thrilled to be able to outfit her children so that they appear "fresh and dainty and new for once in their lives," Mrs. Sommers experiences a sense of restlessness about her impending shopping trip. Mrs. Sommers notes that the children have never before looked as "fresh" and "new" as they soon will, emphasizing how long the family has experienced financial hardships; they apparently have been struggling for the duration of the children's lives. It comes as no surprise, then, that Mrs. Sommers recalls the way the neighbors "sometimes talked of certain 'better days' that little Mrs. Sommers had known before she had ever thought of being Mrs. Sommers." The story was published in 1897, at the end of a long period of economic recession in the United States. The fact that Mrs. Sommers and her neighbors have experienced an apparently long stretch of economic hardship corresponds with the story's historical context. Yet Mrs. Sommers, whose children have grown up in a household characterized by privation and have never experienced those wealthier times, refuses to dwell on the contrast between the abundance of the past and the austerity of the present, although the prospect of future poverty haunts Mrs. Sommers like a "gaunt monster."

Although she previously enjoyed some sort of wealth and status, in the days before she was married with children, Mrs. Sommers has learned from her circumstances and has developed frugal habits; she "knew the value of bargains" and could wait in line for hours to acquire something on sale. Armed with her money, her plan for its prudent expenditure, and her ability to ferret out bargains, Mrs. Sommers ventures out on her shopping trip, but fades quickly with hunger. She soon recalls that she failed to eat lunch. Fatigued, she rests at a counter where her hand unknowingly falls onto a pile of silk stockings. Unable to help herself, she caresses the "soft, sheeny luxurious things—with both hands now, holding them up to see them glisten, and to feel them glide serpent-like through her fingers." Deprived for so long of such luxury, Mrs. Sommers loses herself for a moment, until she is overcome with a new desire—to indulge herself. As "two hectic blotches came suddenly into her pale cheeks," Mrs. Sommers begins to acquire items that signify wealth and a certain social standing, things that make her feel important. She begins with the stockings, proceeding quickly to a changing room where she puts them on. Now, Mrs. Sommers functions instinctually:

> She was not going through any acute mental process or reasoning with herself.... She was not thinking at all. She seemed for the time to be taking a rest from that laborious and fatiguing function and to have abandoned herself to some mechanical impulse that directed her actions and freed her of responsibility.

Guided by impulse, perhaps by the instincts she had honed in her former, wealthier days, Mrs. Sommers proceeds to buy new shoes and gloves. Each purchase is accompanied by an instance of public appreciation for her wise selections, for her sense of style, for her fine appearance. The clerk notices her silk stockings and cannot figure out how a woman with those stockings, and the desire to get the stylish fit she sought regardless of cost, appeared initially in the old, worn shoes. When Mrs. Sommers purchases the new kid gloves, both she and the sales girl "lost themselves for a second or two in admiring contemplation of the little symmetrical gloved hand." When she purchases two expensive magazines, "such as she had been accustomed to read in the days when she had been accustomed to other pleasant things," Mrs. Sommers carries them "without wrapping." In this way, her expensive tastes may be admired by passersby. Her desire to have her good taste and wealth approved of publicly is underscored at regular intervals.

As Mrs. Sommers passes through a crowd, the narrator observes that her new clothes "had worked marvels in her bearing—had given her a feeling of assurance, a sense of belonging to the well-dressed multitude." New boots, stockings, and gloves have made Mrs. Sommers feel important once again, just as the initial possession of the money had. Now, however, Mrs. Sommers also has the satisfaction of confidence—confidence that she fits in with the class of people wealthy enough to have fine things in tough times. Her shopping spree has provided her with the confidence to walk among the wealthy with her head held high; she does not have to skirt the well-dressed crowd cloaked in the shame of poverty. That she has felt such shame is suggested when Mrs. Sommers selects an expensive restaurant for lunch. She has previously viewed the restaurant from the outside, has peered into the windows to see "glimpses of spotless damask and shining crystal, and soft-stepping waiters serving people of fashion." Never having entered before, Mrs. Sommers now dares to, noting with some surprise that "her appearance created no surprise, no consternation, as she had half feared it might." Her worries that she might be frowned upon, that she might be perceived as not belonging in an establishment as fine as this, ease, and Mrs. Sommers sits and orders a sumptuous lunch that includes such extravagances as oysters, a chop, wine, and dessert. Her transformation back into a woman belonging to the ranks of the upper class is now complete, and as she tips the waiter, Mrs. Sommers enjoys the fact that he "bowed before her as before a princess of royal blood." The fact that Mrs. Sommers next takes in a play is the icing on the cake that has been her day of decadence. But when the play ends, and the music stops, and the crowd disperses, Mrs. Sommers has the sensation that "a dream ended."

The fervency with which she longs to prolong her escape from her existence is readily apparent. Mrs. Sommers's desire to escape from her life and her responsibilities is a complex one. She has displayed a sense of relief at having been freed from her maternal duties, and she has luxuriated in a few fleeting moments of independence. She has also lived a day that has allowed her to once again feel a sense of prominence that she once possessed but has since lost. She once could claim a place in the upper class, once belonged with the people who purchased stylish clothes and accessories and lunched at extravagant restaurants and spent leisure hours at the theater. Although Mrs. Sommers has assured the reader at the beginning of the story that she does not indulge in "morbid retrospection" about "better days" as her neighbors do, nor does she possess a "second of time to devote to the past," she has spent the day living as she used to and enjoying the sense of belonging and worth that she has purchased with the unexpected sum of fifteen dollars. Although Mrs. Sommers, early in the story, seems to express a sense of genuine devotion to her children, her behavior throughout the story emphasizes that for some women, the often under-appreciated role of mother does not wholly satisfy a woman's need to be regarded as worthy, valuable, significant. Mrs. Sommers uses money to fill this void and to buy a sense of belonging that assuages her dissatisfaction with her life.

Source: Catherine Dominic, Critical Essay on "A Pair of Silk Stockings," in *Short Stories for Students*, Gale, Cengage Learning, 2012.

Allen Stein

In the following excerpt, Stein evaluates the level of conspicuous consumption present in Mrs. Sommers's shopping spree in "A Pair of Silk Stockings."

It is no news that, failing to find fulfillment in their marriages, wives in Kate Chopin's fiction are sometimes driven in their desperation to suicide, adultery, or desertion. But in "A Pair of Silk Stockings," a story too rarely discussed at length, Chopin presents a woman who tries a different expedient to escape the difficulties imposed by her marriage, a brief foray into the

As Mrs. Sommers shops, her self-esteem rises. *(Victorian Tradtions / Shutterstock.com)*

realm of consumerism. The effort fails, as Chopin shows that, however fashionable what Thorstein Veblen called "conspicuous consumption" might seem in the expanding national economy of the late 1890s, it can offer only ephemeral and illusory gratifications for one enmeshed in the enduring constraints imposed by her marriage.

Finding herself "the unexpected possessor" of fifteen dollars, "little Mrs. Sommers," who has known "better days," now long past, "before she had ever thought of being Mrs. Sommers," decides immediately to use the money for children's clothing so that she might have "her little brood looking fresh and dainty and new for once in their lives." On impulse, however, this long-deprived woman spends all the money on herself, striving for one day at least of self-indulgence, one day that might hint of some personal autonomy in a pinched and narrowed existence.

At a quick glance, Mrs. Sommers's effort seems something of a success. She buys herself

"THIS, THEN, CHOPIN ESTABLISHES, IS A WOMAN CAPABLE OF DECISION AND DETERMINATION WHOSE LATITUDE FOR GENUINELY MEANINGFUL CHOICE HAS BEEN REDUCED DRASTICALLY."

a pair of silk stockings and then, to complement them, one pair of costly shoes and one of kid gloves; next, her spree in the store completed, she treats herself to two "high-priced magazines," browses through them while having a pleasant lunch in an upscale restaurant, and closes her day by attending the theater for a matinee performance. She has enjoyed herself thoroughly. Further, as Doris Davis sees it, Mrs. Sommers has used her money "to nurture her sense of esthetics, an action that Chopin seems to suggest is important for this character's development." Davis goes on to argue that "Mrs. Sommers has developed a feeling of independence and fulfillment in her judicious use of money, and might well serve as a model for Edna Pontellier's emerging sense of autonomy" (p. 148). Similarly, Mary E. Papke comments that Mrs. Sommers, "physically and spiritually exhausted, arrives 'at [a] moment of contemplation and action.' In choosing to buy the pair of silk stockings, she 'experiences a sensuous moment' that reawakens her female self."

A close look, though, both at Mrs. Sommers's little rebellious spree and what precedes it, indicates, as I noted, something decidedly less hopeful, and that is that Mrs. Sommers, from the moment she gets the fifteen dollars to the moment that she has spent every bit of it, never has any more autonomy than she has had at any recent point in her married life. Rather than confronting the terrible constraints under which she labors, rather than seeking through such confrontation to forge what Melville characterizes as a "sovereign sense of self," Mrs. Sommers, understandably enough but also sadly, seeks merely escape from her life and from herself through her brief flight into consumerism. Such venturing, Chopin conveys implicitly here, is futile and devoid ultimately of anything approximating meaningful freedom. Peggy Skaggs notes aptly that "the reader feels deep compassion" for Mrs. Sommers. One might add that what is perhaps most poignant, finally, about her situation is that her reaction against her circumstances is both so abortive and so misdirected.

Appropriately, the story opens with an implicit suggestion that this woman is more one caught up in circumstances than a shaper of them—she is, after all, as the first line asserts, one "who found herself the unexpected possessor of fifteen dollars." She does attempt, however, to take charge of this pathetic little windfall, as the "question of investment . . . occupied her greatly," and she is "absorbed in speculation and calculation," lying awake at night "revolving plans in her mind" for "a proper and judicious use of the money." The right use of the money, Mrs. Sommers finally concludes, of course, is to buy much-needed clothing for her children, and she mentally apportions the funds according to their needs. This is typical of her, as invariably "the needs of the present absorbed her every faculty," and she has come to know the "value of bargains" and has learned to "elbow her way" through a crowd "if need be" and to "clutch a piece of goods and hold it and stick to it with persistence and determination till her turn came to be served." This, then, Chopin establishes, is a woman capable of decision and determination whose latitude for genuinely meaningful choice has been reduced drastically.

Nothing that occurs once Mrs. Sommers begins her shopping foray ever really widens this narrow range of actual possibility for her that Chopin establishes at the start of the tale. Arriving at the department store for "the shopping bout," Mrs. Sommers is, Chopin notes, "a little faint and tired," having actually forgotten to eat lunch, "between getting the children fed and the place righted." While seated at a counter, "trying to gather strength and courage to charge through an eager multitude that was besieging breast-works of shirting and figured lawn," she feels an "all-gone limp feeling" come over her, and she rests her hand "aimlessly upon the counter." Gradually, she "grew aware that her hand had encountered something very soothing, very pleasant to touch," the silk stockings that prompt her to the first of the purchases for herself. For a moment Mrs. Sommers tries to resist their soft allure. Thus, when a salesgirl asks her if she wishes to examine the store's "line of silk hosiery," Mrs. Sommers smiles "just as if she had been asked to inspect a tiara of diamonds with the ultimate view of purchasing it." However, as "she went on feeling the soft, sheeny luxurious things—with both hands now. . . . [feeling] them glide serpent-like through her fingers," the "two hectic blotches" that "came suddenly into her pale cheeks" indicate that she has been seized by a yearning more powerful than her commitment to domesticity, and she asks, "Do you think there are any eights-and-a-half among these?"

Mrs. Sommers's first step, then, into an afternoon of self-indulgence begins not with a carefully thought-out decision but with a pleasant physical sensation made all the more appealing by hunger, fatigue, lightheadedness, and a moment's release from the frantic round of responsibility. Further, though Chopin's account of how the "soft, sheeny luxurious" stockings seem to "glide serpent-like through her fingers" is obviously in the traditional language of temptation and thus would seem to invoke moral choice, that suggestion can only be Chopin's ironic reminder that an ethical framework grounded in religious teaching does not apply here, for she shows that choice itself, whether moral or immoral, just does not come into play in this woman's situation. At most, the notion that the temptation to buy for oneself is sinful is merely an irrelevancy that Mrs. Sommers's tired, duty-driven mind conjures up out of habit before impulse carries her along.

Lest there be any confusion about this, Chopin states explicitly that Mrs. Sommers "was not going through any acute mental process or reasoning with herself," indeed "was not thinking at all" and instead "seemed for the time" to have "abandoned herself to some mechanical impulse that directed her actions and freed her of responsibility." Thus, ironically enough, if Mrs. Sommers has little latitude for free choice in her dutiful daily life, she seems to have even less as she yields to the impulse to self-indulgence. In fact, not only do fatigue and long deprivation prompt her to yield to impulse rather than to make conscious choices, the sorts of self-indulgence to which she is impelled to yield seem less a reflection of needs or aspirations intrinsic to her own nature than a reflection of the artificially induced needs and aspirations of a consumer society. The story thus confirms Papke's observation that one of Chopin's primary "general themes" is "the role of social determinism in class and personal crises" (p. 3).

Barbara C. Ewell notes tellingly that "the power of money to enhance self-esteem and confidence is the core of this poignant tale." More specifically, one might observe, Chopin shows that the value society places on having money can foster the insidious and misguided self-esteem that arises merely from believing one has acquired status in the eyes of others. Thus, as soon as Mrs. Sommers has put on the silk stockings that she bought on impulse, she "crossed straight over to the shoe department and took her seat to be fitted," and the fitting itself is manifestly a part of the pleasure she derives in buying the costly pair of shoes she does. With the girl at the glove counter, as we have seen, she had asked timidly, "Do you think there are any eights-and-a-half among these?" Now, though, on the strength of one purchase, one new addition to her wardrobe, her whole demeanor with the store's sales staff changes. Now she is "fastidious," and, noting that "the clerk could not make her out . . . could not reconcile her shoes with her stockings," she shows that "she was not too easily pleased." Trying on shoes to go with her new stockings, she takes satisfaction in observing that "her foot and ankle looked very pretty," and, Chopin relates, she tells "the young fellow who served her" that "she wanted an excellent and stylish fit" and "did not mind the difference of a dollar or two more in the price so long as she got what she desired." Completing her purchase of the shoes, Mrs. Sommers is immediately at the glove counter—Chopin, in fact, does not even describe her getting there; instead she simply notes, "Now she rested her elbow on the cushion of the glove counter," suggesting how swiftly the growing momentum of impulse and the sudden desperate yearning for quickly attained self-esteem are carrying Mrs. Sommers along. At this new venue she relaxes luxuriously when "a pretty, pleasant young creature, delicate and deft of touch, [draws] a long-wristed 'kid' over Mrs. Sommers' hand." So in the space of perhaps twenty minutes Mrs. Sommers's response has undergone a marked transformation. Shyness and insecurity have given way to a certain self-satisfaction and calculated effort to impress and then, finally, to acceptance of attention from the pretty (and no doubt poorly paid) "creature" at the counter as her due—and all because she has spent some money on a few fashionable items of clothing.

In 1899, two years after the publication of "A Pair of Silk Stockings," Thorstein Veblen observed that "since the consumption of . . . more excellent goods is an evidence of wealth, it becomes more honorific; and conversely, the failure to consume in due quantity and quality becomes a mark of inferiority and demerit." Clearly a product of her society, though obviously not of its "leisure class," Mrs. Sommers, Chopin shows, succumbs to the pervasive social pressure and struggles to avoid the stigma of "inferiority and demerit." Similarly, Philip Fisher has noted of the connection between one's sense of self and shopping in modern urban America that "the self-experience and recognition reached earlier by thinking is, under the conditions of the city, obtained by shopping." Further, it is noteworthy, as well, that Mrs. Sommers is shopping in a department store, for as Alan Trachtenberg has observed in his *The Incorporation of America*, department stores have long thrived on inspiring the belief that merely purchasing items in such large, well-run, modern establishments as theirs makes one somehow successful, part of all that is fashionable and therefore estimable. Consequently, though Mrs. Sommers might seem to be suddenly asserting a longing for personal autonomy in the midst of an existence of dreary constraint, she is actually a driven being, prodded by the conspicuous spending of all those about her and, like all of them, manipulated by those who shape the ideology and practice of consumerism. . . .

Source: Allen Stein, "Kate Chopin's 'A Pair of Silk Stockings': The Marital Burden and the Lure of Consumerism," in *Mississippi Quarterly*, Vol. 57, No. 3, Summer 2004, pp. 357–68.

Emily Toth

In the following essay, Toth recounts two interviews Chopin did with the St. Louis Post-Dispatch *in the late 1890s.*

In *The Awakening*, Kate Chopin called Edna's dual life the "outward existence which conforms, the inward life which questions." Two contemporary interviews that I have found in the *St. Louis Post-Dispatch* suggest that while Chopin claimed outwardly that she had no serious ambitions or thoughts, she was inwardly questioning the nature of love and the significance of suicide—while she wrote *The Awakening*.

In her lifetime, Chopin was best known as the author of charming Louisiana stories, especially those in her first collection, *Bayou Folk* (1894). Two personality profiles that year, by her friends Sue V. Moore and William Schuyler, told readers about her St. Louis antecedents, her years of marriage and motherhood in Louisiana, and her embarking on a literary career after the

"CHOPIN'S ANSWER WAS, OF COURSE, CRITICAL OF A DOUBLE STANDARD—OF THE TENDENCY TO ATTRIBUTE PSYCHOLOGICAL PROBLEMS TO WOMEN AND NOT TO MEN."

death of her husband. According to Moore, Chopin was "the exact opposite of a bluestocking," with "no literary affectations" and no "'fads' or 'serious purpose' in life." According to Schuyler, Chopin was a spontaneous writer who often produced a story in one sitting, and "then, after a little, copies it out carefully, seldom making corrections. She never retouches after that."

Like many nineteenth-century women writers, Chopin presented herself as a dilettante rather than as a professional: she claimed in an essay that she wrote any old time, unless more inspired by "the intricacies of a pattern" or "the temptation to try a new furniture polish on an old table leg." She said that she did not know where her ideas came from, and that she did not write "everything that comes into my head." She also emphasized that she did not revise and polish her work, preferring the "integrity of crudities to artificialities."

That point was reiterated by Harrison Clark, who recorded in the *St. Louis Republic* that "Mrs. Chopin writes fluently, rapidly, and with practically no revision." Similarly, Chopin's son Felix recalled that his mother "wrote very fast, and on completion, seldom had to make more than a few slight corrections." Indeed, Chopin's surviving manuscripts at the Missouri Historical Society show very few changes (although they may be final drafts, with earlier ones thrown away).

But the *Post-Dispatch* interviews show that Chopin did indeed revise: she definitely revised part of *The Awakening* for publication. And while she was writing *The Awakening*, she was not just pondering her furniture. She was thinking deeply about her story, and about women, love, and suicide.

By the late 1890s, Chopin was the center of St. Louis' thriving literary colony. At her "Thursdays," weekly salons held in her home at 3317 Morgan Street, artistic and literary guests held forth about politics, current literature, philosophy, and the like. Chopin was more apt to be a quiet listener, so that "one realizes only afterward how many good and witty things she has said in the course of the conversation," Schuyler recalled.

Among her salon visitors were William Marion Reedy, editor of the weekly *Mirror* (later known as *Reedy's Mirror*), and George S. Johns, editor of the *Post-Dispatch*. By January 1898, Chopin had finished writing "A Solitary Soul" (her notebook title for *The Awakening*), which she began in June 1897—and although she claimed that she never discussed her writing with anyone, both the *Mirror* and the *Post-Dispatch* published items that seemed to stem from discussions of her new novel.

On 13 January, Reedy devoted the *Mirror*'s front page to a discussion of "Wives and Husbands": "Woman's latest discovery is that the husband is a drag," Reedy wrote. "Woman has evolved from a doll into a human being"—something he heartily approved of. As for wives like Madame Ratignolle: "Women who submit to complete obliteration in matrimony will find, in time, that they will not need to obliterate themselves, for they will be ignored." Reedy also described Edna Pontellier's central conflict when he wrote that "Woman's truest duties are those of wife and mother, but those duties do not demand that she shall sacrifice her individuality."

Likewise, the proper role of women—especially society women—was a *Post-Dispatch* concern during the social season of 1897–1898. Chopin was very active during that season: newspaper columns mention her presence at numerous receptions, teas, and readings. When the *Post-Dispatch* launched a series of interviews on problems facing St. Louis society women, Chopin's friends were among the first respondents.

One week the contributors answered the question, "What Is the Unforgivable Sin in Society?" One society woman answered, "Lack of wealth"; another cited "the bad behavior that springs from an impure character." "Brains is of more importance in society than money," a third respondent felt—but Mrs. Julius Walsh, a bridge-playing friend of Chopin, claimed bluntly that in society the rule was "Wealth first, brains afterward."

Chopin was just finishing *The Awakening* when the *Post-Dispatch* called on her to answer the question, "Is Love Divine?"

Two other society women answered first, in a column published on 16 January 1898. Mrs.

Shreve Carter said that "all true women must cherish the belief, deep down in their hearts, that there exists, or will exist, some time and somewhere, their kindred soul, their dual spirit." Mrs. Tudor Brooks, Chopin's Morgan Street neighbor and president of the Golden Chain Humane Society, felt that love must be divine: "Certainly it would be difficult and distressing to believe that love, the motive power of the universe, existed as a material something to be idly picked up or wantonly destroyed by creatures incapable of knowing or appreciating so great a blessing."

The *Post-Dispatch* identified Chopin, the last respondent, as someone who "has written stories of Southern life and as a novelist should know what love is." Chopin's answer to the question was two paragraphs:

> It is as difficult to distinguish between the divine love and the natural, animal love, as it is to explain just why we love at all. In a discussion of this character between two women in my new novel I have made my heroine say: "Why do I love this man? Is it because his hair is brown, growing high on his temples; because his eyes droop a bit at the corners, or because his nose is just so much out of drawing?"
>
> One really never knows the exact, definite thing which excites love for any one person, and one can never truly know whether this love is the result of circumstances or whether it is predestination. I am inclined to think that love springs from animal instinct, and therefore is, in a measure, divine. One can never resolve to love this man, this woman or child, and then carry out the resolution unless one feels irresistibly drawn by an indefinable current of magnetism. This subject allows an immense field for discussion and profound thought, and one could scarcely voice a definite opinion in a ten minutes talk. But I am sure we all feel that love—true, pure love, is an uncontrollable emotion that allows of no analyzation and no vivisection.

Chopin's first paragraph quotes from what became part of chapter 26 in *The Awakening*. Mademoiselle Reisz, speaking of Robert, asks Edna, "Why do you love him when you ought not to?" and Edna replies: "Why? Because his hair is brown and grows away from his temples; because he opens and shuts his eyes, and his nose is a little out of drawing." The changes show that Chopin did indeed revise, contrary to her usual claims. (She may have made other changes as well, but the manuscript for *The Awakening* does not exist.) Whether the changes are significant is, of course, a matter of opinion.

A week later, a *Post-Dispatch* editorial—possibly spawned by salon discussions—noted that "Within a month four young women of high social position have committed suicide under circumstances which seemed to indicate sympathetic motives." The writer, probably George S. Johns, listed the incidents: in each case, one young woman committed suicide, and a short time later, her close friend did the same.

According to the editorial, all were "petted daughters of society," not pinched by poverty or overwork. And so Johns mused: "Aside from the possibility of morbid emotional excitement to which all human beings are liable, there was no strain upon them, except the strain of social activity and rivalry. Does the conjunction of suicidal attempts indicate a tendency in that direction among the women of society? Has high society struck the pace that kills?"

Two weeks later, in a roundup society page interview, the *Post-Dispatch* posed the same question—and Kate Chopin was one of those answering.

The other respondents included Mrs. Maria I. Johnston, a lecturer for the Chart Club, "composed of ladies of fashion" for whom Chopin would read her stories, "A Night in Acadie" and "Polydore," two weeks later. Mrs. Johnston said that society women had fewer strains in their lives than poorer women, and she attributed the suicides to "diseases or heredity," rather than environment.

Another respondent, Mrs. John Green, "litterateur, expert whist player and prominent society woman," had been a charter member of the elite Wednesday Club, along with Chopin. Mrs. Green called society "a benefit to women who have no definite occupation.... It keeps their minds active and saves them from ennui. It has been the salvation of many a woman." She also claimed that young women who did commit suicide tended to be "sensitive" and "morbid" (words later applied to Edna Pontellier by hostile critics).

But the third respondent, Mrs. Martha Davis Griffith ("Lecturer, authoress and leader of the Literary Symposium, an organization of society women"), was less sympathetic to women. Society, she said, created strains for those with "a hysterical tendency.... Strong will-power can overcome a woman's inclination to be flighty, whatever her station in life, but women who are so inclined would do well to keep out of society, as nearly as they can consistently with their station in life."

Only Chopin questioned the validity of the question. Identified as "Leader of a literary set in St. Louis society and author of many stories of Creole life," Chopin said:

> Leadership in society is a business. It is a good thing for women who have no other occupation to engage in it and endeavor to keep up with the social whirl. There is nothing about it that I can see that would tend to produce an unhealthy condition of mind.
>
> On the contrary, it prevents women from becoming morbid, as they might, had they nothing to occupy their attention when at leisure.
>
> Business men commit suicide every day, yet we do not say that suicide is epidemic in the business world. Why should we say the feeling is rife among society women, because half a dozen unfortunates, widely separated, take their own lives?
>
> The tendency to self-destruction is no more pronounced among society women than it ever was, according to my observation.
>
> The desire seems to come in waves, without warning, and soon passes away. The mere reading of a peculiar case of suicide may cause a highly nervous woman to take her own life in a similar manner, through morbid sympathy.
>
> But do not men do the same thing every day? Why all this talk about women?

Chopin's answer was, of course, critical of a double standard—of the tendency to attribute psychological problems to women and not to men. But her associating suicide with "a highly nervous woman" and "morbid sympathy," just weeks after she finished writing *The Awakening*, is intriguing.

When *The Awakening* was published, some fourteen months later, one of the many scathing reviews concluded that "Certainly there is throughout the story an undercurrent of sympathy for Edna, and nowhere a single note of censure of her totally unjustifiable conduct." The reviewer was referring to Edna's "openly pursuing the independent existence of an unmarried woman"—which Chopin, indeed, does not condemn. *The Awakening* was greeted with hostile, even brutal reviews, but most were from men: women readers wrote Chopin warm letters of praise and invited her to give readings. (And contrary to long-standing belief, *The Awakening* was never banned.)

But modern readers have long assumed a deep identification between Chopin and her heroine, and in classroom debates about *The Awakening*, students often point out that Chopin makes the ending attractive, maternal, sensuous. Yet the *Post-Dispatch* interview suggests that Chopin's own attitude toward women's suicide was more critical than sympathetic. (And, of course, she was no suicide herself.)

For the *Post-Dispatch* interviews, Chopin was certainly conscious of speaking to several audiences. When she wrote about whether love is divine, she drew on scientific (or pseudo-scientific) discussions in her salon, discussions which influenced her thoughts in *The Awakening*. But when she wrote about the pace of society, her language also drew on popular concepts of women—especially the impact of reading on susceptible minds.

Yet she also bade men to look at their own lives—and as the responses to *The Awakening* showed, that was something that most male reviewers were not yet willing to do.

Source: Emily Toth, "Kate Chopin on Divine Love and Suicide: Two Rediscovered Articles," in *American Literature*, Vol. 63, No. 1, March 1991, pp. 115–21.

SOURCES

Chopin, Kate, "A Pair of Silk Stockings," in *A Pair of Silk Stockings, and Other Stories*, Dover Publications, 1996, pp. 55–59.

Davis, Doris, "The Awakening: The Economics of Tension," in *Kate Chopin Reconsidered: Beyond the Bayou*, edited by Lynda Sue Boren and Sara deSaussure Davis, Louisiana State University Press, 1992, pp. 143–56.

Elliott, Michael A., "Culture and the Making of Native American Literature," in *The Culture Concept: Writing and Difference in the Age of Realism*, University of Minnesota Press, 2002, pp. 124–60.

Good, Alastair, "NYPD Arrest Hundreds of Occupy Wall Street Protestors on Brooklyn Bridge," in *Telegraph* (London, England), October 4, 2011, http://www.telegraph.co.uk/finance/financialcrisis/8802085/NYPD-arrest-hundreds-of-Occupy-Wall-Street-protesters-on-Brooklyn-Bridge.html (accessed October 4, 2011).

Harris, Susan K., "American Regionalism," in *A Companion to American Literature and Culture*, edited by Paul Lauter, Blackwell Publishing, 2010, pp. 328–38.

Inge, Tonette Bond, and William E. Grant, "Kate Chopin," in *Dictionary of Literary Biography*, Vol. 78, *American Short-Story Writers, 1880–1910*, edited by Bobby Ellen Kimbel, Gale Research, 1989, pp. 90–110.

Ireland, Patricia, "Women's Less Than Full Equality under the U.S. Constitution," in *National Organization for Women*, http://www.now.org/issues/economic/cea/ireland.html (accessed October 4, 2011).

"Issues," in *National Organization for Women*, http://www.now.org (accessed October 4, 2011).

"Kate Chopin," in *The Oxford Book of Women's Writing in the United States*, edited by Linda Wagner-Martin and Cathy N. Davidson, Oxford University Press, 1995, p. 63.

McCullough, Kate, "Kate Chopin and (Stretching) the Limits of Local Color Fiction," in *Regions of Identity: The Construction of America in Women's Fiction, 1885–1914*, Stanford University Press, 1999, pp. 185–226.

Penrose, Patricia, "American Realism: 1865–1910," in *National Council of Teachers of English American Collection*, http://www.ncteamericancollection.org/amer_realism.htm (accessed October 4, 2011).

Rich, Charlotte, "Kate Chopin," in *A Companion to the American Short Story*, edited by Alfred Bendixen and James Nagel, Blackwell Publishing, 2010, pp. 152–70.

Snodgrass, Mary Ellen, "Chopin, Kate," in *Encyclopedia of Feminist Literature*, Facts on File, 2006, pp. 107–108.

Stein, Allen F., "The Marriage Stories," in *Women and Autonomy in Kate Chopin's Short Fiction*, Peter Lang, 2005, pp. 9–74.

Whitten, David O., "The Depression of 1893," in *E.H. Net Encyclopedia*, edited by Robert Whaples, Economic History Services, August 14, 2001, http://eh.net/encyclopedia/article/whitten.panic.1893 (accessed October 4, 2011).

FURTHER READING

Bardaglio, Peter W., *Reconstructing the Household: Families, Sex, and the Law in the Nineteenth-Century South*, University of North Carolina Press, 1995.

> Bardaglio studies the way race, gender, and sexuality entered into the legal structures of southern society in the nineteenth century. The author stresses the way southern culture remained preoccupied with rigidly traditional notions of both gender and race in ways that shaped legislation in the aftermath of the Civil War.

Foote, Stephanie, *Regional Fictions: Culture and Identity in Nineteenth-Century American Literature*, University of Wisconsin Press, 2001.

> Foote provides a detailed analysis of the way regionalism was used as a literary strategy by writers in order to depict characters and locales who appear to readers as foreign when contrasted with traditional middle-class notions of culture and identity.

Kearns, Katherine, *Nineteenth-Century Literary Realism: Through the Looking-Glass*, University of Cambridge Press, 1996.

> Kearns analyzes nineteenth-century literary realist works, including works by American and British authors, discussing the numerous variations inherent in this mode, as well as the multitude of purposes to which authors employ the literary tools of realism.

Valenti, Jessica, *Full Frontal Feminism: A Young Woman's Guide to Why Feminism Matters*, Seal Press, 2007.

> Valenti provides both the historical background of the feminist movement and an overview of modern feminist issues. The work is geared toward a young-adult audience.

Walker, Nancy A., *Kate Chopin: A Literary Life*, Palgrave Macmillan, 2001.

> Walker's critical biography offers an overview of Chopin's life and work. It places the author within the context of nineteenth-century women writers.

SUGGESTED SEARCH TERMS

Kate Chopin AND A Pair of Silk Stockings

Kate Chopin AND regionalism

Kate Chopin AND local color

Kate Chopin AND realism

Kate Chopin AND Louisiana

Kate Chopin AND feminism

Kate Chopin AND Mark Twain

Kate Chopin AND The Awakening

Kate Chopin AND short fiction

Kate Chopin AND American South

A Shocking Accident

GRAHAM GREENE

1957

The British author Graham Greene's short story "A Shocking Accident" is a lighthearted meditation on how a youth named Jerome responds when his father suffers a tragicomic death. The story was published originally in the humor/satire magazine *Punch* on November 6, 1957, and subsequently in Greene's 1967 collection *May We Borrow Your Husband? and Other Comedies of the Sexual Life*.

Greene enjoyed a brilliant career that involved extensive travels to oft-tumultuous foreign lands, a prolonged literary investigation into the roles of religion in people's lives, and the near-constant filming of adaptations of his novels. While he was known for his thrilling "entertainments" as well as high literature, his forays into forthright humor writing were relatively few. However, his well-cued wit is on display in "A Shocking Accident," which will likely leave the reader—no matter how sensitive, sympathetic, or politically correct one imagines oneself to be—laughing time and again at the various versions of the tricky tale of death inflicted by unexpected and undignified forces. The story can additionally be found in Greene's *Collected Short Stories* (1986).

AUTHOR BIOGRAPHY

Greene was born on October 2, 1904, in Berkhamsted, Hertfordshire, England, the fourth of six children. His father, a history and classics scholar

Graham Greene *(AP Images)*

who became headmaster of the village school, was not especially close to his son, while his mother was morally pure and aloof. When Greene first learned to read, he did so in secret, enjoying stories by Rudyard Kipling and Beatrix Potter in a secluded attic. He later turned to adventurous tales by H. Rider Haggard and recountings of great historical events like China's turn-of-the-century Boxer Rebellion. In school, Greene felt alienated because of his father's conspicuous authority and was repulsed by the lack of privacy there, which led him to skip school to escape into books. Turning self-destructive, he experimented with swallowing toxic substances, so in 1920, his father enrolled him in psychoanalysis, then a relatively novel practice, in London. Greene thoroughly enjoyed the experience and became expert in recalling and drawing ideas from his own dreams.

From 1922 to 1925, Greene attended Balliol College at Oxford University. During this time he remained in a prolonged adolescence, mired in hesitation and uncertainty with regard to love and beset by manic-depressive tendencies. He even tried solitary Russian roulette, an experience that luckily was not fatal and that gave him a visceral thrill unlike any he had ever felt. Dabbling in literary endeavors at college—editing the *Oxford Outlook* and publishing a modest volume of verse—Greene veered into journalism after graduating, first writing for the *Nottingham Journal*. By the spring of 1926, he had become a subeditor at the London *Times*. He married Vivien Dayrell-Browning in 1927, having converted to Catholicism for the sake of their union. Greene drew on his journalistic work in writing his crime-oriented first novel, *The Man Within* (1929). He subsequently published two mediocre endeavors before hitting upon a successful formula with the crowd-pleasing *Stamboul Train* (1932), which was later made into a film.

Continuing to publish stories and novels, Greene ventured to Liberia and wrote the psychologically attuned travel volume *Journey without Maps* (1936), which explores the profound feelings about civilization evoked in him during his time on the primally rooted African continent. His writings thereafter were marked by added depth, with novels like *Brighton Rock* (1938) and *The Power and the Glory* (1940)—his own most cherished work—investigating the interplay of religion and society. He also wrote thrilling novels that he labeled "entertainments," such as *The Confidential Agent* (1939). In 1941, he was recruited by the British Secret Intelligence Service and stationed in West Africa, where he reportedly mostly did code work and sometimes hunted cockroaches for amusement.

Over the ensuing decades, Greene variously worked in publishing or journalism, traveled to exotic locales like Indochina and Panama, and wrote, adding stage dramas and screenplays to his repertoire. Unabashedly averse to the United States, Greene created American characters that are often shallow or foolish, and in 1967, he expressed that he would sooner live in the Soviet Union than in the United States. That year he published the collection *May We Borrow Your Husband?* which includes "A Shocking Accident" (originally published in *Punch* in 1957). Writing into his eighties, Greene died in Vevey, Switzerland, on April 3, 1991.

PLOT SUMMARY

1

In the opening section of "A Shocking Accident," Jerome is called to the office of his housemaster at his preparatory school between morning classes. Jerome is certain he is not in trouble, and

MEDIA ADAPTATIONS

- Greene's story was adapted as a 25-minute short film in 1982, titled *A Shocking Accident*. James Scott directed this Flamingo Pictures production, with both the adult Jerome and his father played by the English actor Rupert Everett. The film won the 1982 Academy Award for Best Live-Action Short.

Mr. Wordsworth actually seems fearful of him. The housemaster gradually informs Jerome that his father has been in an accident, leading Jerome to imagine that his father—perhaps not just a travelogue writer but also a British secret service agent after all—must have been killed in action. Instead Mr. Wordsworth reports that while walking through Naples, Italy, Jerome's father was struck by a pig that fell from a fifth-floor balcony, killing him; reporting this leaves Mr. Wordsworth stifling laughter. Jerome asks about the fate of the pig.

2

In moving on to secondary school ("public school" in British parlance essentially being what Americans call private school), Jerome comes to realize how comical others find the story of his father's death. He is given the crude nickname "Pig." Jerome remains fond of his father, even in acknowledging that, as reflected in a sedate photograph from Capri, he was surely no secret agent. Listening to his humorless aunt tell the tragicomic story of his father's death to strangers is upsetting to Jerome; he is left to witness the listener's progression from feigned interest to genuine absorption when the fact of the pig is finally breached.

Vainly conceiving that a biographer might come asking after his only slightly accomplished father, Jerome rehearses versions of the story of his death so as to minimize the comedy. He settles on two approaches. The first entails exposing the listener to the fact of the fatal pig so slowly and incrementally that by the time the matter becomes clear, the death itself is actually an anticlimax. The second entails immediately thrusting the pig upon the listener in such a way that one may imagine that the fatality was incurred in the course of "pig-sticking," or hunting wild boars (typically done on horseback), perhaps prompting the listener to ask about the sport of polo.

Becoming a "chartered accountant" (equivalent to a certified public accountant in America), Jerome gets engaged, at a statistically appropriate point in his adulthood, in what is not an especially passionate romantic relationship, to an innocent young woman named Sally. He refrains from explaining his father's death for as long as possible, greatly fearing how her reaction, if she cannot resist amusement, will affect him. He does come near to revealing the truth—near enough, since he mentions a "street accident," to exclude the possibility of resorting to the "pig-sticking" method.

Finally, a week before the wedding, they have dinner with Jerome's aunt, and inevitably the matter of the "shocking accident" comes up. When Sally urges her on, the aunt abruptly reveals that a pig fell on Jerome's father. Miraculously, Sally does not laugh or even smirk but only gravely listens to the story, commenting sympathetically at the end. At last relieved of his tension over how the story would go over, Jerome finds himself feeling especially amorous toward Sally, and they kiss passionately in the taxi on the way home. When he asks what she is thinking, she expresses wondering what happened to the pig. Jerome gladly notes that it was probably eaten for dinner, and he kisses her again.

CHARACTERS

Aunt

Jerome's aunt (his father's sister) is behind the scenes for most of the story, calling the school to communicate the tragic news of her brother's death to the housemaster and then appearing only in voice, through a sample monologue revealing the news of her brother's death to a stranger. Jerome rues how his aunt, being utterly humorless herself, has no sense for how her delivery of the story may enhance, rather than reduce, the comic aspect. When the aunt finally has Jerome and his fiancée over for dinner a week before their wedding, the story eventually comes up—but the aunt happens to relate the death concisely, and Sally never loses her composure.

Father

Characterized no more elaborately than as a "large sad man," Jerome's father was a travel writer who produced titles like *Sunshine and Shade* and *Nooks and Crannies*. His young son came to imagine that he must have been either running guns—that is, illegally dealing in firearms—or doubling as a British secret agent; but he was only going to the Hydrographic Museum when the Neapolitan pig fell on him. From his dowdy appearance in the photograph taken on the island of Capri, Jerome comes to recognize that his father was undoubtedly just a travel writer after all.

Jerome

When yet just a nine-year-old boy holding the modest distinction of "warden" at his preparatory school, Jerome learns of his father's tragic death from his housemaster at school. By this time he has come to romantically imagine that his father, though nominally just a travel writer, is involved in secretive, important international work. The event of his father's death—offering confirmation that one is better off living safe and sound at home than dying in the course of exploring the world—may be what leads Jerome to opt for the mental and financial security of a life immersed in figures, an accountant's life. His relationship with Sally, too, is oriented more toward tranquillity than thrills. Meanwhile, his father's pig-related death further isolates Jerome from society because he can hardly be amiably disposed toward anyone who laughs at the manner of his father's death, yet virtually no one can resist finding his father's death amusing. It is perhaps for this reason, above all, that the unfalteringly sweet Sally, who surely could never glean amusement from the death of a loved one's beloved parent, proves perfect for Jerome.

Sally

Jerome's fiancée is a "pleasant fresh-faced girl of twenty-five" who is still fond of Hugh Walpole—a prolific early twentieth-century author whose works quickly became considered old-fashioned—and adores babies. Like Jerome, she is perfectly content to be in a safe if unexciting relationship, calling her sweetheart the special nickname of "Jemmy" and imploring him, upon the first brief mention of his father's "street accident," never to drive fast. Most critically, just a week before their wedding, she passes the test of learning of the pig-inflicted death without even a snicker. After this fine display of sentimental gravitas, Jerome loves her more than ever.

Mr. Wordsworth

A housemaster at Jerome's preparatory school, Mr. Wordsworth has great difficulty refraining from laughter in telling Jerome the story of his father's death. Where the reader is told he "shook a little with emotion" upon turning his back to Jerome, Mr. Wordsworth is presumably not truly shaken up but is finally releasing his pent-up chuckles.

THEMES

Sympathy

While the tone and structure of "A Shocking Accident" are so comical as to likely distract the reader from any thematic intent, the story says much about the nature and importance of sympathy. Beginning with Mr. Wordsworth and proceeding to Jerome's best friend in secondary school and other peers, the truth about Jerome's father's death leaves most people utterly struck by the comic aspect and unable to demonstrate proper sympathy toward Jerome. Indeed, few people can be capable of offering condolences over someone's death while stifling laughter over the circumstances of that death; instead they must, as the housemaster does, merely try to stay composed long enough to gain an opportunity to turn and release their facial tension while looking in the other direction.

For such people in this situation, their own impulsive sentiments, experienced firsthand, outweigh whatever competing sympathetic sentiments might be felt on behalf of the bereaved. Surely these people do not lack sympathy for Jerome's tragic orphanhood, with his mother having died sometime before. However, the urge to laugh, once felt, cannot be easily suppressed, and because being killed by a falling pig is such an absurd, farcical way to die—with the bloated animal not just crushing the victim but also leaving him utterly devoid of dignity in death—many a person may instinctively respond to the story with wry surprise or amusement.

Although Greene only hints at this notion, the reader may gather that the common response of inappropriate amusement has been conditioned by excessive exposure to trivial, comedic stories. That is, if one sees a film or television

TOPICS FOR FURTHER STUDY

- Think of a time when you or someone else unfortunately could not prevent other people from laughing about something. This may have been an embarrassing moment or simply a product of random circumstances. Reframe this incident (changing all names, and details if appropriate, to protect the innocent), or conceive an original such incident, and write a fictional short story relating it. You may render the incident/story comical or serious as you see fit.
- Use online and print resources to write a research paper on the psychological underpinnings of sympathy. Address the various ways that sentiments of sympathy or compassion benefit the individual who feels them, as well as how such benefits extend to others. Relate philosophical arguments for or against sympathy and consider how the emotion might have evolved. Draw on personal experience to illustrate your points.
- Imagine that you are a great fan of Jerome's father's travel books and wish to honor his life's work on the Internet. Create a Web page that includes an obituary of the man (whom you should assign a name), incorporating as many details as possible from "A Shocking Accident" as well as invented details. Also create capsule reviews of his various books, including the several volumes mentioned in the story and several volumes you invent. If you have the expertise, create covers for each volume, or else simply include photographs taken from the Internet that illustrate the voyages described in each book.
- Read "The Story of an Hour" (1894), a short story by Kate Chopin that is accessible for young adults and that constitutes a much more serious portrayal of someone receiving news of a loved one's death. Write an opinion paper and post it on your Web page or blog in which you consider the merits of Chopin's and Greene's respective approaches to such circumstances. Explore your personal reactions to each story, and relate whether certain aspects struck you negatively and why. Conclude by discussing your reaction to each story and the overall impact each had on your state of mind.

program—or for that matter reads a novel or short story—in which a serious accident is portrayed comically, as intentionally designed to elicit laughter, the audience thus learns to consider such an accident not sympathetically, with a view to the feelings of those involved, but humorously. In a fictional narrative, of course, the people are not even real, and so the audience may have little difficulty forgoing sympathy for the sake of amusement—especially if the auteur encourages that response by employing devices like silly music, unflattering camera angles, or witty dialogue. In sum, any fictional story that capitalizes on a hurtful accident by prompting laughter in the audience is incidentally degrading the audience's natural sense of sympathy. Greene may thus be considered quite devious for fashioning a story that baits the reader into laughing at a comical death, only to portray all those who laugh at that death as the unsympathetic antagonists of the story.

In American cultural history, perhaps the most significant dramatic cohort to exploit the comic potential of violence was the Three Stooges, whose particular style of vaudeville slapstick translated well from stage to screen in the 1930s. However intentionally absurd their abuse of each other might have been, the viewer would nonetheless be laughing at another person's pain. By the time of Greene's story, which might be assumed set in the 1950s, thanks to ensuing acts inspired by the likes of the Three Stooges and the ubiquitous entertainment of network television, the hair-trigger response to an absurd-sounding death would evidently be laughter. The pop-culture consumer's sympathy for unknown others has been compromised. In Greene's story, the one piece of evidence that the author is actually suggesting such a line of thought is the mention of Sally's appreciation for Hugh Walpole, a serious writer who was in time considered too traditional and old-fashioned. The reader may infer that, likely old-fashioned herself, Sally has not been desensitized by modern comic violence, and so she is duly overcome with sympathy, not mirth, upon hearing of Jerome's father's bizarre death.

Innocence

Sally's sympathetic reaction to the news of the shocking accident seems to be rooted in her innocence. Where a more sophisticated woman, socially accustomed to emotional detachment and seeing the droll side of things, might instinctively recognize the humor in the story, the innocent Sally is so attuned to the tragic aspect of her beloved Jemmy's father's death that she never lets on that she sees any cause for laughter. That is, in knowing Jerome intimately, and in knowing of his father's death, she has already classified that death as a tragic occurrence, and whatever the circumstances turn out to be, they will not reframe the death as anything but tragic in her mind. The reader might imagine, moreover, that Sally's response is not dependent on her love for Jerome; being a compassionate person, she probably would not have laughed no matter who was killed by the pig.

Sally's innocence is evoked most in the detail about her having "adored babies ever since she had been given a doll at the age of five which moved its eyes and made water." The appeal of such a doll lies in the sense it gives the child of having another living being under her care, a sense made all the more vivid by the moving eyes. With such a doll, Sally was conditioned to think sympathetically, to see spiritual and emotional need even in a fabricated object showing only the most minimal signs of life.

As a person advances through school and into the real world—eventually suffering ills at the hands of insensitive others, watching others inflict cruelty, and learning not to be overwhelmed by it all—emotions may harden, and such innocence may be lost. One may learn to see the lives of others at the distance of stories, and one need not feel sympathy for mere characters in stories; yet Sally seems to have retained her childlike innocence and appreciation for all life. For others, the story of death by falling pig is no more than a story, and every listener or reader is entitled to his or her own emotional response to a story, but for Sally, owing to her sustained innocence, a story involving another's life automatically inspires her to feel for that life, and if that life is lost, the story will necessarily be seen as not comic but tragic.

Storytelling

Greene provides through this piece of short fiction a modest seminar on the art of storytelling. In light of his experiences with his peers, who quite cruelly nickname him after the animal that killed his father, Jerome finds himself obliged to work out how to relate his father's death with as little humor as possible. His aunt provides an excellent counterexample: embarking on a "rambling discourse" that entails wondering about what is permitted in a civilized society, mentioning the frugality of the deceased, and hailing his carefulness, the aunt then fairly blindsides the listener with the fact of the falling pig, almost as if intentionally delivering the news as a punch line. Jerome takes an alternate approach in not rambling toward a shocking revelation but gradually exposing the listener to the elements of the accident so that there is as little room for surprise as possible.

His second, much briefer approach—"My father was killed by a pig"—effectively shifts the storytelling burden to the listener. Instead of volunteering the details in a coordinated fashion, Jerome thereby leaves the listener to ask questions in search of details—or even independently suggest details, which Jerome may allow to stand even if incorrect—meaning the story will be slightly different, while perhaps being more or less true, with each listener. This is surely a much less stressful way to tell a story, since the teller is not performing a monologue but need only deliver an opening statement and then respond to whatever questions are asked, as honestly (or dishonestly) as he or she is inclined. The reader may thus gather that while a performance-driven story may be the optimal means of amusing an audience, forcing the audience to take part in the creation of the story may be a better means of preserving one's energy or amusing oneself.

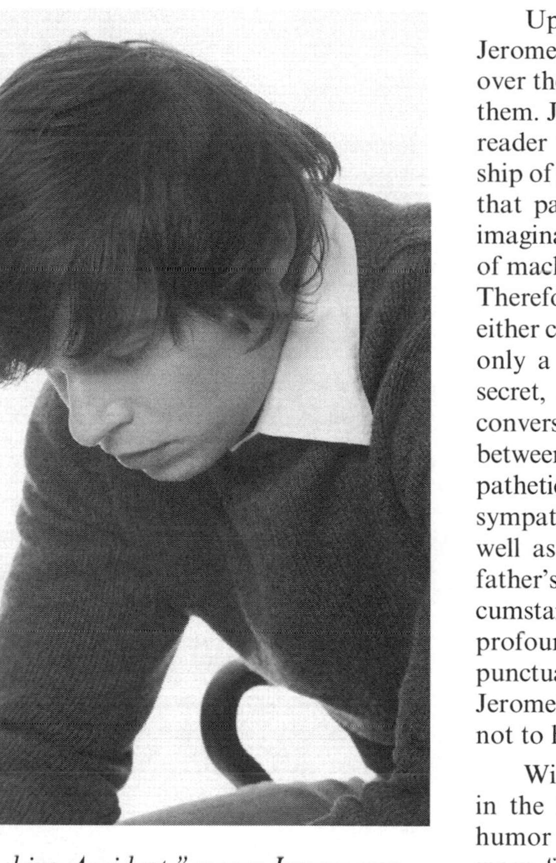

In "A Shocking Accident," young Jerome was forced to face the death of his father and its unusual circumstances. (Piotr Marcinski / Shutterstock.com)

STYLE

Irony

A patently comical story, "A Shocking Accident" derives much of its humor from various instances of irony, when the reader comes across lines that are likely contrary to what is expected. To begin with, Jerome's responses to Mr. Wordsworth's first few statements about his father's accident suggest not concern, fear, or grief—typical responses to news of a loved one's accident—but perhaps intrigued excitement. This irony is quite subtle, as Greene provides no descriptors explaining how Jerome is speaking, or how he is behaving while he is speaking. When the housemaster states, "Your father has had an accident," Jerome simply replies, "Oh." The reader is clued in to the oddness of this flat reply in being told that Mr. Wordsworth then "looked at him with some surprise."

Upon being told the accident was serious, Jerome remarks, "Yes, sir?"—as if not anxious over the details but rather proudly curious about them. Jerome's state of mind is made clear to the reader through the paragraph relating his worship of his father as an imagined secret agent, but that paragraph also makes clear that Jerome's imagination is running wild in picturing "a hail of machine-gun bullets" claiming his father's life. Therefore, the reader expects the death to be either completely mundane, if the father is indeed only a writer, or sensational, if he did have a secret, adventurous life. The remainder of the conversation derives humor from the dissonance between Mr. Wordsworth's efforts at being sympathetic and Jerome's indifference toward that sympathy. Thus, from Jerome's perspective (as well as the reader's), given his notion that his father's death must have been under exciting circumstances, the news that "a pig fell on him" is profoundly ironic. For the reader, the scene is punctuated with one last comical irony, when Jerome's first question about the incident relates not to his father at all but to the fate of the pig.

With the comical circumstances established in the first section, the second section derives humor much less from suspended irony and more from the absurd difficulties encountered by Jerome in light of his father's ridiculous death. What is somewhat ironic in the story's second half is the fact that, in being so concerned with the manner of relating his father's death, Jerome comes across as still indifferent to the death itself. Although he cherishes his memories of his father, having to focus on the precise means of telling the story of his death reduces that death to no more than an element of a story. Jerome thus seems to permanently inhabit a state of ironic emotional detachment from his own father's death.

Tragic Farce

In his review of *May We Borrow Your Husband?* in *Commonweal*, Warren Coffey observes that the collection's stories are largely characterized by varying degrees of balance between tragedy and farce. On the one hand, "A Shocking Accident" can be seen as tragic because the story addresses an orphaned boy's responses to his father's accidental death. On the other hand, Jerome seems to not suffer emotionally in the least over that death or even to grieve at all—Mr. Wordsworth deems the boy's initial response callous or heartless—but rather to be absorbed only by *other* people's responses to the story of

COMPARE & CONTRAST

- **1950s:** Approximately 10 percent of English children are educated in private (independent, or not state-funded) schools.

  Today: Just over 7 percent of English children are educated in private schools.

- **1950s:** Long-distance travel is largely accomplished by ocean liner, with the first reliable passenger jets not running regularly scheduled flights until the mid- to late 1950s.

  Today: Flying is favored as the most convenient mode of international travel, and with enough money, one can easily skip from airport to airport around the world.

- **1950s:** As a result of its attractive location on England's southern coast, direct railway access, and the publicity of hosting the watersports events in the 1948 Olympics, Torquay—Jerome and Sally's planned honeymoon spot—is one of the most popular tourist destinations for English folks.

  Today: Thanks to the ease of international travel and their relative wealth, English people are more likely to travel abroad for vacations, and in turn Torquay sees a greater share of foreign visitors.

his father's death. In the absence of sadness on Jerome's part, the story becomes a farce.

This "tragedy-farce tension," as Coffey calls it, is sustained throughout the story. The title, of course, immediately prepares the reader for some horrifying event that is presumably pivotal to the plot, but in the course of the opening scene, the casual narration supplies none of the dramatic details that the reader might expect to be told in such circumstances, such as Jerome's physical reactions to the news being related. His ironic responses and Mr. Wordsworth's discomfort are played off each other throughout the farcical dialogue. The story leans toward tragedy in alluding to the insensitivity of Jerome's schoolmates and the nostalgia evoked by a photograph of Jerome's father; but the father is characterized in a farcical way, as a dull, even pathetic, mediocre author of forgettable travelogues with insipid titles like *Nooks and Crannies*, and the reader is never led to feel any sadness over his absence in Jerome's life.

Indeed, while duly commiserating with Jerome over the plight he faces in confronting people's responses to the pig episode, the reader is likely laughing all the while at the absurdity and inevitable comedy of every possible version of that episode, adding to the sense of farce. The story leans back toward tragedy in establishing Jerome's serious concern over how his fiancée will react to the pig episode when she hears it, a reaction that could threaten their relationship. But this concern is mercifully nullified when Sally does not laugh or grin at all at the episode and so "appeased his fear for ever." The happy ending, complete with Sally's perfectly matching concern for the fate of the pig, seals the story as tragicomedy, a pleasant tragic farce.

HISTORICAL CONTEXT

Modern Western Civilization

Although "A Shocking Accident" was first published in *Punch* magazine in 1957, the story contains few clues to the historical setting. The one hint comes with the reference to how Sally's "favourite author was still Hugh Walpole," a Briton who was widely read in the 1920s and 1930s but who, by the time of his death in 1941, was already being critically dismissed. The reference thus suggests that Sally perhaps came to appreciate Walpole in his heyday and by the 1940s still appreciated him despite his dwindling literary reputation. With perhaps as much as twenty years separating the first section

In certain neighborhoods in Naples, Italy, families kept livestock in their homes—and that meant sometimes keeping a pig on the balcony. (edelia / Shutterstock.com)

from the second, Greene's story could be understood to take place roughly between the 1930s and 1950s. Meanwhile, in terms of literary sensibilities, the story is not particularly demonstrative of, say, postmodernism (often conceived as achieving cultural prominence after World War II) or any other historic trend in literature.

Perhaps the most significant historical context for the story, then, is the greater context of modern Western civilization. Much of the story's comic tension is founded in the average person's utter surprise that a modern westerner, traveling in a developed Western nation, could possibly die owing to the untimely descent of a pig from a tall building. The aunt expresses this surprise in remarking, "I can't think how such things can be allowed in a civilized country.... I suppose one has to regard Italy as civilized." The housemaster has indicated that keeping pigs on balconies is something done "in the poorer quarters of Naples." Jerome's frank admission that a pig killed his father leads an anonymous listener to ask, "Really? In India?"

The story thus implies that death by pig might be expected in a so-called undeveloped nation like early-twentieth-century India, while an impoverished urban area might also be considered undeveloped or "uncivilized." In this light, the story might be seen as satirizing the unexpected dangers of less civilized places, where building codes and animal-raising regulations may be nonexistent. This sense is heightened by the fact that the accident occurs not somewhere like India or Africa but in the European nation of Italy. In fact, Jerome's father's broader travels could hardly be called adventurous: the "far places" he is said to have visited are mostly delimited by the Mediterranean Sea (Nice, France, and Beirut, Lebanon, being coastal cities, Majorca an island near Spain), with only the Canary Islands, off Morocco (but governed by Spain), being farther afield. Thus, that this relatively timid traveler meets with this uncivilized fate also adds to the satire.

However, with civilization, evidently (judging by Greene's story), comes emotional detachment from the crueler quirks of fate. Indeed, part of the glory of civilization lies in the ways that dangers and accidents are minimized, through infrastructure like roads and telephones (allowing for emergency travel and communication), electricity (keeping perilous darkness at bay), laws oriented toward safety, the enforcement of those laws, and the punishment of criminals. As such, people in a civilized society are conditioned to expect their lives to be generally secured within the boundaries established by that society. Jerome, having attended a "rather expensive preparatory school," may be understood to circulate among the most wealthy and "civilized" of westerners. To such civilized westerners, the notion that someone should die by falling pig is simply ludicrous; the surprise inherent in the event is so strong that instinctive amusement over it may be unavoidable.

One might guess, however, that a member of a less "civilized" society, being more attuned to the myriad ways that fate can sweep lives around—whether through earthquake or fire, famine or war, or the sheer obstinacy or idiocy of other humans—would consider news of death by falling pig as grave as it truly is and would thus prove sympathetically superior to the average westerner. That Greene might be praising (if also satirizing) this sort of instinctive sympathy in the person of Sally is supported by an observation made in *Graham Greene* by Richard Kelly, who notes that Greene's autobiographical *Journey without Maps*—perhaps like "A Shocking Accident"—"can be read as an attempt to recover the sense of innocence that has been blighted by civilization."

CRITICAL OVERVIEW

"A Shocking Accident" is not one of the prolific Greene's most noticed works. In his review in *Commonweal*, Coffey observes that the collection *May We Borrow Your Husband?* was written by a man in his early sixties intending to emphasize the comedic, such that it stirs the reader's blood far less than do his earlier, more thematically ambitious works. The critic states,

> On the whole, Greene seems in these stories to have written his way back to comic North Temperate Zone.... He has perhaps lost something of range and emotional power along the way, but he has certainly gained in control of his matter and even in mellowness.

Coffey is utterly uninspired by "A Shocking Accident," deeming it one of the collection's three "skip stories" (that is, skippable). Referring also to "The Over-night Bag," he writes,

> Stories about dead babies and about people being killed by falling pigs... are a kind of national specialty of the English, and I was more surprised than anything else to find Greene, that most un-insular and un-English of authors, serving them up.

In *Graham Greene* (1984), Kelly reports that Greene was, in his own words, "in a single mood of sad hilarity" when he wrote *May We Borrow Your Husband?* meaning that "A Shocking Accident," already written, fit in well with the collection. Kelly goes no further than to note the "black humor" of the story and classify it among the collection's "trivial works" that "require no comment."

On the other hand, in *Characters and Plots in the Fictions of Graham Greene*, Robert L. Gale notes that Kelly asserts in a later volume, *Graham Greene: A Study of the Short Fiction* (1992), that "A Shocking Accident" reveals Greene's possession of "a comic genius that has never been fully realized or appreciated" and demonstrates "his sense of the absurd and the comic twists of life." In his 1986 revised edition of *Graham Greene*, A. A. DeVitis praises the story as "the funniest of his short fictions," featuring "a delicate balance of farce and pathos" presented through "a macabre incident which builds to an hilarious conclusion."

CRITICISM

Michael Allen Holmes

Holmes is a writer with existential interests. In the following essay, he considers the symbolic value and conceptual resonance of the pig in "A Shocking Accident."

"A Shocking Accident" should surely not be classed among Graham Greene's most profound literary efforts. It is an unapologetic comedy, originally published in a British magazine, *Punch*, whose century-long devotion to satire and comedy had by then rendered it an institution. Even before reaching the story's first sentence, the reader could guess from the context and title that the "shocking accident" in question is going to be the primary source of the comedy. Indeed, the story's subject matter is handled in the lightest, most casual fashion possible.

WHAT DO I READ NEXT?

- Another story in which Greene mixes whimsy with wit is "Under the Garden," found in the collection *A Sense of Reality* (1963). In this story, a boy returns to a place of childhood vacations and finds himself imaginatively transported from a magical garden to a Lewis Carroll–inspired wonderland.
- One of Greene's few explicitly comical book-length works is *Travels with My Aunt* (1969), a novel about a retired banker who learns to love life again by spending time with his spunky seventy-five-year-old aunt.
- A pig-related story that treats the theme of death, one which many young adults have likely seen but perhaps fewer have read, is *Charlotte's Web* (1952), by E. B. White, in which a girl named Fern comes to value the life of one of her father's pigs, Wilbur, who develops a profound relationship with a spider, Charlotte.
- A novel in the Western canon that includes pigs in symbolically rich leading roles is George Orwell's *Animal Farm* (1945), in which a few pigs learn to walk on two legs and decide to rule the farm in cruel (and suspiciously Communist-like) ways.
- In *Beasts of No Nation* (2005), the Nigerian American author Uzodinma Iweala offers a look at the grave consequences of an African man's death as his son is forcibly recruited by militants involved in civil war, including a commander who assumes a dangerously paternal role.
- The English author Roald Dahl, who wrote mostly children's books but also a few aimed at more mature readers, presents in the collection *Kiss Kiss* (1960) a story called "Pig," which, like "A Shocking Accident," is loaded with black humor, addresses the consequences of the deaths of parents, and ultimately conflates the identities of humans and pigs.

"DRAWING ON DE BECKER'S CONCEPT OF DREAM SHADOW FIGURES, ONE MIGHT OBSERVE THAT IN THE STORY, THE PIG FUNCTIONS AS A SHADOW FIGURE OF JEROME'S FATHER, LITERALLY UNITING WITH THE MAN IN PLUMMETING ON TOP OF HIM AND BRINGING ABOUT BOTH THEIR DEATHS."

There is a startling death, but it occurs offstage, so to speak, before the story even begins, and at no point does Greene exploit Jerome's unfortunate circumstances for serious dramatic effect. As far as grief is concerned, Jerome is merely described as not "a boy who cried" but "a boy who brooded." Regarding his orphanhood, the reader is never even told who became Jerome's guardian(s) or how the absence of his parents affected him. Such notions can be surmised from the details of his everyday life, such as his job and the type of person he marries, but his everyday life is contented, not tragic or broken, and the story's ending is a happy one. In sum, there seems to be little room in the story for literary profundity.

Still, whether or not Greene intently infused the text with tangible deeper meaning, he is one of twentieth-century literature's master craftsmen, and the story may hold more than meets the eye. Yvonne Cloetta supports this notion—and hints at a fruitful investigative angle—in remarking, in her foreword to Greene's posthumously published *A World of My Own: A Dream Diary*, "It is well known that Graham was always very interested in dreams, and that he relied a great deal on the role played by the subconscious in writing." In "A Shocking Accident," particularly curious and worthy of closer examination may be the role of the pig.

The pig itself might be understood as the story's primary obstacle to critical appreciation. In his *Commonweal* review of *May We Borrow Your Husband?* Warren Coffey refers to stories "about people killed by falling pigs" as if they constitute a British subgenre, something the average American reader may not have suspected, and on that basis insists on dismissing the story out of hand. In his 1984 volume

Graham Greene, Richard Kelly likewise passes over the story as "trivial." One may suspect that not only is the pig the source of people's difficulty taking Jerome's father's death seriously within the story, but it is also a signal to critics outside the story that nothing serious is contained therein. However, Greene was just the sort of author to set up his audience in such a way—to present a story about people not taking a pig seriously knowing that the people reading the story will also be unable to take the pig seriously.

Interestingly, Greene has used pigs in creative fiction with concealed intentions before. The psychoanalysis he underwent as a teenager entailed recording, sharing, and dissecting his dreams. As A. A. DeVitis remarks in *Graham Greene*, "When he could not remember a dream to please his analyst, he invented one, sometimes bringing a pig into the narration." It is in his autobiography *A Sort of Life* that Greene notes this habitual inclusion of pigs in invented dreams, and he expresses not knowing exactly why he did so. DeVitis further observes that Greene's old habit of pig-related dream invention "may explain the pig incident in the funniest of his short fictions, 'A Shocking Accident.'" The reader is left to conjecture, then, what relevance the idea of a pig held for him, both as muddled youth and as polished author.

Evidently not appearing frequently in real dreams, pigs do not merit much mention in dream-analysis literature. One theorist who does offer helpful perspective is Raymond de Becker, in *The Understanding of Dreams: And Their Influence on the History of Man* (1965). De Becker discusses how shadow figures in dreams, personages paired with but quite unlike the dreamer, often "reveal a dissociated part of our nature and, in fact, a part that has not acceded to genuine humanity. And indeed their appearance is often accompanied by non-human animal figures." It follows that "every dream animal is the animal in us, the nonhumanized part of our being, an ancestral root, a totem, a primitive identification." As his first illustration, de Becker formulates, "If I dream of a pig, it is because there is a pig in me."

Now, Greene did not actually dream about pigs but only compulsively imagined dreams of pigs when prompted by his analyst to invent dreams on the spot. This might suggest that either he wanted to be dreaming about pigs or, perhaps more probably, he imagined that he *ought* to be dreaming about pigs. In fact, Greene seems to have conceived of the school environment he hated being mired in—one of the factors leading to his psychoanalysis—as something of a giant pigsty. In his words, he felt as though in entering school he "had left civilization behind and entered a savage country of strange customs and inexplicable cruelties," a place where he was overwhelmed by "the sense of continuous grime, of unlocked lavatory doors, the odor of farts" (quoted by Kelly). Thus, Greene was likely making associations between the conception of the pig as an animal that gluttonously devours all manner of slop while wallowing in its own filth and the unclean side of human nature, as found in others as well as in himself.

Returning to "A Shocking Accident," one might further suspect that Greene intends in the story to associate uncivilized places especially with pigs, because civilized life is typically conceived as being more dignified and cleaner, with hard footwear and flooring helping humans stay a degree removed from the muck of the earth. Drawing on de Becker's concept of dream shadow figures, one might observe that in the story, the pig functions as a shadow figure of Jerome's father, literally uniting with the man in plummeting on top of him and bringing about both their deaths. As the father's shadow figure, the pig would represent qualities within him. Considered in this light, the father does have a sort of civilized piggishness about him. Physically, he is characterized only as "large," presumably reflecting a predilection for the sorts of gourmet local meals and wines one would expect a travel writer to seek out. In the one photograph described, he does not wallow in the mud to keep cool, but he does shield himself from the sun with an umbrella. Emotionally, he is only "sad," despite being privy to so much of the world's natural beauty through his vocation. While one should not assume that pigs are sad creatures, the idea of living one's uneventful life in the confines of a sty only to be butchered at the end—the fate of most pigs—surely evokes feelings of despair. Jerome's father, by virtue of his writing, is the opposite of physically trapped, but perhaps he should be understood, like many a civilized person, to be trapped in his identity and his routines, which leave him eating even if he is not hungry and unhappy even in the most beautiful places. Turning to the ill-fated pig itself, one might observe where it originates: not in a sty or a barn or a mudhole, but on a fifth-floor balcony in the middle of a city—as if it were an ordinary inhabitant of that city, living side by side with humans. In one of his versions of his father's death, Jerome makes an observation about such pigs that could easily apply to many a cooped-up human—even to his own father, who likely managed to find cheap local transportation far more often than he walked: "Of course the pigs get no exercise whatever and fatten all the quicker." Given the various resemblances, the falling pig indeed seems to be a sort of shadow figure, a spiritual double, of Jerome's father.

One last aspect of the role of the pig that merits examination is its own uncertain fate. Jerome's initial responses to the news of his father's death are fairly quirky: at first he seems mostly excited to hear of the heroic manner in which his father has quit this world, imagining the clichéd but nonetheless dramatic "hail of machine-gun bullets." Even as Mr. Wordsworth suggests otherwise, Jerome simply adapts the housemaster's comments to the mystery-shrouded scheme he has conceived in his mind. When Mr. Wordsworth finally makes the matter clear by fully explaining the pig's mortal descent, Jerome seems to immediately close the book, so to speak, on his father; it is as if he is forced by the bizarre circumstances, which his rational mind wants to interpret as comical but his emotional self insists cannot be, to consolidate a belief in fate, an acceptance of what he calls "the mystery of life."

An acceptance of fate can mitigate the mourning process by allowing the survivor to come to grips with the fact that what has happened has happened, and the past cannot be changed; everyone goes sooner or later, and a person who is gone is simply gone. Once Jerome grasps the quotidian truth of his old man's demise, his attention shifts, and he asks, "What happened to the pig?" If the pig is understood as becoming, in their shared death, the father's shadow figure, this question is indeed entirely natural; the fate of one reflects on the fate of the other. The housemaster surely did not have a reply to this question, and one might presume (based on the story's closing sentence) that no one was ever able to answer this question, whether Jerome never asked it again, or no one was ever bold enough to explain, or no one he asked ever knew the truth.

Thus, while on the surface Jerome becomes obsessively concerned with the precise telling of the pig-death story, perhaps what is really plaguing him is the uncertainty about the pig; not fully understanding the pig's fate, it is as though he does not yet fully understand his father's fate. But by the time he and Sally are engaged to be married, he has had plenty of time to consider the circumstances; surely he has come to his own conclusion about the event. If his poor father—an overweight man, wealthy enough to send his son to elite schools yet sad even in the sunshine of Capri, destined only to wallow and consume, wallow and consume—has met with an ironic and yet fitting end, struck down in the course of his professional, careful, well-fed travels in civilized society by the crashing descent of an overfed pig, then the pig ought to meet with an ironic yet fitting end as well.

The beauty of Sally's final question about the incident—"what happened to the poor pig?"—lies not only in the fact that it mirrors Jerome's response, proving that the minds of this soon-to-be-married couple will make perfect echo chambers for each other, but also in that it allows Jerome to finally answer the question himself, thus articulating the thought that, in being spoken, will at last put to rest the uncertainty that has been nagging him ever since he first heard the news. The ironic yet fitting fate for a pig who became fat so successfully that he caused his own confines to collapse, leaving him to fall five stories but, miraculously, not be utterly destroyed upon striking the ground but be saved for consumption by the ample cushioning of a passerby—the fitting end for this pig is that "they almost certainly had it for dinner." With that affirmation of fate, the perfectly matched Jerome and Sally—one ostracized from pigheaded civilization by the circumstances of his father's death, the other essentially an outcast owing to her permanent state of innocence—can be happy that everything is in its place.

Source: Michael Allen Holmes, Critical Essay on "A Shocking Accident," in *Short Stories for Students*, Gale, Cengage Learning, 2012.

Ann M. Begley

In the following essay, Begley argues that while Greene vacillated in his spiritual beliefs, "the work he produced is, paradoxically, that of a Catholic writer."

As soon as Graham Greene—an English writer of international status and perhaps the most celebrated Catholic layman of the 20th century—died in 1991 at the age of 86, the presses

Pigs can't fly . . . and that was an unfortunate fact for Jerome's father. (Morgan DDL / Shutterstock.com)

began churning out conflicting accounts of who and what he was. It is a widely held view that to fathom Greene's life, one need only decode his fiction. Indeed, as the Joseph Conrad scholar Norman Sherry illustrates in his authorized biography of Graham Greene, there is a strong affiliation between the personal history of the novelist and the fictive world he created. As he himself proclaimed, "I am my books."

The problem is that the lens through which a reader peers is unique, invariably coated with prejudice of one kind or another: Whereas the Rev. Leopoldo Duran's account (*Graham Greene: Friend and Brother*) approaches hagiography, Michael Sheldon has written (*Graham Greene: The Enemy Within*) what Joyce Carol Oates would call a "pathography," a sinister portrait of a dishonorable man whose entire life was based on deception, his Catholic faith being nothing more than one of the multiple masks that he wore.

Just as the dust had settled and we had come to believe that we—each with his own clouded glass—knew all that we were going to know about the author of *The Heart of the Matter* (1948), along comes *Graham Greene: A Life in Letters* (W. W. Norton, $35). A biography of sorts, constructed in

"CONSIDERED TO BE ONE OF THE GREATEST CATHOLIC WRITERS OF THE CENTURY, GRAHAM GREENE CONTINUALLY DISPUTED CHURCH TEACHING, CHAFING UNDER PAPAL INFALLIBILITY."

part out of the novelist's own words and replete with photographs, this collection of personal letters (including many that were unavailable to his official biographer) is edited, well documented and engagingly annotated by Richard Greene (no relation), who points out that his subject once estimated that he wrote about 2,000 letters a year. Greene's prose here—in striking contrast to his published writings—tends at times to be flat. We are reminded that letters are generally written in a single draft, and many in this book were actually dictated and later transcribed by a secretary. They nonetheless are of great interest in that they reveal the novelist's personal, literary, religious and political concerns over a period of 70 years. Greene discusses the craft of writing with some of the outstanding literary figures of his day and describes in detail his travels around the world. The letters also give evidence of his anti-Americanism, his support of the infamous traitor Kim Philby, his inexplicable fondness for certain Latin American dictators and his involvement with British Intelligence—which engendered both *Our Man in Havana* (1958) and *The Human Factor* (1978).

The portrait painted is of an elusive and exceedingly complex, enigmatic, courteous and caring man, an inveterate traveler who was torn apart by longing and brought low by bipolar disorder—which is probably what prompted Malcolm Muggeridge to remark that Greene had a dual personality that he was unable to fuse into any kind of harmony. "Graham was a man of strong appetites," the editor of this volume comments, "often made utterly unmanageable by bipolar illness."

To escape the spiritual angst that tormented him from boyhood on, an inner void bordering on despair that Baudelaire termed ennui and Sherry describes as "a fall in spirit of an unalterable intensity, a kind of plague spot," Greene resorted to a variety of diversions—alcohol, opium, tawdry sexual adventures, attempted suicide and voyages to dangerous areas of the world, "where life," he observed, "was reinforced by the propinquity of death." Writing also was an escape from "the madness, the melancholia, the panic fear which is inherent in the human situation." It was perhaps this spiritual blackness—a major theme in this book—together with his sporadic lack of orthodoxy that led some to conclude that Greene's faith was a sham. The love letters—first to Vivien, who became his wife after a two-year courtship, then to the beautiful American Catherine Walston, who pervaded his thoughts for more than a decade—manifest a painful longing for a lasting, reciprocal passion.

Greene's Catholicism has engendered endless controversy. An atheist, he took instruction in the faith—which he would later describe as "a malign virus from which one could never be cured"—to understand better the beliefs of his fiancée and, in short, to please her. Accepting Catholicism on an intellectual level, he was received into the church when he was 22. As he matured, however, he was often referred to as a religious maverick who kept one foot in the church while identifying with such ecclesiastical dissidents as Hans Kung and liberation theologians in Latin America. His fiction reveals a vacillating belief that was, as the author himself strongly suggests, undoubtedly affected by his continual disregard of the church's moral precepts regarding sexuality. With increasing doubt as to the existence of a loving God, he nonetheless continued to attend Mass periodically, eventually describing himself as a "Catholic agnostic." It is worth noting that the unnamed minor character in *The Quiet American* (1955) who, fearful of an imminent death, seeks out a priest to hear his confession, is, Greene's diary reveals, the novelist himself.

Early on, Greene took to writing fast-paced thrillers—"entertainments" he called them. The best known among these are *A Gun for Sale* (1936; U.S. title, *This Gun for Hire*), *The Confidential Agent* (1939) and *The Ministry of Fear* (1943). His first novel with a Catholic theme, *Brighton Rock* (1938), is at the same time an exploration of good and evil and a psychological thriller. In it the author probes "the appalling... mystery of the mercy of God" moving through a ravaged world. It was undoubtedly T. S. Eliot's support of the thriller as a reputable literary form that encouraged Greene to experiment with it.

The travel book *The Lawless Roads* (1939; U.S. title, *Another Mexico*), a report on the persecution of the church in the states of Chiapas and Tabasco by the Socialist government in power, became a sketch book for *The Power and the Glory* (1940), a serious novel that employs all the conventions of a first-rate thriller. In both the fictional and the historical accounts, any semblance of religious adherence is outlawed, and priests who do not submit to laicization and marriage are summarily executed. It is through the moving story of a priest on the run—the so-called whiskey priest who in a moment of loneliness has fathered a child—that the novelist examines the function of the priest-hood as a medium of grace, placing in relief the distinction between the man and his office. *The Power and the Glory* was condemned by the Holy Office on the grounds that the work was injurious to the priesthood and that the book "portrays a state of affairs so paradoxical, so extraordinary, and so erroneous as to disconcert unenlightened persons, who form the majority of readers." The author was instructed not to permit further editions or translations. Greene composed a "casuistical" response, pointing out that he had already sold the translation rights and so no longer had any control over them. He sent a copy of his response to the influential Monsignor Montini (later Pope Paul VI), who defended the book, shielding Greene from the Holy Office. During a private interview, Pope Paul VI told the novelist that there would always be things in his books that some Catholics would find offensive, but that he should not let that bother him. The aim of his novel, Greene explained, was "to oppose the power of the sacraments and the indestructibility of the Church on the one hand with, on the other, the merely temporal power of an essentially Communist state."

The Vatican quietly dropped the matter. In his lecture "Virtue of Disloyalty" (1969) Greene affirms the necessity of the artist's freedom. Literature has nothing to do with edification, he insists. Catholic novelists (he prefers to say novelists who are Catholic) should, he urges, take Newman as their patron. When defending the teaching of literature in a Catholic university, the cardinal declared that "...if Literature is to be made a study of human nature, you cannot have a Christian Literature. It is a contradiction in terms to attempt a sinless Literature of sinful man."

Greene was sometimes accused of heresy when his characters espoused an unorthodox interpretation of the Catholic creed or value system. The publication of *A Burnt-Out Case* (1961) distressed Evelyn Waugh immensely: he viewed the novel as a confession of disbelief and strongly suggested that the author was "finished as a Catholic." Greene wrote to his friend of many years to assure him that this was not the case; he merely wanted to give expression to various states of belief and dis-belief. "If people are so impetuous as to regard this book as a recantation of faith, I cannot help it. Perhaps they will be surprised to see me at Mass."

The End of the Affair (1951), clearly a close transcript of Greene's relationship with Catherine Walston, deals with the secret love affair of a middle-aged novelist, who narrates the story, and a married woman. A third protagonist, though invisible and mute, the Deus Absconditus, plays the strongest role. As in Paul Claudel's *The City*, some of the writings of Evelyn Waugh and Marguerite Yourcenar, as well as much of the work of François Mauriac—who maintained that there is only one Love—*The End of the Affair* expresses the belief that human love, which cannot satisfy the universal inner longing, is in some arcane way a search for God.

For tax purposes, reasons of health and a desire to be closer to Yvonne Cloetta, with whom he had formed a relationship that lasted over three decades, Greene moved to France in 1966, maintaining apartments in Paris and Antibes as well as a house in Anacapri. Shedding dogma after dogma, he was wont to say that he had "excommunicated" himself and joined "the Foreign Legion of the Church." In his old age, however, Greene returned to the sacraments and together with Duran made an annual retreat at a Trappist monastery. (It is their friendship that forms the basis for the picaresque novel *Monsignor Quixote* [1982], a work that deals with age, death and illusion.) The editor remarks that there are those who are of the opinion that Greene did this just to please his clerical friend. Perhaps. Months before he died, the novelist confided to the literary scholar Alberto Huerta, S.J., whose opinions about politics in Central America he shared, "Really the only link I feel I have with the Catholic Church now is the Jesuit Order." Nevertheless following Greene's instructions, as he lay dying of leukemia at a hospital on the shores of Lake Geneva, Duran was summoned to his side to administer the last rites of the church.

Graham Greene's vast oeuvre consists of more than 25 novels or entertainments, novellas, short stories, plays, children's books, numerous literary and political essays, a biography, screen scenarios, travel books, hundreds of book and film reviews and two volumes of autobiography (in which very little of his personal life is revealed). Although he explored a variety of genres, it is mainly for his fiction that he is known—as well as the masterly film scripts for *The Fallen Idol* (1948) and *The Third Man* (1949). The recipient of a plethora of awards, he was repeatedly considered for the highest literary honor, the Nobel Prize, but each time, this editor notes, his nomination was blocked by "the anti-Catholic Artur Lundkvist." Still, François Mauriac's Catholicism did not stop him from receiving this honor. There is another explanation: some academic critics, ignoring Greene's deep spiritual insight and artistic intensity, dismiss his work as mere entertainment because he used the thriller as a vehicle of serious thought.

Considered to be one of the greatest Catholic writers of the century, Graham Greene continually disputed church teaching, chafing under papal infallibility. He disapproved of the liturgical reforms of the Second Vatican Council, but was drawn to the Mass. As he aged he explained that he had less and less belief every day but more and more faith. Eventually even that seemed to slip away. The malign virus seemingly cured, or almost so, he nonetheless repeatedly declared, "I don't believe that death is the end of everything." Readers of this volume may find Greene's spiritual ambivalence unsettling, but whatever his personal spiritual struggle was, the work he produced is, paradoxically, that of a Catholic writer.

Source: Ann M. Begley, "A Vacillating Believer," in *America*, Vol. 200, No. 11, March 30, 2009, pp. 27–30.

R. H. Miller

In the following excerpt, Miller analyzes three of Greene's stories which he believes represent the themes and techniques of Greene's short fiction as a whole.

Graham Greene is one of the most successful short story writers of all time. Very few writers achieve the ability to rivet readers' attention to a dramatic situation, turn it into meaning through ingenious manipulations of plot, and in the end leave them astonished, breathless. His range is extensive, moving from the introspective to the bizarre to the shocking. Greene's output is contained in five collections, issued from 1935 through 1967: *The Basement Room and Other Stories* (1935), *Nineteen Stories* (1947), *Twenty-One Stories* (1954), *A Sense of Reality* (1963), and *May We Borrow Your Husband? and Other Comedies of the Sexual Life* (1967). These were subsequently brought together into one volume, *Collected Stories* (1972). In addition, several uncollected stories have appeared. Eighteen of the stories were filmed for the series *Shades of Greene*, produced by Thames Television in 1976 and shown over the Public Broadcasting System in the United States, with the simultaneous publication of a collection by that title. Three of the stories may suffice to reveal the prevailing techniques and themes of Greene's short fiction: "The Basement Room," "The Destructors," and "Under the Garden." All three were made into films for the *Shades of Greene* series.

"WHAT IS MORE IMPORTANT TO ONE'S UNDERSTANDING OF IT IS ITS WAY OF DEALING WITH REALITY AND THE RECONSTITUTION OF REALITY THROUGH ART."

"The Basement Room" first appeared as the lead and title story in Greene's first published collection, in 1935. In 1948 it was released as a film, and a highly successful one, under the title *The Fallen Idol*, directed by Carol Reed, who also directed *The Third Man*. "The Basement Room" serves as a guide to the major themes of many of Greene's novels: the innocence of childhood and its subsequent corruption when it confronts the adult world; the insidious nature of evil and its mixture with good; the relative impotence of good in the face of evil; and, most significantly, the inevitability that trust will be rewarded with betrayal, no matter how unintended that betrayal might be.

Greene chooses to narrate this story from a third-person-limited point of view, from the vantage point of the main character Philip's deathbed, sixty years after the events of the story, and to focus subtly one's attention on the life-long impact of this episode on Philip, who has never forgotten it and who must live with its effects until his dying day. In "The Basement Room" the situation concerns then seven-year-old Philip and two household servants, Baines and Mrs. Baines, to whom he has been given over during "a fortnight's holiday." Philip is isolated from his parents and "between nurses," which means that he must, from the context of childhood, deal prematurely with an adult world of marital hatred, duplicity, and adultery, and must make crucial choices as to how to maintain allegiances that the adults require of him.

With its five sections the story is reminiscent of Renaissance tragedy, carrying its construct of rising action, crisis, falling action, and catastrophe, out of which a new awareness, however dim, arises for both protagonist and reader. The story focuses on one crucial event, the accidental death of Mrs. Baines, and its test of Philip's loyalty and his ability to interpret the event within the context of adult morality. The crisis occurs with the surprise return of Mrs. Baines to the house, where she catches Baines and Emmy *in flagrante*. It only remains for the catastrophe of Philip's betrayal to occur, and its result: the misinterpreting of Mrs. Baines's death by the police and the downfall of Baines and Emmy.

The focus of the story is on Philip; its narrative technique binds the readers to him, although they do not discover fully the narrative situation until the close of the story. What happened there on that day succeeded in some unconscious way of killing all Philip's innocence and destroying his childhood love of life. His innocence has no difficulty dealing with Mrs. Baines's clearly malicious nature; it fears it, while it betrays Baines both at the end of the story and earlier, when Mrs. Baines discovers the crumb of pink sugar on his lapel. Emmy, the young girl who is Baines's lover, is a great mystery to Philip throughout his life, and he dies with the question on his lips he has asked himself over and over again for the past sixty years: Who is she? The answer is that she is, like her descendant Rose in *Brighton Rock*, the potentiality for love and happiness, but she is so frail and identityless that she cannot survive in a world in which the force of evil is so strong that it traps the good (Baines) and subverts the innocent to its own cause (Philip). Philip dies an old, loveless man, never having created anything, and carrying with him the unforgettable memory of Mrs. Baines's shrill voice, a voice he could mimic with devastating effect.

The story closes with the death of innocence, the powerful sickness of the heart induced by Philip's betrayal, and foreshadows future stories to be written: *Brighton Rock* and Rose's goodness, that also of Sarah Miles in *The End of the Affair* and of Bendrix's opacity; of Scobie's innocence in *The Heart of the Matter*, and that of Pyle in *The Quiet American*, the deadliest innocent. Philip, too, as a child foreshadows all Greene's children, from the childlike Pinkie and Rose, to Coral Fellows and the Mexican boys, to the shrieking child in *The Third Man*, who almost does in Rollo Martins.

"The Destructors" first appeared serialized in two parts in *Picture Post*, July 24 and 31, 1954. Its first appearance in a collection was in *Twenty-One Stories* in 1954. Perhaps no story since Shirley Jackson's "The Lottery" appeared in the *New Yorker* in 1948 has produced such a disturbing effect on readers. Next to "The Basement Room" it has attracted more critical attention than any other story by Greene, and is his most frequently anthologized story. "The Destructors" may be Greene's best story and perhaps one of the finest in the language. It has all the qualities that have come to be expected in the short story: focus, compression, pace, and that element of surprise, that epiphany that brings one to recognizing a powerful truth. It works as both parable and allegory, parable in the sense that it is a narrative in a relatively contemporaneous setting that makes a clear moral point, allegorical in the sense that it "signifies" on several levels.

As parable the story is a mirror of experience which reflects the condition of England during the immediate postwar period, at a time when England was only gradually recovering from the destruction of the blitz and the ravages more generally of the war. The locale, Wormsley Common, has been bombed, and the house of Mr. Thomas (a.k.a. "Old Misery") sticks up like one last sound tooth in a rotten mouth. More significantly, the house symbolizes the traditions of civilization, having been designed and built by the distinguished seventeenth-century English architect Christopher Wren; yet these traditions have not been upheld over the years, and readers know that Old Misery has been sadly remiss, as have others before him, in their obligation to maintain the edifice in its proper style. The young protagonist, Trevor, or T., as he prefers to be called, sees the rude absurdity of the grand house, and he persuades his gang of boys to set themselves the task of reducing it to rubble, not by destroying it but rather by systematically gutting it and weakening its structure, so that at the close of the story it only requires the tug of the lorry at one corner of the foundation to bring the whole structure down. Old Misery, locked in his outdoor toilet, emerges to find complete destruction. It is a horrendously cruel trick to pull on an old man, but the lorry driver says at the end, "There's nothing personal, but you got to admit it's funny." The younger English generation has succeeded in extending the actions of the older to their logical conclusion, and the landscape of Wormsley Common has rational consistency now that the Wren house is gone.

At one level readers, especially older readers, with their powerful sense of the sanctity of property, react in horror to what the gang achieve. But a deeper reading of the story reveals that much more is at stake here than property; it is the loss of a work of art, the destruction not just of a building but of a wonderful idea poorly stewarded, the loss more generally of an entire culture, not to war alone but to the wanton destructiveness of a new generation who are products of that war and have no understanding of and little stake in preserving that which they do not love.

What is perhaps more appalling than the destruction is the manner in which it is carried out. T. is caught up in both a struggle for and an exercise of power and in a rejection of his heritage, of his father, a former architect, and of his mother, with her class snobbery. Politically the story is a microcosm of the acquisition and uses of power as T. succeeds in wresting control of the gang from Blackie and shapes it and motivates it to carry out his plan. What is most unsettling is that such skill and intellect are exercised by the gang in carrying out their plan. The dinnertime harangues from parents about the value of work and of dedication bear ironic fruit in their efforts.

Most powerful in the story's impact is its multilayered allegory that allows readers to see this not only as a parable on the bitter fruit of the postwar generational struggle; in a broader context it represents the death of property in a class struggle between the custodians of that property and a newer generation that sees the absurdity of that concept. On a political level it is an allegory on totalitarianism and the fruits of power, and the way in which that power, once unleashed, is difficult to control and assumes a life of its own. In another sphere it is the corruption and destruction of the good by a Manichean evil that is present in the world, ready to use those who have some small impulse toward harm and to assume a power even greater than that of those who pursue evil ends. In "The Second Coming" Yeats says, "The best lack all conviction, while the worst / Are full of passionate intensity." Greene's story is saying much the same thing here. "The Destructors" will remain a disturbingly powerful story and take on even more significance as time passes.

"Under the Garden" is Greene's longest story and, given its length, ought perhaps to be thought of as a novella. It first appeared in 1963 in *A Sense of Reality*. This story is as seminal a piece of Greene's fiction as any he has written. It brings together motifs of childhood and adulthood, of the meaning of literature and art, of the interplay of the conscious and unconscious life and the significance of dreams as clues to a character's nature, of the nature of myth and its meaning in real life—all major concerns in Greene's work. Additionally, it combines the strategies of three of Greene's favorite works, two of them, appropriately, children's books: the geography of *Alice in Wonderland*, the escape motif of Henry James's "The Great Good Place," one of Greene's favorite stories, and the romance of Robert Louis Stevenson's *Treasure Island*. It is at the same time one of Greene's most puzzling stories and one of his richest.

Structurally the story is multilayered. It relies on three separate narrations: that of the writer Greene, following his character William Wilditch through the trauma of learning that he has life-threatening, probably terminal lung cancer and his escape to his brother's estate, Winton Hall; that of Wilditch as a thirteen-year-old, recapturing and romanticizing a childhood dream through his story "The Treasure in the Island," printed in his school magazine the *Warburian* under the nom de plume "W. W." (for which one may surely substitute "G. G."); and that of Wilditch as an adult as he rewrites the childhood story into a new version, the product of accretions over the fifty years since the time he had the original dream about his subterranean experience. Three separate voices, three separate stories, all drawn from one source: a dream of a most compelling kind, one that has drawn its dreamer back to it time after time, since the age of seven to the present, when he is now past fifty-seven.

The geography, taken as it is from Lewis Carroll's story, provides a parallel to the dream, for it is a journey into a new land, a timeless underground world that exists below the estate garden, accessible only by squeezing into an entrance beneath a tree root on an island in the middle of a lake. It is also an escape in the Jamesian tradition because it represents a release from the pressures of the world above, where life sucks out vitality and where, in the final version of the story, Wilditch, like his author Greene, looks back over a life of travel to escape and confront certain realities, only to wonder if he has lived at all.

In the original story—that is, the childhood story of part 1, section 5—W. W. moves quickly through the experience to the discovery of treasure, but in his later version the treasure Wilditch discovers is of little avail. The "golden pot" turns out to be an old chamber pot, painted yellow. In the second story the adventure of the cave far overshadows the treasure. The cave is inhabited by primeval parents, Javitt and Maria, both eternal but both maimed physically and symbolically, Javitt by being partially immobilized because he lacks one leg, Maria lacking the power of speech because of her lack of a palate. The one sits and speaks wisdom from his toilet seat, as Wilditch says, like a great prophet; the other races about screaming nonsense. And all this is the product of a childhood dream, written up some years later by the dreamer, mulled over during a lifetime and then rediscovered and written up again. What began as a relatively straightforward but imaginative adventure story has turned into a Freudian fable of significant proportions. Wilditch, facing what seems to be his imminent death, after a lifetime of travel in all parts of the world returns to this single experience to find meaning in it. What he discovers is that he has taken the "facts" of reality and converted them into a new reality for himself. Ernest the gardener becomes the source for much of Javitt, the garden becomes the world, and Friday's Cave and Camp Indecision become efforts on Wilditch's part, at two separate times in his life, to analyze his life and re-create that analysis as narration.

Efforts have been made to unravel this seemingly slightly disguised roman à clef, and most certainly will continue. What is more important to one's understanding of it is its way of dealing with reality and the reconstitution of reality through art. What Greene does here is remarkably similar to what one sees in the allegorical layerings of his best novels. To put it in Wilditch's own words (hence Greene's): "A puddle can contain a continent, and a clump of trees stretch in sleep to the world's edge." In other words, one can sense a truth as broad as the world in a story as confined as Wilditch's. More importantly, it is the life of art and the making of it that is most important, as the story proves its own point. Wilditch's mother, determined to kill all vestiges of the imaginative impulse in him, failed miserably, where the gardener Ernest succeeded by providing him with a character, and the pond and the little hillock provided a place for a powerful creative experience. And at the end of the story Wilditch, having returned to his island and found the old chamber pot, is overcome by a curiosity that can only be satisfied by rethinking and rewriting his story, yet again. A new understanding and new experiences demand a new narration. "Across the pond the bell rang for breakfast and he thought, 'Poor mother—she had reason to fear,' turning the tin chamber-pot on his lap."

Source: R. H. Miller, "Short Stories, Plays, Essays," in *Understanding Graham Greene*, University of South Carolina Press, 1990, pp. 149–76.

Richard Kelly

In the following excerpt, Kelly discusses the stories contained in May We Borrow Your Husband? *as Greene's escape from writing novels.*

. . . In the Introduction to his *Collected Stories* Greene describes his tales as "a collection of escapes from the novelist's world." The short story, he feels, allows him to escape from having to live with another character for years on end, "picking up his jealousies, his meanness, his dishonest tricks of thought, his betrayals." Whatever his motivation, Greene has produced three volumes of short stories: *Twenty-One Stories*, *A Sense of Reality*, and *May We Borrow Your Husband?* A number of the stories are trivial, some are sketches of characters and events for his novels, and some are clear works of art. Greene himself writes that "I believe I have never written anything better than *The Destructors*, *A Chance for Mr. Lever*, *Under the Garden*, *Cheap in August*."

. . . *May We Borrow Your Husband?* was written, according to Greene, "in a single mood of sad hilarity, while I was establishing a home in a two-roomed apartment over the port in Antibes." The setting for many of the stories is Antibes, and the narrator is often an observant writer who, like Greene, overhears the tales of the strange lives going on about him.

Three of the stories deal with homosexuality. In the title story two interior decorators, Tony and Stephen, try to seduce a young man away from his new bride during the couple's honeymoon. They manipulate the narrator to entertain the bride while they drive off with her husband. At the end of the story she naively announces that Tony will visit them in London for several months in order to decorate their house. Greene depicts Tony and Stephen as cruel, witty, and self-indulgent creatures who hunt their prey with the cunning of animals. He extends his dislike of homosexuals in "Chagrin in Three Parts," in which a lesbian named Madame Desjoie seduces Madame Volet shortly after her husband deserts her. "Two Gentle People" continues with this theme of sexual disappointments by recording the brief encounter of a man and woman who realize that they might be happy together, but because they are already married they return to their ordinary lives—he to a dumb American girl named Patience and she to a husband engaged in a homosexual relationship with a stranger.

These three tales exhibit an aura of decadence and concealed bitterness at the waste of female sexuality in the sophisticated and exotic world of Antibes. There is a rich irony in the final comment of the narrator of "Chagrin in Three Parts" when he says of Madame Volet: "I was glad that she was in the kind reliable hands of Madame Desjoie." One recalls the pathetic attachments of Mabel Warren in *Stamboul Train*.

Some or the other stories deal with different abnormalities. "The Over-night Bag," for example, is about a man who carries a mysterious bag that contains, he claims, his wife's dead baby. "A Shocking Incident" [Accident] is a piece of black humor about a boy who discovers that his father was killed when a pig fell from a balcony and landed on him. And "Doctor Crombie" presents a physician who claims that sexual intercourse causes cancer. They are trivial works, however, and require no comment.

Greene's finest piece of writing in this collection is "Cheap in August," a surprisingly tender and compassionate story in light of the cruelty and superficiality of the stories that surround it. An Englishwoman named Mary Watson is on vacation in Jamaica because it is "cheap in August." Although she loves her American husband, an English professor, who is at home working on a study of James Thomson's "The Seasons," she decides that she wants to have an affair, an adventure. She quickly discovers, however, "the essential morality of a holiday resort in the cheap season; there were no opportunities for infidelity, only for writing postcards."

Thirty-nine years old, she feels it is absurd not to be content, but her restlessness is not due simply to physical desires, she argues, but represents "the universal desire to see a bit further, before one surrendered to old age and the blank certitude of death." As fate would have it, she is soon involved in the most unlikely, bizarre affair, one she never planned but that profoundly affects her life.

At the swimming pool she meets an American named Henry Hickslaughter. Greene describes him as "a solitary elephant," an old man with "rolls of fat folding over the blue bathing-slip." They have lunch together, and before long Mary "began to feel oddly at ease with the old man." In a way, Henry is like herself. He came to Jamaica because it is cheap in August, and he appears lonely and unfulfilled, and with little time in life remaining to find happiness. That evening she goes to his room for a drink, and they discuss a variety of subjects, from Longfellow to their family lives. They then go down for dinner, after which he invites her back to his room because, as he says, "I don't sleep well." She refuses at first, afraid that perhaps even at his age Henry might have some sexual designs on her. These thoughts make her feel ignoble, however, and she feels unjustified in refusing him a half-hour's companionship; and so, she goes to his room with a bottle of sleeping pills to help him sleep.

When she enters she is startled to find him crying. "I wanted company," he says, and she reassures him. He admits that he is afraid of being alone and that he would have paid the maid to stay with him if necessary. At this point Henry is no longer described as an elephant but as a geographical region to be explored and marveled at: "It was as if she were discovering for the first time the interior of the enormous continent on which she had elected to live." The stereotyped American turns out to have a tender soul, scarred by failure and dread. "But here, stretched on the bed . . . failure and fear talked to her without shame, and in an American accent. It was as though she were living in the remote future, after God knew what catastrophe."

Like an anxious and troubled child soothed by his mother, Henry finally falls asleep. Mary lies on the bed beside him outside the sheet, and he is lying away from her so that their bodies do not touch. But filled with pity and compassion she arouses his sexuality, and they make love. She feels no guilt but weeps a little at the temporary nature of this meeting. And when "His body began to slip out of her, . . . it was as if he were carrying away her unknown child, in the direction of Curaçao, and she tried to hold him back, the fat old frightened man whom she almost loved."

On one level this story makes one think of Henry as Greene himself, in need of a loving younger woman to reassure and comfort him in a terrifyingly impersonal world. Over and over again Greene has presented heroes, such as Fowler, Scobie, and Castle, with similar needs. There is also an ironic sense of sexuality and motherhood fused in the women of these works; the men are old enough to be fathers to the women but they frequently present themselves as frightened children who need these females to comfort and nurture them.

There is a wonderful innocence about Henry. The fact that he is an American is important, for

Greene has frequently presented the American as an innocent but never so sympathetically. The Smiths in *The Comedians* are well-meaning fools and Alden Pyle in *The Quiet American* is unthinkingly cruel, but Henry Hickslaughter, despite his name, is vulnerable, tender, and compassionate. He is the lost child seeking a home and never really finding it, except for the brief encounter in Jamaica. He is the unknown child who irrevocably slips away from Mary. She has discovered America and lost it in the same night.

In his short stories, then, Greene has shown us children without innocence, such as Trevor and the children in "A Discovery in the Woods" and adults who embody innocence, such as Henry Hickslaughter and William Wilditch. Many of these stories are very contrived or self-conscious escapes from reality, but several of them—such as "The Destructors," "I Spy," "The Basement Room," "A Hint of an Explanation," "Under the Garden," and "Cheap in August"—stand in relationship to the others as Greene's novels do to his entertainments.

Source: Richard Kelly, "Short Stories," in *Graham Greene*, Frederick Ungar, 1984, pp. 145–66.

SOURCES

Abrams, David, "Who Is Hugh Walpole and Why Has He Invaded My Library?," in *The Quivering Pen*, May 25, 2010, http://davidabramsbooks.blogspot.com/2010/05/who-is-hugh-walpole-and-why-has-he.html (accessed August 19, 2011).

Cloetta, Yvonne, Foreword to *A World of My Own: A Dream Diary*, by Graham Greene, Viking, 1994, pp. vii–xii.

Coffey, Warren, Review of *May We Borrow Your Husband? and Other Comedies of the Sexual Life*, in *Commonweal*, Vol. 86, No. 1, August 25, 1967, pp. 527–28.

de Becker, Raymond, *The Understanding of Dreams: And Their Influence on the History of Man*, translated by Michael Heron, Hawthorn Books, 1968, pp. 355–57.

DeVitis, A. A., *Graham Greene*, rev. ed., Twayne Publishers, 1986, pp. 18, 179.

Falk, Quentin, *Travels in Greeneland: The Cinema of Graham Greene*, Quartet Books, 1984, pp. 216–17.

Gale, Robert L., *Characters and Plots in the Fictions of Graham Greene*, McFarland, 2006, pp. 284–85.

Greene, Graham, "A Shocking Accident," in *Collected Short Stories*, Penguin, 1986, pp. 331–36.

———, *A Sort of Life*, Bodley Head, 1971, pp. 99–101.

Kelly, Richard, *Graham Greene*, Frederick Ungar, 1984, pp. 1–22, 160–62.

———, *Graham Greene: A Study of the Short Fiction*, Twayne Publishers, 1992, p. 53.

"Pupil Numbers," in *Independent Schools Council*, http://www.isc.co.uk/FactsFigures_PupilNumbers.htm (accessed August 20, 2011).

Siddiqi, Asif, "The Opening of the Commercial Jet Era," in *U.S. Centennial of Flight Commission*, http://www.centennialofflight.gov/essay/Commercial_Aviation/Opening_of_Jet_era/Tran6.htm (accessed August 20, 2011).

"Torquay History," in *Torquay International School*, http://www.tisenglish.co.uk/torquay-the-english-riviera/torquay-history/ (accessed August 20, 2011).

FURTHER READING

Abrams, Rebecca, *When Parents Die: Learning to Live with the Loss of a Parent*, Psychology Press, 1999.

Abrams draws on her personal and professional experience in exploring the ways that people can emotionally adapt to the death of a parent.

Cross, Julie, *Humor in Contemporary Junior Literature*, Taylor & Francis, 2010.

In this academic investigation, Cross dissects the humorous approaches used in a range of texts aimed at elementary-age children, considering how the humor affects developing and maturing minds.

Lancaster, Jordan, *In the Shadow of Vesuvius: A Cultural History of Naples*, I. B. Tauris, 2005.

This historical guide to the Italian city of Naples brings its long history to life, covering its famous international appeal as well as its crime and controversy.

McFarlen, Arie, *Pigs: Keeping a Small-Scale Herd for Pleasure and Profit*, BowTie, 2008.

In this instructional volume, McFarlen offers all the advice one could ask for with regard to how to raise pigs on a limited scale. She suggests using enclosures situated at ground level.

SUGGESTED SEARCH TERMS

Graham Greene AND A Shocking Accident

Graham Greene AND May We Borrow Your Husband

A Shocking Accident AND May We Borrow Your Husband

Graham Greene AND humor

Graham Greene AND short stories AND comedy

Graham Greene AND Roald Dahl

Roald Dahl AND dark humor

pigs AND civilization

pigs AND literature

Graham Green AND death

Graham Green AND dark humor

The Street of the Cañón

JOSEPHINA NIGGLI

1945

"The Street of the Cañón" is a short story originally published in Josephina Niggli's influential collection *Mexican Village* in 1945. *Mexican Village* contains ten different short stories that are woven together around the village of Hidalgo, Mexico. This was the first "literary work by a Mexican American to reach a general American audience," according to Joseph Henry Dvorkin's *Voices from the Gaps* essay. The book was later adapted into the movie *Sombrero*.

"The Street of the Cañón" is set in 1923 and explores the themes of love and courage. The two main characters, Sarita and Pepe, fall in love and take a risk to reunite two neighboring villages that have been feuding for a decade. The setting and culture of "The Street of the Cañón" are specific to Mexico, but the idea of forbidden love is universal.

AUTHOR BIOGRAPHY

Josephine Niggli was born in Monterrey, Nuevo León, Mexico, on July 13, 1910. She would later write under the names Josephina Niggli and then Josefina Niggli. Niggli's role in Mexican American literature is unique. Although she was born in Mexico, her parents were not Mexican but Caucasian Americans. Her father, a cement-plant manager in Hidalgo, Mexico, was from Texas, and her mother was from Virginia.

Two Mexican villages are engaged in an age-old feud in the story. (Pinkcandy | Shutterstock.com)

Mexico was politically volatile when Niggli was young. The family left Mexico in 1913, after President Francisco Madero was assassinated. They returned to Mexico in 1920, but Niggli was sent to San Antonio, Texas, in 1925, in the wake of the Mexican Revolution. She attended the University of the Incarnate Word, where she majored in philosophy. Niggli won several writing competitions while there. Her interest in writing led her to the University of North Carolina at Chapel Hill in 1931, where she began her literary career and obtained a master's degree in drama.

Niggli became known for her plays and poetry throughout the 1930s. She was awarded Rockefeller fellowships in 1936 and 1938. Her first collection of poetry was *Mexican Silhouettes* (1931). The 1945 publication of *Mexican Village*, however, distinguished her from other writers at the time with its narrative of village life in Mexico. Her first novel, *Step Down, Elder Brother*, was published in 1947. *Miracle for Mexico*, her last book, was published in 1964.

Along with poems, plays, and fiction, Niggli worked in radio, films, and television. Films she worked on included *The Mask of Zorro* (1940) and *Sombrero* (1953), which is based on *Mexican Village*. She also wrote for the *Twilight Zone*. Her nonfiction work includes *Pointers on Radio Writing* (1946). Along with her literary career, Niggli taught at the University of North Carolina and later at Western Carolina University. She retired from teaching in 1975. Niggli died in Cullowhee, North Carolina, in 1983. She did not consider herself Chicana, but her stories about Mexico helped to pave the way for future Mexican American writers and the Chicano movement.

PLOT SUMMARY

"The Street of the Cañón" is a story about a rivalry between two villages and the forbidden love that brings them together. The story begins on a Wednesday evening. Pepe Gonzalez is from Hidalgo. He travels to the neighboring village of San Juan Iglesias, where he is careful to hide his identity because of a feud. Don Roméo Calderón is hosting a party for his daughter's eighteenth birthday and welcomes the stranger. Pepe

MEDIA ADAPTATIONS

- The 1953 movie *Sombrero* is loosely based on *Mexican Village*. Niggli wrote the screenplay. The MGM film, starring Ricardo Montalbán and Cyd Charisse, is available online at OVGuide (http://www.ovguide.com/movies_tv/sombrero_1953.htm#). The film includes the characters from "The Street of the Cañón." Running time is 103 minutes.

places his father's cheese on the table with the food for the party while no one is looking.

Pepe sees Sarita, and she flirts with him using fan language. He charms away Sarita's chaperone and dances with her. He causes a stir when he requests the song *Virgencita*, or "The Shy Young Maiden." Sarita quickly changes the request to *Borachita*, or "Little Drunken Girl." *Virgencita* is the favorite song of Hidalgo, and it is not played in San Juan Iglesias because the villages have feuded for ten years.

Sarita tells Pepe that people in Hidalgo "are wicked monsters." She explains that six months before, men from Hidalgo tried to steal the bones of Don Rómolo Balderas. Don Rómolo Balderas was a famous historian who was born in Hidalgo, but he died in San Juan Iglesias. The two villages have feuded over his bones for a decade. Pepe knows that the attempted theft was only three months before because he was one of the men who tried to steal the bones. Pepe has a bad reputation in San Juan Iglesias because of this attempt, but no one knows who he is. He asks Sarita to walk around the plaza with him on Sunday. She refuses because "to walk around the plaza with a girl means a wedding." They are interrupted when Tío Daniel discovers the cheese from Hidalgo. Pepe disappears, and Sarita immediately knows the identity of her dance partner.

On Sunday, Sarita is walking around the plaza with her friends, and everyone is talking about Pepe's visit. The drummer walks next to her, but it is Pepe in disguise. She tells him her name and where her bedroom is. That night, Pepe comes to see Sarita. She believes he is after the bones of Don Rómolo Balderas, but he explains that he only brought the cheese to tempt the people of San Juan Iglesias to buy cheese from his father again. They agree that the best thing would be to end the feud and reunite the villages.

While they are talking, an eagle attacks Don Roméo Calderón's roosters. Don Roméo Calderón's birds are known as prized fighters. Sarita tells Pepe that their fathers used to cockfight together. This gives Pepe the idea to use a cockfight to end the feud. Hidalgo could win the bones, or San Juan Iglesias could win the cheese trade. He persuades Sarita to give him a bird.

Pepe shows the bird to his friends in Hidalgo and tells them his idea. They are impressed with the bird and agree to help him. They do not ask Pepe how he came to have a bird from Don Roméo Calderón, but they all know that Don Roméo is the only one capable of training his birds not to kill each other. Unfortunately, the bird, Satan, is easy to recognize because of his green hue. The men of the town keep Pepe's secret, but Father Zacaya becomes suspicious.

Father Zacaya travels to see the priest in San Juan Iglesias to discover if anything strange is occurring in the rival village. His trip appears uneventful until he meets Sarita on the Street of the Cañón on his way back. She begs him to take the fifty pesos she saved for her wedding and buy her a statue of Don Rómolo Balderas. She tells him that there is a statue of Caesar available in Monterrey for forty pesos, and a stonecutter can change the name on the statue for ten pesos. She says that she needs the statue for the fight and mentions Pepe before realizing that Father Zacaya does not know about the plot. Father Zacaya runs into Abel, the *árabe* trader, who is nervous because he has signs from the men of Hidalgo that he was told to put up in San Juan Iglesias that night.

The signs challenging San Juan Iglesias to a cockfight for the bones of Don Rómolo Balderas and the cheese trade of Hidalgo are seen the next morning. Don Roméo believes that it is a trick, but he and the other men agree to the fight. Sarita will perform the dance of the Spur at the fight.

St. John's day is two weeks before the fight, and Father Zacaya notices that the whole town turns up for the ceremony and festival. He has the statue by now. He attempts to discover what Pepe has planned, but no one will tell him. Over the next week, the people are more devout, which makes him happy. A note, however, comes from the priest in San Juan Iglesias, who tells Father Zacaya that the men of his town are praying to Michael and Raphael. Prayers to the archangels leave Zacaya concerned that the men are plotting "a miniature frontier war."

Pepe comes to Father Zacaya to ask him about dyeing birds, which is the priest's hobby. Father Zacaya is able to deduce the plan when Pepe asks him about dyeing black and green feathers red. Pepe tells him everything, including Sarita's role in the plot. Pepe, however, does not know anything about the statue. Father Zacaya is initially angry because "cockfights are wicked and terrible things." He agrees with Pepe, however, that feuds are also wicked and terrible, and he agrees to dye Satan.

Both villages come for the fight. The birds, however, refuse to fight each other: "As far as the two cocks were concerned, they were simply two brothers meeting after a long separation." Don Roméo accuses Pepe of stealing, but Sarita says that she gave Satan to Pepe because her father had told her that she should give her husband his finest bird. Don Roméo is furious that she would marry Pepe, and the villages divide over whether or not she should.

Father Zacaya asks Sarita to explain the statue. She confesses that she knew the birds were "taught to love each other," and she was concerned that dyeing Satan might not be enough to make them fight. Pepe initially feels betrayed, but he listens to her explanation. She remembered seeing in Monterrey a statue of Father Hidalgo, who is buried elsewhere. Seeing that situation as parallel, she says of Don Rómolo Balderas, "If Hidalgo has a statue, what difference does it make if San Juan has the bones?" Pepe argues that Don Rómolo Balderas does not belong to a single village, and the man himself would be ashamed of the feud. The people of Hidalgo agree to take the statue in exchange for the cheese trade, and Don Roméo agrees to let Sarita marry Pepe. The feud ends with Father Zacaya calling the people to pray and telling them to remove the dividing line the next day.

CHARACTERS

Abel

Abel is a trader who is an Arab. He is a Muslim who manages to avoid taking sides in the feud between Hidalgo and San Juan Iglesias. He does put up the signs from Hidalgo challenging the people of San Juan Iglesias to a cockfight.

Don Rómolo Balderas

Don Rómolo Balderas is dead when the story begins, but he is pivotal to the plot. He is a famous historian who was born in Hidalgo and died in San Juan Iglesias, where he is buried. The feud begins when both villages demand his body. The feud ends after ten years when Pepe convinces the people that Don Rómolo Balderas belongs to everyone, arguing, "how ashamed he must have been of us while he looked down on our petty little feud."

Don Roméo Calderón

Don Roméo is known for his prized fighting birds. He has a secret skill in training that makes his birds love each other but still win cockfights. Don Roméo is Sarita's father, and he promises that he will give his best bird to her husband at the beginning of the birthday party. This is why Sarita gives Satan to Pepe. Don Roméo is furious at the idea of Sarita marrying Pepe, but he gives his consent in the end.

Sarita Calderón

Sarita is the beautiful eighteen-year-old daughter of Roméo. Pepe falls in love with her "black eyes." She flirts with Pepe using fan language and is embarrassed when she realizes that he understands what she communicated. She agrees to help Pepe end the feud by giving him her father's prize bird, Satan, for a cockfight between Hidalgo and San Juan Iglesias. The bird is part of her dowry, and Sarita believes that she has the right to give him to Pepe.

Concerned that Satan will not fight, Sarita gives Father Zacaya fifty pesos to buy a statue to be relabeled as Don Rómolo Balderas, for Hidalgo. She hopes that the statue will take the place of Don Rómolo Balderas's bones for the citizens of Hidalgo and bring peace to the two villages. Sarita is chosen to be the dancer who will perform the dance of the Spur and trample the birds' blood into the ground. She defies her father and her village when she announces her decision to marry Pepe.

Tío Daniel

Tío Daniel is the village wise man of San Juan Iglesias. He is the one who identifies the cheese that Pepe brings to Sarita's birthday as being from Hidalgo. He bullies Sarita when she announces her engagement to Pepe.

Pepe Gonzalez

Pepe has a reputation for being both wild and eloquent. He is able to talk his way out of trouble. He is handsome and charming, but it is dangerous for him to travel to San Juan Iglesias because of the feud between that village and his home of Hidalgo. He failed in an attempt to steal the bones of Don Rómolo Balderas from San Juan Iglesias three months before the story begins.

Pepe initially wants to end the feud for the sake of his father's cheese business. Later, he wants to end the feud so he can marry Sarita. He plans to end the feud by wagering the Hidalgo cheese business against the bones of Don Rómolo Balderas on a cockfight. Sarita gives him one of her father's birds, and he is able to persuade everyone in Hidalgo to go along with his plan. When the cockfight is not successful, Pepe uses his eloquence to persuade both villages to end their feud.

Don Timoteo Gonzalez

Don Timoteo is a cheese maker from Hidalgo and is Pepe's father. He does not approve of Pepe's wild life. Pepe brings his father's cheese to San Juan Iglesias, hoping that it will help create interest in the neighboring village and lead to trade. Don Timoteo agrees to accept the statue of Don Rómolo Balderas on behalf of the village of Hidalgo. He is impressed that Sarita thought of the statue in the first place.

Doña Juanita

Doña Juanita hides Satan for Pepe. She is a childless widow who treats Pepe and his friends like family.

Little Doctor

Little Doctor is a friend of Pepe's who helps him hide Satan and plan the cockfight.

Porfirio

Porfirio is a friend of Pepe's and the wood-carver in Hidalgo.

Rubén

Rubén makes candy in Hidalgo. He breaks his arm trying to steal the bones of Don Rómolo Balderas with Pepe.

Satan

Satan is Don Roméo's best fighting bird. He is black with a green sheen. Father Zacaya and Pepe dye him red to hide his identity the day of the cockfight. Having been trained to love his brothers, Satan does not fight.

Don Saturnino

Don Saturnino is the richest man in Hidalgo. Pepe persuades him to allow the cockfight. Don Saturnino is a friend of Father Zacaya's, but he does not tell the priest Pepe's secret.

Bob Webster

Bob is the quarry master and a friend to Father Zacaya. He keeps Pepe's secret about the cockfight.

Father Zacaya

Father Zacaya is the priest for Hidalgo. He does not approve of cockfighting, and the villagers keep Pepe's plan a secret from him. At Sarita's request, he buys a statue of Caesar to convert into a statue of Don Rómolo Balderas. Father Zacaya is concerned when he realizes that the entire village is hiding something from him.

Pepe persuades Father Zacaya to dye Satan red for the cockfight. In turn, Father Zacaya persuades the villagers to listen to Pepe and Sarita. At the end of the story, he announces that the line dividing the villages will be removed.

THEMES

Love

Love, both romantic and brotherly, is a main theme in "The Street of the Cañón." This classic story of forbidden love largely mirrors William Shakespeare's *Romeo and Juliet*. Sarita meets and flirts with Pepe without knowing that he is the infamous man from Hidalgo and her enemy. For Pepe, it is love at first sight. He first sees Sarita before the story begins, while he is trying to steal the bones of Don Rómolo Balderas. He eventually tells her, "For three months I've remembered your face." When she flirts with him at her birthday party, Pepe takes the opportunity to dance with her.

Despite the bitter feud between Hidalgo and San Juan Iglesias, Pepe risks coming back

TOPICS FOR FURTHER STUDY

- Read *Koyal Dark, Mango Sweet* (2006) by Kashmira Sheth. This young-adult book tells the story of Jeeta, a teenage girl in India who questions the custom of arranged marriages. Create social network pages (Twitter, Facebook, Myspace, Google+) for Jeeta and Sarita, and with a friend, conduct a conversation between them. What would Sarita tell Jeeta about falling in love? What would Jeeta tell Sarita about her culture and traditions?
- Research the aftermath of the Mexican Revolution from the 1920s to the 1950s. What societal changes occurred during this time? Create a video or multimedia presentation on this time period that focuses on these sociological changes. Include the life of Josephina Niggli in your presentation. Explain why you think she remained in America.
- Research American stereotypes of Mexicans and Mexican Americans in the early twentieth century using print, media, and online resources. Create a time line in a Web site that explores the evolution of these stereotypes. Include Niggli's work and influence. In your opinion, did Niggli succeed in changing the way Americans saw Mexican people and Mexican culture? Write a personal opinion essay and link it to the end of the time line. Ask classmates to comment.
- Read José Antonio Villarreal's *Pocho* (1959). Villarreal is considered the father of the Chicano movement. Write a one-act play in which Villarreal and Niggli work together. How do you think the authors would relate to each other? Ask a classmate to perform the play with you. Record the performance, and post it on a Web site or blog.
- Read Shakespeare's *Romeo and Juliet*. Write a paper comparing the play with "The Street of the Cañón." What are the similarities and differences in the characters, plots, and themes? Explain why you think Niggli chose to depart from this traditional story of forbidden love.

to see Sarita on Sunday. Both Sarita and Pepe express their desire to be together, although Sarita needs some convincing. Motivated by their love for each other, they plan to end the feud. Pepe prepares for the cockfight with the bird Sarita gives him. Sarita plans to give a statue of Don Rómolo Balderas to the citizens of Hidalgo. Together, they are able to unite their two villages.

As well as romantic love, "The Street of Cañón" shows brotherly love. Don Roméo's birds are famous for not killing each other. He trains them to love each other. At the fight, Satan does not attack his brother: "As far as the two cocks were concerned, they were simply two brothers meeting after a long separation." The fighting birds are symbolic of the separation between Hidalgo and San Juan Iglesias. Before the argument over where Don Rómolo Balderas should be buried erupted, the neighboring villages were close. Sarita's father was a friend of Pepe's father. Pepe argues that Don Rómolo Balderas may have used the birds to teach the people a lesson in brotherly love.

Courage

Both Pepe and Sarita are courageous. Pepe has a reputation "for doing the impossible." Sarita has heard that Pepe caught a mountain lion using only a rope. He crosses the border into San Juan Iglesias repeatedly. He takes risks to see Sarita despite the feud. His courage, however, is reckless. Don Saturnino believes that "men like Pepe live fast and die young." Sarita is just as courageous as Pepe, but she is not as reckless.

Pepe, from Hidalgo, visits San Juan Iglesias and walks into a party at a home. (*Travel Bug / Shutterstock.com*)

Niggli is known for creating strong female characters. Sarita's courage and intelligence are critical in reuniting Hidalgo and San Juan Iglesias. Sarita has the foresight to create an alternative plan to the fight, as she asks Father Zacaya to purchase the statue of Don Rómolo Balderas for Hidalgo. She admits her love for Pepe before both villages at the cockfight. In declaring her intention to marry Pepe, she risks the anger of her father and the people of her village. The fact that she is a woman also places her at risk, but she refuses to be bullied. The exchange between her and Tío Daniel over her declaration illustrates her courage: "'You are a woman,' called out old Tío Daniel, 'and the words should be dry in your throat.' 'Dry it for me,' Sarita snapped."

Sarita's confession to Pepe that she knew there was a chance the birds would not fight is another act of courage. She knows that her honesty could cost her Pepe, and indeed, Pepe initially views her actions as betrayal. Her idea about the statue, however, inspires him to convince the people that Don Rómolo Balderas is greater than their two villages. His argument that Don Rómolo Balderas would be ashamed of their prejudice against each other ends the feud and reunites the people.

Prejudice

After ten years of feuding, the villagers of San Juan Iglesias and Hidalgo are willing to believe the worst about each other. They develop unreasonable prejudices. In fact, a visible line divides the two villages. Sarita tells Pepe how men from Hidalgo "are wicked monsters." After it becomes known that she danced with Pepe Gonzalez, a man from Hidalgo, the boys tease her: "Take care, Sarita, a devil doesn't snatch you from your house." Sarita does not lose her prejudice quickly. She still assumes that Pepe wants to steal the bones of Don Rómolo Balderas when he first comes to her window. She loses her blind prejudice against Hidalgo as she falls in love with Pepe. The relationship that develops between Pepe and Sarita is an example for both villages and teaches the people to release their intolerance.

STYLE

Short Story

A short story is a brief narrative that typically has a clear plot with a progression and resolution. A true short story should be short enough to read in a single sitting. "The Street of the Cañón" is a story that introduces a conflict that comes to a resolution by the end. The volume *Mexican Village* is sometimes referred to as a novel. This book, however, is a really a collection of short stories that weaves the same characters throughout different narratives.

Omniscient Third-Person Narrator

An omniscient narrator, who speaks in the third person, tells the story of "The Street of the Cañón." The narrator provides information to the readers by explaining the thoughts of the characters. For example, when Sarita tells Pepe that it has been nearly six months since there was an attempt to steal the bones of Don Rómolo Balderas, "The man started to point out that the space of time from February to May was three months, but he thought it better not to appear too wise."

A third-person omniscient narrator provides information without unnecessary dialogue, which can slow the plot's progression. For example, the change in Hidalgo after Pepe plans the cockfight is succinctly described: "The month of May and part of June passed in a male whisper. Father Zacaya was worried. For the first time his good friends... were keeping a secret from him."

HISTORICAL CONTEXT

Mexican Revolution

Niggli's work typically represents life in Mexico both during and after the Mexican Revolution, and *Mexican Village* is no exception. The Mexican Revolution began when Francisco Madero ran against President Porfirio Díaz in 1910. Under Díaz, most companies operating in Mexico were foreign, and racial discrimination forced many people into poverty. Díaz jailed Madero when his opponent became popular. Madero escaped to Texas; he later returned to Mexico, advocating revolution.

In 1912, Madero and other revolutionaries such as Pancho Villa, Emiliano Zapata, and Pascual Orozco forced Díaz's resignation. Madero was elected president, but disputes between the revolutionaries led to the establishment of different factions in Mexico. In 1912, conservatives revolted, led by General Félix Díaz, who was captured. General Victoriano Huerta was assigned to handle the revolt in 1913, after Díaz escaped during a coup d'état. Huerta killed five thousand civilians. He then captured Madero and took control of the presidency.

Huerta came to an agreement with Díaz and the U.S. ambassador. President Woodrow Wilson, however, never recognized Huerta's government. Madero was murdered in 1913. Huerta's harsh actions, such as limiting the press, led to further revolutionary activities. Zapata and Pancho Villa were particularly dynamic opponents.

Venustiano Carranza overthrew Huerta in 1914, but Villa and Zapata broke ties with Carranza. Wilson threatened American interference in 1915 if the chaos continued in Mexico. Carranza was officially elected president in 1917. Zapata was killed in 1918, and Villa was murdered in 1920. That year Carranza fled with funds from the treasury and was murdered. Adolfo de la Huerta became the interim president until Álvado Obregón's election. Shortly after the election, de la Huerta revolted against Obregón, unsuccessfully.

The Mexican Revolution had a profound impact on life in Mexico. Many people involved in the revolution viewed the Catholic Church with suspicion because it was supported by conservative regimes. Catholicism, however, was an integral part of the country's culture. There were attempts to remove Catholic influence in schools and secularize the country in the 1930s and 1940s, according to Alan Knight in the *Hispanic American Historical Review*. The attempts at molding citizens were not always successful. Knight points out that the aftermath of the revolution "strengthened national integration and national markets." The "home, the 'movies,' the press, and so on," however, were stronger influences on culture than the government.

Mexican American Literature

Mexican American literature is also known as Chicano literature. Early Mexican American literature was typically written in Spanish. "Niggli is the only writer of the 1930s and 1940s who

COMPARE & CONTRAST

- **1920s:** The effects of the Mexican Revolution are altering Mexican culture and society. After years of bloodshed and chaos, people are choosing to emigrate to America for their safety and security.

  1940s: Mexico joins the Allies in World War II. Mexico's industry supports the American war effort, and many people from Mexico cross the border to America to work in light of the labor shortage. Under the Bracero Program, a government-sponsored effort to bring temporary workers to the United States, more than four million Mexican farmworkers come to work the fields.

  Today: The 1990s brought a financial crisis and hardships to Mexico. People still emigrate to the United States for a chance at a more secure future.

- **1920s:** In the United States, stereotypes of Mexican and Mexican American characters are dominant. There are few genuine representations of Mexicans in films, literature, or the media.

  1940s: Mexican Americans continue to face discrimination, and stereotypes still dominate the media. Fictional Mexican American characters speak broken English and are described as weak or lazy. Caucasian actors play many lead roles for Mexican American characters. Niggli attempts to displace some of these stereotypes with realistic representations in her writing.

  Today: Stereotypes still exist, but there are more opportunities for Mexican Americans to represent their culture in mainstream American society. For example, schools teach Mexican American literature. Additionally, adapted *telenovelas*, such as *Ugly Betty*, are popular with American audiences. Most large cities have Hispanic television and radio stations.

- **1920s:** Only a small percentage of the population in Mexico lives in cities. Most people reside in villages, such as the ones that Niggli describes in *Mexican Village* and her other works.

  1940s: Mexico's import substitution industrialization (ISI) policy focuses on developing local industry and production. Industry begins to grow in Mexico, and the landscape changes and urbanizes.

  Today: The country is more industrialized. A majority of Mexican citizens live in cities. Many villages are now popular tourist destinations.

revealed Mexican life and culture from an insider's point of view, in English," according to Elizabeth Coonrod Martínez in *Josefina Niggli, Mexican American Writer: A Critical Biography*. Eventually, authors such as Maria Crístina Mena also began writing in English. Niggli's *Mexican Village*, however, was the first Mexican American work to gain popularity with an English-speaking audience. Most critics agree that Niggli helped to pave the way for writers such as Rodolfo "Corky" Gonzáles and José Antonio Villarreal.

Modern Mexican American literature developed with Villarreal and his 1959 novel *Pocho*. The civil rights movement of the 1960s led to a Chicano literary movement called the first wave. Writers and artists in the first wave typically focused on political themes. The first wave did not include many female writers. The second wave of Chicano literature occurred in the 1980s, and female artists, such as Alma Luz Villanueva, Gloria Evangelina Anzaldúa, and Pat Mora, became influential with themes of personal identity.

Pepe leaves a mysterious package at the party. (Yuri Arcurs / Shutterstock.com)

CRITICAL OVERVIEW

Niggli was one of the first writers to create stories about people in Mexican villages for American audiences. Critics acknowledge that she paved the way for future Mexican American writers, but reviews have frequently been mixed. For example, Agapito Rey's review of *Mexican Village* in the *Journal of American Folklore* concludes that "it is an interesting and well written book with live pictures of a typical Mexican village." On the other hand, Claude Kean argues in the *Americas* that the book is "tedious" and that the author "steers a reader's sympathy to the evil and away from the good."

Modern critics, too, admit that her work is not without flaws. María Herrera-Sobek, in her introduction to *Mexican Village*, points out that "humorous scenes will be laced with Mexican stereotypes that to our modern, critical, and politically conscious eye detracts from her work." Although her work was predominantly written in English, Niggli was bilingual, which affected her style, a style that Mexican American writers in the future would copy. Regardless of her flaws, there is no denying her impact on Mexican American literature. As Yvette Fuentes says in her *Quadrivium* review of Coonrod Martínez's biography of the author, "Niggli's work must be taken into account in any study of the literature and culture of U.S. Latinos."

CRITICISM

April Dawn Paris

Paris is a freelance writer who has an extensive background working with literature and educational materials. In the following essay, she examines how

WHAT DO I READ NEXT?

- Translated from Spanish to English in 2005 by Ramón Layera, *The Impostor: A Play for Demagogues* (1944) is a play by Rodolfo Usigli. Usigli was a Mexican playwright whose drama influenced the work of Niggli.
- Mitali Perkins's young-adult novel *Secret Keeper* (2009) was named a 2010 Amelia Bloomer Book by the American Library Association. This book explores the themes of love and courage as Asha, a teenage girl in 1970s India, makes decisions about her future and the future of her family.
- *Beyond Stereotypes: The Critical Analysis of Chicana Literature*, by María Herrera-Sobek, is a nonfiction book published in 1985 that explores female authors and their influence on Mexican American literature. Herrera-Sobek, who wrote the introduction to the 1994 edition of *Mexican Village*, examines Niggli and other Chicana authors.
- *Mexican Folk Plays* (1938), by Niggli and Frederick Koch, was republished in 1976. This book provides examples of Niggli's skill as a playwright.
- *Post-revolutionary Chicana Literature: Memoir, Folklore and Fiction of the Border, 1900–1950*, by Sam López, examines the roles of women in Mexican and Mexican American literature. Published in 2007, this book explores Mexican American literature before the Chicano movement.
- Written by Michael J. Gonzales in 2002, *The Mexican Revolution, 1910–1940* is a nonfiction book that explains the events of the Mexican Revolution and their impact on Mexican society. The book gives background on the setting and culture of "The Street of the Cañón."
- *The House on Mango Street*, by Sandra Cisneros, is a 1984 novel that tells the story of Esperanza as she develops her personal identity as a Mexican American in Chicago. Cisneros's work is an example of Mexican American literature after the Chicano movement.

"UNLIKE THE SUBSERVIENT OR SELFISHLY SUBVERSIVE STEREOTYPES, SARITA IS A STRONG WOMAN WHO IS WILLING TO DEFY CONVENTION AND FOLLOW HER HEART; SHE ACTS SELFLESSLY AND CONSIDERS THE WELFARE OF THOSE AROUND HER."

Sarita manages to be a strong female character without descending to the stereotype of the subversive female in "The Street of the Cañón."

In a letter to Maren Elwood, quoted in William Orchard and Yolanda Padilla's *Women's Studies Quarterly* essay on Josephina Niggli's historical relevance, Niggli expressed her original goal in writing. She claimed that her goal was to "present Mexico and the Mexicans as they had never before been presented." In her fiction, Niggli attempts to portray Mexican characters who do not reflect the Hollywood stereotypes of her time. She was particularly skilled at accomplishing this goal with female characters such as Sarita. Unlike the subservient or selfishly subversive stereotypes, Sarita is a strong woman who is willing to defy convention and follow her heart; she acts selflessly and considers the welfare of those around her.

Given her wit, intelligence, and temper, Sarita is definitely not a stereotypical submissive female. María Herrera-Sobek, in her introduction to Niggli's *Mexican Village*, argues that Sarita "subverts" the people around her. The character, however, is not a stereotype. Her subversive behavior is not selfishly motivated. Rather, Sarita rebels against the authority of her father, her town, and her future husband to end a feud between the villages of Hidalgo and San Juan Iglesias. Her actions are rewarded in the end when peace is attained and Don Roméo gives his permission for her to marry Pepe. Niggli does not reward other subversive female stereotypes in her literature. For example, Herrera-Sobek points out that Nena in "The Chicken Coop" is "selfish, petty, petulant and is given her comeuppance at the end."

It is important not to confuse confidence with subversive behavior. Sarita is confident from the beginning of the story, and she knows exactly what she wants. She flirts with Pepe by closing her fan to her face while looking at him. This action is a type of fan language that indicates an invitation to dance. Although she likes Pepe, Sarita does not give him his way. For example, she changes his song request when they dance, and she refuses to walk in the square with him the following Sunday. Sarita wants Pepe to work for her love.

When it becomes clear to Sarita, and everyone else in San Juan Iglesias, that she danced with the infamous Pepe Gonzalez at her birthday, she is not afraid or appalled. She is excited. Sarita secretly hopes that Pepe will meet her in the square that Sunday, but she scolds him when he does, calling him a fool. His request to see her at her window that night is met with a stern reply: "Now you are twice a fool. Do you think I would talk to you?" Pepe, however, speaks to her own sense of adventure, and she tells him her name and where she lives.

Sarita is not welcoming when Pepe first arrives at her window. She angrily accuses him of trying to use her to steal the bones of Don Rómolo Balderas. After listening to Pepe's explanation, however, she agrees with his view of their situation. Pepe gives Sarita the opportunity to voice her true feelings, and she says, "It makes no difference to me whether he is buried in San Juan Iglesias or Hidalgo, and that is the truth." He tells her that most of the young people in Hidalgo likewise do not really care about the bones of Don Rómolo Balderas.

Sarita and Pepe agree to try to end the feud together. She mocks Pepe when he tells her that ending the feud will help them marry. Again, Sarita will have to be persuaded to do what she really wants. When Pepe comes up with the idea of a cockfight, Sarita is not immediately convinced. She insists that she is a "good daughter," and she initially refuses to give Satan to Pepe. Sarita relents, but she thinks better of it later. In the story, Sarita proves herself to be a good daughter but not an obedient one. She is strong willed, and she will always do what she believes is best.

Sarita does not tell Pepe that Satan might not engage his brother in a cockfight. Unwilling to crush Pepe's hopes and dreams, Sarita devises a backup plan. She remembers seeing a statue of Father Hidalgo in Monterrey, where Hidalgo is not buried. Therefore, Sarita decides that giving the village of Hidalgo a statue of Don Rómolo Balderas is the best way to end the feud between the two villages: "If Hidalgo has a statue, what difference does it make if San Juan has the bones?"

In choosing to pursue her own plan to unite Hidalgo and San Juan Iglesias, Sarita takes Father Zacaya into her confidence. She asks him to take the fifty pesos she saved for her wedding and purchase a statue of Julius Caesar in Monterrey for her and have a stonecutter change the name on the statue to Don Rómolo Balderas. Although Father Zacaya does not know Sarita or understand the purpose behind her request, her selfless sacrifice makes a profound impact on him. He buys the statue for her and keeps it in his home. Father Zacaya is part of Sarita's plan long before he becomes involved in Pepe's plot for a cockfight. When someone wonders what motivates Pepe, Zacaya remembers Sarita and says, "I think I can imagine the spirit."

When the cockfight is not successful, Pepe realizes that Sarita's plan was more effective than his. A fight would have only brought further anger and rivalry: "Suppose we had won—or the men of San Juan Iglesias. The anger would still be there, worse even on the part of the loser." Pepe is not the only one to respect Sarita's wise decision in purchasing the statue of Don Rómolo Balderas. Pepe's father is the first one to inform Sarita that Pepe will forgive her deception because "you thought of the statue." Earning the respect of the villagers from San Juan Iglesias and Hidalgo, however, does not come easily. She first has to confront the prejudice that she faces as a woman.

When Sarita announces her engagement to Pepe, her father and the villagers of San Juan Iglesias perceive her as a rebellious female. She only speaks to protect Pepe from her father's accusations of theft, but Don Roméo responds in anger. He says that he will put her in a convent and that Sarita will marry Pepe over his dead body. Sarita is unmoved by Don Roméo's threats. She insists, "I am the bride, and I have the right to say." The idea of a woman refusing to be guided by her father enrages old Tío Daniel. He tells her, "You are a woman, and the words should be dry in your throat." Sarita simply dares the old man to "dry it for me."

Father Zacaya persuades Sarita to explain her plan regarding the statue to Pepe. The crowd is angry when they hear her say that the bones are not important. When Tío Daniel hears Sarita's reasoning behind purchasing the statue, he mocks her: "Don Roméo, you should lock this girl safe in a convent to save the world from women's brains." Sarita does not pay attention to the jeers. She knows that she cannot persuade people like Tío Daniel to listen to her. She is focused on persuading Pepe to understand her: "She was looking imploringly at Pepe, her eyes begging him to understand. 'Please, Pepe. Don't you see?'"

As someone who values Sarita and does not belittle her for being a woman, Pepe is able to see the brilliance of her plan. This understanding inspires him to make a brilliant speech that successfully ends the decade-old feud between their villages. He even uses the roosters' failure to fight as a symbol for the brotherly love that should exist between the neighboring villages. When his speech is complete, Sarita remarks, "How wonderful you are."

Even though Pepe's speech is the same message that angered the crowd when Sarita spoke, the people are willing to listen to him. Pepe's success is due to the fact that he is male and a proven orator who could "argue Grandfather Devil out of an eon in Hell." The people are not willing to accept the suggestion that a woman's idea could be valuable. Sarita, however, knows from personal experience how convincing Pepe can be valuable. She is also aware of how the villagers feel about "women's brains." Persuading Pepe to accept the symbolism of the statue is the best way to persuade the villagers to end the feud. By allowing Pepe to make the argument for her, Sarita successfully defies convention without being a stereotypically subversive female.

Throughout the story, Sarita remains a strong, independent woman. She does defy convention, but she is selfless in her actions. For example, Sarita is willing to sacrifice her wedding in order to reunite the feuding villages. She only speaks out to save Pepe from her father's attack and at the request of Father Zacaya. She is successful at convincing Pepe of her plan, however, and this leads to the end of the feud. Sarita is rewarded for her selflessness and courage when the villages are reunited in friendship and her father gives her his blessing to marry Pepe.

Source: April Dawn Paris, Critical Essay on "The Street of the Cañón," in *Short Stories for Students*, Gale, Cengage Learning, 2012.

"THE MULTILAYERED LENS THROUGH WHICH NIGGLI SEES MEXICO INFORMS HER VERSION OF MEXICAN NATION-BUILDING, RESULTING IN AN IMMIGRANT NATIONALISM THAT NECESSARILY REFLECTS THE NUMEROUS CULTURAL AND POLITICAL CONTEXTS THAT SHAPED THE MEXICAN AMERICAN EXPERIENCE, WHILE ELUCIDATING THE TRANSNATIONAL NETWORKS THAT CONSTITUTED LIFE ON THE BORDER."

Yolanda Padilla

In the following excerpt, Padilla contends that the narrative in Mexican Village *"engages in much more than simple escapism" as it is a "serious attempt to examine the issues" of the border.*

BETWEEN AMERICAN FANTASIES AND MEXICAN REVOLUTIONARY NATIONALISM

...*Mexican Village* is composed of ten interrelated short stories that are anchored by the saga of the Texan-Mexican protagonist, Bob Webster. His character is motivated by the rejection he endures in the United States because of his mixed-race ancestry, indicating the larger societal rejection of those of Mexican and/or Indian descent. The product of an affair between an Anglo American and his Mexican maid, Bob is left alone in the world at a young age after his mother's death. When he honors his mother's dying request that he go to his father to see if they can build a relationship, the elder Webster cruelly rebuffs him, exclaiming "admit an Indian is a son of mine? Damn it, I'm a white man!" (Niggli 1994 [1945], 453). This moment is a formative one for Bob; it initiates years of aimless wandering, of searching for a place that might accept him. He finds this in Hidalgo, in the northern Mexican frontier country that his grandmother had described lavishly when he was a child. After a process of many years that encompasses his initial resistance and ultimate embrace of a *mestizo* identity, Bob finally finds peace and is able to move beyond the rejection that had been his life's torment.

Mexican Village was enormously successful. It was widely reviewed by many of the nation's premier arbiters of taste in venues such as the *New York Times*, the *Saturday Review*, and the *Commonweal*, and was almost universally praised as a kind of apolitical ethnography, one that infused enough sentiment into its pages to capture the "spirit" of the Mexican people. The emphasis of these reviews on the narrative as a source of ethnographic charm with little historical or political content reflects the period's enthusiasm for local color writing, with its focus on exotic and picturesque representations of regional culture. As my brief summary shows, however, the narrative engages in much more than simple escapism. Rather, it proves to be a serious attempt to examine the issues facing the proto–Mexican American border subject through an engagement with political and cultural contexts in the United States and Mexico.

Niggli imagines Mexico both in terms of the local color fantasies the United States had projected onto the country *and* the Mexican revolutionary nationalism so influential in her thinking about the nation's future. Her ongoing interest in Mexican politics and culture was not unusual; many Mexican immigrants remained deeply invested in their homeland long after they had settled to the north, paying close attention to the direction the burgeoning nation was taking (G. Sánchez 1993, 9; Márez 2004, 130). While versions of Mexican nationalism that coupled nation-building and race were far from a new phenomenon in Mexico, this iteration reached its greatest level of influence in the years following the Mexican Revolution, at the same moment that hundreds of thousands of Mexicans were immigrating to the United States. Niggli herself remained committed to Mexican affairs even as she evinced a growing preoccupation with emerging Mexican American subjectivities in the United States. The racialized rhetoric of nation that was prominent in Mexico shaped her thinking both about the future of the Mexican nation and about the place of the Mexican immigrant in U.S. culture, driving the deep interplay of U.S. and Mexican contexts that is a hallmark of her writings, and that marks Mexican American writing more generally.

One can trace the rise of Mexican revolutionary nationalism to 1916, the year that Manuel Gamio, an anthropologist, published his highly influential book, *Forjando patria*. He crafted a narrative of the Revolution that positioned nation-building as its ultimate goal, consequently obscuring the rebellion's agrarian origins and demands, and initiating the process of its appropriation by the Mexican Left. Gamio believed that the Indians were the primary impediment to the country's becoming unified (Hewitt de Alcántara 1984, 10–13). In elaborating on his stance, he set the terms for what would become official *indigenismo*, a tricky balance of valorizing Mexico's indigenous heritage as central to the nation-building project while insisting on the imperative of Indian assimilation. The result was that even as Mexico's indigenous ancestry was to be fundamental to the nation, Indians of the day had to be "de-indianized" and incorporated into the culture. This is where Gamio's plan shifts from *indigenismo* to *mestizaje*, a complementary concept that indicates the mixing of races, and that Gamio used as the basis for his evolutionary logic: that while the Indian was essential to a unified understanding of the nation, the *mestizo* was the nation's ideal for the future (Saldaña-Portillo 2003, 206–12; Bonfil Batalla 1996, 113).

Gamio's ideas quickly achieved prominence, and Niggli's thinking was shaped by this postulation of revolutionary *mestizaje*, with many of her writings foregrounding the centrality of the *mestizo* to the past, present, and future of Mexican society. This nationalist agenda combines with the inevitable influence of U.S. cultural and political contexts in her work, producing a text marked by moments of thematic fragmentation that, I argue, point to the various contexts that shaped her worldview and to the related issue of the numerous audiences she felt compelled to address. The narrative's contradictions signal that Niggli's work, like the work of so many Latina/o writers, is never reducible to a single literary tradition, cultural sensibility, or national allegiance. In *Mexican Village* the internal tensions stem from the array of imperatives that pull the narrative in a number of directions at once—including its concern with Mexican politics, its attempt to change stereotypes in the United States about Mexico, and its drive to grapple with the situation of the border subject. The first of these narrative divergences centers on the text's evaluation of the Mexican Revolution and its consequences.

Niggli sets *Mexican Village* during the ten years following the Mexican Revolution, between 1920 and 1930. This was a period of great uncertainty about the direction the embattled and weary country would take, and marked the height of the employment of nation-building strategies by Gamio and other Mexican officials. Niggli indicates late in the novel that through her narrative she too is imagining the terms and conditions of Mexico's transformation from a "geographical expression" to a full-fledged nation (Knight 1986, 2). As Bob Webster asserts in his assessment of the family politics that animate the tension in the novel, "here is a microcosmic bit of Mexican history being played out in terms of family rather than of nation" (Niggli 1994 [1945], 453). He refers to the great Castillos, the family that has ruled the region for centuries. We encounter them in a time of crisis, just as the Revolution has dismantled the *cacique* or overlord system that historically ordered Mexican society, and the novel proceeds as Bob suggests, through an allegorical narrative in which family intrigues have national resonance.

Although the crumbling of the Castillo power is a consequence of the Revolution, the family patriarch, Don Saturnino, believes that he has only to find the proper heir to restore his family to its place of preeminence. His son, Joaquín, should by right be that heir; however, he and Don Saturnino had a falling out many years earlier, when Joaquín decided to fight on the rebel side of the Revolution. In explaining his decision to Bob, Joaquín articulates the Revolution's most noble aspirations:

> My ancestors for over three hundred years have ruled this valley. In the beginning they had the power of life and death. Their word was law.... And in spite of revolutions and the breaking away from Spain, and later from Maximilian, the outside world had little to do with the Castillo power in the Sabinas. The Great Revolution changed all that. It was time to change. It was not good for one man to say, "This one shall be rich and that one poor—this one shall live and that one die."

This emphasis on the egalitarian spirit of the Revolution is a major theme in the novel, one that is elaborated on in the middle chapters with an insistence that demands attention. For example, references to numerous village committees (building committees, a saloon committee, among others) abound, underscoring the importance of the group over the individual when decisions must be made. Most notably, a long section on the town's beauty contest, which I return to below, painstakingly describes the voting process in detail, demonstrating a young but increasingly confident democracy at work.

Combined with Niggli's assertion that the distinction she was most proud of was that her *Mexican Village* had helped end the "banana republic" view of Latin America (Eberly 1982, 37), the amount of space the narrative devotes to the relationship between revolution and democracy becomes pointed, suggesting a connection with long-standing debates in the United States that made democracy a racial issue. Hubert Howe Bancroft, the wealthy book dealer and publisher, declared in 1912 that Porfirio Díaz had no choice but to impose dictatorial rule on Mexico because "a nation of *mestizos* was not, like the Anglo Americans, predisposed toward democratic institutions" (in R. Sánchez 1995, 30). Madison Grant—whose *Passing of the Great Race* was among the most influential expressions of the rising eugenic view of immigration in the 1920s—argued that the true achievement of the "melting pot" was best exemplified by "the racial mixture we call Mexican, and which is now [through the Mexican Revolution] engaged in demonstrating its incapacity for self-government" (in Jacobson 1998, 81).

Mexican Village responds to the biases against the democratic possibilities of a *mestizo* populace with numerous scenes that emphasize democracy as an important element of village life. These references run counter to the idea of Mexico as a premodern society too hampered by racial impurity to organize itself around a system of democracy. Such ideas are most clearly articulated in the section about the town's beauty contest. The young women of Hidalgo submit photos of themselves that are judged by the men:

> The voting was laborious, requiring much wetting of lead pencils and scratching of ears, but finally the last ballot had been thrust into the box, and it remained for the committee to sort and count them. To keep from showing any hint of favoritism, Alejandro [one of the Castillo sons] had invited three of his Monterrey friends to make up the committee.

The narrative emphasizes the lengths the village goes to in its efforts to ensure that not even the slightest hint of fraud can mar the integrity of the voting process.

The vote-counting scene that follows further illustrates the still-precarious but important place of democracy in the village. The committee members react with horror when they realize that Maria, an orphaned woman the town regards with distrust, has won by a landslide. They plead with Alejandro—the younger of the Castillo sons, who dies midway through the narrative—to disregard the results of the vote and to name instead a "reputable" woman as the winner:

> "No," Alejandro said thickly. "This Maria won the contest. Her name shall be declared as the winner in Hidalgo. The counting of the votes will be kept secret. . . . You were asked to count the votes that was all. I am Chairman of the committee. We shall simply announce that Maria won the majority of the votes."

Rather than simply assert his will by virtue of his standing in the village as one of the great Castillos—the usual recourse in an earlier era—Alejandro appeals to the democratic process as the final arbiter of justice.

Although the elaboration of democracy through a beauty contest might seem to trivialize the matter, Rita Barnard reminds us that such contests have often been a site where ideas about cultural values and national identity are revealed and contested. They "transform one of the participants," she writes, "by imbuing her with a new and communally significant or representative status," and the almost inevitable controversy surrounding pageants suggests their "overdetermined signifying capacity" (2000, 348). Niggli invests her representation of the beauty contest with the gravity of such issues, even as she packages them within the picturesque rubric most recognizable to readers in the United States. Thus, Maria comes to represent both the quaint values of a traditional society scandalized by even the appearance of impropriety and the embrace of a democratic system that allows for the movement into modernity. Even more, when read against Bob's treatment as a mixed-race subject in the United States and against U.S. skepticism about the democratic possibilities of a *mestizo* nation, the narrative's theme of a democratic Mexico denaturalizes U.S. conceptions of race, showing Mexico to be a more egalitarian society as a consequence of the very Revolution many North American commentators derided on racial grounds. Appropriating the United States' iconic imagery of fairness and democracy, the narrative undercuts the notion of Mexico as a "banana republic," while calling into question U.S. claims of republican superiority.

At the same time, however, the first and last chapters, which are much more explicit in their political concerns, are in tension with the text's democratic themes, focusing instead on the plot elements that complicate or at times undermine Joaquín's judgment of the achievements of the Revolution. In those chapters, the village engages the consequences of the fighting in a way that signals that assessments of the war are ongoing, and that the narrative sees itself in conversation with continuing debates in Mexico about the war's meaning and about the future of the Mexican nation. The Indian characters in particular are forthright in their assertions of the meaningless loss and betrayal caused by the Revolution. Don Anselmo, the elderly Indian who greets Bob when he first arrives in the village, seamlessly introduces the topic almost immediately and without prompting:

> The Great Revolution was a grand thing. Don Nacho, who is Alcalde, says so. Also Don Rosalio and the little Doctor, and even the priest, say so. They are all very wise. But me, I stayed safe from the battles in the hills, and now that the fighting is two years done, I say to them, "Of what good is the Great Revolution save to hang people and burn buildings? If it was so fine, why do they not bring people back to life and give us new buildings?" They answer me with pretty words that mean nothing.

Later, as the Indian quarry workers rest, their talk drifts again to the subject:

> After awhile there was talk of the Great Revolution and what it would mean to the Inditos, if it meant anything at all, which the old ones doubted; for, as the wisest said, through all the years there had been so many promises and so many do-nothings. Now the Great Revolution was two years finished, and it, too, seemed to end in do-nothing.

Comments such as these act as a counterpoint to the turmoil that the Revolution has caused for the Castillo family, and which is presented as symbolic of a deeper societal transformation. The novel's competing discourses about the war together make the case that both things are true at once; that while the fall of the Castillo family and the larger fall of the landed elite that it represents constituted a major reordering of Mexican society, for those on the bottom, Indians and peasants in particular, the things that mattered most remained largely unchanged.

This instance of narrative tension points to the thematic negotiations the text attempts as it addresses itself to very different audiences. They show that the book is as much a serious engagement with some of the most urgent issues facing postrevolutionary Mexico as it is about indulging in static representations of the Mexican folk. Such tensions are also prominent in the narrative's elaboration of the Mexican Left's nation-building program, which is necessarily shaped by Niggli's intimate knowledge of the place of

"CURIOUSLY, WHAT SHE NEVER ATTEMPTED DIRECTLY, WHAT HER WORK ALTOGETHER FAILS TO ACKNOWLEDGE, IS AN EXPLORATION OF NIGGLI'S OWN DILEMMAS AS AN ENGLISH-LANGUAGE WRITER *IN* THE UNITED STATES."

Mexico in the U.S. imaginary. At some times, that knowledge produces in her work familiar images of an exotic Mexico. At others, it prompts an engagement with such images, one that complicates or rebuts their logic. The multilayered lens through which Niggli sees Mexico informs her version of Mexican nation-building, resulting in an immigrant nationalism that necessarily reflects the numerous cultural and political contexts that shaped the Mexican American experience, while elucidating the transnational networks that constituted life on the border. . . .

Source: Yolanda Padilla, "The Transnational National: Race, the Border, and the Immigrant Nationalism of Josefina Niggli's *Mexican Village*," in *New Centennial Review*, Vol. 9, No. 2, 2009, pp. 45–72.

Ilan Stevens

In the following essay, Stevens argues that Niggli's work is important because "it showcases the way ethnic literature has often emphasized the stereotypes it seeks to undermine."

A successful author of one-act plays, novels, and poetry in the 1930s and 1940s, Josefina Niggli (1910–83) is undergoing a revival. Since the mid-1990s, her work has been featured in anthologies, some of her books have been reprinted, and she's been the subject of scholarly examinations. The overall impetus of this revival is to discover her as a forerunner of multicultural literature in the United States, a "woman of color" whose oeuvre is a pathbreaking herald of things to come.

This approach, clearly, is flawed. It reveals a lack of serious critical thinking. Niggli, it strikes me, is applauded more for having come first than for offering a profound exploration of the cultural mores of the Mexican characters that populate her imagination. This assessment of her contribution is lopsided. Plus, she wasn't actually a woman of color. But her vision is important for another reason: it showcases the way ethnic literature has often emphasized the stereotypes it seeks to undermine.

Born in Monterrey, in the Mexican state of Nuevo León, just as La Revolución, the first armed peasant struggle of the twentieth century, erupted, Niggli spent her life feeling like an outsider. Her parents were European Americans. Frederick Ferdinand Niggli, her father, came from a family of Swiss and Alsatians who immigrated to Texas in 1836. Goldie (Morgan) Niggli, her mother, was a well-known violinist in the Southwest, whose ancestors came from Ireland, France, and Germany. The multiplicity of Niggli's background resulted in what today is called a hyphenated identity. (This is clear in the spelling of her name, at times showing up as Jose*ph*ina and others as Jose*f*ina, and in her middle name: María.)

Niggli's father was in charge of a cement factory in Mexico. As a young girl, she spent her time in a large hacienda in the state of Nuevo León that was called La Quinta del Carmen and was filled with servants. In terms of formal education, for four months she was sent to the American School in Mexico City; otherwise, she was homeschooled before enrolling at the Main Avenue High School in San Antonio, Texas. She used English with her parents and American friends and Spanish with Mexican people.

Niggli attended the College and Academy of the Incarnate Word, where she was mentored by R. E. Roehl, a professor in the English department. She graduated in 1931. Even though her first publications are dated at least three years prior, it was in college that she committed herself to a career in letters. Writing in general, and writing about her knowledge of and experience with Mexico, made her feel justified. She wanted to be an interpreter of the people she was acquainted with in the hacienda, to allow others to understand what they felt and how they thought. She was especially interested in Mexican history and folklore, topics into which she delved in her sophomore year. As Niggli recalled years later, one of the sisters at the college locked her up until she finished a piece for *Ladies' Home Journal*. Emblematic of her literary approach throughout her life, her first poem, "Tourist in a Mexican Town," a rather one-dimensional exercise, appeared in the *Denver Echo*. It places the narrator in the position of an outsider looking in: Mexico, for Niggli, is a source of nostalgia, a quaint, postcard-like landscape with which she's infatuated.

Her first book, *Mexican Silhouettes*, a collection of poetry underwritten by her father, appeared in 1928. The poems in it engage in a *costumbrista* style popular at the time among émigrés. An appropriate example is the poem "Mexico, My Beloved" included in the *North American Review*, which serves as the epigraph to the present volume. In it, Niggli reacts against clichés ("the clashing of cymbals" and "vermilion sails / over the heart / of the wind") and then outmaneuvers herself by talking of Mexico as "my beloved," of the moon that "touches the silken waves" of the Lerma River. The impression the reader gets, not only in these early efforts but in the narratives she produced in the 1940s also, is of a romanticized Mexico.

Restless and unhappy with poetry as a form, Niggli began experimenting with radio. Before and after college, she worked for KTSA in San Antonio. The experience defined her. Niggli's approximately one dozen plays have a radio-like quality; the plotline develops based less on physical movement than on anecdotal exchanges, and the cast rarely consists of more than half a dozen actors. Niggli also was involved with the film industry, albeit anonymously—at least at first. She worked for 20th Century Fox and Metro-Goldwin-Mayer in Hollywood. Among the movies in which she was involved is *The Mark of Zorro*—again, a romanticized version of its colonial-period New Mexican hero. Nevertheless, it was theater that most attracted her. In the early 1930s Niggli collaborated with San Antonio Little Theater. She then opted for graduate school, moving to Chapel Hill to enroll in a program with the Carolina Playmakers, which was part of the University of North Carolina. She devoted herself fully to writing plays. It was a prolific period. Her teachers were Samuel Selden, Frederick H. Koch, Paul Green, and Betty Smith. Her thesis for the degree of Master in Drama was a three-act play called *Singing Valley*, written in 1936.

The five one-act pieces that constitute the present volume belong to this period. They were all published in 1938 in a single book called *Mexican Folk Plays* by the University of North Carolina Press. Niggli's themes echo her interest while she was in college: Mexico, from the pre-Columbian past to its tumultuous present (now past). One is about the Aztecs, another about the female soldiers in La Revolución, "for whom there was no blazing patriotic fire," for "they were 'broken shells whose only desire was revenge for all they had suffered . . . '" The settings are mostly rural. The casts are invariably small. The plays do not explore the inner selves of their characters as much as they pigeonhole them. The fact that they aren't staged any more reflects the fact that their value is less as drama than as cultural artifact; they allow us a window through which to appreciate the way Mexico has been perceived—that is distorted—by American eyes. As a concept, "folklore" emerged in the nineteenth century in the context of romantic nationalism. Each nation, it was suggested, has its own culture, expressed in literature, art, music, cuisine, and religion. By stressing these expressions, one nation emphasizes its differences from the others. Mexico, in Niggli's eyes is sharply unlike the United States. But in depicting this uniqueness she succumbs to mannerisms. For one thing, she portrays Mexicans as stereotypes: Anselmo "a barber," Adelita "a young girl," Concha "the revolutionary leader," Esteban "who longs to own a goat." Each character is reduced to a single characteristic. And in some cases, the stereotypes become symbols: the naive girl turns out to be näivetée itself, the wealthy owner is also evil incarnate, and so forth.

Plus, Niggli falls prey to misconceptions and false assumptions. For instance, the author's note to *Azteca* places the action in "the year of the Christian calendar 1412." It adds that "the opening of the curtain reveals four young priestesses kneeling in the garden making flower wreaths for their hair. The four girls are pretty little things whose lives have been dedicated by their parents to the temple which they serve. If it were a Christian country, they would be called nuns. They are dressed in pink, blue, yellow, and white. The one dressed in white is a novitiate." Niggli states, "Her name is Xochitl, which means 'a flower,' and she has the serene beauty of a white rose. Seeing her, one thinks of a mountain in the far distance, placid and distinct against the sky, yet capable of a dark and terrible aspect with the setting sun." And the appendix to *Mexican Folk Plays* states, "Like the United States, Mexico is a melting pot of all nations: Irish, German, and Spanish being the three most popular foreign strains. However, I have yet to meet a man with possibly no more than a single drop of Indian blood who does not say proudly, 'I am a true Mexican!'" *Yo soy puro mexicane* . . . Niggli is arguably an optimist, but she's also near-sighted. Her view of Mexico is rosy. While the country has had a receptive policy toward immigrants, it is far less heterogeneous than she suggests. At least that was the case when she was active as a playwright. Plus, she ignores the widespread sentiment of *malinchismo*, the *anti-mexicanismo* embedded in the nation's psyche, dating back to the encounter of Hernán Cortés and his mistress and translator Doña Marina, aka La Malinche.

Niggli's penchant for exploring folklore on stage continued until the mid-1940s. She wrote several more comedies and tragedies, mostly on a historical note, among them *The Cry of Dolores*, *The Fair God*, *This Is Villa!* and *The Ring of General Macías*. They have now been collected (along with *Mexican Silhouettes*) in a volume called *The Plays of Josefina Niggli*, edited by William Orchard of the University of Chicago and Yolanda Padilla of the University of Pennsylvania. The topics are similar: one addresses the struggle for independence of Father Miguel Hidalgo y Costilla in 1810, while others are about historical figures like Emperor Maximiliano I and Pancho Villa. Around the time she worked for the Carolina Playmakers, Niggli became acquainted with Rodolfo Usigli, one of Mexico's most important playwrights in the 1940s, responsible for the 1938 classic *El gesticulador* (*The Impostor*). Usigli was also the author of *Relato de un crimen* (*Rehearsal for a Crime*), a novel adapted to the screen by Luis Buñuel in a film called *La vida criminal de Archibaldo de la Cruz* (*The Criminal Life of Archibaldo de la Cruz*). Usigli's own background was similar to Niggli's: he was born in Mexico City of European parents (his father was Italian, his mother Polish), and he longed for a national theater able to reflect the challenges of Mexico as a modern nation. In a comment on Niggli, Usigli talks about the absence of a native theater in Mexico. "Mexican folk drama does not really exist," he says. "Or rather it does not exist as drama but as a casual accumulation of external, picturesque facts poorly woven into a dramatic plot. In fact drama does not seem to be, up to now, the most adequate literary expression for Mexico." He emphasizes his point by talking of "a four-centuries-old theatrical wasteland." Furthermore, Usigli imagines Niggli's career south of the border. His conclusions are sorrowful: "I cannot help thinking... that had Miss Niggli written her plays here for our commercial theater, she would have encountered the obstacles which we are trying at present to overcome, instead of the cordial reception which she found in Chapel Hill." Still, he isn't altogether happy with her work. In a word, he finds her "foreign."

In the 1950s, Niggli turned to the novel, publishing two in quick succession: *Mexican Village* in 1945 and, two years later, *Step Down, Elder Brother*. Clearly fiction allowed her to be more expansive, to flesh out her symbols, making them more believable. In *Mexican Village*, Niggli's alter ego of sorts is Robert Webster, a Texan interloper who moves to Hidalgo, in Nuevo León, where he is the quarry master at a mine. There's a cast of almost one hundred characters who cover the wide range of classes in Mexico. The effort results in caricature. At a time when William Faulkner was already engaged in mapping his imaginary southern county, Yoknapatawpha, Niggli took a similar approach in *Mexican Village*: the creation of a self-sufficient community. In a review published in the *New York Herald Tribune*, Joseph Henry Jackson described the volume as "a document... without a peer in its field... an utterly faithful, wholly convincing portrayal of Mexican village life as it is." A forgettable Hollywood movie based on it, *Sombrero*, with a screenplay by Niggli, was made in 1953.

Niggli's second novel feels like John Steinbeck's *East of Eden*, published half a decade later. It takes place in Monterrey, Mexico, as well as in Saltillo, Santa Catarina, and Nuevo Laredo, and portrays the ethnic and class rivalry between *criollos* and *mestizos*, among the aristocracy, the bourgeoisie, and the poor masses. While it remains one of the least read of Niggli's books, *Step Down, Elder Brother* strikes me as the most ambitious and demanding, and the one in which she came closest to realizing her artistic potential. The ample cast of characters highlights the battle for power in Mexico during its emergence as a modern nation. It is important for the reader to keep in mind that, as Niggli's two novels appeared, fiction about the neighbor to the south was a fixture in the United States. These books range from D. H. Lawrence's *The Plumed Serpent*, published in 1926, to Graham Greene's *The Power and the Glory*, from 1940, about a drunken priest in Tabasco during the reactionary war against Catholic bishops in the 1930s, and Malcolm Lowry's semi-autobiographical *Under the Volcano*, released the same year that *Step Down, Elder Brother* came out. Collectively, the portrait is daunting: Mexico comes across as a version of Dante's hell. Particularly in her second novel, Niggli also attempts—far less successfully, though—to portray Mexico as a place where history and myth collide.

A third and last novel by Niggli appeared in 1964: *A Miracle in Mexico*. She also wrote a couple of instructional manuals (she called them "pointers") for playwrights, one in 1945, a sequel in 1967. It is important to place Niggli's fiction in context. The last three decades of Niggli's career are marked by stasis. In 1950 she worked at Dublin's Abbey Theatre. In the mid-1950s, she started teaching English and drama as an instructor at Western Carolina University, where she remained for twenty years, until her retirement in 1975. (Her papers, which include correspondence, newspaper clippings, journals, manuscripts, and classroom notes, are located at the institution's Hunter Library.) She continued writing for radio and movies, and she also tried her hand at television, for shows such as *The Twilight Zone* and *Have Gun, Will Travel*. She died in 1983.

Curiously, what she never attempted directly, what her work altogether fails to acknowledge, is an exploration of Niggli's own dilemmas as an English-language writer *in* the United States. She always looked to Mexico for inspiration, not to her immediate surroundings. Why then present her as at the forefront of Latino literature? My explanation is straightforward: such is the hunger of the current crop of Latino authors to find a place in the American canon, one with roots in the past, that quality and vision are often put aside in the scramble to find antecedents. As a female novelist, Niggli has even been compared to Willa Cather (in *Death Comes for the Archbishop*) and other classic authors. The evidence doesn't withstand such comparisons: Niggli is parochial, a mere tourist guide. She ought to be read on her own terms, for the interest of the scenery she provides and the thoughts on "tourist art" she generates.

Source: Ilan Stevens, Foreword to *Mexican Village, and Other Works*, Northwestern University Press, 2008, pp. ix–xv.

Elizabeth Coonrod Martínez

In the following essay, Martínez claims that despite writing in English, Niggli portrayed Mexican life from an insider's point of view.

Just as the current boom of Latino music in the United States has its roots in dance rhythms that gained popularity in the 1920s, Latino literature is hardly a recent arrival. An early Mexican American writer with an unusual name blossomed in the US literary world during the era that Carmen Miranda was performing her fusion of Argentine, Brazilian, Mexican, and Caribbean dances, the trio Los Panchos came on the scene with songs of Mexican romance and nostalgia, and Hollywood featured (often stereotypically) passionate "Latin" characters. With internationally recognized plays in the late 1930s and best-selling novels a decade later, Josefina Niggli introduced Mexican thought and culture to US readers.

> "WITH THE EXCEPTION OF A FEW MINOR SHORT-STORY WRITERS, NIGGLI IS THE ONLY MEXICAN AMERICAN WRITING IN ENGLISH DURING THE MID-TWENTIETH CENTURY WHO CREATED AUTHENTIC STORIES BASED IN MEXICAN CULTURE."

The trajectory of Niggli's life reflects both Mexican and US history during the first half of the twentieth century. Born in Monterrey, Nuevo León, the same year as the inception of the Mexican Revolution—1910—she grew up in the countryside, her favorite pet a burro. As a child, she was occasionally summoned urgently into the house as shots were heard in the distance. As the years of battle dragged on, in 1925 Niggli and her mother joined other refugees who set up new lives across the border.

Josefina had celebrated her quinceañera at the family ranch, and as is typical, prominent members of society were invited to the gala affair. In her case, the governor of Nuevo León attended and asked what she would like for a present. The fifteen-year-old quickly responded, "All of Monterrey." Years later, she would recount this anecdote to illustrate her great fondness for her birthplace, that sense of *patria*—both homeland and region—often professed in Mexican songs and poetry. The story also demonstrates the ardent desire that infused her creative works, to carry Monterrey with her, always. As a writer, she strove to reveal the complexities and beauty of the people of northern Mexico to the English-speaking world.

While Diego Rivera was creating his murals in the Mexican capital and being invited to major US cities, Niggli finished high school, published poetry, and completed a bachelor's degree at Incarnate Word College in San Antonio, Texas. As it was for others in northern Mexico, this city was a logical choice, an environment that had always been half-Mexican, half-Anglo. San Antonio had maintained a steady but small population during the previous century, then grew quickly to 160,000 by 1920, with the influx of Mexicans fleeing a civil war that killed more than a million people. For the next two decades, Josefina and her mother would go back and forth between San Antonio and the family ranch near Monterrey, where her father continued to work.

Some of Niggli's Mexican contemporaries have names currently more recognizable. Dolores del Río, Anita Brenner, and Frida Kahlo were also born during the first decade of the twentieth century and reached their heyday in the same period as Niggli. Kahlo, who had begun painting self-portraits in 1926, declared herself a child of the Mexican Revolution (changing her year of birth from 1907 to 1910), but Niggli more appropriately deserves that designation.

During the 1930s, Kahlo's unique paintings took on a bolder tone, and Niggli began creating her Mexican folk plays. Del Rio, born in the state of Durango, was from the north like Niggli; her film career was launched in Los Angeles in the late 1920s, and in ensuing decades she produced films in both countries. Brenner published journalistic works about the success of the Mexican Revolution, garnering attention in New York City. Born in Aguascalientes, Brenner also left her home for Texas when revolutionary fighting heated up; like Niggli, she always considered herself Mexican. Brenner and Kahlo died in Mexico, but Del Rio and Niggli had been living in the United States at the time of their decease and can be categorized as both Mexican and US Latinas.

Although she wrote in English, because of her themes and her birthplace Niggli belongs to the Mexican literary generation of Mariano Azuela, Martín Luis Guzmán, and Nellie Campobello. The great intellectual Alfonso Reyes was also born in Monterrey, a couple of decades earlier.

In 1935, Niggli headed to the University of North Carolina, Chapel Hill, to pursue a master's degree through its prestigious Carolina Playmakers. A cutting-edge theatrical company, its director's emphasis on folk—the authentic people of the countryside, not cosmopolitans was a perfect fit for her purposes of adapting small-town Mexican life to dramatic presentations. Niggli was the only member of the company (which included such luminaries as Thomas Wolfe and Paul Green) whose themes featured Mexican culture and folklore. After earning her master's, Niggli intended to return to Monterrey and set up her own theater, but world economic and political conditions altered her plans. The proximity to New York City and the publishing world also provided opportunities she needed as a writer. She received fellowships to create plays and took further writing classes at Columbia and other universities.

By the late 1930s, Niggli was widely acclaimed for her one-act folk comedies and some of her historic plays, centered on themes of the Mexican Revolution and the portrayal of mestizo consciousness. Two comedies, *Sunday Costs Five Pesos* and *The Red Velvet Goat*, became so popular that they were staged throughout the United States and England for many years. During the 1940 blitz in London and throughout World War II, *The Red Velvet Goat* was said to have been performed in the bomb shelters each night, to hilarious reception.

In 1938, Niggli published her first book, *Mexican Folk Plays*, a selection of five of her works. Her close friend Rodolfo Usigli, for whom she had worked as stage manager for a Villaurrutia play in Mexico City, wrote the foreword to her collection, lauding her as one of only three dramatists of that era who are "essentially" Mexican. He makes note of her humor and sensitive portrayal of folk life. Usigli laments that she does not write in Spanish, noting that "Mexican folk drama does not really exist.... In fact drama does not seem to be, up to now, the most adequate literary expression for Mexico." But he adds that Niggli's excessive descriptions would be "unnecessary" should her plays be rendered in Spanish. Years later, in an interview, Niggli stated that had she written her plays in Spanish, they would have been written in exactly the same manner. She then pointed out that Usigli was raised in Mexico City "on the myth of the Revolution" and had not known the experiences of northern Mexico and country folk as she had. Thus Niggli displays—along with characteristic conviction and confidence—a regional perspective of her country, much like Nellie Campobello and other northerners. In terms of her choice of language, Niggli said she knew Mexico needed playwrights, but she felt strongly that people in the United States had a greater need to learn and understand Mexican culture.

Niggli, who had taken classes in broadcast journalism, was hired by NBC International to write radio messages in Spanish, which were transmitted to Latin America during World War II. The war years opened the opportunity for women to hold (temporary) university teaching positions for the first time, and Niggli excelled in teaching Shakespeare and drama during the early 1940s. Soon a publisher commissioned an instructional text, *New Pointers on Playwriting*, which was reissued for years.

Niggli's attention also turned to creating novels. These garnered considerable attention in the New York scene; in newspaper photos, Niggli appears very much the debonair author, wearing fashionable hats. Her first novel, *Mexican Village*, was even made into a Hollywood movie, *Sombrero*, starring Ricardo Montalbán. The book saw five subsequent reprintings, selling nearly 23,000 copies within the decade following its release in 1945, and continued to be recommended by academic journals for years. With a dearth of cultural and literary texts on Mexico in that era, her novel filled a niche.

She had written the book over a period of several years that she spent between the Hidalgo ranch near Monterrey and the kitchen table of her mother's home in San Antonio. At first considered nonfiction, *Mexican Village* in fact provides a historical portrait of small-town Mexican life between 1910 and 1920, depicting philosophical lore and practices, and featuring characters of both mixed US-Mexican heritage and of mixed indigenous-Spanish heritage. The main character is modeled on Niggli's father, the manager of a cement plant, where many characters work. In the quaint village of Hidalgo—named, like many things in Mexico, for the hero of independence—the community relies on the local *curandera* for medical needs and the priest for spiritual matters, and espouses a hybrid practice of indigenous and Catholic beliefs. The plant manager is unaware of his Mexican mother's indigenous background (denied by his father, who is of Texan and European origin) until later in the story.

Niggli's real family heritage is not indigenous, but with this character she elucidates the experience of many Texans, immigrants of a variety of backgrounds. Her parents were not born in Mexico; however, Niggli described the Mexico of her own experience. Her father, Frederick, whose grandparents had immigrated to Texas in the 1840s, was of Swiss-Alsatian heritage. Josefina's mother, raised in Missouri, was a concert pianist who met her future husband in San Antonio, during a winter engagement with a string ensemble. They married in 1909, and Josefina was their only child.

Frederick Niggli lived in or near Mexico for most of his life. When he was nine, his father—a sheriff of Medina County, west of San Antonio—was shot and killed by a recent immigrant from Germany. With three children to raise, Frederick's mother joined Niggli relatives in the border town of Eagle Pass. Many Texans had moved there—and to Piedras Negras, just across the border in Mexico—during the US Civil War years, seeking haven from marauding sympathizers of the South.

Frederick's older brother found work as an auditor for the Mexican International Railroad Company, and in 1893 he hired the younger Niggli as an office boy. Within a few years Frederick had risen to the position of general agent at the Torreón station, where US and Mexican railroads had first been connected in 1884. In 1906, he was hired away as the general manager of the newly created Cementos Hidalgo by the successful Torreón businessman Juan F. Brittingham. That company later merged with another to form Cementos Mexicanos, or CEMEX, which would become one of the world's largest cement makers. Niggli's novel depicts the first stages of this major enterprise.

Monterrey had been a political stronghold for those opposed to Porfirio Díaz, and after the Revolution it became even more significant for its economic expansion. Niggli's second novel, *Step Down, Elder Brother*, published in late 1947, relates that history through a particular family, but the city itself is a significant element of the story. In its opening pages, the novel states that "when the fighting days of the Great Revolution finished, Monterrey shook herself, exchanged her rags for a free new dress, and strung a chain of factories about her neck." It contrasts and portrays the old-fashioned elitist class system with the new social awareness of the mestizo, while richly describing the geography and climate of the region, as well as Monterrey's historic background and economic success.

Of great importance to the main character is the city's indigenous tradition, as well as the books on Maya heritage that he reads in his spare time. The protagonist's nature is that of an elder son who demonstrates a strong sense of respect and duty to family. His uncle is a ruthless politician who operates real-estate and banking businesses. While the novel reflects her eyewitness experience, Niggli's records show that she also did extensive research.

The novel contrasts the city's pursuit of modernization with the danger of losing its inherent beauty. Niggli perceived that the city would lose its uniqueness as it grew; thus she captured its heritage and customs at that particular moment. Critics at the time, and later, salute the novel's historic value as well as its literary quality. A *New York Times* critic, who found it important to note that the novel was not a translation, found the book so extraordinary, he stated the following:

The measure of our northern culture may well be the reception we accord this fine novel. Whether a public punch-drunk with second-rate historical fiction will perceive its qualities is not certain. This reviewer remains hopeful. Niggli sweeps into the discard a whole library of books by Americans purporting to tell us of Mexican life. We can see them for what they were, pretentious pseudo-romances which left the real Mexican culture untouched because their authors had never known it so as to understand it.

David Toscana, a contemporary novelist and native of Monterrey, was so impressed when he discovered Niggli's novel in the 1990s that he created a translation, in order to rescue it for Nuevo León literary history. He considers it "testimony," since only a native could so skillfully describe the city's climate and geography and portray its rapid move to industrialization. In 2004, proclaiming it the important recovery of a novel "unknown to us for decades," the prestigious Nuevo León Council for Culture and Arts (CONARTE) released *Apartate Hermano* with great fanfare.

The 500-page novel was highly touted during several months of publicity. An ongoing series of articles in the newspaper *El Norte* stated that no other novels depicted Monterrey's transformation following the Revolution and its ethnic and cultural history. Writer Hugo Valdes, also of Monterrey, calls Niggli the "invisible precursor" of *regiomontana* women writers from Mexico's northeast region. Daniel de la Puente noted "the need to reexamine one of the most significant and yet most overlooked female authors of Mexico's literary history."

Niggli's first novel had also seen translation, in abridged form, commissioned by her publisher and released in 1949. But Niggli was not at all pleased with it, because the translator, a Spaniard and professor at an East Coast university, had changed grammar and other aspects of the story, removing its Mexican authenticity.

During the 1950s, Niggli traveled to Hollywood and Mexico City to film the movie based on her first novel. She received a fellowship to study in England in 1950; years later she was invited to teach at the Old Vie Theatre in Bristol. She also began teaching fulltime at Western Carolina University, where she was in charge of her own theater program. By her late 40s, Niggli was ready to settle down. The San Antonio home was sold in 1957; after her father's death in 1945, the family ranch in Hidalgo is no longer mentioned in her letters or papers. Her mother lived with her in North Carolina until her death in 1968; Niggli never married.

She continued to travel at least once a year to San Antonio, visiting her cousins and always stopping at its landmark Mexican market—not to purchase anything but simply to smell the genuine leather and watch passersby. Niggli created a new historical novel, Beat the Drum Slowly, but it never saw publication. Set in the late 1700s, an apt period for the emergence of the mestizo, the story line develops between Europe and northern Mexico, and contrasts dark- and light-skinned male characters. Her notes demonstrate substantial historical and geographical research.

Niggli did publish a third novel, however. In 1964 she released *A Miracle for Mexico*, the first creative text in English to depict Mexico's iconic symbol. Its focus is the inception of mestizo consciousness through the appearance of the Virgin of Guadalupe in 1531. This new publisher wanted to market a line of juvenile books and decided to classify Niggli's as such. It is accompanied by several exquisite color drawings by Mexican artist Alejandro Rangel Hidalgo, whose depictions were extremely popular during the mid-twentieth century, appearing on postcards and on named prints in hotel rooms in Mexico. Because they are childlike figures, they support the idea of a children's book, but Niggli's narrative is a rich rendering of history. Her story depicts the making of a new society, with Africans, Nahuatl-speaking Indians, mestizos, and Spaniards. It is not elementary reading at all.

Even though most reviewers declared that it was not a book for children, *A Miracle for Mexico* has since its publication been shelved in the children's section in libraries, and biographical notations on Niggli seldom include it. If the title had stated "Guadalupe" it may have received greater attention once the Chicano movement began to emerge in the following decade. It is a valuable Mexican/Chicano text for its historic characters, including an excellent three-dimensional depiction of la Malinche, intelligent and enchanting, rather than the negative stereotype history has given Hernán Cortés's companion. The events surrounding the Virgin's appearance are related through a fictional thirteen-year-old main character who serves as interpreter between Juan Diego and the bishop, an effective bridge between indigenous culture and the new Spanish colony.

Today, Niggli's novels are generally found in most US libraries; they are worth reading for their revelation of mid-century Mexico from an insider's point of view. With the exception of a few minor short-story writers, Niggli is the only Mexican American writing in English during the mid-twentieth century who created authentic stories based in Mexican culture. Mexico's history, from Independence to the Revolution, its myths and lore, the lives of its campesinos, the mestizo's rise in Mexican society, and feminist ideals, are all revealed in her works.

Her first play, *Cry of Hidalgo*, is set on the evening of September 15—the date of the famous rallying cry for independence from Spain—and highlights the heroic woman Josefa Dominguez. While this one has received little attention, her two historic plays that are most often staged by college and community groups are *Soldadera* and *A Ring for General Macías*, which was translated into Spanish. *Soldadera* is the first depiction in English of the valiant Adelita woman of Mexican lore. The second play is a work of irony, vengeance, and honor, a very astute rendition of civil war. The three-act *Singing Valley*, which served as her master's thesis in 1937, could easily represent the first Mexican *telenovela*—a solid historical drama, including reverence for the Virgin, with a side comedic element.

Mexican by birth and American through her parents, Josefina María Niggli lived between two cultures and two nations. She preserved and presented the basis of Mexican cultural history to English-language readers—and shines as an outstanding woman writer of the first half of the twentieth century.

Niggli died in 1983, bequeathing her possessions and her future royalties to a foundation for student scholarships at Western Carolina University, where a theater bears her name. In San Antonio, Texas, a centennial ceremony is being organized for 2010 to commemorate the year of her birth.

Source: Elizabeth Coonrod Martinez, "Josefina Niggli: Daughter of the Mexican Revolution," in *Americas*, Vol. 59, No. 6, November/December 2007, pp. 46–53.

SOURCES

Cumberland, Charles C., Review of *Mexican Village*, in *Southwestern Historical Quarterly*, Vol. 51, No. 2, October 1947, pp. 194–96.

Dvorkin, Joseph Henry, "Josephina Niggli," in *Voices from the Gaps*, University of Minnesota, http://voices.cla.umn.edu/artistpages/niggliJosephina.php (accessed September 5, 2011).

Fuentes, Yvette, Review of *Josefina Niggli, Mexican-American Writer: A Critical Biography*, by Elizabeth Coonrod Martínez, in *Quadrivium*, Vol. 2, Winter 2010, http://www.fcas.nova.edu/faculty/publications/quadrivium/issue2/mexican_american_writer/index.cfm (accessed September 6, 2011).

Herrera-Sobek, María, Introduction to *Mexican Village*, University of New Mexico Press, 1994, pp. xvii–xxix.

"Josephina Niggli," in *The Border*, Public Broadcasting System, http://www.pbs.org/kpbs/theborder/history/timeline/18.html (accessed September 6, 2011).

Kean, Claude, Review of *Mexican Village*, in *Americas*, Vol. 2, No. 4, April 1946, pp. 534–35.

Knight, Alan, "Popular Culture and the Revolutionary State in Mexico, 1910–1940," in *Hispanic American Historical Review*, Vol. 74, No. 3, August 1994, pp. 393–444.

Martínez, Elizabeth Coonrod, *Josefina Niggli, Mexican-American Writer: A Critical Biography*, University of New Mexico Press, 2007, pp. 2–3.

"Mexican Immigrant Labor History," in *The Border*, Public Broadcasting System, http://www.pbs.org/kpbs/theborder/history/timeline/17.html (accessed September 23, 2011).

"The Mexican Miracle: 1940–1968," in *Emayzine.com*, http://www.emayzine.com/lectures/MEX9.html (accessed September 6, 2011).

"Mexican Revolution Time Line Revolución Mexicana, 1910–1920," in *MexicanHistory.org*, http://mexicanhistory.org/MexicanRevolutiontimeline.htm (accessed September 5, 2011).

Niggli, Josephina, "The Street of the Cañón," in *Mexican Village*, University of New Mexico Press, 1994, pp. 173–219.

Orchard, William, and Yolanda Padilla, "Lost in Adaptation: Chicana History, the Cold War, and the Case of Josephina Niggli," in *Women's Studies Quarterly*, Vol. 33, Nos. 3–4, Fall/Winter 2005, pp. 90–113.

Rey, Agapito, Review of *Mexican Village*, in *Journal of American Folklore*, Vol. 60, No. 237, July–September 1947, pp. 326–27.

FURTHER READING

Augenbraum, Harold, and Margarite Fernández Olmos, eds., *The Latino Reader: From 1542 to the Present*, Houghton Mifflin, 1997.

This reference book examines the history of Mexican and Mexican American literature. The compilation shows Niggli's role in the genre and its evolution over the centuries.

Champion, Laurie, ed., *American Women Writers, 1900–1945: A Bio-bibliographical Critical Sourcebook*, Greenwood Press, 2000.

This book is a collection of essays devoted to female writers from the early twentieth century. Champion includes Niggli and other Mexican American authors in this volume.

Laurens, Jennifer, *Falling for Romeo*, Grove Creek, 2011.

This young-adult novel explores the theme of love as two teenagers discover their feelings toward each other. This is another example of a romance of a seemingly mismatched couple.

Linhard, Tabea Alexa, *Fearless Women in the Mexican Revolution and the Spanish Civil War*, University of Missouri Press, 2005.

Linhard's nonfiction book studies the role women played in the Mexican Revolution. This volume provides insight into Niggli's view of Mexican society.

Niggli, Josephina, *Step Down, Elder Brother*, Rinehart, 1947.

Step Down, Elder Brother is Niggli's first true novel. In the work, published shortly after *Mexican Village*, Niggli again attempts to show Mexican culture to American audiences.

Strehle, Susan, and Mary Paniccia Carden, eds., *Doubled Plots: Romance and History*, University Press of Mississippi, 2003.

This diverse collection of essays presents the argument that romantic stories reflect the histories and cultures of different writers. The romances of *Mexican Village* are specifically addressed in this volume.

SUGGESTED SEARCH TERMS

Josephina Niggli

Josefina Niggli

Josephina Niggli AND biography

Josephina Niggli AND Mexican Village

Mexican Revolution

Mexican American literature

Mexican American literature AND history

Mexican American history

Josephina Niggli AND criticism

The Street of the Cañón AND Josephina Niggli

A Sunrise on the Veld

DORIS LESSING

1951

"A Sunrise on the Veld" is a story by the distinguished British writer Doris Lessing. Lessing has been publishing fiction for over half a century and won the Nobel Prize for Literature in 2007. This is one of her earliest short stories, published in her first collection, *This Was the Old Chief's Country*, in 1951 in London and in 1952 in the United States. It was reprinted in *African Stories* in 1964 and *The Doris Lessing Reader* in 1989 and is currently in print in the reissue *This Was the Old Chief's Country*, volume 1 in Lessing's *Collected African Stories*.

The story is set in Southern Rhodesia (now Zimbabwe) sometime between the 1930s and 1950s, when the country was still a British colony. Lessing lived in Southern Rhodesia during her childhood and early adulthood, so the setting came naturally to her. The story covers just a few hours in the life of a fifteen-year-old Caucasian boy who gets up at four thirty in the morning to go hunting on the nearby veld (grasslands). He is full of life and energy, feeling as if he can control everything about his life. But his exuberance is curbed when he encounters a wounded buck that is being devoured by ants, and he is forced into a new, more mature understanding of life. With its rich sensory language that brings the setting to life, and with its careful development of the boy's new understanding, this coming-of-age story is an ideal introduction to one of the most celebrated writers of the twentieth century.

Doris Lessing *(AP Images)*

AUTHOR BIOGRAPHY

Lessing was born Doris May Taylor in Persia (present-day Iran) on October 22, 1919. Both her parents were British. In 1925, the family moved to Southern Rhodesia, now Zimbabwe, which was then a British colony. Her father, formerly a bank official, became a maize farmer. Doris was sent to a convent school and later a high school in Salisbury, the capital city, which was about one hundred miles from the family farm. However, she hated the convent and dropped out of the high school when she was fourteen. She received no more formal education. She was, however, a voracious reader, especially of the great European and Russian novelists, such as Charles Dickens, Honoré de Balzac, and Leo Tolstoy.

Doris left home when she was fifteen and worked as an au pair. She also began writing short stories, two of which were published in a magazine in South Africa. She moved to Salisbury and worked as a telephone operator. At the age of nineteen she married Frank Wisdom, a civil servant. They had two children, but Doris left the family after a few years, while still living in Salisbury; she divorced Wisdom in 1943. Always interested in politics, she moved in left-wing circles, where she met and later married Gottfried Lessing, a German who shared her Marxist political beliefs. They had one son, but the couple divorced in 1949.

Lessing moved to London with her son later that year and published her first novel, *The Grass Is Singing*, in 1950. The novel was an immediate success. Her first collection of short stories, *This Was the Old Chief's Country*, was published a year later in London and in 1952 in the United States. This volume contains the story "A Sunrise on the Veld." Much of Lessing's writing from the 1960s and 1970s is set in Africa and exposes the injustice of white-minority rule. During this time she was banned from entering Southern Rhodesia or South Africa because of her writings. In 1962, she wrote *The Golden Notebook*, the novel for which she is best known. Notable novels of the 1970s included *Briefing for a Descent into Hell* (1971) and *Memoirs of a Survivor* (1974). Lessing also wrote many short-story collections during this period, including *To Room Nineteen: Collected Stories, Vol. 1* (1978) and *The Temptation of Jack Orkney: Collected Stories, Vol. 2* (1978). Her five novels collectively known as *Canopus in Argos: Archives* were published from 1979 to 1983.

She published in 1985 the novel *The Good Terrorist* and three years later *The Fifth Child*, which received the Grinzane Cavour Prize in Italy and was nominated for the 1988 Los Angeles Times Book Award. Another novel, *Love, Again*, appeared in 1996, and in 2000, Lessing published a sequel to *The Fifth Child* titled *Ben, in the World*.

Lessing has also published plays, an autobiography, and two opera libretti (in collaboration with composer Philip Glass). She has won many literary awards, including the David Cohen Prize in 2001 for her lifetime contribution to British literature. In 2007, she was awarded the Nobel Prize in Literature.

PLOT SUMMARY

"A Sunrise on the Veld" is set in Southern Rhodesia (now Zimbabwe), one early morning on the veld. A *veld* is an area of grassland with scattered trees and shrubs. The term is usually applied to areas in southern Africa. Literally, the word means "field."

The story, which has only one character, begins at four thirty on a winter morning. The protagonist, a fifteen-year-old boy, wakes at exactly the time he determined he would when he went to bed. He does not even need the alarm clock to wake him. He has trained himself to sleep for exactly the time he wants to. As he wakes he is pleased to have it confirmed that he can control every part of himself, including his brain.

He jumps out of bed in the cold room and dresses quickly. It is still two hours before sunrise. He ventures out of the house; it is still night, and the stars are visible. He creeps past the window of his parents' bedroom; they have no idea that he rises so early and is going out. From inside another window he retrieves his gun that he placed there the previous evening. Then he goes to the room where the dogs sleep. He takes them with him, making sure they stay silent until he is a hundred yards from the house. Then they race off into the bush.

He hurries on his way, feeling energetic. He has some miles to travel and he wants to do it before sunrise. The dogs run ahead of him. He breaks into a run and soon leaves the cultivated area of the farm behind him, with acres of long grass stretching ahead of him. The birds wake and begin their calls, and other creatures in the bush soon follow. He hears the guinea fowl and knows they will soon be hidden in the grass, and he will be unable to hunt them. But he does not mind. He is just filled with joy to be out there, and he runs as fast as he can, shouting as he runs for two miles through grass that is waist high. He stands on a rock looking down at some water and is still feeling exhilarated, intoxicated with the joy of life. He feels there is nothing he cannot do. He feels he can become anything he wants and even change the direction of the world depending on the choices he makes, what he decides to do. He starts to sing and listens to the echoes of his voice.

Then he hears another voice that he does not recognize. It is not a bird nor the sound of cattle. He hears it again and realizes it is a shout of pain, a kind of scream. He calls for the dogs, but they have gone off on their own trails. He walks toward some trees to investigate.

He finds a young buck staggering about in pain, covered by black ants. Thousands more ants are in the grass heading for the buck. The buck falls and stops screaming, silently writhing on the ground. The boy thinks at first he should shoot the animal to put it out of its misery. Then he decides the buck is already beyond feeling anything, and anyway, there is nothing he can do about it. This is the way life is in the bush. Animals die in pain all the time. The realization comes to him with some force, that this is an unalterable law of life. Life is cruel. He feels angry, but he is also satisfied that he has understood something about life and knows he cannot alter it. He watches the ants as they devour the carcass, and he is aware of tears cascading down his face.

The sun rises, and the ants devour the carcass completely, leaving only a skeleton. The boy swears and stands over the skeleton, and tells the ants that are still there eating the meat to go away. They cannot have him as well, he says. He bends over and touches the bones, thinking about how only an hour or so ago the buck was as full of life as he himself was.

He wonders what could have happened to the buck. Could it really have been brought down by an army of ants? He then notices that the bone in one of the back legs is broken, and he realizes that this was the reason the crippled animal could not escape the ants. He wonders about how the animal broke its leg. He thinks it unlikely that it just fell, and decides that some of the local people must have thrown stones at it in an attempt to kill it so they could have the meat.

He remembers earlier mornings in which he went hunting and shot at bucks, never knowing whether he might have hit one and going home to have breakfast before ever finding out. This thought troubles him for a moment.

The anger he had been feeling fades. He picks up his gun and starts to walk home. He is tired, and he knows that he will have to do a lot more thinking about the death of the buck before he can feel at ease again. He resolves to go again to the bush the very next morning and try to figure it all out.

CHARACTERS

The Boy

The boy who goes out hunting in the early morning is not named. Few details are given about his circumstances in life. He lives with his parents on a farm somewhere in southern Africa. He is most likely white, since he refers to the people who may have attacked the buck as "natives" and "Africans." He is independently minded and gets up before his parents are awake, without their knowledge, to go hunting. It seems likely that the boy's father must have trained him in how to use a gun and how to hunt, since he seems very familiar with the practice. It appears that he has been out hunting on the veld many times before. He is a very healthy, energetic boy who is full of a sense of adventure and is confident in his own youthful powers. He feels he can control his environment and mold it how he pleases, because he has never known anything to the contrary. This gives him a feeling of power, and he indulges in little exercises, such as training himself to wake up at an early hour every morning, that confirm his belief that he is very much in control of all aspects of his being and his life. It seems that this boy has never known adversity or defeat. So one might conclude that he has had a happy childhood, without any rude shocks about the unpredictable turns that life can take. His expedition on the veld on this particular morning, however, changes that feeling in him. The boy then shows himself to be thoughtful, adventurous but reflective, and with a developing desire and ability to puzzle out for himself some of the mysteries of life. He is emerging into adulthood.

THEMES

Coming of Age

Coming of age is a common theme in literary works. The novel or story in which such a theme occurs will usually feature a young protagonist, likely in his or her teens, who over the course of the story goes though an experience that may be uncomfortable or troubling but which reveals something about life that he or she had not known before. It could be any of life's complexities or mysteries that the protagonist will have to learn about as part of the passage to adulthood. Sometimes such stories are called initiation stories, in which a child or teenager is in some way initiated into a deeper, more mature understanding of life. The maturing boy or girl loses the innocence of childhood and takes a big step into adulthood.

"A Sunrise on the Veld" has all the hallmarks of a coming-of-age story. On the veld that he knows well, the carefree boy witnesses the cruel death of the buck, something he has not had the chance to observe before, and this sets him thinking about the inherent cruelty of life, the inevitability of it. At first he thinks he will shoot the dying buck to put it out of its misery, but then he decides that there is no reason for him to interfere because such things happen all the time in nature and they are beyond his control. For the first time in his life he has an understanding that there are some things he cannot control. Life on the veld is cruel, but that is just the way things are. It seems that this is the first time he has conceptualized such a thought, and he finds it satisfying.

A few moments later, however, he remembers that he himself has been a hunter, and he might very well in the past have shot and wounded a buck and left it to a similar fate as he went home to eat breakfast without giving it a second thought. This realization troubles him, and for a moment he does not want to think about it. But then he realizes that he is going to have to think about it. He has to make a moral decision about whether he is right to shoot and hunt, whether he will be an active participant in the cruelty of the veld or not. Whereas a moment before he had thought the buck's death was really nothing to do with him, now he knows that is not true: "The death of that small animal was a thing that concerned him, and he was by no means finished with it." In other words, he has to face up to the fact that he as a reasoning human being can make ethical choices, unlike the other creatures that live and die on the veld. He is now at a pivotal moment in his development as a person as he starts to think about the values he will choose to live by.

Mortality

When the boy runs in the veld in the early morning, he feels exhilaratingly alive. He feels as if there is nothing he cannot do, nothing he cannot control. He has a superabundance of life; he runs and runs and shouts just for the joy of it. He is conscious only of life, how it courses through him, and what he can do with it. He feels he can bend the entire world to his will: "If I choose, I can change everything that is going to happen: it depends on me, and what I decide now." But as

TOPICS FOR FURTHER STUDY

- Write your own coming-of-age story. Show a character encountering a situation or an event that forces him or her to come to a new understanding of life. The story can be autobiographical (that is, something you have experienced yourself) or something that you invent. When you are finished, post the story to your Web log and invite comments from friends and classmates.
- Consult *Taking Off, and Other Coming of Age Stories by American Teen Writers*, by Kathryn Kulpa (1996). This book, which was nominated by the American Library Association as a "Best Book for Young Adults" in 1996, contains fourteen stories written by teenagers. Read several of these stories and then select two. In a short essay, describe in your own words why these stories are classified as coming-of-age stories. What do the characters learn? How do their experiences help them grow from childhood into a more mature awareness?
- Read Lessing's short story "The Old Chief Mshlanga," which is another of her African stories. Like "A Sunrise on the Veld," it is a coming-of-age story, although what the protagonist, a fourteen-year-old white girl, learns is rather different from what the boy in the other story learns. Give a class presentation on this story, explaining what it shows about the relations between the colonial rulers and the Africans in Southern Rhodesia at the time.
- Do an Internet search on the "scramble for Africa" and create a time line that shows about twelve to fifteen key dates in the colonization of Africa by the European powers in the late 1800s. Give a class presentation in which you explain how the scramble for Africa is the context for understanding the history of Zimbabwe from colonial days to the present. In your presentation, explain in brief what the scramble for Africa was, why it took place, and what its consequences were.

---

he listens to his echoing voice across the veld, he hears another voice that is certainly not his. He soon realizes that the sound is that of a dying animal. As he investigates and finds the stricken buck, he contemplates the scene, and it has a deep effect on him. Not only is this something he cannot control, but it also opens up a dimension of existence he had not considered before: everything is mortal; everything dies. The other side of the exuberant life he feels within himself is death, and he, too, will eventually share that fate.

There are several references in the story to similarities between the boy and the buck. The first is when he has a fleeting awareness, which he immediately dismisses, that as he runs wildly through the veld, he might fall and break his ankle. This is much like what has happened to the buck: he somehow broke a bone and was crippled, becoming an easy kill for the ants. Later in the story, the boy draws an explicit comparison between himself and the buck. He realizes that the dead buck, only an hour or so ago, "had been stepping proud and free through the bush, feeling the chill on its hide even as he himself had done, exhilarated by it." Just like the boy, the buck had walked "like kings and conquerors . . . through this free-held bush, where each blade of grass grew for it alone." This is like the boy's belief that the world exists entirely for him to enjoy and control. But now he knows that he and the buck share another similarity: they are both subject to mortality. The inevitability of death is one thing that he cannot control, and as he walks home he realizes he is going to have to do some more thinking about this new realization.

In "A Sunrise on the Veld," Doris Lessing spins a tale of the anticipation of an early morning hunt by a young British colonist in Africa. (Nici Kuehl / Shutterstock.com)

STYLE

Setting

When the boy sets off over the veld, the descriptions of him emphasize how full of life he is. He revels in his youth, his strength, and his endurance. The descriptions of the perfection that he feels in his own life are mirrored in the descriptions of the veld that take on an almost paradisal flavor. The veld seems like a kind of idyllic place, especially as it greets the dawn. In the veld there are lakes (*vlei*), "acres of long pale grass that sent back a hollowing gleam of light to a satiny sky. . . . Thick swathes of grass were bent under the weight of water, and diamond drops sparkled on each frond." It is almost as if the veld is newly created each morning as a paradise. When he runs down to the lake or river he runs "under a tumult of crimson and gold, while all the birds of the world sang about him." This paradisal scene suggests his oneness with all of creation. However, when he spots the wounded buck, the images become darker. For example, he first sees the buck "against a background of gaunt black rocks." However, somewhat paradoxically, although the images may darken, they are nonetheless part of the boy's necessary awakening, the expansion of his awareness. This is the reason for the title of the story, since the rising sun acts as a metaphor for the rising of greater self-consciousness within the boy. When he sets off he is literally and figuratively in the dark, but during the course of the morning, a new awareness dawns in his mind along with the sunrise on the veld.

Figurative Language

One of the themes of the story, the boy's discovery that he and the buck share more than he had previously realized, is also conveyed by the use of figurative language. Before the boy finds the stricken animal, the narrator explicitly compares him to a buck or duiker (a small antelope found in Africa): "He cleared bushes like a duiker, leapt over rocks." The use of the word "like" indicates the presence of the simile, in which two different things are described in a way that brings out the similarity between them. A more subtle example of figurative language that emphasizes the link between boy and buck comes later, after he has witnessed the animal's death: "His clothes were soaked with the sweat of that other creature's pain." Literally, this means that the boy's clothes are soaked with the sweat that he produced as he observed the struggles of the stricken animal. But the actual words say something a little different: the sweat is presented as produced by the pain of the animal itself, somehow transposed onto the boy's skin. The trick with language accomplishes in a much more visceral way the same idea as the earlier simile: the buck and the boy are sympathetic in some way; they participate in the same process of living and dying that the boy has not yet fully conceptualized.

Another relevant image, this time an auditory one, shows the moment when the boy has to take notice of something that does not fit into his confident, self-assured world. When he first goes out hunting, he feels a certain oneness between himself and the veld, as part of his joyful realization that "there is no country in the world I cannot make part of myself, if I choose." This intellectual realization or belief is then illustrated by an auditory image. He sings at the top of his voice and listens to the echo as it reverberates around the river gorge. It is as if he really does have the ability to make the environment part of himself as he hears his own voice echoing all around him. But suddenly that changes, and he hears a new sound, which is quite different from his own voice: "It seemed as if there was a new voice. He listened, puzzled, for it was not his own." The new sound he hears is the wounded buck, screaming in pain. The auditory images convey the shift that is about to take place in the boy's awareness; from being carefree and joyful, as if he owns the whole veld and is part of it, he discovers something that has up to this point been beyond his realm of understanding: the suffering and death of the buck, and what this means for him, emotionally and intellectually.

HISTORICAL CONTEXT

Early Southern Rhodesia

At the time Lessing's story takes place, Southern Rhodesia was a self-governing British colony. Rhodesia was founded by the British businessman Sir Cecil Rhodes (1853–1902) and named after him in 1895. Rhodes was a believer in British imperialism who dreamed of bringing Africa under British control from Cairo in the north to the Cape of Good Hope in the south. This was during the period when the African continent was subject to colonization by the major European powers. Rhodes was especially interested in the area to be named Rhodesia because of its mineral wealth. Several hundred British settlers arrived in the early 1890s, protected by a force of mercenaries. Soon they had taken over much of the land previously ruled by African chiefs. The Africans were resettled in areas the whites did not want. In 1896, there was a rebellion by the African tribes, and 10 percent of the settlers were killed. The rebellion was soon put down with the aid of British soldiers.

Soon after its founding, the country was split into Southern Rhodesia and Northern Rhodesia. In its earliest days, Southern Rhodesia was administered by the British South Africa Company, but it became a self-governing British colony in 1923, just two years before Lessing's family moved there. Political power was firmly in the hands of the whites, who formed only a small minority of the people in the country. Voting rights were given to blacks and whites, but the requirements to be met in order to qualify for the vote, based on property ownership and annual income, in practice excluded the vast majority of blacks.

Plight of African Farmworkers

As a child in the 1920s and 1930s in Southern Rhodesia, Lessing observed the plight of the African farmworkers. Lessing's father employed between forty to sixty Africans, so as a child she had plenty of opportunities to observe the conditions under which they lived. As Carole Klein observes of such workers in *Doris Lessing: A Biography*, "Their living conditions were patently abysmal. They were given only a day to build a makeshift hut and they were given meagre foodstuffs in comparison to the white farmers." African workers were often abused. Klein points out that "slaps and kicks, withholding of wages to insure against defection, and endless fines for the smallest infraction were habitual ways of keeping workers in line." In *Going Home*, an account Lessing wrote in 1957 about her trip back to Southern Rhodesia in 1956 (excerpted as "The Fruits of Humbug" in her volume *A Small Personal Voice*), she recalls an incident between a white maize farmer and a discontented black worker that she witnessed when she was about twelve, which would have been in the early 1930s. The man was required to work, performing hard physical labor, from six in the morning to six at night, with an hour's break. One day he was an hour late, and the farmer

COMPARE & CONTRAST

- **1950s:** Southern Rhodesia is a self-governing British colony, ruled by a prosperous white minority of Europeans, mainly of British origin. Whites dominate the political and economic life of the country. In the 1950s, as Britain readies to give independence to African colonies, such as Ghana in 1957, there is increasing pressure from black nationalist movements within the country for independence and majority rule. However, whites resist the idea of "one man, one vote" and strive to preserve white minority rule.

  Today: Zimbabwe is an independent nation under the rule of President Robert Mugabe, who has been in power since Zimbabwe's independence in 1980 and rules as one of the world's most oppressive dictators. In 2009, Mugabe, who is accused of rigging elections to guarantee his reelection, agrees to accept a power-sharing arrangement with opposition leader Morgan Tsvangirai.

- **1950s:** Southern Rhodesia is a prosperous country for many of the white minority, but there are huge inequalities of wealth based on race. Whites occupy the most desirable farmlands.

  Today: After a decade of severe economic contraction, the Zimbabwean economy is growing. Growth of 5.9 percent is recorded in 2010. However, the economy is still burdened by high unemployment and debt. Also, the farming sector has been damaged by land-reform programs. The programs were designed to remove the inequities of land distribution under colonial rule, but they leave the country as a net importer of food.

- **1950s:** White immigration to Southern Rhodesia continues to rise. In the 1950s, white immigration doubles to over 200,000 people per year. Immigrants are drawn to what they see as a prosperous, stable country. However, as in its southern neighbor South Africa, a system of racial segregation, known as apartheid, operates in Southern Rhodesia. Not only are blacks discriminated against in politics and employment, but also the races do not mix socially, and many amenities, such as swimming pools, libraries, and department stores, are for whites only.

  Today: In racially integrated Zimbabwe, the number of whites in the population has fallen dramatically, and they now account for less than 1 percent of the population of just over 12 million. Most of those who remain are elderly. The majority of young whites leave the country for destinations such as South Africa, Britain, the United States, Canada, Australia, and New Zealand. Many of the whites who remain live in poverty because runaway inflation has destroyed the value of their pensions and life savings.

---

fined him the equivalent of one-sixth of his month's wages. The man objected to the fine and said he was leaving, but the employer insisted that he had signed a contract and must stay. Lessing recalls that in such circumstances it was customary for the employer to take the African worker to the local police station, where he would be offered a choice between paying a fine and being beaten. On this occasion, the farmer claimed he had no time to take the man to the police, so he asked the worker whether he would agree to allow the African "boss-boy" on the farm to whip him so they could settle the matter. The man refused to accept such a punishment and kept insisting that the employer take him to the police instead. Lessing does not say how the incident was resolved, but the story gives firsthand insight into the kind of treatment that African workers at the time had to endure.

Farmers such as these are the "natives" who are just glimpsed in "A Sunrise on the Veld"; the boy imagines they have chased and hurled rocks at the buck in order to kill it for food. (It appears that only the whites had access to firearms.) The

The African bush is the setting for "A Sunrise on the Veld." (Pichugin Dmitry / Shutterstock.com)

situation for the Africans had been made worse by the Land Apportionment Act of 1930, which restricted their access to land, meaning that more had to seek work as laborers on white-owned property. The act also meant that there was greater segregation of the races. As Klein points out, at this time whites, though they made up only 5 percent of the population, were completely dominant. Few blacks met the qualifications to be eligible to vote, and blacks "were also blocked from most union jobs, commercial transactions or access to public places like restaurants or hotels."

Pressure for Change

By the 1950s, when she had moved to England and "A Sunrise on the Veld" was published, Lessing was a distant observer of the country in which she had spent most of her youth. When she returned to Southern Rhodesia in 1956 she found that social and political conditions there had not changed much. At the time, the British government had set up the Central African Federation, comprising Nyasaland (now Malawi), Northern Rhodesia (now Zambia), and Southern Rhodesia (now Zimbabwe). There was increasing agitation among the African population for independence and majority rule, and they opposed the formation of the federation. However, any progress toward majority black rule was resisted by the white minority in an atmosphere of increasing repression. In "The Fruits of Humbug," Lessing gives a fierce indictment of the system as it existed in the federation at that time. As a British citizen addressing British readers, Lessing states,

> We are responsible for one of the ugliest social systems in the world, where seven million Africans live in conditions of extreme poverty, ridden by disease, malnutrition, illiteracy, kept in segregated townships and reserves, deprived of even the pretence of liberty. They are ruled by 300,000 whites, whose standards of living are higher than those of all but a tiny minority of the British people, and who are prepared to do anything to maintain their privileges.

CRITICAL OVERVIEW

Fiona R. Barnes, writing in the *Dictionary of Literary Biography*, discusses "A Sunrise on the Veld." She describes how "a boy's initial romantic idealization of the rural world that surrounds him" is changed following his encounter with the fatally wounded buck: "This countervision confronts him with the impersonal power of nature and the knowledge of his own fragility and mortality." Barnes also sees the initial attitude of the boy toward the land—his belief that he can control everything and shape it however he wants—as reflective of a recurring theme in the collection *This Was the Old Chief's Country*, in which "A Sunrise on the Veld" first appeared, namely, whites' possessiveness toward the land and even the Africans themselves:

> The high-handedness of the white settlers' attitudes toward their adopted country is seen in their dealings with the land and its people. The male settlers, mostly farmers, view the land as a challenge, their own virgin territory to conquer and control.

Mary Ann Singleton, in *The City and the Veld: The Fiction of Doris Lessing*, views the story as exploring a recurring motif in Lessing's work, that of the veld itself. According to Singleton, the veld represents for Lessing "the unity of nature, whole and complete, but in which the individual counts for nothing." Out of that undifferentiated condition, humans develop self-consciousness. The story, then, "charts the fall from a mythic unity of man and the universe to the fragmentation and responsibility of consciousness."

CRITICISM

Bryan Aubrey

Aubrey holds a Ph.D. in English. In the following essay, he discusses the transformation the boy goes through in "A Sunrise on the Veld," with some reference to the background of white colonial rule.

"A Sunrise on the Veld" is an early story by Doris Lessing, set on the Southern Rhodesian veld that she got to know so well as a child and adolescent in the 1920s and 1930s. The family farm was close to the veld, and the young Lessing would spend hours wandering in the veld by herself, sometimes carrying a rifle, like the boy in the story, ready to shoot game. Later, as a young writer, Lessing wrote many stories set in Southern Rhodesia in which she shines a light on the injustices, both overt and subtle, of white colonial rule in that country, something that no other fiction writer at the time was attempting. Although "A Sunrise on the Veld" does not focus on the social system in Southern Rhodesia or relations between the races, such issues can still be glimpsed in some of Lessing's other African stories, which depict not only white privilege but male privilege, also. As Clare Hanson points out in her essay "The Woman Writer as Exile: Gender and Possession in the African Stories of Doris Lessing," in these stories,

> The men characteristically feel that they own Africa in both the literal and the metaphorical sense: they organize it, partition it, drive roads and railroads through it, imposing European notions of order on it. Men are associated with the hunt, the chase, guns and dogs.

In this respect, the boy in "A Sunrise on the Veld" appears, at least at first, as a perfect young colonial-in-training. As he runs joyfully through the long grass of the veld, he expresses exactly those beliefs about the unlimited power he is able to assert over his environment:

> All the great men of the world have been as I am now, and there is nothing I can't become, nothing I can't do; there is no country in the world I cannot make part of myself, if I choose. I contain the world. I can make of it what I want. If I choose, I can change everything that is going to happen: it depends on me, and what I decide now.

Like other men in Lessing's stories, he too is going hunting, armed with a gun and with dogs at his side. And yet there is a difference in this story that serves to undermine this stereotypical

"ALTHOUGH THE FOCUS OF 'A SUNRISE ON THE VELD' IS THIS SUNRISE IN CONSCIOUSNESS—THE AWAKENING TO A FULLER KNOWLEDGE OF WHAT LIFE IS—RATHER THAN ON THE SOCIAL ASPECTS OF THE COLONIAL WORLD THE BOY LIVES IN, IT IS PERHAPS NOT WITHOUT IMPLICATIONS FOR THAT COLONIAL WORLD."

WHAT DO I READ NEXT?

- *Stories* (2008), by Lessing, is a recently published edition of a selection of her short stories and two novellas, with an introduction by Margaret Drabble. The collection ranges over several decades in Lessing's career and includes the well-known coming-of-age story "Through the Tunnel," first published in 1955, in which an eleven-year-old boy plans a risky swim through an underwater passageway in the ocean.
- *The Doris Lessing Reader* (1989) contains a representative selection of Lessing's work, chosen by the author herself. It includes excerpts from several novels, fourteen short stories, and some of Lessing's nonfiction, including *Going Home*, the memoir she wrote in 1957 of a return she made to the place of her former home in Africa, where she spent much of her childhood and early adulthood.
- *Mukiwa: A White Boy in Africa* (2004), by Peter Godwin, is a memoir by a white journalist who was a child in the 1960s when Southern Rhodesia unilaterally declared its independence. A long guerrilla war followed that eventually resulted in uncontested independence in 1980. Godwin describes what it was like to be a child in Rhodesia at the time, and he reports his later experience as a policeman committed to defending the country against black African guerrillas. Godwin later left the country but returned as a journalist to cover the transition to black majority rule.
- *Robert Mugabe's Zimbabwe* (2007), by James R. Arnold and Roberta Wiener, is a political biography of Zimbabwe's president written for young adults. It shows the difficulties of the transition from white to black rule and traces the path Mugabe took toward a virtual dictatorship while preserving the trappings of democratic rule. There is also a very useful chapter, "Zimbabwe's Past," which explains the colonial background, the days of Southern Rhodesia and white minority rule. Also included are a time line, a glossary, and suggestions for further reading.
- *Out of Shadows* (2010), a novel for young adults by Jason Wallace, is set in a boarding school in Zimbabwe in the 1980s, at the dawn of the country's new era. The novel won the prestigious Costa Children's Book Award in the United Kingdom. The story is about a white British boy who emigrates to Zimbabwe and is bullied at the school he attends.
- *Kaffir Boy: The True Story of a Black Youth's Coming of Age in Apartheid South Africa*, by Mark Mathabane, made a big impact when it was published in the United States in 1986. Mathabane is a black South African, born in 1960, who moved to the United States in 1978 on a tennis scholarship. His book explains what it was like for a black youth to grow up in an impoverished ghetto under the apartheid system of racial segregation that existed in South Africa through the 1980s. The book became a national bestseller.
- *Nervous Conditions* (1988) is a novel by Zimbabwean author Tsitsi Dangarembga. Set in the 1960s and early 1970s, the novel takes place in Zimbabwe while it was still known as Southern Rhodesia and later Rhodesia. This semiautobiographical novel centers around several female characters as they confront the patriarchal structure of their society. One of the few novels written by a black Zimbabwean about this period in Zimbabwe's history, it contributes to postcolonial literature, works by authors from countries once colonized by the European powers.
- *Coming of Age in America: A Multicultural Anthology* (2007), edited by Mary Frosch, is a wide-ranging collection of more than twenty previously published coming-of-age stories and novel excerpts by authors including Tobias Wolff, Paule Marshall, and Dorothy Allison.

picture of the young colonial. The dogs soon disappear entirely from the story, running off on their own trails, and the boy also soon decides that this is not to be a hunting trip, since he realizes he has come too late to accomplish his original intent of shooting guinea fowl. His gun itself proves no use to him either, since when he discovers the wounded buck he decides not to shoot it to put it out of its misery because he realizes that the scene is unfolding exactly as nature has decreed it should and needs no assistance from him. This is one thing he cannot control.

Here, then, is this fifteen-year-old boy, suddenly left without the masculine props of the colonial world he has grown up in: no dogs, no chase, no hunt, no game, no sense of power or control, and a gun that can accomplish nothing for him. But it is in this stripping away of what the boy is used to, the extremely subtle undermining of the masculine colonial enterprise, that the seeds of growth and transformation lie. The moment when transformation is at hand is clearly heralded in the story. It comes almost immediately after his triumphant declaration of his own power. He feels so exultant that he starts to sing, and for a little while he hears only the echo of his own voice. It is as if he does indeed fill the environment with himself. And then he hears some other sound, a voice he does not recognize and which puzzles him. There is a moment of silence that is pregnant with meaning; it is "the deep morning hush that held his future and his past." It is as if everything stops for a moment, and he is on the brink of some revelation. The sound that heralds the revelation comes out of the silence, and it is the sound of pain, a scream. Just in that moment, the pain of the entire world, of existence itself—for that is what is signified, far more than the mere cry of a small animal in distress—begins to make its way into his consciousness, and it will likely never leave him. He has known joy, the supreme delight of being alive in the moment, but now he is to come face to face with pain and cruelty, the ruthlessness of life as it is experienced on the veld, which he has never noticed in the past. As a result, the common fate of all sentient beings dawns in his awareness: "The knowledge of fatality, of what has to be, had gripped him and for the first time in his life." The revelation is so stunning that for a moment he can neither think nor move.

Before this happened, the boy's perception of the world was quite different. Out on the veld, as Mary Ann Singleton observes in her book *The City and the Veld: The Fiction of Doris Lessing*, the boy experiences an untroubled oneness with nature, a kind of ecstasy which causes him to shout and sing with delight. Singleton attaches great importance to this in Lessing's work as a whole, arguing that the veld represents a kind of primordial state in which there is no division between subject and object, between the human being and the world he or she inhabits. Self-consciousness has not yet emerged, so humans are not in some fundamental way at odds with their environment. There is no split in their awareness, no sense of separation between consciousness and nature. Singleton further likens this state of being to *participation mystique*, a term invented by the anthropologist Lucien Lévy-Bruhl in the early twentieth century and used usually with reference to so-called primitive societies. The psychologist Carl Jung, in *Psychological Types; or, The Psychology of Individuation*, defines *participation mystique* as a condition in which "the subject is unable to differentiate himself clearly from the object to which he is bound by an immediate relation that can only be described as partial identity." Jung describes this as characteristic of the state of infancy and as a condition that is occasionally, though seldom, found in modern society. Those who know English literature may think immediately of the poetry of William Wordsworth, whose descriptions of his boyhood and youth in the English Lake District suggest both *participation mystique*—the individual is absorbed as part of the great oneness of the natural world—and of the veld in Lessing's works, especially for the boy in "A Sunrise on the Veld," the veld fulfilling the same function for him as the Lake District did for the young Wordsworth.

The term *participation mystique* should not be overused in this context, however. It is certainly true that the boy exults in the veld as if he is romping in some primordial paradise, and when he shouts and sings and listens to the echo of his voice coming back to him from all directions, it is indeed as if there is no separation between himself and his environment, and there are certainly no troubling thoughts in his mind about the paradoxes or mysteries or cruelties of life—just unadorned bliss in a world that belongs to him so closely he can barely be said to be separate from it. However, it is as well to remember that even while he does this, he also delights in conceptualizing ideas of power and control and sees the world as a challenge; it is his to possess and do with as he pleases, like an external object that can be manipulated for his enjoyment. This suggests that in some respects he has already moved beyond the *participation mystique* stage of consciousness. Nonetheless, the scope of the boy's awareness is of a limited kind, untempered by any knowledge deeper than a young boy reveling in nature can acquire. Then, suddenly, within the space of a few moments, he acquires this thing called deeper knowledge, and it knocks him clean out of his known moorings as far as his understanding of life is concerned. Now he must dig out a deeper truth than he has formerly known, and it will take much pondering. He discovers himself, as so many have done before him, as a being who exists in two worlds, as both a part of nature—he will share the same fate as the buck—and apart from nature, because unlike other creatures of the natural world he has the gift of reason, the ability to think philosophically, to ponder, to make choices, to bear the weight of responsibility, to live by a system of morals and ethics. In this way he is challenged to exert a new kind of control over his life, a kind that is very different from his earlier childish fantasy of never-ending power and control, because he is now aware of some brutal facts of life and implications that had never before entered his mind.

Although the focus of "A Sunrise on the Veld" is this sunrise in consciousness—the awakening to a fuller knowledge of what life is—rather than on the social aspects of the colonial world the boy lives in, it is perhaps not without implications for that colonial world. The boy has become more aware than before of the consequences of his actions. He realizes that there have been many days when he walked casually home to breakfast having shot at a half-glimpsed buck without ever knowing whether he hit it. Now he knows that he might have condemned an animal to a similar fate as that of the buck he just witnessed, wounded, crippled, and devoured by ants. The boy does not want to think about this but knows he must. And once he starts thinking about that, who knows what else will occur to him to question, such as, perhaps, why he lives in a comfortable house on a farm while the "natives" who work on the farm live in mud huts? (This is not actually shown in the story but is likely the case.) Lessing leaves such questions unanswered, but is it not likely that this young boy, now learning to reflect deeply on his actions and on the nature of life, may start to question other things that go way beyond the death of a buck? He might of course conclude that relations between the races are just another aspect of life that he cannot control and that cannot be altered. Or he might conclude something else entirely, as Lessing herself did.

> "THE SPATIAL AND VERBAL STRUCTURES LIKEWISE ECHO LESSING'S FICTIONAL STRATEGIES AND SUGGEST THAT SHE MUST BE READ WITH CLOSE ATTENTION TO NUANCE AND GESTURE."

Source: Bryan Aubrey, Critical Essay on "A Sunrise on the Veld," in *Short Stories for Students*, Gale, Cengage Learning, 2012.

Jane Hotchkiss

In the following excerpt, Hotchkiss provides a stylistic and thematic analysis of Lessing's African stories.

When Doris Lessing's collection of African stories first appeared in 1951, white South African reviews revealed the peculiar double vision of colonial settlers. Her sketches of Southern African societies were applauded for their realism, yet the urgent issues they raised were left lying, as if inert, and the urgency was evaluated as a "bitterness" that spoiled her "art." Lessing's work was often regretfully dismissed as "promising but artistically flawed" by her tendency to "standardiz[e] human beings to serve abstract ideas." Her brief return to Africa in 1956 elicited a sharper response. Journalist Oliver Walker confidently claimed, in an article ominously titled "Novelist Given a Tarred White Feather in Bulawayo," that black Africans preferred apartheid to "British hypocrisy" regarding race relations, but Lessing, a "prohibited immigrant" at that time and permitted to cross the border only by mistake, was kept under surveillance throughout her trip and, as Walker put it, "accused of putting ideas into the munts' heads" (47). Her meticulous representation of the monstrous quotidian was recognized, examined in aesthetic terms, and tidily discounted, while her possibly subversive presence stimulated the usual official response of vigilance and control.

More recently, Lessing's work has been found flawed in a different regard; it is neither too bitter nor realistic but rather too "romantic." In her 1991 article "*Veldtanschauung*: Doris Lessing's Savage Africa," Eve Bertelsen cites the need to consider "the ways in which literary tradition and its forms impose upon the writer, defining in advance the range of her creative freedom, and often seriously contradicting or undermining an explicit social or political project." Bertelsen is speaking of the way the romantic/primitivist view of Africa pervades Lessing's early novel *The Grass Is Singing*; specifically, she draws a parallel between Lessing's writing of Africans and Africa and Conrad's in *Heart of Darkness*. Both writers present a "vision of Africa" that relies on "a set of literary conventions and a cultural myth that appears to be stronger than conscious intent" (p. 658). Zimbabwe critic Anthony Chennells has also criticized Lessing's early work for its perpetuation of a romantic view of "darkest Africa." Questioning Lessing's inclusion in the literary canon of Zimbabwe by the *Tabex Encyclopedia Zimbabwe*, Chennells writes: "If one reads Lessing's stories as produced by a European romanticism rather than as the products of a liberal settler, the distinction between herself and writers who wrote Africa as primitive may not be as valid as the Encyclopedia entry assumes."

It is not difficult to find passages that support such a view in Lessing's early stories, collected in the anthology *This Was the Old Chief's Country* and published a year after *The Grass Is Singing*. But I would argue that the early work as a whole demonstrates Lessing's awareness of the problem presented by the literary tradition she is writing her way out of and that many occasions of "romantic primitivism" in that work are deliberately ironic. The story she chose to open the collection, "The Old Chief Mshlanga," confronts the problematic of literary tradition and political intent which Bertelsen finds in the earlier novel. Through its implicit involvement with Conrad's representations of "savage Africa," the text both recognizes and critiques the seductions of romanticism and writes the confrontation with that tradition as integral to the constitution of self-irony in the liberal settler. One might use Homi Bhabha's metaphor of the "tethered shadow" to describe the relationship of Conrad's text to Lessing's—*Heart of Darkness* dogs her discourse, and she deals with its inevitable echoes through parodic repetitions that underline the collusion of belated romanticism in the pathology of colonialism.

In addition, Lessing's African story suggests, *avant la lettre*, postmodern formulations of "identification," in which apparent binary oppositions actually include a third aspect or property, the betweenness itself or "fissure," the reciprocity of difference that both threatens and makes possible the identification. It is this fissure Lessing maps as the territory inherited by the African-born settler awakened to political awareness. Gilles Deleuze, in *Logique de sens*, posits "two readings of the world," the first the mimetic type, which "asks us to think of difference on the basis of pre-established similitude or identity," and a second which "invites us on the contrary to think of similitude and even identity as the product of a fundamental disparity." The first "establishes the world as icon," the second "presents the world itself as phantasm," or, as Walter Benjamin put it, allows "the true surrealist face of existence [to break] through."

In the apparently faithful social realism of Lessing's early work, surrealism consistently breaks through; icons are subverted, phantasms shimmer on the surface of the prosaic. The permeability of the boundary between real and surreal, sanity and schism, was, for Lessing, fundamental: in her own words, "the quintessential eccentricity of the human race was borne in upon me from the beginning." Lessing was no distanced academic observer of the dis-ease of patriarchal imperialism; she learned it at her father's knee. She "concluded at the age of about six" that her father was "mad"; she describes his "splendidly pathological character" as something she "spent a good part of [her] childhood coming to terms with."

> It was [my father's] wont to spend many hours of the day seated in a rickety deckchair on the top of the semi-mountain on which our house was built, surveying the African landscape which stretched emptily away on all sides for leagues. After a silence which might very well have lasted several hours, he would start to his feet, majestically splenetic in shabby khaki, a prophet in his country, and, shaking his fist at the sky, shout out: "Mad! Mad! Everyone! Everywhere! Mad!" (p. 7)

The young Doris May Taylor learned how the skewed double standard of colonial "moral sense" worked. One early lesson, "comparatively uncomplicated, not to say banal," as she puts it, occurred on a windless day when her father was burning a fireguard to protect the cowshed from the wild veld fires common in the dry season in Southern Africa. The fire burned slowly, "yet it was in the nature of things that any small animal, grounded bird, insect or reptile in the 200-yard-wide, mile-long stretch of fire would perish, not presumably without pain." When a large field mouse ran out of the burning grass in front of Lessing's father, the "boss-boy," an African man,

> brought down a heavy stick across the mouse's back. It was dying. The boss-boy picked up the mouse by the tail, and swinging the still-twitching creature, continued to stand beside my father, who brought down his hand in a very hard slap against the boss-boy's face. So unprepared was he for this, that he fell down. He got up, palm to his cheek, looking at my father for an explanation. My father was rigid with incommunicable anger, "Kill it at once," he said.... The boss-boy flung the mouse into a nest of flames, and stalked off, with dignity. "If there's one thing I can't stand it's cruelty of any kind," my father said afterwards, in explanation of the incident. (pp. 9–10)

This autobiographical anecdote bears some of the hallmarks of Lessing's fiction. She attempts no explication or analysis of the incidents; she merely presents it to the reader and moves on to another "more obliquely rewarding in its implications" (p. 10). One is left to imagine the child observing these "lessons" unprotected by the seasoned irony of the adult relating them: the successive shocks to her sensibility, her puzzling over "implications," her gradual deconstruction of rank hypocrisies presented to her as self-justifying truths.

The spatial and verbal structures likewise echo Lessing's fictional strategies and suggest that she must be read with close attention to nuance and gesture. The two men stand side by side watching the controlled destruction of a landscape now inhabited only by "small animals," creatures considered insignificant; yet the narrative voice posits their "presumable pain." The men stand together but are differentiated by their designations as "my father" and "the boss-boy"; then they are once again aligned by the repetition of the phrase "brought down" to describe their actions. The contrast of those actions directly relates to the matter of "dignity." Through the intimacy of the employer's gesture, the blow of hand against face, the suggestion of a father punishing and instructing a wayward child, Lessing extends the figure of her father to encompass colonial patriarchy and the "white enlightenment" of people of color. Through his wordless demand for an explanation and his silent gestures of refusal—"he flung the mouse... stalked off, with dignity"—the African man constructs an alternative discourse that rejects the colonizer's language and, to use Homi Bhabha's words, "deflect[s] the dominating ideologies being imposed on him." The farmer's final pompous remark lamely follows the expressive gesture, and Lessing underlines the irony with her repetition of the word "explanation"; this delayed and oblique "reply" to the African's unspoken question inadvertently comments on the white man's actions as much as on the African man's.

...There are no easy resolutions in Lessing's tales of colonial "Zambesia," the fictional name she derived to represent both Rhodesia and South Africa, "two countries... similar in atmosphere and political structure" in the time of which she wrote and for some time thereafter. After long struggle, those times have changed, and settlers' stories like Lessing's have become part of history. It is appropriate that even liberal "settler ideologies" be marginalized in an era when Africans write "themselves as subjects of African discourses." The question arises, then, whether it is of any use to retain in social memory—in the literary canon, for example—white liberal stories of the era of white hegemony in Africa and elsewhere. I would reply that, in a postcolonial age more accurately characterized as neocolonial, examples of the art of bearing witness to political oppression are still of value, for that art is one we all must master. It would be romantic to suppose otherwise.

Source: Jane Hotchkiss, "Coming of Age in Zambesia," in *Borders, Exiles, Diasporas*, edited by Elazar Barkan and Marie-Denise Shelton, Stanford University Press, 1998, pp. 81–91.

Ruth Whittaker

In the following excerpt, Whittaker argues that in her African stories, Lessing "works both within and beyond the colonial experience."

Doris Lessing has written numerous short stories about Africa and in nearly all of them she describes a conflict between white sensibility (or lack of it) and African culture. We are shown both the European and the African experiences of exile and alienation. The European exile causes the Africans' displacement, forcing then to leave their tribal lands, and to live apart from their families. Underlying her narratives is Mrs Lessing's implacable message that Africa belongs to the Africans, so that there is never a 'happy ending' for the settlers in the sense of unconditional acceptance. Any coming to terms with their

"'A SUNRISE ON THE VELD' IS A VERY GOOD EXAMPLE OF HOW DORIS LESSING GIVES A LOCAL SITUATION OR INCIDENT A WIDER, EVEN UNIVERSAL APPLICATION, WITHOUT EXPLICITLY ANALYSING THE POINT OR COMMENTING ON THE MORAL."

new country is provisional or a compromise, or indeed, occasionally an awareness of the impossibility of 'settling.' Even those Europeans who feel themselves to be liberal and enlightened are not exempt from Mrs Lessing's strictures. Some kinds of liberalism, as shown in 'Little Tembi' or 'A Home for the Highland Cattle' are seen to be as ineffectual as the most common attitudes of racial prejudice.

Some of the African stories are told from the point of view of a child or an adolescent, and through their openness to their surroundings we see the dawning realisation of strangeness, of differences, of unbridgeable gulfs. The child's perception is a useful device for the author because it enables her to show the registering of new awareness, a process not often made available to her adult characters who are too fixed in their views to see freshly. The stories about adult settlers concentrate more on their efforts to subdue the alien culture to their own. 'This Was the Old Chief's Country' is one of Mrs Lessing's best known stories in which the action is seen predominantly through the eyes of a 14-year-old girl. Although the child has lived in Africa for many years, she has inherited an English tradition of landscape and literature, so that oak and ash trees are more familiar to her than the African shrubs all around her, and her fairy tales are Northern—of witches and woodcutters and snow. Walking in the bush she meets some natives and is struck by their dignity. She is introduced to the oldest of them, who is a tribal chief. She learns that the district she lives in once belonged to this chief and his ancestors, and this knowledge gives her a new perspective on Africa and her attitude to the natives: 'It seemed it was only necessary to let free that respect I felt when I was talking with old Chief Mshlanga, to let both black and white people meet gently, with tolerance for each other's differences: it seemed quite easy' (*Collected African Stories*).

After discovering that their cook is the chief's son and heir, the girl decides to visit his home, out of curiosity. On the long walk to his village she travels through unfamiliar country and experiences terror of the bush for the first time. Here, Mrs Lessing suggests that the strangeness of Africa is unable to be alleviated because the folklore and culture which might make it accessible are not available to the white settler. Northern forests can be rendered harmless, made familiar, through stories of woodcutters and fairies. The African bush stays unknowable, a distance which is echoed by her reception at the village. On arriving she notices the difference between the village with its beautifully decorated, thatched huts, and the dirty, transient atmosphere of the native compound at the farm. She is welcomed distantly and formally by the chief, and can think of nothing to say to him. She returns home, feeling excluded: 'there was now a queer hostility in the landscape, a cold, hard, sullen indomitability that walked with me, as strong as a wall, as intangible as smoke: it seemed to say to me: you walk here as a destroyer' (*Collected African Stories*).

The story ends with a row between her father and the old chief. A herd of goats has damaged one of her father's crops, and he keeps the goats in compensation. The native people were relying on the goats for food in the dry season, and their loss is serious. The chief says, in effect, that the white people have no right to his land, and both he and his son return to the bush. As an indirect result of this altercation the villagers are moved from their kraal to a distant native reserve. Thus, in miniature one might say, Doris Lessing illustrates the colonial takeover. Her protagonist, however, is more clear-sighted than the majority of colonials she writes about. The girl moves from total ignorance of the country and the people around her to the false impression that there is room for everyone, given a little mutual respect. Her final realisation is that no easy apologies will make her any less of a usurper, neither will Africa ever belong to her.

A similar story is revealed in 'A Sunrise on the Veld,' which is told from the viewpoint of a boy of 15. He goes hunting on the veld in the early morning with his gun and his dogs. He feels strong and invincible: 'there is nothing I can't become, nothing I can't do; there is no country in the world I cannot make part of myself, if I choose' (*Collected African Stories*). He hears a noise like a scream, and finds a dying buck being eaten by swarms of ants. He is appalled, but accepts this grim knowledge as part of the 'vast unalterable cruel veld.' Then he realises that the buck had had its leg broken by native hunters, which is why the ants attacked it. And he thinks of the times he has taken a shot at a buck, not always bothering to find out whether or not he has killed it. This shifts the responsibility from the impersonal forces of the veld to man's involvement with it, and he is left to contemplate the difference. During the narrative his mood changes from one of wild exhilaration in his own strength (dismissing the thought that he could ever break his ankle), to impersonal stoicism, to the gradual unwelcome awareness of his own potential to cause much suffering. It is a short and economically told story, but it resonates with meaning like an allegory. In a few minutes, the boy goes through stages of revelation that may not be universally learnt in generations. 'A Sunrise on the Veld' is a very good example of how Doris Lessing gives a local situation or incident a wider, even universal application, without explicitly analysing the point or commenting on the moral.

Many of Mrs Lessing's short stories show the ways in which the settlers are changed in their attempts to adapt to Africa. 'Leopard George' is such a story. From the beginning we see that George feels an affinity with Africa and its wildness. When choosing his land he rejects a beautiful, lush farm for five thousand acres of bush, and settles there. He builds himself a large house and a swimming pool, and employs native people whose leader formerly worked for George's father. Mrs Lessing describes the mutual respect between George and his 'bossboy,' and adds, in parenthesis: 'This was in the early 'twenties, when a more gentle, almost feudal relationship was possible between good masters and their servants: there was space, then, for courtesy, bitterness had not yet crowded out affection' (*Collected African Stories*).

George is unmarried, and both his bossboy and his neighbours urge him to take a wife. He is considered slightly eccentric because he will not allow any animal to be killed or hunted on his farm, which 'was as good as a game reserve.' He appears to be satisfied with his solitary life, though we are not shown his interior thoughts. The narrator admits a diffidence in intruding on George's privacy:

> But it is not easy to ask of such a man, living in such a way, what it is he misses, if he misses anything at all. To ask would mean entering into what he feels during the long hours riding over the ridges of the kopje in the sunshine, with the grass waving about him like blond banners. It would mean understanding what made him one of mankind's outriders in the first place. (*Collected African Stories*)

Thus Mrs Lessing suggests the sort of person George is, without analysing for us the psychological basis of his character, or his motivation. The narrator says of George: 'Perhaps he really did feel he ought to marry.' The 'perhaps' refuses the authorial privilege of absolute knowledge, and the unknowability of a character is more realistic than if we wholly understood all George's innermost thoughts and impulses.

At weekends George holds bathing parties, where the young girls of the neighbourhood flirt with him. At one of these parties a native African girl appears, wanting to talk to him. She gives the clear impression of being his mistress; his white guests notice this and feel 'an irritation which was a reproach for not preserving appearances.' George is very angry with the girl. She is the daughter or grand-daughter (again, the narrator is uncertain) of his bossboy, Smoke, and her liaison with George has lasted for five years. He sends for Smoke and complains that the girl is making trouble. George arranges for her to be sent to a mission school to get her out of his way. A few weeks later another, younger girl presents herself to George. He tries to make the arrangement perfectly clear. He pays her and insists that she return home after their love-making, even though she is terrified of the bush at night. The next day Smoke is very upset, and George realises with horror that the young girl is his new wife. When she comes to him again, he sends her straight home. She is too frightened of the bush to go on her own, and George cannot understand this. He is not frightened of the bush, and he feels obscurely that the girl should not be afraid of her natural habitat. In the morning Smoke comes to tell George that the girl has not arrived home. For the first time George feels fear growing inside him, a fear of the African landscape. He takes his gun and kills a leopard. In the morning he finds its cave, where there are fresh human bones amongst the other debris.

Killing the leopard in revenge is not enough, however: 'He did not know what satisfaction it was he needed.' Neither are we told. The narrator says only that 'there was a hurt place in him, and a hungry anger that no work could assuage.' After this episode George fills his stables with horses and dogs, and establishes regular leopard hunts. He kills a wounded leopard with the butt of his rifle, and eventually his body becomes covered in scars from his wounds. He marries a woman with grown-up children, and the story ends abruptly.

Significantly it is the omissions in this narrative that are the most potent carriers of meaning. We are not told specifically why George does not marry a suitable young white girl early on, or why he gets impatient with his house parties and rides off alone into the bush. But it is implied that he feels more akin to Africa and the African than to his white compatriates. Thus he oversteps the unspoken boundaries of the white/black division. Mere prostitution of the native girl would have been acceptable, it is suggested, a business-like arrangement understood by everyone. But George muddles it by affection. He sometimes allows the girl to spend the night with him, and buys her presents in addition to paying her cash. She in turn breaks the rules by allowing herself to be seen by his white visitors at a weekend party. The second girl expresses her fear of the bush, and George is impatient because she feels fear and he does not. But of course her fear is based on an intimate and realistic knowledge of its dangers. Again, we are not told why her death completely changes George's life. Her disappearance engenders in George a new and stark recognition of the African bush, which mocks his former affinity with it. He feels guilt for sleeping with Smoke's wife, and he feels guilt when the girl is killed by the leopard, but he displaces his anger from himself to the animals. His earlier feelings about Africa are destroyed: 'For him, now, thc landscapc was simply a homc for leopards.' For all his sense of belonging, for all his love of its wildness, and his irritation with white 'civilisation,' George is finally frustrated by the Africa he thought he knew. It seems almost that he is punished for his arrogance in having assumed such knowledge. He cannot, ultimately, transcend his foreignness; he cannot become part of Africa because his skin is white and his ways are essentially European.

In her African writings Doris Lessing works both within and beyond the colonial experience. She understands the rigorous limitations of colonial society which is formed and kept cohesive by maintaining its own narrow boundaries. But she has also achieved the feat of imaginatively stepping outside its borders—and this does not automatically follow her literally having done so by leaving Africa for England. This extended vision enables her to see beyond the false colonial myths of white superiority and the necessity of blacks and whites remaining separate. Hence her African short stories arise from a kind of irony engendered by perceiving the gap between the myths and the African reality. The price of 'settling' is an acceptance of the myths, of making a home amongst them. But Doris Lessing's home has long since been reclaimed by the bush, and appropriately, for she has always been engaged in the process of making herself homeless, of leaving, of moving on.

Source: Ruth Whittaker, "The Colonial Legacy," in *Modern Novelists: Doris Lessing*, St. Martin's Press, 1988, pp. 17–34.

Mona Knapp

In the following excerpt, Knapp uses "Sunrise on the Veld" to illustrate Lessing's lessons on dignity and justice in the face of oppression.

... "Sunrise on the Veld" establishes an intrinsic tie between a fifteen-year-old boy and the entire African landscape, through which he roams in the early morning hours. It traces the boy's three steps toward mature vision, expressed by the symmetrically placed words "eternity," "fatality," and "responsibility." The first section is devoted to the boy's exultant sense of power as he bounds over the waking veld. The sight of a buck being eaten alive by ants fills him with a distinct sense of fatality: "If I had not come it would have died like this: so why should I interfere?... this is what happens, this is how things work... *it was right and nothing could alter it*" (emph. orig.). Only on closer inspection of the animal's soon clean-picked carcass, whose broken leg bone must have prevented its escape from the ants, does it dawn on the boy that he himself took a potshot at just such a young buck some mornings past. He realizes that, in his drunken joy of life, he must have inflicted the wound that predetermined a painful death. In short, Lessing draws a thumbnail sketch of the cycle of life, suffering and death, and hinges the whole picture on the consciousness of one adolescent: who may or may not, in time, rework the incident into ethical conviction.

The child on the veld represents the yet-intact bond between human beings and nature, an ideal aspired to by most of Lessing's characters. This perspective is complemented by that of children who observe adult society from the fringes, narrating with the heightened sensibility of adolescence ("Old John's Place," "The New Man," "Getting Off the Altitude"). These child narrators are still suspended between nature and society, aware of the conflicts and injustices involved in adult life, but not yet bent into conformity. As we know from *The Grass is Singing*, whose protagonist goes directly from pink-pinafored childhood into oppressed middle age, this state of innocence is tenuous, the step into downtrodden adulthood swift and inevitable.

Lessing's African stories are among modern literature's most compelling delineations of individual fate against the tableau of historical circumstance. It is their rare achievement to show the individual "as a microcosm and in this way to break through the personal, the subjective, making the personal general, as indeed life always does. . . . " The stories' given societal framework denies their characters a mature, fulfilled adult existence. Once they leave childhood behind, they must choose between two paths: either to adapt to the status quo or to evade social integration altogether. The path of conformity is ruinous. It leads to brutal white supremacy (Mr. Slatter, Mr. Macintosh), exploited femininity (Molly Slatter), prostitution ("A Road to the Big City"), and crime ("Hunger"). But neither can the individual be saved by resisting integration. This is demonstrated by "Leopard" George in the story of the same name, a settler who becomes a guilty party in the life-death cycle despite all his efforts to remain uninvolved, or by the "Non-Marrying Man," who drifts back and forth between stifling white society and the native bush. He is an African Wandering Jew who will never fit into either realm. And the children of the veld, as shown above, are granted only a temporary reprieve.

The logical conclusion of Lessing's African stories is that human beings, if they are to save their dignity and sense of justice, must escape from the "disgraceful scene" of a society whose very existence depends on violent segregation and exploitation of the weak. It was undoubtedly in this spirit that Lessing herself left Africa before her thirtieth birthday. The gradual sequestration of the individual from an oppressive society, arrived at only by implication in these stories, will be carried out step by step by a single figure, Martha Quest, in *Children of Violence*. . . .

> **"FOR LESSING, THE AFRICAN VELD IS THE UNCONSCIOUS, PHYSICAL WORLD OF NATURE THAT NOURISHES MANKIND WITH ITS UNITY BUT ALSO INFLICTS ITS OWN MINDLESS REPETITION AND, IN HUMAN TERMS, CRUELTY AND INDIFFERENCE."**

Source: Mona Knapp, "A Splendid Backdrop to a Disgraceful Scene: African Fiction, 1950–1965," in *Doris Lessing*, Frederick Ungar, 1984, pp. 19–48.

Mary Ann Singleton

In the following excerpt, Singleton examines the dual concepts of city and veld—or hope for an ideal future as opposed to the unconscious, physical world of nature—as central to Lessing's fiction.

[Doris Lessing] believes (with many others) that our civilization is slipping ever-faster toward the precipice. Almost from the beginning, her work has explored what in human nature is causing this catastrophe and what, if anything, can be done about it. . . .

Lessing's attention is always turned toward humanity's destructive weaknesses and potential strength, and it is essentially these that I have called the two *cities* and the *veld.* For Lessing, the African veld is the unconscious, physical world of nature that nourishes mankind with its unity but also inflicts its own mindless repetition and, in human terms, cruelty and indifference. The city is half-evolved consciousness, the destructive fragmentation of partial awareness. The ideal City is a hope for the future: the unified individual in a harmonious society. To impose such an intellectual scheme upon Lessing's work goes against its spirit; however, if it leads to increased understanding of her writing, perhaps to do so is forgivable. . . .

The ideal of the City stands behind everything Lessing has written, an expression of her firm sense of purpose, put most explicitly in an important essay, "The Small Personal Voice." There she affirms a belief in "committed" literature, in which the writer considers himself/herself "an instrument of change." For if the ideal of the City stands in the background of Lessing's work, the Armageddon of technological disaster looms there as well....

Lessing believes that mankind is at a crucial point in history and that artists must paint the possible evil as well as strengthen "a vision of good which may defeat the evil"; that is, art for society's sake. Lessing's criteria for art fit her own work. Not simply an artist, she is also critic and prophet, dissecting in minute detail the faults of a society "hypnotized by the idea of Armageddon" and prophesying the calamitous results of those faults. At the same time, she attempts to delineate possible solutions to the world's problems.

There are three main motifs in Lessing's work, which I have called the two *cities* and the *veld*, and they are apparent in her themes, imagery, and structures. The veld represents the unity of nature, whole and complete, but in which the individual counts for nothing. Before the birth of self-consciousness, as it is known today, mankind readily participated in this natural world and at times was scarcely differentiated from it; but the price of unity was to be caught in the ceaseless round of natural repetition, all instinct with no reason.

The city represents modern consciousness, expressed in a strife-torn society. Its origins are the loss of mythic consciousness that prevailed in early, simpler cultures; its power, the ability to use the tools of reason; its culmination, the achievements and excesses of the last two hundred years, when logic and reason have come to be valued by society as a whole almost to the exclusion of other modes of perception. Reason has the power to raise mankind above the brute, instinctual level, but in its present form it is partial, fragmented.... According to Lessing, such fragmented perception is presently leading mankind to certain disaster—much like fire in the hands of a child—causing unbalanced, private lives and conflict in society. As citizens of the contemporary city, mankind is a victim of a second type of repetition, not of natural cycles this time, but the constant replaying of destructive patterns of behavior. Both here and in the veld he has no hope of change except from natural evolution, in which he is simply acted upon: Jude rather than Prometheus.

The third motif is the ideal City, a new and more unified form of consciousness,... expressed as a harmonious society of unified citizens. The human imagination holds the key: "[we must] force ourselves into the effort of imagination necessary to become what we are capable of being." Nature's harsh unity is no longer compatible with human self-consciousness and values. Partial truths have proved disastrous. The next step is to create new, whole forms that will somehow contain intuition along with reason, both myth and logic, with all the complexities the terms suggest. When—and if—this new unity is accomplished, the ideal City will be possible, the Golden Age finally at hand. The City in the veld is a man-made harmony—part of nature, yet at the same time separate from it, as consciousness is of and yet above nature.

Most of Lessing's fiction may be seen within this overall pattern. For the most part, Lessing depicts the psychically warped citizens of the city, all inexorably headed for disaster. The early *The Grass Is Singing* concerns Mary Turner's complete destruction by social and psychic forces of which she is not even aware, and many of the short stories dramatize the fragmented lives of people who have varying degrees of awareness. *Retreat to Innocence* shows Julia Barr's refusal to leave the superficial life of the city.

After *The Grass Is Singing*, Lessing's major protagonists and more visionary characters search for ways to integrate the city and the veld, even while they are inextricably caught in the tangles of the mass psyche and society. *The Golden Notebook* is an odyssey of the individual in search of wholeness, and while Anna Wulf's story is central, the reader sees beyond it to the society that conditions her and limits what she can be. "Children of Violence" is Lessing's most complete portrait of the fragmented city. Here, half a century passes before one's eyes, as Martha and her closest friends search in vain for inner and outer versions of the City, as society races with increasing speed toward its destruction. In "Children of Violence" Lessing comes closest to the first half of her criterion for the committed writer—to paint a vision of evil; her view of the good that may defeat it has evolved slowly and is therefore more clearly presented in the later works....

There is a substantial difference between Lessing's view of humanity's possibilities and the predominant attitude of most twentieth-century novels, in which the hero is perforce an anti-hero, stumbling gallantly through the world. Certainly Lessing's view of man in his present condition is bleak: in these lost generations, too, everyone is sick. Nevertheless, she extends a glimmer of hope that somewhere latent in man is, after all, the possibility of psychic health. . . .

Lessing is a writer of great variety. Her short stories are usually economical and carefully crafted, while "Children of Violence" sprawls over five long novels, finally moving away almost entirely from customary narrative techniques . . . . But if her forms vary, her metaphysic, which I have summed up in the images of the two cities in the veld, remains essentially the same. . . .

Most of Lessing's fiction deals with the need to join the mythic and discursive, the veld and the city—to be in touch with the mythic state, unified and close to experience, yet without losing the uniquely human values of ego-consciousness and logic. It is to be a hard-won wholeness based on a joining of reason and myth: something new. This is the unity suggested by the image of the City in the veld. The ideal City represents a man-made achievement, a triumph of consciousness and mental and physical harmony, standing apart from and yet integral to the cruel, unconscious, yet harmonious veld.

Lessing has said that people must force themselves, through effort of imagination, to become what they are capable of being; her image of the City, superimposed upon her picture of fragmented and violent society is such an attempt, as are all descriptions of Utopia . . . .

If Lessing shares in this Utopian dream, she usually describes the world of here and now, trying to analyze what is going wrong. As a result, she seems to combine two extreme views of man. On the one hand, . . . mankind seems always to be a victim of "grim fatality." From this point of view, if a finer consciousness should arise, willed human creativity will have no hand in it: at the end of *The Four-Gated City* Martha writes of the new children who are mutations, affected by the radiation of the catastrophe. Their consciousness is a product of natural evolution, comparable to the first sea creatures who crept up to land. On the other hand, Lessing's work never quite relinquishes the possibility that a "willed mutation" will be possible, that through new modes of perception men and women have the power to catapult themselves back to the top of the great chain of being; this time even higher than the angels and perhaps on a godly level themselves, as their own creators. . . .

Source: Mary Ann Singleton, *The City and the Veld: The Fiction of Doris Lessing*, Bucknell University Press, 1977.

SOURCES

Barnes, Fiona R., "Doris Lessing," in *Dictionary of Literary Biography*, Vol. 139, *British Short-Fiction Writers, 1945–1980*, edited by Dean Baldwin, Gale Research, 1994, pp. 159–72.

Fletcher, Martin, "Should I Stay or Should I Go: What Every White Zimbabwean Asks," in *Times* (London, England), February 18, 2009.

Hanson, Clare, "The Woman Writer as Exile: Gender and Possession in the African Stories of Doris Lessing," in *Critical Essays on Doris Lessing*, edited by Claire Sprague and Virginia Tiger, G. K. Hall, 1986, p. 111.

Ingersoll, Earl G., ed., *Doris Lessing: Conversations*, Ontario Review Press, 1994, pp. 134, 214.

Jung, Carl G., *Psychological Types; or, The Psychology of Individuation*, translated by H. Godwin Baynes, Harcourt, Brace, 1926, pp. 572–73.

Klein, Carole, *Doris Lessing: A Biography*, Duckworth, 2000, pp. 17–45.

Lessing, Doris, "The Fruits of Humbug," in *A Small Personal Voice: Essays, Reviews, Interviews*, edited by Paul Schlueter, Vintage Books, 1974, pp. 164–66, 171.

———, "A Sunrise on the Veld," in *African Stories*, Simon and Schuster, 1981, pp. 59–66.

Norman, Andrew, *Robert Mugabe and the Betrayal of Zimbabwe*, McFarland, 2004, pp. 43–45.

Pickering, Jean, *Understanding Doris Lessing*, University of South Carolina Press, 1990, pp. 1–17.

"Rhodesia—Mzilikaze to Smith," in *Africa Institute Bulletin*, Vol. 15, 1977, http://www.rhodesia.nl/mztosm.html (accessed September 10, 2011).

Singleton, Mary Ann, *The City and the Veld: The Fiction of Doris Lessing*, Bucknell University Press, 1977, pp. 19, 23.

"Zimbabwe," in *CIA: World Factbook*, https://www.cia.gov/library/publications/the-world-factbook/geos/zi.html (accessed September 10, 2011).

"Zimbabwe Profile: Timeline," in *BBC News*, http://news.bbc.co.uk/2/hi/africa/country_profiles/1831470.stm (accessed September 10, 2011).

FURTHER READING

Barclay, Philip, *Zimbabwe: Years of Hope and Despair*, Bloomsbury, 2010.

Barclay is a British diplomat who witnessed the precipitous decline of Zimbabwe after the country attained independence in 1980. Readers of

Lessing's African stories, noting the injustices of colonial rule in Southern Rhodesia, will be interested and surely saddened to know that so soon after independence, one form of injustice was replaced by another.

Brewster, Dorothy, *Doris Lessing*, Twayne Publishers, 1965.
This study, though it only covers Lessing's work up to 1965, remains useful for its biographical information about the author's early life and analysis of the early short stories.

Lessing, Doris, *Under My Skin: Volume One of My Autobiography, to 1949*, HarperCollins, 1994.
In this acclaimed autobiography, Lessing describes her life in Southern Rhodesia during her childhood on the family farm and as a married woman in Salisbury, followed by her embrace of Communism during World War II. The descriptions of her early years are important for understanding not only "A Sunrise on the Veld" but all of her African stories.

Maslen, Elizabeth, *Doris Lessing*, Northcote House, 1994.
With a writer as prolific as Lessing, who in her long career has written so much in many different genres, it can be difficult for the newcomer to know where to start. Maslen's concise introduction to Lessing covers a wide range of her work, including novels, short stories, and essays.

SUGGESTED SEARCH TERMS

Doris Lessing

A Sunrise on the Veld AND Doris Lessing

Southern Rhodesia

Rhodesia

colonialism

scramble for Africa

Cecil Rhodes

Zimbabwe

participation mystique

coming-of-age story

initiation story

Doris Lessing AND South Africa

Doris Lessing AND colonialism

Glossary of Literary Terms

A

Aestheticism: A literary and artistic movement of the nineteenth century. Followers of the movement believed that art should not be mixed with social, political, or moral teaching. The statement "art for art's sake" is a good summary of aestheticism. The movement had its roots in France, but it gained widespread importance in England in the last half of the nineteenth century, where it helped change the Victorian practice of including moral lessons in literature. Oscar Wilde and Edgar Allan Poe are two of the best-known "aesthetes" of the late nineteenth century.

Allegory: A narrative technique in which characters representing things or abstract ideas are used to convey a message or teach a lesson. Allegory is typically used to teach moral, ethical, or religious lessons but is sometimes used for satiric or political purposes. Many fairy tales are allegories.

Allusion: A reference to a familiar literary or historical person or event, used to make an idea more easily understood. Joyce Carol Oates's story "Where Are You Going, Where Have You Been?" exhibits several allusions to popular music.

Analogy: A comparison of two things made to explain something unfamiliar through its similarities to something familiar, or to prove one point based on the acceptance of another. Similes and metaphors are types of analogies.

Antagonist: The major character in a narrative or drama who works against the hero or protagonist. The Misfit in Flannery O'Connor's story "A Good Man Is Hard to Find" serves as the antagonist for the Grandmother.

Anthology: A collection of similar works of literature, art, or music. Zora Neale Hurston's "The Eatonville Anthology" is a collection of stories that take place in the same town.

Anthropomorphism: The presentation of animals or objects in human shape or with human characteristics. The term is derived from the Greek word for "human form." The fur necklet in Katherine Mansfield's story "Miss Brill" has anthropomorphic characteristics.

Anti-hero: A central character in a work of literature who lacks traditional heroic qualities such as courage, physical prowess, and fortitude. Anti-heroes typically distrust conventional values and are unable to commit themselves to any ideals. They generally feel helpless in a world over which they have no control. Anti-heroes usually accept, and often celebrate, their positions as social outcasts. A well-known anti-hero is Walter Mitty in James Thurber's story "The Secret Life of Walter Mitty."

Archetype: The word archetype is commonly used to describe an original pattern or model from which all other things of the same kind are made. Archetypes are the literary images that grow out of the "collective unconscious," a theory proposed by psychologist Carl Jung. They appear in literature as incidents and plots that repeat basic patterns of life. They may also appear as stereotyped characters. The "schlemiel" of Yiddish literature is an archetype.

Autobiography: A narrative in which an individual tells his or her life story. Examples include Benjamin Franklin's *Autobiography* and Amy Hempel's story "In the Cemetery Where Al Jolson Is Buried," which has autobiographical characteristics even though it is a work of fiction.

Avant-garde: A literary term that describes new writing that rejects traditional approaches to literature in favor of innovations in style or content. Twentieth-century examples of the literary avant-garde include the modernists and the minimalists.

B

Belles-lettres: A French term meaning "fine letters" or" beautiful writing." It is often used as a synonym for literature, typically referring to imaginative and artistic rather than scientific or expository writing. Current usage sometimes restricts the meaning to light or humorous writing and appreciative essays about literature. Lewis Carroll's *Alice in Wonderland* epitomizes the realm of belles-lettres.

Bildungsroman: A German word meaning "novel of development." The *bildungsroman* is a study of the maturation of a youthful character, typically brought about through a series of social or sexual encounters that lead to self-awareness. J. D. Salinger's *Catcher in the Rye* is a *bildungsroman*, and Doris Lessing's story "Through the Tunnel" exhibits characteristics of a *bildungsroman* as well.

Black Aesthetic Movement: A period of artistic and literary development among African Americans in the 1960s and early 1970s. This was the first major African-American artistic movement since the Harlem Renaissance and was closely paralleled by the civil rights and black power movements. The black aesthetic writers attempted to produce works of art that would be meaningful to the black masses. Key figures in black aesthetics included one of its founders, poet and playwright Amiri Baraka, formerly known as Le Roi Jones; poet and essayist Haki R. Madhubuti, formerly Don L. Lee; poet and playwright Sonia Sanchez; and dramatist Ed Bullins. Works representative of the Black Aesthetic Movement include Amiri Baraka's play *Dutchman,* a 1964 Obie award-winner.

Black Humor: Writing that places grotesque elements side by side with humorous ones in an attempt to shock the reader, forcing him or her to laugh at the horrifying reality of a disordered world. "Lamb to the Slaughter," by Roald Dahl, in which a placid housewife murders her husband and serves the murder weapon to the investigating policemen, is an example of black humor.

C

Catharsis: The release or purging of unwanted emotions—specifically fear and pity—brought about by exposure to art. The term was first used by the Greek philosopher Aristotle in his *Poetics* to refer to the desired effect of tragedy on spectators.

Character: Broadly speaking, a person in a literary work. The actions of characters are what constitute the plot of a story, novel, or poem. There are numerous types of characters, ranging from simple, stereotypical figures to intricate, multifaceted ones. "Characterization" is the process by which an author creates vivid, believable characters in a work of art. This may be done in a variety of ways, including (1) direct description of the character by the narrator; (2) the direct presentation of the speech, thoughts, or actions of the character; and (3) the responses of other characters to the character. The term "character" also refers to a form originated by the ancient Greek writer Theophrastus that later became popular in the seventeenth and eighteenth centuries. It is a short essay or sketch of a person who prominently displays a specific attribute or quality, such as miserliness or ambition. "Miss Brill," a story by Katherine Mansfield, is an example of a character sketch.

Classical: In its strictest definition in literary criticism, classicism refers to works of ancient Greek or Roman literature. The term may also be used to describe a literary work of recognized importance (a "classic") from any time period or literature that exhibits the traits of classicism. Examples of later works and authors now described as classical include

French literature of the seventeenth century, Western novels of the nineteenth century, and American fiction of the mid-nineteenth century such as that written by James Fenimore Cooper and Mark Twain.

Climax: The turning point in a narrative, the moment when the conflict is at its most intense. Typically, the structure of stories, novels, and plays is one of rising action, in which tension builds to the climax, followed by falling action, in which tension lessens as the story moves to its conclusion.

Comedy: One of two major types of drama, the other being tragedy. Its aim is to amuse, and it typically ends happily. Comedy assumes many forms, such as farce and burlesque, and uses a variety of techniques, from parody to satire. In a restricted sense the term comedy refers only to dramatic presentations, but in general usage it is commonly applied to nondramatic works as well.

Comic Relief: The use of humor to lighten the mood of a serious or tragic story, especially in plays. The technique is very common in Elizabethan works, and can be an integral part of the plot or simply a brief event designed to break the tension of the scene.

Conflict: The conflict in a work of fiction is the issue to be resolved in the story. It usually occurs between two characters, the protagonist and the antagonist, or between the protagonist and society or the protagonist and himself or herself. The conflict in Washington Irving's story "The Devil and Tom Walker" is that the Devil wants Tom Walker's soul but Tom does not want to go to hell.

Criticism: The systematic study and evaluation of literary works, usually based on a specific method or set of principles. An important part of literary studies since ancient times, the practice of criticism has given rise to numerous theories, methods, and "schools," sometimes producing conflicting, even contradictory, interpretations of literature in general as well as of individual works. Even such basic issues as what constitutes a poem or a novel have been the subject of much criticism over the centuries. Seminal texts of literary criticism include Plato's *Republic,* Aristotle's *Poetics*, Sir Philip Sidney's *The Defence of Poesie,* and John Dryden's *Of Dramatic Poesie*. Contemporary schools of criticism include deconstruction, feminist, psychoanalytic, poststructuralist, new historicist, postcolonialist, and reader-response.

D

Deconstruction: A method of literary criticism characterized by multiple conflicting interpretations of a given work. Deconstructionists consider the impact of the language of a work and suggest that the true meaning of the work is not necessarily the meaning that the author intended.

Deduction: The process of reaching a conclusion through reasoning from general premises to a specific premise. Arthur Conan Doyle's character Sherlock Holmes often used deductive reasoning to solve mysteries.

Denotation: The definition of a word, apart from the impressions or feelings it creates in the reader. The word "apartheid" denotes a political and economic policy of segregation by race, but its connotations—oppression, slavery, inequality—are numerous.

Denouement: A French word meaning "the unknotting." In literature, it denotes the resolution of conflict in fiction or drama. The *denouement* follows the climax and provides an outcome to the primary plot situation as well as an explanation of secondary plot complications. A well-known example of *denouement* is the last scene of the play *As You Like It* by William Shakespeare, in which couples are married, an evildoer repents, the identities of two disguised characters are revealed, and a ruler is restored to power. Also known as "falling action."

Detective Story: A narrative about the solution of a mystery or the identification of a criminal. The conventions of the detective story include the detective's scrupulous use of logic in solving the mystery; incompetent or ineffectual police; a suspect who appears guilty at first but is later proved innocent; and the detective's friend or confidant—often the narrator—whose slowness in interpreting clues emphasizes by contrast the detective's brilliance. Edgar Allan Poe's "Murders in the Rue Morgue" is commonly regarded as the earliest example of this type of story. Other practitioners are Arthur Conan Doyle, Dashiell Hammett, and Agatha Christie.

Dialogue: Dialogue is conversation between people in a literary work. In its most restricted sense, it refers specifically to the speech of characters in a drama. As a specific literary genre, a "dialogue" is a composition in which characters debate an issue or idea.

Didactic: A term used to describe works of literature that aim to teach a moral, religious, political, or practical lesson. Although didactic elements are often found inartistically pleasing works, the term "didactic" usually refers to literature in which the message is more important than the form. The term may also be used to criticize a work that the critic finds "overly didactic," that is, heavy-handed in its delivery of a lesson. An example of didactic literature is John Bunyan's *Pilgrim's Progress.*

Dramatic Irony: Occurs when the reader of a work of literature knows something that a character in the work itself does not know. The irony is in the contrast between the intended meaning of the statements or actions of a character and the additional information understood by the audience.

Dystopia: An imaginary place in a work of fiction where the characters lead dehumanized, fearful lives. George Orwell's *Nineteen Eighty-four,* and Margaret Atwood's *Handmaid's Tale* portray versions of dystopia.

E

Edwardian: Describes cultural conventions identified with the period of the reign of Edward VII of England (1901–1910). Writers of the Edwardian Age typically displayed a strong reaction against the propriety and conservatism of the Victorian Age. Their work often exhibits distrust of authority in religion, politics, and art and expresses strong doubts about the soundness of conventional values. Writers of this era include E. M. Forster, H. G. Wells, and Joseph Conrad.

Empathy: A sense of shared experience, including emotional and physical feelings, with someone or something other than oneself. Empathy is often used to describe the response of a reader to a literary character.

Epilogue: A concluding statement or section of a literary work. In dramas, particularly those of the seventeenth and eighteenth centuries, the epilogue is a closing speech, often in verse, delivered by an actor at the end of a play and spoken directly to the audience.

Epiphany: A sudden revelation of truth inspired by a seemingly trivial incident. The term was widely used by James Joyce in his critical writings, and the stories in Joyce's *Dubliners* are commonly called "epiphanies."

Epistolary Novel: A novel in the form of letters. The form was particularly popular in the eighteenth century. The form can also be applied to short stories, as in Edwidge Danticat's "Children of the Sea."

Epithet: A word or phrase, often disparaging or abusive, that expresses a character trait of someone or something. "The Napoleon of crime" is an epithet applied to Professor Moriarty, arch-rival of Sherlock Holmes in Arthur Conan Doyle's series of detective stories.

Existentialism: A predominantly twentieth-century philosophy concerned with the nature and perception of human existence. There are two major strains of existentialist thought: atheistic and Christian. Followers of atheistic existentialism believe that the individual is alone in a godless universe and that the basic human condition is one of suffering and loneliness. Nevertheless, because there are no fixed values, individuals can create their own characters—indeed, they can shape themselves—through the exercise of free will. The atheistic strain culminates in and is popularly associated with the works of Jean-Paul Sartre. The Christian existentialists, on the other hand, believe that only in God may people find freedom from life's anguish. The two strains hold certain beliefs in common: that existence cannot be fully understood or described through empirical effort; that anguish is a universal element of life; that individuals must bear responsibility for their actions; and that there is no common standard of behavior or perception for religious and ethical matters. Existentialist thought figures prominently in the works of such authors as Franz Kafka, Fyodor Dostoyevsky, and Albert Camus.

Expatriatism: The practice of leaving one's country to live for an extended period in another country. Literary expatriates include Irish author James Joyce who moved to Italy and France, American writers James Baldwin, Ernest Hemingway, Gertrude Stein, and F. Scott Fitzgerald who lived and wrote in

Paris, and Polish novelist Joseph Conrad in England.

Exposition: Writing intended to explain the nature of an idea, thing, or theme. Expository writing is often combined with description, narration, or argument.

Expressionism: An indistinct literary term, originally used to describe an early twentieth-century school of German painting. The term applies to almost any mode of unconventional, highly subjective writing that distorts reality in some way. Advocates of Expressionism include Federico Garcia Lorca, Eugene O'Neill, Franz Kafka, and James Joyce.

F

Fable: A prose or verse narrative intended to convey amoral. Animals or inanimate objects with human characteristics often serve as characters in fables. A famous fable is Aesop's "The Tortoise and the Hare."

Fantasy: A literary form related to mythology and folklore. Fantasy literature is typically set in non-existent realms and features supernatural beings. Notable examples of literature with elements of fantasy are Gabriel Gárcia Márquez's story "The Handsomest Drowned Man in the World" and Ursula K. Le Guin's "The Ones Who Walk Away from Omelas."

Farce: A type of comedy characterized by broad humor, outlandish incidents, and often vulgar subject matter. Much of the comedy in film and television could more accurately be described as farce.

Fiction: Any story that is the product of imagination rather than a documentation of fact. Characters and events in such narratives may be based in real life but their ultimate form and configuration is a creation of the author.

Figurative Language: A technique in which an author uses figures of speech such as hyperbole, irony, metaphor, or simile for a particular effect. Figurative language is the opposite of literal language, in which every word is truthful, accurate, and free of exaggeration or embellishment.

Flashback: A device used in literature to present action that occurred before the beginning of the story. Flashbacks are often introduced as the dreams or recollections of one or more characters.

Foil: A character in a work of literature whose physical or psychological qualities contrast strongly with, and therefore highlight, the corresponding qualities of another character. In his Sherlock Holmes stories, Arthur Conan Doyle portrayed Dr. Watson as a man of normal habits and intelligence, making him a foil for the eccentric and unusually perceptive Sherlock Holmes.

Folklore: Traditions and myths preserved in a culture or group of people. Typically, these are passed on by word of mouth in various forms—such as legends, songs, and proverbs—or preserved in customs and ceremonies. Washington Irving, in "The Devil and Tom Walker" and many of his other stories, incorporates many elements of the folklore of New England and Germany.

Folktale: A story originating in oral tradition. Folk tales fall into a variety of categories, including legends, ghost stories, fairy tales, fables, and anecdotes based on historical figures and events.

Foreshadowing: A device used in literature to create expectation or to set up an explanation of later developments. Edgar Allan Poe uses foreshadowing to create suspense in "The Fall of the House of Usher" when the narrator comments on the crumbling state of disrepair in which he finds the house.

G

Genre: A category of literary work. Genre may refer to both the content of a given work—tragedy, comedy, horror, science fiction—and to its form, such as poetry, novel, or drama.

Gilded Age: A period in American history during the 1870s and after characterized by political corruption and materialism. A number of important novels of social and political criticism were written during this time. Henry James and Kate Chopin are two writers who were prominent during the Gilded Age.

Gothicism: In literature, works characterized by a taste for medieval or morbid characters and situations. A gothic novel prominently features elements of horror, the supernatural, gloom, and violence: clanking chains, terror, ghosts, medieval castles, and unexplained phenomena. The term "gothic novel" is also applied to novels that lack elements of the traditional Gothic setting but that create a similar atmosphere of terror or dread. The term can also be applied to stories, plays, and poems. Mary Shelley's *Frankenstein* and Joyce Carol Oates's *Bellefleur* are both gothic novels.

Grotesque: In literature, a work that is characterized by exaggeration, deformity, freakishness, and disorder. The grotesque often includes an element of comic absurdity. Examples of the grotesque can be found in the works of Edgar Allan Poe, Flannery O'Connor, Joseph Heller, and Shirley Jackson.

H

Harlem Renaissance: The Harlem Renaissance of the 1920s is generally considered the first significant movement of black writers and artists in the United States. During this period, new and established black writers, many of whom lived in the region of New York City known as Harlem, published more fiction and poetry than ever before, the first influential black literary journals were established, and black authors and artists received their first widespread recognition and serious critical appraisal. Among the major writers associated with this period are Countee Cullen, Langston Hughes, Arna Bontemps, and Zora Neale Hurston.

Hero/Heroine: The principal sympathetic character in a literary work. Heroes and heroines typically exhibit admirable traits: idealism, courage, and integrity, for example. Famous heroes and heroines of literature include Charles Dickens's Oliver Twist, Margaret Mitchell's Scarlett O'Hara, and the anonymous narrator in Ralph Ellison's *Invisible Man.*

Hyperbole: Deliberate exaggeration used to achieve an effect. In William Shakespeare's *Macbeth,* Lady Macbeth hyperbolizes when she says, "All the perfumes of Arabia could not sweeten this little hand."

I

Image: A concrete representation of an object or sensory experience. Typically, such a representation helps evoke the feelings associated with the object or experience itself. Images are either "literal" or "figurative." Literal images are especially concrete and involve little or no extension of the obvious meaning of the words used to express them. Figurative images do not follow the literal meaning of the words exactly. Images in literature are usually visual, but the term "image" can also refer to the representation of any sensory experience.

Imagery: The array of images in a literary work. Also used to convey the author's overall use of figurative language in a work.

In medias res: A Latin term meaning "in the middle of things." It refers to the technique of beginning a story at its midpoint and then using various flashback devices to reveal previous action. This technique originated in such epics as Virgil's *Aeneid.*

Interior Monologue: A narrative technique in which characters' thoughts are revealed in a way that appears to be uncontrolled by the author. The interior monologue typically aims to reveal the inner self of a character. It portrays emotional experiences as they occur at both a conscious and unconscious level. One of the best-known interior monologues in English is the Molly Bloom section at the close of James Joyce's *Ulysses.* Katherine Anne Porter's "The Jilting of Granny Weatherall" is also told in the form of an interior monologue.

Irony: In literary criticism, the effect of language in which the intended meaning is the opposite of what is stated. The title of Jonathan Swift's "A Modest Proposal" is ironic because what Swift proposes in this essay is cannibalism—hardly "modest."

J

Jargon: Language that is used or understood only by a select group of people. Jargon may refer to terminology used in a certain profession, such as computer jargon, or it may refer to any nonsensical language that is not understood by most people. Anthony Burgess's *A Clockwork Orange* and James Thurber's "The Secret Life of Walter Mitty" both use jargon.

K

Knickerbocker Group: An indistinct group of New York writers of the first half of the nineteenth century. Members of the group were linked only by location and a common theme: New York life. Two famous members of the Knickerbocker Group were Washington Irving and William Cullen Bryant. The group's name derives from Irving's *Knickerbocker's History of New York.*

L

Literal Language: An author uses literal language when he or she writes without exaggerating or embellishing the subject matter and without any tools of figurative language. To say "He ran very quickly down the street" is to use literal language, whereas to say "He ran like a hare down the street" would be using figurative language.

Literature: Literature is broadly defined as any written or spoken material, but the term most often refers to creative works. Literature includes poetry, drama, fiction, and many kinds of nonfiction writing, as well as oral, dramatic, and broadcast compositions not necessarily preserved in a written format, such as films and television programs.

Lost Generation: A term first used by Gertrude Stein to describe the post-World War I generation of American writers: men and women haunted by a sense of betrayal and emptiness brought about by the destructiveness of the war. The term is commonly applied to Hart Crane, Ernest Hemingway, F. Scott Fitzgerald, and others.

M

Magic Realism: A form of literature that incorporates fantasy elements or supernatural occurrences into the narrative and accepts them as truth. Gabriel Gárcia Márquez and Laura Esquivel are two writers known for their works of magic realism.

Metaphor: A figure of speech that expresses an idea through the image of another object. Metaphors suggest the essence of the first object by identifying it with certain qualities of the second object. An example is "But soft, what light through yonder window breaks? / It is the east, and Juliet is the sun" in William Shakespeare's *Romeo and Juliet.* Here, Juliet, the first object, is identified with qualities of the second object, the sun.

Minimalism: A literary style characterized by spare, simple prose with few elaborations. In minimalism, the main theme of the work is often never discussed directly. Amy Hempel and Ernest Hemingway are two writers known for their works of minimalism.

Modernism: Modern literary practices. Also, the principles of a literary school that lasted from roughly the beginning of the twentieth century until the end of World War II. Modernism is defined by its rejection of the literary conventions of the nineteenth century and by its opposition to conventional morality, taste, traditions, and economic values. Many writers are associated with the concepts of modernism, including Albert Camus, D. H. Lawrence, Ernest Hemingway, William Faulkner, Eugene O'Neill, and James Joyce.

Monologue: A composition, written or oral, by a single individual. More specifically, a speech given by a single individual in a drama or other public entertainment. It has no set length, although it is usually several or more lines long. "I Stand Here Ironing" by Tillie Olsen is an example of a story written in the form of a monologue.

Mood: The prevailing emotions of a work or of the author in his or her creation of the work. The mood of a work is not always what might be expected based on its subject matter.

Motif: A theme, character type, image, metaphor, or other verbal element that recurs throughout a single work of literature or occurs in a number of different works over a period of time. For example, the color white in Herman Melville's *Moby Dick* is a "specific" motif, while the trials of star-crossed lovers is a "conventional" motif from the literature of all periods.

N

Narration: The telling of a series of events, real or invented. A narration may be either a simple narrative, in which the events are recounted chronologically, or a narrative with a plot, in which the account is given in a style reflecting the author's artistic concept of the story. Narration is sometimes used as a synonym for "storyline."

Narrative: A verse or prose accounting of an event or sequence of events, real or invented. The term is also used as an adjective in the sense "method of narration." For example, in literary criticism, the expression "narrative technique" usually refers to the way the author structures and presents his or her story. Different narrative forms include diaries, travelogues, novels, ballads, epics, short stories, and other fictional forms.

Narrator: The teller of a story. The narrator may be the author or a character in the story through whom the author speaks. Huckleberry Finn is the narrator of Mark Twain's *The Adventures of Huckleberry Finn.*

Novella: An Italian term meaning "story." This term has been especially used to describe fourteenth-century Italian tales, but it also refers to modern short novels. Modern novellas include Leo Tolstoy's *The Death of Ivan Ilich,* Fyodor Dostoyevsky's *Notes from the Underground,* and Joseph Conrad's *Heart of Darkness.*

O

Oedipus Complex: A son's romantic obsession with his mother. The phrase is derived from the story of the ancient Theban hero Oedipus, who unknowingly killed his father and married his mother, and was popularized by Sigmund Freud's theory of psychoanalysis. Literary occurrences of the Oedipus complex include Sophocles' *Oedipus Rex* and D. H. Lawrence's "The Rocking-Horse Winner."

Onomatopoeia: The use of words whose sounds express or suggest their meaning. In its simplest sense, onomatopoeia may be represented by words that mimic the sounds they denote such as "hiss" or "meow." At a more subtle level, the pattern and rhythm of sounds and rhymes of a line or poem may be onomatopoeic.

Oral Tradition: A process by which songs, ballads, folklore, and other material are transmitted by word of mouth. The tradition of oral transmission predates the written record systems of literate society. Oral transmission preserves material sometimes over generations, although often with variations. Memory plays a large part in the recitation and preservation of orally transmitted material. Native American myths and legends, and African folktales told by plantation slaves are examples of orally transmitted literature.

P

Parable: A story intended to teach a moral lesson or answer an ethical question. Examples of parables are the stories told by Jesus Christ in the New Testament, notably "The Prodigal Son," but parables also are used in Sufism, rabbinic literature, Hasidism, and Zen Buddhism. Isaac Bashevis Singer's story "Gimpel the Fool" exhibits characteristics of a parable.

Paradox: A statement that appears illogical or contradictory at first, but may actually point to an underlying truth. A literary example of a paradox is George Orwell's statement "All animals are equal, but some animals are more equal than others" in *Animal Farm.*

Parody: In literature, this term refers to an imitation of a serious literary work or the signature style of a particular author in a ridiculous manner. Atypical parody adopts the style of the original and applies it to an inappropriate subject for humorous effect. Parody is a form of satire and could be considered the literary equivalent of a caricature or cartoon. Henry Fielding's *Shamela* is a parody of Samuel Richardson's *Pamela.*

Persona: A Latin term meaning "mask." Personae are the characters in a fictional work of literature. The persona generally functions as a mask through which the author tells a story in a voice other than his or her own. A persona is usually either a character in a story who acts as a narrator or an "implied author," a voice created by the author to act as the narrator for himself or herself. The persona in Charlotte Perkins Gilman's story "The Yellow Wallpaper" is the unnamed young mother experiencing a mental breakdown.

Personification: A figure of speech that gives human qualities to abstract ideas, animals, and inanimate objects. To say that "the sun is smiling" is to personify the sun.

Plot: The pattern of events in a narrative or drama. In its simplest sense, the plot guides the author in composing the work and helps the reader follow the work. Typically, plots exhibit causality and unity and have a beginning, a middle, and an end. Sometimes, however, a plot may consist of a series of disconnected events, in which case it is known as an "episodic plot."

Poetic Justice: An outcome in a literary work, not necessarily a poem, in which the good are rewarded and the evil are punished, especially in ways that particularly fit their virtues or crimes. For example, a murderer may himself be murdered, or a thief will find himself penniless.

Poetic License: Distortions of fact and literary convention made by a writer—not always a poet—for the sake of the effect gained. Poetic license is closely related to the concept of "artistic freedom." An author exercises poetic license by saying that a pile of money "reaches as high as a mountain" when the pile is actually only a foot or two high.

Point of View: The narrative perspective from which a literary work is presented to the reader. There are four traditional points of view. The "third person omniscient" gives the reader a "godlike" perspective, unrestricted by time or place, from which to see actions and look into the minds of characters. This allows the author to comment openly on characters and events in the work. The "third person" point of view presents the events of the story from outside of any single character's perception, much like the omniscient point of view, but the reader must understand the action as it takes place and without any special insight into characters' minds or motivations. The "first person" or "personal" point of view relates events as they are perceived by a single character. The main character "tells" the story and may offer opinions about the action and characters which differ from those of the author. Much less common than omniscient, third person, and first person is the "second person" point of view, wherein the author tells the story as if it is happening to the reader. James Thurber employs the omniscient point of view in his short story "The Secret Life of Walter Mitty." Ernest Hemingway's "A Clean, Well-Lighted Place" is a short story told from the third person point of view. Mark Twain's novel *Huckleberry Finn* is presented from the first person viewpoint. Jay McInerney's *Bright Lights, Big City* is an example of a novel which uses the second person point of view.

Pornography: Writing intended to provoke feelings of lust in the reader. Such works are often condemned by critics and teachers, but those which can be shown to have literary value are viewed less harshly. Literary works that have been described as pornographic include D. H. Lawrence's *Lady Chatterley's Lover* and James Joyce's *Ulysses.*

Post-Aesthetic Movement: An artistic response made by African Americans to the black aesthetic movement of the 1960s and early 1970s. Writers since that time have adopted a somewhat different tone in their work, with less emphasis placed on the disparity between black and white in the United States. In the words of post-aesthetic authors such as Toni Morrison, John Edgar Wideman, and Kristin Hunter, African Americans are portrayed as looking inward for answers to their own questions, rather than always looking to the outside world. Two well-known examples of works produced as part of the post-aesthetic movement are the Pulitzer Prize–winning novels *The Color Purple* by Alice Walker and *Beloved* by Toni Morrison.

Postmodernism: Writing from the 1960s forward characterized by experimentation and application of modernist elements, which include existentialism and alienation. Postmodernists have gone a step further in the rejection of tradition begun with the modernists by also rejecting traditional forms, preferring the anti-novel over the novel and the anti-hero over the hero. Postmodern writers include Thomas Pynchon, Margaret Drabble, and Gabriel Gárcia Márquez.

Prologue: An introductory section of a literary work. It often contains information establishing the situation of the characters or presents information about the setting, time period, or action. In drama, the prologue is spoken by a chorus or by one of the principal characters.

Prose: A literary medium that attempts to mirror the language of everyday speech. It is distinguished from poetry by its use of unmetered, unrhymed language consisting of logically related sentences. Prose is usually grouped into paragraphs that form a cohesive whole such as an essay or a novel. The term is sometimes used to mean an author's general writing.

Protagonist: The central character of a story who serves as a focus for its themes and incidents and as the principal rationale for its development. The protagonist is sometimes referred to in discussions of modern literature as the hero or anti-hero. Well-known protagonists are Hamlet in William Shakespeare's *Hamlet* and Jay Gatsby in F. Scott Fitzgerald's *The Great Gatsby.*

R

Realism: A nineteenth-century European literary movement that sought to portray familiar characters, situations, and settings in a realistic manner. This was done primarily by using an objective narrative point of view and through the buildup of accurate detail.

The standard for success of any realistic work depends on how faithfully it transfers common experience into fictional forms. The realistic method may be altered or extended, as in stream of consciousness writing, to record highly subjective experience. Contemporary authors who often write in a realistic way include Nadine Gordimer and Grace Paley.

Resolution: The portion of a story following the climax, in which the conflict is resolved. The resolution of Jane Austen's *Northanger Abbey* is neatly summed up in the following sentence: "Henry and Catherine were married, the bells rang and every body smiled."

Rising Action: The part of a drama where the plot becomes increasingly complicated. Rising action leads up to the climax, or turning point, of a drama. The final "chase scene" of an action film is generally the rising action which culminates in the film's climax.

Roman a clef: A French phrase meaning "novel with a key." It refers to a narrative in which real persons are portrayed under fictitious names. Jack Kerouac, for example, portrayed various friends under fictitious names in the novel *On the Road.* D. H. Lawrence based "The Rocking-Horse Winner" on a family he knew.

Romanticism: This term has two widely accepted meanings. In historical criticism, it refers to a European intellectual and artistic movement of the late eighteenth and early nineteenth centuries that sought greater freedom of personal expression than that allowed by the strict rules of literary form and logic of the eighteenth-century neoclassicists. The Romantics preferred emotional and imaginative expression to rational analysis. They considered the individual to be at the center of all experience and so placed him or her at the center of their art. The Romantics believed that the creative imagination reveals nobler truths—unique feelings and attitudes—than those that could be discovered by logic or by scientific examination. "Romanticism" is also used as a general term to refer to a type of sensibility found in all periods of literary history and usually considered to be in opposition to the principles of classicism. In this sense, Romanticism signifies any work or philosophy in which the exotic or dreamlike figure strongly, or that is devoted to individualistic expression, self-analysis, or a pursuit of a higher realm of knowledge than can be discovered by human reason. Prominent Romantics include Jean-Jacques Rousseau, William Wordsworth, John Keats, Lord Byron, and Johann Wolfgang von Goethe.

S

Satire: A work that uses ridicule, humor, and wit to criticize and provoke change in human nature and institutions. Voltaire's novella *Candide* and Jonathan Swift's essay "A Modest Proposal" are both satires. Flannery O'Connor's portrayal of the family in "A Good Man Is Hard to Find" is a satire of a modern, Southern, American family.

Science Fiction: A type of narrative based upon real or imagined scientific theories and technology. Science fiction is often peopled with alien creatures and set on other planets or in different dimensions. Popular writers of science fiction are Isaac Asimov, Karel Capek, Ray Bradbury, and Ursula K. Le Guin.

Setting: The time, place, and culture in which the action of a narrative takes place. The elements of setting may include geographic location, characters's physical and mental environments, prevailing cultural attitudes, or the historical time in which the action takes place.

Short Story: A fictional prose narrative shorter and more focused than a novella. The short story usually deals with a single episode and often a single character. The "tone," the author's attitude toward his or her subject and audience, is uniform throughout. The short story frequently also lacks *denouement*, ending instead at its climax.

Signifying Monkey: A popular trickster figure in black folklore, with hundreds of tales about this character documented since the 19th century. Henry Louis Gates Jr. examines the history of the signifying monkey in *The Signifying Monkey: Towards a Theory of Afro-American Literary Criticism,* published in 1988.

Simile: A comparison, usually using "like" or "as," of two essentially dissimilar things, as in "coffee as cold as ice" or "He sounded like a broken record." The title of Ernest Hemingway's "Hills Like White Elephants" contains a simile.

Socialist Realism: The Socialist Realism school of literary theory was proposed by Maxim

Gorky and established as a dogma by the first Soviet Congress of Writers. It demanded adherence to a communist worldview in works of literature. Its doctrines required an objective viewpoint comprehensible to the working classes and themes of social struggle featuring strong proletarian heroes. Gabriel Gárcia Márquez's stories exhibit some characteristics of Socialist Realism.

Stereotype: A stereotype was originally the name for a duplication made during the printing process; this led to its modern definition as a person or thing that is (or is assumed to be) the same as all others of its type. Common stereotypical characters include the absent-minded professor, the nagging wife, the troublemaking teenager, and the kindhearted grandmother.

Stream of Consciousness: A narrative technique for rendering the inward experience of a character. This technique is designed to give the impression of an ever-changing series of thoughts, emotions, images, and memories in the spontaneous and seemingly illogical order that they occur in life. The textbook example of stream of consciousness is the last section of James Joyce's *Ulysses.*

Structure: The form taken by a piece of literature. The structure may be made obvious for ease of understanding, as in nonfiction works, or may obscured for artistic purposes, as in some poetry or seemingly "unstructured" prose.

Style: A writer's distinctive manner of arranging words to suit his or her ideas and purpose in writing. The unique imprint of the author's personality upon his or her writing, style is the product of an author's way of arranging ideas and his or her use of diction, different sentence structures, rhythm, figures of speech, rhetorical principles, and other elements of composition.

Suspense: A literary device in which the author maintains the audience's attention through the buildup of events, the outcome of which will soon be revealed. Suspense in William Shakespeare's *Hamlet* is sustained throughout by the question of whether or not the Prince will achieve what he has been instructed to do and of what he intends to do.

Symbol: Something that suggests or stands for something else without losing its original identity. In literature, symbols combine their literal meaning with the suggestion of an abstract concept. Literary symbols are of two types: those that carry complex associations of meaning no matter what their contexts, and those that derive their suggestive meaning from their functions in specific literary works. Examples of symbols are sunshine suggesting happiness, rain suggesting sorrow, and storm clouds suggesting despair.

T

Tale: A story told by a narrator with a simple plot and little character development. Tales are usually relatively short and often carry a simple message. Examples of tales can be found in the works of Saki, Anton Chekhov, Guy de Maupassant, and O. Henry.

Tall Tale: A humorous tale told in a straightforward, credible tone but relating absolutely impossible events or feats of the characters. Such tales were commonly told of frontier adventures during the settlement of the west in the United States. Literary use of tall tales can be found in Washington Irving's *History of New York,* Mark Twain's *Life on the Mississippi,* and in the German R. F. Raspe's *Baron Munchausen's Narratives of His Marvellous Travels and Campaigns in Russia.*

Theme: The main point of a work of literature. The term is used interchangeably with thesis. Many works have multiple themes. One of the themes of Nathaniel Hawthorne's "Young Goodman Brown" is loss of faith.

Tone: The author's attitude toward his or her audience maybe deduced from the tone of the work. A formal tone may create distance or convey politeness, while an informal tone may encourage a friendly, intimate, or intrusive feeling in the reader. The author's attitude toward his or her subject matter may also be deduced from the tone of the words he or she uses in discussing it. The tone of John F. Kennedy's speech which included the appeal to "ask not what your country can do for you" was intended to instill feelings of camaraderie and national pride in listeners.

Tragedy: A drama in prose or poetry about a noble, courageous hero of excellent character who, because of some tragic character flaw, brings ruin upon him- or herself. Tragedy treats its subjects in a dignified and serious manner, using poetic language to help evoke pity and fear and bring about catharsis, a purging of these emotions. The tragic form was practiced extensively by the ancient Greeks. The classical form of tragedy was revived in the sixteenth century; it flourished especially on the Elizabethan stage. In modern times, dramatists have attempted to adapt the form to the needs of modern society by drawing their heroes from the ranks of ordinary men and women and defining the nobility of these heroes in terms of spirit rather than exalted social standing. Some contemporary works that are thought of as tragedies include *The Great Gatsby* by F. Scott Fitzgerald, and *The Sound and the Fury* by William Faulkner.

Tragic Flaw: In a tragedy, the quality within the hero or heroine which leads to his or her downfall. Examples of the tragic flaw include Othello's jealousy and Hamlet's indecisiveness, although most great tragedies defy such simple interpretation.

U

Utopia: A fictional perfect place, such as "paradise" or "heaven." An early literary utopia was described in Plato's *Republic,* and in modern literature, Ursula K. Le Guin depicts a utopia in "The Ones Who Walk Away from Omelas."

V

Victorian: Refers broadly to the reign of Queen Victoria of England (1837-1901) and to anything with qualities typical of that era. For example, the qualities of smug narrow-mindedness, bourgeois materialism, faith in social progress, and priggish morality are often considered Victorian. In literature, the Victorian Period was the great age of the English novel, and the latter part of the era saw the rise of movements such as decadence and symbolism.

Cumulative Author/Title Index

C

N

O

P

Y

Z

Cumulative Nationality/Ethnicity Index

African American

American

Antiguan

Argentinian

Asian American

Australian

Kenyan

Mexican

Native American

Nepalese

New Zealander

Nigerian

Peruvian

Philippine

Polish

Portuguese

Puerto Rican

Russian

Scottish

Sierra Leonean

South African

Spanish

Swedish

Trinidadan

Welsh

West Indian

Subject/Theme Index

T

U

V

W